BECOMING MAE WEST

Mae in Chicago, ca. 1914, while touring on the Keith circuit with Deiro.
She billed herself as "The Original Brinkley Girl"

BECOMING

Mae West

Emily Wortis Leider

FARRAR STRAUS GIROUX

New York

Farrar, Straus and Giroux
19 Union Square West, New York 10003

LIBRARY OF CONGRESS CATALOGING-IN-PUBLICATION DATA
Leider, Emily Wortis.
    Becoming Mae West / Emily Wortis Leider. — 1st ed.
      p.   cm.
    Includes index.
    ISBN 0–374–10959–1 (alk. paper)
    1. West, Mae.   2. Motion picture actors and actresses—United
States—Biography.   I. Title.
PN2287.W4566L44   1997
791.43'028'092—dc20
  [B]   96–43803

ACKNOWLEDGMENTS

Without the generosity of many, I could not have written this book. My thanks go first to my twin, Avi, for suggesting that I write about Mae West. To Andrew Wylie, for proposing that I focus on the first half of her life. To Farrar, Straus and Giroux for its editorial support. To the Roger Richman Agency for permission to quote from Mae West's books and scripts. And to Sarah Chalfant for her unstinting enthusiasm and professional savvy.

Among informants who knew Miss West, Jack Allen has been bountiful with his time, knowledge, and collection. So has Chris Basinger. Thanks go as well to Kevin Thomas of the *Los Angeles Times*, Robert Duran, Tim Malachosky, and Karl Fleming, a writer and consultant formerly with *Newsweek* and CBS. Also to Andrew Stone, Rona Barrett, Frank Cullen, Floyd Hall, Eric Concklin, Scott Eyman, and Stephen Longstreet.

I also would like to thank Fay Wray, Ron Fields, Betty Lasky, Michael Saltz, Gene Feldman, *Remember That Song*, Richard Lamparski, Miles Kreuger, Marc Wanamaker, David Thomson, Steven Bach, Michael Kaplan, the late George Eells, Peter Manso, and Leonard Maltin—they shared memories, facts, insights, or contacts.

Among librarians, collectors, and archivists, my thanks go especially to Sue Presnell of the University of Indiana's Lilly Library and Madeline Metz of the Library of Congress Motion Picture, Broadway and Recorded Sound Division; to Charles Kelly of the Library of Congress Manuscript Division, and to Kristine Krueger and Sam Gill at the Margaret Herrick Library, Academy of Motion Picture Arts and Sciences; to Kenneth R. Cobb of New York City's Municipal Archives; Georgia Leigh and Robert A. McCown of the University of Iowa Library, Special Collections; to Maryann Chach of the Shubert Archive; Mary Corliss of the Museum of Modern Art; Jonathan Rosenthal at the Museum of Television and Radio;

Crystal Hyde of the Wisconsin Center for Film Research; Elizabeth White of the Brooklyn Public Library; Ned Comstock at the University of Southern California's Cinema and Television Library; the staffs of the Harry Ransom Humanities Research Center, the British Film Institute, UCLA Film and Television Archive, the American Film Institute and the Billy Rose Theater Collection, New York Public Library; Linda Dobb and Karen Alman for help with legal research; Marty Jacobs at the Museum of the City of New York; Kay Bost of the DeGolyer Library, SMU; Jeanne T. Newlin, formerly of the Harvard Theater Collection; genealogical researcher Ann Holohan Ross; Helen Whitson of Special Collections at San Francisco State University Library, and Archive Film, for showing me rare clips; sheet music collectors Sandy Marrone, Bob Johnson, Wayland Bunnell, and much-missed Nelson Rice; Jin Auh for help with permissions; and Drew Borland, who on my behalf rewound endless reels of microfilm.

It's my pleasure to publicly thank Harry Schwartz for a guided tour of the Bushwick section of Brooklyn; Katherine Murphy and Richard Leider for research assistance; Amy Saltz for exploring Cypress Hills Cemetery with me; photographer Elena Sheehan; Ben Schwartz, Betty Crews, Diana Cavalieri, Eric Solomon, Ann Marshak, Susan Brody, Leon Friedman, Diane Wortis, Joe Bozza, Jean Leider, the late Dr. Joseph Wortis, Lillian Schlissel, for miscellaneous acts of generosity; and always, William Leider, for holding my hand through Los Angeles monsoons, Washington heat waves, and London larks.

Finally, thank you, Mae West, for making me laugh out loud in hushed sanctuaries.

FOR THE HOME TEAM:

JEAN, RICHARD, AND MY BILL

CONTENTS

BECOMING MAE WEST

INTRODUCTION

$\mathcal{M}$AE West courted excitement. She loved big cities, form-fitting clothes, lipstick, jazz, sex in taxis, intrigue, gun-toting bootleggers, boxers lathered in sweat, and cops who read her the riot act. Her stunning success as a performer came as a by-product of her megawatt energy, which she learned, during a gaslit girlhood, to channel and transmit. The chronicle of her evolving performance style is in part a story about how she learned to harness that energy, turning her baby shouts into an internationally recognized womanly purr.

Casting herself in the role of health guru, she recommended as part of a surefire fitness regimen that "a thrill a day keeps the pill away," one of her many quotable lines. For audiences lucky enough to have watched her strut her stuff on American burlesque or vaudeville stages, in legitimate theaters, or on movie screens all over the world, "Flaming Mae"—the way she moved, the way she looked, the words she spoke and the way she spoke them—provided a pleasurable kick, a rush that mingled comic and erotic juices. Slow-moving, fast-comeback Mae, a crafty and hardworking pro, kept ticket holders coming back for more and guaranteed employment for bluenosed sentries.

Sixty-plus years after a screen debut that turned her into an "instant" star, the name Mae West still spells danger to some. When I visited the elementary school she briefly and infrequently attended, near the Brooklyn-Queens border, a school secretary who proved extraordinarily helpful looked a bit uncomfortable as she asked me why I had chosen to write a book about such a woman. Did I *like* (read "approve of") Mae West? "She's a lot of fun," I offered by way of explanation. "And interesting." "But don't you think . . . ?" Her voice became hushed. "Don't you think she was a little bit *wild*?"

More than a little wild, Mae West devoted her young and less than young womanhood to raising Cain, eyebrows, and other body parts. The provocative comedienne, deftly manipulating her sultry voice and figure like an accomplished musician with an instrument, titillated or amused some members of the audience while inflaming the wrath of moral guardians. Her phrases, which she in time became adept at turning, also got her into both laugh heaven and hot water.

In the 1920s, as she broached her thirties, she began to describe herself as a writer, a calling not common among sex queens. Her name appears as the author of plays, screenplays, novels, magazine and newspaper articles, an autobiography, and a book of advice on sex, health, and ESP. For her, being a writer meant taking control of her professional vehicles. By creating or participating in the creation of her own material, sometimes co-producing her own plays, and consistently minimizing or denying credit to writing collaborators, she could literally run the show, which mattered more to her than anything else. Her ability and need to dominate and claim full credit would color her relations with co-writers, directors, and indeed with every performer who appeared with her in her vaudeville, Broadway plays, or Hollywood movies.

Most people who think at all about Mae West think of her as active rather than contemplative. She *was* a woman in perpetual, provocative motion, and some of her early performances involved strenuous gyrations. But even when she cut loose, wiggling for a bunch of Yalies in New Haven or shimmying to wild applause on Broadway in *The Mimic World of 1921*, she did so with premeditated abandon, calculated for maximum shock or showstopping effect.

Her first writing efforts—skits and then "comedy-dramas"—could have used more premeditation. The existing scripts of such efforts as *The Ruby Ring*, *The Hussy*, and *Sex*, preserved in the Manuscript Division of the Library of Congress, are, despite help from professional writers, crude, jerry-built affairs that nevertheless manage to offer clues about Mae West's preoccupations, vitality, and nerve. As her performance technique matured, her public moves and spoken lines acquired finish, less often suggesting spontaneity or careening energy. They had been precisely choreographed and rehearsed to convey voluptuous nonchalance.

Few today are aware of Mae West's inwardness, disciplined work habits, and social reticence; few remember her meticulous honing of verbal inflection, rhythm, and delivery style. Because she decked herself out glitzily with diamonds, sequins, and heavy makeup, high heels and furs, people don't associate her with economy of any sort. ("I like restraint," she once said, referring to the ornate decor of her Hollywood apartment, "if it doesn't go too far.") In fact, the body language she perfected over the years wastes no leer, side-of-the mouth crack, or hip swing; and her screen one-liners showcase succinct, pared-down wit that seems effortless but is anything but.

When Mae West finally achieved a success that had long eluded her, the new celebrity coincided with her mastery of slow motion. Her first performances were frenetic, scattershot efforts; but after her 1928 Broadway sensation *Diamond Lil*, her speech and movements became measured, leisurely, and highly stylized. Her laugh lines were now spoken with a languorous drawl which later, in her Hollywood days, became familiar to the world as one of her trademarks. She was quick with an improvised riposte but, once she thought of a snappy comeback line, would polish it to perfection before huskily intoning it on the stage or on camera.

Before she started writing she had experimented early on by custom-fitting scripted dialogue for her small part as an Irish maid in a 1911 Broadway musical revue, making the lines she had to project—but another had written—funnier, more flippant, and more in keeping with her style. Later, in the last stage of her vaudeville career, she wrote the act she performed with Harry Richman.

She'd entered vaudeville—which trained her for future stage and screen stardom—after a brief, never admitted apprenticeship in burlesque. It was in vaudeville that Mae West began to see herself and be seen by others as a comedienne; in vaudeville she became a character actress, fashioning and learning to put over her "eccentric" persona, that of an outrageous, self-mocking, tough-talking, and sultry New York vamp. In vaudeville, abandoned for the legitimate stage at a time when radio and movies were taking over American popular entertainment, she mastered the split-second timing of her laugh lines and learned to make her statement quickly, with broad strokes that would be hard to erase and were unforgettably vivid. And on vaudeville's Keith Circuit she faced her first censorious opposition.

Her young career in vaudeville was dogged by dry spells, obscure billing, and negative reviews, but after the mid-1920s, in her third decade on the boards, she finally hit her stride when she began to appear in her own plays. From then on she worked tirelessly, with steady focus, only occasionally forgetting her mother's counsel that playing around with men should come second to seeking out the stage spotlight and advancing her image.

Following her mother's hunch that fame could be found in the pursuit of the outlandish or risqué, she became an onstage scofflaw, proclaiming with every move and syllable her indifference to social and sexual decorum. She still occupies a place where excess meets control, and manages to defy the canons of propriety whenever her films are shown. Her audience still divides into opposing factions: fans who admire her craft and find her outrages entertaining, and those law-abiding citizens who either take offense at these excesses or are turned off by them.

Her record as a performer and writer for the stage offers a primer in American censorship history. From the day of Baby Mae's first stage triumph at a Brooklyn theater's amateur hour—when raucous spectators threw coins at the little darling—she challenged the prevailing Christian norms of feminine propriety. At the vaudeville houses she once toured, she got tired of hearing worried managers turn strident as they warned, "You can't sing and move that way," or, more sympathetically, "Sorry, Mae, it's great . . . but it's too hot." Her practices onstage often found her caught in the cross fire between, on one side, the champions of restraint and gentility and, on the other, enthusiasts of a new culture that endorsed pleasure seeking, acquisitiveness, self-centeredness, and freedom from constraints.

Controversy pursued her through her brief and much publicized jail term for indecency in her raunchy play *Sex*, continued through her experiments with homosexual stage comedy, and culminated, on an international scale, in the late 1930s, the end of the Paramount phase of her movie career. After a period as a top box-office attraction as Lady Lou in *She Done Him Wrong* and Tira the lion tamer in *I'm No Angel*, she was attacked by the Hays Office, which was empowered to ensure moral conduct on screen.

While scandal during her New York stage years had made her famous, landing her photo on the front page of the *Evening Graphic* in a hot embrace from *Sex*, scandal prompted by her filmwork proved truly harmful. The Hays Office badly damaged her movie career. Especially after 1934, when Joseph Breen, head of its Production Code Administration, became the enforcer of the Production Code, Mae West movies were subjected to microscopic scrutiny and were vigorously revised, bowdlerized, and cut. Many Hollywood-watchers believe that the Hays Office's rigid administration of the Production Code became Mae West's undoing—not a view Miss West herself shared. She went to her grave convinced that nothing could stop her, and that nothing ever had.

She was the first to point out that the censors who plagued her also contributed enormously to her good fortune. "Censorship *made* me," she once told an interviewer to whom she was reminiscing about her jail term and explaining her reasons for favoring film industry regulation of taste and permissiveness. Outraged in the 1970s by the post–Hays era fashion in Hollywood and Europe for screen nudity, violence, and four-letter words, she had come to view censors the way she looked at corset stays: necessary restraints that could help define and sharpen the profile of what was being contained.

Up to a point. When the Hays Office succeeded in placing her film career on hold in the late 1930s, and effectively severed her connection with Paramount, the studio that had presided over her stardom, she responded with confusion, hurt, a desire to accommodate, and, finally, a muffled, rarely voiced-in-public anger. It's hard to know whether she ever fully came to terms with what had hit her; nothing she ever said in public addressed the issue squarely. When she came back into view in the 1960s and '70s, she insisted that she was not making a comeback.

Those later years will only tangentially engage my attention here. The story of her life and career up until the time early in 1938 when Paramount ceased either making or distributing her pictures is the one I undertake to tell.

Few lives divide as neatly into segments as does Mae West's. In the first part of her life, she rises from not altogether respectable Brooklyn roots to forge a unique identity, initially on the stage, then in movies, as a taboo-breaking, slangy, singing and dancing New York hussy; an amiable underworld type (often a prostitute) who flourishes on her own terms, escaping a honky-tonk past to walk off, center stage, in triumph with at least one smitten prince, preferably one with a British accent.

Mae West's affection for plots that mimic "Cinderella," tracing an ascent from sneered-upon lowdownness to palatial splendor, springs directly from her own life experience. Despite her testimony to the contrary, in her ghost-written autobiography, *Goodness Had Nothing to Do with It*, she was not born with anything resembling a silver spoon in her mouth, nor did she exhibit from day one the attributes of an outrageous, teasing seductress. She learned very early to become one.

If any one person served as midwife to her transformation, it was her Bavarian mother. Matilda Delker Doelger West possessed a sexual morality code more European and relaxed than American puritan, and she instilled it in her daughter. As an immigrant she quickly acquired an altogether American ambition for social and material betterment (for her child if not for herself) that combined practicality and zeal. Matilda devoted her life to her favorite daughter's career, and did much to determine and advance its course.

Mae West's father, too, a brawling ex-boxer who hung out with punks, bodybuilders, two-bit gamblers, and racetrack touts, exerted a magnetic pull, though sometimes, as in the case of his working (not very hard) and drinking (hard) habits, the pull was in the opposite direction.

Her parents' union, an unhappy one, also provided a negative example. Mae West opposed marriage, at least for herself. She equated wifehood with constricting domesticity, which held no allure. Monogamy struck her as a bad bargain. "Haven't you ever met a man that can make you happy?" Cary Grant, as Captain Cummings, asks her Lady Lou in *She Done Him Wrong*. "Sure," she answers. "Lots of times." Her real-life marital adventure, her 1911 exchange of vows with dancer Frank Wallace on tour in Wisconsin when she was a few months shy of eighteen, proved immediately to be a serious misstep. Although she and Frank Wallace never lived together as man and wife, and she never told her parents about the match, the early marriage would come back to haunt her.

Her Irish-American father's easy socialization with African-American men, highly unusual for its time, paved the way for Mae West's frequent crossovers into black blues, jazz, and dance idioms; and sanctioned her interest—one she often acted on—in black men as lovers.

These liaisons with black men (such as chauffeur-boxer Chalky Wright), like all her many intimate encounters, remain largely inaccessible and unknowable in any detail because there are no letters, confessions, or diaries to consult. But we do know from observers on the scene, from the occasional kiss-and-tell lover, and from her own rare admissions in interviews that they took place. Mae West remained an extremely private person, but one who wanted people to know that she'd had countless affairs. (Someone once said she took lovers the way another person would send out for pizza.) She tried her damnedest to keep the names of her lovers (with a few exceptions, like George Raft) and the details of her relationships with them to herself. Very often, it appears, there was not a great deal to tell about her trysts, beyond the facts that they occurred and were mostly mutually enjoyed. (A few men seem to have found her sexual aggressiveness a turnoff.) But when there *was* something to tell, she preferred not to tell it. She wanted everyone to know the wisecracking, sashaying, public Mae West, but did her best to guard her intimate life and keep it hidden from view.

To piece together the puzzle, a Mae West biographer must scrounge, winnow, weigh credibility, and read between the lines—relying on published interviews Mae West granted to numerous applicants, which are forthcoming only some of the time; on accounts, both published and not, from people who knew her, sometimes a more trustworthy source; and on public documents like the U.S. Census, neighborhood directories, newspapers, and court records. Her autobiography, *Goodness Has Nothing to Do with It*, is often most reliable as an exercise in mythmaking. Frequently it tells us what she wants us to believe rather than what actually happened, and what she wants to believe herself. What she wanted us to believe, what she needed to believe about herself—these, too, are essential to her story.

Manipulating the truth was something she learned early, also from her mother. This tendency surfaces in her plays and movies as a penchant for masking and unmasking. Captain Cummings is really "the Hawk." Klondike Annie was once Frisco Kate. A list of the characters in her scripts who change or disguise their identities would be a long one.

In the 1930s, Mae West's first smash-hit movies swiftly lifted her to a place at the head table, among Hollywood's most popular and highly paid celebrities. She was credited with having miraculously cured a sick box office in the worst years of the Depression, with bringing dead theaters to life and causing blood to race once more in hardened arteries. "From nothing in the movies," wrote a Los Angeles reporter, "she rose in a single twelvemonth to a spot among the ten brightest stars. Nothing has been heard of like it since Rudolph Valentino won overnight acclaim."

She didn't exaggerate when she likened her fame to that of the grandest, most towering and legendary figures in history, Napoleon, Lincoln, Cleopatra. Like them, she became an icon. Her image was installed in wax at Madame Tussaud's and copied in cartoons. Her face adorned soap ads, her figure perfume bottles. Little children could imitate her voice, wiggling as they placed hands on hips to extend the famous invitation, a variant on the one Mae West extends to Cary Grant in *She Done Him Wrong*: "Why don't you come up and see me sometime?"

She knew better than anyone that her success and renown, sudden as they may have appeared to be as they crested, had been long in the making and hard-won. Mae West arrived in Hollywood in 1932, not as an obscure, undefined nobody, but as a veteran professional with thirty-five years of stage credits behind her and a decade-long record as her own chief scriptwriter. She departed her home city of New York to embark for California a mature woman, close to her fortieth birthday, packing in her baggage, along with her diamonds, furs and silks, the scripts of several of her plays—a few would be used for her movies—and notoriety. With a string of scandalous and/or celebrated Broadway performances in self-created plays in her past, a long history in vaudeville, and a fat file of newspaper clippings in tow, culled from her various encounters with the police and other moral watchdogs, she was already, as she put it, "a finished product" who deserved—but didn't immediately get—star treatment from the public, Paramount, or from the press.

The script for her first movie, *Night After Night*, offered her the role of Maudie Triplett, which she initially rejected as too small and too lackluster. When the producer, William Le Baron, gave his okay to her plan to rewrite Maudie's role to her specifications and liven it up, she reconsidered. Her performance in the resulting script sparkled, propelling her to stratospheric stardom.

Seven more Paramount pictures followed. After the sensational *She Done Him Wrong* and *I'm No Angel* came *Belle of the Nineties*, which, although a financial success, suffered from the first substantial interference from the Hays Office. *Goin' to Town* has some wonderful moments, but failed to match her earlier triumphs. *Klondike Annie* tried to mollify the Hays Office, but only brought down the wrath of religious and conservative leaders. In *Go West, Young Man* and *Every Day's a Holiday*, her last two Paramount-distributed pictures, which Emanuel Cohen produced, she shows definite signs of wear and tear. The jokes have begun to get old.

After *Klondike Annie*, in which half the time she acted someone different from her usual character, the icon became Jenny One-Note. World-famous, a creature of myth, but underemployed for long stretches of time once she left Paramount, when she did work she compulsively repeated her own best lines and flaunted the glittering, larger-than-life personality, the raunchy, irresistible-to-men persona that she worked so hard to create and promote. She prized that persona and fought to protect it from unauthorized imitators in the same way a successful manufacturer would a company's product, advertising slogans, logo, and brand name. In these later years Mae West became as repetitive and predictable (and foolproof, she fondly believed) in her public outings as the formula for Coca-Cola. Tamper with a proven winner at your peril, she staunchly believed. Beginning as the Depression gave way to the World War II era, and continuing until shortly before her death at age eighty-seven in 1980, she served herself up defrosted instead of fresh. The daredevil of the 1910s, '20s, and early '30s dwindled into a no-surprises performer shackled to the tried and true.

*   *   *

I consider the first four decades in Mae West's life, from the 1890s through the early Paramount years, when she was still honing her performance style and still taking risks, to be, hands down, the most dynamic decades in an iconic life. They also happen to be pivotal decades in the development of the United States into a predominantly urban population, one that took many of its cultural cues from New York City. Without that change, Mae West, a quintessential tough New Yorker in speech and manner, might never have become a national star.

The same decades saw momentous, accelerated changes in the world of American entertainment. In following Mae West's course, we can at the same time track a not always sequential transformation from a period when local stock theater companies, music halls, and rough saloons predominate to the era of powerful syndicates that oversee tours in burlesque, theater, and vaudeville. We can share in the shifts in popular dance and music: from ragtime to blues and jazz, from the 1890s "kootch" through the pre–World War I dance craze to the shimmying teens and Harlem-drenched twenties and thirties. We can travel with her from vaudeville to the prestige of the legitimate Broadway stage, watching in the wings as audiences respond— not always favorably—to daring sexual suggestion. At last we make the leap with her from New York theater to Hollywood movies, which, when they aren't banned, are distributed all over the world.

We also usher her from a time when actresses were social pariahs to the era when they walked with royalty, and from a community-centered sphere of entertainment to one that is a mega-business with international reach. Along with changes in the industry itself come shifts in the advertising, management, agenting, and public-relations practices within show business, all reflected in Mae West's own career. Beginning as a child performer handled by a pushy stage mother instead of an agent or a manager, she came to rely in her twenties on the aggressive management style of the devoted Jim Timony, who gave up a lucrative, possibly shady law practice to shepherd her career and help produce her plays. Later still, she would rely on the negotiating clout of the burgeoning William Morris agency, on producers William Le Baron and Emanuel Cohen, and on the network of entertainment reporters who were fed press releases by professional publicists.

The first half of Mae West's life also takes us through shifts in American ideals of feminine beauty. Voluptuous Lillian Russell was the standard-bearer for womanly pulchritude of face and form during the turn-of-the-century years of Mae's childhood. At that time, prevailing notions of propriety insisted that a woman's body be clothed from head to toe. At various moments in her young career, Mae West challenged the increasingly precarious assumptions about decency in women's dress and demeanor by displaying, sometimes shaking, her shoulders, breasts, and legs—till then discreetly sheathed portions of the female anatomy.

In those younger, dancing days, she was slight of figure, even boyish. But by her early thirties, the time of her first major successes in *Sex* and especially in *Diamond Lil*, she had ballooned into the curvaceous woman most people remember as Mae West. As Diamond Lil, her signature role, she revived the corseted, covered-up turn-of-the-century mode that better suited her present ample proportions than the sleek contemporary fashions. *Diamond Lil*, a hit on Broadway, brought back the Lillian Russell style—hourglass shape, huge picture hats—to an audience that included stick-figured flappers in cloches. *Diamond Lil* followed Mae West's unconvincing and some said ludicrous appearance on stage, in her play *The Wicked Age*, overflowing a one-piece bathing suit in the role of a plump flapper. She learned from her error and did not perform in a bathing suit again.

In Hollywood, after her stunning success in the *Diamond Lil* adaptation, *She Done Him Wrong*, Mae West would be credited with banishing the svelte Garbo look in favor of full-figured bombshell curves. Wealthy New York and Beverly Hills fashionables, along with high school coeds, abandoned diets designed to keep pounds off in favor of malted milks and banana splits, which they hoped would promote Westian roundness of bosom and hip.

Mae West's reputation has survived many revisions. From total obscurity, she attained an infamy that peaked after her arrest, trial, and imprisonment for *Sex*. That scandalous reputation in New York evolved into mainstream stardom on Broadway, which, in turn, after a setback or two, landed her her first motion picture role. From an interlude as an omnipresent, much quoted, wisecracking Hollywood glamour queen, she evolved into the scourge of the Hays Office, the incarnation of screen immorality whose smart mouth had to be muzzled. After World War II, she emerged as the empress of camp, reprising her *Diamond Lil* performances, appearing as Catherine the Great, and accepting roles in two films that rival each other in unfunny sleaze, *Myra Breckinridge* and *Sextette*.

Now, more than fifteen years after her death, her Paramount films, from *Night After Night* to *Every Day's a Holiday*, have all been reissued on video, and show up often on television. Popular culture currently enjoys favor among scholars, and the academic community is cranking out Ph.D. dissertations that examine Mae West's significance vis-à-vis America's shifting sexual attitudes and within the entertainment industry. Social historians hail her liberating influence on women's sexuality, but some feminists have decried her layers of makeup, male orientation, and hyper*femme* style as retrograde. Pop stars who make a point of hypersexuality (like Madonna), ambiguous sex (like David Bowie), or full-bodied, outrageous fun (like Bette Midler) compliment Mae West by following her lead. Whatever the take, she is spoken of, imitated, enjoyed, and written about.

As one indicator of the present status of Mae West, the following seems to me telling: at a New York bookstore specializing in the performing arts, I asked the proprietor for books pertinent to Mae West. I had already checked the shop's obvious categories: Biography, Cinema History, Vaudeville, Broadway. "Have you tried this section?" He indicated a corner in the back of the shop. I checked it out. It was a section on Female Impersonators.

When George Davis described Mae West in 1934 as the greatest Female Impersonator of all times, he was merely putting into quotable form a perception of her that many shared: her exaggerated femininity crossed the line into self-parody and exuberant kitsch. Early in her performing life, and continuing throughout her career, Mae West befriended, imitated, enjoyed, and defended many a drag queen and backstage homosexual; she often performed in vaudeville with female impersonators who in the early decades of this century were not marginal but in the theatrical mainstream. At least once as an adult and often as a child, she performed in male attire. She enjoyed queer camping comic turns, inviting effeminate men home to fix her mother's hairdo.

Her complex attitude toward homosexuality was flawed, by today's standards. She disliked lesbians and tended to group all male homosexuals together as women trapped in men's bodies; she thought they needed to be "cured." Nonetheless, she had and still has a devoted gay following. Among cross dressers, she was (and in some quarters still is) imitated and idolized, even fetishized as a cult diva. She enjoys such ranking not just among female impersonators but among all mavens of popular culture who find the sexual margins engrossing.

Her 1927 play, *The Drag*, attempted to bring to Broadway a cast of forty gays. Subtitled "a homosexual comedy," it was closed by a screening committee after opening in Bridgeport, Connecticut. The following year, she reprised the same theme on Broadway with *Pleasure Man*, exciting the tabloids and purity crusaders to a white heat and guaranteeing herself a second trial and months of front-page headlines that would ultimately pay off at the box office.

Intrinsic to her comic appeal was her ability to distance herself enough from everything in her path to make a joke of it, to put quotation marks around her objects of affectionate derision, deflating balloons of high seriousness, pomposity, or hot air with the pinprick of parody, even *self*-parody. Nostalgically turning back the clock for the outré 1890s costume roles that made her famous, her getups, as opposed to her words, created distance from the present. She was no secondhand Rose, but her love for fashions from the past made her a prophet of today's retro chic.

Her gift for distancing also allowed her to view her stage persona with enough detachment to allow a separation between "Me" and "She." The legend, the public Mae West, could be viewed and spoken of in the third person by the private woman. The one time in her career when she risked discarding the distancing device and attempted to appear "sincere," as repentant, black-clad, religious do-gooder Sister Annie in the film *Klondike Annie*, her inconsistency confused her audience. It was hard for a public trained to expect kidding to distinguish the repentant soul saver Sister Annie from the familiar outsized vamp she played half the time in the very same movie; or to believe for one moment in a serious, religious, conscience-stricken Mae West.

The private Mae West circa 1936 didn't "take religion for a joke" any more than Sister Annie did, but she was more drawn to spirituality than to organized religion. Catholicism nonetheless plays a major role in her biography. She had a judgmental Catholic aunt and Catholic cousins. When she first came to Hollywood, she regularly attended Mass with her devout manager Timony, explaining that it was a good way to begin the day. Such devotions carried little weight in the eyes of the Catholic Church, which led the opposition to her screen "immorality." Over the years, she became more and more drawn to the occult. Séances, gurus, and contact with the dead became mainstays of her life.

Others who have written about Mae West have commented on her Lone Star isolation and singularity. John Mason Brown called her a soloist in a duet world. Colette hymned her on-screen independence of entangling alliances: "She alone has no parents, no children, no husband . . . [and is] in her style, as solitary as Chaplin used to be."

My lens sometimes will zoom close in, trying to penetrate the layers of makeup to probe the elusive, singular woman. It will also seek a framework, from time to time employing a lens wide enough to take in other stars who were her contemporaries, rivals, and sometimes models; to include not just the star but the co-stars (George Raft), supporting players (Harry Richman, Cary Grant), associates (Marlene Dietrich), musicians (Duke Ellington), other performers she copied and learned from (Eva Tanguay, Texas Guinan), and the many behind-the-scenes participants—directors, producers, managers, theater and film executives, costume designers, cameramen, and fan magazine writers—who helped create her.

Even her talent for tongue-in-cheek can be understood as both an individual gift and a habit of the theatrical culture she grew up in. Burlesques, travesties, and parodies were after all the lifeblood of New York musical and variety stage in the first decades of this century. Send-ups of popular performers, songs, public figures, and current plays were standard fare. Clyde Fitch's *Barbara Frietchie* was spoofed as *Barbara Fidgety*. Imitations of well-known performers were part of the initiation rite of every newcomer—including Baby Mae, who cut her teeth mimicking her parents' visitors and graduated to onstage takeoffs of the likes of Eva Tanguay, Eddie Foy, and Bert Williams.

Thirty years later, during the Depression, to draw an example from her heyday in Hollywood, her tough-talking, big-city manner fused perfectly with the country's "let's get real" mood. Even her voluptuous body worked to provide reassurance that abundance was around the corner and the sunken cheeks of hard times and breadlines would pass.

But beyond being *of* her times, she remains a phenomenon like no other, uniquely herself. Like the cartoon characters she loved as a kid and later inspired, she leaps out at us, in overstated, indelible outline. Although tiny in height, Mae West the Hollywood legend took on—in common with other American folk figures—a Paul Bunyonesque grandeur, omnipresence, and opulence. She fostered the grand illusion in her screen appearances by wearing stilt-heeled shoes and by avoiding any frame she could not dominate. No director, no leading man, no rival beauty, no co-star called *her* shots. She thought of herself as one of history's commanding feminine presences, a Catherine the Great. Examined as a cultural lightning rod, her Amazonian dimension remains intact. Like any queen, she stands for something mythic beyond her private self.

More than any other theatrical luminary of the earlier decades of this century, I believe, Mae West remains our contemporary. Her impertinent camping and her overbearing demeanor push her into the sexual margins, and for whatever complex of reasons, our contemporary culture has a pre-occupation with border crossings. Mae West's appeal to the camp followers among us assures her place as an American icon combining 1890s stylization and epigrammatic wit with today's "transgressiveness" and gender-bending. Her aphorisms, look, and voice still provoke smiles and tribute.

HER CHRISTIAN NAME
WAS MARY

*I*N 1893, during the summer Mary Jane West was born in Brooklyn, a belly dancer known as Little Egypt created a sensation at the Midway Plaisance of the Chicago World's Fair. Her costume—harem pantaloons, short bolero with coin decorations—set tongues wagging. So did her loose hair, since the current fashion for ladies favored elaborately rolled and pompadoured effects, and in public during daytime hours a hat decorated with ribbons and plumes was considered *de rigueur*. Most startling was the dancer's exposed, undulating abdomen, which she could adroitly activate while hardly moving her feet. The enticing "hootchy-kootchy" presentation at the World's Columbian Exposition—a celebration of the four hundredth anniversary of Columbus's venture into the New World—made Little Egypt both notorious and a leading attraction. Popular with the press as well as among the millions who thronged to the fair, Little Egypt's drawing power rivaled that of the festooned horses of William F. "Buffalo Bill" Cody's Wild West Show, the quick-stepping marches of John Philip Sousa's World's Fair Band, and the display of brute strength by a half-naked strongman, Eugene Sandow, whose manager, a youth named Ziegfeld, would allow society matrons to palpate Sandow's muscles backstage if they contributed handsomely to charity.

"When she dances," announced a barker inviting one and all to sample the wonders of "The Streets of Cairo," "every fiber and every tissue in her entire anatomy shakes like a jar of jelly from your grandmother's Thanksgiving dinner . . . She is as hot as a red-hot stove on the fourth of July in the hottest county in the state."

Of course, outraged guardians of public decency tried to close down "The Streets of Cairo" and its licentious performance. Purity crusader Anthony Comstock, founder of the Society for the Suppression of Vice, special agent of the U.S. Post Office, and tireless protector of the virtue of the nation's young and innocent, shook his ginger-colored side-whiskers and pronounced it "the most outrageous assault on the sacred dignity of womanhood ever endured in this country." The entire Exposition, he fulminated, must be razed to the ground, and its commissioners indicted for keeping a disorderly house. According to Comstock, wanton displays of this kind had long been perpetrated in tawdry dens and infamous resorts. But the exhibition of such lasciviousness in a public arena, in clear sight of uncorrupted, God-fearing American women and children, he adjudged an unspeakable abomination. The Chicago Fair had been designed, after all, to celebrate and proclaim patriotic glories, to demonstrate how far American technology and artistry had progressed since Columbus's discovery, and to call attention to the young nation's mounting ascendance in the international arena. For Comstock, Little Egypt's wantonness reeked of *foreignness*, a word he mouthed with evident distaste.

Mr. Comstock did not, in this skirmish between puritans and pleasure seekers, prevail. Instead, his outcries and the attendant publicity prompted a Little Egypt craze. In cities all over the country, children chirped and giggled as they wiggled their hips, whined exotic Casbah refrains, and incanted jingles: "And the dance that they do/Is the Hootchy-Kootchy Koo." One of many "authentic" and "original" Little Egypts, invited to perform at a ceremonial dinner, induced New York Police Captain Chapman, "Czar of the Tenderloin," to raid the premises, resulting in a front-page news story.

The *National Police Gazette*, ready always to supply an eager readership with racy tidbits, reported that a woman had been arrested for public drunkenness as she demonstrated a dance "that made even the boy on the stone fountain blush," while singing the popular ditty: "On the Midway, the Midway, the Midway Plaisance/Where the naughty Algiers girls/Do their naughty, naughty dance." Songstress Bonnie Thornton echoed the theme, singing about a poor little country maid, innocent of the city's sinful ways, who was lured by a bounder onto the sordid streets of Cairo, where each night she posed in abbreviated clothes: "All the dudes were in a flurry,/For to catch her they did hurry."

From New York to California, as architects in celluloid collars and sleeve garters drew up blueprints for lofty colonnaded buildings redolent of empire, jaunty pleasure seekers outfitted in straw hats and parasols flocked to sportive resorts in pursuit of summer larks. Within a year there were dozens of Little Egypts performing wherever traveling circuses, burlesque theaters, and side-street dime museums could be found. At Coney Island, Brooklyn's teeming and boisterous seaside amusement park, Sunday revelers rubbed shoulders, as camels, elephants, and snake charmers crowded into the narrow "Streets of Cairo."

Perhaps it was there, in the arms of her brawny father or buxom mother, that Baby Mae, future *prima* kootch dancer *assoluta*, Baby Vamp and prodigy of the swiveling hip, heard her first exotic strains and caught the rhythm of a drumbeat that beckoned oglers into a tent to see a show more suited to shade than the blaze of daylight.

"Mae" was, in the 1890s, a frequent nickname for "Mary," as a popular song of the day attests. In Brooklyn vaudeville theaters, singer Lydia Barry intoned "Her Christian Name Was Mary," while manipulating a large fan with the letters M A R Y printed thereon. As she proceeded through the song's several verses, Lydia's person became gradually more visible as "MARY" dwindled on the fan to MA, with MAY intervening:

> Her Christian name was Mary
> But she took the R away
> She wanted to be a fairy
> With the beautiful name of May
> But a young man came to wed her
> In a year or so he was a Pa
> So they took the Y away from May
> Which made little Mary Ma.

Mae West never seems to have been addressed by the prim name her parents bestowed in honor of her Ireland-born paternal grandmother, Mary Jane Copley. She was sometimes called "May," sometimes "Mayme," and finally "Mae." (She chucked the "y" in Mae, she said, because she didn't like to see it drooping below the line: "I don't like anything downbeat.") That she would never choose to realize the song's transition from "May" to "Ma"—that she would deliberately and happily shun motherhood—might have been predicted early on, for she had in Matilda West a mother deeply invested in her own plans for Baby Mae, big plans that left no place for the girl's eventual marriage, bearing of children, or forging any other binding ties that might divert her darling's unimpeded pursuit of stage stardom.

Mae, a cuddly, cheerful, and robust moppet with a round "full moon" face, fair skin, an upturned nose with wide nostrils, plump and curvaceous lips, and golden hair that would darken to brunette, was not her parents' first-born. A sister, Katie, preceded her, but survived only a few months. Like little Mae, Katie had breathed her first breaths in the punishingly hot dog days of a Brooklyn August. A midwife assisted at the home birth, for young mothers of the 1890s considered it immodest to have a male physician attend them and female physicians were almost unknown.

Two years later, delivered by an aunt who was a midwife, along came blue-bonnet-eyed Mae: "I was born on August 17 [1893] at 10:30 p.m. on a cool night of a hot month, so I can expect anything," she would report. Unlike her siblings', Mae's birth went unrecorded. She lacked a birth certificate, but 1893, a year in which the euphoria of the World's Fair was undermined by economic panic, depression, and massive unemployment, was the one she eventually acknowledged as her first.

Leo, her astrological sign, marked her, she came to believe, as a lioness and a fighter—qualities the adult Mae would prize and endow with high significance, as she would also weight the determining energy of her rising planet, Venus. The Leo and Venus factors worked in concert, she concluded, to assure her destiny as a *femme fatale*. "Since lions travel in prides," she would write, "don't be surprised if as a Leo woman you find yourself surrounded by men."

But her older sister, Katie, also a Leo and presumably also a fighter, lost her battle against respiratory disease. Profoundly mourned, the departure of Katie assured Mae's privileged place in her mother's affections and in the family galaxy. Matilda West was determined that her second baby, by heaven, was going to survive and flourish. She treated Mae "like a jewel."

Mae spent her first five and a half years a pampered only child. Her sister Beverly, whose given name was actually Mildred Katharina, didn't arrive until 1898, and a brother, John Edwin, was born two years later. Although her sister and brother remained securely fastened at the core of Mae's emotional life, and although the West household functioned as part of a large extended family replete with aunts, uncles, and cousins (Matilda had six living siblings in 1900), those first five years of doting, undivided maternal attention established her as an eternal soloist and a law unto herself. She was excused from mundane chores, like picking up after herself. She delighted in her own reflected image, caught in storefront mirrors as she passed by: "I'd pose as I'd walk along and look at myself." Liking what she saw, she remained enthralled by mirrors and images of herself captured by lenses. Her photograph appeared on a calendar before her sixth birthday.

Parental dictates that applied to sister Beverly and young John Edwin didn't affect her. "I was different from my sister and brother. My mother had to use the strap or show it to 'em to make 'em mind. But if she gave me an unkind word I would sulk for days." "Mother knew how to get me to do anything and everything by usin' the right tone. She'd never say, 'Go and shut that door,' y'know what I mean? But: 'Dear, wouldya mind shuttin' the door please?' Then I'd shut it."

Mae was so special she didn't even get sick the way other kids did, nor did she ever suffer from a toothache or a cavity. She came to believe that her hardiness signified more than good genes or extra-attentive mothering; she felt "protected" by something out there she would eventually speak of as "the Forces."

Matilda ("Tillie" to her family) had suffered the loss of Katie when she was barely out of her teens. She transmuted her grief into an extravagant dedication to Mae—whose whims were indulged like the commands of a diminutive czarina—that lasted as long as she lived. Did Mae covet a blond, blue-eyed doll dressed in lilac-pink satin on the topmost shelf of a neighborhood department store? Fear not, the saleslady will find a nice man with a big ladder who will fetch it down for you.

If her father, as Mae once reported, voiced regret that she wasn't born a boy, Tillie delighted in Mae's winsome, pink-ribbon femininity. She lavished attention on her exquisite skin, sewed her lace-edged petticoats and frilly frocks, curled her hair and tied it with a big satin bow: "Mother dressed me in dainty light clothes and fabrics much like the clothes she herself wore."

Her diet was closely monitored. Chocolates were *verboten*, fresh fruit and vegetables prized. But sensual pleasures, the infant's first banquets of touch, were bountifully indulged. Mae's earliest memory was of her mother massaging her with baby oil. She would never stop delighting in the luxurious feel of lotion, scented oil, or cocoa butter smoothed on her naked skin— preferably by someone else.

Matilda herself, a soft-spoken native of Bavaria whose stunning hourglass figure reminded people of the ripe and rounded opulence of reigning New York beauty, actress Lillian Russell, had married after a brief stint modeling corsets, a scant seven years after her arrival in America. She had once harbored hopes for a stage career of her own, but her respectable merchant family, kin to proprietors of a New York brewery renowned for its lager, forbade it. They probably had also discouraged her forays into the corset-modeling profession, which she glamorized with a French word, *modiste*. More acceptable was another vocation she had taken some training in— fashion design, which taught her dressmaking, educated her eye, and would help her engender in Mae "a lasting appreciation for the best of everything in clothes," a lifelong partiality for silk and chiffon in creamy white and pastel tones. And for fur: a baby picture shows a languorous six-month-old Mae enthroned on a bear rug. Growing up, little Mae always carried a muff during the winter, and when snow blanketed the Brooklyn streets she was pulled along in a horse-drawn, fur-lined sleigh.

The undulating shape of her mother's corseted body seemed to find echo everywhere in the material world—on Brooklyn stoops, with their sinuous cast-iron rails; in the curlicued lettering of street signs; in Swan Boats afloat on a lake in Prospect Park; indoors, on wooden chairs that had been carved with a scroll saw, or upholstered pieces, plushly pillowed. Opulence was in fashion. Nothing succeeded, as Oscar Wilde put it, like excess. Too much of a good thing, Mae would later put it, can be wonderful. Skirts for dresses that touched the floor required yards and yards of fabric. Hips and bosoms stinted by nature had to be fleshed out into roundness with padding. Wide-brimmed picture-book hats were piled high with what one wag called "delirium trimmings." The fashionable "look" of Mae's childhood years, and in particular of her mother, would leave an indelible stamp. She would return to it again and again in her performing career, recalling in her own plumed sinuousness a past she cherished and idealized. "Aubrey Beardsley might have drawn the canary-white tendrils weaving over the hourglass figure as a landlocked mermaid," wrote Cecil Beaton about the look she made her billowy signature.

If they knew about it, Matilda's family almost certainly would have attempted to thwart her impetuous marriage at age eighteen to John "Battlin' Jack" West, a cigar-chomping, street-smart tough. The marriage certificate of Tillie Delker and John West, dated January 19, 1889, in the city of Brooklyn—a separate city then, not yet a part of metropolitan New York—lists the groom's age as twenty-two, his birthplace as New York City, and his occupation: "mechanic."

His parents' names are entered in the appropriate slots: Father, also John West, a native of New York (the U.S. Census for 1920 contradicts this, naming Newfoundland as his father's birthplace); and Irish-born mother, Mary Cobley, a misspelling of Copley. Copley is also the name listed for one of the witnesses (E. Frances). The second witness was Julia West.

The presence of two witnesses standing up for the groom and none from the bride's family supports the theory that while his family favored the marriage, hers did not. Perhaps the young couple's decision to marry had been made in such haste there wasn't time to arrange a full-tilt Event. Perhaps, fearing obstruction, Tillie didn't inform them of the wedding until afterward. Very likely, Tillie's father, a former chemical engineer at a sugar refinery in Germany, Mae claimed, who had a liquor business in 1892 and whose occupation in the 1900 census was given as "salesman—coffee," disdained the modest earning capacity of a mechanic son-in-law. The Doelgers, at least some of them, were substantial property owners whose successful lager beer enterprise had made them wealthy. When Peter Doelger, a cousin, died in 1912, he left an estate valued at more than one million dollars.

Whatever her family may have thought of the match, Tillie herself soon came to regret it. "My father had swept her off her feet," Mae once told a reporter, "and she always felt she had made a big mistake, marrying him. She didn't want me to make the same mistake." Mae's unproduced autobiographical play, *The Hussy*, includes some domestic scenes that may mirror her parents' interactions. The father in that play, a rough-hewn, exuberant loudmouth, comes home from a day at the track boasting about his near big win and throws his hat on the table; his wife puts the hat on the rack. When he deposits his cigar butt on the table, she again corrects his boorish gesture, placing the cigar on an ashtray. Her reproaches are silent, but it's clear she considers him coarse, oafish, and underbred.

A worldly, competent, and ambitious woman, Matilda yearned for a role outside the home, but for a married woman with young children a job was out of the question as far as her husband was concerned. Dissatisfaction with a mate who wouldn't think of allowing his wife to work only fortified the bond between Matilda and her children, especially Mae.

The Wests' marriage license gives the bride's birthplace as Germany, lists her father as Jacob Delker and her mother as Christiana Brimier, which sounds French, and may explain why Mae so often told people she was of French or Alsatian extraction. The family name on Mae's mother's side, then, was Delker, but the family business, the brewery founded by cousins in New York in the 1840s, was Joseph DOELGER & Sons. Perhaps Delker and Doelger were one and the same, with variant spellings; an immigration clerk may have written "Delker" for "Doelger." Mistakes in the transcription of foreign names happened routinely at Castle Garden, at that time New York's immigrant port of entry. In her autobiography Mae gives both names, introducing her mother as Matilda Delker Doelger.

Mae West never addressed in public the oft-repeated rumor that on her mother's side she was part Jewish. Many have testified that when she was with someone Jewish she privately confessed that she was, as she privately also acknowledged being left-handed. Despite the admissions, the partially Jewish ancestry remains unproven, a matter for speculation; if true, the fact that it remained a secret rather than a freely acknowledged part of her heritage suggests that Tillie may have imparted to her daughter a sense of shame about her Jewish ancestry, perhaps animated by anti-Semitic experiences and reinforced by an immigrant's eagerness to shed any markings of a foreignness that might impair assimilation into the American mainstream. When their brother, Jack, married a Jewish woman in Los Angeles in the 1930s, both Mae and Beverly considered that he'd married "outside."

Tillie herself, from all indications, functioned as a Christian and a German-American whose parents continued to reside, in the years of her young motherhood, on a Brooklyn street surrounded by other German-born citizens of modest means but eminent respectability: clerks, salespeople, engravers, retired bakers. Hungry for success, she conveyed to her daughter the lesson that altering the truth to further one's private agenda is perfectly okay. Mae learned at her mother's knee to be "secretive, almost to the point of mystery."

In Brooklyn, "City of Churches," Matilda attended church, not synagogue, sometimes Lutheran, sometimes Catholic, but always Christian. But writer Ruth Biery, who knew Mae well, described her mother as "that shrewd, at least partially Jewish woman." *The New Yorker* reported in the twenties that "the Jewish publications claim Miss West as a member of their faith, but she says that her grandmother was a Copley"— a name that often turned up in newspaper society columns—"and claims Harry Thaw as her relative."

Boasting of a connection with Harry Thaw—the wealthy wastrel husband of the beautiful model Evelyn Nesbit, and murderer of Nesbit's lover, architect Stanford White—suggests a willingness to accept wealth and fame as signifiers of merit, even when the wealth is inherited and the fame infamy. Harry Thaw, whose sensational 1906 crime made him one of the most talked- and written-about men of this century's first decade, was famous even before he killed White—as a philanderer, drinker, and spendthrift who once drove an automobile through a New York display window and reportedly lost $40,000 in a single poker game. Matilda would pass on to her daughter—along with voluptuous proportions, theatrical aspirations, and a penchant for mystification—an appreciation for names everyone recognizes and luxuries only the rich can afford. It was Matilda who presented Mae with her very first diamond, and her drink of choice was champagne. ("Champagne Till," her husband sometimes called her.) Mae's father, on the other hand, didn't give a fig for luxury or social position, and it was he, not Matilda, who might have legitimately claimed kinship with Harry Thaw. Thaw's mother had been, like John West's mother, a Copley.

Mae bragged of an even grander patrimony. "Just because I was born in Brooklyn some people figure the West family tree [is] a rubber plant," she complained. "We were descended from Alfred the Great on my father's side," she claimed. Her father was "one of a long line of John Wests" originally from Long Crendon in Oxfordshire, England. A concern with pedigrees, a need to legitimize her claim to a distinguished heritage, would follow Mae to Hollywood and be summoned to shield her from the wounding charges of commonness often hurled in her direction. Like her character Cleo in *Goin' to Town*, she bristled when high hats put her down as "rather crude oil."

The Anglo-Irish Wests were Anglicans, not Catholics; but either through intermarriage or conversion, there were Catholics on the West side of the family. The midwife aunt who assisted at her birth, Mae once told Stanley Musgrove, was "a very Roman Catholic woman who later must have wished she'd dropped [me] on the head at birth, because she avidly disapproved of [my] stage and screen characterizations." The aunt came to see Mae as " 'Old Ned—the Red Devil, himself.' "

Religion, in the West household, provided a confusion of identities rather than one central, defining one. Mae said she attended both Protestant and Catholic churches as a child—but Sunday school always gave her a headache. Organized religion contributed little that was positive to her sense of self.

Mae's grandfather West had been a whaling captain, and may have served in the Civil War as a stock keeper. If her autobiography can be trusted on this, Mae's father was the only one of several brothers who did not go to college. Grandfather John West, a religious Protestant who prayed before taking dinner, had speculated in real estate and prospered. But his renegade son, Mae's father, Jack, displayed no appetite for piety, schooling, or genteel company. He preferred to move freely, at Gravesend, Brighton Beach Fairgrounds, or Sheepshead Bay racetracks, among turf touts, swells, and bookies; and amid the roughnecks, sharpies, gamblers, and confidence men of Coney Island, where he had once worked as a bouncer and where he often had entered the square ring, fists raised, to demonstrate his prowess in the "manly art."

John "Battlin' Jack" West was a man of pungent odors: cigars, horses,

sweat, whiskey. He had been a bare-knuckle featherweight prizefighter before his marriage, at a time when, in New York and its environs, prizefighting outside of private athletic clubs was illegal and was suffused with
underworld notoriety and cachet. "Prize-fighting," the somber and sober
New York Times editorialized in 1893, is "an evil every Christian must ab-
hor." Theodore Roosevelt, who as President would bring boxing to the
White House and make a fetish of "the strenuous life," while a mere civil-
service commissioner, in 1890, characterized people who attend fights and
make heroes out of fighters as "men who hover on the borderline of crim-
inality."

Powerfully built, short and compact, fit and "all knobby with muscles,"
Battlin' Jack was infamously hot-tempered and vengeful, prone to settling
disputes with his fists at a time when masculine American culture was recoiling *en masse* against the confinement of rooms cluttered with Victorian
bric-a-brac and the constraints of tedious urban routines. A street brawler,
he once beat a neighborhood cop fighter, the Iron Man of Dutchtown, so
brutally the man required thirty-two stitches in his head. When, before their
marriage, he took Tillie out to a social club where another man paid too
much attention to her, he responded by knocking his rival out with a single
punch, then breaking two beer steins, whacking them together, and cutting
his way through the fray. "He'd go to a drawer and when he couldn't find
what he wanted, he'd pull the whole drawer out and dump it on the floor
and swear—and my mother would have to come and find things for him."

In all her accounts of her father's brutality, Mae never mentioned the
part liquor may have played in fueling his wrathful fires, but most likely he
became belligerent when in his cups. A gregarious man and a sports fan,
he would seek out a saloon for some rowdy conviviality, to hear the latest
telegraphed results from ball games or championship boxing matches, and
to place a bet. The swinging doors, polished wood, and hammered brass of
the saloon—plus the promise of free lunch by day and musical entertainment at night—beckoned from many a Brooklyn corner. They "all had
'Family Entrances.' Inside, each one had a long bar, with sawdust on the
floor . . . All around the place were shining brass cuspidors, with a sign over
them on the wall reading DONT SPIT AT EM, SPIT IN EM . . . Against the side
wall opposite the bar would be an old upright piano . . . The walls would
be covered with pictures of naked queens and . . . big time prize fighters."

Finding a saloon was never a problem. "In 1897 there were 8,316 liquor
licenses issued in New York . . . In Brooklyn in the same year there were
4,129 licenses issued." This many watering holes required staffs to service

them. According to one account, Jack was employed when Mae was a baby as a bartender in Greenpoint.

Prizefighting and drinking had long been boon companions. John L. Sullivan, the bare-knuckle heavyweight champion from Boston whose portrait adorned every barbershop and saloon, began as a "booze" fighter and roisterer in the days when boxing matches did not end until one contender had been punched, scratched, bitten, and kicked unconscious. To keep going, fighters anesthetized themselves with alcohol through endless rounds in the ring. Physical prowess, drinking, and bravado all ranked high in the masculine Irish urban subculture John L. Sullivan and Battlin' Jack shared.

Mae, in any case, came to despise excesses of alcohol, though her sister, Beverly, became an alcoholic. As an adult, she shunned drink. Drunk men, she once said, were the only kind she didn't like. She held W. C. Fields's drinking against him. And she despised cigars—the smoke she associated with Battlin' Jack made her ill. She cringed when her father came close to her.

His rages must have terrified her, but she was not cowed by them. She even, before she hit her teens, considered retaliating against him with physical force if he ever struck her—evidence of her extraordinary guts, gall, and self-assurance. "Nerve," her father called it. Once, when she was twelve, he flew into a temper after she stayed out late with some boys. "He came home and I picked up an iron rod he kept near his bed. I thought he was going to hit me and I was going to hit him first, but he never touched me."

She kept her father at arm's length, but at the same time identified with him, telling one interviewer that she believed she was more like her father than her mother, although she was much closer to and more openly affectionate with her mother. "I was always more like my father than like my mother, more like a man." Like him, she seethed with impatience when looking for things she couldn't find. Like him, she remained a stranger to the kitchen, her mother's realm, and to any menial task performed to serve another. She set her sights on the bustling world outside and, with her father, marched to an up-tempo city beat.

Battlin' Jack was the one with the slangy, wiseacre sense of humor, the one who grabbed the Sunday funnies for the latest antics of the Katzenjammer Kids, and quipped, when he saw a shiner on someone, "He forgot to duck." He blazed the path she would follow—as the family outlaw, the one who did as he pleased and heeded the calls of the wild.

It was Battlin' Jack who took her to Coney Island to see Frank Bostock's lions, which so thrilled Mae she started to dream of one day becoming a lion tamer, a whip-snapping, daredevil showman whose fitness, strength, and authority would compel attention and proclaim her mastery over the beast.

Accompanying her father to the gym and watching him work out with weights, she appropriated his no-one-pushes-me-around attitude, his athlete's obsession with what the late nineteenth century called "physique" and a life devoted to "banging physical action." She would remain partial to men who were muscular brawlers, especially those strongmen willing to exchange punches over her. Asked by a movie magazine what kind of man she would have been, she guessed she would have followed her father into the ring and become a prizefighter.

Battlin' Jack hung up his gloves, Mae said, when he married. He opened a livery stable, offering carriages, surreys, light rigs, or winter horse-drawn sleighs for hire, and bringing horse stands to beach resorts during the summer. As a child she and a girl friend would go to the stable and ride the elevator used to store carriages at different levels. The gym and the livery stable—where stable hands and neighborhood retirees gathered among the harnesses, whips, and horse blankets—were male sanctuaries to which few women ventured; they awakened her appetite for the salty company of men released from the social niceties of mixed company.

But awareness of her resemblance to Battlin' Jack came slowly and didn't make him easier to love. "I was crazy about my mother. But I never liked my father much when I was small. I don't know why, 'cause he never laid a hand on any of us . . . and he always provided good for us."

Without fail, Mae depicted her childhood as one plush with lace-curtained stability and comfort, and her father as the provider of that comfort. But various Brooklyn directories and public documents hint at a more turbulent course, full of zigzags. A mechanic when he married, two years later—at the time of Katie's birth, in 1891—Jack gave his profession as "bridle maker." Further down the line, when Beverly was born in 1898, John West gave his occupation on her birth certificate as "laborer." That same year Lain's Brooklyn Directory found him still at 308 Humbolt Street, which is in Greenpoint, but now employed as a "watchman." From "watchman," it was for Mae, years later, just a small mental jump to "detective." She would recall for Karl Fleming that her father had "a big detective agency in Brooklyn. He was the one who started the night patrols" that protected warehouses and stores from night raiders. No Brooklyn directory of the day corroborates this, though it seems likely that a "big agency" would have been listed. King's 1893 *Handbook of New York City* reports on the proliferation of private detective agencies and private watchmen enlisted to protect the buildings being erected by new millionaires, but hints darkly that "the uprightness of many of them is questionable."

By the 1920s Mae was regularly telling people who asked about her father, "He's a doctor now, practicing medicine in Richmond Hill." This was her embellishment of the fact that he sometimes operated health-related businesses: he once ran an herb store, soon after they moved to Queens, and the 1920 U.S. Census lists his profession as "masseur."

For at least the earliest years of her childhood, then, Mae apparently knew prosperity only intermittently, or via some source other than her father, such as grandparents. What Jack West did for a living in his first decade as a family man was, like Damon Runyon's Feet Samuels, "the best he could." Like Feet Samuels, he may have "hustled some around the race tracks and crap games and prize fights, picking up a few bobs here and there as a runner for the bookmakers, or scalping bets." The explosive, cigar-chomping father in Mae's unproduced autobiographical play *The Hussy*, spends his days at the track, where he rarely picks a winner. The neighbors, behind his back, brand him a layabout who never worked a day in his life, and his seductive daughter tells him she's glad his parents bypassed him in their wills and instead left bequests to the grandchildren. If this is a picture of Battlin' Jack, it goes a long way toward illuminating his blurry and various work profile.

Along with the many shifts in his occupation came frequent changes of address—all within North Brooklyn or adjacent Queens, but ranging from Meeker Avenue in Greenpoint to Bushwick to Ridgewood, a neighborhood of modest two-family homes on the border of Queens. The family kept relocating—from Varet Street to Humbolt to Conselyea Street, then to a six-family house on St. Nicholas Avenue near Bleecker and Seneca, and eventually to a substantial house on Linden Street, which may have been shared with or inherited from relatives. Mae told several interviewers in her pre-Hollywood days that they used to live with her rich grandmother.

North Brooklyn, except for the grandeur of Bushwick Avenue, a wide, tree-shaded thoroughfare where the mayor lived in a stately brownstone, was a bustling lower-middle- and working-class enclave of "horse-plagued streets," German beer gardens enlivened by strolling street bands, breweries redolent of malt and hops, and modest brick apartment buildings and wood-frame houses, some adorned with wrought-iron gates and fences. Occupied by German, Irish, Polish, and Italian families, many of whom worked in nearby rope, glue, sugar, and oil factories, in breweries, or at the thriving Brooklyn

Navy Yard, the district's population swelled as new immigrants arrived from Europe. Manhattan, a burgeoning port and commercial center, was a long bicycle or a short trolley ride away over the still-new Brooklyn Bridge, or you could take one of thirteen steamer ferries plying the East River. For those who worked in Manhattan, Brooklyn served as a convenient dormitory. It was the "baby carriage and rubber plant" borough.

The landscape was changing quickly. Gaslight was giving way to the newfangled Edison carbon-filament lamp. Cobblestone streets were being paved with asphalt. Stores attracted consumers with newly available inexpensive plate-glass windows enticingly displaying their abundant wares. Mae, a precociously material girl, remembered peering at a beautiful diamond hung on black velvet and coveting it. A memorable sequence from one of her movies set in the 1890s, *Every Day's a Holiday*, shows her cutting through a department store's glass window and appropriating the manikin's elegant attire.

Appeals to the eye proliferated. Advertisements—for Pears' Soap, Castoria, or Pink Pills for Pale People—beckoned from the sides of wagons and the walls of buildings; advances in printing, especially in color lithography, made the billboard, the handbill, and the poster omnipresent.

With the shorter workday, people had more leisure time than in the past, and shopping for goods and good times became consuming occupations. Opulently appointed vaudeville theaters were cropping up, and the first kinetoscope parlors for peep-show sightings of Annabelle in a serpentine dance or Sandow flexing his biceps appeared.

In Manhattan, the theater district inched northward from Fourteenth Street along Broadway. At Twenty-ninth Street, the Weber and Fields Broadway Music Hall, a small colonnaded structure ornamented with wreaths and a lyre, brought immigrant-accented humor from the Lower East Side into the main stem. Its Victorian architecture spoke of bygone days, but its rollicking polyglot productions announced a new kind of American musical theater. Close at hand, steel-framed buildings were introduced, and skyscrapers began lording it over church steeples on the horizon, blazoning a new kind of aspiration, a new ethic of success, based not on rectitude, piety, and self-control but on individual initiative, consumption, expressiveness, and upward striving. "I was a child of the new century just around the corner," Mae would sense, "and I ran toward it boldly."

BABY MAE

$\mathcal{T}$HE polyglot, immigrant-swelled New York Mae West grew up in housed more Irish than Dublin, more Jews than Warsaw, as many Germans as Hamburg. New citizens from Europe joined Afro-Americans from the South and country dwellers lured to the urban hub in an economic scramble. The confident boom years that followed the Spanish American War found young women flocking into the workplace, leaving behind grandmotherly standards of propriety that would have kept them indoors, chaperoned and shielded from the public arena. As women trooped to work—a majority of those between sixteen and twenty held jobs in 1900—they became more casual about mingling with the men they might encounter (on the El or a ferry, in a department store or an office), more interested in buying things, having fun, and looking pretty. Glamour was now something you could purchase in a store. Cosmetics, previously applied only to the faces of actresses or prostitutes, now reddened the lips and blushed the cheeks of respectable young misses.

Shop girls, factory hands, and piece workers, after toiling all week in confined spaces, when at leisure craved amusement, the outdoors, and exercise. On pleasant Sundays, young women picnicked in city parks, rode the trolley to the beach, danced on ferries, bicycled in divided skirts and bloomers, or window-shopped in ankle-length skirts and shirtwaist blouses. New York women, "daughters of liberty and commercial democracy," as they promenaded down Broadway, offered up "an unending variety of feature, complexion and personality," pleasing to one contemporary, and carried themselves with a characteristic audacity, an "easy hauteur": "They made no hypocrisy of meekness, but marched along alluringly, emphasizing their physical graces by their carriage and gathering their skirts about them with a frankness astounding to the foreigner."

Young Mae, who had an aunt employed as a midwife, a girl cousin in show business, and a mother chomping at the domestic bit, announced herself a child of the new century by her kinetic verve and relentless physicality. She roller-skated, went sledding in winter, and worked out with weights, training in gymnastics and acrobatics with her father to develop her strength to the point where, as a teenaged member of Tenni's Arab Acrobatic Troupe, she was able, she claimed, to lift five hundred pounds and support three men in pinwheel formation on her sturdy shoulders.

Outgoing Mae made a game of studying the quirks and mannerisms of people she encountered, winning kudos from her father for her on-target impressions. When guests visited, she'd zero in, watching them intently enough to be able to mimic them after they had left, "saying everything they'd said in the same voice" and aping their gestures. Destined to become one of the world's most imitated and impersonated women, she started out doing "travesty" impressions of others that spoofed as well as copied their subjects. Her send-up of W. C. Fields, in the final take of My Little Chickadee, preserves a sample of this craft; her wicked burlesque of Sarah Bernhardt—complete with rolled *r*'s and exaggerated postures—survives in the merry account of John Kobal.

On the strength of her evident flair, Tillie signed Mae up for dancing lessons with "Professor" Watts, who had a studio on Fulton Street, Brooklyn's bustling commercial thoroughfare. Watts promptly entered his nimble new charge, who was seven, in a Sunday-night amateur competition. Mae had sung and danced previously at church socials, but never before a paying audience or accompanied by an orchestra. The amateur contest would mark her true initiation as a trouper.

Battlin' Jack protested rushing her onto the boards while she still had her baby teeth, but Tillie's assurances quieted his doubts. Mae would do fine. She would not, Tillie insisted, suffer stagefright. And Tillie would stand beside her in the wings. She would literally push her onto the stage, when the moment came.

Clubby and community-minded, Brooklyn boasted almost as many fraternal benefit societies as it had churches: the Grand Order of Odd Fellows, Knights and Ladies of the Golden Star, the United Order of Druids, each donating prizes and patronage for youngsters who proved themselves worthy. This particular amateur night was sponsored by the Benevolent and Protective Order of Elks. The theater—the Royal, on Willoughby Street, near Fulton—was no great shakes, though large. It seated about seven hundred people. One vaudevillian characterized it as a "dingy spot," but Mae up-

graded it in her fond recollection to a well-appointed house with two balconies, boxes, and its own twelve-piece orchestra.

"Baby Mae—Song and Dance," outfitted in a pink-and-green satin dress
with gold spangles, a large white-lace picture hat with pink buds and pink
satin ribbons, pink kid slippers and pink stockings, waited, poised, in the
wings, as the orchestra oomphed her introduction. "The actor ahead of me
finished on the left side of the stage and my mother was waiting on the
right to push me on. But the 'spot' was way over on the other side. I
wouldn't budge. The orchestra played my introduction again and someone
yelled to the man with the spotlight. When I saw it comin' for me I ran
out to meet it."

The spot caught her display of pique, which charmed the audience into
laughter and applause, and she gamely launched into her song and dance,
never skipping a beat. Her cheeks flushed and the adrenaline pumped, producing a delicious rush of elation that she would later associate with erotic
arousal. "I fell in love on that stage," Mae remembered. The audience's
applause and the warm glow of the lights engulfed her, she would recall, in
an overwhelming embrace that felt "like the strongest man's arms around
me, like an ermine coat."

For her debut she sang "Movin' Day," a comic "coon" song that played
on the stereotype of the chicken-stealing black man, down on his luck,
while expropriating the infectious syncopated rhythms of ragtime. The
slangy lyric, told from the woman's point of view, closes in on a lady and
her honey as they are about to be put out on the snowy city street by their
landlord, who says he "wants ma rooms or else I wants my dough." Unless
they can pay up—

> It's movin' day.
> Pack your foldin' bed and get away,
> If you've spent every cent,
> You can live out in a tent,
> It's mooo-oo-oo-oo-ovin' day.

The comic effect got a boost from the incongruity between Mae's ultra-
feminine getup and her surprisingly masculine-sounding "female baritone"
voice. "I had a deep, rough voice for a child. The audience started laughing
when they heard my first powerful tones."

After the song, she executed a skirt dance that mingled the tiptoeing of ballet with the spirited kicks and swings of folk-style "clog." The crowd gave its ringing approval.

The debut at the Royal forecasted much that would become signature Mae West: the gritty city street scene and colloquial lingo put to comic effect, the easy appropriation of the black idiom, the stylized rhythmic movement, a costume that heightened her femininity, a tilt toward gender-bending, the sensual warmth of the lights and of the audience's embrace. Even her stubborn insistence on the proper spot cue anticipates her later fastidiousness about the details of production, especially lighting. "She would come off stage," director Herbert Kenwith recalls of a much later day, "saying, 'Herbert, lights number 1, 12, 13 and 26 need gels.' And she was absolutely correct."

What counted for the present, at the Royal the night of her debut, was that Baby Mae had scored a hit. Still glowing, she went home in triumph, clutching a first-prize gold medal to show off to the neighbors and relatives.

"Papa was proud," Mae knew. His misgivings about the hazards of the theatrical life don't seem to have counted for much or cut very deep. Within his family, a let-me-entertain-you precedent had been set by his niece Marie Ellmore, who as "Marie DeVere" strutted in chorus lines, acted in sketches, and posed with her sisters, their ankle-length tresses resplendent, in ads for Seven Sutherland Sisters Hair Tonic (Marie would later find employment as a sword swallower at Huber's Museum, Coney Island). And the world prizefighting Battlin' Jack inhabited often spilled over into show biz, when former champions exploited their fame by appearing in plays designed to showcase their pugilistic prowess: Bob Fitzsimmon as *The Honest Blacksmith*, John L. Sullivan as a blacksmith in *Honest Hearts and Willing Hands*, or Jim Corbett as *Gentleman Jack*, removing his top hat and kid gloves to face down a kidnap gang, his fists raised menacingly in a classic boxing stance. Fighters also turned up in Bowery joints like Harry Hill's, where boxing matches were featured entertainment, and in vaudeville, not always to deafening acclaim. The *New York Dramatic Mirror* pummeled "Philadelphia Jack" O'Brien's attempt to turn himself into a monologist: "He appeared in evening clothes, and related incidents which he said he had gathered as a prizefighter. He finished with a pathetic recitation, written by himself."

Mae's father settled for a supporting role. He built her a basement stage—white, with a white curtain—to practice on at home. He squired her to the theater in one of his rigs when she performed, lugging her makeup, costume, and dance shoes in a leather grip. When Mae balked onstage one night, at having to bend down to pick up coins the approving audience tossed her way, he dispatched two of his buddies and had them fill their derby hats with the offerings. One of his many jobs along the way was ticket taker at a theater.

Matilda, for her part, eagerly assumed the duties of stage mother, accompanying Mae to classes and contests, searching out the best teachers, carrying Baby's muff and scarf when they weren't needed, and eventually hand-picking her stage partners and manager. "Mother was always talkin' to me about bein' an actress. We went to all the shows and we talked about nothin' but what I was going to be." Neighbors were scandalized by Mrs. West's willingness to let her daughter wear makeup and to subordinate everything else to the stage. Matilda, too, wore makeup, and kept herself apart, appearing to "hold herself above others." She seems to have displaced onto Mae all her own frustrated hopes for a theatrical future.

Mae was stagestruck, to be sure, but both her parents invested heavily in her promise. When she arrived in Hollywood in the early thirties, Paramount's publicity department issued a hokum-filled studio biography that claimed "Miss West made her professional debut in her parents' vaudeville act." They came closer to striking the truth than they knew.

Not every wannabe star embarks with her parents' backing or prodding. Lillian Gish, born in Ohio the same year Mae came into the world, was taught from the cradle that acting was shameful. She and her sister "were billed as 'Baby Alice,' baby something . . . just so we could keep the name from being used and not disgrace the family." Cabaret singer Sophie Tucker, who, like Mae, started out as a "coon shouter," had to reckon with a mother convinced that being a wife, a mother, and a helpmate to her husband's career were all a woman needed. And a decade later, Brooklyn-born Clara Bow's deranged mother threatened her stage-struck daughter with violence, shouting, "You ain't gonna be no *hoor*."

"Don't Put Your Daughter on the Stage, Mrs. Worthington," warns a comic Noël Coward song, perpetuating a persistent, puritan-based suspicion that a woman who treads the boards must be a woman of no character. Protestant clergymen pointed to the stage as "the porch of pollution" and labeled performers "the very offal of society." Social leaders turned up their noses, relegating players to the low tier "somewhere between that of a gypsy fortune teller and a pickpocket." Suspect in part because they kept to themselves, show folk shared a free-and-easy subculture, rife, supposedly, with temptation and depravity. Actors, after all, trafficked in illusion and emotion, where carefully monitored ladies and gentlemen feared to tread. They lived out of trunks, kept irregular hours, paraded in wigs and makeup, donned tights that exhibited their bodies. Males and females dressed, re-hearsed, and traveled together; they consorted without scruple.

Even offstage, performers transgressed by calling attention to themselves. Actresses, complained the *New York Dramatic Mirror*, are known "by their saffron hair, painted eyes and eyebrows, flaring hats, gorgeous-hued gowns and other tokens of loudness." In other words, they looked like harlots. And they seemed to behave without a thought to what others might think. A young newcomer to the Daly touring company complained in her diary about some sister female troupers: "I don't see why they think they must be so loud just because they are on the stage, and so bold and free with the young men of the company, when they never met any of them before. We have actually heard some of them swear; they use awful slang, and their grammar—well it isn't there!"

A Texas preacher fulminated that celebrated leading ladies Sarah Bern-hardt, Lillie Langtry, and Lillian Russell "are but leaders in the vast army of fallen women." Girls brought into regular contact with actors, warned the protectionist Elbridge T. Gerry, could be expected to follow the path of sin. They "lose all modesty and become bold, forward, and impudent. When they arrive at the limit-age of the law, they have usually entered the downward path and end in low dance-houses, concert-saloons, and the early grave which is the inevitable conclusion of a life of debauchery."

In nineteenth-century America's early decades the link between acting and harlotry had signaled a more than metaphoric bond. Theaters reserved their third tiers for prostitutes and their clients; they were scorned as "lust palaces." Unescorted women entered via a separate door, so as to spare the sensibilities of respectable wives, daughters, mothers, and sisters. This prac-tice ended by the 1870s, but by that time actresses on the legitimate stage were often grouped with winking music-hall can-can dancers and soliciting waiter girls in concert saloons: rough, all-male enclaves dispensing liquor and sex for purchase, along with entertainment. At Volk's Garden, in New York's infamous Bowery, "actresses leaned out of the balconies between performances, exposing their breasts and urging men to come up and 'have some fun.' "

By the 1880s, New York concert saloons were losing ground to vaudeville theaters, which catered to mixed sex audiences, proscribed the sale of liquor except during intermissions, and censored blue material. Tony Pastor's the-ater on Fourteenth Street lured respectable women patrons by scheduling afternoon performances and giving away groceries, coal, dress patterns, and dishes as prizes. "He advertised clean shows that were first-rate entertainment." Rupert Hughes, reporting on the New York scene in 1904, seemed disheartened by the new epidemic of public decency. "Vaudeville theaters," he wrote, "have become family resorts, and the performances are . . . 'such as any young girl can take her mother to in safety.' The continuous performance lasts from two in the afternoon to ten-thirty at night . . . [since they appeal] to a variety of taste, ranging from the weary shoppers to the younger children, only the most inoffensive humor is permissible."

By 1900, performers were enjoying improved social status. Members of New York's elite society now sought them out, inviting the most celebrated of them to hobnob over teacups on Fifth Avenue. Entertainers who were successful enough to do so affected the opulent lifestyle of aristocratic swells, and through ostentatious display became "shills of the consumer culture." Leading men donned silk top hats, sported diamond stickpins, and carried gold-headed canes. Lillian Russell's admirer Diamond Jim Brady presented her with a gold-plated bicycle with mother-of-pearl handlebars and diamonds, sapphires, and rubies set in the spokes. She moved into a new home decorated by Duveen and photographed by Byron so that the public could partake in its splendors: a Louis XVI music room, a Marie Antoinette drawing room, a Turkish den. Her ample body was always "royally gowned." The less regal Eva Tanguay cavorted in one costume made entirely of sewn-together one-, five-, ten-, and fifty-dollar bills. Known for her lavishness, Tanguay earned three thousand dollars a week and spent a thousand dollars a month just on gloves and hose.

Even chorus girls who were paid eighteen dollars a week could trade up, exploiting their good looks and visibility to acquire the accoutrements of wealth and social status. Rich stage-door Johnnies proffered jewels, or hundred-dollar bills, imbedded in bouquets; they provided bottle-and-bird suppers at Rector's lobster palace, and equipped their favorites with private carriages, fur wraps, even townhouses. "I got a whole diamond necklace out of an oyster at Rector's," ran a popular gag line of the day.

The chorus girls in the sextette of *Florodora*, an English-import musical that opened in New York in 1900, became the toasts of the town. Paired with young men in gray frock coats and gray silk top hats who sang, "Tell me, pretty maiden, are there any more at home like you?," they answered in song as they promenaded in frilly pink walking costumes, black ostrich-plume hats, and parasols. Gay blades like Diamond Jim, Stanford White, and Freddie Gebhard attended nightly. All of the original six chorus girls in *Florodora* left the show to marry millionaires.

Newspapers boosted the celebrity status of actresses by using the newly developed cheap photoengraving process to adorn their theatrical pages with actress portraits, enclosed within decorative scrolls. Theater columns, especially in weekend editions, assumed places of prominence, and New York trade weeklies, the *Clipper* and the *Dramatic Mirror*, later supplanted by *Variety*, devoted themselves exclusively to news of the popular performing arts. The tabloid *Police Gazette* featured gossip of the Rialto and images of Footlight Favorites. Photographs of actresses like Lillie Langtry and Maude Adams could be purchased and collected; they adorned cigarette cards, cigar rings, and soap wrappers.

Responding to the hype surrounding theater people, Matilda West saw the stage as an avenue to success, which to her meant money, renown, and assimilation into the American mainstream. She signed Mae up for singing lessons and brought home sheet music for her to learn. She sought out a dancing teacher named Ned Wayburn, who opened a Times Square studio, charged one dollar an hour, and advertised: "Ned Wayburn's Training School for the Stage. Practical Instruction by the Most Successful Stage Director in the World. Stage-Dancing, Acting, Make-Up, Costuming. Classes for Adults and Children. Special Course for Vaudeville. Engagement Contracts Given All Graduates From $25. to $50. per week."

Wayburn, who would help Mae land her first Broadway role, became famous for grooming chorus girls known as "stepping ponies" for the *Ziegfeld Follies* and other revues. He drilled his chorines in perfectly timed ensemble work, and taught them to "make the fullest possible revelation of their physical charms." Male dancers in productions he staged tended to take subservient, supporting roles; it was the American *girl* he and Ziegfeld wanted to glorify. Credited with bringing both tap dancing and ragtime to the New York stage, he had learned ragtime's rhythms as a boy, from banjo players in Alabama, and once produced an all-female minstrel show, *Ned Wayburn's Minstrel Misses.*

When Mae wasn't rehearsing songs, lines, or steps she was dreaming of a glittering future: "I was always imagining my name up in lights. I would fall asleep at night seeing my name up there . . . I used to sit and practice my autograph for hours." She didn't mingle much with other children: "I was so carried away with myself, my dancing, my singing, that I didn't need other kids around." She did her best to ignore her sister Beverly, five years younger: "We never had much in common as children." Baby John was another story. She doted on him.

School took a back seat. Mae attended the local public school, but only when her schedule of dancing and singing classes and performances allowed—which, beyond third grade, amounted to hardly at all. "I hated school—I ducked more often than not," she would confess. A former classmate at P.S. 81 in Ridgewood, Queens, remembered the teacher sternly admonishing Mae on one of her rare days behind a classroom desk: "How do you expect to amount to anything if you don't come to school?"

Truant officers don't seem to have plagued her, but the Gerry Society, New York's Society for the Prevention of Cruelty to Children (which believed that applause "overstimulates the nervous system of the child"), sometimes did, providing Mae her first outings as an outlaw. Although children under sixteen were allowed to act children's dramatic parts, they could not sing or dance unless specifically licensed to do so. Buster Keaton, who toured in vaudeville with his family, sometimes had to pretend to be a midget to ward off Gerry Society hounds. Mae learned she must on occasion revise her act, excising songs and dances to rely entirely on her talking imitations. At times she had to shun New York City venues and seek theaters out of the city, where the law didn't apply. She readily falsified her age, which would become a habit.

Mae's dearth of formal schooling would become another of her closely guarded secrets and a source of private embarrassment. "She was terribly sensitive about her lack of education," a co-worker from the 1920s testified, and being in the presence of educated people pressed her defensive buttons. She fabricated stories about private tutors instructing her in French and German, but broached the truth when she said, "I speak two languages, English and Body." As soon as she could afford to, she would, as an adult, hire a secretary to correct her misspellings and weed out grammatical glitches that held less appeal in writing than in her gloriously unreconstructed speech: "I could have went and put this show on cheap, but I didn't." When, after she was established as a movie star, a professor and self-appointed chief of police for standard English proposed that a "speech dictator" be installed in Hollywood to foster proper usage among the masses, and take a broomstick to the "ain'ts" and dropped g's of types like Mae, she snappishly allowed as how she'd been "talkin' Brooklyn" for a long time and was being well paid for it, and was "gonna continue talkin' it."

Like other future headliners—Fanny Brice, Eddie Cantor—Mae used amateur contests as a springboard. She trotted out her well-rehearsed routines whenever she could compete for a prize. Waiting in the wings, she watched the trick bicyclists, the Irish and "Dutch" (German) comics, jugglers, whistlers, acrobats, dancing dogs, and song-and-dance men in straw hats. When the professional vaudevillians had completed their turns, there would be a chord of horn music, a role of the snare drum, and the audience would be invited to cheer and throw coins at hopeful newcomers: maybe a juggler, a buck-and-wing dancer, a blackface comic, a quartet of singing newsboys.

For her amateur outings, Mae never chose to sing the flowery sentimental storytelling sob ballads like "After the Ball" or "The Fatal Wedding," which were still popular in the first years of the new century. Her songs were up-tempo comic "novelties" that used dialect to establish a character and catchy rhythms—rather than singable tunes—to snag the listener. One such, "Mariutch Make-a the Hootch-a-ma-Kootch," told the tale of a nice Italian girl who winds up making "hootch-a-ma-kootch at Coney Island," suggestively swaying her hips "like-a this, like-a that." Mae's sister Beverly said, "Even as a little girl, Mae's character songs were risqué."

The summer Mae sang "Mariutch," 1907, the Brooklyn police raided midway booths at Coney Island, charging that the dancers were violating obscenity laws. Raids, shutdowns, public outcry over moral transgressions played a constant obbligato in Mae's years of growing up, as they would in her future career. As sexual expressiveness increased in commercial culture, as titillation and voyeuristic pleasure become staples in advertising and en-tertainment, so did strident cries of outrage and alarm. Incensed clergymen clamored to have Sunday closing laws invoked; progressive reformers added their voices, causing nickelodeons and vaudeville theaters to temporarily go dark in 1908. On the legitimate stage, Olga Nethersole got herself arrested for allowing herself to be kissed and carried aloft by her lover to an upstairs chamber in *Sapho* (sic); Shaw's play *Mrs. Warren's Profession*, which con-cerns a madam and her several disorderly houses, prompted the arrests of both the producer, Arnold Daly, and the leading lady, and inspired Shaw to label the outcries of vice crusader Anthony Comstock "Comstockery."

The furor over *Mrs. Warren's Profession* triggered a stampede to the box office. "So many came to the first performance that it was necessary to call out the reserves to dispel the crowd [of] disappointed prurients." No one could help noting that a well-publicized hue and cry over alleged immorality provided the kind of advertising producers and leading ladies dreamed about. After Richard Strauss's *Salome* was shut down at the Metropolitan Opera, a Salome dance craze ensued, and in some places the discarding of gauzy layers by a sinuous dancing temptress prompted arrests—several of which were staged by press agents to garner notice.

For her amateur outings, in addition to songs, Mae did imitations of per-formers she'd watched so many times she had them down cold, copycatting the fey clowning of Eddie Foy; the cocky, high-stepping, cane-twirling, big-city, Yankee Doodle impudence of George M. Cohan; the dizzy shouts and gyrations of Eva Tanguay; or the funny-sad lamentations of Bert Williams.

Williams, a mocha-skinned West Indian who sang, danced, and panto-mimed with his face darkened by burnt cork, was a comic genius who was able to break the color line and penetrate to mainstream white audiences—he became the first black recording artist and an acclaimed Broadway star—only at enormous cost to his integrity. Well-spoken and educated, he portrayed a type familiar to white audiences, a ragged, loose-limbed, shambling man with "discouraged shoulders," a loser dogged by bad luck and trouble. Mae learned his theme song, "Nobody," and took in the nuances of timing and gesture that worked to dramatize the doleful words.

Bert Williams completely captivated young Mae; he was her favorite comic. Knowing how much she idolized him, Battlin' Jack made Williams's acquaintance and invited him to the West home for dinner. For a white man to extend hospitality to a black man—even one as celebrated as Bert Williams—was no everyday occurrence in those racially polarized days, when blacks at the theater could sit only in the cheapest gallery seats and at hotels were restricted to the freight elevator. When Williams and his partner, George Walker, brought their all-black *In Dahomey* to Broadway, *The New York Times* reported incipient race war. After Williams joined the *Ziegfeld Follies* in 1910, the cast protested, threatening to strike. To his credit, Mae's father had no truck with bigotry. Renowned in the thirties for her path-breaking insistence on racially integrated casts, Mae clearly was shown the way by her father.

Introduced to Bert Williams before dinner, ten-year-old Mae screamed, "It's not! It's not!" and retreated in tears to her room. (This is the sole tearful outburst the preternaturally sunny Mae ever acknowledged in speaking of her childhood.) She hadn't recognized him without his black-face makeup. Williams, according to Mae, calmed her down when he "stood outside my door and started to sing," which convinced her of his authenticity. She emerged from her room and they all sat down to dinner.

Matilda followed with avid attention the progress of one of the most daring and flamboyant of vaudeville and musical comedy headliners, Eva Tanguay. "Mother took me to see Eva Tanguay again and again and told me I could be important like that." Ardent fanship resulted in friendship between the star and Mrs. West. Tanguay told Louella Parsons in Holly-wood, decades later, that she had known and liked Mae's mother: "I used to visit her and continued to be close to the family up to the time Mrs. West died."

Described variously as the "I Don't Care Girl," the "Cyclonic Comedienne," "Evangelist of Joy," and "Queen of Perpetual Motion," Tanguay thumbed her nose at pious killjoy managers, making her tousled-hair abandon, riotous dancing at a feverish pace, flamboyant costumes, and explosive, shouting delivery of provocative songs like "I Don't Care," "Go as Far as You Like" and "I Want Some One to Go Wild with Me" pay off in box-office bonanzas. Her byword was energy. She was never silent, never still. "She screams, she shouts, she twists and turns, she is a mad woman," one critic wrote, "a whirling dervish of grotesquerie."

Tanguay promoted herself tirelessly, taking out huge ads in *Variety* to answer critics and contriving stunts, such as hiring a trained elephant to stand with her on street corners, to catch the public eye. She called a press conference to display her new Salome costume but, when a gaggle of reporters had gathered round, opened her fist to display two pearls. One Tanguay publicity stunt that would find an echo in Mae's subsequent career involved posing at Bostock's animal exhibit at Coney Island's Dreamland with a cub lion and then entering a den of tigers.

All the entertainers Mae chose to impersonate stood out not as actors but as "personalities," creators of vivid, exaggerated, and highly individual stage personas that bordered on caricature and blurred distinctions between on- and offstage roles. Instead of submerging their identities to become Hamlet or Hedda Gabler, each forged a stylized, larger-than-life self, developing a signature speech, bearing, or prop, and putting together routines that telegraphed news about that self. As "personalities," they shone with a special luminosity, what Mae called "the glitter that sends your little gleam across the footlights." According to Mae, no one could teach you personality. You either had it or you didn't, and it originated in your individual thoughts, feelings, and personal style. "You can sing like Flagstad or dance like Pavlova or act like Bernhardt, but if you haven't personality you will never be a real star."

Her impressions of Bert Williams and Eddie Foy at one amateur outing happened to be witnessed by Hal Clarendon, an actor and manager who was forming his own Brooklyn-based stock company at the Gotham Theatre. After seeing Mae cop another prize, he came backstage to offer her, if her father consented, a place in his company, which would be needing someone for child roles. Clarendon, a well-established stock-company regular, was a veteran of the Brooklyn-based Spooner Company, where he had played two hundred different roles, and had also taken minor roles on Broadway.

Mae's parents couldn't quarrel with Clarendon's terms. As a pro, Mae would begin at eighteen dollars a week. Since the average working-class family earned fifteen dollars a week at the time in New York, this was nothing to sneeze at. Mae never spoke of the money she earned as part of the lure of the stage, but it's hard to believe her salary didn't factor in. In the twenties, she spoke of her satisfaction in being able to provide her mother with luxuries she otherwise would have lacked. Only after her spectacular successes on the screen, she told a reporter in Hollywood, did she begin to feel "anything like secure" financially. "My folks made a lot of sacrifices for me when I was a kid . . . I had obligations as long as my mother and dad were alive."

A major "show town," Brooklyn in the early years of this century supported five resident stock companies, where the top ticket price was fifty cents, as well as large houses like the Amphion, where touring headliners could pull in 2,000 spectators a night. The *New York Dramatic Mirror* for March 30, 1907—a day picked at random—lists for Brooklyn a lecture on Shakespeare, a mounting of *Julius Caesar*, and nine other productions, ranging from George M. Cohan's *Little Johnny Jones*, about an American jockey falsely accused of throwing the English Derby, to the melodrama *Parted on Her Bridal Tour* and the more lurid *Queen of the White Slaves*; not to mention half a dozen vaudeville houses and four burlesque joints, which offered bawdy comic entertainment for male audiences and generous displays of female flesh. At a theater called the Star, John L. Sullivan headlined, backed by the Blue Ribbon Girls Burlesque.

Clarendon's stock company, formed in 1907, was outranked by two other Brooklyn stalwarts—the Corse Payton Company at the Lee Avenue Theatre and the Spooner Stock Company at the Park, both of which rated far more press coverage. Mae sometimes appeared with each of these more recognized troupes and their touring satellites, although at Spooner Stock she met major competition for child roles from Cecil Spooner, the founder's daughter.

She couldn't have joined the Clarendon troupe until after she had turned thirteen, since it didn't exist before then, but she remembered otherwise, recalling for John Kobal that by age twelve "I had gotten too mature for children's parts, so I went back to living at home . . . till I was sixteen, when I could get a work permit and go back on the stage."

At the cheaper neighborhood theaters like the Gotham, hushed decorum did not prevail. Boy sopranos sang as they passed glasses of water between acts or sold sheet music a music publisher had hired them to plug. "Matinee girls" presented gifts to the favorite leading men—fudge, pencils, shoelaces, even diamond-studded shoelace snaps. Gallery "gods" hurled jeers, spitballs, and rotten fruit at the heavies, whistling while the orchestra played the chorus and stamping their feet when they approved. At the Lee Avenue Theatre, Hal Clarendon was so roundly hissed as the villain in *Hearts Aflame* that a policeman had to be hired to keep order in the gallery. At the Gotham one night, during a performance of *The Silver King*, police ejected two "unruly" boys for shouting "Fire" during a dark scene and causing a panic in the theater. FOOL BOYS START PANIC IN THEATER ran the headline in the *New York Telegraph*. No fire materialized, but half a dozen women and children were scratched and bruised and "many were on the verge of hysteria." To re-establish calm, the orchestra started to play "Waltz Me Around Again, Willie."

With Clarendon, Mae became a journeyman in stagecraft who grew savvy about audience reaction, blocking, pacing, and interactions with other play-ers. "I played . . . the moonshiner's daughter in grim dramas of the Kentucky hills. I stopped the express train with an oil lamp when the bridge was washed out. I was the poor little white slave in Chinatown." She was Lovey Mary in *Mrs. Wiggs of the Cabbage Patch* and Little Mother in *The Fatal Wedding*, Little Nell in an adaptation of Dickens's *The Old Curiosity Shop*. "No actress ever had a better school."

She worked hard, but wasn't above invading Clarendon's dressing room once when he was sleeping and using greasepaint in assorted colors to pro-vide him with a beard, mustache, and red nose.

A new role had to be learned every week, and between shows Mae was forever studying and memorizing her lines, which she did by hearing them rather than reading them. "They used to tell me the lines, and I'd say 'em over. I was always doin' something while I said them—hangin' over the arm of the chair or something." Alexander Walker speculates that the way she later handled dialogue—lingering over the rhythms of her lines and dividing long words into syllables like "fas-cin-at-in' "—might owe some-thing to her old habit of breaking down a line her mother was helping her commit to memory.

Mae played boy parts as readily as girl roles—the prince in *Richard III*; Cedric, who becomes Little Lord Fauntleroy and dons velvet knickerbockers and a white lace collar; Little Willie in *East Lynne*, wringing hearts by dying in the arms of his repentant disguised mother as he affirms, "It is nothing to die when our Saviour loves us." Often cast as the angelic innocent, as Mary in *Ten Nights in a Bar-room* she tugged the coattails of her inebriated father, begging in song:

> *Father, dear father, come home with me now;*
> *The clock in the steeple strikes one*
> *You said you were coming home from the shop*
> *As soon as your day's work was done.*

before she dies piteously, struck down by a misdirected whiskey tumbler sent flying through the murky air at Slade's saloon.

Dying piteously was a specialty. The last scene of *Uncle Tom's Cabin* lifted her little Eva into heaven, a golden halo encircling her curls; in a white robe, she sat astride a milk-white dove.

Melodramas, sometimes called "mellers," fleshed out a family-centered sphere of neatly polarized moral extremes: dastardly villains and saintlike, long-suffering heroines whose goodness will ultimately shine through and meet its just reward. Children, wise and pure, were usually presented in peril—orphaned, enfeebled, abused, or neglected. A fallen woman could win sympathy only when she demonstrated remorse and endured the retribution of degradation and decline.

Mae would eventually turn this moral universe upside down, making a heroine of the fallen woman and a heavy of the goody-goody. But she retained the binary vision of melodrama, locking herself into a mindset which labels women either "good" or "bad," either "angel" or "devil," Snow White or Scarlet Woman.

She also would draw on melodrama's love of sensation—hair-trigger escapes, thundering storms, hidden daggers, concealed identities, nefarious schemes, sudden reversals of fortune and attitude—when she came to write plays and filmscripts. Margy, in *Sex*, recalls melodrama's unmotivated transformations when she suddenly reforms at the end of the play and selflessly renounces her "clean" and wealthy true love because her wicked past would besmirch him. Diamond Lil offers a melodramatic flourish when she covers the dead body of Rita by letting down the corpse's hair and calmly combing it as the police break in. So does the scene in the unproduced *Frisco Kate* that traps the heroine in the evil captain's cabin as the boat springs a leak. Ace Lamont in *Belle of the Nineties* reprises melodramatic villainy when he prepares to set fire to Sensation House, imprisoning his former love in a closet so that she will be engulfed by flames.

In stock, Mae appeared in literary European plays—English drawing-room dramas, French farces bowdlerized for Brooklyn audiences, and Shakespeare, which Clarendon called "high class royalty plays"—but didn't take to any of it. Shakespeare's "thees" and "thous" seemed high-toned and artificial, and the tragedies licensed actors to ham it up, "wave daggers and chew out the big scenes in the style of a man fighting off a beehive." She favored a natural style and was given license to alter a line or word that felt awkward. From the start, Mae shied from the highfalutin and gravitated toward popular vehicles in the vernacular idiom, with broadly democratic appeal. She once told a columnist she was working on a comedy version of *Macbeth* and was planning, for the role of Lady Macbeth, to "spice up the old girl, loosen her up."

Mae earned her stripes as an actress in stock just as melodrama was losing its hold. Movie theaters were cropping up in neighborhoods all over. The tide in American popular theater was shifting: audiences wanted stars in lavishly mounted hits; they wanted variety, and they wanted comedy. Local managers like Hal Clarendon couldn't compete with powerful theatrical magnates like Marc Klaw, A. L. Erlanger, and Charles Frohman, who, joining a trend toward centralization and consolidation, formed a theatrical syndicate that hogged most of the entertainment pie, or the syndicate's up-and-coming archrivals, the Shubert brothers.

The Gotham Theatre, like so many others once dedicated to the repertory system, which used a permanent company and a home theater to showcase ever-changing productions, converted to vaudeville. Even when it housed the Clarendon stock company, vaudeville intruded at Gotham shows when variety acts—such as Mae impersonating Eva Tanguay—were slipped in during the intermissions.

Baby Mae put her angel wings in mothballs. She had gotten too big for child roles anyhow. At sixteen, she would be able to get a work permit and leave home, perhaps as a soubrette on the stage or in vaudeville as a singing and dancing comedienne. Meanwhile, she was discovering boys.

[3]

"I LOVE IT"

*A*T age nine Mae got her first lesson in sex, not from a person but from a book—some kind of medical text—she found at the home of a friend who was a doctor's daughter. "After I read it I had a funny feeling about my parents . . . disgust, you might say."

The queasiness soon evaporated, giving way first to a lively curiosity, then to an unblushing hypersexuality that rarely confused love and lust, and put a high premium on variety. Instead of feeling ashamed of her body, she reveled in it, exhibitionistically inviting others to share her delight. "She'd drop her clothes at the drop of a hat," Hollywood photographer George Hurrell attested. Maria Riva, the daughter of Marlene Dietrich, recalled her in a Paramount dressing room, in the early thirties, nonchalantly lifting one alabaster breast out of its whalebone corset. Stephen Longstreet, ghostwriter of *Goodness Had Nothing to Do with It*, reports that on his first day at work Mae greeted him in her Ravenswood apartment in a negligee. Indicating her chest, she invited him to "feel these, they're hard as rocks."

Mae claimed she escaped completely the puritan association of sex with sin and guilt. "Sex is no more vulgar than eating," she would say, "vulgar only to vulgar people. Why is it necessary to weep or gnash teeth over the processes of nature?" She credited her mother's permissiveness as the liberating agent. "My mother thought I was the greatest thing on earth and she liked me to play with the boys." The more special and unique she made Mae feel, the more Mae exempted herself from religious or social constraints that keep other people from doing exactly as they please.

Matilda shared in the Bavarian pleasure ethic, a relaxed *gemütlich* enjoyment of living that smiled on beer drinking, hearty sauerkraut-drenched dinners, music making, and mixed-sex conviviality—when it followed, rather than displaced, the day's pursuit of money or success. Lots of boyfriends for Mae threatened her ambitions far less than her pairing off as half of a steady couple. The message she conveyed to her favorite daughter was *Feel free, enjoy yourself, but keep it a sideline.* She encouraged Mae's sensuality, so long as it didn't impede her competition for the golden ring of stardom— never to be mistaken or exchanged for a wedding band.

At the cusp of adolescence Mae awakened to a taste for male company that went along with a competitive frostiness to friends of her own sex and age. She stated many times that she had no taste for female friends, and she for the most part held to that stance. Paramount costume designer Edith Head, one of the few exceptions Mae made to this rule, said it surprised her when Mae took to her, "because she really didn't like women." As Mae put it, "I always went with the boys. Girls seemed a foolish investment of my time." Rona Barrett, who knew the mature Mae well, believes that because of Mae's experiences with a demanding mother and dependent sister, Mae considered women excessively needy—a partial explanation of her distancing.

Male gallantries and favors in deference to her sex pleased her no end: "Boys could hold me up as I skated or assist me down from trolleys or wipe off park benches with their caps." Eager for proof that the strong sex *was* physically stronger, she'd ask to feel boys' biceps—the brawnier the better. They called her "Peaches," in homage to her fine complexion, a name she would recycle for her character in *Every Day's a Holiday*.

From day one, she accepted male chivalries and tributes in the form of gifts as her due, but fought the double standard that gave boys the upper hand in matters sexual, granting them the exclusive right to experiment, take the initiative, and play the field, while restricting girls to the role of passive receptor. "I was liberated," Mae said, "before anybody even used the word. I thought to myself, 'If boys can do it, why can't I?'" "Even as a child it struck me as odd that a man could go out, have his fun, and be thought of as a regular guy, but the girl he had fun with was called a tramp." The single standard to her meant, not continence for both sexes, as most reformers proposed, but all for fun and fun for all.

The double standard was undergoing attack in the wider world from feminists and progressive social-hygiene advocates who were convinced that white-slave traders were luring young women into prostitution against their will, concerned about the acceptance of prostitution as a sexual outlet for men, and alarmed about the risks of venereal disease. If men were going to shun prostitutes, reformers thought, their sexual needs were going to have to find release among "decent" women—wives and girlfriends.

The purity campaign launched in many cities around 1910 targeted "immoral" working-class women and immigrants, but the hue and cry inadvertently encouraged all women to express their sexuality and helped break down reticence about sex. Magazines began publishing articles on birth control, divorce, "the social evil," and changing sexual mores. Words like "prostitution," previously excluded from polite discourse, became common coin.

Freud, who came to lecture at Clark University in 1909, helped raise American consciousness about sex, although his views were less well known in prewar America than those of Havelock Ellis, whose *Man and Woman* went through multiple American editions and who extolled sex as "the chief and central function of life." Anarchist Emma Goldman also fostered a new permissiveness; she toured the country, lecturing on such subjects as "The Limitation of Offspring" and "Is Man a Varietist or a Monogamist?" She challenged feminists who advocated chastity, insisting that liberated women faced more danger from too little sexual experience than they did from too much.

Nickel movies were also undermining hush-hush attitudes by offering suggestive films, rife with sexual innuendo, images of half-dressed women, and passionate embraces. "For the first time in the history of the world it is possible to see what a kiss looks like," the New York *Evening World* commented. "What the camera did not see did not exist." Lurid titles like *White Slaves* and *Traffic in Souls* sounded an alarm while cashing in. In 1900 there had been fifty nickelodeons in New York City; by 1908 there were more than five hundred, all of which were briefly closed down that year shortly after the release around Christmas of a film that graphically re-enacted the notorious outcome of Stanford White's love affair with showgirl Evelyn Nesbit: his murder by Harry Thaw.

On Broadway, playwrights took new liberties. Several people in an opening-night audience fainted in shock at the profanity uttered by a stage dope fiend in Clyde Fitch's *The City* (1909) who shot his wife as he exclaimed, "You're a God damn liar." The same year, David Belasco's production of *The Easiest Way* presented a heroine accused by her fiancé of being "not immoral . . . just unmoral," a new kind of distinction. Instead of repenting, as she would have in an old-fashioned melodrama, she parts company with him, promising to live to the hilt: "I'm going to Rector's to make a hit, and to hell with the rest."

Mae remembered this play. And she borrowed a leaf from singers of double-entendre songs whose lyrics pulled in two directions, one polite and the other risqué. English music-hall stars like Alice Lloyd and Vesta Victoria made these hugely popular in America, performing songs like "Stockings on the Line," "Who You Looking At?," and "You Can Do a Lot of Things at the Seaside."

Pubescent Mae relished and sought out occasions that allowed her to be the only female in an otherwise all-male party. "Evenings the gang would gather at somebody's house, the six boys and I, with perhaps another girl. We'd sit close together, sing, talk and enjoy ourselves. This included catch-as-catch-can kissing. I was quite impartial. I liked all the boys." It also included sex play. "I'd play with their—umm, *you* know."

Her father, working at this time as a watchman on night patrol, was away from home during these parlor sessions and knew nothing about them until he was tipped off by a tattletale niece. He flew into a rage, but was eventually quieted by Matilda's gentle insistence that no harm had been done, Mae should be left alone. "Oh, let her go, Mae's different. She isn't like other girls." In Mae's play *The Hussy*, when the father complains that their daughter's carryings-on are bringing disgrace to the family name and inciting gossip, the mother intercedes, "People are always talking about this one or that one."

Matilda ran interference, protecting Mae when she could from neighborhood busybodies and family finger pointers, but there was a trade-off: Matilda had to sit at the controls. Mae had a free hand as long as she didn't get too attached to a particular fellow. "But when one of 'em began to interest me too much—I could tell by my mother's face . . . I could see if she was hurt. I couldn't stand to see her worried."

Matilda registered disapproval both by signaling her own distress and by finding fault with the object of Mae's affections. "She would point out some little flaw he had, like big ears that stuck out."

The freedom Mae enjoyed to entice and experiment with many boys, untroubled by guilt, did not, oddly enough, extend to permission to talk about it. Although she would eventually take credit for relaxing American gag rules and opening up closed bedroom doors, she somewhat inconsistently maintained for herself a ladylike reticence, which her upbringing insisted on. "I never used bad language, and I never liked to listen to dirty stories. We . . . were very proper people." Sex was an embarrassing subject, unmentionable at home, she reported, and she never ever discussed it with her sister, even when as adults they were living under the same roof. She remained, according to Karl Fleming, "careful to an almost Victorian degree about the words she chose to describe the most earthy functions." Her ability to suggest, without explicitly stating, would serve her well in the future, becoming a hallmark of her comic art.

Mae's first steady beau, Joe Schenck, a pianist and singer who would became well known as half of the harmonizing vaudeville team called Van and Schenck, was the trolley-conductor son of a nurse who came to the West home to attend Mae's brother, John, when he had pneumonia. Handsome, blue-eyed, and nineteen, he took fifteen-year-old Mae for rides in his Model T Ford, sent her flowers, and brought his band over for Saturday-night ragtime sessions, where they rehearsed instrumental numbers like Scott Joplin's classic "Maple Leaf Rag." Mae joined in with vocals, singing "Beautiful Ohio" or "Marie from Sunny Italy," the first song published by Irving Berlin.

Joe Schenck was soon displaced by Otto North, a light-heavyweight prize-fighter who belonged to a gang, the Eagles' Nest. When a member of a rival gang, the Red Hooks, made a pass at Mae during a date at Coney Island, a vicious gang fight in which rocks were hurled and clubs wielded erupted near her home the next night. Battlin' Jack joined the fray and got himself bloodied. Mae couldn't have liked it more. Triggering a testosterone war was her idea of fun.

Mae first experienced orgasm, she later said, in a dream featuring a huge, furry brown-black bear who entered her bedroom and then her body. She gave contradictory accounts of her first *human* lover, telling Karl Fleming she had lost her virginity at age thirteen, before she started menstruating, when an actor, about twenty-one years old, walked her home after an amateur show and made love to her on the stairs in the vestibule of her house, with her fur coat wrapped around her; subsequently, she told Fleming, she slept not only with Joe Schenck but with his trumpet player and drummer as well. But in other interviews she said the affair with Joe Schenck "wasn't a *sex* love affair" and that she postponed intimate sex until after she married Frank Wallace in 1911. Karl Fleming remains dubious about the story she gave him. "It didn't wash," he says. "She was a complete invention of herself."

In her mid-teens, Mae's stage appearances became scattered and irregular. She appeared briefly with an acrobatic act, sang in Sunday concerts for groups like the Knights of Columbus, and toured the smallest of small-time vaudeville theaters around New York as a sun-bonneted and lace-bloomered Sis Hopkins type, a farm girl matched with a hayseed Huck Finn type, played by Willie Hogan in a red wig, with blacked-out front teeth. A New

York theatrical manager who claimed he booked "Hogan and West" described it as a "Bowery act," defining it by the neighborhood of cheap theaters, saloons, dance halls, dime museums, penny arcades, and gambling dens in lower Manhattan that provided venues. Her mother or an aunt chaperoned these Bowery outings, as one of them always had her stage appearances in past years.

Matilda, who so greatly admired Eva Tanguay, also allowed Mae to try out provocative adult fare: a fan dance that made the young men in the audience stamp their feet and yell for more. "The fan was big and red and she shook her bare body behind it. Her body was simply saturated with powder. When she shook herself, the powder would fly all over the stage, down onto us in the front rows."

Mae always denied that she'd ever appeared in burlesque, which catered to male audiences who counted on generous displays of female flesh along with comedy, and which after the twenties meant déclassé striptease. Perhaps she did do the fan dance, as she reported to Ruth Biery, as a vaudeville headliner paid a salary of $115 a week. More likely it was a burlesque house. Without question, when she eloped with her song-and-dance partner, Frank Wallace, in 1911, they were playing at the Big Gaiety Theater in Milwaukee, part of the Columbia Amusement Company, the Eastern burlesque wheel run by Henry Jacobs and John Jermon.

Frank Wallace, a dark-haired, wiry acrobatic dancer and a less handsome Gene Kelly look-alike whose real name was Frank Szatkus and whose father was a Lithuanian tailor in Queens, had shared the bill with Hogan and West in Brooklyn at Canarsie's Waldo Casino. According to Wallace, it was Matilda, not Mae, who suggested he team up with Mae as a "double." "A swell looking woman came around back stage and told me she had a daughter who was a comer. She had seen my act, she said, and thought I could help her kid. Well, she brought the kid in, and I want to tell you she was one classy little dame. The brunette youngster was Miss West.

"Mae was a sweet little kid . . . about sixteen. I took her mother up and we went into rehearsal—in the cellar of her Bushwick Avenue house." Sometimes Frank would be invited to stay for a dinner, cooked by Matilda, of pigs' knuckles and sauerkraut. "After a few weeks' rehearsal, we went on the Fox circuit. Later we signed with Jacobs and Jermon, the burlesque producers."

Mae was credited by Frank Wallace's mother, Mrs. Anna Szatkus, with looking out for her. Mae would tell Frank, "Here, now, you stop playing cards all the time and save a little money and bring it to your ma." She would take five dollars out of his pay envelope and bring it to his mother now and then.

At the time Mae West and Frank Wallace put their act together, the quickening pace and restlessness of city life were infusing popular culture. Critics lauded vaudeville acts that had "zip," "go," and "rush." Ragtime, known as "feet-moving music," had completed its transition from red-light districts to the urban mainstream and was at its commercial zenith as the American dance craze gathered steam. "The public of the nineties had asked for tunes to sing. The public of the turn of the century had been content to whistle. But the public from 1910 on demanded tunes to dance to." Broadway lobster palaces and restaurants like Rector's, Bustanoby's, and Reisenweber's would soon begin moving out tables to make room for dancing. " 'Rag' strains will empty the tables for the glazed floor," *Variety* reported, "while the well known two-step or waltz air receives little attention . . . Not to dance a 'rag' is to be distinctly out of it." Tin Pan Alley obliged with syncopated songs with snappy, colloquial lyrics and a marchlike beat, like "When Ragtime Rosie Ragged the Rosary," "Yiddle on Your Fiddle Play Some Ragtime," "Alexander's Ragtime Band," and "Everybody's Doin' It."

"It," intentionally ambiguous, could be taken to mean more than one thing, but the official definition of what everybody was doing was ragtime dancing. "I Love It," one of the songs Mae West and Frank Wallace rehearsed for their act, insists via short, jerky, rhyme-rich phrases that the finger-snapping ragtime beat can't be resisted; it *forces you* to move:

> Ain't that some band? That rag is grand,
> I could keep on glidin' till I drop.
> Law, oh pshaw, they're goin' to stop,
> Tell all the boys to make a noise,
> Make 'em play it some more . . .
> Go on and rag it, drag it . . .

When singing ragtime, West and Wallace consciously imitated black performers: "It was the black man's sound and we copied it because it was the greatest." After they sang, they demonstrated the song's swaying power, sliding, shuffling, and stepping in a "sultry, passionate and so smooth" style that brought them bookings in Brooklyn, New Jersey, and Philadelphia.

Much to the distress of churchmen, social reformers, and uplifters alarmed about the shedding of inhibitions and the erosion of formality, the new dances licensed couples to snuggle daringly close—a departure from past practices in social dancing, which had kept partners separated by several inches, the woman's left hand on the man's shoulder and her right hand extended out from her body. If you did the new Grizzly Bear, you imitated a bear hug, holding your partner with both arms, "close to your baby." Mae's number "Honey Man" invites the man who calls her "cutey, sweety, Oh, You Kid" to hold her tight: "And when that man does kiss/I shake with bliss." In a year or two, as a sheet-music cover girl, she'll issue invitations to "Smooch Around" and "Cuddle Up and Cling to Me."

To make like an animal and abandon yourself to the wild seemed exciting and glamorous. Readers of Elinor Glyn's novel *Three Weeks* encountered unmarried lovers dallying on a tigerskin rug. At the *Ziegfeld Follies* Sophie Tucker, soon after Teddy Roosevelt returned from an African hunting trip, sang "Moving Day in Jungle Town," surrounded by big game and outfitted in a leopardskin—an idea Mae reprised a few years later when she posed as "the Cave Girl" and sang "I learned to dance/When I saw the tiger prance" in a similar getup. If dancers tired of the Grizzly Bear they could attempt the Turkey Trot, the Bunny Hug, the Chicken Scratch, or the Kangaroo Dip. The New York *Sun* editorialized that these animal dances constituted "a reversion to the grossest practices of savage man. They are based on the primitive motive of the orgies enjoyed by the aboriginal inhabitants of every uncivilized land."

When Mae West and Frank Wallace signed on, early in 1911, with Jacobs and Jermon to tour on the Columbia burlesque circuit, the Eastern wheel was undergoing one of its periodic self-cleansings, playing down the girlie-show format in favor of "book" shows that rivaled traveling musical comedy combinations. "A Florida Enchantment," part of the Big Gaiety lineup, resembled a revue more than a book musical. It was a loose-jointed assemblage of sketches (one about two woman haters who turn into skirt chasers, another prophetically called "Fun in Jail"), songs (Shelton Brooks's "Some of These Days," which became Sophie Tucker's theme song was here sung by Barry Melton), and recitations (Eddie Lovett intoning "The Girl of My Dreams," as chorus girls travestied first Ethel Barrymore, then high-kicking Bessie McCoy), animated by a chorus line whose "clothes look ever so much better than the girls in them."

Variety knocked "A Florida Enchantment" as "pretty bad," and suggested that the ushers and orchestra be put on double salary for having to sit through the Big Gaiety show twice daily. But "Sime," the reviewer (who was *Variety's* founding editor, Sime Silverman), singled out "May" West, in an olio turn with "Fred" Wallace, as "the only likely looking one" among the women. "Miss West may develop," he predicted, but she didn't need to wear those tights; she *did* need a course in enunciation. "Of the songs sung by her and Mr. Wallace, no words were distinguishable." Her partner, "Fred," rated no mention at all, except to say that when he joined in "The Draggy Rag" he and Mae "draw pretty close to the line"—of good taste, presumably.

Mae's tour with the Columbia wheel marked her first long separation from her ever-watchful mother. She celebrated by getting married in Milwaukee, on the morning of April 11, 1911.

What she wanted to do with Frank Wallace was sleep with him, not marry him: "I told him, 'There's just this physical thing between us.'" But an older woman on the bill with them, a singer named Etta Woods, whose comic tag line was "I drink my sandwich and eat my beer," persuaded Mae she might get pregnant and shouldn't put herself at risk. "Something may happen to you one of these days, and you won't be married, and then what will your parents think?" Mae maintained she was tricked into marrying. "I did it because I was scared . . . Getting pregnant was a great disgrace in those days. I had a very beautiful close relationship with my mother and I never wanted to do anything to hurt her."

She took pains to avoid getting pregnant, several years before Margaret Sanger coined the term "birth control." She chose a venerable method, in use among ancient Jews several thousand years before the birth of Christ and still being suggested at American birth-control clinics as late as 1930: a "little silk sponge with a string on it. You wet the sponge in warm water and then put it in and it worked fine—you just pulled it out and washed it." Condoms were a later favorite. (From her twenties on she seems to have taken care to avoid contracting VD, though it's hard to believe someone as sexually active as she totally escaped it. As a mature woman she liked her prospective lovers to be tested for VD. One of them reportedly assumed, when she asked him to be tested, that she meant a screen test.)

Mae insisted that the marriage be kept a secret; disclosure would have dire consequences, she felt certain, for both her family and her career. Managers, she worried, would steer clear of a married actress, on the theory that audiences liked to think of temptresses as available. Her mother had harped on this, using it to bolster her own fear of having to relinquish authority where Mae's career was concerned. She never learned the truth, and Mae would have carried her secret with her to the grave if a worker in the office of Milwaukee's County Register of Deeds hadn't discovered the marriage license (which gives her age as eighteen, the age of consent in Wisconsin—a year older than she actually was—and occupation "actress") in May 1935.

She and twenty-one-year-old Wallace never co-habited; they stayed together only a few months, the length of their tour in "A Florida Enchantment," and even during that time Mae tormented Wallace—who truly cared for her—by stepping out on him, staying out late with various men she met in the towns they passed through. After the tour, she encouraged him to join a different road company, and she returned to her parents' home in Brooklyn. Wallace claimed she wrote him letters addressed "My dear husband" and signed "Your little Mae." The Wests were not a family of letter writers, but when they did write they addressed each other in a florid, nineteenth-century style. Mae's brother, John, addressed their sister Beverly in writing as "My Darling Sister Beverly."

Neither partnership nor monogamy suited Mae ("I was born to be a solo performer, on and off stage"), and she never promised Wallace she would be his alone, she said. The notion of an all-surrendering love held no appeal: "I saw what it did to other people when they loved another person the way I loved myself, and I didn't want that problem." Rona Barrett theorizes that the inability to commit had its origins in emotional pain inflicted very early, probably by her father. "Mae's heart was broken very early on" and she could not afford to have it broken again.

Nor did she ever want children, since she feared motherhood would change her mind, body, and outlook. Being a mother was a career in itself. A married woman who had children couldn't be a sex symbol; men sensed she was unavailable.

Although she quipped that no family should be without a marriage, she made the institution the butt of many jokes, usually equating wifedom with drab domestic servility. "I'm not the cottage apron type," she'd say. "Marriage is a great institution, but who wants to be in an institution?" Margy, her character in *Sex*, refuses to sew buttons on the pimp Rocky's shirt: "What do you think I am, your wife? . . . If there's any waiting on around here, I'm the one that's going to get it." When the Chump in *I'm No Angel* says to Tira, "I don't suppose you believe in marriage," she answers witheringly, "Only as a last resort."

Performed in haste and repented at leisure, the marital misadventure served only one good end, as far as Mae could tell: it prevented her from marrying anyone else.

4

"PRESIDENT OF THE FEMALE 'NUT' CLUB"

*T*HE theater that introduced Mae West to Broadway, the Folies Bergère, owed its existence to the notion that Europe, and Paris in particular, held the patent on sophisticated nightlife, and that New Yorkers out on the town were ready—on home turf—for lavishly mounted cosmopolitan revues, featuring lovely pseudo-Continental chorines in various states of undress. An Anglo-American woman, the thinking went, promised no particular allure. Mary, in the George M. Cohan song "Mary's a Grand Old Name," has honesty and a no-frills plainness going for her, but it's pretty Marie, a dissembling coquette with dyed hair, who breaks men's hearts.

Florenz Ziegfeld, Jr., helped set the Gallic trend in motion with his wildly successful *Follies,* staged on the rooftop garden of the New York Theatre, which he converted to a Parisian-style café and named Jardin de Paris. Ziegfeld's private tutoring in French came via his Parisian wife, Anna Held, a bosomy, wasp-waisted music-hall beauty renowned for taking milk baths and fluttering thick lashes as she warbled, in fetching Frenchified English, "I Just Can't Make My Eyes Behave."

Jesse L. Lasky, a vaudeville producer who would become a founder of Paramount Pictures, followed Ziegfeld's lead. He decided to build in the Times Square area, which since the advent of the subway in 1904 had burgeoned as New York's entertainment hub. "The Times Square section of New York is seemingly show-mad," *Variety* reported. "There are eleven theaters in course of erection or proposed between 42nd and 49th streets." He selected a site on Forty-sixth Street, west of Broadway, across the street from Charles Dillingham's Globe and adjacent to the Gaiety, managed by George M. Cohan and his partner.

At Lasky's Folies Bergère, a restaurant as well as a cabaret that offered two completely different shows nightly, every detail bespoke luxury. The

New York *Clipper* had no need to elaborate, only to report: "The house will have a rich front of glazed tiles set in Louis Seize designs, and inset with an eight-thousand dollar mural painting . . . This colorful outside will be lit at night by blazing gas torches softened with steam." Inside were movable glass-topped tables, each with its own silent flag signal mounted on a silver ashtray, for summoning a waiter without making a distracting noise. There was a balcony promenade, a gold champagne bar, and there were boxes, each with a table, chairs, and "more Parisian than Paris" three-dimensional nude murals. "An expanding stage slid out over the orchestra pit and put the performers on hand-shaking intimacy with the first-row patrons."

The intimacy of the space had appealed to Mae West, who depended on the audience's ability to see her facial expressions, gestures, and comic mannerisms. She had insisted on visiting the theater, auditioning it, so to speak, before accepting her role in the Folies Bergère's *A La Broadway*.

Her casting resulted from a Sunday-night concert showcase attended by Broadway and vaudeville producers that took place at the Columbia Theater, flagship of the burlesque wheel she had joined with Frank Wallace. Matilda attended, as did such luminaries as Florenz Ziegfeld and Mae's former dancing teacher, Ned Wayburn, who was staging *A La Broadway* for Lasky and his partner, Henry B. Harris. According to Mae, Ziegfeld was impressed enough to ask her to call at his office; when she did, she claims he offered her a spot in his *Follies*, which she brazenly turned down on the grounds that his theater, the New York Roof, would swallow her up: "It's too big, too wide, there isn't much chance for a personality—I need people close to me." Her story loses credibility when you remember that she next—less than two months later—took a role in a revue destined for the Winter Garden, which has a seating capacity of 1,700. And she would soon appear in a Ziegfeld production in the very same theater she said she found wanting, the New York, renamed the Moulin Rouge "to provide an added spice of naughtiness."

A La Broadway introduced Mae to the man who twenty years later would surface in Hollywood as the producer of six out of eight of her Paramount pictures, William Le Baron. Le Baron, who wrote the *A La Broadway* book, started out penning shows as a college senior and went on to write playlets he and Lasky produced for the vaudeville stage. Shy and urbane, with a "small smile and a recessive manner," he would remember the Mae he first knew as "a peppy, vivacious 'tomboy' who was slightly and very delicately formed" and whose "hoydenish routine and remarkable delivery of the songs stopped the show." His portrait of Mae in her late teens matches that of

Frank Wallace, who said, "As for those curves, she was more on the lean side then—slinky and peppy."

A *La Broadway* initiated a practice Mae would continue throughout her career: altering lines written by others to suit her own conception of what "worked," what would make her stand out and stamp her performance with individuality. She added extra choruses to her song, "They Were Irish," delivering each in a different ethnic dialect. And she changed her part as Maggie O'Hara, a spying Irish maid, turning her into "a flip, fresh, lazy character who acted as a maid shouldn't." The critic for the *Evening World* praised her "amusingly impudent manner and individual way of making her points," pronouncing her a female George M. Cohan—a comparison that would be repeated.

Her ragtime number, "The Philadelphia Drag," scored comic points with a costume that combined and contrasted the sedate grayness of a Quaker dress with the cut-loose abandon of red harem trousers, which were currently fashionable. The Belle Epoque look of recent decades, with its corsets, pastels, lace, and feathers, was giving way to Orientalism in fashion—vivid colors, beads, fringes, loosely draped garments in a Turkish or Persian mode. In Mae's number, Quaker propriety serves as a foil to a steaminess implied in her costume's evocation of a seraglio and underlined by snappy American colloquialisms and churning Afro-American–derived rhythms and steps. "That is some dizzy-like busy-like Philadelphia drag," she sang.

> Even the sleepiest creepiest feet have to wag
> That slumber city awakens when they hear that rag
> Come on get up and be dancing the Philadelphia Rag.

Even though several reviews singled out Mae West as a hit, and theater tycoons like Ziegfeld and the Shubert brothers applauded her opening night, *A La Broadway* and its companion piece, *Hello, Paris,* survived for only eight performances. The general public, convinced the Folies Bergère had been created to serve the wealthy, at prices only they could afford, kept away. The theater's seating capacity was fatally small, while overhead in the posh operation soared so high, Lasky reported, "that in order to break even we had to keep the theatre in almost continuous operation from noon until early morning with capacity crowds," which never materialized. And it ignored the latest trend. At a time when patrons wanted to participate in dancing, not just watch, the space lacked a dance floor. After only six months, the Folies Bergère closed permanently at the end of September 1911, to be converted into a conventional theater drably named the Fulton.

Despite all the building under way in the Times Square area, the fall of 1911 proved a slow theater season. "The legitimate houses in almost all sections of the country are complaining bitterly about the business this season," *Variety* reported. Some were blaming the popularity of the automobile, which made car owners hanker for the road and correspondingly less likely to stay put, during leisure hours, in a costly theater seat. Many actors, despairing of finding work on the stage, were trying for far less prestigious jobs in motion pictures.

Among the shows that did prosper that fall, however, were two that open windows on prevailing anxieties about ambiguous or redefined sex roles: *The Fascinating Widow*, a vehicle for the elegant female impersonator Julian Eltinge in a dual role as both the male suitor, Hal, and Hal disguised as Mrs. Monte, exposing his rivals in courtship as fops and two-timers. And Lew Fields's *The Never Homes*, which, at a time when women's suffrage debates, demonstrations, and legislation dominated the news, spoofs a feminist takeover of a town.

After the demise of *A La Broadway*, Mae West's next break came in a revue for the Shuberts, *Vera Violetta*, one-third of a program that also included an Annette Kellerman vehicle called *Undine*, featuring the shapely swimmer as a water nymph, toe dancing and diving in "a champagne colored union suit worn without corsets." Kellerman, a champion diver and swimmer from Australia, had created a sensation a few years back when she appeared on a Boston beach in a brief one-piece bathing costume instead of the conventional shirt and bloomers that entirely covered and effectively concealed the female form from neck to knee. Arrested for indecent exposure, Kellerman became a headliner in vaudeville and revues, making a specialty of her diving prowess—tanks for her act were installed onstage—and showing off her beautiful figure in daring skin-tight suits. Shocking at the beach, her revealing attire was acceptable on the legitimate stage.

Vera Violetta, destined for the huge new Shubert flagship, the Winter Garden, starred Al Jolson in blackface as Claude, a singing American waiter employed at a Paris skating rink, and featured Gaby Deslys, a flamboyantly costumed singer and dancer newly arrived from France—with twenty-five trunks and a million dollars in jewelry—as a professor's old flame whose interpretation of "the Gaby Glide" brought down the house. The Shuberts' publicist, the wonderfully named A. Toxen Worm, drummed up interest in

Gaby Deslys, who had to justify (and repay) the Shuberts' investment in her of $4,000 a week, by planting stories about her romance with the recently deposed King Manuel of Portugal.

Mae played Angélique of the Opera Comique, a dancer hired to give lessons in love to an American professor while his wife is away. The plot turns on a theme that crops up repeatedly in scripts of this era—spouses tempted to stray when they are apart. Gaby Deslys says to an American husband in Paris, "You married?" He answers, "Not particularly. You see my license is only for Newark."

Reports of dissension in the cast leaked to *Variety* while the show was in rehearsal. Gaby Deslys, the story went, insisted on reducing the parts of other players to bit roles. Stars like Frank Tinney and Louise Dresser protested, and in Dresser's case bolted. "Outside of Mlle. Deslys, whose turn will consume over an hour, no one will have a part of any size. Later it was arranged for Tinney to appear in his specialty only."

Mae surely did not endear herself to the diva-ish Gaby Deslys by strutting onto the stage during tryouts in New Haven in a getup designed to make her resemble the star. She emerged in a big headdress and fancy gown, and the audience mistook her for Gaby. "When she came out . . . they didn't know whether to applaud or not."

Gaby Deslys was probably miffed enough, and powerful enough, to get Mae sacked. The official explanation was that Mae West had been "stricken with pneumonia upon arriving in New York" and for that reason did not open at the Winter Garden. In an interview, "jolly little" Mae laughed it off, kidding about opening and closing in a single week and again asking to be compared to Gaby Deslys: "I believe I'll go to Paris and get myself a king. See my diamond pins. Gaby has nothing on me with her pearls."

At the New Haven opening, Yale students, many of them drunk after a football game at which Yale lost to Princeton, created mayhem by rushing onto the stage and then wrecking the theater, which then had to close down for several days. *Variety* faulted the show for being merely a musical sketch that provided an occasion for Al Jolson to sing "Rum Tum Tiddle" while running to the rear of the house and back again. "After seeing Vera Violetta . . . one can hardly blame the Yale boys at New Haven for having torn up the furniture of the Hyperion theatre last Saturday." A few months later, when Mae had long since left the show, *Variety* speculated she might even have instigated the student riot: "It is said Mae was right in the middle of the fray, if she did not start it."

The volatile pairing of Mae West with an audience of out-of-control

Yalies again proved explosive five months later at Poli's Palace Theater in New Haven when she appeared in vaudeville with the Girard Brothers, two dancers in evening clothes, Bobby O'Neill and Harry Laughlin, who had been in the chorus of *Vera Violetta*. During the act Mae addressed the crowd in a sultry tone of voice, sang "Cuddle Up and Cling to Me" (which Charles K. Harris published as sheet music, with a picture of Mae and her partners on the cover), and danced provocatively, shaking her body in "dev-astating slow motion." On her first outing the gallery merely clapped and cried out; on the second, the next day, young men marched into the front orchestra section just as she was about to appear, singing "Boola Boola." After the third, she and the Girard Brothers were fired—HER WRIGGLES COST MAE WEST HER JOB, the headline went—and the Yale students tore the place apart.

Mae and the Girards took their act to New York, where they were greeted critically with an encouraging but patronizing pat on the back: "Miss West exhibits a nice wardrobe, wearing a nifty harem outfit at the close. She works hard. The boys dance well but their voices hold them back. Miss West is a lively piece of femininity . . . [but she and] the brothers need a lot of 'pop' circuit and 'big small time' work to put them in any kind of stride for faster company." No trace of condescension colors the response to their turn at the American Roof two months later: "Mae West Monday evening was as far above the heads of the American Roof clientele as the roof was above the street. Mae is there." As "a wiggly sort of rough soubret" she and her partners danced a rag on chairs "that was a peach, and funny." But after tipping his hat to her, *Variety*'s Sime lectured Mae for fussing with her dress strap—something you'd expect from a burlesque queen—onstage: "It isn't necessary, especially when a décolleté gown starts something on its first appearance."

The Girards were consistently ignored, or shrugged off as mere window dressing, and Mae began to wonder if she really needed them. When they worked as a "three" act they earned $350 a week (more than double the amount *Variety* quoted as average for a trio), out of which Mae had to finance meals and travel expenses for everyone, the commission for her agent, Frank Bohm (no more than 5 percent, according to a new New York State law), bankroll musicians accompanying her, and underwrite wardrobe costs, which for her ran high. Mae had extravagant taste in clothes and could indulge it with the rationale that women in the audience expected displays of feminine finery and were disappointed if those expectations were dashed.

Mae took her cue from popular female impersonators like Eltinge, who was always elaborately turned out—coiffed, hatted, and robed—in the latest styles. She plunked down $200 for a plain satin gown, and considerably more for another gown of solid rhinestones and a brocade coat draped with white fox. When Frank Bohm assured her he could book her as a "single" for as much as she made with the Girards, she sent them packing.

Bohm, according to Mae, had personal as well as professional reasons for wanting her to be unencumbered; he was, as she put it, "in trouble" over her. After insulting her at their first interview in his Broadway office by failing to remove his hat in her presence, he had turned to mush. He took her out to dinner and gave her a diamond ring when she promised she would discourage the attentions of a rival admirer, Loew's circuit booking manager Joseph M. Schenck (not the Joe Schenck of her puppy-love days). The Hungarian-born Bohm was a charmer, "generous, vital, and adoring," and he and Mae developed an "intimate, warm understanding."

Mae's memoir fails to record a salient fact about Frank Bohm: he had a pregnant wife about whom he didn't trouble himself much. When his son was born, Bohm celebrated "by winning three games of pinochle at the Comedy Club the same night." Mae during her Hollywood years made a point of steering clear of married men, or at least paid lip service to that ideal as part of her strategy of appealing to women fans. But while she was launching her career she seemed free of such scruples, especially in instances where the man in question wielded power in the entertainment world. "I learned that one man was about the same as another. I learned to take 'em for what they were. Stepping stones. If a man could help me— . . . Men can be a lot of help to a girl in more ways than one."

Frank Bohm began as an agent for small-time three-a-day acts, specializing in theaters on the Loew circuit—which owned Manhattan's American Roof, where Mae had appeared with the Girards. He widened his sphere of influence when he announced an agreement with the powerful Keith circuit, which controlled the octopus-like United Booking Office. After two years with UBO he returned to Loew, claiming that he found their personnel more congenial and considered the Keith circuit too political and too greedy. He brought suit against them for recovery of commissions they withheld. These changes in Bohm's affiliation had a direct impact on Mae, because when he, her agent, went with Keith or Loew she followed.

While Bohm worked on getting her booked in big time, Mae took a part in a Ziegfeld revue called *A Winsome Widow*, a new musical version of an 1890s hit, Charles Hoyt's *A Trip to Chinatown*. Put down by *The New York*

Times as "just another of those composites of girls and clothes and song and dance which have come to be expected," and by *Variety* for its excessive length, the show pleased the audience—which in tryouts had included producer Marc Klaw, Ziegfeld, composer Raymond Hubbell, and Bert Williams, now a Ziegfeld star. They applauded the stunning women, gorgeous costumes, and magical staging. In one scene, skaters on real ice spun around as daylight succumbed to moonlight against a backdrop of huge black-and-lavender windows. "The tunes won't last long," commented the *Globe*. "But there was movement, color, brilliant dancing, clever lines."

Mae West, as La Petite Daffy, won plaudits for her vivacity and saucy appeal. "All curls and wiggles," said the *World*, she "cut a funny figure." "Mae West assaults the welkin vigorously," the dignified *Dramatic Mirror* reported. Only *Variety*'s Sime took exception, assuming the scolding tone he had used before to protest that " 'Piccolo,' a pretty melody, [was] spoiled in the singing by Mae West, a rough soubret who did a 'Turkey' just a bit too coarse for this $2 audience."

Even though news of the sinking of the *Titanic* cast widespread gloom immediately after *A Winsome Widow* opened, the show broke box-office records, perhaps benefiting from publicity about a divorce action against Ziegfeld that Anna Held had just initiated. In its first three days, it collected $8,900, and went on to enjoy a long run. But it flourished without Mae West, who, three days after the opening, without explanation "abruptly left the cast and prepared to return to vaudeville. She will play Hammerstein's May 20," *Variety* announced. In a span of a year and a half, Mae had appeared in three different Broadway productions, not making it through two weeks in a single one of them. She would not return to the Broadway stage for more than six years.

Vaudeville, she must have calculated, beat out the musical revue as the place to cut a swathe and make her name. For one thing, it offered more opportunity, wider exposure, than "legit." In 1912, there were about five thousand vaudeville theaters in the United States, four thousand of them small-time. A Sage Foundation survey estimated that 700,000 people in New York City attended forty low-price theaters every week. The audience was estimated to be 60 percent working class (compared to 2 percent at the legitimate theater) and 64 percent male. While a Broadway revue ticket in 1912 would set you back two dollars, the top price in big-time vaudeville ranged from about seventy-five cents to a dollar, much less in the neighborhood houses.

Vaudeville grew up in cities and made virtues of those urban necessities:

speed, excitement, diversity, and discontinuity. Like the department store, it paraded a tempting array of appealing displays vying for attention. Like the sensational press, it told its story quickly and graphically. One acute observer compared vaudeville to a wolfed-down meal: "It may be a kind of lunch-counter art, but then art is so vague and lunch is so real." A rapid-fire sequence of about a dozen unrelated acts, each between ten and fifteen minutes in length, it "whizzed before the audience like the view from an elevated railroad."

Within three hours, on a vaudeville program, a one-act play "gives way to the trapeze artist, the trapeze artist to the sleight-of-hand Houdini, Houdini to the Singing Midgets and the Midgets to the Elephants." "Vaudeville," said E. F. Albee, who played Richelieu to United Booking Office king B. F. Keith and took over as manager after Keith's 1914 demise, "suits the American nature; it is quick, various and to the point. The people who build great office buildings in a few months and change the skyline of a city have no time for long dragged out entertainment . . . Every artist must have his or her act boiled down to the essentials, and the appeal must be direct, sudden and unmistakable."

Compression was at a premium. In comedy, the one-liner enjoyed a heyday, at the expense of the extended story. "Within fifteen minutes, the audience had to be pumped into a state of contagious mirth." City slang and the mangled English of immigrants still struggling with their new language set the tone, but the rube's homespun regional accent was also good for a laugh. Performers tried to link themselves with a tag line, slogan, or descriptive epithet that would capsulize their fame. Buster Keaton was "the Human Mop." Sophie Tucker "the Mary Garden of Ragtime," evolved into "the Last of the Red Hot Mamas." The Cherry Sisters had to settle for "America's Worst Act."

Vaudeville artists competed fiercely among themselves—for bookings, for top billing, for a good dressing room, a choice venue, a high salary, or a desirable spot in the lineup. Before performing, a small-timer "examined the front of the theatre to check the size of his name and his position in the list of acts. Seeing his name in runt letters could catapult [him] into a three-day funk."

Managers, booking agents, critics, and the performers themselves constantly monitored how an act was doing. Drawing a packed house and holding its rapt attention were gauges of success. An invisible applause meter measured approval for all acts, and laughs—big ones, in the right places—propelled the comics. As a performer, your job was to "get over," "sell" your song or routine, and make the audience beg for more. Just like a baseball player, you "scored," or failed to score, a hit. Like a race horse, you ran for the finish. *Billboard*'s critic describes Mae West in a Union Square Theater outing "coming under the wire an easy winner." One New York newspaper ran a "Vaudeville Chart," where players were rated according to the salaries they fetched. It was a thrill, Sophie Tucker said, watching the chart move her from fourth, to third, then second place, then at last the delicious summit: headliner.

After the Palace Theatre opened in New York in 1913, a booking at the Palace signified arrival at "the Topmost Rung." "Here Genius not Birth your Rank Insures," *Billboard*'s regular feature on the Palace proclaimed. Before the Palace opened, Hammerstein's Victoria, "the Corner," on Forty-second Street and Seventh Avenue, "a big, tinkling pearl box—all in white and gold with the opals of electricity studding it in profusion," held the top position. An act booked there had it made, old-timers agree. But any spot in the big time carried trophy status. A cartoon in *The Player*, the publication of the Vaudeville Union, showed performers climbing up into a water tank labeled "The Goal—Big Time," then falling through it onto rocks marked "small-time," "$25," "8-a-day."

Although Mae West's big-time appearances in New York were the ones that got written up in *Variety* and *Billboard*, those dates were hard to come by, and about as frequent as the Fourth of July. She didn't have the pulling power of a top-ranked headliner. Among the male competition, luminaries like Houdini, Will Rogers, Eltinge, and W. C. Fields—at this stage a juggler known as "the Silent Humorist"—outranked her. Among the women, Nora Bayes, Belle Baker, Sophie Tucker, and Fanny Brice had bigger names and played New York more often. They got booked into the Palace, which didn't touch Mae until the 1920s.

Eva Tanguay continued to reign as queen of vaudeville and its surest feminine draw, even when she broke with the Keith circuit in 1912 and toured for two years as an independent, before rejoining Keith for a triumphant sell-out run at the Palace. She took out full-page ads in *Variety* to keep the entertainment world apprised of just how great she was. When Mae brags in her autobiography that she was booked once, on the Keith circuit, in direct opposition to Eva Tanguay, she leaves the impression that she had gained equivalent celebrity, but that was still far from the case.

Starting in 1913 and continuing for the next several years, Mae earned her bread and butter—and helped her mother buy a house in the Wood-haven section of Queens—by touring the country, first on the Keith and then on the less prestigious Loew circuit. (Occasionally, too, on the Orpheum and Interstate routes.) She didn't travel to the Far West but otherwise pretty much covered the North American map, from Philadelphia to Baltimore to Atlanta, Norfolk, Virginia, Texas, Cincinnati, Cleveland, Detroit, and Chicago. She even played in Montreal and other Canadian locations. She was working steadily now, but not as a headliner.

In Newark, New Jersey, she appeared on a bill with Minnie Palmer's Four Marx Brothers and ex-heavyweight champion James J. Corbett. In New York she warmed up the crowd for Evelyn Nesbit and the Three Keatons. In Brooklyn she preceded Fred and Adele Astaire. In Scranton, Pennsylvania, she supported headliner Emma Carus, who sang songs in several dialects—Scotch, Dutch, British, and black American, and billed herself "the Human Dialect Cocktail." In Louisville, Kentucky, she performed on a program with comic acrobat Stan Stanley, whom she would later cast as the stage manager in *Pleasure Man*. And in Baltimore she shared the spotlight with Apdale's Zoological Circus, featuring eight dogs, three monkeys, four bears, and one Brazilian anteater.

More and more often, films, or "flickers," were cropping up on vaudeville bills. A Philadelphia program for 1913 included, along with Mae West, both a Pathé kinetograph of current events—a newsreel—and a comedian who did a travesty on motion pictures. The entertainment form that would eventually destroy vaudeville began as a kind of kid brother, always welcome to tag along but never, at this juncture, the main attraction.

These circuit-route tours weren't the glamorous excursions in posh private rail cars that the biggest stars commanded. Second-string players bought their own train tickets, put up with dirty, crowded, ill-equipped dressing rooms, paid for their own rooms in inexpensive boardinghouses or hotels, and also carried freight charges for costumes, drops, and props. When the "jumps" from one stop on a tour to the next involved long distances, players endured endless hours in transit, sometimes on the milk train, and contended with awkward transfers at odd times of day. Mae adopted her lifelong habit of giving herself a daily enema in response to theater bathrooms that were "so filthy I couldn't face them." Trouping tested any performer's mettle.

Because of the uncertainties they faced and the risks they took, vaudevillians tended to be a superstitious lot. Wishing someone good luck, whistling in the dressing room, allowing peacock feathers in a theater were all tabooed as invitations to bad luck. When he met her in the early thirties, Paramount costume designer Travis Banton found Mae West's caution about umbrellas, mirrors, ladders, and black cats, her belief that pearls brought sorrow and that eight was her lucky number, amusing and idiosyncratic; he might not have if he had spent more time with other former vaudevillians.

Audiences remained confounding, mysterious, whimsical. To please them, it seemed, required divine intervention, as well as talent. A player never knew when or where they might throw her a curve. Of course, crowds varied from one region to another, even from one night to the next, and Mae learned to study them and adapt herself to their responses. "I would try to figure out what the audience looked like, what they did, what problems of life they faced. I would ask a lot of questions of the stage manager. 'What kind of people do you get on Monday night?' . . . I learned to adjust the mood, tempo and material of my act." Her least favorite "house" contained society types at a charitable benefit. She found them stiff, self-conscious, and reserved.

She also disliked some fellow performers, especially "artistes," actors and actresses from the legitimate stage who were appearing in dramatic vaudeville playlets and looked down their noses at mere vaudevillians, who ranked much lower in the entertainment world's social hierarchy. In the Mae West play *Pleasure Man*, set backstage and offstage with variety players as characters, a snooty British or pseudo-British couple called the Hetheringtons, "two up-stage legits," exemplify this obnoxious breed. They revile the swish female impersonators in the bill because they "lack perception . . . of the finer qualities which go to make up the true artist of the legitimate drama," and disparage pretty young "singles." "Isn't it disgusting?" Mrs. Ripley Hetherington remarks to her equally affected husband, "how brazenly and boldly some women in vaudeville conduct themselves before others." A couple of amiable small-timers in *Pleasure Man*, a married couple whose comedy act involves cross-fire talk and kicks in the face, make a sympathetic contrast to the Hetheringtons. They josh good-humoredly, float bad jokes (Q: "How did you get on stage? A: I fell out of the balcony"), groan about playing Peoria, and hope for no opposition on the bill—so that they can make a hit.

Vaudeville bills were carefully structured in a way that highlighted certain spots in the lineup. Since audiences didn't necessarily arrive on time, remain for the whole show, or sit still for every attraction, first and last acts on the program were usually "dumb," designed to be seen and not heard—animals, acrobats, or dancers. The most sought-after spots on the bill came right before intermission, or second to last, which was called "next-to-closing."

A disadvantageous spot could make your job difficult, as it did for Mae West at Hammerstein's, when she opened right after intermission to an unsettled, inattentive house and "some of her very good material went for naught." It was also considered fatal to share a bill with a number of acts too close in type to the one with which you hoped to score. Frank Bohm took out a big ad in *Variety* to pitch "Mae West, 'The Scintillating Singing Comedienne,' Late of Ziegfeld's Moulin Rouge," and the long program did offer a range of acts, from Adonis, a contortionist who worked with a trained dog, to Master Gabriel, a midget comedian, to a Wild West act featuring bucking broncos and rope twirling. But three "single" women singers crowded the bill: Mae West, Blossom Seeley, and Ethel Green. In the sixth spot, Mae West nonetheless held her own. *Billboard* reported that she "registered a most emphatic hit," singling out for special mention her closing number, "Rap, Rap, Rap," during the rendition of which "Miss West sits and uses the 'bones' in a manner that might be envied by a [blackface] minstrel end man." Her remarkable sense of rhythm was beginning to be noticed.

Especially if you worked solo, as Mae West preferred to do, in vaudeville you wielded considerably more power than the legitimate stage allowed, choosing and shaping (unless censors interfered) your own songs, costumes, dances, patter, stage maneuvers, and—all-important for Mae—tempo. A Keith circuit theater manager suggested in his Monday report on a Philadelphia performance by Mae West that she should not be billed, as someone suggested, as the "Harum-Scarum"; that would be a mistake, "as she is not volcanic in style and manifests no inclination to whoop things up. She is quiet in style and the 'Nonchalant, Unique Artiste' would be more like my idea of billing her." Another manager, this time in Cleveland, also dwelt on her languid pace: "This hunk of humanity is evidently somewhat of a hypnotist. She remained on the stage for sixteen minutes, didn't do much of anything, but still she made the people laugh. She talks about herself, sings a few songs and stalls around the stage, but still the people laugh and applaud."

Working at a languorous pace came naturally to sultry Mae and became a defining trait of her vaudeville personality. It marked a departure from her own peppy Broadway characterizations and heightened the contrast between her slow motion and the speeded-up tempo of her vaudeville model and now rival, the frenetic Eva Tanguay; and with the full-tilt acts that often surrounded her on a vaudeville bill. The same distinction between her pacing and that of surrounding players would serve her again, splendidly, onstage in *Diamond Lil* and later in the movies.

The need to "wow" the audience inclined her to costume herself oddly and outlandishly—in silver harem pants or a cerise chiffon coat and hat over a "flashy purple velvet gown"—justifying the label "eccentric." She would cut out the crown of her velvet hat, allowing her own hair to come through, and top her creation with a large plume that enhanced her height. In Philadelphia, appearing on the same bill with clothes-horse Valeska Suratt, who was the headliner, Mae wore "some clothes that give Valeska Suratt a grand race. She still wears that fur animal that seems to be nibbling at her left hip, but it's shrunk and has been dyed red."

According to her sister Beverly, Mae's bizarre, can-you-top-this outfits were sometimes chosen by Matilda, whose study of Eva Tanguay had taught her how crucial "extreme" clothes can be in furthering an outlandish image and forging an indelible impression. A Chicago critic wrote: "Mae West is nearly an Eva Tanguay. She acts the part and wears the same style costumes, though she doesn't fill them so completely as does . . . Eva."

The tilt toward the bizarre was not lost on *Variety*'s Sime, who found it unseemly. (It was probably Sime who inspired *Billboard*'s quip "*Variety* leaves no turn unstoned.") When Mae West got her first major vaudeville break, a spot on the bill at Hammerstein's Victoria, he applauded her strength of character for breaking free of Ziegfeld, and then knocked her for lacking "that touch of class." "The girl is of the eccentric type," Sime wrote. "She sings rag melodies and dresses oddly . . . She's one of the many freak persons on the vaudeville stage, where freakishness often carries more weight than talent."

Cousin of the circus freak acts and the old dime museum that exhibited two-headed babies and bearded ladies, the vaudeville "nut" act sanctioned off-the-wall attitudes and conduct—within a structured and miniaturized frame. Eccentricity onstage carried to its logical conclusion the notion that comedy and exaggeration go hand in hand. Willie Hammerstein, next-to-oldest son of impresario Oscar and father of the second Oscar, the lyricist, made Hammerstein's Victoria a showcase for all kinds of stunt and oddball acts; he especially favored newsmakers who generated publicity and could create "living tabloid"—star athletes, participants in sex scandals like Evelyn Nesbit, women who had shot their lovers or husbands, anyone who'd gained notoriety or made headlines. When she appeared at Hammerstein's

Victoria, Mae highlighted her outrageous quality on one occasion with a group of songs tied together with a common thread of craziness, culminating with "Everybody's Ragtime Crazy." She let loose so persuasively, a critic for the New York *Telegraph* anointed her "that Cohanesque, Tanguayish president of the female 'nut' club."

Even when they slammed her indifferent singing, managers and critics acknowledged her flair as a comedienne. *Variety*'s Jolo was pleased to see Mae West moving away from the song-and-dance routine she had tried with the Girard Brothers. "She is doing less 'singing' and has a lot of new 'kidding' talk that is very good. She put it over to unmistakably indicate that this is her forte." To help her get laughs, she hired Tommy Gray, a comedy writer who had a weekly column, "Gray Matter," in *Variety*, and had many sketches, songs, and monologues to his credit. He supplied lyrics for several comic songs: "Good Night, Nurse" (which allowed her to pose for the sheet-music cover costumed in a white nurse's cap and apron), "Isn't She a Brazen Thing?," and "It's An Awful Easy Way to Make a Living."

Gray was not amused when Mae failed to pay him in full for his services, and he sued her for $169. Stiffing a writer for *Variety* was not a good idea. Of course, his suit found its way into print, and—as *Variety* duly reported—she promptly coughed up the cash. She didn't need a reputation as a deadbeat, especially when things seemed to be starting to go her way.

Audiences and critics for the most part concurred: she was funny, alluring, and she had style. "Miss West can't sing a bit," said the New York *Morning Telegraph*, "but she can dance like George Cohan, and personality just permeates the air every minute she is on the stage. In other words, it isn't what Miss West does, but the way she does it that assures her a brilliant career on the stage." In case the crowd didn't pick up on her highly stylized attitudinizing and coolly self-mocking manner, her preening hand-on-hip poses and diva-like red carpet entrances, Mae helped them along with reminders. Before an appearance in Philadelphia she flooded the downtown area with circulars announcing her specialty, "A Muscle Dance in a Sitting Position," and trumpeting, "It is all in the way she does it and her way is all her own." She soon began opening her act with a song called "I've Got a Style All My Own" (her variant on Eva Tanguay's "It's All Been Done Before But Not the Way I Do It") and concluding with a little speech: "It isn't what you do, it's how you do it."

In all this focusing on the triumph of an artificial, outré manner over matter, she recalls the dandified, "too utterly utter" Aesthetes of the Wildean 1890s, for whom the embossed and scented envelope counted far more than its contents, and beckons to "nance" inheritors of the dandy's torch. Frankly effeminate vaudevillians were familiar figures, both before the foot-lights and backstage, and Mae gravitated toward them, finding them "hu-morous, sweet, talented." They, in turn, relished her outlandishness and were inspired by it: "It's easy for 'em to imitate me, 'cause the gestures are exaggerated, flamboyant, *sexy*." After a New York or Brooklyn matinee sometimes "I used to take some of the chorus boys home. My mother loved 'em 'cause they'd fix her hair and her hats."

Paradoxically, at the same time she was making such a pitch for the high-gloss stylization of her act, Mae West was advertising herself to vaudeville audiences as the embodiment of and model for a much imitated fashionable type distinctive for her naturalness and pert informality, the "Original Brinkley Girl." All but forgotten today, the Brinkley Girl became famous in the 1910s as the successor to the tall, athletic, shirt-waisted Gibson Girl created in the *Life* magazine lithographs of Charles Dana Gibson. The in-vention of a woman cartoonist named Nell Brinkley, she came to life in lacy pen-and-ink drawings that appeared regularly in Sunday newspaper supplements. Where the corseted Gibson Girl had been coolly aristocratic, holding her chin high with an aloof and commanding air and walking with a forward bend, the Brinkley Girl's turned-up nose, puckered lips, and fluffy, wind-blown hair conveyed flirtatious ease, spontaneity, and lack of pretense.

Mae West started billing herself as "the Original Brinkley Girl" around 1913, but as early as 1908 the *Ziegfeld Follies* had featured a song about the Nell Brinkley Girl, "with her hair all in a whirl," who wears the smartest clothes and doesn't mind if the wind blows her skirt and allows her to show off her silken hose. Annabelle Whitford played the Brinkley Girl first in the *Follies*, then in her vaudeville act. A publicity piece for Whitford an-nounced that the Gibson Girl had passed majestically away and that her replacement, the Brinkley Girl, would be appearing next week at the Or-pheum. "The Brinkley Girl is lithe and lithesome and willowy. She is a thing of continuous curves and shapely lines and she bends forward at the middle in a sort of tired way, a very careless, piquant way. Her mouth is a pucker and her hair, oh goodness—it's all tangled, and it blows down her face and neck." The Brinkley Girl marks a local stop on the ride from Gibson Girl to flapper.

In pressing herself into the Brinkley mold, twenty-year-old Mae calls at-tention to her free-and-easy girlishness. She isn't yet the full-bodied sex goddess, or even a woman of the world. One manager, in fact, labeled the carelessness she projected "boyish." But flirtatiousness and nonchalance—

two Brinkley Girl hallmarks—meshed perfectly with her innate provocativeness. "The men like her better than the women," reported a Keith
circuit manager in Philadelphia; he recommended she cut her line letting
the audience in on the secret that the manager had promised to take her
out to lunch "and see what was doing for me."

Vaudeville no longer squeaked as loudly with cleanness as it once had.
Standards for all kinds of variety acts had relaxed. "Vaudeville has started
on the downward path, where burlesque left off," *Variety* lamented. Where
once the word "damn" raised hackles and could cost a performer's job, now
"lewd dances" and "tainted sketches" were standard fare in big time.

"Sex o'clock" had struck in America, as a journalist observed with dismay. "A wave of sex hysteria and sex discussion seems to have invaded this
country." On Broadway, Eugene Brieux's *Damaged Goods*, a play about a
married man with venereal disease, which included parts for prostitutes that
were difficult to cast (presumably because actresses feared being tainted),
ran for twenty-two months, spurring a rush of "vice plays" and ending up
as a film. Although *Variety* issued an edict prohibiting ads in its pages for
films sensationalizing vice, such films continued to be made and to draw
audiences hungry for thrills.

Taste in screen heroines also signaled a change. After her 1915 film
debut, Theda Bara—who would play Carmen, Cleopatra, Salome, and
DuBarry—created a foil to the virginal goody-goody screen heroine of the
Mary Pickford variety. Shortening the word "vampire" to "vamp," she em-
bodied libido rampant, a carnivorous sexual appetite, and allure that seemed
to justify the dire premonitions of vice crusaders. Her frank wantonness,
although as exaggerated as Mae West's screen image would be, lacked any
note of lightness or self-parody. Bara's true *femme fatale* promised gratifica-
tion at her lover's peril; her brand of sex, swathed in spiderwebs, metal, and
curved asps, augured something dark, ominous, predatory. The note of
mockery she failed to sound would be supplied by others, eventually doing
her in as a screen idol. Her silent command "Kiss me, my fool," in *A Fool
There Was*, almost as famous in its day as the misquoted "Come up and see
me sometime" would become, turned into a campy comic tag line. But in
1915 her vogue was burgeoning.

As world war broke out in Europe, the American dance craze reached a
feverish pitch, and afternoon *thé dansants*, at which daring middle-class
wives could rent a male partner, took hold. Vaudeville managers, *Billboard*
reported, "are meeting the dance craze more than half way by filling their
bills with all sorts of dancing acts." Irene and Vernon Castle became top-

dollar stars; their style, sophistication, and stepping set a standard for millions. Hotels provided spaces in which ordinary mortals could strut their stuff: "Married and single, bachelors and spinsters, old men and elderly ladies, the clerk, the stenographer, the merchant, the printer, foundry employee, the banker, the actor, the actress, the truckdriver and the street-car conductor, any and every class and strata of humanity have taken to the waxen floor."

As in other periods of galvanic social upheaval in America—the 1890s, the 1920s, the 1960s—change in the direction of greater sexual expressiveness met not only with sensationalized exploitation but also with repressive clamp downs. A New York grand jury condemned the Turkey Trot as indecent, and public dancing thereafter had to be licensed. A curfew was established at New York cabarets. At Hammerstein's, an Apache dance in which the male partner fondled and ripped off the dress of his female partner brought out the police; the act wasn't shut down but "had a muffler placed on it." And New York City canceled showings of Chaplin's film *A Night Out* because it showed the comedian in a hotel room with another man's wife.

Movie censorship, up to now a matter for the individual states, went national with the formation of a National Board of Censors, which laid down very specific guidelines for presentation on film of the "wanton heroine." It forbade "the extended display of personal allurements, the exposure of alleged physical charms, and passionate, protracted embraces." It also condemned "the showing of men turning lightly from woman to woman, or women turning lightly from man to man in intimate sexual relationships."

The Supreme Court, in the wake of controversies provoked by *The Birth of a Nation*, ruled in 1915 that motion pictures were not "free speech," that they "may be used for evil," that "the exhibition of moving pictures is a business pure and simple," and that censorship of films was constitutional.

On vaudeville's Keith circuit, the Monday manager's report listed the specific offending lines that had to be cut from each act. Blue envelopes containing directives about cutting naughty bits of business or dialogue would be placed in a vaudevillian's mailbox after a matinee but before the night show. A performer had no voice or choice. You obeyed, quit, or risked being canned. In Cleveland, for instance, Mae was ordered to remove the word "chicken"—used as a synonym for "pretty young girl"—from her act.

Managers not only tried to uphold the Keith tradition of moral uprightness, they lived in fear of offending the church, most particularly the Catholic Church. In rehearsal, or after Mae performed something they considered beyond the limit, they'd get after her with "My God, you've got to change that song, the churches will be after us." ("They were never worried about the police, just the churches," she remembered.)

Mae dealt with censorship by trying to work around it. "To get away with what I wanted to do on stage," she wrote, "I had to pull every trick I could think of. When I rehearsed my material, I'd do my utmost to tame it down—then, at my first show, I'd pull out all the stops. When audiences lined up with ticket money, most managers began to see things my way." As she would rediscover in films, she could take an innocent-sounding line and, through voice inflection, timing, facial nuance, and body language, give it an erotic charge. Sometimes she'd hand a worried manager the sheet music to a song he'd asked her to cut, asking him to be specific. "He'd read it and re-read it, and of course there was nothing to delete. It was all in the voice, in the attitude, in my personality."

She did manage to incorporate some blatantly suggestive lyrics that somehow slipped by the censors, like the step-by-step account of the cozy aftermath of a date in a song called "And Then":

> First we had a talk—and then,
> We sat by the fire and then,
> It was getting warm and so,
> We drew our chairs away from the fireside glow.
> Mother said: "Good night"—and then,
> We turned down the light—and then,
> We cuddled close together,
> And we talked about the weather,
> Yes we did (Yes we did!)—not then.

A critic in Detroit was shocked by this. "The big hit of the bill is Mae West," he wrote, "who is, plainly, vulgar. This woman is all that is coarse in Eva Tanguay without that player's ability. Yet the audience howled for more. It hardly seems possible that Miss West will be allowed to sing her song "And Then" the rest of the week by the Temple [Theater] management, usually so careful to eliminate the objectionable."

A pattern had emerged: while audiences loved her, managers and critics regularly cried foul. It's hard to calculate to what extent Mae's willingness to "overstep the line between facetiousness and freshness" sabotaged her rise to the pinnacle of vaudeville stardom. Undoubtedly it played some part.

She seems to have made at least a fleeting effort to broaden her acceptability by lowering the temperature of her act. Back at the American Roof in New York in early 1915 after a long absence, she was reported by Sime to have "repressed her exuberance somewhat, but could stand just a trifle more repression."

After two years of hard traveling on the vaudeville circuit, although she'd gained immeasurably in self-definition and performing finesse, and garnered some excellent notices, she now lost ground, at least in the recognition department. She faced cuts in pay and demotions in billing. Her name appeared less frequently in the trade papers, and when it did turn up, a reader, with rare exceptions, would require a magnifying glass to decipher it. Her career—apparently set so surely on course toward the "Topmost Rung" a few years back—had lost its moorings.

5

ALLIES AND LIMITED PARTNERS

$\mathcal{M}$AE West's career floundered in part because of looming ominous conditions beyond any single performer's control. War in Europe and an American economic slump had combined to effectively let the air out of the balloon that floated the entertainment business. Even before war erupted in the summer of 1914, vaudeville had endured a season of shrinking profits, a decline attributed to an unfortunate convergence of bad weather, overbuilt theater districts and competition from movies, whose appeal was widening. Now, in addition, European acts, and American acts that had been touring in Europe, all sought bookings in the relative safety of the States. A surfeit of talent combined with a dwindling market, in an atmosphere of fear and uncertainty, meant cuts in pay and all-around retrenchment.

The coincidental deaths in 1914 of both B. F. Keith, the little-loved founder of the Keith circuit, and much-missed Willie Hammerstein, showman par excellence and creator of the Hammerstein Victoria Theater's wildly successful "living tabloid" formula, seemed to mark the end of vaudeville's frisky young adulthood. "Since the death of William Hammerstein," *Billboard* reported, "business has fallen off and 'the Corner' has lost its Individuality." Heralding a future era, and sounding a warning bell for vaudeville, Hammerstein's Victoria was leased in May 1915 to the Rialto Theatre Company as a picture house.

The Keith circuit announced performers' salary reductions of 15 percent, eliciting shrieks of protest from the hard hit. Loew, "the Henry Ford of show business," promised no cuts, but offered its acts arduous three-a-day schedules and long routes, according only limited glory to the overworked troupers. The White Rats—the American Federation of Labor–affiliated union for variety artists, which took its animal name from "star" spelled backwards—led the fight for some kind of contractual protection, and for a time they had the support of *Variety*. But as yet union membership among the performers was far from universal. Mae West (later an early supporter of the Screen Actors Guild) seems not to have heeded organized labor's first rallying cry, although the president of the White Rats made a special bid for more "girl members," promising that in the organization's clubhouse "we will gladly set aside hours for you in the gym and swimming pool." Even before the Affiliated Actresses of America joined forces with the White Rats, British comic singer Alice Lloyd's name appears on the roster of the White Rats' lifetime members, but not Mae West's.

Never much of a brooder about world or national issues, Mae seems not to have been fretting much about the fight for entertainers' economic security, or about the European war, although her mother's German accent must have caused worry as American anti-German sentiment burgeoned. To Mae and many others in the States the war initially felt "far away and still remote," distant enough to joke about. Tommy Gray wondered in his *Variety* column: "With Russia, Germany and Austria-Hungary mixed up in a war, what are we going to do for Russian dancers, acrobats and hotel orchestras?"

References to the war inevitably found their way into American popular songs and some vaudeville acts. Comedians referred to orchestra members in the pit as "you boys down there in the trenches." Supporters of pacifist or non-interventionist policies sang "I Didn't Raise My Boy to Be a Soldier." Interventionists came up with their own song, "I'd Be Proud to Be the Mother of a Soldier." Al Jolson sang "Sister Susie's Sewing Shirts for Soldiers," and the marching song of British enlisted men on the front, "It's a Long Way to Tipperary," became a hit. Nazimova appeared in *War Brides*, and *War Babies* depicted a woman whose grief after seeing her baby killed by random shelling converts her to militant pacifism.

The official policy of the Woodrow Wilson government was at first neutrality, a position that found some support in the theater trades. At the White Rats' clubhouse, the time-honored camaraderie among players of varying nationalities still prevailed. German acrobats could be seen "helping to lift the rigging of an English team, or a Russian dancer chatting with an Austrian animal trainer." The virulent anti-German fervor that would soon sweep the United States did not take hold until after Germany torpedoed the *Lusitania* in May 1915, killing more than a thousand civilians, an event re-created on the New York vaudeville stage in a "mechanical" production that showed the launching of the torpedo boat, the SOS call by wireless operator, and the giant craft's sinking beneath the surf.

*　　*　　*

In August 1914, when England declared war on Germany after its invasion of Belgium, Mae was in Texas, performing vaudeville on the Interstate circuit. She remained unruffled by what she considered faintly audible drums, having thrown herself into a passionate and, for her, long-lasting love affair whose fervor wholly consumed her. Her lover was Guido Deiro (sometimes spelled Diero), a handsome Italian accordion player with a shock of black hair whom she'd met in 1913 at a Detroit vaudeville theater. The man she calls "Mr. D." in her autobiography had "a terrific personality and sensual Latin charm." Jealous, ardent, and possessive, he once bribed a hotel phone operator to monitor Mae's calls, and would attempt to demolish rivals with menacing looks and gestures that threatened "swords, daggers and blood." When a man in a restaurant insulted Mae after a performance by calling her "just a dressed up chippie," he responded as Battlin' Jack would have, with a "clip right on the chin." He ended up having a plate of spaghetti hurled in his face.

Mae usually avoided romantic entanglements with performers, especially those better known and more established than she was. In her idealized version of herself—presented, among other places, in the novelization of *Pleasure Man*—she swears off male performers in general as lovers: "There was never a bill she was on that the men performers, young and old, didn't go on the make for her. But she never played around in the profession. She chose her amours in the wide world outside the stage door. They could be bankers, brokers, or merchant chiefs, or maybe just a push-face truck driver with oversize muscles."

Deiro, however, most definitely belonged inside the stage door. Although she underplays his professional prominence when writing about him in her memoir, he had already made his name in vaudeville and had a devoted following when they met. He had appeared at the Palace, and had been described as "a New York favorite who needs no commendatory notice. He is a real musician." In San Francisco, where he performed everything from "the classiest classic to the raggiest rags, injecting a swing and dash to his numbers," he had "evoked the wildest enthusiasm." Mae would issue no recordings at all until after her arrival in Hollywood, but Deiro had scored a recording contract on the Columbia label. (His brother Pietro, with whom he had a publicly rivalrous relationship, also played piano accordion in vaudeville and recorded for Victor.)

Since power issues always top Mae West's agenda, she makes it seem, when writing about her affair with Deiro—one of the *grandes amours* of her life—that *she* always held the trump card. As she reports it, *he* was the one besotted by love and desire, half crazed to make her his forever through marriage; *he* was the one allowing his career to backslide, willingly demoting himself from a headliner to her bandleader, so long as they could travel and stay together. But at the beginning she was equally unhinged, and overwhelmed by desire for him. For once her career came second. "The sex thing was terrific with this guy. I wanted to do it morning, noon and night, and that's all I wanted to do." For the first time, physical desire met its match in emotional intensity. This affair went "very deep, hittin' on all the emotions. You can't get too hot over anybody unless there's somethin' that goes along with the sex act, can you?"

Throughout 1914 and into the early part of the next year Mae West and Deiro traveled together and appeared all over the country on the same vaudeville stages. More often than not, although crowds enjoyed her act, *he* was singled out as the hit of the evening. In Texas, at San Antonio's Majestic, he took top honors for his temperamental and talented display, and Mae West, "the Eva Tanguay of vaudeville," was listed off-handedly among "six other acts." In New York at the American Roof, Deiro scored "the applause hit in the first half," while Mae West was placed "next to closing, a position Deiro should have had." At Chicago's Palace, when their romance was young, Deiro "came near stopping the show, while Mae West, despite "spots of fun, lets down." After they split up as a couple, Deiro went back to the major-league Keith circuit and signed with top agent Max Hart, while Mae had to settle for the relative obscurity of the Western Vaudeville circuit, based in Chicago. She appeared in such venues as Peoria and Des Moines, as well as Chicago itself.

The split-up came in the spring of 1915, just months after they had announced their partnership to the show-biz world in a big ad, featuring photographs of both of them, in the Christmas issue of *Variety*: Deiro, "Master of the Accordion, Incomparable in His Line," and Mae West, "The Original Brinkley Girl, A Style All Her Own," were, the ad told readers, under the auspices of Frank Bohm, "engaged jointly as headline features" for forty weeks on the Loew Circuit. They jointly wished the entire world a Merry Christmas and a Happy New Year. Their offstage partnership became so well known in the profession that Nils Granlund, a publicist for the Loew circuit, writes in his memoirs that Mae West and Deiro got married. Since Mae had not divorced Frank Wallace, who when last heard from was dancing in a Brighton Beach, Brooklyn cabaret, she could not have married again without committing bigamy.

Deiro was—at least at the time they met—not free to marry either, since he apparently had a wife from whom he was separated when he took up with Mae. She was Julia Tatro, a musician he'd met in Spokane, Washington. Julia Tatro, according to *Variety*, accused him of statutory rape before their 1911 marriage, but withdrew the charge when he agreed to marry and support her. He failed to stay with her, or satisfy his financial obligation, and she took legal action. When Deiro was playing the Chicago Palace, on the same bill with Mae, he was arrested on a fugitive warrant issued by Spokane authorities. After posting $2,500 bail, he left town for Erie, Pennsylvania, where he had a booking. Mae took off in another direction, to Indianapolis, but they reconnected soon again, after the commotion had settled down. It's not known whether Deiro ever divorced this wife, or even if her claim of obligation had merit. An earlier complaint she'd filed in San Francisco was dismissed because of lack of evidence. In any case, their respective marital entanglements neither prevented Mae and Deiro from getting together nor drove them apart.

Mae and Deiro broke up, after two years of high-intensity togetherness, because she found monogamy too constricting and wanted to get her career back on track. Once again, Matilda played a pivotal part in shaping her daughter's destiny. Mae's closeness to the accordionist alarmed her, and his threats of violence if he couldn't have Mae all to himself instilled maternal terror. "My mother didn't like it. She had ambitions for me. She said I was only interested in myself and not in my career." To Matilda, Mae's preoccupation with love signified selfishness, while interest in her career signaled unselfish, thoughtful consideration of Matilda's wishes. When Mae showed no inclination to leave Deiro's side, "Mother pointed out other married couples to me . . . showed me how their lives were wasted." Without nagging, she silently conveyed her disapproval and made it apparent that Mae's lovesickness and distraction were making her devoted mother miserable. Mae came around to seeing that Matilda "was right, and when I realized that, I got rid of him."

Matilda finally spoke up, actually asking Mae to break with Deiro. When she saw an opportunity to slip away, without so much as a parting word or a farewell embrace, Mae abruptly departed for Chicago. "It almost killed the poor guy. He started to drink. He would come around to our house looking for me, and my mother would say she didn't know where I was. He would cry and cry and say he was going to kill himself." He also threatened to kill any man who displaced him in Mae's affections, which prompted Mae's father to remark, "None of those Italian knife tricks."

Mae suffered deeply as well. She told Ruth Biery she went through a desolate period when she was just marking time. "Waiting until she could forget *love*. 'From that time on, I have thought only of Mae West. Men have been important only as they could help me to help Mae West.' " She was already beginning to see herself in the third person, as a persona separate from the private woman.

Between appearances all over the Midwest on the Western Vaudeville circuit she consoled herself in Chicago with a new lover, the man she calls "Rex" in her autobiography and likens to a character out of F. Scott Fitzgerald. Handsome, wealthy, and from a socialite family, he, too, wanted to marry her, a possibility Mae says she considered. "I felt that Mother would be happy with a marriage of this kind." She contemplated making a clean breast of it, confessing to Matilda about her marriage to Frank Wallace and getting an annulment, on the grounds that she had been underage when she married; this would free her for Rex. Instead, she decided that Rex was too domineering, too bent on insisting she give up show business for him. She preferred to give up Rex, but in time would base several characters in her plays and screenplays on him: Reggie Muchcash in *The Ruby Ring* and the socialite Stanton in *Sex*; wealthy Wayne Baldwin in *The Constant Sinner*; the Cary Grant role, Jack Clayton, in *I'm No Angel*; and Paul Cavanagh's Edward Carrington in *Goin' to Town*.

In Chicago (she called it "Chi") Mae straddled both the right and the wrong side of the tracks, finding pleasures to be savored among upscale high-livers and down-and-dirty lowlifers alike. Socialites didn't faze her—she loved luxury—nor did an opera singer with whom she enjoyed a fling. But for an after-the-show blast, nothing compared to the black-and-tan nightclubs on South State Street, where "racial and sexual tolerance was shockingly loose for the times." Here she picked up "low husky blues" and "wild shouting laments of love and pleasure," and learned dances labeled "vile" by the Chicago Morals Commission, like the bump, the jelly roll, and "shakin' the shimmy," or "shimmy sha-wobble." At the Elite No. 1 she saw "big black men with razor-slashed faces, fancy high yellows and beginners browns—in the smoke of gin scented tobacco" dance to the "Can House Blues." "They got up from the tables . . . and just shook their shoulders, torsos, breasts and pelvises . . . There was a sensual agony about it . . . and if you ever saw it performed, you would know that no white person could create such a dance."

Mae already had displayed a knack for what jazz dance historian Marshall Stearns calls "vernacular hip movements," and inserted the shimmy into her vaudeville act; "it like to tore the house down," even though the manager hesitated to let her go on with it. Not for her the genteel adaptations of Irene and Vernon Castle, whose 1914 dance-instruction book for the social set advises, "Do not wriggle the shoulders. Do not shake the hips. Do not twist the body. Avoid low, fantastic, and acrobatic dips." Mae tried to duplicate exactly what she saw in the Chicago clubs, and took credit as the first to initiate what would become a new shimmy dance fad, the first to smuggle that African-derived New Orleans black dance form, kin to the Shake and the Quiver and linked in some minds to Little Egypt's hootchy-kootchy, across the border into "respectable" white venues.

In Chicago she also met the white comic dancer Joe Frisco, a stuttering Chicagoan soon (at Mae's urging) to drop his Chaplin imitation and crash New York clubs as an innovative jazz dancer. Frisco had heard a jazz band headed by white trombonist Tom Brown in New Orleans, and had helped bring that band, the first to be billed as a "jass" band, to Chicago in 1915. Now he helped Mae work out her new dance routine and advertised in *Variety* that Sophie Tucker and Mae West numbered among his jazzing dance students. Frisco, like Mae West, sometimes seemed to travesty the dances he presented, shaking his shoulders and pelvis while his tongue lodged in his cheek. "You can't tell whether he's on the level or kidding," said Sime of Frisco, as others would later say of Frisco's student Mae West.

The Windy City served as a workplace and song-publishing site for the creator of the "Darktown Strutters' Ball," black composer Shelton Brooks, who conducted the orchestra and played his own pieces at the Pekin Theater on South State Street. Brooks, who also appeared as a comic in New York vaudeville, composed both music and lyrics for "Some of These Days," the song Sophie Tucker took as her theme. Mae liked the relaxed, finger-snapping Shelton Brooks sound; she adopted his "They Call It Dixieland" and "Walkin' the Dog"—Tucker also performed the latter—for her own act. (In 1933 she would sing Brooks's "I Wonder Where My Easy Rider's Gone" in *She Done Him Wrong*.)

Mae West and Sophie Tucker, who made many appearances in Chicago big-time vaudeville during the war years, undoubtedly knew each other, although professional rivalry precluded friendship; neither's memoir mentions the other. They shared burlesque roots, East Coast urban and immigrant origins, a sexually aggressive stance, a fondness for furs, diamonds, and double-entendre lyrics that turned sex into a laughing matter, and an affinity with Afro-American musical idioms. They worked with similarly named bands, Tucker with her Five Kings of Syncopation; Mae West, ten years later in *Sex*, with the Fleet Syncopators, and used some of the same songs and songwriters. But Tucker, a hefty woman, lacked Mae's dance skills and sexual allure. "I Don't Want to Be Thin," one of her songs proclaimed, insisting (as Mae West never would) that fat women have more fun. As Robert Allen says, Tucker's girth limited her transgressiveness. Tucker belted her songs with raucous powerhouse pipes, and none of Mae West's vocal nasality. She would and did play the victim and the jilted lover far more convincingly, when she sang bluesy he-done-me-wrong lyrics, than could Mae, and Tucker became a star of the cabaret scene—something Mae West postponed until the 1950s. At this juncture, before the United States entered World War I, Sophie Tucker took first place, among white singers, in the Red Hot Mama sweepstakes.

Mae said she felt an instant affinity for jazz. "I had graduated from ragtime to the new music from New Orleans . . . Jazz suited me—I liked the beat and emotions." Although neither an improvisor nor a prober of deep emotion, she fell right in with the swinging dance rhythms, blues intervals, and syncopations that were already familiar to her from coon shouting and ragtime. The introduction of brass instruments in her backup complemented her own brazen insolence.

As she made the rounds of the various nightspots, she picked out the best musicians and the best-looking men for a jazz band that she formed to back her new act, becoming one of the first in white vaudeville to use jazz musicians. She doesn't say whether her band was racially integrated, but if it was, that would have been radical in the vaudeville of that era, a time when the White Rats union formed a separate Colored Branch, when race riots were breaking out in response to the pro-Klan sentiments of *Birth of a Nation*, and when in most vaudeville theaters blacks sat upstairs, segregated. Irene and Vernon Castle, before their duo divided because Vernon went to war, had used the black James Europe band; but it was *all* black. Mae West's Chicago band definitely did use at least one white musician, because Jules Stein, the founder of MCA, remembered playing in it.

Because jazz was considered too hot, too tainted by its association with "pernicious" red-light districts for elites to handle, Mae West branded herself as a scarlet-lettered outsider when she jazzed before the new music had established a foothold in the popular music business. The Chicago Musicians' Union denigrated it as "nothing but cheap and shameless." Even the word "jazz" could scandalize; it came into use around 1915, and initially meant "screw," in its crude, slangy sexual sense. Middle-class blacks, as well as establishment whites, kept jazz at a distance. Ralph Ellison's parents considered it a "backward, low-class form of expression." "The word jazz," F. Scott Fitzgerald wrote in *The Crack-Up*, "in its progress toward respectability has meant first sex, then dancing, then music. It is associated with a state of nervous stimulation, not unlike that of big cities behind the lines of a war."

After the Chicago interlude, Mae turned up in Pittsburgh with the Victoria Burlesquers, not exactly a four-star attraction. In short order, she returned to New York and volunteered to appear on a bill presented by the White Rats for prisoners at Sing Sing in a Decoration Day show, suggesting that she did feel some solidarity with her unionized fellow vaudevillians; and with prisoners, as she would later make abundantly clear.

Back home after an absence of more than a year, she once more accepted the dictum that mother knows best. Matilda's advice, by now a predictable refrain, was: Marry your career, not a man. Since Deiro had dropped out of the picture, and Mae had spent some time traveling, absorbing exciting new moves and tonalities into her act and strewing some wild oats along the way, she now seemed ready to regroup. In addition to focusing on her career, there was one other thing Mae could do to make Matilda happy: look after her younger sister, Beverly.

Five and a half years younger than Mae, Beverly had bloomed into an attractive young woman who, like her older sister, sang, danced, loved clothes and men, and dreamed of stardom. But Beverly struggled against several handicaps. She walked with a slight limp, the result of a childhood injury, and wore an orthopedic shoe. Although she was pretty, bright, and talented, she was not as pretty, bright, and talented as Mae, who had the advantage of a running start in all endeavors and always took first place in her mother's thoughts and affections. Moreover, Beverly, who probably gave up very early any hopes of outstripping her older sister, had a besetting sin. Much as she enjoyed the glow provided by theatrical limelight, or a man's warm embrace, these paled compared to the flush produced by a few drinks. By the time she entered her late teens, booze had become Beverly's truest and most treasured companion.

Mae acknowledged that she had done her best to ignore her sister as a youngster. When she did take notice, she often saw her as a rival who needed to be reminded who was fairest and sexiest of them all. In addition to feelings of competition, Mae must also have harbored a guilty sense of responsibility for her younger sister's problems. In some corner of her heart, not one she examined too searchingly, she may have feared that she had either caused or assisted Beverly's downslide.

Beverly sang well, and shared the family's theatrical bent. During her vacations from high school, she succeeded in getting booked at Manhattan and Brooklyn vaudeville houses on the Loew circuit. "But we never did much of a sister act," Mae wrote in her autobiography. "I always liked to go it alone." In the telling opening scene of her first play, *The Ruby Ring*, two young women compete for the attention of a handsome foreign officer who has promised to tell one of them, Alice, how he won the Croix de Guerre. Not being able to choose between them, he forsakes both, and Alice wryly comments, "You can't get a man by making a sister act of it." The play's heroine, Gloria, a stand-in for Mae, doesn't have to worry about sister acts; she works solo, and succeeds in making every man she meets want to marry her.

A sister act was exactly what Matilda urged Mae to undertake with Beverly. Underscoring her superior drawing power, Mae billed the act "Mae West and Sister," denying Beverly the distinction of a separate identity. For Mae this outing carried weight, since it marked her return both to New York City and to the big-time United Booking Office. Frank Bohm had died, still a young man, of tuberculosis of the spine, and she no longer had an agent. Joseph M. Schenck, manager of the Loew circuit, had married screen actress Norma Talmadge and turned his attentions more and more to film work; things between him and Mae were less chummy than they had been. To make it as a vaudeville headliner, she needed steady dates in UBO's big-time.

The sisters appeared at the Fifth Avenue Theater, located around the corner on Broadway and Twenty-eighth Street, in a lineup that included a Keystone comedy flicker, *The Bright Lights*, with Fatty Arbuckle. The Fifth Avenue, according to Fred Allen, was known as a "show house," where new acts presented themselves at cut rates in order to be seen by Keith bookers who attended and later appraised the acts at weekly meetings. The sister act shaped itself around two major contrasts, juxtaposed: between the old-fashioned girl (a forerunner of Diamond Lil) and her modern counterpart; and between young men and young women, "chappies" and "chippies." For their first number, "I Want to Be Loved in the Old Fashioned Way," Beverly and Mae both appeared (for Mae, prophetically) in Edwardian picture hats and flowing skirts, and together sang the first verse. Then, during the applause, in the wings, Mae tore off the old-fashioned dress and came out in a modern fringed number and frizzed hair, cutting loose with a shake dance, while spelling out her preference for the modern way of loving: in a car, with plenty of wine to keep things going and flowing. As early as 1916, precocious Mae was presenting herself as a petite version of the quintessential hell-bent flapper, gyrating her way to ecstasy, breasts unbound.

She and Beverly sang a song about a premarital quandary: which man should a girl marry, the rich suitor or the likable lad who's broke? That's an easy one, Mae allowed; Sister should marry the poor one and retire to a cottage; Mae will gladly take the rich one—in the act, a male dummy with whom she dances as the lights dim—for herself.

Next they did two black-inflected Shelton Brooks songs, both currently popular, "They Call It Dixieland" and "Walkin' the Dog." For the latter, their dancing finish, Mae appeared in drag, in top hat and tux. Women dressed as men were pretty standard fare in vaudeville, almost as popular as men dressed as women. Just recently "Miss Hamlet," a travesty musical comedy, had shown at the American Roof, allowing the young woman in the title role to display what *Variety* judged a shapely pair of legs in black silk tights. An act called Tempest and Sunshine, which featured Marion Sunshine in an enormous hat à la Gaby Deslys, and Miss Florenz Tempest in a man's dress suit, pleased President Wilson so much when he caught it in Washington that he arranged to have the performers presented to him at the White House.

The crowd at the Fifth Avenue applauded the West sisters enthusiastically, and Mae responded with a closing word: "I am very pleased, ladies and gentlemen, you like my new act," she began. "It's the first time I have appeared with my sister. They all like her, especially the boys who always fall for her, but that's where I come in—I always take them away from her." One can only imagine how Beverly felt.

Sime, who wrote the review in *Variety*, did not share the crowd's enthusiasm. Mae West riled him. It was not her appearance in drag that offended his moral sensibilities and piqued his critical ire, although he sarcastically proposed, "Perhaps if Miss West would wear men's dress altogether while upon the stage and stop talking, she would appear to better advantage." It was the shoulder-shaking, gold-digging, wine-drinking, meet-me-in-the-back-seat-of-a-car routine that made him wince. (Although Mae drank hardly any alcohol herself, the character she played usually did imbibe, and—right through her first two movie roles—frequented a smoky watering hole. She acted the bad girl, and liquor and lust belonged together as the "Devil's Siamese Twins.")

Sime's *Variety* roasting must have hurt. For starters, it suggested that Mae West deluded herself by thinking of herself as a "big time act and trying to make vaudeville accept her as such." It then compared the sisters: "Sister's hair looks very much like Mae's, and there the family resemblance ceases . . . for 'Sister' isn't quite as rough as Mae West can't help but being." Finally, it branded Mae West as too vulgar for vaudeville: "Unless Miss West can tone down her stage presence in every way she just [might as] well hop right out of vaudeville and into burlesque."

Although Mae and Beverly toured their sister act in the New York area for several weeks, it failed to provide a springboard for bigger and better vaudeville opportunities. Beverly would show up drunk at the theater, and Mae, fit to be tied, finally refused to continue performing with her. She told her mother she could no longer be expected to assume a quasi-parental role and take care of Beverly; being responsible for herself was a big enough job in itself. In a move that may have been designed to shield her from Sime's poisoned darts, she announced in *Variety* that her next appearance in vaudeville would disguise her identity in two ways: not only would she masquerade as a male in an act written by Blanche Merrill—a songwriter who wrote for Eva Tanguay, Belle Baker, Trixie Friganza, and Fanny Brice—she would use an assumed name as well.

The difficulty of tracking Mae West at this interval is compounded by the fact that not only did she at least announce she would be hiding behind a different name but another Mae West emerged on the vaudeville scene. The Christmas *Variety* issue in 1916 contains an ad for Gene Frawley and Mae West, "Advanced Comedy Gymnasts." A published roster of members of the National Vaudeville Artists lists Gene Frawley and Mae Frawley, and this comic gymnast was almost certainly the wife of Gene and not our Mae.

Within months of the sister act's dissolution, Beverly married the first of her two Russian-born husbands, Serge Treshatny, an inventor—he designed and manufactured air-cooled motors—who came to the United States in 1916 as a member of the Imperial Russian Munitions Commission. At the time of Beverly's 1917 marriage, her sister Mae, according to *The New York Times*, was employed as an entertainer in a Paterson, New Jersey, cabaret. No job description was provided for Beverly herself.

The Keith circuit did not sign Mae West for a route, nor was it likely to do so after *Variety*'s public tongue-lashing for her suggestiveness onstage. When "preparedness" replaced "neutrality" as President Wilson's watchword, the official moral atmosphere again tightened. The Keith's United Booking Office announced a major clean-up order; its acts could no longer include blue material or swear words, not even a single "hell" or "damn." The Broadway Association in New York followed suit. Backed by the police, it announced a campaign to rid the Gay White Way and its cabarets of vice, part of a nationwide clean-up of red-light districts.

At the same time, the Keith organization was moving to destroy the White Rats union and replace it with a manager-sanctioned alternative, a company union called the National Vaudeville Artists. Keith's UBO, together with other managers, created a blacklist: if a vaudeville artist was found to be a member of the White Rats, or to have performed at a theater the managers didn't recognize, his or her contract would be automatically canceled.

Not surprisingly, vaudevillians fled the White Rats in droves and signed with the National Vaudeville Artists, the company union. The New York *Telegraph* editorialized: "Actors do not work like other men; their efforts are classified under amusements or art—anything but labor." *Variety*, long sympathetic with the Rats, withdrew its support when it judged the Rats' leader, Harry Mountford, tyrannical and the union—especially when it called for a strike, pushing for a closed shop—unrealistic. Even the White Rats' lawyer jumped ship when the going got tough. He resigned as counsel, *Variety* reported, "through being unable to secure his claim for services," although he did secure $3,000 after the furnishings of the White Rats' clubhouse were sold.

The lawyer in question, the one who took his $3,000 and ran, was a man destined for a major role in the biography of Mae West. When he died in 1954, *The New York Times* gave him credit for Mae West's development "from a relatively obscure singer and dancer into an internationally known prototype of the American siren." His name was James Timony.

Just out of Brooklyn Law School—the 1916 Trow's Directory of Manhattan lists him as a law student—James A. Timony quickly set up shop in an office at the Longacre Building, right at Broadway and Forty-second Street, as a lawyer specializing in real estate and investments, and catering especially to clients in the theatrical profession. He took out big ads in *Variety*, offering to invest his clients' money ("denominations of eight hundred dollars upwards") for them in "guaranteed mortgage bonds paying five percent per annum," or to drive them himself to view North Shore Long Island property, twenty-five minutes from Times Square, offering swimming, fishing, and hunting. "Make small payment and the balance to be paid off in rent. Actors, Listen to This!"

Before Mae met him, Matilda had hired Timony as her attorney, which suggests that she must have come into some money from her family, independent of her husband. Shrewd Matilda thought he could be helpful to Mae and introduced them. According to Mae, there was instant mutual attraction. An affair ensued that would prove more durable than any of Mae's previous liaisons, partly because Matilda had given it the green light.

Stocky, built like the football player he had been, with a florid, round, Irish face, Timony was the son of a Tammany politician. Raised a Roman Catholic in Brooklyn, where he still resided, he continued to attend Mass regularly and carried a rosary. In common with Mae and her father, he loved sports, speed, and games combining chance, prowess, and skill. According to Mae, he owned a baseball club and a Brooklyn airfield, and was among the first New Yorkers to fly his own private plane. He also owned a $35,000 racing car, "piloted to fame by the great Ralph DePalma in 1915."

Not conventionally handsome, the young Timony nonetheless appealed to Mae physically. She went for "the guys with busted noses and cauliflower ears and scrambled pans especially . . . guys with faces that ain't handsome, but strong. Guess it's because I been in shows so much with handsome men around me . . . that I go for the ugly ones who got something more than a face." A flamboyant dresser, he favored bow ties, wing collars, boutonnieres, diamond-horseshoe tie pins, a neatly folded white triangle of handkerchief peeking out of his left upper suit-jacket pocket. An observer in the thirties describes him carrying a cane with an elk's tooth embedded in the handle. "His overcoat was of the light tan early Mackintosh style; his open coat revealed an expansive bright-hued waist-coat; his suit was a loud black-and-gray checkered pattern." His walk, said the same observer, "was a swaying counterpart" of Mae's. He limped, but since he had once played football, his disability must have been acquired rather than congenital. Someone floated a rumor that he had been shot in the leg.

Timony certainly knew his way around Murderers' Row, or came to know it. Mae told one of her Hollywood secretaries he had won several murder cases in the 1920s. Andrew Stone, a movie producer who knew Timony well, said he had once visited San Quentin prison with him; Timony was warmly greeted, addressed by his first name ("Hi, Jim!") by many inmates there.

By the mid-1930s the balance of power between Mae West and Timony would completely reverse itself. She would become dominant, a powerful bestower of favors. But early on, he was the high-roller, the one with the bulging wallet, the flashy car, the powerful contacts, the can-do credo she equated with virility. A character modeled on herself, Gloria in her 1921 play, *The Ruby Ring*, succeeds in beguiling businessman R. John Broad Wall by telling him she finds his drive, his energy, pep, ambition, and "push" a turn-on. "Your power—your force—your ability to *do* things—*big* things! The whirl and rush of the City is in the snap of your voice."

One of Timony's first efforts as an attorney on her behalf, however, misfired, resulting in a costly fiasco. Mae confided in him about her marriage to Frank Wallace, and he undertook divorce proceedings on her behalf, perhaps hoping that once free she might marry him. Frank Wallace told the press in 1935, after a clerk in Wisconsin discovered the 1911 marriage certificate and went public with it, that some time soon after Mae met Timony he, Wallace, saw her riding in regal splendor—bejeweled and befurred—in the back seat of Timony's "fine, big automobile." Timony pulled over and addressed Mae's nominal husband: "He said I ought to realize my marriage to Mae was a fizzle and that she could not afford to be married because there was a future waiting for her in show business." Not long after, Wallace saw Timony again and was told divorce proceedings had been initiated. Wallace revealed he was going through a nervous breakdown at the time, "and while I was in the middle of it, Mae's sister Beverly came to my room in the Chesterfield Hotel and gave me a paper. I was in no condition to know what it was. It might have been a complaint, summons or a divorce decree . . . Later, Timony telephoned me that the divorce had been granted. He asked me to tear up the paper and I did."

But a glitch occurred somewhere along the line, and no evidence of a 1916 or '17 divorce ever surfaced. Whether Timony, Beverly, Wallace, or some anonymous clerk was responsible will probably remain a mystery. Unfortunately for Mae West, her marriage to Wallace lingered on the books, even after he married Rae Blakesley in 1917.

Crazy about Mae, Timony soon realized that the surest way to link their lives was for him to make her professional life his business. Little by little, he allotted more time to looking after her career, until, in the mid-1920s, she became a full-time job.

But right now he felt she was starting almost from the ground floor. All the years she had devoted to the stage thus far hadn't made much of a splash. Audiences loved her, but management ran scared. She had been savaged by the most influential critic in the New York entertainment world. The question was: Where, exactly, should she set her sights? Big-time vaudeville was treating her to a frigidly cold shoulder, and besides, she wasn't certain she really wanted to go back on the road. "I didn't like to travel. I was too high-strung to adjust myself easily to new surroundings in hotels, on those old un-airconditioned trains." To make matters worse, the war effort was curtailing fuel supplies, which meant fewer trains and higher rates for every kind of transportation.

Moreover, since America had joined the Allies and begun sending its sons overseas to fight, the war was exacting a heavy toll on the entertainment industry. Many male performers enlisted or were drafted, creating a paucity of male dancing partners and a glut of sister acts. A popular song lamented, "I'm dying for one little dance,/But my dancing partners are somewhere in France." The cost of living had spiraled up. People were reducing their pleasure budgets and investing what they had in Liberty Bonds. What with the war tax, the liquor tax, a rule requiring weekly lights out, and the enforcement of 1:00 a.m. closings in cabarets, "Broadway," reported *Billboard*, "was wearing a grouch."

The climate for entertainers looked grim, but Timony had a few ideas for boosting his young protégée. Although he by no means "created" Mae West in the way that von Sternberg may be said to have created Marlene Dietrich, Timony's devotion to her certainly catalyzed Mae's determination to zero in on her future success and buttressed her belief in herself at a time when it needed buttressing. As soon as he met her, he latched on to the notion that her unique style, good looks, talent, and personality needed a push; publicity would be her ticket to stardom.

While E. F. Albee, manager of the Keith circuit, and critics like Sime viewed Mae's shamelessly lubricious comic vamping as a liability, Timony saw it as an asset that should be exploited to the hilt. One of his early efforts on her behalf was to use his contacts in the newspaper business to get her some exposure that would titillate, and perhaps generate useful publicity. Titillation, shock, and sensation sold newspapers, and they could sell Mae West.

Timony brought her to meet his friend Ned Brown, sports editor for the New York *World*, asking, "Can you get this little girl's picture in your Sunday theatrical section?" Brown, "a Broadway rounder, said he thought so and suggested she wear a bathing suit for the camera study." (Things had changed in the decade since Annette Kellerman got herself arrested for appearing in public in a bathing costume considered scandalously scanty. Kellerman appeared in the altogether, with only her tresses to protect her modesty, in the 1916 film *Daughter of the Gods*, and Mack Sennett's bathing beauties were creating a market for the type.) Mae rejected the bathing suit idea. She had something else in mind. "She took her coat off. The dress she wanted to be pictured in had a round piece cut out of the upper section, exposing the entire left breast."

Of course the exposed breast photo, if taken, never appeared in the *World*, nor could it. But the anecdote demonstrates Timony's willingness to manipulate the press and to capitalize on Mae's lack of shyness about usually tabooed behavior. Still fumbling during the war years, he would become a master of publicity by the mid-twenties.

Mae West wasn't the only performer in New York willing to display half of her delectably naked upper torso. In the 1917 *Ziegfeld Follies*, Kay Laurel stood before French and American flags with her blouse torn open to expose one breast. After the United States joined the fighting Allies, the gesture could be deployed in the service of patriotism, the female form presented as a kind of living statue of heroic proportion. Isadora Duncan, from the stage of the Metropolitan Opera House, after dancing the "Marseillaise," explained her dance as a call to the boys of America to rise and protect the highest civilization of our epoch. She bared her shoulders and one breast, representing a figure on the Arc de Triomphe. In another instance, Isadora draped herself in the Stars and Stripes, a pose many other performers found timely.

Also in favor, not necessarily with any component of nudity, were human renderings of the Statue of Liberty, the posture that Mae West would make famous in one tableau from the opening sequence of *Belle of the Nineties*. In 1917, said Mae, "I put some flag waving into my act to match the torso waving." She also had herself photographed in a straw hat, as a "farmerette" planting a Victory garden.

Patriotism, wedded to kill-the-Hun fervor, had turned into a growth industry. In Detroit, a July Fourth vaudeville program flashed screen images of Teddy Roosevelt, McKinley, and President Wilson on a background of Stars and Stripes. New York Theatre ushers sported military-style uniforms, and the Fifth Avenue Theater pulled in crowds by running a patriotic song contest. Nationwide, George M. Cohan's "Over There" ranked second in popularity only to the "Star Spangled Banner." Sophie Tucker belted "Follow the Flag You Love," Van and Schenck scored a hit with "The Ragtime Volunteers Are Off to War," and Tommy Gray wisecracked about Mary, who "had a little voice,/She couldn't sing a 'Rag,' " but turned her act into a riot by singing about the flag.

To head off egg throwers, German acts in vaudeville changed their names, while the United Booking Office prohibited both peace songs and joking references to the fuel shortage. Government encroached behind the stage door, insisting via its Bureau of Military Intelligence that vaudeville and the legitimate theater be purged of German propaganda and issuing dire warnings about the dangers of "vicious" jests, songs, sketches, and pictures. Newsreels, censored by the federal government, gained places of prominence on vaudeville bills. At the Jefferson Theatre, *Variety* reported, "an episode of the German's Retreat followed, with the Sixteen Navassar Girls in the next position." At the Palace, Trixie Friganza presented a novelty number based on the premise that the Kaiser had been captured, taken to Coney Island, and had his head thrust through a hole in a canvas sheet. "She chirped about heaving balls at the Hun's head," as the audience was invited to hurl rubber pellets at a paper effigy of Kaiser Wilhelm.

Both movie and vaudeville theaters beat the drum for the war effort by converting their stages and lobbies into recruiting stations. At the Palace, an actual young sailor in uniform, introduced by his chief quartermaster, sang "It's Time for Every Boy to Be a Soldier" and appealed to American parents to give up their sons to military service.

Once denigrated as the dregs of the acting profession, movie stars now commanded huge salaries and wielded wide influence, which they now enlisted to promote the sale of Liberty Bonds. Mary Pickford, Douglas Fairbanks, and Chaplin (who had been called a "slacker" when he failed to return to England to volunteer to fight) all pitched in. Pickford auctioned off one of her curls in a Chicago theater benefit, for $15,000. Douglas Fairbanks, a living advertisement for the strenuous life, raised over $8 million for the bond campaign, by leading parades, allowing his name to be used by a Red Cross chapter, and serving as emcee for benefits and rodeos.

As sons departed for the front, mother love came back into fashion as it had not been since the 1890s, with songs like "Just Break the News to Mother" and "America Needs You Like a Mother (Would You Turn Your Mother Down?)." The apple of Mom's eye, her son in uniform, was depicted as defender of all that was sacred: flag, home, women's honor, men's decency, and righteousness itself. The marauding Hun and his Kaiser became "the greatest white slaver of them all." France, Belgium, and Democracy were likened to innocent Woman, crying out for rescue and the restitution of Honor. Irene Castle, whose husband and dance partner, Vernon, enlisted as a pilot, appeared in the film serial *Patria*, depicting womanhood's heroic resistance to Germans and sensuality. Mary Pickford's film *The Little American* showed her being rescued in the nick of time from the rape and plunder of enemy troops. "A French spy arrested by the Germans, she demands an explanation of their savage action in raping a fellow-prisoner. The Prussian colonel, with a sneer under his waxed mustache, tells her that 'My men must have relaxation.' "

Wives and girlfriends back home were also bathed in the purifying waters of official reverence. "You're a real girl . . . the kind that's worth working and fighting for," says Reggie to Gloria, the Mae West figure in her *Ruby Ring*. Artists performing for troops "Over There" were instructed not to make jokes derogatory of women, since "absence from home has surrounded women in the boys' eyes with a sentimental halo." A comedian in the States who joked that his version of the Home Guard meant "I take care of the soldiers' wives while the soldiers are in France" got the back of a censor's hand. The Chief of Military Intelligence sternly admonished, "This is no time to make jest of the uniform, [or to] disgrace soldiers' wives by making them a subject of ridicule." Federal officials in Chicago confiscated copies of a song Eva Tanguay had sung to riotous applause in New York, "It'll Be a Hot Time for the Old Boys When the Young Men Go to War."

But while they were being sanctified, American women also were seizing the reins of power. They did continue to play supporting roles, as fund-raisers, canteen workers, or bandage rollers for the Red Cross. But they also carried banners in suffrage demonstrations and streamed into the labor market, occupying jobs vacated by men at war. They drove cars, worked machines in factories and offices. The next thing you knew, they might be flying airplanes; a vaudeville girl act sang a song called "Since Katie the Waitress Became an Aviator." Competence, independence, strength, and even toughness were not just tolerated among women now, they were positively encouraged as a patriotic duty. New York formed a women's police unit, and a women's motor corps transported injured soldiers to and from theaters. A cartoon in *Life* showed a child crying to its mother, shown in work overalls and cap at the wheel of a steamroller, "Mother, dear Mother, come home with me now."

Mary Pickford, America's Sweetheart, made it clear that a woman could combine feminine appeal with power and business savvy. She boosted women's financial independence, saying, "I think I admire most in the world girls who earn their own living. I am proud to be one of them." Of course, she earned more money than just about everybody, close to a million dollars—an unheard-of sum in 1917. She selected her own stories, costumes, and co-players and headed her own film production company.

Stage women also strutted a new kind of quasi-military might. At New York's American Roof an act called "What Women Can Do" featured sharpshooter Anna Vivian in khaki and breeches. A skit, "Nowadays," included women dressed for their newly active roles: a conductorette, a coppette, and a letter carrierette. Showgirls in Ziegfeld's *Midnight Frolic* masqueraded as Zeppelins. One vaudeville act, "The Aeroplane Girls," turned female acrobats into whirling dervishes. Another featured a nurse just back from Rheims; appearing in uniform at the Palace, she sang and addressed the crowd in an "explosive manner, with some hells and damns," displaying some (presumably deactivated) German bombs. Everyone cheered.

Especially in cities, women's increased autonomy, the emotional volatility unleashed by war, and the mobility and privacy that autos made available created a climate hospitable as never before to sexual freedom and experimentation. "Making love lightly, boldly and promiscuously seems to be part of our social structure," columnist Beatrice Fairfax wrote in 1917.

Both high and low cultures registered a new permissiveness for women. A play produced by Greenwich Village's Provincetown Playhouse and later as a vaudeville playlet, Susan Glaspell and George Cook's *Suppressed Desires*, satirized a post-Freudian wife's notions about repression, and libido as the center of the soul's energy. A movie based on the scandalous cavorting of one Mary MacLane, *Men Who Have Made Love to Me* (1918), depicted a woman's six affairs, one with a married man, and her view of each lover "as a specimen to be stuck on pins and examined under a microscope." The film was banned in Ohio.

A song publisher, Leo Feist, Inc., advertised its sheet music for "There's a Little Bit of Bad in Every Good Little Girl" with quips like "Even Mother Eve raised Cain" and "Most every girl that's proper has someone she calls 'Papa.' " Another song, "Skirts Are Getting Shorter All the While," heralded the changes in women's fashions as they became freer and less covered up.

Birth control grabbed headlines as debate about it reached a high pitch. The subject found its way into film. A dramatic feature directed by Lois Weber, *Where Are My Children?* (1916), portrayed a rich woman consulting an abortionist without telling her husband. Margaret Sanger, arrested and imprisoned shortly after she opened the first American birth-control clinic in the Brownsville section of Brooklyn, toured the country with her six-reel feature, *Birth Control*, and was praised in the columns of *Variety* for her placid, clear-eyed presentation. "There is not a suggestive scene in the picture," the reviewer clucked.

Men, too, wrestled with changing definitions of their proper role. Those males who dodged the draft or advocated peace were savaged, their manliness impugned, by no less a standard-bearer for American virility than Teddy Roosevelt; he called them "flubdubs," or "mollycoddles." The experience of war was advertised as a curative for weaklings, cowards, and "lounge lizards." The battlefield became a proving ground, guaranteed to temper a flaccid wrist (by implication, phallus) into steel. Even little boys on the home front got into fights on city streets to prove they weren't sissies. A woman writing for *The Dial* complained about the paucity of real men onstage. "As show girls have become more showy," she maintained, "leading men have become steadily more insignificant."

Victorian moral rectitude made an attempted comeback, with purity crusaders and social hygienists organizing to keep the American military man safe from obscene thoughts and acts, and to render the fighting force "the cleanest group of young men ever brought together outside a monastery." The Secretary of War, just days after Congress declared war in April 1917, formed a Committee on Training Camp Activities to protect young men who had been drafted from the degradation of drink and the temptations of the flesh. Liquor was banned near the camps, and state after state jumped on the Prohibition bandwagon. A government pamphlet called *Keeping Fit to Fight* characterized women who solicited soldiers for "immoral purposes" as "DISEASE SPREADERS AND FRIENDS OF THE ENEMY." Posters announced, "A German Bullet Is Cleaner than a Whore."

The campaign to keep "our boys" pure may have boosted morale at home, but it did not keep soldiers—either the ones in American training camps or those facing machine-gun fire and poison gas at the front—chaste. As they hummed "Goodbye Broadway, Hello France," our boys did some serious stepping out, availing themselves freely of the services of prostitutes. In the Dos Passos novel *1919*, Fred Summers of the U.S. Ambulance Corps in France says, "Fellers, this ain't a war, it's a goddam whorehouse."

Within the military, the VD rate soared. Officers responded by distributing condoms (Mae West always called them "protectors") as well as pamphlets. Many American women first learned about birth control from husbands or lovers who had served in the Army or Navy. "The availability of contraceptives licensed sexual activity and the new acceptability of sexual activity licensed contraception." The Great War, in short, helped make the States safe for carnality.

A man's military uniform itself worked as an aphrodisiac, spurring young women who saw men on leave wearing them to "lose their heads in a whirl of emotion." Del, a young wife in *1919*, has a tendency to "disappear into a phone booth with anything she could pick up so long as it had a uniform on." A colonel, one popular song averred, might wear an eagle on his shoulder, but a private has a chicken on his knee.

Mae would remember "the French in crayon blue, the British in khaki and swagger sticks," and she performed gratis at a Sunday show for soldiers and sailors at the Casino Theater. Her Diamond Lil falls instantly for Captain Cummings, whose Salvation Army uniform looks just like one for the military, purring, "You know, I always liked a man in uniform, that one fits you marvelous."

With the end of the war in sight, American soldiers and sailors on leave in New York—just like the ones in *On the Town*, one world war later— wanted a good time, which often meant sex, drinks, and taking in a show. They, along with civilians hungry for escape and enriched by a demand for American-made goods, helped create a Broadway boom as Armistice approached. The depression of the earlier war years had been routed.

The way had been cleared for Mae West finally to hit it big.

6

THE SHIMMY TRIAL

*W*HEN Mae West debuted as a sassy servant or a wriggly soubrette on the New York legitimate stage in the early 1910s, she struggled against built-in limits on an actress's ability to control her own onstage destiny. Although she did revise some of her lines and stage business to suit herself, she found that producers, directors, writers, and stars with top billing pulled too much weight. Back at the beginning of the decade, vaudeville seemed to offer a wider berth, more freedom to select her own material and custom-fit it. Now, with the end of the long war in sight, the tables had turned. It was vaudeville, which Albee and the UBO struggled to keep clean enough to qualify as middle-class family entertainment, that represented constraint; by contrast, the Broadway stage, whose more affluent audience cultivated a taste for Ziegfeld-style titillation and the opulently daring, instilled hope for a shot at unfettered glory.

During the war, the American musical stage had briefly turned away from what had been a wellspring, the Viennese operetta tradition; recoiling from light opera was part of the purge of anything slightly inflected with a German accent. At a time when even dachshunds smacked of the unpatriotic, the American nativist impulse gained momentum. Actors no longer declaimed; they got familiar, with audiences and one another, adopting a naturalistic, conversational speech. Home-grown cultural products of all kinds got the nod, especially those alive with the genuineness and spunk of a regional, vernacular idiom.

For dwellers in the big city, that meant giving the go-ahead to the vibrant, smart-alecky talk and gritty sights of the streets, with their raffish characters, garish neon signs, and shady back alleys. The humble ashcan lent its name to an entire school of painting. "Well bred people," said artist Reginald Marsh, "are not fun to paint."

W. C. Fields, now a *Ziegfeld Follies* star, agreed; he developed a skit about the subway. Jack Lait wrote a playlet in Chicago about a lady crook, "Diamond Daisy," whose talk was rife with "tough" dialogue and "wise comebacks." Mark Linder, later connected with *Diamond Lil*, wrote a skit about Sing Sing prisoners just sprung from "the crib," or jail. Before "Street Scene" became the title of a play, it was the name of a preoccupation, one that was fueled by the movement of more and more Americans into urban centers. "Until the 1920 census, population demographics preferred the country to the town, but as of 1920 the majority of Americans dwelled in cities."

In May 1918, as the scent of imminent victory for the Allies suffused the air, Broadway producers looked forward to a record-breaking season. With the advent of peace, they reckoned, every mother, father, and relative, no matter what part of the country they hailed from, would somehow scrape up the coin to buy train fare or gas money to New York to greet returning doughboys at the pier, and they'd stay to celebrate their homecoming with a few days—and nights—on the town.

Arthur Hammerstein, the producer brother of the late lamented Willie, chose this moment to cast Mae West in his forthcoming production of a Rudolf Friml musical, *Sometime*. The Bohemian-born Friml, a Broadway veteran, had written enough musical hits to gain a place at the light-operatic high table near Victor Herbert and Sigmund Romberg. His librettist in this endeavor, a talented woman named Rida Johnson Young, had collaborated with Victor Herbert on the 1910 light-opera success *Naughty Marietta*, a nostalgia-steeped romantic confection lacking any role Mae West could conceivably have played. Unlike *Naughty Marietta*, *Sometime* takes its tone from right here, right now: New York City in 1918, with flashbacks to other times and places. (It borrowed the technique from the movies, something many stage productions were doing, in an increasingly movie-saturated climate.)

Mae West was a perfect fit for the role of Mayme Dean, a "flip" and forward chorus girl wise in the ways of the city, the polar opposite of the Sis Hopkins country-rube role she'd once played in sunbonnet and gingham. Mae's Mayme Dean borrows a little something from the stage "tough girl," who first surfaced in turn-of-the-century Harrigan and Hart productions, and another something from the stereotyped stock character of the chorus girl (not to be equated with actual chorus girls, who often didn't fit the cliché).

The "tough" or "hoodlum girl," made famous in earlier days by the character actress Ada Lewis, talked with a funny, slangy Bowery or servant-girl accent; her tenement upbringing and foreign-born parents taught her faulty English: "He brung it and when he bringed it I was sorry dat he brang it." She wasn't sexy; she wore raggedy dresses and ill-fitting gaiters.

The chorus-girl stock character, on the other hand, was emphatically sexy. Although she worked for a living, earning just enough "jack" to pay the rent on a furnished room, the jewels, furs, and deluxe cars she fancied came to her by way of rich Sugar Daddies or well-heeled stage-door Johnnies, presumably in return for sexual favors—a matter of a woman on the take connecting with a man on the make. Her idea of a good time combined garish sensuality bordering on the tacky, easy virtue, and pricy fun. She helped bring the term "gold digger" into currency, and employed her own expressive argot to further her getting and spending interests. If "gimme" did not always find its way to her lips, the sentiment was never far from her thoughts. The chorus girl, according to newspaperman O. O. McIntyre, "takes her sweetie buy-buy."

In announcing the casting news for *Sometime*, *Variety* forgot about Mae West's previous appearances years ago in *A La Broadway*, *Vera Violetta*, and *A Winsome Widow* and blithely announced that in *Sometime* she would be making her Broadway debut:

> Mae West, known in vaudeville for some seasons as a "single," is going into Arthur Hammerstein's forthcoming musical play *Sometime*, which starts rehearsals in July . . . It will be her first appearance in the legitimate.

It was not her first appearance, but it proved to be the one that put her on the Broadway map.

When the call went out for *Sometime* chorus girls, three hundred young women showed up to be auditioned, two of them, *Variety* reported, in uniform. The girls in uniform were told by the manager, "No female impersonators [are] wanted." A spirit of anxiety about what exactly befit each sex had taken hold. Smoking, for example, used to be a male prerogative. Now so many women were picking up the habit that Jack Benny kidded onstage that he'd been forced to stop—it was too effeminate. Jokes about cross dressing and mixed sexual cues were making the rounds. Sample: According to female impersonator Bert Savoy, of the celebrated comedy team Savoy and Brennan, Greenwich Village was a place where the men sang tenor, the women bass. When Savoy (born Everett McKenzie) sued his wife for divorce, he quipped in court that she'd been wearing his clothes.

The script of *Sometime*, a story about a touring theatrical company, gives additional testimony that the war's recasting of sex roles had provoked a measure of bewilderment and, in some quarters, discomfort. Ed Wynn, who after tryouts in Atlantic City replaced Herbert Corthell in the role of *Sometime*'s Loney Bright, revised the part Rida Johnson Young had written to add a lavender tinge. Loney's effeminacy is hinted at by more than Ed Wynn's lisping delivery of lines like "What is a man to do in wartime when he can't make both ends meat? Make one end vegetables!" Wynn's domestically talented Loney Bright once ran a theatrical boardinghouse and now has the job of property man, stage manager, and wardrobe master for a show in which the company's leading lady (played by Dorothy Bigelow) stars. He's a vegetarian bleeding heart ("I'm no cow to graze on spinach," Mae's character kids), worried, as no he-man would be, about the unfortunate birds killed to furnish ladies with hat feathers. Way back when, he used to perform in a stock company, donning tights and doubling in a girl's role:

> I used to be an acrobat, oh girls, and what a figger!
> I used to pose at all the shows in tights which were de-rigger
> I graduated soon from that and played as Romeo
> In tank towns on a branch line of the lovely B. & O.
> When quite a child in Uncle Tom I worked just like a
>   beaver
> In doubling up a blood-hound with the part of little Eva.

Ed Wynn may not have realized that Mae was studying his comedy technique and learning from it. "He helped me the most," she told a reporter. When she and Wynn were onstage together in the show's opening weeks, he always grabbed the audience's attention "by his clowning. I found I was throwing away all my lines. So I learned to catch the eye of the audience first—usually with some movement. Everything I do and say is based on rhythm."

Although *Sometime* scripts a boy-girl romance between an aviator back from the war and his actress heartthrob, it hints that the course of true love sometimes can't even find an outlet to get started, never mind about running smooth. Mae's character, Mayme Dean, details a sexy lady's frustrations. Her comically wistful lament—Where are the men?—must have resonated on the distaff side of the war-weary audience. For the one and only time in her career, Mae West plays a vamp whose command of Theda Bara tricks fails to bag her a single lover; dressed to kill in a slinky black velvet halter-top sheath that's cut at the calf to show some leg, she's a teasing chorus girl who writes mash notes to herself to keep the others from guying her. "I see all these dames getting their Packards," she moans, "but I can't land even a Buick. What do you have to do to get it?" she wonders as she sidles into her first song, "What Do You Have to Do?":

> *I wonder why these dames can reign as lobster palace queens*
> *While I go home and o'er the gas warm up a can of beans.*

When the company tour takes Mayme to a posh Buenos Aires racing club (a scene Mae West will return to, on film, in *Goin' to Town*), she pouts that she can't hope to land a man while surrounded with people who don't speak her "42nd Street language." Mayme's speech brands her as an American version of Shaw's cockney Liza Doolittle, street-smart and unschooled, but colorful, comical, astute, and completely natural. The wisecracking New York dame who says "goin' " for "going" was headed for a very long run: Mae would continue to play her, even when costumed as a St. Louis woman, a Texas rancher, a Frisco doll, or a Russian empress, for the rest of her career.

Praying for the attentions of "Any Kind of Man" (the name of her second song), she wails: "I don't talk Spaghetti or Wop or Parley Vous . . . Here's this wonderful tropical country, palms, flowers, a moon. All the tools for love-making . . . [I'm a] 'Vampire with No One to Vamp.' " The song she sings has lyrics by Rida Johnson Young (who'd loosened up considerably since writing "Ah, Sweet Mystery of Life" in 1910) that Mae delivered "tough girl" style, to make that "42nd Street language" sound realer than real:

> *I was born a scamp*
> *Meant to be a vamp*
> *If I'd had a chance I could have did*
> *Theda Bara tricks,*
> *Paralyzed the hicks*
> *Nothing could have stopped me but the lid*
> *But somehow my style has got a cramp*
> *Can't find a single soul to vamp.*
>
> *All I want is just a little loving*
> *Just a little spooning and a squeeze*

I was really meant for turtle doving
Lead me to it, let me do it please

. . .

If the boob can walk, he don't have to talk
Send me any kind of man.

At the end of this number, stage direction indicates, Mayme falls into the leading man's arms—but it's just a momentary coupling; he's to marry another.

If her energetic vamping harvested no conquests for Mae's character, Mayme, it scored with audiences and some reviewers. Leonard Hall, who became a columnist for the New York *Telegram*, remembered how, as a mildewed show-hungry soldier just off a transport, he'd headed straight for Ed Wynn and Mae West in *Sometime*. "A whippet tank and eight Missouri jug heads couldn't have tugged me north . . . Along came a shapely, flashy young specialty . . . Mae at that time had not yet begun to expand and billow—she was a slim and flaring flame," and he was smitten.

"Mae West gave a capital characterization of a chorus girl in search of temptation, but never finding it, which toward the close of the show was marred by vulgarity," the *Tribune* opined. Shockable Sime, in *Variety*, had to admit Mae West bowled them over with her dance—she "stopped the show with it, then made a speech, and then made another"—but he couldn't pass up another opportunity to scold, this time about the shimmy, which he diagnosed as that old bugaboo the kootch dressed up in new clothes. "Miss West has improved somewhat in looks," he conceded, "but is still the rough hand on hip character . . . that she first conceived as the ideal type of woman single in vaudeville."

The charges of vulgarity only helped *Sometime* at the box office. Despite its inauspiciously timed opening at the peak of the Spanish influenza epidemic (one reviewer called the show "catchy as the grip"), when thousands of New Yorkers were succumbing each week, and theaters in many parts of the country had to close down, the production survived for eight months, becoming the season's longest-running musical.

Its term finally ended as the season wound down, in June, in its thirty-sixth week, well before the start of the actors' strike that would close the New York legitimate theaters, force managers to recognize Actors Equity, and educate the public about prevailing injustices in the way actors had traditionally been treated. *Sometime*'s Ed Wynn served as an Equity organizer. (Wynn was a scrapper. Although he was making $800 a week—

considerably more, we can assume, than Mae West was earning—he demanded 1 percent of the gross of *Sometime*, claiming he'd rewritten his role.) Mae West played no visible role in the Equity struggle, but she surely benefited from new contracts that required managers to pay for transportation and costumes. When she created a union hothead in her play *Pleasure Man*, she made him a crude goon. (On the other hand, she showed some empathy for socialist and presidential candidate Eugene Debs, who went to jail for his antiwar beliefs. According to Milton Berle, she wrote to President Harding congratulating him for commuting Debs's sentence after he'd served three years in the pen.)

Having opened at the Shubert Theatre, *Sometime* moved on after demonstrating its staying power to the famous Casino, a turreted, high-Victorian, pseudo-Moorish extravaganza whose boards had been seasoned by the likes of Lillian Russell and the Florodora sextette. The move took place on a momentous day: November 11, 1918, the day the war came to its official end.

Armistice Day in New York began with sirens blaring and bells ringing. Mobs of cheering, horn-tooting, flag-waving celebrants streamed into Times Square, where the Times Tower was festooned with electric lights spelling out the word "Victory." Downtown on Wall Street a dummy of the Kaiser was washed along with a firehose. "I was happy we won," remembered Mae, who had seen friends and relatives go off to battle, "but I was young and busy, and I excused myself with the old corny but true idea—the show must go on."

The public had overdosed on deprivation and sorrow. Now it wanted to wash its cares away, obliterate the ugly stain of war in a shower of ticker tape, confetti, and frothy entertainment, for which it was willing to pay top dollar. Consumption went haywire in a decade-long shopping spree that of course left many Americans behind. Inflation accompanied the rush to good times. PUBLIC TURNING AWAY FROM WAR PLAYS AND PICTURES, *Variety* reported. "Weary Nation Wants Happiness and Gaiety. Continuous Joy Centre Predicted for Broadway." The Fuel Administration's lights-out policy came to an end: Broadway again blazed with electricity, and gaudy signs ballyhooed Four Roses whiskey and Canadian Club.

The enactment of Prohibition would soon change the signs—" 'Squibb's Dental Cream' will be the most intoxicating product recommended," and restaurants replace "Ales, Wines, Liquors" with "Soda, Ice Cream, Pastry"— but it wouldn't eliminate public drunkenness. "Prohibition appears to be increasing the number of drunks around Broadway," *Variety* reported.

The shimmy, the dance Mae West transported from Chicago's South State Street to New York's Broadway, captured and capsulized the frenzied, youth-worshipping, hedonistic, hip-flask fueled, scofflaw spirit of the moment. Women's skirts climbed upward, to allow for greater freedom of movement and a better view for gapers. The Westian languor, for now, waited in the wings; this was not the moment for "a guy what takes his time." Speedy motion was the thing, whether on the road in a spiffy Pierce Arrow, in the air (flying ace Eddie Rickenbacker's stock as a hero-performer soared), or in jazz-filled clubs on the dance floor:

> Honey baby, won't you come and take a chance,
> Sweet Patootie, can't you hear my plea
> That nervous sort of movement is the latest dance
> Oh how that dance appeals to me.

Unlike the Turkey Trot of old or the soon-to-conquer Charleston, the shimmy required athletic and aerobic capabilities only professionals and the most energetic, gifted—and uninhibited—amateurs possessed. The wider public danced "to saxophone-shrill foxtrots, in cheek-to-cheek, body-to-body clutches." The shimmy was primarily an exhibition dance.

Other white performers just in from Chicago—Joe Frisco, and Sophie Tucker's two protégées, Gilda Gray and Bee Palmer, also came on the scene as shimmying dynamos. (So did female impersonator Bothwell Browne.) Gilda Gray wowed them in the Shubert's *Gaieties of 1919*, when she did the shimmy to the "Balstreet Blues." Blond Bee Palmer brought her shimmying wild woman to the *Ziegfeld Follies* and then the Palace, prompting "The Skirt," in *Variety* to snipe: "It rather surprised me to see a shimmy dancer headlining at B. F. Keith's Palace, but I suppose the box office equalizes everything, even in vaudeville, refined or otherwise."

Generous and affectionate toward Frisco, and also toward George Raft, who was making his way as a vaudeville and club dancer with a mean tango and an even meaner shake, Mae considered both Gilda Gray and Bee Palmer to be trespassers on her turf and stealers of her thunder. She stakes her claim as the mother of all shimmy dancers in *Goodness Had Nothing to Do with It*: her shimmy in *Sometime* came eight months before Sophie Tucker brought Gilda Gray to New York as a shimmy artist. Mae, Gilda Gray, and Bee Palmer, all white dancers scoring on Broadway and vying for the shimmy crown, seemed to forget that they had first learned the shake from unnamed black dancers in Chicago, who had in turn brought it from the South, where it had evolved from its African roots.

From Harlem to Coney Island, in New York clubs and restaurants with dance floors, talented young dancers shook the shimmy; others sang about it. Sophie Tucker released a recording on the Aeolian label of "Everybody Shimmies Now," and Mae West's picture adorned the cover of the sheet music for the same song. Frances White, in Ziegfeld's *Midnight Frolic*, sang "The World Is Going Shimmy Mad." Bootleg alcohol was a suspect when-ever people at leisure pulled out all the stops; they must be under the influence, the thinking went, to cut loose with such abandon. Bert Williams made the assumption explicit when, in the *Ziegfeld Follies of 1919*, he sang Irving Berlin's "You Cannot Make Your Shimmy Shake on Tea."

Free-flying steppers who actually danced the shimmy brought down the wrath of the morals detail of the New York City police and other defenders of right conduct, like the Committee of Fourteen. They agreed that the shimmy was not a "ladylike way of prancing," listed 114 locations in New York where it was indulged (including Luna Park's "Shimmyland," in Coney Island), and pushed for a bill outlawing the dance as a "shameless evidence of debauchery." At its Chicago meeting, the National Association of Danc-ing Teachers voted the shimmy "the most vulgar and dangerous of all Amer-ican dances," and passed a resolution that "all dancing should be done from the hips down." A Chicago judge closed a jazz and shimmy club, declaring: "The evil genius of this place has artfully combined the grossness of prim-itive sensuality with the gilded refinement of modern licentiousness." Even burlesque theaters on the Columbia wheel forbade the shimmy.

At New York restaurants where jazz bands were featured, inspectors were deployed with instructions to watch out for couples shimmying the night away with more enthusiasm than was deemed suitable; delinquent couples were told to "either cut the wiggle or quit the floor." Dance venues were warned by police "that if the shoulder and body movements are permitted during dancing, their dancing licenses may be revoked."

Monitors of stage morals in several Eastern cities, convening in New York's Astor Hotel, ruled to bar the shimmy and kootch dances, along with several other incendiary acts: baring your legs (or other, usually covered parts of your anatomy), swearing, mingling too intimately with the audi-ence, portraying the ingestion or inhaling of dope, and depicting the "nance" or "sex pervert" type of man. Censors, it was announced, would be making weekly reports on any infringements of these standards. "There is less psychology than physiology on the American stage today," playwright Channing Pollock lamented.

The shimmy, like jazz, saloons, women who smoked, and blatantly effeminate prancing, threatened and sabotaged the "normalcy" the postwar middle-class standard-bearers so desperately tried to foster. In Mae West's play *The Ruby Ring*, Mae's stand-in, the irresistible Gloria, pretends at one point to be a proper ingenue; having bet that she can make any man propose to her within five minutes, her Little Miss Innocent refuses to dance the Chicago, preferring the waltz, or a quiet evening at home reading Booth Tarkington. But when Gloria tries to get a repressed professor to propose, she pulls out those Theda Bara tricks, teasingly displays her leg, and promises to try out the act Mother Eve used on the Genesis Circuit, "before we had a National Board of Censorship."

Under attack by censors, shimmying also found its defenders, especially among savvy, cynical, citywise gentlemen of the press. The roguish Jack Lait kidded one manager who'd read the riot act to shimmy dancers, accusing the man of "giving the cold shoulder to the hot one," and begging him not to be so buttoned up. "Tempus fugits . . . Gout sets in . . . Oh Doc, dear Doc, leave us have our shimmy in peace. Go after them as shakes other things."

Mae had no inclination, for the present, to shelve her shimmy act. On the contrary, the prospect of a police raid or a close-down only fanned her flame. She found a niche for the dance in a new vaudeville act, directed by Ray Hodgdon (who also directed Sophie Tucker and was the son of the Keith office's head booker) and unveiled to a house "packed from pit to dome" with "six rows of standees decorating both orchestra and balcony rails." She returned to the Fifth Avenue Theatre, where she'd tried her sister act with Beverly back in 1916. Presumably the Fifth Avenue, a Keith house, decided Mae West had built enough of a following by now to make her a moneymaker, and they caught the UBO censors looking the other way when they booked her. It may have helped that Timony was doing legal work for the Keith circuit.

The reception that greeted her left no doubt that the crowd had been wowed. *Variety*'s Bell reported that, after a two-year absence from New York vaudeville, she "was accorded a reception on her entrance," and that her shimmy "got 'em, and she closed to a whirlwind of applause." More forgiving than Sime, Bell said the shimmy "seems a bit broad for vaudeville, but can readily be tempered down for the better type of houses."

Accompanied by a male pianist (probably Arthur Franklin) and a jazz cornetist who filled in while she changed from a black-and-white outfit ("very tasteful") to "a silver jet that looks like a million dollars," she opened with a "vamp" medley that included a French dialect number, a comedy Indian song ("Indian Water"), and a rag. "Miss West shows a marked improvement in method and delivery since last appearing in vaudeville," the critic allowed. The whole turn lasted all of sixteen minutes.

This favorable notice did not land her headliner status on the Keith circuit, but it did lead to a good but short-term singing and shimmying part in the elaborate stage show that accompanied the grand opening of the Capitol Theatre, on Broadway and Fifty-first, a huge movie palace built to challenge the Hippodrome. The Capitol had royal aspirations: it had a marble entrance, a marble staircase, French rock-crystal chandeliers, and 5,300 seats. Movies were big business now, and posh theaters encouraged the public to feel like classy participants, not mere spectators, in a glamorous world. The days when a "flicker" served as filler for a full program of live entertainment had long passed.

Her former dancing teacher, Ned Wayburn, now both portly and famous for his *Ziegfeld Follies* stagings, was the one putting together the stage show for the Capitol opening, to be called *Demi-tasse Revue*, and he hired Mae in September 1919 (when *Sometime* went on the road with Ida Mae Chadwick in the role Mae West had played).

Following a screening of the Douglas Fairbanks feature film, *His Majesty the American*, a film that showed the swashbuckling Fairbanks quashing rebellion in a small kingdom in Europe, the two-hour revue laid it on thick. Sixty chorus girls wearing electric bulbs in their slippers high-kicked synchronously. Will Crutchfield, a Will Rogers knockoff, twirled his rope, accompanied by a chorus of cowboys and girls, the Bronco Bucks. The Capitol Band played "I Promessi Sposi," and Lucille Chalfant sang Gounod. Gershwin's "Swanee"—soon to become a sensational Jolson hit—was premiered: something for every taste.

For her turn in *Demi-tasse Revue*, Mae West reprised her recent vaudeville act, repeating the songs "Laughing Water" and "Oh, What a Moanin' Man," the latter in a scene billed "Vampires." *Variety* reported she "scored as a single with a burlesque 'shimmy,'" but judged the whole revue guilty of overkill. "The settings are lavish and there are several novelties worthwhile. By itself it would furnish sufficient entertainment, but preceded by pictures and a band concert, it partakes very much of surplus entertainment."

After repeating the same performance at the Winter Garden on a Sunday night, Mae began putting together a new act, one based on her realization that the shimmy alone would not set her apart: "Who wants to make a career of the shakes?" She needed to frame her seductive body work with good comic material—song lyrics and patter between the songs—that would showcase her talents as a laugh vamp (Jack Lait's term). As she had done before, she turned to one of the best skit, comic song, and gag writers in the business, Tommy Gray, who still wrote a column for *Variety*. Gray had become one of the busiest, funniest, and best-known writers on the New York scene, hired by the likes of Bert Williams, Savoy and Brennan, Trixie Friganza, and Gus Edwards for his Kid Kabaret. "SERIOUS about making others FUNNY," his ad promised. "In nominating Harding and Coolidge," he joshed in his column during the presidential campaign, "the Republicans showed a great disregard for the lyric writers—what can you rhyme with names like those?"

Known as a quipster, Gray was an Irish-American denizen of the Broadway and Forty-second Street hub, a waggish, well-liked punster with an office in the Palace Theatre building. (He would soon take off for a season in Hollywood, writing scenarios for Buster Keaton, but return like a homing pigeon to New York.)

Paving the way for future newspaper wits of the twenties like Damon Runyon and Walter Winchell, Gray kept his phrases quotable, short, breezy, and peppered with New York irreverence. He thumbed his nose at the straitjacket of formal or official-sounding lingo, and kept his ear cocked for fresh and colorful lines, sometimes called "nifties." He always carried a pencil, so that when a laugh line came to him, he could jot it down as it "flashed through his thinkery." Mae West would soon adopt the same jot-'em-when-you-think-'em habit.

The act Gray created for her—eighteen minutes at the Colonial, a Keith house famous for its rowdy claque—opened off season in sweltering, booze-less August. The Volstead Act, which extended wartime Prohibition into the postwar era, was a few months old, and one of the turns on the same bill featured a medley "mourning the passing of Barleycorn."

Soar Mae did, at least for the moment, and she shared the honors with Tommy Gray, credited in Bell's *Variety* review for creating "Miss West's new singalong." Initially, according to Bell, the audience was as cold as the night was hot, sitting through the first three acts "in a listless daze that bordered on a trance." Mae West, fourth on the bill, caused them to forget fanning themselves with their programs, sit up and take notice.

She wore the same silver-jetted one-piece dress she had worn a year ago at the Fifth Avenue, supplementing it with a full wardrobe of hats and a silver cloth cape. Her several songs, accompanied ably by pianist George Walsh, each won applause, and she finished, shimmying "expressively" but "nicely kept within bounds," with enough of a wow to justify a brief speech. Her first two songs, "I Want a Cave Man," and "I'm a Night School Teacher," furnished "the necessary contrast of style," the latter offering lyrics "full of 'wisecracks' and sophisticated comedy allusions." The patter between songs also scored as "100% funny." With her clincher, "The Mannikin," she introduced three comic characters, each of course played by herself: a slangy shopper, a simpering bride-to-be, and a Broadway tough girl or "broiler." *Variety*'s Bell applauded the "ease and legitimate repose in character comedy" she'd developed since last seen; she got "every point across without the slightest effort and for full value." He praised her fidelity to Gray's material. "Thanks to Tommy Gray and her own comedy ability, Miss West looks set as a big time feature."

But it didn't quite happen that way. She failed to even complete her Colonial date. After the review appeared she withdrew, pleading illness. We will never know for sure whether she in fact did fall ill, or whether (more likely) the Keith office or Colonial manager pressured her to tone down her shimmy even more than she had, demanding more compromise than she was willing, at this juncture, to concede.

In the fall she took her act to upstate New York, far from the madding crowd, and in March of 1921 landed a role with a touring Shubert revue, *The Whirl of the Town*, that became *The Mimic World of 1921* when it opened in New York. In the interim she worked on her first play, *The Ruby Ring*, coming to grips with the possibility that if she wanted to start really climbing, she might just have to create her own vehicles and her own opportunities.

She was also working on a new look for herself. Her appearances in *Sometime* and the *Demi-tasse Revue* had given her her first magazine cover. She gazed out smokily from the front of the *Dramatic Mirror*, by this time a much less widely read theater-trade publication than *Variety* or *Billboard* but still a cover any actress would have been delighted to appear on, looking like Theda Bara, with a curly upswept brunette do and heavily kohled eyes and brows. The mouth is small, barely smiling. She looks terrific, but not yet distinctive. The attempt to copy Theda Bara is clear. Within a year she will emerge as a sultry blond siren, availing herself of the advances in hair coloring and cosmetic art that were turning the beauty industry into a major player, and leaving behind any traces of lingering girlishness. She was now a woman of twenty-seven, putting on a little weight and adding curves. Thirty was sneaking up on her.

Even with a hit musical and a trade-paper cover to her credit, Mae West did not work in any highly visible venues again for months. How did she survive during the long layoffs so common in these and earlier years? Timony was undoubtedly one source of support; Mae may have been living with him some of the time—at least Frank Wallace accused her, decades later, at the time of the highly unpleasant Wallace–West divorce, of having cohabited with Timony. In 1921 she still maintained her legal residence with her parents on Boyd Avenue, using their address in Woodhaven, Queens, when she registered the copyright of *The Ruby Ring*.

Her attachment to Timony did not prevent her from accepting gifts from other male admirers. Mae collected diamonds as tokens of esteem; they were more durable than men, she maintained, and provided proof of a man's regard. "Most men value you by what they spend on you" were words she first put in the mouth of her character Nona in *The Hussy* (1922) but would repeat later as Mae West. Like Tira in *I'm No Angel*, she held to a belief that the way to live was to "keep cool and collect." But she joked she'd never been a gold digger. "I take diamonds. We may be off the gold standard some day."

She also liked to play the horses. Clues about this habit come to us in her autobiographical second play, *The Hussy*. In that drama, Mr. Ramsey, the father who resembles her own, accuses his vivacious gadabout daughter Nona of spending too much time at the racetrack with rich Sugar Daddies. "She's got too damned many clothes for a girl that don't work," he roars, as he claims he spotted her at the track with a man old enough to be her grandfather. Nona makes no effort to deny this, though she mocks men who think they can buy any girl they see just by flashing rolls of bills at her; love comes first, Nona rather unconvincingly insists. She was indeed at the racetrack with a banker one day, with another sport the next, every day a different man—but he shouldn't worry, there's safety in numbers, and public places are not where young women face danger, anyhow. What's more, when it comes to horses, she, unlike her loser of a loutish father, knows how to bet on winners.

It turns out that Nona is never wholly dependent on her male admirers or her racetrack winnings, having earned some of her money as a cloak model (a job also held by Babe Gordon in *The Constant Sinner* and very likely at some point by Mae herself), and having also accepted help from her mother, who takes in boarders and sews to supplement her income. In the play, Nona is very good to her mother when she finds herself in the chips, dressing her up, buying her furniture and a phonograph; in addition, she pays for her brother's piano lessons and sends him to prep school, even though he's decided "I don't want to be no doctor or lawyer." Like Mae's actual brother, John, he's endearing but laid-back. If his sister buys him a garage, the brother in the play says, he'll hire people to do all the work.

Economic insecurity is one of the things the play is about, as it was one of the central issues in Mae's life at this time. *The Hussy*, dramatized by Adeline Leitzbach from material Mae West supplied, addresses the perennial Mae West themes of class difference and social climbing, focusing on gossipy, snobbish, you're-not-good-enough-for-us neighbors, on people who want more and pretend to be higher-toned than they are, and the various wiles lovely young women and their conniving mothers use to snag trophy husbands who have fancy ancestors and social status as well as money. Several women characters devote themselves to their climb up the economic and social ladder, which Mae (speaking for Tira in *I'm No Angel*) would one day claim she climbed "wrong by wrong." The father of one of Nona's friends, a former pickle man, has become a millionaire grocer, snagged by a socially ambitious widow.

Nona has grown up poor, scraping for pennies, and her desire for money is made sympathetic, not grasping, because it's based on her understandable wish to have the same things fine folks have. She wins the heart of a prize catch, Bob Van Sturdivant, a much pursued young man of Dutch, Old New York ancestry, who owns an estate and a manor house with Rembrandts on its walls. Trying to pass himself off as an aristocrat (to impress Van Sturdivant before he marries Nona) in one comic scene, Nona's blunt, rough-hewn (and in this scene, likable) father replaces Rembrandts with his family portraits, to make himself feel less like an imposter.

The Hussy is also a corrective to the part Mae had played in *Sometime*. Mayme Dean begged for a man, any kind of man, but Nona, like her predecessor Gloria in *The Ruby Ring*, picks men off like flies—they all want to marry her. A stage direction in *The Ruby Ring* when Gloria enters reads: "The more men on this scene, the better the entrance will be."

Although she hoped to make money writing the plays Timony's secretary would type, neither of these first two playscripts was ever produced. Mae West still needed income from performing, and she usually came up with something, even if she had to settle for dates at less-well-paying neighborhood houses like Loew's Delancey Theatre (where Fred Allen said he worked with her in 1919) or bookings outside Manhattan, far off the main drag. She also made a little money with sheet music that featured her on the cover—but not enough to make a real difference.

Big-time vaudeville would remain inhospitable so long as it continued to ban blue material. The Keith office, still monarch of the big-time, gave no indication that it was lowering its guard against infractions of conventional standards of decency. "Stringent Methods for Clean Shows Vigorously Undertaken by Keith Office," *Variety* reported. "Acts Called into Presence of Keith Executives—Personally Told What to Eliminate of Dialog and Songs in Acts." Slang expressions like "That's the cat's meow," "the cat's pajamas," "hot dog," and "hot cat" were forbidden. Offending artists in New York were taken to task by Albee himself. Groucho Marx likened Albee to the owner of a large cotton plantation where actors served as slaves.

The overall moral climate was deteriorating, the UBO maintained. The "flip style of act" was gaining popularity, "following its lead through the latitude allowed shimmy and jazz dancers." Vaudevillians were picking up a blue style, they suggested, from Broadway musicals and roof shows, "where liberties are allowed in talk and song found nowhere else." Irving Berlin's song "I'm Gonna Do It If I Like It, and I Like It" was one of the offending numbers, and was ordered off Keith time.

Some New Yorkers felt that the theater, in particular, showed signs of deplorable moral laxity. "The public likes its dirt. Don't mistake that," *Variety* editorialized, blaming the war and, above all, the box office. "The trend of the day has been toward a freedom in the theater that one formerly looked for in a gin mill." Nudity, ribald gags, suggestive lyrics, the shimmy, and jazz dancing came up for a rigorous drubbing. Musical comedies and revues seemed especially prone to these infractions of decorum.

A revue for the legitimate stage again came to Mae's rescue. A Shubert production, *The Whirl of the Town*, opened its tryout tour in Washington, D.C., in March 1921 to mixed reviews. "Huge, gigantic"—the words the Shuberts applied to the revue in their ads—were, denuded of advertising hype, euphemisms for shapeless and unwieldy. This revue, more like a vaudeville bill than a unified musical, was bursting at its hurriedly basted seams; with a book by Harold Atteridge (one of the adaptors of *Vera Violetta*) and music by Jean Schwartz, it spilled over into twenty-five scenes, not all of them up to snuff. The *Variety* man in Washington predicted—

Little Egypt, ca. 1893
(Harvard Theater Collection, Houghton Library,
Bequest of Evert Jansen Wendell)

LITTLE EGYPT.
13 AND 15 WEST 24TH ST. N.Y.
·MADISON SQUARE·

Joseph Doelger's Sons, 1899; from a
calendar *(Brooklyn Historical Society)*

Bert Williams
(Courtesy Library of Congress)

Eva Tanguay
*(San Francisco Performing Arts
Library and Museum)*

Gotham Theatre, Fulton Street and Alabama Avenue, Brooklyn. This postcard photo is probably from about 1902, era of the Hal Clarendon stock company (*Brooklyn Historical Society*)

In Milwaukee, April 11, 1911, newlyweds Mae West (her age was seventeen, but she said she was eighteen) and Frank Wallace (*né* Szatkus, age twenty-one)
(*Wisconsin Center for Film and Theater Research*)

Cover, sheet music for 1912 song "Cuddle Up and Cling to Me," published by Chas. K. Harris. Cover designer was Starmer. The Apeda Studios photo shows dancing vaudevillian Mae West with "Girard Brothers" Bobby O'Neill and Harry Laughlin *(Private collection)*

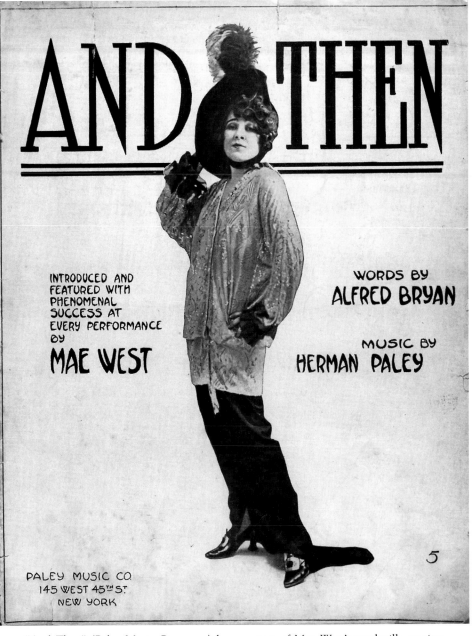

"And Then" (Paley Music Co., 1913) became part of Mae West's vaudeville routine around 1913. This photo marks the first record of the famous hand-on-hip gesture and signature picture hat *(Courtesy Starr Sheet Music Collection, Lilly Library, Indiana University)*

"Good-night, Nurse" (1912, Jerome H. Remick & Co.) marks Mae's first use of material by comedy and lyric writer Tommy Gray, and her debut photo as a dressed-in-white tease. Composer W. Raymond Walker worked briefly as her pianist

(Courtesy Starr Sheet Music Collection, Lilly Library, Indiana University)

Heartthrob accordionist and lover Deiro in Apeda Studio portrait, ca. 1915

(Harry Ransom Humanities Research Center, Theatre Arts Collection, University of Texas at Austin)

A favorite Keith circuit venue in New York City for Mae West and other sensational or freakish vaudevillians, Hammerstein's Victoria (1899–1915) occupied the northwest corner of Forty-second Street and Seventh Avenue

(Photo by George P. Hall, ca. 1905, New-York Historical Society)

Mae West as a "Farmerette"
planting her Victory garden
during World War I
*(Museum of Modern Art Film Study
Center)*

A pensive Mae West cos-
tumed as a sailor girl, around
1918 *(Private collection)*

erroneously, as it turned out—that "sooner or later it will be a good show. Sunday night, it wasn't."

One player, anyhow, scored a bullseye:

There was one outstanding feature that caused a riot—men actually stood up and yelled—namely, Mae West when she shimmied. Miss West simply shook the house from its seats, as well as shaking herself from her neck to her toes and then back again.

So great was her triumph that when the show traveled to Philadelphia, where it ran for three weeks at the Chestnut Street Opera House, Mae West rated billing as a feature, along with Shubert leading man Jimmy Hussey. The other actresses in the cast, according to Mae, resented the amount of applause and attention she was generating. J. J., the Shubert brother she liked best, told her just what she wanted to hear: "All these girls are afraid to appear in the same show with you." Real life, as Mae perceived it, came amazingly close to the plot in her earliest plays: no other woman stood a chance next to Mae West.

The shimmy in this revue climaxed a sketch—the first of many such, set in courtrooms, scripted for her—called "The Trial of Shimmy Mae." In it, her character, who's "pretty strong on looks," is accused by the police of killing the shimmy, after originating it ("It came natural") in a Chicago cabaret: "You know my home is the Bronx/But these Western honkytonks/ Lured me from the lights of Old Broadway." While she was dancing, her song says, the cops raided the place and she was busted. When delivering its verdict at her trial, the uproarious jailhouse jury comes out shimmying.

The shimmy's outlaw status was reinforced, in the Boston tryouts, by a blackout at the first shake of her shoulders that rendered her invisible. Boston censors were notoriously exacting, and the Boston Shubert contingent weren't willing to take any chances. They also cut a Jimmy Hussey–Mae West scene, "The Bridal Suite," which insulted the sanctity of marriage. In it, after her youthful husband leaves their hotel room on an urgent business matter, the bride receives a gaggle of male callers, lovers all.

The show that survived the tour to open as *The Mimic World of 1921* in New York at the new Century Roof still featured Mae West, but not Jimmy Hussey, who quit in a last-minute set-to with the Shuberts over billing and "other mooted matters." In the rush to reassemble, several vaudeville acts were thrown in to fill the gaps in the program. On opening night the dismembered revue concluded with Mae West's blacked-out-in-Boston shimmy, and earlier on featured her in several comic roles: as "Jazzimova," in a spoof of sinuous screenstar Nazimova, who had just appeared on screen as the demimondaine Camille opposite Rudolph Valentino's Armand; in a travesty Shakespeare piece ("Shakespeare's Garden of Love") in which she vamped in a Cleopatra getup, the first of Mae's several Cleo roles. (W. C. Fields decades later would privately describe Mae West as "a plumber's idea of Cleopatra.") She also played a Frenchy temptress named Madelon who never kisses anyone until after the check is paid, and another version of her New York scamp, this one called "Shifty Liz."

The Shifty Liz bit introduced an underworld milieu that Mae West would return to again and again, and make her own. It's midnight on Times Square, and gangsters, card sharks, and other lowlifes prowl for victims. Mae's Shifty Liz poses—posing always figures in Mae West roles—as an ingenue, lost in the big city without even carfare money to get her home to Jersey. Presumably her ploy has already worked many times; she's found plenty of suckers willing to fork over some cash to help out a poor little waif in trouble. Her cover is broken by a Salvation Army man (an embryonic prototype of Captain Cummings in *Diamond Lil*), who reveals that the day before she'd stolen his bass drum and robbed him of a thousand dollars. As soon as he exits, Shifty Liz validates the Salvation Army man's story, indirectly; she approaches a broker and says she wants to invest a thousand dollars she just happens to have in gilt-edged motorcar stocks.

The Shuberts had hoped for a big hit with *The Mimic World of 1921*, which inaugurated their new roof theater, the Century, featuring a restaurant and promenade overlooking Central Park. But they didn't get one. Revues are by definition miscellaneous, but this one's messy mix overstepped even that flexible line. *The New York Times* called it a hodge-podge, and a mediocre one at that. James Hussey's last-minute pullout, despite the attempts to patch it, left a gaping hole obvious to all; though Hussey's name appeared on the program, a last-minute substitute, James Burton, filled in for him in the burlesque boxing match. On opening night, Jack Dempsey livened things up by engaging in improvised, onstage comic fisticuffs, but that was only one performance. He wasn't about to return every night. The Jean Schwartz songs, all critics seemed to agree, were nothing special, conventional but peppy. "They give ample opportunity for the display of the chorus and their gowns—or lack of them." A scene in which close-ups of chorus girls were projected from a screen won praise for its production values, but that wasn't enough to carry the whole.

Although *The Mimic World* closed after just a few weeks, Mae West was definitely garnering notices, not always favorable. The more morally upright critics hurled her way their familiar charges of coarseness and vulgarity. Susceptible to her charms, *Variety*'s Jack Lait found her kootch and wriggle in skin-tight clothes "pretty snappy." Her featured song, he reported, failed to ring the bell, but her Fatima work in the finale demanded several curtain calls.

The *World* said her dancing "looked more as if it were an attempt to get out of a straight jacket without the use of the hands" and *Women's Wear* commented on her daring black velvet dress, which was "not only décolleté to the waistline at the back but is cut at either side to display her bare hips." Months after the show had closed, glossy and prestigious *Theatre Magazine* published a picture of Mae West, blonder than she had been in years, gazing fetchingly while seated before a crystal ball. The caption described her as the "leading woman of many musical comedies whom those who do not know African tribal customs credit—or damn—with the invention of the shimmy" and "the particular star of *The Mimic World*."

One person with plenty of cachet found Mae West's shimmy a knockout: Jack Dempsey, the Manassa Mauler. Described by Mae as a shy young guy with muscle appeal, the handsome heavyweight was at the peak of his fame, having recently defeated Georges Carpentier with a fourth-round knockout in a widely publicized Jersey City bout. The once illegal sport of boxing had become a mainstream big business, with a newly formed state commission governing it in New York. Under the spanking-new, spanking-clean Walker Law, bouts of up to fifteen rounds, which could end in a decision, were permitted, and a huge public that included the middle class, not just lowlifes and slumming aristocrats, thronged to major events. Scalpers were able to sell ringside seats at championship bouts for eighty-five dollars a pop.

Definitely a part of show business—Dempsey appeared in both vaudeville and newsreels, and charged admission for a peek at him working out—major fights were media events, and sports heroes ranked with the idols of the entertainment world as popular icons. At the Dempsey–Carpentier fight, according to Tommy Gray in *Variety* (which now ran a weekly sports column), 91,000 people attended, and 89,000 of them were "shot" (photographed) by the news weeklies. Sports heroes were masculine models of how to be, what to strive for, what men want to imitate and women desire. In *The Ruby Ring*, Gloria describes today's ideal man as a combination of Jack Dempsey, tenor John McCormack, and Babe Ruth.

Dempsey had weathered a siege of bad publicity resulting from his failure to enlist during the Great War. Excused from the service because he was the sole support of his mother, he was nonetheless charged after the war with feloniously evading the draft, and branded a slacker. Prizefighters were supposed to come across as walking vials of testosterone, embodiments of virility. When Rudolph Valentino's masculinity was publicly questioned, especially after his success in making women swoon over him in *The Sheik*, Valentino responded in *Moran of the Lady Letty* by "hoisting up his [sailor's] bellbottoms like a street tough spoiling for a fight." Showing he could fight would prove he was a real man—like Douglas Fairbanks or Jack Dempsey.

But because Dempsey had failed to fight in the war, columnist Grantland Rice in the New York *Tribune* published a wounding column in 1919, contending that, morally speaking, Dempsey had not won the world's championship, "not by a margin of 50,000,000 men who either stood or were ready to stand the test of cold steel and exploding steel. He missed the big chance of his life to prove his own manhood." But having been exonerated by the court in 1920, Dempsey was riding the crest of his post-Carpentier-bout popularity when he joined the fun onstage in *The Mimic World*.

Dempsey had an eye for the ladies ("They call me honey: I get stung so often," he kidded in his stage act), and in Mae West he more than met his match: she had an eye for fighters. After the show, he and his manager, Jack Kearns, came backstage and offered her a screen test for a Pathé film serial they were once again planning, *Daredevil Jack*. The *Daredevil Jack* plan had been in the works for a while but had been shelved when Dempsey faced the slacker charge.

Mae agreed to be tested for the part: in a love scene she urges him to hold her tighter. "Look, Champ, I won't break." The test went well, but since the movie deal with Dempsey involved a pre-filming vaudeville tour with him on the Pantages circuit, she reluctantly backed out—under pressure. Timony, jealous and protective, didn't think she should be touring with three shows a day, and he obviously saw Dempsey as a sexual threat. (In her memoir, Mae reports that the film was never made, but Dempsey's memoir states that he did complete *Daredevil Jack*, co-starring Josie Sedgwick.)

Mae wasn't one to look back wistfully at what might have been. She got busy working on a new vaudeville act featuring a new piano player and love interest, Harry Richman. Later famous as host of his own nightclub, as a Jolson sound-alike on the radio, as the straw-hatted singer of "Puttin' on the Ritz," and in Hollywood as one of Clara Bow's lovers, Richman was an obscure piano player when Timony approached him about auditioning for the job of Mae's accompanist, and to fill in as a singer while she changed costumes.

Richman says in *A Hell of a Life* that Timony warned him not to try romancing Mae: "Falling in love with Mae, if you're working with her, always breaks up the act." In his written version of the story, he suggests he heeded Timony's warning. But according to Milton Berle, Richman was boasting to his cronies at the Friars Club that he and Mae were rehearsing more than a stage act; he said they made love often, once with the radio broadcast of a baseball game as a background, to help her concentrate; she needed "something," and music made her drowsy.

When he auditioned, Richman sat down "under an electric light bulb hanging from the ceiling on a cord" and talked his way through some songs, lisping nervously. Mae told him not to worry about it, the lisp could turn out to be the making of him, it was distinctive. She turned down the other contender for the job—Jimmy Durante—and hired Richman, who spoke his first-ever lines on stage in a sketch in which he played an impresario to Mae West's diva.

A diva Mae certainly was from day one, in his eyes. He says she already dressed in the style of the movie siren she would become: "tight-fitting dresses, lots of plumes, glittering fabrics," long, low-cut gowns. In one scene they played together, she even portrayed an empress, one who wanted to hire a gladiator dressed in nothing but a squirrel skin. Let *him* show some skin. But this was a diva with a difference. She wanted more than top billing and sexual control, though to be sure she wanted those. She had written some of her own material, and she pushed for more money, holding out for $750 a week from Albee, who was offering $500 a week tops. Even with bill collectors harassing her, Richman says, and her telephone disconnected, she preferred not working to working on someone else's terms.

When a manager balked at a blue line in a song she sang—"If you don't like my peaches, don't shake my tree"—Mae was called in to do her act at the front office, for B. F. Albee himself. Consummate performer that she was, Mae was able to deliver the line to Albee as an ingenue—as Little Eva in *Uncle Tom's Cabin* would have, casting her eyes upward mournfully as she clasped her hands close to one cheek. Albee fell for it, declared that even a priest would not be offended, and allowed her to continue both the line and the act. Onstage, the Little Eva delivery disappeared.

Although the writing for the vaudeville act she and Harry Richman performed was credited to song lyricist Neville Fleeson, Mae herself wrote one of the featured routines—the one she incorporated into both *The Hussy* and *The Ruby Ring*, about how different styles of *femme* vamping can be adapted to suit a variety of male types—"how different types of vamps put the bee on their heavy Johns," Conway put it in *Variety*. Another skit drew on her training in melodrama, placing her in a sequence of lovers' parting scenes—as various Juliets saying goodbye to various Romeos. Jack Lait found her "alarmingly legitimate and astonishingly satiric."

The reviewers heaped plaudits upon her in a way they never had before. She was called "classy," "strong," "a hit," praised for cutting out the shimmy and keeping things clean. She had, finally, been willing to compromise for the UBO. Conway, in *Variety*, hailed her transition from a girl who could shake a wicked shoulder to a "delineator of character songs, a dramatic reader of ability and a girl with a flair for farce that will some day land her on the legitimate Olympus." Mae West was being recognized as something considerably more than an escaped burlesque queen, misfiled in vaudeville or a revue. She was applauded as a virtuoso comic actress, a *farceuse* right up there with Fanny Brice, but less ethnic and more glamorous.

She at last reached the vaudeville pinnacle, getting booked with Richman at the Palace, where "she took the track like a flash of lightning" and "cooked all the eggs in the big crowd." Word went out that she had Arrived and could look forward to a stream of successes that might run as long as she continued to make people laugh; a laugh vamp could last forever, it was averred, while a mere shimmy dancer would have a stage life "just as long as the shimmy lasts." Show masters were upbraided for having "let that blonde baby get away from them so long." "We say it was the best thing of her career, for we remember when Miss West did most of her acting with her hips . . . and she shook the meanest hip that ever concealed a flask." The public, as well as critics, were pleased: "She made a world of friends. People don't beat their hands off clapping as they did for her unless they like you."

After angling for top UBO recognition for years and not getting it, she now turned down a three-year contract because it involved—for starters—a long jump to San Francisco and she had decided she'd had her fill of touring in vaudeville. She told Albee she'd be glad to accept dates in the New York area but would sign no long-term contracts. She may also have cannily sensed that big-time vaudeville was already losing out—to small-time, to movies, cabarets, and the booming Broadway stage.

The Shuberts were looking for a script for her, they kept telling her. But if they didn't come up with one, she would write one, she told herself, and get it produced by hook or by crook. Meanwhile, she pinned her hopes on a promising prospect. A writer named Paul Dupont had a starring comic role for her in something called *The Ginger Box Revue*.

7

PENCIL-PACKIN' MAMA

*T*HE *Ginger Box Revue* certainly sounded promising. If only things went right, it might transform Mae West from an also-ran into a star. Here at last was a showcase for her various talents: singer, stepper, looker, comedienne, and self-mocking temptress. Here was a chance to shine that would quicken the pulse of any ambitious young musical comedy actress in New York at the time of the revue's golden age. Fanny Brice, Gilda Gray, and Marilyn Miller were just a few who had already traveled the revue route to huzzahs, earning Broadway celebrity via Ziegfeld's elaborately mounted musical extravaganzas. Ann Pennington, "the girl with the dimpled knees," had made a name for herself in George White's *Scandals*; and uptown at Daly's 63rd Street Theatre, the very place where Mae West would one day star in *Sex*, Florence Mills had dazzled audiences, singing and dancing her way to glory in the all-black Eubie Blake–scored musical favorite *Shuffle Along*.

Downtown, Bert Savoy had become the riotously campy favorite in the *Greenwich Village Follies*, scoring laugh after laugh with his drag impersonation of a hussy who shared a lot with Mae West's future stage and screen persona: an overdressed, mincing, New York dame of exaggerated curves, with a flouncing walk, a fondness for enormous picture hats, suggestive, double entendres, and leisurely, leering glances. Savoy's floozy called everyone "Dearie" and had a repertoire of favorite, much repeated catch phrases in choice Times Square slang that many theater lovers knew by heart: "That ain't the half of it, dearie," "My nerves is all unstrung," "I'm glad you asked," and, most famously, "You *must* come over." In the company of Savoy's hussy, Edmund Wilson wrote after Savoy's sudden death in 1923, "one felt oneself in the presence of the vast vulgarity of New York incarnate and almost heroic."

Mae West, a quick study, surely trained her own gimlet eye on Bert Savoy, appropriating for her later use some of the expressions and campy hyper-*femme* mannerisms, which blended seamlessly with her own strutting style. (The line "Come up and see me some time," which echoes Savoy's "You *must* come over," did not become Mae West's tag line for another decade, after her first movie starring role in *She Done Him Wrong*.) For the present she had yet to make her name synonymous with the wisecrack, and had still not committed herself to playing a single character. She fastened her hopes on the musical revue, which would let her exploit the spectrum of theatrical skills at her command.

The Ginger Box served up wall-to-wall Mae West. In addition to featuring her as Circe, turning her lovers into swine, it presented Mae West as a Broadway vamp (played to Harry Richman's victim), Mae West singing "I Want a Cave Man," Mae West clowning Tommy Gray's "I'm a Night School Teacher," and torching a song whose regretful tone she would later rule out, "Sorry I Made You Cry."

A sketch provided a perfect podium for her adroit spoofing: in a send-up of the Eugene O'Neill play *The Hairy Ape*, which had recently opened at Greenwich Village's Provincetown Players, impressed the New York critics as an innovative masterpiece, and moved uptown to Broadway, she burlesqued O'Neill's tragic hero Yank Smith. The stoker on a luxury liner, Yank Smith is sweaty, foul-mouthed, burly, primal: "I'm steel and steam and smoke and de rest of it." Yank was the very sort of brutish cave-man type Mae West favored as a foil to play against, onstage and off: in O'Neill's hands a somber and powerful Jungian archetype, and in hers a comic cartoon rendered with broad strokes. Backed by the Stoker Girls' chorus line, and by the black orchestra called the Cleff Club, she sang "Eugene O'Neill, You've Put a Curse on Broadway," bellowing, Yank-style, "She don me doit! Lemme up! I'll show her who's an ape!"

The Ginger Box Revue introduced her to a mandolin-playing comedian, Dave Apollon, whose fractured, "sour cream heavy," Russian-Jewish accent she and audiences found a crack-up. At the tryouts in Connecticut, he was the one elected to go out in front of the curtain and make apologies to the opening-night crowd for the woeful absence of scenery in the show they were about to see, muttering under his breath, "It was better with the Czar and the lousy pogroms." His mangled English got so many laughs, according to Mae, that the paucity of scenery and costumes was almost forgiven.

But the skimpy scenery and costumes turned out to augur more than a temporary glitch. Major production troubles were afoot. Although his cast

didn't know it, the producer, Edward Perkins, had established an unfortunate track record; he had a habit of launching productions and then leaving
them stranded on the road, which had happened with his luckless mounting
of *The Red Moon*. In New York, his *Suzette* ran for two days at the Princess
before he skipped out. On a wing and a prayer, he had booked *Ginger Box*
into New York's Greenwich Village Theatre, but as he did so was fast running out of funds for maintaining the production, for actors' salaries, stagehands, set builders, and electricians, and for the rent on the theater. A
slippery fish, Perkins also had a fondness for pseudonyms. "Paul Dupont,"
listed in the program as librettist, was alleged in a newspaper exposé to be
"one of five names used by Perkins."

The bankrupt revue took a critical drubbing for its scrawniness and obviously premature birth. The show at the Connecticut tryout looked more
like a vaudeville lineup than a scripted stage piece, and what there was of
a "book" cried out for revision. The "wiseacres" who journeyed to the preview held out little hope for the show in New York "in anything like the
form it showed there."

The out-of-town tryout lasted all of two days. In mid-August 1922, Perkins pulled another disappearing act and vanished from sight. GINGER RE-
VUE NOW A PEPLESS STEW AS PROMOTER DISAPPEARS, the *Daily News*
reported, referring to him as "Shoestring" Perkins and ridiculing his smooth-
talking boast to the cast and anyone else within earshot that he would out-
Ziegfeld Ziegfeld. "A lot of sadder and wiser stage people are ready to admit
that Edward Perkins, alias Roy Dixon, alias Fred Carroll, Paul Dupont, the
Prince of Bunk of impresarios, took them in like the city slicker selling gold
bricks to a visiting backwoods farmer. Despite warnings against him they
were won by his smooth way, his many plausible tales, his flattery, his read-
iness to concede their ability and promise the salaries they wanted." He
sounds like the kind of character Mae would mock in *Every Day's a Holiday*,
the sort who like flim-flam showman Nifty Bailey constantly cadges the
money he needs to mount his underfunded productions.

Thirteen Equity actors in *The Ginger Box* sued Perkins for recovery of
their salaries: PRODUCER OF FLOPS SUED. Mae West, Harry Richman, and
Dave Apollon were not among those bringing suit; in fact, Mae, who was
to have received a percentage of the receipts of the show, told a reporter
she found Perkins a likable man: "I think he was all right, but just couldn't
get the money he needed." She did express a "warm desire" to reach a
settlement with him.

Perkins also faced a claim for $1,000 rent from the Greenwich Village Theatre, where the show rehearsed but never officially opened. "The electric sign for the Ginger Box Revue, starring Mae West, is still up on the façade of the Greenwich Village Theatre, but current will never light it. A few days ago in Tinpan Alley folks were saying the name alone was worth a quarter of a million. Today in the open market it wouldn't bring thirty cents."

Not one to give up easily, tenacious Mae gamely tried to interest another producer, Earl Carroll, in taking over the revue. Carroll had his own uptown theater, where his risqué *Vanities of 1923*—lots of scantily clad chorines and blue lines to titillate its "tired business man" audience—would later score a hit. When Mae approached him he was shopping for a show for his Carroll Theatre, and she tried to convince him that *The Ginger Box* would fit in perfectly. "There he was with a show house that wasn't doing so good, and there I was with a play that I was certain would make him money. He wouldn't take it. He wouldn't even read it. And did I badger him?" Her all-out campaign came to naught and *The Ginger Box* vanished from the boards. She obviously had staked much on this vehicle, and to see it die so ignominiously—and in full view of the public—must have hurt.

When she came, in the late 1950s, to write about *The Ginger Box* in her memoir, Mae left out the part about the bankruptcy, the failure to open in New York, the flimflam man producer, and the Equity lawsuit. She considered dwelling on misfortune to be a capitulation to "negativity," a violation of her credo that one's well-being is best served by accentuating the positive and banishing all dark or downcast thoughts. For her, acknowledging a defeat was the equivalent of zooming in with a camera on shadows that mar an otherwise flawless complexion. Airbrushing away unpleasant memories could make them vanish. And besides, she reasoned, the public who knew her as a knock-'em-dead movie star associated Mae West with success, not failure: "Mae West always triumphs," she insisted, characteristically referring to the persona she eventually fashioned on the stage and screen in the third person, as a being with an independent existence.

As 1922 wound down, Mae West returned briefly to vaudeville, where her teamwork with Harry Richman had brought her more plaudits than any previous outing of hers had ever garnered. Maybe she could squeeze more mileage out of it. But her temperament was that of a soloist, and even this winning alliance proved fragile. She and Richman were booked on the

Keith circuit in Pittsburgh and Syracuse for a split week in the beginning of September 1922, but they never appeared at either place. Around the time of her twenty-ninth birthday, their partnership abruptly ruptured.

There are several versions extant of the story of the breakup between Mae West and Harry Richman. Mae says in her memoir that they split because he got an offer he couldn't refuse, to go into nightclub work, where he did indeed make a success, eventually running his own Club Richman. She disliked nightclubs, she avers, although later in her career she certainly overcame that bias and in her post-Paramount years developed a celebrated nightclub act, starring herself, backed by a chorus line of hunky, half-naked muscle men.

Richman confided to a friend that he and Mae couldn't stay together on the stage once they became lovers—unconvincing, in light of his prior boast that they bedded down soon after they met, well before their triumphant opening on the Keith circuit.

Variety reported—in a version that sounds like the one designed for public circulation—that Richman had suddenly quit to join Nora Bayes's show. MAE WEST, AUTHOR, LOSES HER PIANIST. Early in 1923 he would take to the vaudeville stage on the Keith circuit as a headliner himself, aided by a midget in burnt cork, and later the same year appeared in a Brooklyn cabaret revival of Wayburn's *Demi-tasse Revue*, with Arthur West, not Mae, as his partner. Miss West, meanwhile, was looking for a new accompanist.

Soon she appeared at the Colonial with not one but two male teammates, a pianist named Leon Flatow (who wrote the music for her song "I Never Broke Nobody's Heart When I Said Goodbye") and an operetta singer named Joseph Lertora. This three-person act recycled much of the material Mae West had used with Harry Richman: a vamp number, a Frenchy bit, a shimmy ballad, and the Gladiator song that cast her as an empress snapping her whip at a love slave. Sime, who remained deaf to Mae West's music and blind to her charms, complained in *Variety* that the act had lost "the little touch of finesse that made her before," and needed less brass. She should trade in the two men for the one Richman.

Mae must have taken this to heart, for a few months later she was back with Richman at the Colonial, as part of a vaudeville bill that included the world-class triple-time tap dancer Bill ("Bojangles") Robinson and featured the Harold Lloyd movie *Safety Last. Variety*'s Conway reported that the Mae West–Harry Richman routine had remained pretty much the same since its earlier outing, although a new bit of business introduced a police dog carried on by a "colored maid in the French number," the first of Mae's many stage maids. She was also flashing some new getups: a silver décolleté gown was a "knockout beneath her blonde hair," ditto a black velvet train gown, paired with a white aigrette and silver headdress. "Miss West's suppressed sophistication, her mastery of the last trick of jazz delivery and her wicked send-up of a temperamental French prima donna" prompted many bows and a curtain speech of the "Thank you, ladies and gentlemen" type.

But this date at the Colonial would be the last stand for Harry Richman with Mae West. Nils Granlund, a friend of Richman's who was a press agent, radio star, and cabaret owner, reports that Mae fumed when the crowd at the Colonial called back Richman, who'd been hired to serve as her pianist, for some solos after she had exited to cheers and taken her bows. He'd moved in on her territory, singing "There's No Hot Water in the Bronx" and carrying on for another fifteen minutes, until the audience stood up and cheered. This was supposed to be *her* act; according to Granlund, a steamed Mae, taking a cue from the temperamental prima donna she'd just spoofed so hilariously, fired Richman on the spot.

Mae West was never much for co-starring. Whether the man she played opposite happened to be Deiro, Harry Richman, Cary Grant, Victor Mc-Laglen, or W. C. Fields, things went smoothly with her only when, diva feathers unruffled, she clearly functioned as the limelight-grabbing top-billed headliner and he as a supporting player, one acolyte among many.

Variety had announced after Harry Richman first went his own way, back in 1922, that while Mae West was planning to recast her vaudeville act with a new piano player, she was collaborating with a playwright on the writing of a farce in which she herself planned to star. The reference was clearly to *The Hussy*, written with an experienced but obscure scriptwriter, Adeline Leitzbach, who wrote for the screen as Adeline Hendricks. Since neither directors like Edward Perkins nor accompanists like Harry Richman could be relied on, and since the Shuberts kept stringing her along, telling her they were looking for a play for her but never finding anything suitable, it became more and more clear that if she wanted stardom she was going to have to take control of her stage vehicles. With a little help from her friends Mae West intended to reinvent herself as a triple threat: her own producer, leading lady, and writer.

The transition from struggling performer to creator, producer, and star of her own scripts came slowly, and required a major mobilization; getting there took concentrated energy, belief in her own abilities, sweat, and well-worked connections. It also took timing—something she became famous for.

Her prospects, after the failure of *The Ginger Box* and the breakup of her act with Richman, seemed anything but promising. Nobody was buying. She spent the later half of 1923, and most of 1924 and 1925, in comparative obscurity, away from the glare of the highly visible New York stage and its attendant publicity.

Where, exactly, did she go during this interval? What was she doing? Trying to sell sheet-music songs with her picture on the front cover, for starters. The songs she pitched (none of which she recorded) kept her image before the public even when she wasn't performing regularly, helping to put over the style and personality she wanted people to identify as Mae West's. One song, "Hula Lou," with lyrics by Jack Yellen, brought back a variant of the perennial Mae West kootch: "She does her shakin' where the shakin' is best." It told about a hula dancer with a form that was so "perfect every place;/You never get a chance to look her in the face."

Another of her sheet-music covers, "Big Boy," also featuring lyrics by Yellen, situates her smiling face and décolletage next to a drawing of an outsized man sporting a cane and dressed dapperly in felt hat, white dress shirt, striped tie, and wide-shouldered brown suit. The man's face is pink, but the lyric daringly adopts the persona of a black woman singing about a hulking, dark-skinned stud who drives the ladies so wild they're willing to slave all week as chambermaids to buy him shirts and socks. Toying with mixed-race sexuality—an explosive issue for mainstream audiences—would continue to be a hallmark of Mae West's risky try-and-stop-me posture.

Throughout the twenties she treated herself to occasional late-night visits to Harlem "black-and-tan" clubs, like the Nest (whose co-owner Johnny Carey was a buddy), where she heard black musicians play and sing jazz, and blues laced with suggestive, double-entendre ("My Handy Man Ain't Handy Anymore") lyrics. The Harlem scene awakened her long-established sense of kinship with African-Americans and their music. She had been singing ragtime for years, and now extended her love affair with the black vernacular idiom to the frankly sexual blues-woman singing style that was crossing over to white audiences, though she stopped short of the explicitness of something like Bessie Smith's "Copulatin' Blues." According to Barry Singer, she often visited black Gaiety Building publishing offices "throughout the Twenties in search of fresh bawdy song material for her repertoire."

Another Mae West sheet-music lyric from this interlude, "Down by the Winegar Woiks," picks up where her comic tough-girl stage roles left off, but instead of dropping her onto Times Square places her with the shanty Irish and right-off-the-boat Swedes, down by the railroad tracks in the down-and-out part of town:

> *You've read about rough men and places*
> *In books that you keep on the shelf.*
> *Well, say, I'm so rough, and at times I'm so tough,*
> *That I must be polite to me-self.*
> *Me pals is a couple of bulldogs*
> *With mustard I sweeten me tea—*
> *There's only two guys in this world who is tough*
> *And both of them babies is me.*

Chorus: *I live over the Wyaduct*
> *By the Winegar Woiks . . .*

How else was she occupied during these post–*Ginger Box*, post–Harry Richman years of lying low, when vaudeville, because of the proliferation of movie theaters, suffered a general decline? Jon Tuska's *The Films of Mae West* conjectures that she may have resorted to bit parts in burlesque, on the raunchy Mutual Circuit, where, according to *Billboard* route lists, there *was* a May or Mae West in the chorus of several shows at Brooklyn's Star Theatre. It seems unlikely, however, that the chorus girl in *French Models* was our Mae; if she were, would the *Billboard* reviewer have grumbled about how young and inexperienced the chorus was? A return to burlesque after she'd appeared at the Palace, and received accolades for her work in a long-running Broadway hit, and while she still maintained a tenuous connection with the Keith circuit, doesn't seem plausible. Mae West had demonstrated her aversion to poorly paid supporting roles and displayed a willingness to turn down parts she considered bad career moves and to wait for the right one.

Although she was surely struggling in the years between the failure of *The Ginger Box* and the sensation that *Sex* became, we know that at other times when the going was tough in show business she had no trouble finding alternative means of support. Timony adored her, lending abundant material as well as emotional help (he probably paid the rent on her Jersey City apartment), and there were always additional men in the wings who wanted to buy her diamonds. Her mother wasn't going to let her starve, either.

Matilda was willing to chip in funds, when she could, so long as the money was going to advance Mae's career.

Mae briefly returned to vaudeville in 1924 on the Interstate Circuit, where she'd toured exactly ten years earlier with Deiro. In Houston, away from the watchful eyes of both Matilda and Timony, in March she fell hard for a Texas-based *Variety* reporter named Bud Burmester, even going so far as to risk a bigamy charge by letting him take out a marriage license, which was never signed by a minister or recorded. Mae was smitten. "No One Does It Like That Dallas Man," she'd sing in the pre-censored *I'm No Angel*. "He's a wild horse trainer/With a special whip." But the romance quickly cooled. The *Los Angeles Examiner* reported in 1935, when Mae's 1911 marriage to Frank Wallace was getting a great deal of press play, that Burmester was an also-ran in the Mae West husband stakes; they quoted him calling their brief, intense escapade and charade march to the altar "a distorted publicity gag."

After her Texas fling, and a short detour to a Keith vaudeville theater in Detroit, Mae returned to New York, Mother, and Timony. When he wasn't closing a real-estate deal or defending a bootlegger in trouble with the law or serving as counsel for a producer run afoul of censors, Timony was spending some time looking for a script Mae could develop as a stage vehicle, something steamy enough to create the sensation needed to carry her over the top. He had served as Earl Carroll's lawyer, and he had learned a thing or two about how censors' attacks and court battles reported in the tabloids can spur a box-office boom. When Earl Carroll was acquitted of charges that he had displayed "immoral" pictures of actresses in the lobby where his *Vanities* was playing, "business jumped smartly," going to nearly $20,000 in one week. Newspaper stories of the court's decision concerning the pictures resulted in a rush to the theater lobby for a peek.

During Prohibition, lawlessness had acquired a new cachet. Partying New Yorkers, thumbing their noses at the Volstead Act, regularly got "lit," "loaded," "stewed," or "cockeyed," and other laws that curbed indulgence were honored more in the breach than in the observance. According to *Variety*, there were seventeen times more "booze joints" in Prohibition America than there had been before. Around Broadway, hip flasks and gin in teacups were as common as wristwatches. Drug abuse was also on the rise: BOOTLEG DRUGS AT HIGH RATES IN TIMES SQUARE. Heroin, cocaine, and morphine could be had readily for $40 an ounce. Gambling flourished as well; shell games, pitch men, and Runyonesque floating crap games crowded into Times Square.

Small-timers were overshadowed by gun-toting bootleggers in slouch hats and chalk-striped suits who played for high stakes and cleaned up financially, moving in on the world of nightclubs and commercial entertainment. They invested in theatrical productions, bought cabarets whose liquor they supplied, and became chummy with many of the show-business people—actors, musicians, dancers—they encountered. The new brand of gangster lived high. Theater builders complained they had trouble obtaining marble for their posh interiors because so many bootleggers who had made a bundle were building themselves marble palaces.

Discreet and elegant East Side Manhattan brownstones (like the one George Raft would preside over in Mae West's first movie, *Night After Night*) became private "social clubs," many run by former saloonkeepers. Hotels in the midtown theater district, deprived of liquor-related profits, began to allow prostitutes and speakeasies on their premises. Restaurants folded and were replaced by cabarets which for a cover charge of fifty dollars would provide a chorus girl for each table.

Gangsters, now that they had wealth and power, became celebrities, people you hoped to catch a glimpse of, read about, or see represented on the stage. Some high-rolling mobsters, instead of cowering in obscurity, actually sought the visibility and notoriety tabloid coverage could guarantee. Bootlegger Dutch Schultz, born Arthur Flegenheimer, changed his name because "it was short enough to fit in the headlines. If I'd kept the name of Flegenheimer, nobody would have heard of me." The man in the street got a yak out of seeing or reading about big-shot tough guys of humble origin, dressed more flashily than the President or Henry Ford, making monkeys out of pretentious and privileged dullards who played by the rules. "Legs Diamond," Mae wrote, "a gangster and blonde chaser, made bigger headlines . . . than a great many Broadway shows."

The Broadway theater, enjoying a boom, reflected the popular glorification of gun- and slang-slinging underworld types. "It was a wild, raucous period in American drama," Mae remembered, "and we all tried to give the theatre patrons the feel and taste of the times . . . Plays like *Chicago, Broadway, The Racket* . . . showed that crime was a national sport like baseball."

The theater showed itself able to absorb shock waves, while vaudeville tolerated little deviation. The Keith-Albee circuit, squeezed by both movies and the burgeoning popularity of radio and phonograph home entertainment, became more and more repressive, issuing edicts on what could and could not be mentioned from the stage. Jokes about Prohibition, for instance, were taboo. It was on the legitimate stage, more prestigious and upscale than all but the top vaudeville houses, and now less polite, that Mae West set her sights.

Two trends were about to collide on Broadway: on the one hand, greater permissiveness about nudity, profanity, and subject matter; on the other, a spiraling campaign launched by church groups, women's clubs, reformers, and politicians for a clean-up. The clash between moral guardians and theatrical risk takers, many of whom hoped to cash in by catering to the taste for anything shocking, made for a heated public dialogue similar to the one between drinkers and "dry" agents.

New York City District Attorney Joab Banton spearheaded the crackdown on stage immorality. Responding to vice crusaders, he went on the warpath against nudity, miscegenation, illicit sex, and profanity—what the press called "dirt shows." Banton convened and impaneled a "Citizen's Jury," made up of representatives from churches, reform groups, and Actors Equity, which supported efforts to clean up Broadway. In some instances, script or costume changes were demanded. Recommended cuts in O'Neill's *Desire under the Elms* were refused, on the grounds that O'Neill's artistry exempted him from such tinkering and the play had been independently produced. But *Good Bad Woman* and *Ladies of the Evening* did accept revisions that complied with "decency" edicts.

Those opposed to theater censorship hoped that Jimmy Walker, elected Mayor of New York City in 1925, would side with them and stand up to the uplifters. As a state senator he had charged moralizing politicians with hypocrisy for preaching one way (pro-Prohibition) and acting another (imbibing alcohol). "No woman," he'd said when state censorship of books became an issue in Albany, "was ever ruined by a book." A debonair *bon vivant*, Jimmy Walker had written popular songs and kept a mistress who was an actress. He patronized speakeasies, tippled, sported spats and derbies, frequented the racetrack, and made the rounds with the likes of Walter Winchell, a former vaudevillian and man-about-town newly appointed critic-at-large for the *Graphic*. With Walker at the helm, things looked auspicious for theatrical scofflaws and bad for the bluenoses.

When she looked around and surveyed the Broadway scene, Mae West made no distinction between serious dramas breaking new ground and frankly exploitative vehicles. By her lights, the successful playwrights of the day had all succeeded because they brought thrills and the vitality of raw experience to the stage. Even a literary giant like Eugene O'Neill, she claimed, derived his power not from formal education or insight into the human condition but from "the fact that he went to sea and led for several years a knockabout life."

O'Neill's thundering impact on the New York theater in the early twenties helped direct her course toward playwriting. Even if she never attended a performance of one of his plays, she knew that he helped legitimize a raw realism that fed on the seamy side of life and expressed itself in the "vulgar" idiom. Said *Variety*'s critic, "Mr. O'Neill always takes for his plays' subjects the sordid, bitter things of life."

On the New York stage, plays about prostitutes and other lowlifes continued to proliferate. There were legions of them: *A Good Bad Woman*, *The Shanghai Gesture*, *Ladies of the Evening*, and David Belasco's racially mixed production of *Lulu Belle*, which starred Lenore Ulric as "a mulatto courtesan reeking with Billingsgate." O'Neill's *Anna Christie*, which opened in 1921, starring Pauline Lord in the role that eventually, on the silent screen, became Blanche Sweet's, and then Garbo's first talkie, focused on a blond, "fully developed," and heavily made-up Swedish farm girl from Minnesota who winds up in New York after escaping from a St. Paul brothel and seeks out her hard-drinking seaman father.

Sadie Thompson, as portrayed rivetingly, to wide acclaim, by Jeanne Eagels in *Rain*, supplied another illustration of the way a Jezebel's unleashed sexuality could work on the stage to rouse the public into a frenzy of ticket buying. All about repression and its devastating toll on the life of a South Seas missionary, it placed Eagels at the top of every theatergoer's list as a tawdry, raucous tart: sin incarnate, repression's polar opposite. Wanted in San Francisco and on the lam from a Honolulu brothel, she finds the "primitive" instinctiveness of the steamy Pago-Pago setting a perfect backdrop for her jazz-fed carnality. Wrote John Mason Brown: "Jeanne Eagels in *Rain*, with her plumed hat, cheap finery, parasol, highbuttoned shoes, raucous voice, and ready oaths, still wages, as Sadie Thompson, her own kind of war in the Pacific."

Rain, a dramatization by John Colton and Clemence Randolph of W. Somerset Maugham's short story, was the hit of the 1922–23 season, which also offered *The God of Vengeance*, a drama by Sholem Asch that had been produced in Berlin by Max Reinhardt; about a brothelkeeper and his lesbian daughter, it earned its players convictions for giving an immoral and indecent performance.

Characters like Sadie Thompson, Anna Christie, and Lulu Belle struck a chord in Mae West because they glamorized, popularized, and made commercial hay out of the kind of role she knew she could play, that of a tawdry but alluring strumpet who shows herself capable of goodness. For the actresses who preceded her in portraying fallen women on the New York stage, these roles brought major recognition, stellar status on Broadway, at a time when prostitution—the real thing, not the stage version—after a period of decline was again on the rise in New York City. The Committee of Fourteen, watchdog of vice, reported a 31 percent increase in the number of cases of delinquent women, attributing the outbreak to the proliferation of nightclubs and speakeasies.

The 1920s saw a consumers' feeding frenzy, fueled by both advertising—by now a major industry—and the movies, which millions of Americans attended weekly. "For the first time, 'jest folk' could glimpse silken drapes, Louis Quinze sofas, and gilded society lilies" and stylishly clad and coiffed stars. Buy it on the installment plan, the advertisements and screen images urged, but buy it: a car, a radio, silk hose, a beauty-parlor makeover, a new nose via plastic surgery (Fanny Brice bought one of these, as did Jack Dempsey; *Variety* started printing tidbits about numerous show-business face lifts). Looking young and sexy—having "It," like Elinor Glyn's heroine, who would be fetchingly brought to the screen by Clara Bow—became the thing. Having "It" put you in the running, and everyone wanted to run—toward freedom, fun, and newly available creature comforts.

Young women paid close attention when alluring Gloria Swanson, who in *Why Change Your Wife?* had asked for a sleeveless, backless, and skirtless dress that "goes the limit," issued her "Seven Deadly Whims":

> New Lips to Kiss
> Freedom from Conventions
> A New World for Women
> No More Chaperons
> Life with a Kick in It
> The Single Standard
> Our Own Latchkeys

Among those who craved Gloria Swanson–style glamour but lacked her budget were some who became easy marks for the prostitution trade. Working women's wages were 60 percent less than men's for performing the same job; but those without money found doors to stylish company closed in their undercoiffed and insufficiently powdered faces. In the New York area, "working roadhouses and nightclubs, hardly distinguishable from the mad-cap flapper crowd surrounding her, the professional could make easy money. Lots of money."

In *Sometime*, Mae West had played a slinky, tough-talking New York chorus girl; in *The Mimic World of 1921* she'd been a kiss-and-collect French vamp and Shifty Liz, a Forty-second Street scam artist. She'd been busted in a staged police raid and gone to trial as farcical Shimmy Mae. She'd experienced the wrath of puritanical critics, Keith circuit vaudeville managers, and a Boston theater censor's preemptive strike. In her own unproduced plays she'd created the role of a flippant, winningly upbeat, sexual hunter who collects men for sport, the way hunters bag game. On the vaudeville stage she'd shimmied, jazzed, and torched her seductive, stag-pitched message across the footlights. All of this constituted an extended prologue. Now came the feature. At the height of the jazz age, she shifted into an even more daring, racy, and frankly illicit mode, choosing as her stage persona's preferred neighborhood the red-light district, where the unapologetic consumerism of the booming, buy-your-way-to-joy postwar economy fell right into step with the age-old sex trade.

Mae West liked to repeat the story of how she got the idea for the play that became *Sex*, whose leading character, Margy LaMont, is a prostitute. One evening, Mae would say, down by the West Side Manhattan waterfront, she saw a cheap woman with frizzy bleached hair, a wrinkled coat, and runs in her stockings wearing an expensive Bird of Paradise plumed hat, surely the gift of one of the two sailors who had their arms around her. Mae was riding in a car at the time, and a companion identified the streetwalker as the sort who gets paid fifty cents to two dollars a trick. "When I went home I kept thinking, 'Fifty cents! How many guys would she have to have to pay her rent, buy her food?' I thought, 'Jeez, this dame is stupid.' I thought if I could only talk to her, she could always get one or maybe two guys to keep her if she was too lazy to work at anything else . . . I was making her over in my mind; figuring how am I going to get her out of the gutter, and [in the play] I finally brought her practically into society."

The waterfront scene sparked her imagination because it found her in an already receptive state. She'd always been drawn to her father's rough-and-tough world of brawlers, cardsharps, and racetrack touts. Encouraged by her mother, she'd grown up pressing the borders of propriety, prizing people who manage to flout the conventions and still come up winners. Those who cashed in on their sex appeal didn't have to offer explanations. It wasn't selling yourself that bothered her; it was selling yourself short or cheap.

She latched on to the idea of a plot tracing the course of a prostitute's rise from the gutter. To Mae West, *Sex* wasn't just an exploitation piece about a hussy; it was a tale of upward mobility, chronicling a woman's all-American ascent from a sordid Montreal brothel to Westchester's poshest quarter. "There's a chance of rising to the top of every profession," says Mae's character Margy LaMont, a tough but sympathetic strumpet who has followed the fleet from Montreal to Trinidad. (*Rain* and *Anna Christie*, not coincidentally, also involved soldiers or sailors.) In Trinidad Margy meets a rich man's son, Jimmy Stanton, who's come from suburban New York to oversee his father's plantations. Jimmy falls in love with Margy and wants to marry her after bringing her home first to be introduced to his well-heeled and apparently ultraconventional parents.

Unbeknown to the naïve Jimmy, who doesn't even realize the bombshell Margy has a "past," his own mother has had an ill-fated fling in Montreal, and turned up in the very Montreal brothel Margy and her sisters in sin share with the roughneck pimp Rocky. Whereas Mrs. Stanton, Jimmy's mother, is a hypocrite who tried illicit sex only because her high-society marriage bored her, Margy turns tricks to earn a living. At least she isn't two-faced. With the rough charm of Mr. Ramsey in *The Hussy*, replacing Rembrandt portraits on the walls of a borrowed mansion with pictures of his family, Margy wipes her hands carelessly on her hostess's Marie Antoinette brocade.

Even though Margy finally decides—in a sudden change of heart right out of the kind of melodrama Mae West cut her teeth on—that she can't marry Jimmy Stanton because her past would catch up with her and tarnish him, the fact that he begs for her hand assures her moral triumph. She's been received as an equal in the most exclusive social enclaves, been waited on by the Stantons' butler and maid, and along the way has knocked phony Mrs. Stanton off her high horse. She's also stood her ground against the bullying pimp Rocky, threatening to turn him over to the police if he doesn't skidoo. "Don't think I'm afraid of you," she warns when he tries to browbeat her. She knows he has committed murder—"croaked a guy"—and "If I start talking, I can put a rope around that . . . neck of yours." By the time the final curtain comes down, Margy LaMont has bested all of them. Her rise to the top provided the kind of street-smart Cinderella story people liked to hear and Mae West would never tire of telling.

Sex was neither a wholly original play nor the work of Mae West alone. In 1924, Timony paid J. J. Byrne of East Orange, New Jersey, $300 for the production rights for *Following the Fleet*, which appears to have been written to order. Mae West told Byrne she needed a play in the style of *Rain*, explaining that "the leading character in *Rain* was that of a loose woman who made her living from soldiers. I told him I had an idea of a girl who made her living from sailors—and to call the play *A Sailor's Delight* or *True to the Navy*, sayings I had previously used in a song." The play, originally titled *The Albatross* and written by Mae West masquerading as "Jane Mast" (Jane was her middle name, and Mast combined the first and last letters of "Mae West") with uncredited Adeline Leitzbach as collaborator, became a *succès de scandale* called *Sex*.

When *Sex* began making money, J. J. Byrne sued, accusing Timony and Mae West of play piracy. Attempting to paint himself as a man of impeccable moral integrity, he accused Timony of stealing his original, which he insisted was meant to teach a moral lesson, and of altering it in a way calculated to make it "a subject of moral gossip." Byrne testified in Federal Court that he took exception to Timony's plan to spice up the play. "I told him that if those suggestions were adopted, the play would be as objectionable as *God of Vengeance* and that someone might be arrested. He said that was what he hoped for, that he wanted the play so 'raw' that the police would make some arrests, which would give the play more publicity than any newspaper advertisements or dramatic comments." Byrne complained further that Timony had advised him "to give up trying to write plays and go into the real estate business."

Federal Judge Charles W. Goddard eventually dismissed Byrne's complaint and demand for half a million dollars in punitive damages, on the grounds that trashy plays of this ilk warrant no legal defense. He said both plays in question, *Following the Fleet* and *Sex*, "were palpably designed for salacious appeal, and . . . no author of a work of this nature can expect a court of equity to support him when he does not come into court with clean hands." Adeline Leitzbach, called as a witness for the prosecution, testified that she had collaborated with Mae West on the revision of Byrne's play. She presumably never pressed her claim as co-author, after Mae copyrighted the play in her name only, figuring, perhaps, that a similar dismissal in court would have resulted. Maybe she felt less than proud of her contribution to *Sex* and was content to settle for relative anonymity. She did squawk about being overlooked as co-author of *The Hussy*.

* * *

From the early 1920s until the end of her life, Mae West, a savvy grammar-school dropout whose ear for the perfectly pitched, precision-timed one-liner did battle with a shaky grasp of the fundamentals of structure, grammar, spelling, and punctuation, staked her claim as a credited member in good standing of the writing trade. Over the years she signed her name as author to eleven plays, published three novels, took credit for her own screenplays, an autobiography, and a book of advice about sex, health, and ESP.

Matilda, the instigator, judgment caller, and prime mover of so many events and maneuvers in her favorite daughter's early career, took the lead in starting Mae to thinking about trying her hand as a playwright. "My mother had watched me . . . putting in punch lines, rewriting my parts . . . and she told me 'You can write your own play.' " The impetus to write grew out of a general need for maximum control of any vehicle she used, a desire to hold the spotlight for hours rather than vaudeville's minutes, and a particular need for authentic-sounding dialogue that suited her personality. The more clearly she defined the "Mae West" character, the more essential it was for that character to talk, sing, dress, gesture, and even walk in a droll, come-hither, street-smart way that conveyed her individuality.

Initially, Mae's written efforts were hesitant and fragmentary. She said she valued her jottings so little that she scribbled on little scraps of paper—"a paper bag maybe at breakfast . . . I gave it to my mother's attorney [Timony] . . . to have it typed at his office."

Timony's secretary, to judge from the copies of the plays deposited at the Manuscript Division of the Library of Congress, could herself have used a brush-up course in writing fundamentals. The scripts are oddly punctuated, favoring the dash as a substitute for commas and periods, and full of misspellings, inconsistencies (a character like Mrs. Stanton, in *Sex*, changes from Clara to Caroline in midstream), and gaps in continuity. Stage directions can be elaborate some of the time, rudimentary—or simply absent—at others. Often the only clue to the action is the word "business"; presumably the actor in that scene would be counted on to supply the necessary movements and bits of dialogue as they came up, in improvisatory fashion.

Rarely did rehearsals begin on a Mae West play with a finished script in hand. "When the play is put in rehearsal she has but a bare outline of the plot and dialogue. As the rehearsals progress she throws in a line here, a speech there. She jots them down on stubs of tickets, the backs of programs, on bags that contained ham sandwiches on rye. In the evening her stage manager collects these pieces of paper and [his secretary] types them. The play is built on the stage."

The pearls of wit that dropped from the lips of her screen characters became synonymous with the Mae West whose movies would ravish the world. But except for *Diamond Lil* and *The Constant Sinner*, her stage plays of the twenties—"sex-dramas," she called them—offer few of these polished and quotable ripostes. They are rough-hewn artifacts in which the situations and the performers' exaggerations, not the lines, create most of the laughs: for example, Mr. Ramsey, in *The Hussy*, hits a golf ball through the minister's window. The few attempts at wordplay come across as pretty rudimentary: "Which do I throw," the cowboy in *The Ruby Ring* asks Gloria, "the lariat or the bull?"

The plays, novels, and screenplays all do agree on one point, however. In every case where there is a part written for Mae West, that woman is a tantalizing siren before whom legions of men fall like wheat before the scythe. Bold, self-assured, unflappable, quick-witted (Mae West never scripted herself as a *dumb* blond), good-hearted, fun, she is defined not only by her frank interest in men, sex, and luxury but by her dominating power and astuteness. Where men are concerned, she's not just lucky; she's a seasoned expert who savors the control that her mastery confers more than any single object of her attention, affection, or interest. Her success in manipulating her silky allure never fails to arouse a man's desire; it often excites a woman's envy, adulation, or wish to serve her as well. No other person in the world she creates, male or female, can match her. None is her equal. Although tiny in stature (a fact she concealed whenever possible), the self-created Mae West towers over everyone.

As a writer of her own quips and laugh lines for the Paramount talkies of the 1930s she would work alone splendidly, infusing the American language with as many quotable sayings as Dorothy Parker, Groucho Marx, or W. C. Fields. The popularity and pervasiveness of oft-repeated advertising slogans ("They laughed when I sat down at the piano") may have bolstered the twenties' fashion for wisecracks. But there's also a nostalgic strain present that looks backward toward the 1890s. More than one Mae West admirer has crowned her the American Oscar Wilde, his equal in mannered, aphoristic humor. But unlike Wilde or Dorothy Parker, who defined themselves as *writers* first—albeit writers whose witty conversation required an audience and aped the qualities of a performance—Mae West was first a showman, a virtuoso entertainer who veered into writing in order to extend her sphere of influence, enlarge and enhance her limousine-scale celebrity profile, and expedite delivery of her letter to the world.

When it came to extended writing in forms longer than the quip—plays, articles, movie scripts, novels, autobiography, even letters—she generally relied on help from a better-schooled hand, someone more practiced than she in getting words onto the page in readable, literate fashion. Playwrights J. J. Byrne and Adeline Leitzbach deserve more credit than they got for their contributions to *Sex* and *The Hussy*. Lawrence Lee assisted with the novel *Pleasure Man*, Howard Merling with *Babe Gordon* (whose title later became *The Constant Sinner*), and Stephen Longstreet ghosted *Goodness Had Nothing to Do with It*. "She did none of the writing—but we talked for weeks," he reported. Numerous screenwriters, some uncredited, shaped the screenplays attributed to her. Whether she acknowledged it or, more often, failed to do so, Mae West's literary endeavors were usually collaborative. "I'm fast as a thinker, but slow and lazy as a writer, so I just throw up the ideas while somebody else gets them down," she admitted to W. H. Mooring.

Sometimes, as with Adeline Leitzbach, the scriptwriter developed situations and characters that Mae West supplied. (The title page of the script of *The Hussy* lists Mae West and Adeline Leitzbach as co-authors. Crossed out are the words: "Dramatized by Adeline Leitzbach From material supplied by Mae West.") Other times, as with *Sex*, she doctored someone else's script until, as she persuasively argued in court, it took on her unique voice and became more hers than anyone else's. With *Pleasure Man*, she relied on actors to supply much of the dialogue and action. She grew fanatical about taking credit, *all* the credit, for what she wrote, even in the many instances when a co-author, ghostwriter, or script doctor contributed a major share of the work she signed "by Mae West." Extraordinarily generous with money—there are endless accounts of her bountiful openhandedness to people in need—she was greedy to an almost larcenous degree in the matter of attribution.

Once, in the 1960s, the composer John Corigliano came up with an idea for a comic and risqué version of *Peter and the Wolf*, to be narrated by Mae West. Mae read the script, liked it, and invited Corigliano and his collaborator to come to Hollywood to discuss it with her. When they arrived at her apartment, she informed them that the project could go forward only if they agreed to credit her as sole originator and author. She would pay them for the script, but then they had to vanish—a condition they would not accept.

She usually got away with hogging writing credit for a variety of reasons, the main one being that no one could deny that, once she altered and acted in a script supplied or enhanced by another, her unique performing style and personality were what carried the day, what audiences paid to see. As John Mason Brown put it, she created "a category of [her] own which can only be described as a Mae Western. Without her it would be nothing. With her it is Mae West."

Unlike self-educated wits like Groucho Marx and W. C. Fields, Mae West never developed much of a taste for reading. "I'm too nervous to read much," she told Karl Fleming. "Good reviews is my favorite reading matter." More at ease with the spoken than the written word, she liked to have someone read and summarize books for her, and often dictated her words to a scribe of some sort, first Timony's secretary, then her own co-author or secretary/assistant. She told Malcolm Oettinger she wrote the novel *The Constant Sinner* with the help of a dictaphone. "I had one with me all the time, see? Whenever an idear struck me I just talked it into the thing. Then my sec'atary would piece the different parts together and arrange chapters and things . . . This sec'atary changes the word where I've used the same ones too often. He's a college man and he puts in high-class words, see?"

Defensive about her comparatively unlettered state, she took the position that people who had book learning but scant life experience were the handicapped ones, not she. Her caricatured Professor Thinktank, in *The Ruby Ring,* may get the world's respect as an eminent psychologist, but he's actually a ridiculous, sexless nebbish, a bookworm with owl-like horn-rimmed spectacles and prissy hair parted in the middle, who knows "everything about books and nothing about life."

Mae West, by contrast, trumpeted the fact that she came up in the school of theatrical hard knocks and lusty living. Her scripts and novels verified that she had pursued experience with gusto: "I write in my books what I learned myself, from life," she explained. "I've never studied construction, continuity and all those things. I just write as I feel; the same way as I live."

"People come to my plays," she claimed, "because they know they are . . . full of action, with real personalities, and devoid of long drawn-out preachments." A woman playwright's raw experience counted for more than formal education, she told a *Brooklyn Eagle* reporter, because women were more likely than men to be hobbled by the limitation of having led sheltered lives. Not Mae West. She adopted an outlook that in the past had generally been reserved for men but as the twenties roared along had gained flapper esteem: life was meant to be lived as a catapulting adventure in which risks and thrills are pursued rather than shunned; a life of caution and reflection was dismissed as a crashing bore.

Mae West turned thirty in 1923, the year before Timony acquired the rights to *Following the Fleet*. She was too old to be counted a genuine flapper, and too shapely, to boot. Career goals loomed larger in her life than they did in the lives of most flappers, anyhow. Pleasure counted for plenty, but it had to be shoehorned amid long hours devoted to rehearsing, writing, performing, visiting song publishers, and making rounds to the theaters. So long as she maintained this discipline, kept fit, shunned alcohol, saw her mother, kept appointments with the hairdresser, and got her beauty rest, she went after a good time. She saw herself as one who lived to the hilt, gulping rather than sipping life's brew: clandestine trysts, speeding sedans, laughs by the bushel, glamorous furs, days at the races, prizefights, Harlem late nights, bee-stung lips, jazz, and diamonds.

This gulping, thrill-seeking energy is what propels her plays. She began writing for the legitimate stage after years as a vaudeville trouper, and her plays draw directly from that experience. Subtlety finds no place. "In vaudeville you learn to put your stuff across quickly and surely. You've got to hit them in the eye with it. That's the training I brought with me to the legitimate theater." Her earlier work as a child actress in melodrama fostered the same impulse toward a theater of bold strokes, biff-bang action, and sensational, rip-roaring effects. At the opposite extreme from closet drama, which is all writing and no stage action, her plays are long on flash and short on literary finesse. They are not the work of a woman of letters, but rather that of a supreme performer bent on expanding the territory at her command and making money at it, to boot: "My first thought, frankly, is the box office. I'm not interested in art but only in giving the people what they want."

She set out to feed the public taste, not form it. "People want dirt in plays, so I give 'em dirt." In her movies she relied on innuendo and suggestion to convey her sexual message. The plays, from *Sex* onward, are frankly raunchy. Torrid embraces and sultry kisses abound. When she auditioned a then still-wet-behind-the-ears Nebraskan named Lyle Talbot for a sailor role in *Sex*, she scared him off by putting her hand on his butt and commanding, "Get close to me!" A nightclub dancer named George Raft refused a part in *Sex* on the grounds that he wasn't "ready."

She always seems to have enjoyed making out with actors in front of an audience; turning a lot of people on turned her on. "Mae West herself, not to be outdone by Sadie Thompson, kissed hither and yon with abandoned passion," reports a review of *Sex*. One scene at the Stanton home has her necking with Jimmy before going up to his bedroom. She helps him take off his collar and tie.

In *Sex* and *The Wicked Age*, she flaunted her body, just stopping short of nudity. The New York *Mirror*'s review of *Sex* comments: "She undresses before the public, and appears to enjoy doing so." In the opening act of *Sex*, set in a Montreal brothel, according to Zora Neale Hurston, Mae played "Honey Let Yo' Drawers Hang Low" on the piano, a song not named in the script that was lifted whole from black brothels, or "jooks." Her performance, wrote Hurston, "had much more flavor of the turpentine quarters than . . . of the white bawd. I know that piece she played . . . was a very old Jook composition." In the cabaret scene she sang two Harlem favorites, "Sweet Man" and "Shake That Thing" (a song associated with Ethel Waters), and did a belly dance to the "St. Louis Blues." In the last act, set in the Stantons' posh Westchester mansion, she sits down at the piano and begins to play "Home Sweet Home," but abruptly switches to a blues. "That's more like you, Marge," says her admirer, Lieutenant Gregg.

Director Edward Elsner, a veteran of Charles Frohman productions who had directed Maude Adams and the Barrymores, encouraged Mae to make her sexiness the focus of *Sex*, rather than a mere condiment. In rehearsal, he spoke words to her she would cherish for the rest of her life, and often repeat: "You've got a sex quality, a *low* sex quality—something I've never seen in anyone before. It even mocks you personally." Elsner named, sanctioned, celebrated, and endowed with trademark status the sensual quality she always knew she had, but had so often been asked to downplay.

Sex appealed to the public appetite for sleaze and sensation. In addition to prostitutes caught in arousing embraces, it includes guns, knockout drinks, a jewelry heist, cops, an offstage suicide, bribery, and the threat of a shootout. Rocky the pimp tries to shake down Mrs. Stanton by blackmailing her. He has murdered someone, has unabashedly lived off women, and now threatens to "plant Margy under the daisies" if she tries to break free of him. She refuses to sew his buttons and threatens, "If I didn't have a certain amount of refinement, I'd kick your teeth all over this floor. Now blow, bum, blow." Better yet, in the last act she pulls a gun on him.

This was surefire stuff. A writer for the theater, Mae West told interviewers, must not only have *lived*, she needs to make the audience feel fully alive as well: give them kicks, an experience that's the opposite of ho-hum, something sensational like the latest edition of the tabloid *Graphic*, which shouted to all and sundry the latest spine-tingling doings of murderers, kidnappers, nudes, and sheiks. "People . . . can be dull at home," Mae maintained, "but in the theater they want excitement. They want to feel, not think, know what I mean?"

Tabloids supplemented the lurid details of the latest news-making scandal with huge, attention-grabbing press photos that told the story vividly and quickly, and sold papers. The *Mirror*'s reporting on a party at which Earl Carroll dumped a teenaged chorine into a bathtub of champagne generated a huge jump in circulation—and revenue. A 1926 issue of *Life* magazine that appeared soon after *Sex* opened made fun of the tabloid credo: "Blessed are the prurient in heart, for they shall know what the public wants." It featured a cartoon drawing of a newsboy hawking copies of the *Evening Grabit*, crying "Sextra! Sextra!" *Sex* was tabloid drama in an era of tabloid supremacy.

The publicity shots for *Sex* fit perfectly into the tabloid format. Mae West appears on the front page of the New York *Evening Graphic* (which played at being outraged by such liberties) as a slinkily provocative hussy in a spaghetti-strap slip dress that's falling off one shoulder, caught in an intimate moment with a good-looking, fully clothed man (Lyons Wickland, the actor who played Stanton) who seems to like her as the one on top. The headline reads, IS THE STAGE JAZZING DOWN TO HELL? When *Sex* toured in Chicago, the ad that boomed it in newspapers warned, "If you cannot stand excitement—see your doctor before visiting Mae West in *Sex*."

No chances were taken with the publicity for *Sex*. Placards were placed everywhere. "I sent boys all over town with stickers. If you stopped for a minute when one walked by, why you got a sticker stuck clean across your back, with SEX printed on it." The sticker gag would find its way into *Every Day's a Holiday*, where Nifty Baily borrows the same technique.

The title *Sex* had been chosen for its socko shock appeal. Who could forget it? Mae often took credit for having single-handedly brought the word "sex" into the bright light of common American use; before her play, she said, the term was only whispered in hushed tones or medical texts. But in fact, as early as 1913, the article called "Sex O'Clock in America" had been published in *Current Opinion*. In 1916, a movie called *The Sex Lure* had appeared, and in 1920 Fred Niblo's film *Sex* featured a wild party scene in which a drunken businessman dons a tigerskin and crawls on the floor, biting a chorine's ankle. Just at the time when Timony acquired *Following the Fleet*, attacking suggestive film titles became a high-priority item on the agenda of Will Hays, since 1922 the head of the Motion Picture Producers and Directors Association. Among the titles Hays cited as objectionable were: *Manhandled, A Woman of Fire, The Female, The Café of Fallen Angels,* and *The Enemy Sex.*

Choosing *Sex* as a title was part of Mae and Timony's strategy to stir things up. Even people who couldn't afford the price of a theater ticket would know about Mae West if she created enough of a buzz to get herself photographed and written about in the press. In court following a police raid, and in the headlines, she could star in an offstage spectacle, the theater of hyper-real life. "Let 'em close the show," puffed Timony. "I hope the police do get after it. That'll mean business."

Sex would never have opened without the financial backing of the Morals Production Company. Founded and headed by Timony, it including other backers: co-producer Clarence William Morganstern, former manager of a Pittsburgh vaudeville theater in which Mae had played way back when; a clothier named Harry Cohen, who anted up an initial $2,500, and another $1,500 to carry the play during rehearsals and Connecticut tryouts; and Harry Cort, manager of Daly's 63rd Street Theatre.

Timony remained Matilda's favorite among Mae's many lovers. Completely devoted, he had assumed a quasi-parental role in Mae's life. He looked out for her, put her career first, pulled what strings he could on her behalf, and especially while she was working on a script did his best to steer her away from other men. "Timony used to lock her up when she had to write a new act and he wouldn't let her out until the work was done. She submitted because she saw the results." She readily conceded that sex could be a time- and energy-consuming distraction from whatever else she needed to accomplish; along with Timony, she had become convinced that until the play was ready, she needed to throw all her superabundant energy into it.

Matilda pitched in with funds, becoming a silent partner in the Morals Production Company (Mae West—read Matilda—reportedly held a 40 percent interest in the show). No longer just an ambitious stage mother, Matilda had gone into business, and was now the sub rosa operator of three successful Long Island roadhouses: the Royal Arms, the Blue Goose, and the Green Parrot, all of them on Long Island's Merrick Roadway. She also, according to *Los Angeles Times* journalist Kevin Thomas, owned an interest in the presidential-sounding Harding Hotel, on Broadway and Fifty-fourth Street in Manhattan, where Mae would reside at the time she was working on, and in, *Diamond Lil* ("Single Room with bath $3.95; Special Induce-ments to Artists").

According to Thomas, whose informant was silent film director and one-time Harding Hotel resident Alan Dwan, Matilda's financial partner in the Harding Hotel venture—a man who may also have been involved in her roadhouses—was none other than underworld big-wig Owney ("the Killer") Madden.

Yorkshire-born, Liverpool-raised Owney Madden, "Duke of the West Side" during the 1920s, moved to Manhattan's Hell's Kitchen district as a youth, "a banty rooster out of hell," and there joined the infamous gang known as the Gophers. By the time he turned twenty-three he had chalked up five murders, and had proven his mastery of the revolver, the blackjack, brass knuckles, and the lead pipe wrapped in newspaper. Convicted of man-slaughter in 1914 for the death of a Gopher rival, Little Patsy Doyle, he went to Sing Sing prison and served seven and a half years of his term. When he emerged, a slim, soft-spoken, and dapper parolee "with the gentle smile of a cherub," Prohibition had been launched and he found his golden opportunity. Rumrunning, beer-brewing, coal and laundry rackets kept him in the chips. He bought into the famed Harlem night spot the Cotton Club (presenting the likes of Duke Ellington, "the cream of sepia talent"), and into other clubs, like the midtown Silver Slipper. Business flourished. He drove a bulletproof Duesenberg (he'd already been shot up so many times police nicknamed him Clay Pigeon), and moved into a penthouse apart-ment in Chelsea, near his Phoenix Cereal Beverage Company, where hun-dreds of thousands of gallons of beer, "Madden's No. 1," were produced daily.

Mae West became one of Madden's amours, and remained an affectionate chum even after his move to Hot Springs, Arkansas, and hers to Hollywood. He treated her with respect, did her many favors, and made a classy ap-pearance, always turned out as a perfect gentleman, with a gray fedora pulled low over one eye, a black shirt, white tie, and (because of his horror of germs and fingerprints) white gloves. He had power, wealth, and a quietly menacing air—a devastating combination, she found. "So sweet," she'd say of him, cooing appreciatively; "so sweet and so vicious." "He's a bad man," she'd croon in *Belle of the Nineties*, "but he treats me good."

Madden relished the company of many entertainers and prizefighters (Primo Carnera and Joe Louis were later interests of his); he found he had much in common with show people. They were "for real." As Madden's biographer, Graham Nown, explains, "They were open and genuine. Like them, he followed a precarious calling, and they seemed to understand each other." As Mae West would say in a movie magazine questionnaire, "Gangsters, as a rule, have a very deep respect for persons in my profession." Madden also fancied newspaper people, who of course were in a position to drum up business in the clubs he owned by plugging them. Walter Winchell and Madden went to cabarets and prizefights together regularly. Another columnist, Ed Sullivan, said of him, "It was like knowing the mayor to know Madden. You just had to ask Owney for anything you wanted, and you'd get it." Madden also knew the mayor.

Matilda, like her daughter, had no quarrel with lawbreakers if they had class and clout. Roadhouses in the Prohibition era were speakeasies on roadsides outside the central city; they were illicit operations that depended on bootleg alcohol, either smuggled in across the border or illegally manufactured in the United States, usually provided by the mob. Said Jimmy Durante, who worked in clubs and knew the scene so well he wrote a book about it, roadhouses "all had plenty of parking space for cars, and necking space for couples. There were orchestras in the bigger places, and phonographs in the smaller ones, so you could flip your tootsies around between drinks. A lot were pretty raw."

Mae West disliked drinking, but she did appear now and then, on the arm of a dapper escort, at the Silver Slipper. She wasn't a regular, but places where drinkers gather keep turning up in both her family saga and her scripts. Her most famous play, *Diamond Lil*, takes place in a rowdy saloon, and her 1927 fiasco, *The Wicked Age*, has scenes set in a roadhouse. The movies *Night After Night*, *She Done Him Wrong*, and *Belle of the Nineties* all use saloons or clubs as settings. *Klondike Annie* begins in a San Francisco dive. Her father once tended bar; her mother's family were brewers; her mother kept roadhouses and used her profits to help finance Mae's plays.

Texas Guinan, also a non-drinker, became so closely associated with speakeasies she was thought of as the personification of the outlaw spirit of the twenties in New York City. Crowned "Queen of the Nightclubs," the former stage and screen actress became a celebrated emcee and nightclub hostess supreme. "She favored picture hats two feet wide, from which dangled ribbons of yellow, blue, purple, and pink . . . Her laugh rattled the rafters. The bright blond hair was tightly waved, her mouth a smear of blatant lipstick."

With backing from rumrunner Larry Fay, a partner of Owney Madden in his sideline taxi business, Guinan presided with raucous high spirits over a series of speakeasies, one of which, the El Fey Club on West Forty-fifth

Street, opened just about the time Mae West got back from Texas in 1924. Another, the Club Abbey, took up a corner of the Hotel Harding at the time Mae West was living there. "Hello, Sucker," Guinan would offer by way of greeting. "Give this little girl a big hand," she'd coax, introducing the members of her chorus line. Everyone knew her tag lines. An ad for one of her clubs crowned her "the World's most charming Hostess. Her bright sayings quoted by millions." Her rowdy, wisecracking style suited her chum Mae to a T, and taught her plenty. Advice Guinan proffered could have served as Mae West's apologia: "Exaggerate the world. Dress up your lives with imagination . . . don't lose that purple mantle of illusion."

Newspaper types like Walter Winchell and Heywood Broun showed up regularly at Guinan's night spots, out for a sure good time and a shot at great copy. Rudolph Valentino might drop by to dance, and George Raft appeared regularly on the entertainment bill; more than likely a well-heeled businessman from the Midwest, the kind Texas christened the "butter-and-egg" man, would be there, too, and would cheerfully shell out the cash for the exorbitantly priced drinks. News footage exists showing Mae West celebrating at one of Guinan's clubs one night alongside Guinan herself.

When the El Fey was raided and padlocked, Guinan moved on to another venue. For her, getting busted by Prohibition agents, or raided by the police, became so routine and caused so little alarm, it took on the feeling of a popular road show, all the more fun for being free, colorful, and unpredictable. Getting padlocked, to the woman who made "The Prisoner's Song" her theme, became the high point of the party.

If Texas Guinan had gangsters bankrolling her in the nightclub business, why shouldn't her friend and admirer Mae West on the legitimate stage? And if Texas made capital out of flouting the law, getting busted, and going to jail, why Mae West could, too.

[8]

PRISONER'S SONG

*A*LTHOUGH the Morals Production Company raised enough money to pay actors, a band (The Syncopators), and rent on rehearsal space for *Sex*, it could hardly be called a flush organization. Prior to its opening, *Sex* barely squeaked by. The production values it could finance were "shoe-stringed"—the set for the Westchester mansion used in the last act was borrowed from an old production of *Mutt & Jeff*; and before the play opened, rehearsals at Bryant Hall had to be suspended for two weeks because of the backers' inability to post a bond with Actors Equity, as required. The funds were scraped up—thanks to Harry Cohen, the lower Manhattan clothier—and rehearsals resumed at the end of March 1926. (Harry Cohen later sued, claiming he was being cut out of the profits.)

Previews began in Stamford, Connecticut, in April 1926 and went on to Waterbury and then New London, a town on Long Island Sound where, according to Mae, only eighty-five brave souls showed up for the first per-formance. Word of mouth soon filled the theater to overflowing with bois-terously enthusiastic sailors on shore leave. Men in uniform and Mae West maintained a mutual-admiration society that lasted throughout her career, peaking during World War II, when the British Royal Air Force delighted her by christening its pneumatic life jackets "Mae Wests."

In New York the theater booked for *Sex* was Daly's, run by John and Harry Cort—partners who agreed to a percentage of the profits in lieu of rent. Situated uptown at Sixty-third Street, a mile from the theater district clustered around Times Square, Daly's location caused some apprehension. Would the droves of New Yorkers they hoped to attract find their way there? As it happened, after the reviews appeared, they did.

Not that *Sex* met with reviews that could be characterized as raves. Some of them resembled gasps of horror. A sampling of review headlines: "SEX"

WINS HIGH MARKS FOR DEPRAVITY, DULLNESS (*Herald Tribune*); "SEX" A
CRUDE DRAMA (*The New York Times*); "SEX" AN OFFENSIVE PLAY, MON-
STROSITY PLUCKED FROM GARBAGE CAN, DESTINED TO SEWER (*Daily Mir-
ror*); FUMIGATION NEEDED (*Milwaukee Sentinel*).

The New Yorker wondered "how anything so undressed in its intentions
can manage [to be] so dreary," and judged it a turnoff: "*Sex* would turn any
Mr. Casanova into a Mrs. Grundy."

"Disgraceful," not "dreary," was the more common complaint, and some
particularly venomous attacks issued from within the show-business community, not provincial outsiders. *Billboard* angrily pronounced *Sex* "the
cheapest, most vulgar, low 'show' to have dared to open in New York this
year," a "disgrace to all those connected with it . . . Poorly written, poorly
acted, horribly staged." *Variety*'s Bob Sisk concurred. "Never," he lamented,
"has disgrace fallen so heavily upon the 63rd Street Theatre." Its three hours
of "nasty, infantile, vicious dialog" would be tolerated in just a few burlesque
houses. Many in the audience left in disgust during the first act, he reported.
As for the audacious Mae West, she inspired gratitude for any "repression
that may have toned down her vaudeville songs in the past." He concluded:
"A police pinch or a flood of publicity on its dirtiness is the sole salvation
of *Sex*." *Variety* wanted no part of any box-office boom generated by publicity. Its reviewer, along with two others who covered *Sex*, agreed "not to
cover its filth."

This attempted conspiracy of silence failed utterly. In and out of the
newspapers, tongues wagged. A few published commentators actually hyped
the play's brash vulgarity, despite an opening night jinxed with minor mis-
haps: a window shade would not stay down, and a cork's "pop" occurred
several seconds after the wine had been opened. "A more flaming, palpi-
tating play has not been seen hereabouts for some time," said the man from
William Randolph Hearst's New York *American*, completely won over by
the star and oblivious of his boss's contempt for "dirt" plays and all things
Westian. Mae West's "slouching, whiskey tenor manner" also found a champion at the *Sun*, even if her writing failed to please: "[It] ranges," he said,
"from the undeniably adroit to the unbelievably inept—to moments when
characters are hauled on and off the stage rather as though hooks had been
inserted in their coat collars."

Walter Winchell, in the *Graphic* (sometimes called the *porno-Graphic*),
pounced on the amateurish script but extolled Mae West's brazen performance style. "She has an amazing degree of self-assurance and convincingly
portrays the tough-stuff assignment," he reported; but he found she lost

credibility as "the goody-goody character in the last scenes, when she turns pure and wears white." He ended by praising the play—"*Sex* is a bold and cheeky enterprise"—while holding his nose to escape its "stench." Morally he judged it "unpardonable."

Variety's Jack Conway, parting company with his *Variety* colleague Bob Sisk, who'd done his best to torpedo *Sex*, waxed hyperbolic several weeks after the opening in his piece about Mae West. She slayed him. Donning the mask of a prizefight insider writing to his buddy Chick, he crowned the star "the Babe Ruth of the Stage Prosties," and urged friend Chick to grab a look-see—and he'd better bring along his sweatshirt:

> Chick, Mae is hot. In the second act, a cabaret scene in Trinidad, she turns in "Sweet Man," very Harlem . . . Some of her lines knock the peasants into the aisles. She sure saxes sex, and how that blonde baby knows her stuff. The production is just so so, but nobody pays any attention to it . . . Mae's conception of Margy LaMont will sentence her to the scarlet sisterhood artistically for life. She's the type from now on, and good enough to fool a traveling salesman's convention.

Jack Conway got it right. Mae West was, after *Sex*, "sentenced to the scarlet sisterhood" onstage for life. After all her innings spent making rounds and beating the drum in pursuit of stardom, she now emerged, in a role that fit her as snugly as one of her slinky dresses, as the New York stage sensation of the moment.

A huge ad adorned the side of a city bus hired by the Keith-Albee organization for an afternoon to house a band that serenaded ticket buyers at the Palace Theater. Occupants of nearby theatrical offices, on hearing the music, poked their heads out of their windows to read: MAE WEST, STAR OF "SEX," AT DALY'S. A *Variety* reporter savored the irony in this coincidence; the Palace, linchpin of the Keith circuit, had opened its doors to Mae West only once, in more than a decade. "Miss West has been in vaudeville off and on," *Variety*'s Inside Vaudeville column reminded readers. "Every time she got a new act it seemed she would be 'off,' until Miss West decided to do dramatic playing." She had become, with *Sex*, the Talk of Broadway, if not quite the Toast of it. The "Babe Ruth of the Stage Prosties" had vaulted decisively into fame.

Notoriety sells theater tickets, and the Morals Production Company found it had a hit on its hands, much to the dismay of naysayers like Robert

Benchley. Writing for *Life*, Benchley reported that he'd trotted up to Daly's to see *Sex* soon after the first reviews had appeared, expecting to find himself sitting in a half-empty theater. Instead, he encountered an enormous queue at the box office. "At first we thought that [co-producer] Mr. C. William Morganstern was being inserted in the stocks by the authorities," he deadpanned, but he soon realized that the people on line were clutching dollar bills in their hands; they wanted tickets to a hot show. A play he scorned as utterly banal, a piece of work he considered far inferior, technically, to *The Shanghai Gesture* or *Lulu Belle*, scored as "a whacking hit solely because the papers had said that it was 'vulgar' and 'bold' and because someone had the genius to think of its name." It irked him no end that this calculated attempt to shock had perfectly realized its goal, creating a *succès de scandale* that cut across class lines. "The sudden rush to see *Sex* is not confined to the *canaille*. The agencies are hot after tickets and each night soft purring limousines roll up with theatre parties of gentry, out 'just for a lark.' " There were some socialites who returned to see it again and again.

By its third week, *Sex* was raking in $10,000 a week. In its seventh week, it hit the $16,500 mark, then leveled off at a steady $8,000. As a money-maker, it couldn't match a blockbuster like *Broadway*, which grossed $31,000 in a single week, but it was holding its own nicely as a durable steady earner despite repeated mutterings that it should be closed down. It wasn't the play people came to see; it was Mae West. When a production of *Sex* opened in Los Angeles with another actress in the role of Margy LaMont, a critic compared it to "Hamlet without the Dane."

Convened by the district attorney, a volunteer Play Jury that included one woman, one physician, and two Brooklynites (the rest were male residents of Manhattan) in June, by a vote of 8 to 4, "cleared" *Sex* and *The Shanghai Gesture* of the charge of indecency, while urging that *Bunk of 1926* be closed and that the nude choristers be dropped from *Great Temptations*. *Variety* hinted darkly in an editorial that the actors in *Sex* must have been tipped off in advance to tone things down for the jury's benefit, but the fact remained that *Sex* had been absolved of the charge of salaciousness, and the district attorney agreed to comply with the Play Jury's decision. A long run for *Sex* seemed a shoo-in.

But incensed vice crusaders could not allow what they considered an orgy of theatrical indecency to continue unchecked. John Sumner, heir to the puritanical legacy of Anthony Comstock, referred to Broadway as a "sewer." He used his Society for the Suppression of Vice to pressure New York City officials to bypass the Play Jury and go on the warpath. The Catholic Church and other religious organizations lent their powerful voices to the chorus of the outraged. In District Attorney Joab Banton they knew they had a staunch ally. The State Penal Law contained a section, numbered 1140-a, that could be invoked to enforce moral standards, if only the police and the district attorney would act. This clause in the Penal Code held accountable not only performers in any "obscene, indecent, immoral or impure drama" but all who aided and abetted such performances: theater owners, managers, directors, or agents. Violators could be found guilty of a misdemeanor punishable by imprisonment for up to one year, a fine of $500, or both.

Sex continued its profitable run through the exceptionally hot summer of 1926, the summer in which Rudolph Valentino died following surgery for a ruptured appendix. His extraordinary funeral and lying-in-state—bally-hooed by publicists from both the movie studios and the Frank E. Campbell funeral parlor—turned Manhattan into a cortege of epic proportion. More than 100,000 mourners packed the sidewalks. Women fainted. Rioting broke out and many were injured. The tabloids faked photographs of Val-entino in surgery and drummed up a story that "the Sheik" had been poi-soned.

One week after Valentino died, according to a columnist for the *Phila-delphia Inquirer* named Whitney Bolton, a séance arranged jointly by Texas Guinan and Mae West took place in a Manhattan loft; Owney Madden and Tommy Guinan, the nightclub-owning brother of Texas, also graced the occasion, and an Italian medium officiated. The purpose of the séance was to determine whether Valentino had in fact been murdered. A death from natural causes seemed inconceivable to this bunch, and much too tame.

The weeks that culminated with Valentino's untimely and melodramatic death rekindled public debate about the manliness of the American male, a debate that had erupted during World War I, when men who did not serve in the military were branded "slackers" and "mollycoddles." Muscular, passionate, and often violent in his on-screen pursuit of women, Valentino was resented by many American men because of his ability to quicken the collective pulses of legions of women; and because of the androgynous sex-uality he projected. Floppy harem pants, slave bracelets, a smooth, powdered complexion, slicked-back hair, mascaraed eyes, a swarthy exoticism, even his prowess at the tango all flew in the face of the rough-and-tough, tall-in-the-saddle, 100 percent American he-man ideal. Would a real American man recline languorously, costumed as a bedizened Young Rajah, in a swan-boat barge?

A widely quoted *Chicago Tribune* editorial, "Pink Powder Puffs," blamed Valentino for the rapid feminization of American men. Deploring the presence of men's-room powder-vending machines, it questioned whether women really like "the type of 'man' who pats pink powder on his face," and sneered, "Why didn't someone quietly drown Valentino years ago?" Wounded by this derision, Valentino challenged his accuser to a boxing match. On his hospital bed, after his surgery, he reportedly asked, "Doctor, am I a pink puff?"

But while effeminacy was officially decried, and the word "homosexuality" rarely used in polite, non-medical company, a thriving gay subculture flourished in New York City, especially around Times Square, in Greenwich Village, and in Harlem enclaves where gays sought (relatively) safe haven and same-sex bars and drag balls proliferated. Harlem's Hamilton Lodge Ball—a yearly drag extravaganza called the Dance of the Fairies or the Faggots Ball—drew 1,500 guests in 1926, many of them "straight" spectators. *Variety* likened the drags to gala society events, noting "an increasing number of the entire group." At the balls, "beautiful cars of the most expensive make roll up to the doors and deposit the 'boys' in the most gorgeous feminine creations."

As the "pansy craze" swept the city, while she continued to play the prostitute Margy LaMont in *Sex*, Mae West began making plans with Timony and the same group of investors (minus Cohen) who'd helped her before, to write and stage a play on a homosexual theme. Members of the "third sex" and prostitutes shared much more than the fact that both subcultures flourished on the borders of the theater district; they shared outcast status, police and court disapprobation, a strategy of sexual aggressiveness directed at men, and a common definition of what a seductive woman should look like. The sexual attributes of both hookers and drag queens were highlighted and heightened, outlined in black or underlined in red. Heavy perfume, furs, lots of lipstick, form-fitting clothes, and high heels broadcast the come-and-get-me message. "The fairy's most obvious attribute, his painted face, was the quintessential mark of the prostitute."

As *The Drag* took shape, *Sex* inched toward its one-year anniversary at Daly's, and District Attorney Banton hinted he was about to make a move against perpetrators of indecency on Broadway. He distanced himself from the Play Jury system, revealing that he had sent police officials to view some plays about which he had received numerous recent complaints. Mayor Walker, with an eye on the upcoming election, entered the fray, warning that unless producers voluntarily cleaned up Broadway, censorship would inevitably result. The New York *Journal*, targeting Walker as "the man who frequents night clubs and prize fights so much that his nocturnal excursions are a scandal," suggested he would lose his Catholic constituency unless he responded with action to Cardinal Hayes's recent call for a Broadway purge. The Hearst press cheered him on. DONT RELAX MAYOR, the headline on the New York *American* urged, WIPE OUT THOSE EVIL PLAYS NOW MENACING FUTURE OF THEATRE.

All this commotion was good for business at Daly's, the theater Timony considered so "lucky" he wouldn't think of leaving it for a better-located one farther downtown. Although *Sex* tickets were now being offered at cut rates for what had turned into a long run, they were selling briskly after a summer slump. *Variety* reported that in its thirty-ninth week, *Sex* continued raking in profits at a steady clip, grossing $10,500 in a week: another bitter pill for reformers.

In February 1927, while Mayor Jimmy Walker left New York for one of his frequent junkets, this time to Florida, Acting Mayor Joseph V. ("Holy Joe") McKee instituted police raids on three Broadway shows, including *Sex*. The New York *Herald Tribune* headline blared: THREE SHOWS HALTED, ACTORS ARRESTED IN CLEAN-UP OF STAGE. Even *The New York Times* rated the story important enough for a front-page spot. Mae West, James Timony, and Morganstern, along with twenty-one members of the *Sex* cast, the press reported, had been charged with "corrupting the morals of youth, or others" and arrested by Deputy Chief Inspector James S. Bolan and a squad of ten policemen after the Wednesday-evening performance. The arrested actors were permitted to go to their dressing rooms and remove their greasepaint and change into street clothes before being booked.

A rumor had circulated that arrests were about to be made, and an excited crowd, eager to witness the anticipated "pinch," had gathered outside the 63rd Street Theatre. A battery of cameras and about a thousand onlookers stood at the ready. "There were faint cheers and murmurs as twelve policemen and twenty-three victims made their way through the crowd in ten taxicabs, which had been hastily summoned. Etiquette prevailed . . . The policemen handed the women of the company into the cabs with ceremonious gallantry." VICTIMS NOT UNWILLING, SUBMIT CORDIALLY TO AR-

RESTS. (*The Drag* anticipates this scene when one of the queens tells what fun it was to get "pinched": "The police were perfectly lovely to us . . . Why the minute I walked into jail, the captain said, 'Well Kate, what kind of cell would you like to have?' "

At West Side night court Mae West, smartly dressed in a black cloche hat and a knee-length fox-collared fur, was fingerprinted and booked, along with others, and released on bail: $1,000 each for Mae West, Morganstern, and actors Barry O'Neill, Warren Sterling, Lyons Wickland, and Daniel Hamilton; $500 each for minor players. Timony, Elsner, and John Cort, overlooked in the first sweep, were later hauled in and released on bail of $1,000 each.

The other plays raided during the same February night sweep were *The Virgin Man* and *The Captive*. *The Virgin Man*, a lightweight comedy about the attempted seduction of a Yale undergraduate, was about to close when the raid saved it. It moved from the Princess Theater, which seated 300, to a house with more than a thousand seats. And *The Captive*, a much-praised, "highbrow" French import by Edouard Bourdet, starred Helen Menken (who had recently married Broadway actor Humphrey Bogart) in the role of a married woman pursued by a female admirer, and featured Basil Rathbone. It had opened in October 1926 and, having struck an especially raw nerve, had been playing to packed houses ever since; its lesbian theme was considered even more daring than the story of a woman who sells her body to men. It was branded by the former president of the Colonial Dames of America "an affront to American womanhood."

Mae West confessed that even she found *The Captive* unsettling: "You may think I'm kidding, but plays like *The Captive* make me blush," she told a reporter. When, in "a flurry of bondsmen" at night court, she met *The Captive*'s star, Helen Menken (who played her role in exceedingly white makeup, to heighten her character's unnaturalness), Mae West is said to have "gathered her ermine about her" and remarked, 'Well, anyhow we're normal!' "

Although she saw the folly of sweeping it under the carpet, ignoring it, and pretending it wasn't there, Mae West regarded homosexuality as abnormal and harbored a particular distaste for women who loved other women. She befriended—and hired—many gay men, but nevertheless referred to the 5,000 homosexuals who she said had tried out for parts in *The Drag* as "perverts," victims of a "tragic" disease that needed to be treated, like cancer, and openly faced. "Some homosexuals are not to be blamed for their condition," she would write. "They are inverts or the ones born that way . . . Some, however, are perverts—become that way because of weak character or desire for new thrills."

She and Timony knew from responses to *The Captive* that because it was both explosive and swathed in secrecy, "inversion" was a surefire attention-grabber as a dramatic subject. They also knew of comic possibilities that had never been tapped on the legitimate stage.

Not by coincidence, it was soon after *The Captive* opened that Mae and Timony undertook a production of their "homosexual comedy." "Jane Mast" would again be the pseudonym of the author, recognized by one and all as Mae West. Initially announced as *The Wicked Queen* and timed to capitalize on both the "pansy craze" in New York and the heady controversy over *The Captive*, *The Drag* concerned men who love men, not women who love women. (At the drag party in the second act, when the Duchess goes to the piano, Clem makes reference to the Bourdet play when he says, "Play 'The Woman Who Stole My Gal' from *The Captive*.") Instead of featuring heterosexuals portraying gays, its cast would spotlight the real thing, "about forty young men from Greenwich Village." It was slated for Daly's 63rd Street Theatre after *Sex* completed its run.

These were jam-packed, hectic days. Mae was performing in *Sex* eight times weekly, and at the same time trying to create a script for her new play. In wanting to produce "a realistic drama of the tragic waste of life," a wish to shock and to make money by creating a sensation topped her agenda, but her motives may have been more complex. A once-married bisexual man whom she'd found attractive helped fuel her interest in the subject, but the matter didn't end there. Queers fascinated her. She personally "liked her sexes stable," but found herself curiously drawn to the flaunting, preening, suggestive speech and campy put-ons of drag queens. She spoke that language, too.

Intrigued and puzzled, she looked into the literature on homosexuality. "I read [had someone read to her] Freud and [Karl] Ulrichs [a nineteenth-century German who'd written a learned tome on homosexuality], "who called gays *Urnings*. I learned a lot about the yearnings of urnings." Ulrichs shared her belief that an invert possessed a woman's soul trapped in a man's body. When she happened to see a bunch of cops roughing up some "boys" after a matinee, she intervened. "Remember," she told the police, "when you're hitting one of the gay boys you're hitting a lady."

Scheduled to open in Stamford, Connecticut, *The Drag* opened instead— just a week prior to the New York raids of *Sex*, *The Captive*, and *The Virgin*

Man—in Bridgeport after being banned in Stamford. *The New York Times* described Jane Mast's new effort as the play that "caused the sudden action . . . toward cleaning up the stage." It dismissed the characters' talky but earnest medical and legal discussions of the homosexual's outcast status as nothing more than an attempt to "sterilize" the rest of the action. "The play purports to put across the message that certain persons are more to be pitied than censured."

The Drag is a strangely divided play, part a serious plea for openness and toleration, part campy, sensationalized free-for-all. In the first act, David, a homosexual who is addicted to drugs, visits a physician to confess his misery and seek help. "I'm one of those damned creatures who are called degenerates and moral lepers for a thing they cannot help," he tells Dr. Richmond, sobbing. "Always, from the earliest childhood . . . my mind has been that of a female." David confesses further that he'd found a man he loved, and briefly enjoyed happiness with him, but now that man, capitulating to family pressure, had married a woman. Worse, the beloved married man had fallen for another, a "normal" man. David would kill himself if he had the courage.

The compassionate and learned doctor—who keeps a copy of Ulrichs's treatise on homosexuality close at hand—gives David a shot, suggests he "try athletics," and preaches self-acceptance. "One man is born white, another black—neither man is born a criminal." He deplores the folly and futility of a legal system that forces a man "born with inverted sexual desires . . . to become something which his soul will not permit him to become."

At the end of *The Drag*, when David has confessed to the murder of his ex-lover, who happens to be the son of a judge who is the good doctor's best friend, and the nominal husband of the doctor's daughter, the plea for acceptance and understanding is repeated: "A judge's son can be just the same as another man's son—yes a king's son, a fool's son."

The earnest and thoughtful—but uncharacteristically solemn, stilted, and wholly undramatic—exchanges that frame *The Drag* are Mae West's. But the dialogue comes alive only during the drag party that takes over the second act, where the wisecracking repartee developed out of the gay cast's frolicsome improvisations. At rehearsals, according to *Variety*, director Edward Elsner "permit[ted] the 'our sex' members to cavort and carry on as they like. Results are more natural and spontaneous."

The actors in drag and those who were outrageously swish made a huge contribution to Mae West's evolving style. As Pamela Robertson said, "The characters in West's scripts who sound most like [her] film persona are the gay men in *The Drag* and the female impersonators in *Pleasure Man*." Just like Mae West, the character named Clem addresses everybody as "Dearie"; as she would, he tells a hunk of a taxi driver (described as "rough trade"), "Ride me around a while, dearie"; as she might, he adeptly assumes a "rather artistic pose" when seated. The drag artist known as the Duchess always fusses with a powder puff and dresses à la Mae West, in "black satin, very tight, with a long train of rhinestones." But it's Winnie who anticipates Lady Lou's celebrated invitation to Cary Grant's Captain Cummings in *She Done Him Wrong*: "So glad to have you meet me. Come up some time and I'll bake you a pan of biscuits."

The essential quality Mae West came to share with drag queens is a fluency in diva-speak, what Wayne Koestenbaum calls a "succinct, epigrammatic language of vindication and self-defense." Every line, every move, is a put-on. ("All my life I've been a put-on," Mae West once said.) Speech becomes a vehicle for flaunting, "a way of asserting power, pre-eminence and invulnerability." To Mae West, "camp" meant "bein' funny and dishy and outrageous and sayin' clever things." The diva—whether Mae West or a drag queen—finds an identity "only by staging it . . . throwing it—as the ventriloquist throws the voice." The line dividing show from substance vanishes. The show *is* substance.

In the 1930s and after, in response to many observers who pointed out her resemblance to female impersonators, Mae West thought about the comparison a good deal and came to some understanding of the whys and wherefores. When George Davis emblazoned her "the greatest female impersonator of all time," she said she didn't like it at first, but "I guess he meant it as a compliment and I can kind of see what he meant, I guess. I lived like a man, in some ways—decided what I wanted and went after it." She could acknowledge that she had some attributes commonly associated with masculinity, and could also readily see why the "boys" in the chorus were crazy about her exaggerated gestures and flamboyant costumes, why they loved to imitate her.

But she remained uncomprehending of same-sex attraction. And in 1927 her ability to identify with her gay cast members was limited by her "us-and-them" mentality. However much she enjoyed kidding with them and questioning them about their lives, she continued to see homosexuals as objects of pity who were more often sad than gay. She believed that doctors should study the homosexual in an attempt to change him, and that society should be protected from the ones who "became that way because of weak character or desire for new thrills." In *The Drag*, she explained, "I wanted to show the tragic *waste* that was spreadin' into our society when people were shocked by it . . . but didn't do anything to cure them."

Attempting to head off the attacks that might prevent *The Drag* from opening, Mae West and the producers claimed that the play offered the public instruction as well as entertainment. Morganstern told the press that *The Drag* "has a moral just like *Sex*. It deals with the discussion of a disease." *Variety* reported that an invitation-only dress rehearsal, solely for physicians and city officials, would take place at midnight on February 8, 1927, in New York at Daly's, and that the producers were angling for endorsements from the medical community and city officials to the effect that *The Drag* was "an educational and a remedial gesture on behalf of the 'Homos.' According to the 'author' of *Sex*, the Homos number one male in twenty in the United States and a larger percentage in Europe."

The *Graphic*'s reviewer—who attended a preview in Bridgeport—was the only critic to find merit in the claim that the play had something worthy to say: WENT TO BE SHOCKED; FOUND "THE DRAG" CLEAN. Crediting the author as the first to cast "such a calcium light" on those "who will never get over to greet St. Peter—unless they fly over," the review praised her daring:

> The blood-red subject was laid bare with a scalpel of the surgeon, but done so nicely that it drove home a lesson. The scoffers remained to praise. There were a dozen curtain calls after each of three acts.

Audiences at the out-of-town previews also gave *The Drag* thumbs-up. At Bridgeport, where many ticket seekers had been turned away, the crowd "laughed immoderately. During the 'drag' scene they were convulsed with mirth." In Paterson, New Jersey, two days later, six patrolmen had to be dispatched to the theater to handle the predominantly male crowd that stormed the door.

The police and most representatives of the press thought otherwise. Rush, in *Variety*, dismissed *The Drag* as "a deliberate play for morbid interest," a "jazzed-up revel in the garbage heap," and a vulgar exercise in capitalizing filth. He claimed to have approached the performance with an open mind, in the belief that "sex perversion" was as old as history and that bringing it out into the open couldn't be any worse than the silent treatment. But the subject, he insisted, demanded discretion and tact. Instead, he was shown "a grand and glittering spectacle" in the manner of P. T. Barnum, something that could have been titled "The Destruction of Sodom." "All hands are rouged, lip-sticked and liquid whited to the last degree," he reported, adding that he didn't believe Mae West wrote it. "It has all the earmarks of being the work of a boss hostler in a livery stable. If it ever gets to Broadway, it would be a calamity."

William Randolph Hearst used *The Drag* to sound a rallying cry for state censorship. In a New York *American* editorial that presages future Hearst attacks on Mae West, he grandstanded: "We see where the lack of censorship is bringing us." Never naming her or the play that so incensed him, he referred to it obliquely as "a disgusting theatrical challenge to decency just revealed at Bridgeport, where the foulest use of sex perversion for dirty dollars is being polished for a metropolitan run."

The Drag became a symbol of stage prurience run amok. Neither the politicians nor the theatrical big wigs wanted it to open; they felt it wantonly overstepped the line, inviting the righteous indignation of moralists, justifying agitation for censorship, and branding the legitimate theater with a bad name. "The men who ran New York were afraid," Mae said, "that my play would start a riot!"

Alarm was rampant. *The New York Times* published a letter from a Jackson Heights mother asking the mayor to ban sex perversion as a stage subject: "Perversion is a horror and social smallpox" that should be banished to the pest house. Public opinion seemed to concur.

A group of theatrical managers, actors, and authors convened, in an effort to head off legislative and police attacks on "dirt" plays which were obviously being planned. *Variety* reported that the group, including the distinguished producer-director Winthrop Ames, Eugene O'Neill's producer Arthur Hopkins, and representatives from Equity and the Theatre Guild, had agreed not to permit *The Drag* to open on Broadway. Timony cried foul; what about the Bourdet play, he wanted to know. He reportedly offered to withdraw *The Drag* if *The Captive* was taken off, but when no deal was struck he turned grandiose, insisting, "We are going forward with both shows. We are seriously considering hiring Madison Square Garden for *The Drag*."

Sex had been running for forty-one weeks when the bust on it took place. There was much discussion about why it had been allowed to run unmolested for all these months, only to be suddenly subjected to a crackdown by the authorities. Said Morganstern, "If they are right now, they confess that they have been negligent for eleven months." District Attorney Banton explained that he was responding to a public that was "thoroughly aroused."

The real reason was panic about the imminent New York opening of *The Drag*, characterized by the *Times* as "the last straw."

After the arrests, word went out that *Sex* and the other two raided plays would continue to be presented nightly; but so, the *Times* reported, would the arrests be repeated until the offending plays were withdrawn or modified to comply with standards of decency. Daly's box office was barraged with phone calls and ticket seekers, many of whom had to be turned away. RAIDED SHOWS PLAY TO CROWDED HOUSES, ran the *Times* headline.

Meanwhile, the out-of-town reviews for *The Drag* had come in, along with stories of lines for tickets that went around the block, ovations after each act, and banners stretched across thoroughfares touting it as MORE SENSATIONAL THAN "RAIN" OR "SEX." But *The Drag* would soon be history. Not a single New York theater was willing to book it. PRODUCER DROPS "THE DRAG." Morganstern announced that the company had been paid and disbanded, and that efforts to stage *The Drag* in New York had been abandoned.

The day following the theater raids, a justice of the State Supreme Court, Aaron J. Levy, granted an injunction under which all three of the plays that had been raided were allowed to carry on. "It is necessary to protect the stage against persecution," he said. A lively debate about the pros and cons of government censorship ensued. A group of dramatists including George Abbott, Marc Connelly, and George S. Kaufman voiced their opposition; the theater should keep its own house clean, they maintained. Actor Otis Skinner condemned New York's campaign to purge the theater as "indiscriminate slaughter," and Anne Nichols, author and producer of the long-playing *Abie's Irish Rose*, berated the arresting police. Joseph Wood Krutch of *The Nation* argued that standards of decency are relative, not absolute: in Dickens's day, it was considered scandalous to mention ankles; "knees and thighs are today what ankles were in Dickens's time." A lawyer compared the present trial for alleged indecency with the recent Scopes trial concerning the teaching of evolution in Tennessee: "Down in Tennessee," he said, "they thought they would save their souls by keeping people ignorant. Here in New York some people think that if you keep people ignorant, you will save their morals."

Mayor Walker, in Miami, issued an ambiguous statement from his private box at the Hialeah racetrack. "While I am back of Acting Mayor McKee in anything he has done," Walker said, "I do not believe in censorship in any of its forms and I believe the producers will clean their own house."

The governor of New York, Al Smith, stated that he, too, opposed stage censorship, in part because he believed it simply would not work.

The *Sex* trial began on February 15, 1927, with the eyes and ears of New York glued to it. In West Side Special Sessions Court, police inspector James S. Bolan was called as a witness for the prosecution. "He produced a sheaf of yellow paper, adjusted his eyeglasses and read in a solemn tone that suggested a church service. The inspector's lean, grave face ministered to the effect." Too embarrassed to quote the rough language of *Sex* directly, Inspector Bolan made an attempt to improve its tone when he read from the text, changing the word "joint" to "place" (as in "Don't call this joint a dump") and converting "sugar daddy" to "sugar dandy." When he did use "plain roadhouse language" to describe one scene, titters erupted in the courtroom. The magistrate pounded his gavel. "If there is anyone who thinks this is funny," he warned, "I want him to get out and stay out. This is not a show. It's a trial."

Trials in general were providing the press and the public with no end of entertainment fodder. The tabloids had a field day, just as the "sewers of Broadway" brouhaha was breaking, with the Peaches Browning story: a mercenary young girl's extremely public marriage to and subsequent separation from a much older, wealthy realtor—"Daddy" to his many friends—with a taste for nymphets. The New York *World* insisted that it made no sense to censor the theater if the press was going to be given carte blanche. The courts and the tabloids, according to the *World*, were matching and surpassing the sleaziness of the stage. The "Peaches and Daddy" circus had followed fast on the heels of other courtroom and tabloid scandals: screen comedian Fatty Arbuckle's shameful party in San Francisco back in 1921, which ended with a starlet's death; the arrest of Mrs. Frances Hall in the love-triangle murder of her minister husband; the sensational hammer-murder charges brought against Mrs. Ruth Snyder and her lover, Judd Gray. "What we have here is a series of national spectacles put on for the amusement of the crowd," the *World* editorialized. "They are produced by swindlers for suckers."

Playing the publicity angle for all it was worth, the producers and cast of *Sex* applied for, and were granted, a jury trial instead of a trial before three judges in Special Sessions. In early March (1927) the grand jury returned an indictment against the management and part of the cast. Mae West and the other indicted cast members entered their plea: Not guilty.

Norman P. Schloss, chief counsel for the defense, argued in the Court of General Sessions that current, not outdated, standards of morality should be applied to any judgment of *Sex*; times and moral norms had changed since the law now being invoked to close the play had passed more than twenty years ago, he maintained. Prostitution, once a taboo subject, was now openly discussed. "Twenty years ago women on the streets in knee-length skirts . . . smoking, would have been considered immoral, but our wives do this same thing today and we think nothing of it." Judge Don-nellian broke in, "It doesn't make any difference if Adam and Eve wore a figleaf 2,000 or more years ago."

Defense attorney Harold Spielberg tried to show that *Sex* had already been cleared of obscenity charges by the volunteer Play Jury, and that the district attorney had vowed to support the jury's findings. A member of the Play Jury, Raymond Hood, was summoned. He testified that he and his wife had not found either the dances or the love scene between Margy LaMont and Jimmy Stanton, which the prosecution claimed suggested sexual inter-course, offensive.

Detailed examination of Mae West's second-act *danse du ventre*, per-formed as a sailor's jazz band played the "St. Louis Blues," ensued. Miss West testified that what she did onstage "was nothing more than an exercise involving control of my abdominal muscles, which I had learned from my father when I was a child, along with other body-building exercises." The courtroom audience roared when, questioned about the visibility of the star's navel, one of the arresting officers stated he had seen "something in her middle that moved from east to west." The "east to west" image would find its way into the opening sequence of *I'm No Angel*.

Yet another defense attorney, Noah Stancliffe, tried to reason that the play had already been widely viewed, with no apparent damage to civili-zation at large. He pointed out that if you added up the numbers attending the Connecticut tryouts and then in New York, at Daly's, you'd get a total of "300,000 persons, including members of various police departments." At-torney Harold Spielberg pitched in: "Judges of the criminal courts have visited this show, one of them six times." The courtroom's rafters again rocked with laughter.

Meanwhile, *Sex* closed voluntarily. (*The Captive* had already been shut down by Adolph Zukor, whose Famous Players owned Charles Frohman, Inc., which had brought the play to Broadway.) The reason given for closing *Sex* was that Mae West's health was suffering. "STAR IS SAID TO BE ILL/Mae West Tired After Year's Work in Show, Lawyer Declares." Af-ter the final curtain at Daly's on Saturday night, March 19, 1927, C. Wil-liam Morganstern announced from the stage that the play was ending its run. "Miss West could not be reached in her suite at the Mayflower-Plymouth Hotel."

The scuttlebutt among Broadway insiders was that the real reason behind the decision to close *Sex* was shrinking ticket sales, and a belief on the part of those standing trial that they would receive more lenient treatment from the court if the play shut down. At the peak of its long run, the show had grossed $17,200 weekly, but not recently. The play needed to pull in $7,000 a week to break even; it grossed only $6,000 in its last week. The actors rejected management's suggestion that, in light of a falling box office, they should accept salary cuts.

Although Mae had made a bundle—$30,000—during the brief run of *The Drag*, her expenses were mounting. The legal defense team she mobilized for her day in court didn't come cheap; Mae estimated that when she included legal costs she ended up spending $60,000 on *Sex*.

One reason the public may have stopped lining up to see *Sex* was that the best show in town was playing, for free, in court and was being followed assiduously in the press. Mae West's trial received front-page treatment, not just once, but for weeks. "Had the public exhibited as much interest in the show when it was running at Daly's as it has during the trial," *Variety* wryly observed, "the drama would still be hanging out the SRO [Standing Room Only] sign." During jury selection and throughout the trial, the courtroom was packed to the doors.

One of the stars of the proceedings was Sergeant Patrick Keneally of Inspector Bolan's midtown vice squad. The first witness called by the prosecutor, Keneally spoke with a broad Irish brogue. "He showed a remarkable memory of the lines and scenes of the play, frequently . . . assuming poses to demonstrate the manner in which members of the cast delivered their lines."

The assistant district attorney, James G. Wallace, in his final argument took the moral high road, pretending that prostitution had been wiped out but now stood in danger of being brought back. New York City, he said, had years ago banished its scandalous red-light district, but the theater had created a replacement, out of sheer greed. "We've got red lights on the stage." The jurors, he contended, had a duty "to prevent a continuance of such objectionable presentations on the stage to protect the youth of the city from their influence."

By the time Mae West and the cast faced the verdict, a state law had been passed in New York, the Wales Padlock Act, which gave the police the right to arrest the producers, authors, and actors of plays that showed "sex degeneracy or perversion" or that they considered indecent, obscene, or immoral, and to padlock the theater for a year if the courts found the defendants guilty. In response, Texas Guinan took to wearing a necklace strung with little gold padlocks, and she displayed a diamond bracelet from which dangled a small gold police whistle; within a few months she would open in a revue—produced by C. William Morganstern—called *Padlocks of 1927*. During a brief interlude before it opened, when Guinan refused to show up for rehearsals, *Variety* reported that "Mae West is being readied to jump in."

One part of the charge against *Sex*—the accusation of maintaining a nuisance—was dismissed by the court, but the indecency rap stood. A defense motion for permission to put on a special performance of *Sex*, solely for the benefit of judge and jury, was denied after Assistant District Attorney Wallace protested that the defendants would be free to change the play from the one police had raided back in February.

The day of reckoning came in April, nearly two months after the arrests. The *Sex* jury, after receiving instructions to the effect that it could judge the whole show obscene if one portion of it was, returned a guilty verdict. They had deliberated for five and a half hours, and night had fallen on the Tuesday the trial came to an end. SEX CAST GUILTY, TWO BACKERS, 22 FACE JAIL TERMS. In their concluding arguments, Norman Schloss, lead defense counsel, and ADA James G. Wallace had almost come to blows. "You've made enough speeches," Schloss hissed. "You're a cheap, arrogant, insolent dog," Wallace returned, only to be invited outside for a showdown. "I'll take care of you," he threatened Wallace.

Before the verdict came down, according to *The New York Times*, Timony, Morganstern, and the actors displayed high spirits, but their mood darkened as the decision became imminent. "Timony, large of stature, was seen to take from his pocket a rosary as the jury filed out, and began to finger the beads in prayer."

Barry O'Neill, the actor who played the British lieutenant Gregg, received special mention in the *Times* because of his war record; he held the King George Medal for bravery during a mine sweep. As the jury foreman prepared to speak, O'Neill's face took on "an expression of fear in contrast to the display of levity which had characterized his attitude during the trial. Mae West, seated beside him, endeavored to hearten the leading man with remarks such as 'Don't worry, Barry, it'll come out all right.'" When the guilty verdict was pronounced, O'Neill's face turned a deep red. "He leaned over and buried his face in his hands. Mae patted him on the back and spoke more words of consolation, and when he raised his head tears welled in his eyes."

Stage manager Alfred Rigali protested, "Why should I, trying to make an honest living on a salary, be branded the same as a second story man?"

An actress in a supporting role jumped to the defense of the cast, insisting to a reporter that between scenes they discussed Beethoven, Bach, Shakespeare, "and all the world's most famous philosophers and literati."

Mae West stood apart from the others. "Assuming the hard-boiled manner she played in the play, [she] did not wink an eyelid when the sentence was pronounced." She never lost her composure but emerged from the courthouse fighting mad. "We are not through with this case. We'll fight this on an appeal," she promised. "You've got to fight in this world. You got to fight to get there and fight to stay there. *Sex* as given at Daly's was a work of art."

Sentencing took place two weeks later. Judge Donnellian praised the guilty verdict as just, "based on the moral standards of today. Obscenity and immorality pervaded this show from beginning to end. Since Mayor Gaynor's time a certain form of vice has been driven from our streets. The producers of *Sex* paraded this vice upon the stage." He reproached Mae West for collaborating in the writing, participating in many of the objectionable scenes, and going "to extremes in order to make the play as obscene and immoral as possible." Sounding a personal note, the judge revealed that he had been born on the site of the Metropolitan Opera House, had lived in the theater district his entire life, and "never did feel that the success of the stage depended on the capitalization of filth." A play like *Sex*, he averred, would work no harm on the sophisticated and worldly, but has "a most inimical effect upon the youth of our city." Brimming with self-congratulation, he pronounced New York "the most moral city in the universe."

Chief counsel for the defense, Norman Schloss, pleaded for lenient sentences on the grounds that all the defendants had clean records. The district attorney had recommended mercy for all but the prime movers, and his wishes prevailed: the players, except Mae West, received suspended sentences. But the culprits had to be taught a lesson. Mae ("modishly attired"), Morganstern, and Timony ("fashionably dressed with a spring coat over his left arm and a blue flower in his lapel") each had to pay a fine of $500 and serve a sentence of ten days in prison.

Timony was marched off to the Tombs, where his "initiative and ambition" soon won him the top position on the mop-and-broom squad.

Mae West spent her first night under lock and key in Greenwich Village at Jefferson Market Prison, where her sister inmates both moved and shocked her: tattered drug addicts, wasting away and prematurely aged; "a spinster type, with a long scar on the side of her face and neck . . . spoke with an Irish accent. She had been sentenced to ten days for stealing a $3.89 pair of shoes." A black woman possessed of a "comedy personality, with Bert Williams speech and delivery," provided the only note of levity. Her presence gave them all a lift, as did Mae's. "The other inmates were so enthusiastic and elated over my being there . . . They continued to shout my name, asked me how I like the place, and repeated different lines from my show *Sex*, in order to let me know they had seen it. They sang for me and told some jokes, before the matron intervened, ordered them to their cells and locked them in for the night."

She slept in a tiny, barred room equipped with an iron cot. Achy after an uncomfortable night, she downed a breakfast of eggs, bacon, German fried potatoes, and coffee.

She was driven over the Queensborough Bridge, en route to what is now called Roosevelt Island but was then Welfare Island Women's Workhouse, in a Black Maria, accompanied by two other prisoners. MAE WEST GOES TO WORKHOUSE IN VAN WITH TWO NEGRESSES. In the middle of the bridge, a huge elevator lowered the vehicle onto the island, a narrow strip in the East River, once a pasture for swine called Blackwell's Island that had become a city-owned repository of lost souls, "a place of quiet reformatory meditation for the vicious." The grim granite structures, turreted like medieval fortresses, had been built by convicts: a charity hospital, penitentiary, workhouse, and at one time a hospital for incurables and an asylum for the insane. Boss Tweed once did time there.

Mae West betrayed no trace of contrition or dejection as she faced her induction as a prisoner. "I expect it will be the making of me," she jauntily informed a reporter. "I expect to employ my time to good advantage on the island getting material for a new play." She later rated the term she spent in jail as "about the most profitable days of my life," estimating that the publicity alone was worth a million dollars.

At least half of that million went toward printed chatter about her prison wardrobe. "MAE WEST WEARS WORKHOUSE GARB / Finds Blue Cotton Dress Is Uncomfortable As She Does First Day's Tasks / MAKES BEDS AND SWEEPS." She would recall: "A matron took my purse, my valuables and my pedigree . . . Everything but my enviable reputation, at the same time displaying a piece of blue material that looked like two aprons sewed together, with two holes for the arms. I didn't like it at all; no *lines* to it. I was handed underwear of very coarse material, almost like canvas. Then came cotton stockings and the flat slippers that were too large." The *Times* reported that she griped to the warden that she found the prison clothes uncomfortable, "the only complaint she voiced during her first day." Said the *Times*: "Although the clothes are coarse, faded and darned, they are clean. For Miss West the change from the silks, crepes and sheer stockings of the average well-dressed woman . . . to the prison outfit was a shock."

The warden, Henry O. Schleth, announced that he planned to find "sufficient for her to do to keep her in a healthy mental state . . . and to make it possible for her to do work without too much or too close contact with the general run of prisoners, many of whom are old and hardened offenders." He assigned her to a private cell, rather than the dormitory, and to work duty consisting of making beds, sweeping up, scrubbing down the corridors, and dusting the scant prison library. The warden seemed to agree with her that he had more than enough help in the laundry and cooking brigades. Mae informed him that in any case she would have been little use in those capacities, "never having had any experience" performing such tasks.

Permitted to take her meals in the warden's home, she became acquainted with the women prisoners assigned to work there and questioned each about her path to prison. "Three were colored, three white. The cook . . . named Marie, was a very likable colored girl from Puerto Rico. I learned she was quite a racehorse fan. Another colored girl, Mary F., was a drug addict and had just taken the narcosan cure. Her daily task was ironing. Lulu, the third of the colored women . . . was a stick-up woman. I liked Lulu very much, for it required a lot of nerve to 'stick-up' a man."

A "dainty little white girl" named Adele, a waitress at the warden's home, taught Mae a lot about the way fur thieves operate—information she would draw on for *Diamond Lil*. "If I had ever wanted to get local color, I sure got it there." During coat season, Adele would enter a fur shop, bringing with her friend "who had 'collateral' on her—one who would look like a likely purchaser of expensive garments. She would thus encourage the salespeople to bring out the most expensive pieces of fur, such as silver foxes, sable, mink and ermine." Adele would seize a moment of privacy to cram one of these choice furs into an ample pair of bloomers, worn under a flaring coat, and, with her accomplice, make her exit—a maneuver she pulled off successfully every time but the last.

Although Mae West thought of herself as a "man's woman," her interest in and compassion for these sister prisoners ran deep. She wouldn't forget the eighteen-year-old Chinese girl on the narcotics ward whose father had forced her to bring him his opium pipe, or the fifteen-year-old vagrant who'd stowed away on a boat from Savannah. Some of the women on the sick ward, which she was allowed to visit, were former beauties, prostitutes who had syphilis. "Honest to God, when I heard that I just . . . left them each some money." She believed most wanted a different life but couldn't break the cycle: "These girls are willing to work, but how can they when the law is always ready to pounce upon them and send them back to the Workhouse?"

She identified with the prostitutes, believing "there but for the grace of God go I." "If I hadn't started writing plays . . . I think I could have gone the other way and wasted my whole mentality and life on sex."

She summed up the whole experience in a song:

> As I was walking down the street
> Detective Flynn I chanced to meet
> He took me down to Jefferson Jail
> And there they kept me without bail
>
> Next morning at eight o'clock
> They took us down to Twenty-sixth Street dock
> Miss Mulry next to us on the other side
> When I saw the Workhouse I nearly died
>
> They marched us into the Slattery
> Where she took our history;
> They gave us a dress the color of blue
> And a pair of shoes, size sixty-two
>
> We have a matron by the name of Vaughn;
> All she says is, "Keep on goin,'
> Get your pail and scrub the floor,
> Or I'll lock you up in eighty-four"
>
> We got a matron by the name of Mack
> You'll see her in the bums' room when you get back
> She sits behind the desk in a little wooden chair,
> And all she says is, "Quiet there!"

We got a matron, name of Smith;
She takes everything she catches you with;
She locks you up in a coal-black cell.
I wish the old bird was in h— —

Bootleg in the morning, bootleg at night
Beans on Sunday and then out of sight;
They serve 'em in a little tin dish.
Friday you get potatoes and fish.

Ten more days and I'll be free
From this place of misery—
No more lock-up, no more mail,
No more scrubbin' in the iron pail.

Sentenced to ten days, Mae West was released from the workhouse a day early for good behavior. Reporters and photographers gathered to record the moment, and Warden Schleth gratified them with a statement. "Mae West," he declared, "is a fine woman—and a great character." Miss West informed the press that she had not suffered unduly. "I expected to find harsh guards and unsympathetic matrons. Instead I found kindness and understanding." She said she had gathered material for "a dozen plays," and that her experience in jail had given her a new angle on life. "She announced that hereafter she would devote some of her time to philanthropy, especially to getting jobs for some of the unfortunates whom she met on Welfare Island." She would start by donating the $1,000 she was to receive for a magazine article on her prison experience to the prison library.

After buying herself a pair of white stockings at the commissary, "the actress was met by her mother, her sister, Beverly West; her negro maid and a young man [brother Jack?] wearing a white carnation. They accompanied her from the island on the municipal tug . . . across the East River, and escorted her in a taxicab to her apartment in the Mayflower at Central Park West and 61st Street."

A few weeks later she returned to Welfare Island as guest of honor for a group of clubwomen from the Women's National Democratic Club and the Penology and Delinquency Division of the New York Federation of Women's Clubs. She and the clubwomen—some of them very likely former activists against the "dirt plays"—posed together for press photographers. They never repeated their display of mutual goodwill, however: clubwomen became more and more vociferously incensed about Mae West as her fame increased.

Her imprisonment left an indelible mark on Mae West, one she proudly displayed—almost as a badge of honor. The affectionate warden and the coarse underwear were incorporated as vital and colorful details of the official Mae West Saga.

The New York public didn't really need a reminder, so close on the heels of the event, but got one anyhow when the *Grand Street Follies* opened in May. Among the revue's satirical interludes was a send-up of sex-show crusades called "Stars with Stripes." Decked out in prison stripes, a "Mae West" (actress Mae Noble) commiserated with "La Prisonnière" (the French title of *The Captive*), complaining about playhouse padlocks. "Mae West" then set about seducing "The Virgin Man" as "The Captive" lamented that her "Hellenic habits made the Broadway Babbitts squirm." The Babe Ruth of stage spoofers had graduated to spoofee.

9

PLUMP FLAPPER

$\mathcal{T}$O make the most of her new fame, Mae West had to work fast. She needed a new vehicle to keep her name afloat. She'd toyed with the idea of staging her still unproduced play *The Hussy*, but felt she needed something more topical, more of the moment. On the double she tumbled into a new play about the twenties, *The Wicked Age*.

Broadway was booming; an unprecedented number of shows, 268, saw production in 1927, squeezing into sixty to seventy theaters. Neon signs, introduced in 1924, added a garish effervescence, and the new theaters that were still being built signaled bullish faith in the future. But at the same time that giant musical talents like the Gershwins, Jerome Kern, Cole Porter, and consummate performers like the Astaires, Gertrude Lawrence, and Paul Robeson saw their stars rising, concern was mounting about competition from both movies and radio. Radio could claim 30 million regular listeners that year, double that on the night of the Battle of the Century between Dempsey and Tunney, and luxury movie palaces were horning in on the upscale territory previously reserved for the legitimate stage. These incursions, and a backlash against permissiveness in matters sexual, created a climate of caution.

In *Sex* Mae West had played a prostitute. Her new offering, *The Wicked Age*, cast her in the role of a more mainstream flouter of respectability, the flapper. By 1927 the flapper had lost some of the sheen and shock value she once possessed. She had ripened into an established type, the postwar New Young Woman who'd crashed onto the scene, cigarette in one hand, gin-filled teacup in the other, early in the decade. Books like *Flaming Youth* (which was made into a film), plays like *No, No, Nanette*, and movies with titles like *Jazzmania* and *Wine of Youth* gave her wide currency. The sight of a young woman in a knee-length skirt no longer set off alarms.

The flapper made her plea for social freedom, not through her recently won privileges at the voting box, but through fashion: she bobbed her hair, painted her lips scarlet, tossed away her corset, bound her breasts, rolled her stockings, shortened her skirts, and kicked up her heels in an energetic Charleston. Although her signature outfit weighed in at all of two pounds, her pared-down look didn't come cheap. She had to *buy*: silk stockings, cloche hats, fringed chemises, and recordings of jazz bands and boop-a-dooping chantoosies. She paid a hairdresser to curl and color her hair and smoothed her cheeks with pricy youth dew, because she couldn't grow up: she had to remain a jazz baby, like Helen Kane piping "I Wanna Be Loved by You" in the coyest of itty-bitty little-girl voices.

Popular culture's current examples of women, rather than girls, weren't all that joyous. Bessie Smith belted "Sobbin' Hearted Blues," lamented her empty bed, and cursed out two-timing sons-of-guns. Helen Morgan's voice filled with tears as she draped herself over the piano to sob "Why Was I Born?" Ruth Etting shared her misery at the hands of a lover who was "Mean to Me." Even comedienne Fanny Brice turned on the sob faucet when she torched about taking it on the chin from "My Man."

Mae West never liked playing victim, and it's easy to see why she steered clear of such heart-wrenching scripts. She opted for the upbeat every time. But as a flapper in her late teens—the role she took in *The Wicked Age*—she strained credulity. At thirty-four she was no longer in her first youth, a fact she made every effort to conceal. Even her court and insurance documents stated her year of birth as 1900, instead of 1893. Her body had long since shed all traces of boyishness. No longer the sylph who'd shimmied with such abandon in *Sometime*, she'd gained sufficient avoirdupois to be dubbed "a very plump flapper" and risk unfavorable comparison to the slimmer actresses beside her on the stage. Katharine Zimmerman, in the New York *Telegram*, judged Miss West's decision to appear onstage in a woolen one-piece bathing suit, surrounded by other, trimmer bodies that achieved the authentic flapper look, "rather a misguided move."

Beauty contests had been in the news a great deal of late. The spectacle of lined-up young lovelies in bathing suits always promised to deliver a kick to the stag audiences Mae West attracted, and plenty of young women with stage and screen ambitions were willing to bare almost all to compete; they saw the contests as a way to advance their show-business careers. Clara Bow, who along with Gloria Swanson reigned as the current screen goddess, had gotten her first break through a movie magazine's photographic beauty contest. Singer and actress Helen Morgan had once been crowned "Miss 1925"; a month after the opening of *The Wicked Age* she would bring down the house in *Show Boat*, moaning, handkerchief in hand, about that man she can't help lovin'.

The good name of the Miss America Pageant in Atlantic City, an annual event since 1921, was sullied when a scandal hit the papers: the 1925 winner, Fay Lamphier, happened to have a movie contract with Famous Players, and it was hinted that her victory had been prearranged by the filmmakers, who were on the scene with cameras at the ready. (Cameramen also turn up at the beauty contest in *The Wicked Age*.) In 1927, Atlantic City refused to back the pageant, claiming it was staining the resort's reputation.

A fixed beauty contest provided the framework for *The Wicked Age*. Instead of the forty-odd "Greenwich Village types" enlisted for *The Drag*, the cast boasted a troupe of shapely young women in one-piece bathing suits, poised to receive the attentions of the gawkers, mashers, and photographers surrounding them. *The Wicked Age* marks the introduction of what will remain a constant Mae West theme: image making. Posing for close-ups, testing klieg lights, and facing the prying eyes of leering cameramen all find places in the beauty contest setting.

A skin show with a satiric edge looked so promising as an investment that Anton F. Scibilia, one of Texas Guinan's backers in *Padlocks of 1927*, signed on as producer, filling the spot left vacant by C. W. Morganstern, who had bailed out after *The Drag*. Scibilia's pockets soon proved to be not deep enough, and money woes beset the production from the moment it opened in Long Branch, New Jersey. An Actors Equity document tells the sorry tale:

> Show opened Long Branch September 23, 1927. Trouble from first week. Salaries [totaling $1510] for week ending October 1, 1927 were not paid until after the matinees of the Wednesday of the following week; half of the company were let out without notice or transportation, also receiving only part of their salaries for the week they had just worked. After many demands upon Mr. Scibilia, and Mae West . . . cash was deposited at Equity office for all claims but three.

Several actors had to be dropped before the next week of tryouts, and the remaining cast members were notified by Equity that they should not perform until their claims had been settled. Marjorie Main, who played Mae's mother in *The Wicked Age* and later gained fame in the movies as Ma Kettle, was one of the cast members who filed an Equity claim, demanding payment of the $79.35 she was owed.

Mae tried to cut down production costs by accepting underwriting from clothing and shoe companies, which would furnish her costumes and shoes gratis in return for credits in the program and plugs in the dialogue. In the last act she tells her maid she will don her Sam Mayo creations, which were negligees. The printed program credits read: "Costumes worn by Mae West in first and second acts by Russeks, New York. Third act costumes by Lord and Taylor. Bathing creations by Famous Fain Knitting Mills. Negligees . . . designed by Mr. Sam Mayo and executed by Mayo Undergarment Co. Miss West's footwear especially created for her by Cammeyer Shoes by Shanks Boot Shop, New York."

The shoes got an additional pitch via glossy postcards that were distributed between acts; they showed the star in a full-length pose, with the caption "Cammeyer shoe creations have a leading role in my wardrobe."

Despite the frank commercialism, the play never took off. Money woes and flak from Equity were compounded by friction with Raymond Jarno, a screen actor hired to play the romantic lead, the handsome, socially prominent Jack Stratford. Jarno's background was in silent films, not theater, and in performance his voice failed to project beyond the first few rows. (Microphones were not used in the theater then.) He had a contract and could not be fired, but his deficiencies would be less obvious if his part were rewritten and reduced. Anton Scibilia appealed to Equity, asking a representative to attend a performance of *The Wicked Age* to verify that Jarno could not be heard and that a cut in the number of lines he spoke was justified. "While his voice did carry in the rehearsal hall," Scibilia wrote, "it certainly does not on the stage and he has been ridiculed by every audience. Mr. Jarno cannot blame us for his lack of personality and diction on the stage."

But Jarno and the producer had an agreement that he was to play a major role; it had to be honored, Equity ruled, after judging his performance of professional caliber. When *The Wicked Age* opened in New York at Daly's, it featured Raymond Jarno in the role of Jack Stratford—sans cuts.

Daly's 63rd Street Theater, Timony staunchly believed, spelled good luck. But the charm had been broken. Opening night caught the company scrambling to learn last-minute script changes. Some of the scenery had been left outside, where rain the previous day had spoiled much of it. The set proved "too large to get through the stage door in units, necessitating sub-division." The curtain didn't go up until 9 p.m., and the actors, one observer noted, "felt their way as cautiously as a blind man crossing Broadway."

The opening-night audience got bad notices, too. The *Herald Tribune* called them "somewhat dark and saturnine, but apparently harmless" and *Time* magazine referred to a "greasy gathering." The occasion "needs the talent of a police reporter far more than a recorder of theatrical events," one observer noted. The purring limousines of socialites that Benchley had noticed outside the ticket window after *Sex* opened were nowhere in sight.

In her memoir, Mae West described *The Wicked Age* as "a hit and a headache." The headache part sounds right enough. But the hit? The kindest words written about the play were those calling it "a choice piece of limburger that will paradoxically attract shekels at the box office," a show so dirty its ineptness might be overlooked by titillation-seeking playgoers.

Harold M'Gillicudy in the *Telegraph* had nothing positive to say about the production, but did extol its star's bravado: "She stands alone. Yea, bo—she stand alone. She has no counterpart on this or any other stage. Nobody [else] would carelessly run through a show like she does improvising, ad libbing and gagging with whoever happens to be around."

Mae West's performance style had the freewheeling spontaneity of jazz. She danced the black bottom, reaffirming her indebtedness to black idioms; played a "mean blues" on the harmonica, and belted several self-created songs, including "You Can Neck 'Em," "My Baby's Kisses," and "Satisfied," none of which has survived. Many of her lines, quoted in reviews, don't appear in the script, including one ad lib that counted on the public's awareness of Mae West's recent past: "Some of our best people have been in jail."

The boldness of her vamping once again spurred unflattering associations with burlesque: "The clinches, the torso tossing and the racy comedy would make [burlesque impresarios] Scribner and Herk squirm in official trepidation," *Variety* commented. "Miss West is getting away at $3.85 [per ticket] with something the [burlesque] wheels don't dare at $1.65." The scribe from the *Herald Tribune* concurred: "She throws out the right hip and then the left in the fashion which used to be affected by the sirens of "The Tammany Tigers" or "The Creole Belles."

Preview audiences turned thumbs-down. At the New Haven tryout, according to *Variety*, "throughout the performance [they] gave the piece the razz . . . *The Wicked Age* will be fortunate if it holds out long enough to reach New York. There are plenty of legs in the show but the production hasn't a gam to stand on."

The Long Branch, New Jersey, preview fared no better; the local paper branded it "gross, disgusting, tiresome, utterly futile vulgarity, without a single excusing feature or reason for being."

When it opened in New York *Billboard* dismissed *The Wicked Age* as an appeal to "tawdry morons to whom the theater is an intensified and expanded peep show." Without Mae West's notoriety—which, the critic claimed, resulted from generous coverage of her exploits in the scandal columns of the tabloids—it would never, he said, have been either conceived or produced. The *Times* let loose with a fusillade, calling it "incredibly cheap and vulgar trash," the low point of the theatrical season. "The whole was in the best Mae West tradition of playwriting and acting—that of just saying one word after another with no regard for any sort of technique and less for common sense."

Timony tried to salvage something from the ruin by interesting Hollywood in acquiring film rights, perhaps for a talkie, the spanking-new medium. Since the advent of the talkies, Broadway plays—and performers—were often finding their way to Hollywood. A rumor circulated that Clara Bow, Hollywood's flapper of choice, might star in the movie version, but it was not to be. A reader's report on the script survives in Lincoln Center's Billy Rose Theatre Collection: "This as a play is nothing more than a sex play. Desexed it's no great shakes . . . All things about the younger generation have been better said years and years ago."

The Wicked Age was never able to recover from the many body blows it sustained. A week after it opened, a Monday-night performance was abruptly scratched without notice. An explanation that Mae West had been seized with indigestion was put forward: "Failure to pay salaries appears to have been the trouble." The next day the money materialized, Equity gave the nod, and performances resumed—but not for long. The following week, the show closed for good, after only nineteen performances. Mae West announced plans to revive it, but never did.

The surviving script of *The Wicked Age* reads more like a hastily thrown together and disjointed first draft than a finished play. The third act bears little relation to the two preceding it, introducing a transformed protagonist and a new setting, a posh New York apartment. The jokes rarely rise beyond the level of a randy thirteen-year-old. Sample: "Babe, you certainly can neck. You'd make a wooden Indian raise his tomahawk."

As in every other vehicle Mae West created for herself, the leading lady, Babe (Evelyn) Carson, possesses irresistible allure, an independent, buoyant, defiant spirit, and a willingness to shrug her shoulders at those who label her "bad." She tells her fuming father, "I want to be filthy low—vile—call it anything you please—but God I want to live my own life." She juggles rival swains ("You take care of the phone—I'll take care of the men") who ply her with gifts, dominates all scenes, and has a quick comeback line ready for every occasion.

Babe resides in a small, dull New Jersey backwater called Bridgeton, whose leading citizens have decided to boost the town by staging a beauty contest in it. "Success today," says one contest promoter, "is based on the exploitation of the female form . . . Everything is an excuse for a horde of almost naked women to parade up and down the stage, to give the out of town buyers a kick." Although conservatives like Babe's Aunt Elizabeth and father, Robert Carson, consider the beauty contest a sure path to moral ruin, they are overruled and the contest takes place, amid all kinds of behind-the-scenes skulduggery.

Like *The Drag* before it, and *Pleasure Man* and *Diamond Lil* later, *The Wicked Age* includes a murder. Babe's innocent cousin Gloria vanishes during a storm following the contest. She's been strangled, it turns out. Her body is found in the marshes, and an unscrupulous groundskeeper pins the blame on simpleminded Willie, one of Babe's devotees, an affectionate young man of whom she's fiercely protective. (Babe's relationship to Willie resembles Nona's to Tom in *The Hussy*, and Mae's to her own brother, Jack.) Almost as an afterthought, the true murderer emerges in the last act, absolving Willie.

As in melodrama or *The Evening Graphic*, the thrills follow thick and fast. In addition to the murder, there is a lights-out necking party, a near striptease, some steamy clinches; jealous rivals in the fixed beauty contest try to eliminate Babe from the running by stalling her car, ruining her bathing suit, and getting her drunk. In the third act, Babe, now a preening, self-infatuated celebrity, throws away her cocaine because she doesn't want it to mar her beauty. She engages in hand-to-hand combat with Frenchy, the lecherous lout who turns out to be the murderer. Babe scratches, kicks, and beats him, and he slashes her face, but—not to worry—the wound is shallow, she's going to be fine, and as lovely as ever. The shock-saturated, mostly stag audience could not complain of boredom.

Despite its lurid plot, rickety structure, primitive characterizations, unmotivated reversals, and overall crudity, *The Wicked Age* provides many autobiographical clues. Mae honored her past by hiring aged Hal Clarendon, in

whose Brooklyn stock company she had toured as a girl, to act the part of
Mr. Carson, Babe's father. The play itself is full of references to her actual
life. Babe's manager scolds her for getting carried away by her love life, at
the expense of her career, in a way that probably echoes Timony's words
to Mae: "You can't ride two horses at the same time—it's either this guy
or your career."

Babe's stage family bears a striking resemblance to Mae West's: she has
a father who tears into her for picking up men at roadhouses (Matilda's
Blue Goose roadhouse gets a plug) and kicks her out of the house for staging
a wild, gin-soaked, roadhouse-style party at home when he and the missus
are out; a judgmental and prying aunt who thinks Babe has been ruined by
pampering; and an affectionate, indulgent mother, who tries to mediate the
rift between raging father and renegade daughter. Mrs. Carson defends the
"always so generous—so impulsive" Babe by saying she takes after her once-
wild father, pointing out that in his youth he'd been a sower of wild oats
himself, and that "the older generation always thinks the young generation
is all wrong. The children of this generation are not hypocrites . . . They
don't sin behind closed doors." She tries to persuade Babe that, after all,
her father does privately love and admire her, though he doesn't show it;
she caught him reading an article about her in the paper.

Babe even has a younger sister, Ruth, who condemns Babe's riotous living
in the first act but, after the beauty contest, "seems to have taken a new
lease on life—since her sister has become so famous"; Babe demonstrates
her goodheartedness by giving her sister a dress that she wore only once.
(Mae was always giving Beverly her castoffs: first dresses, eventually cars.)
There the resemblance to Mae and Beverly ends. In the play, the younger
sister is a puritanical goody-goody; Babe is the one who gets drunk and who,
according to her aunt, must have been sprinkled with gin at her baptism.

Mae's offstage sister Beverly had recently been sued for divorce by her
husband of more than a decade, Serge Treshatny. The divorce action resulted from a 5 a.m. police raid on director Edward Elsner's room in the
Arcade Hotel, Bridgeport, Connecticut, following the opening of *The Drag*,
when Beverly and Elsner were arrested together for disorderly conduct (read
drunkenness) and disturbing the peace. Although charges were dropped,
Treshatny got hold of testimony in the Bridgeport case and used it against
his wife, who had once tried to sue *him* for divorce, claiming he had posed
as a Russian count and had locked her in, turning her into "a bird in a
gilded cage." She claimed he earned $50,000 a year, but he maintained his
income was only $21.29 a week, and her first application for alimony and

counsel was denied. This time the divorce was granted, and Beverly moved to Floral Park, Queens, to be near her family; on their minds—and hands— once again.

Among the self-reflective elements in *The Wicked Age* are ruminations about the penalties of fame and the fate of aging beauties. The last act finds Babe, so recently a dizzy flapper interested in nothing but having fun, transformed by her bathing-beauty crown into a vain, ambitious, demanding, tantrum-prone, and mercenary prima donna who considers herself "the girl with the most perfect toes in the world," superior to both Sarah Bernhardt and the Queen of Sheba. She demands a gold piano, signs contracts with an ostrich-plume pen, throws the telephone across the room after answering a wrong number, wonders aloud why she was born so beautiful, and treats those around her like slaves: her maid must fan her as she reclines while her mail is read to her. Press clippings about her are her favorite reading matter, and a day when the paper fails to provide some scandalous item about her leaves her threatening to sue the editors. She tells her manager to think of something right away: "Have me married, divorced or kidnapped—or all three."

The Babe Gordon of Act 3 sends up Mae West, exaggerating her self-infatuated diva tendencies and defusing them with laughs. She even has fun at the expense of celebrity testimonials in advertisements, of the very sort Mae's highly glazed giveaway postcards plugging Cammeyer shoes exemplified. Babe Carson's fame as a beauty queen has sent manufacturers scurrying to her doorstep, checkbook in hand, seeking product endorsements in the form of catchy slogans. She proves herself a quick study as a copywriter, coming up with the slogan "Drink Babe Carson's Milk—it never runs dry," for a dairy, and wangling a $10,000 deal for telling the world, "When you start taking Starter's Liver Pills, you start something."

Without warning, *The Wicked Age* moves from farce to melodrama when an old woman named Lottie Gilmore enters, a former actress who now sells lingerie. As Babe the beauty queen tries on lingerie samples, Lottie soliloquizes about her own past glories as a stage belle carelessly squandering her looks on the high life. She recognizes her youthful self in Babe and warns her she must safeguard the asset of her beauty by taking meticulous care of herself: "There is always someone there to take your place, younger, more beautiful, so the thing is to guard it, treasure it, hold on to it as long as you can . . . Don't get old before your time." It is after this encounter that a stricken Babe Carson imagines herself a broken-down crone and dramatically throws away her cocaine.

The monologue about preserving a star's youthful good looks anticipates Mae West's own Hollywood years, when she avoided sun, insisted on bathing in bottled water as well as drinking it, and held to her regimen of administering a daily enema to complete the thorough inside-and-out cleansing she considered essential. Whether she actually experimented with cocaine and later renounced it will never be known, but she undoubtedly had observed drug users similar to Babe, or to David in *The Drag*, firsthand. In her account of her prison days, she casually describes the drug addicts she met, and seems pretty matter-of-fact about the narcosan cure. Karl Fleming, who interviewed her in the seventies, remembers her expressing disdain for the hippies as inventors of nothing new; she'd seen it all decades before. He thought she'd certainly witnessed plenty of drug use—including opium parties in Hollywood in the thirties—and possibly engaged in it briefly herself. Drugs figure prominently in her next two plays as well.

The encounter with the sorry old actress in the last act of *The Wicked Age* triggers a reformation in Babe Carson's character. All of a sudden she turns serious and heroic, discovering the identity of the murderer and doing battle with him. There's even a hint she will settle down as the wife of Jack Stratford. The pasted-on capitulation to virtue may be a concession to the censors. The passage of the Wales Padlock Act meant that another police raid would risk more than a second jail term; it might result in closing down Daly's theater—or whichever theater she played in—for a year, and penalties for theater owner, manager, producer, and cast alike. The virtuous turn also may signal an attempt to attract a wider audience. The mainly stag, burlesque-seasoned audience suited Mae West just fine, but she realized she needed to draw in women as well as men if she meant to become a mainstream star. How to attract women to her shows became something to ponder in depth. "I analyzed it to figure out what was maybe keeping the women away. I'd done a belly dance which might offend them. And then one of my characters [in *Sex*] was this slick-looking blackmailer who got this society woman and pushed her and grabbed her jewels off her, treated her rotten. You'd be surprised how many people sit there and think that's themselves up there."

The play that would break the barrier—attracting women as well as men, the young and the old, slumming socialites and lowlifes on the town—would be her next one, *Diamond Lil*. Her misguided sortie into flapperdom would be filed away as a learning experience. She would never again risk being upstaged by younger, prettier scene stealers.

Mae rang in her banner New York year, 1928, with a one-night stand, hosting a nightclub, à la Texas Guinan, at Park Avenue and Fifty-ninth Street's Club Deauville. A capacity crowd paid ten dollars a head for "A Program of Distinctive and Unique Entertainment Conceived and Directed by the Distinguished Star in Person." She earned $1,700 for a single night's work, but was never tempted to repeat this success. She had bigger fish to fry.

10

DIAMOND MAE

*T*ODAY, if you mention the name Mae West, most people will mentally switch on her screen outing as Flower Belle Lee in *My Little Chickadee*—an irony, since she hated the film and hated the amount of credit and screen footage she had to share with W. C. Fields. Few remember that Flower Belle's period costumes and amorous entanglements with bandits were just variations on an earlier, oft-repeated, and by 1940 all-too-familiar Mae West theme: Diamond Lil. From the late 1920s through the '30s, '40s, and '50s, it was that persona who instantly came to mind when Mae West's name was mentioned. She seemed never to tire of re-creating Diamond Lil, the insouciant, insinuating, sashaying, tough-talking, sultry-voiced, golden-wigged, diamond-encrusted, bone-corseted, wasp-waisted, flaring-hipped, and balloon-bosomed 1890s Bowery saloon hostess and singer she first brought to the stage in 1928. Lil became Mae West's signature role, in effect her trademark, as much a part of her as Ed Wynn's lisping Perfect Fool, Theda Bara's kohl-eyed vamp, Valentino's Sheik, or Charlie Chaplin's Little Tramp. Diamond Lil transformed Mae West from a mere actress into an enduring icon of American popular culture.

Once the play *Diamond Lil* had been transposed into celluloid in the 1933 screen adaptation called *She Done Him Wrong*, the starring role took on the permanence of folk legend. Audiences who came to see Mae West expected some version of the character they already knew, and Mae wasn't one to disappoint them. "If you've found a magic that does something for you, honey, stick to it," she advised. "Never change it."

Even when she wasn't playing Lil, or Lil's cinematic incarnation, Lady Lou, Mae West perpetuated the type by continuing to portray performers. She reaffirmed her link with turn-of-the-century America, and with slangy lines spoken in a languorous drawl—the famous "voice like a kazooka blown through steel wool." She returned over and over again to the opulent costumes of a bygone era—enormous picture hats and floor-length, skin-tight gowns that flattered her hourglass figure—deployed against a colorful underworld background that has been purged of menace, declawed and defanged.

Diamond Lil's white slavers, escaped convicts, dopers, Bowery drunks, and thieves were disinfected for the benefit of slumming theatergoers by infusions of nostalgia and the stagy exaggerations of melodrama. Types, including stereotypes like the tightwad Jewish landlord, Jacobson, inhabited this terrain—not rounded characters. Viewed from a safe distance, the seamy side of life in the Tenderloin, so fascinating to twenties audiences, acquired "the heightened unreality of a waterfront ballad."

As Diamond Lil, Mae West could draw upon her vaudeville character's campy stylization, to which the drag queens in *The Drag* had given fresh impetus. "Rasping and undulating, undulating and rasping," she moved "sullenly about the stage, as if it pained her." Slow motion set her apart from the other players. Critic Stark Young remarked on "that audacity of leisure motion which becomes an intensity of movement by its continuity, but is almost stillness because it is so slow. The whole body—not a beautiful one—is supple, flowing, coolly insinuating, the voice and enunciation only more so." For him, Mae West as Lil was "as remote and purely theatrical as Sarah Bernhardt in *La Tosca*."

Lil marked Mae West's first critical clean sweep, first on April 4, 1928, in Brooklyn, where the play brought down the house at Teller's Shubert Theatre ("You'd have thought that a favorite bootlegger had come back from Atlanta"), then a few nights after as a Broadway attraction at the Royale, a West Forty-fifth Street theater with more than a thousand seats. If Stark Young grouped her with Bernhardt, other journalists ranked her—in popularity, showmanship, and sheer pizzazz—with actresses almost as celebrated: "Mae West . . . is more admired by her public than is Jane Cowl, Lynn Fontanne, Helen Hayes, or Eva LeGallienne," Percy Hammond wrote in the *Herald Tribune*. "She makes Miss Ethel Barrymore look like the late lamented Mr. Bert Savoy," Robert Garland claimed in the *Evening Telegram*. Leonard Hall, also of the *Telegram*, went for broke, rhapsodizing not about her acting ability but her sizzling provocativeness. He crowned her "Flaming Mae, Torchbearer and Good Bad Girl of Broadway." Mae West, he wrote, ". . . is to the New York stage what a match is to a scuttle of gunpowder— what hot fire is to a shivering wienerwurst. . . . She is the prize tang-inserter of the American Theatre."

Like so much that comes to seem inevitable, *Diamond Lil* happened by accident. Jack Linder, a vaudeville agent, approached Timony in 1927 during the run of *Sex*, saying he wanted to produce a Mae West play and that maybe she could do something with a script written by his brother. Back in 1915 his brother, Mark Linder, had created a one-act playlet about a Sing Sing prisoner, called *The Frame Up*, which made the rounds on the burlesque circuit. He then enlarged it into three acts, placed most of the action in the 1890s, retitled it *Chatham Square*, and shopped it around, trying to get it produced.

It was this play that Mark Linder read to Mae, who loved the underworld atmosphere and nostalgic Bowery saloon setting but little else. She obviously had no use for a script with a male lead and no starring role for herself (Linder's script features a pregnant woman who then has a child, something no Mae West character ever does). She decided to create her own Mae West vehicle: "I only go into a play where I can be myself, and strut my stuff." She composed the dialogue, thought up the situations, invented and named every character except Chick Clark, the escaped convict in Linder's original script.

In her autobiography she insists that she was already thinking about writing a play with a Bowery setting at the time she heard Linder's play. If that is so, this is a case of synchronicity. But because the settings and atmosphere echo those in *Chatham Square*, she agreed to give Mark Linder an acting part in the play, a 50 percent financial interest in it, and eventually to credit him for suggesting the period and locale.

Exposure to *Chatham Square* got her thinking about how the Old Bowery atmosphere could be worked to her advantage. As *The Wicked Age* had made abundantly clear, Mae West trying to palm herself off as an eighteen-year-old flapper bathing beauty only invited jeers. The fashions of the 1890s, on the other hand, perfectly suited her body type and taste. Her abundant curves, her beautiful skin, her love of feathers, diamonds, and picture hats could all be indulged without stint. The corset, banished by flappers, could be invited back for a flamboyant last stand. With the help of Dolly Tree, the production's British costume designer, she would deck herself in beige satin, feather boas, a strapless black number trimmed with jet passamenterie, a red show-stopper for the last act, a negligee of "heavy cream lace and yellow chiffon flounces" for the boudoir scenes.

She sensed that a play she starred in that was set in New York in the Gay Nineties would appeal to every age group, attracting three generations: the young, their mothers and fathers, and their grandparents. The young would take to the scandalous heroine, the rip-roaring action, and the rollicking saloon atmosphere. The female audience that had been conspicuously absent before would be drawn in by the period costumes; they'd admire her artfully painted face: darkened eyebrows plucked in an arching line, whitened skin, and bright red Cupid's-bow lips. In the copyright version of the playscript, there is a note attached to a scene in which Diamond Lil sits before her dressing table that says: "This scene can be worked with Lil cold-creaming her face . . . and putting on full make-up, always interesting to women in an audience."

Grandly gowned as a woman of the 1890s, Mae West could finally thumb her nose at the flapper. She lashed out in the press at young women who were deceived into believing that they "looked well by appearing mannish, in sports styles. Naturally, this leads to rough manners and a generally careless attitude. Good lord, if there's anything more awkward than a woman draped over a bar. The speakeasy influence. Sit at a table, dearie, I always say."

The fashions, songs, and ambience of New York in the 1890s, she understood, held enormous appeal for audiences in the late twenties. The Gotham on the far side of the great divide of the world war, before the advent of radio, talkies, and the automobile, seemed quaint, its beer-drenched pre-Prohibition rowdiness innocently endearing. Bartenders with handlebar mustaches and white aprons tucked into their waists, cops twirling nightsticks, couples astride bicycles built for two, Florodora girls trailing long skirts under parasols, and Irish tenors shamelessly plucking the heartstrings had become emblems of the good old days, wistfully remembered by those who had been young in their heyday.

As part of the 1920s backward-glancing disposition, Mark Sullivan published the first volume of his detailed study of the social history of the United States from 1900 on, in 1926. John Held, Jr., did stylized, intentionally dated-looking woodblock illustrations of saloon songs in *Ballads from the Dear Dead Days*. Comic strips like "When Mother Was a Girl" became popular. Fanny Brice sang "I Was a Florodora Baby," and presidential candidate Al Smith tried to link himself with a simpler, more direct era by making "On the Sidewalks of New York" his theme song. Tour operators in Times Square filled their buses with visitors eager for a look at what remained of the fabled, notorious past: "See the Chinese opium dens! The Bowery slums! Coney ablaze with light!"

Although she didn't want it buzzed about that she was herself old enough to have memories of the Bowery at the turn of the century—she claimed she learned it all from a hotel night manager and onetime Bowery cop with a long memory—Mae West once, in an unguarded moment, trumpeted her firsthand knowledge of the scene. (Since she had to have been under the age of ten, these images must have been embellished by secondhand accounts, possibly her father's):

> I recall all the famous places. There were Silver Dollar Smith's, famous Nigger Mike Salter's, where Irving Berlin started as a singing waiter; McGuirk's Suicide Club [prototype of the Suicide Hall setting for *Diamond Lil*], a glittering cheap dive in which many young girls committed suicide from shame . . . and such sordid rendezvous as the Plague and Chick Tricker's Fleabag. Cheap sports, political satraps, barflies, fancy women, gangsters and drug addicts frequented these places.

She claimed to remember Diamond Charley, who "sported a blinding array of gems gotten chiefly through traffic in 'knockout drops' of chloral which he peddled at exorbitant prices to gangsters," and Chuck Connors, a legendary character who, after visiting England, costumed himself in flamboyant costermonger gear. Jim, the piano player in *Diamond Lil*, is dressed "à la Chuck Connors," in a bright-blue flannel shirt covered with white buttons, a white tie, a brown derby hat with a blue quill feather. When the play went on the road, the actor enlisted to play Jim was Chuck Connors, Jr.

When it came to casting and dressing up characters for the crowded Bowery saloon scenes, she opted for authenticity: "She hired real bums: flat-nosed, punch-drunk prize fighters, genuine homosexuals, real alcoholics." One of the singing waiters she cast, Jo-Jo, had been a singing waiter and beer slinger at Nigger Mike Salter's in the days when Irving Berlin was still Izzy Baline. Eighty-two-year-old Ida Burt, who danced at special midnight performances, dated from the days of Tony Pastor.

Mythologizing the old Bowery wasn't new. Even during Mae's girlhood, the honky-tonk neighborhood's garish glories took on a legendary glow. The popular song "The Bowery" enshrined it as a rousing but menacing place where "they say such things, and they do strange things," and a tourist was likely to get swindled—or worse. Countless vaudeville sketches depicted the downtown area near Chinatown as the picturesque hangout of trollops, thieves, con men, and glad-handing Tammany bosses with mutton-chop whiskers, watch chains over their vests, and derby hats.

According to *Variety*, a real-life prototype of the Lil character came to the Bowery from Chicago. Her signature was a diamond set in one of her front teeth. Although Mae West might not have known about it, there had also been a song, "East Side Lil," sung by Ada Lewis, who was playing a Bowery manicurist in the 1905 musical *Fritz of Tammany Hall*. Another forerunner was a stage character named Diamond Daisy in a vaudeville playlet of that name by Jack Lait, a lady crook prone to "wise comebacks" who engages in tough dialogue with a detective.

Re-creating the turn-of-the-century scene sent Mae back to a stylized version of the New York of her own childhood years, to the sinuous curving lines, furbelows, cluttered interiors, and opulence that characterized Victorian taste. Set designer August Vimnera brought them vividly back to life. The boisterous saloon, equipped with a rinky-dink piano, decorated with photos of the boxing champions of yore, with "old time posters and programs," and entered via swinging doors, restored her father's former milieu.

Lil's upstairs dressing room—positioned to provide opportunities for her grand, descending entrances—is "a gaudy, blazing thing, with expensive trappings, jumbled together." (The caretaker at Cypress Abbey, where Mae West's body reposes, claims she once lived in an apartment in nearby Queens, over a bar.) She reclines in a gilded bed, shaped like a swan, that had previously belonged to 1890s actress Amelia Bingham and that Mae bought from the estate of Diamond Jim Brady—erstwhile companion of Lillian Russell, whose buxom beauty Mae made every effort to recapture.

The plush voluptuousness identified with Lillian Russell always made Mae think of her mother, who as a young woman had looked so much like Lillian Russell that she was often mistaken for the star. As Diamond Lil, Mae West summons up the young Matilda. "Diamond Lil," writes Alexander Walker, "is a mother image on whose idealized endowments the daughter superimposed her own post-Freudian sexual freedom and enjoyment."

In other words, Diamond Lil doesn't behave like a woman of the 1890s. Her appeal rested in her ability to straddle two eras, present and past. "While her look was associated with the nineties, her attitudes were recognized as decidedly modern." She sings the blues, while those around her trot out 1890s favorites like "After the Ball" and "More to Be Pitied than Censured." She's sexually liberated, at ease in the arms of the usually Westian passel of men: the crooked politician, ward heeler Gus Jordan, who keeps her; the escaped convict she once lived with in Chicago, Chick Clark; the swarthy and debonair South American, Juárez; the dashing but innocent man in uniform, Captain Cummings from the Salvation Army, who turns out to be a police detective known as the Hawk. Before she falls for Cummings, Lil affirms that she considers men a sorry lot, all alike and not worth working yourself into a lather about. "Married or single, it's the same game. *Their game.* I happen to be wise enough to play it their own way." Even the apparently pure Cummings "can be had."

She's cynical, good-naturedly world-weary; life to her is just a "tiresome performance," a "joke on us all." When her piano player runs low on cocaine, she hands him some from her dressing-table drawer, endorsing his view that "you have to do somethin' ter make yerself think the world is good to live in." Straight-talking Lil takes life as she finds it and calls them as she sees them: "I don't kid myself or nobody else either." Although in the copyright version she instructs women in how to shoplift furs and fancy lingerie, techniques Mae West learned about from fellow prisoners on Welfare Island, her conscience doesn't bother her, she says, because she doesn't have one, and nothing scares her: "I ain't afraid of nothin', God, man or the devil."

In the novelized version of *Diamond Lil*, published in 1932, Lil takes on organized religion and expresses blasphemous views with evident relish. "Who the hell can get worked up about goin' to Heaven where there's a lot o' people lookin' like they was brung up on a dill pickle?" she wonders to Cummings. When Cummings upbraids her for speaking disrespectfully of God, she shoots back, "All I'm interested in is Greek gods. You know, you kinder look like one yourself." Although her infatuation with Cummings ultimately makes her want to prove that she does have a soul and can redeem herself through good deeds, she starts out freely acknowledging that she has no taste for salvation: "I'm the scarlet woman. When I die, I'm goin' to burn in Hell," she shrugs.

In the novel, Lil has the leisure to show off her knowledge of the Bible. Salome, the Whore of Babylon, and Delilah all strike chords in her—they're her own kind. As for the men: "She liked the stalwart David who slew Goliath and she adored Solomon who sang so wonderfully of his love for Shulamith. Lil loved the robust, the sensuous, the strong. The pale Nazarene and His doctrine of self-abnegation were too meek and mild for her. She liked best the Old Testament, whose men and women were of the earth, mighty in war and mighty in love." Her affection for the Old Testament stopped short of the Ten Commandments, however, because they condemned adultery, which she apparently equates with sex unsanctified by marriage. "What was the harm in skin to skin if you had a lot of fun and nobody got cut? It was breaking one of the Ten Commandments . . . But then, Lil had never liked Moses."

Diamond Lil's sinfulness is much more explicit in the novel than in the play, where Lil is certainly a kept woman, but one whose involvement with the South American white-slave traffic and past connection to prostitution is left blurry. (Her training of thieves was deleted from later scripts.) The movie's tribute—"[She's] one of the finest women ever walked the streets"—isn't in the play. She does sing "Frankie and Johnny," a ballad about a black woman who goes to jail for killing her two-timing lover, and "Easy Rider," but not everyone would recognize the term "easy rider" as a reference to a man who lives on a prostitute's earnings. In the book version, Lil's red-light past is spelled out. "True enough," we're told, "she had sold her own body, but she had always been complete mistress of herself." Lil asks, "How'd you think I got all my diamonds, playin' pinochle? You know they don't hand you out diamonds for just lookin' at them."

Lil is a walking paradox, an embodiment of the polar opposites basic to melodrama: she's "the scarlet woman in a setting of white ice," the devil who looks like an angel, the cool one who shows warmth and empathy for a girl in trouble. She mocks the pious Salvation Army psalm singers as "plaster saints, wishin' to God they had somethin' besides a wet string up their back," makes fun of prayer and cowardly goody-goodies, but secretly buys the building the psalm singers occupy so they won't be evicted. ("Would God masquerade behind a devil, to do a good turn?") Passionate in a man's embrace, bold enough to initiate a kiss in public, she's the soul of indifference in her gestures and drawling speech. She lolls in her swan-shaped golden bed reading the *Police Gazette*. After (in the Shubert's stage manager's script) she stabs a woman—the evil South American white-slave recruiter Rita Christinia—in self-defense, she coolly lights a cigarette, covers the corpse's face with her long hair, and calmly continues to comb it after the police enter her boudoir.

Diamonds have triggered the skirmish with Rita. Juárez has given Lil a pin—transmogrified into a pendant later in the script—that Rita Christinia, the sinister older woman who pays his way, had presented to him. Lil adds it to her hoard, and Rita flames into a jealous fury, pulling out a concealed knife, when she recognizes it adorning Lil. Cummings has tipped us off that he's Boy Scout Pure by disdaining diamonds, telling Lil they are cold and without soul, that they're merely "gee-gaws" that make her look like a "glittering palace of ice." After murdering Rita, Lil makes an effort to redeem herself as worthy of Cummings by returning the diamond gift to Juárez, saying, "Take the ball and chain—it has no soul anyway."

Diamonds always carried enormous prestige in the precarious entertainment world, as talismans of value, solidity, and permanence. According to Fred Allen, a vaudevillian who was doing well "wore a large diamond horseshoe in his tie and two or three solitaires or clusters on his fingers; his wife, dripping with necklaces, rings, earrings and bracelets, looked as though she had been pelted with ice cubes that somehow stuck where they landed . . . To the small-timer, a diamond represented security. It impressed the booker, the manager, and the audience, but more important, the diamond was collateral." Sophie Tucker, in her memoir, speaks of her hunger for diamond rings, bracelets, necklaces. "A performer, I told myself . . . has to have diamonds. They make you important."

They also made a woman feel desired and valued. A man's gift of diamonds indicated that his interest was more than casual. The Damon Runyon character Feet Samuels reasons, "Naturally any doll must give serious consideration to a guy who can buy her diamond bracelets."

Mae West amassed a sizable diamond collection herself, and as Diamond Lil—before her miraculous transformation—she confesses in the novel version that she actually prefers diamonds over men. "Men would wither and custom stale them, but diamonds! Ah, they were crystallized immortality! She felt that life would never go out of her while she covered her body with diamonds." When Mae first met Jack and Mark Linder, she decked her arms with $30,000 worth of diamond bracelets.

She pawned them all, one witness recalled, to launch *Diamond Lil*. "I had never before seen a human being place a one hundred percent bet on himself." She waged everything she had on the enterprise. The Linders initially owned half the show, but were ultimately bought out by the Shuberts when the production left New York for the road in early 1929. Owney Madden was again a silent partner, and Tommy Guinan, the nightclub owner brother of Texas, owned 10 percent.

In its ten months at the Royale, *Diamond Lil* earned steadily, peaking at the end of May with a gross of $17,000. In August, the only non-musical on Broadway to top it was O'Neill's *Strange Interlude*. Actors' salaries ran to about $1,800 a week, with the highest salary, after the star's, awarded to Curtis Cooksey, a Shakespearean actor who earned $250 weekly as Captain Cummings, the role taken by Cary Grant in the movie. Four months after it opened, according to *Variety*, the play was yielding a net weekly profit of $6,000. Half that, plus one half the royalty, went to Mae West; the remainder was initially divided between other stockholders and Mark Linder, still being described as "co-author."

Mae was not pleased to see Mark Linder constantly credited as a co-author. In fact, she went on the warpath against both Linder brothers. Backstage, in the presence of a *Variety* reporter, she buttonholed Mark Linder and grilled him: "Did you write one line of the dialogue of *Diamond Lil?*" He said no—that she had completely rewritten his play. "Is there a situation . . . that is in your play?" she pursued. He yelled back, "Atmosphere and locale. It is all mine." Her legendary *sangfroid* abandoned her. "Atmosphere and locale!" she shouted. "You can't copyright atmosphere and locale. There are any number of Bowery sketches with the same atmosphere. I own the copyright to Lil and I wrote every line of it." She continued: "The Linders got a break when they got hooked up with me. I am the one who brings people to this theatre. The atmosphere and locale they yell about have nothing to do with it. I was all ready to change the locale from the Bowery to the Barbary Coast if the public didn't like the Bowery. Tomorrow 'atmosphere and locale suggested by Mark Linder' will go on the program. . . . I have a certain style of writing. I went to jail developing that style of writing, didn't I?" She predicted that once she "got rid of them" no one would hear from the Linders again.

New programs were indeed printed, designating Mae West as sole author and attributing "atmosphere and locale" to Mark Linder. Jack Linder issued a statement accusing Mae West of trying to control the business affairs of the production and "otherwise exceeding her rights as principal player." He filed a complaint with Actors Equity. According to one account, Linder withdrew the complaint, yielding to pressure from Equity to do nothing that would jeopardize the life span of a show that was providing many actors with weekly paychecks.

Mae's already stormy relationship with the Linders deteriorated further after they advertised her and Peaches Browning, tabloid favorite and former wife of "Daddy" Browning, in the same promotional campaign. Peaches was being featured in another show produced by Jack Linder, *The Squealer*, which was bracketed with *Diamond Lil* in newspaper ads. Mae fumed until the copy was changed. "They had her name in the same type as mine, too, and I made them change that. *Diamond Lil* is a different corporation from that of *The Squealer* and they have no right to advertise the shows together. Jack Linder thinks he is another Jed Harris [a producer of multiple Broadway hits] and he is crazy on this 'Jack Linder Presents' stuff. Because they don't know anything about show business, the Linders put a fifty-cent attraction like Peaches on Broadway, where she has no draw." Within weeks after this contretemps the Linders had been bought out by the Shuberts.

Mark Linder went to his grave convinced he had been cheated out of his fair share of *Diamond Lil* bounty. He sued to claim half of Mae West's portion of *She Done Him Wrong* profits, but the case was thrown out of court.

As Mae had hoped, *Diamond Lil's* public appeal cut across class lines, in a way that *The Wicked Age* had failed to do. Jack La Rue, who played Juárez, the South American gigolo, remembered the audience: "Sitting side by side in the same row . . . would be gangsters from the underworld, a group of society people right out of the Social Register, college boys and grey-bearded men."

Just as a throng of actors playing slumming socialites from uptown swarm into Suicide Hall in *Diamond Lil's* saloon scenes, so actual upscale New Yorkers found it chic in 1928 to take in Mae West and company at the Royale Theater, especially the weekly Thursday midnight performances, when real beer—perhaps supplied by Owney Madden's Phoenix Cereal Beverage Company—flowed from the taps at the onstage bar.

For a time Mae employed press agent Wendell Phillips Dodge as special emissary to the limousine trade, on hand "to greet the swanky mob" in the lobby on her behalf at every performance and invite these swells backstage after the show.

The intelligentsia also paid homage, with an earnestness that *Variety* found ridiculous: "There's enough that's funny about Diamond Lil, but funnier still is the arty bunch finally 'discovering' Mae as a great dramatic actress." *The New Republic*, newly recruited to the Mae West camp, published a long and adulatory critique. *The New York Times* validated Mae West's "fine and direct" approach to sex by labeling it "almost Elizabethan," and condescended to rate the play "amply, if somewhat embarrassingly, entertaining." Veteran producer and playwright David Belasco, who had brought *Lulu Belle* to Broadway, came backstage and offered his compliments. Novelist and photographer Carl Van Vechten, an aficionado of Harlem nightlife and friend to the avant garde, attended several performances, and on one occasion brought along John Colton, the co-adaptor of Maugham's *Rain* for the stage; no doubt Colton recognized the echoes of *Rain* in the play: the seduction of a pure man by a scarlet woman, and the use of a storm to build tension during a climactic scene.

Everyone who saw *Diamond Lil* agreed that Mae West was the whole show. Without her "the play would be a rough and interesting phase of American life, Chatham Square thirty years ago—a rather tawdry melodrama. With Mae West it becomes important, amusing . . . almost a bit precious." A critic for the *Brooklyn Eagle* called it a "one-man show," in the same category as vehicles for Buffalo Bill and John L. Sullivan.

As Lil, Mae West dominated the stage with the larger-than-life splendor of a clipper ship in full sail, creating an illusion of grandeur and amplitude— she appeared to stand five feet nine inches and to weigh 160 pounds—via padded floor-length costumes, wide-brimmed, be-plumed hats, and high heels that recast her diminutive five-foot form into that of a Junoesque Jezebel.

She loomed large offstage as well as on. Although Ira Hards, a former actor under Charles Frohman, who had recently directed Bela Lugosi in *Dracula*, was listed as the director, the real boss was Mae West. She picked the actors, she issued the orders backstage, she chose the songs. A theme song written by Robert Sterling, an actor who was one of the initial stockholders, was cut out without explanation; in its place came a thirty-year-old song, "Heart of the Bowery." Sterling interpreted this as Mae West's retaliation for his refusal to insert her name as co-author of his song. It may have been an economy move as well; she probably didn't have to pay royalties on an old song that predated the 1914 founding of ASCAP.

She even fashioned her own corsets—"She would get a regular boned corset, turn it upside down and trim off the top"—and saw to it that the script provided many opportunities for her to display herself in them. "I prefer to talk to men when I am not dressed," Lil announces to an embarrassed Captain Cummings, who has suggested she should not receive him until she has put on some clothes.

A member of the company described her backstage demeanor as "strong and tough." When an actor gave her flak, she snapped, "Well, if you don't like it, just step out in the alley after the show and I'll settle it with you, personally."

After the curtain, Mae held court at the Royale, a Spanish-style theater built by the Chanin Brothers in 1927. "People of every kind, age and class would storm her dressing room door . . . She was as hospitable and as interested in a street cleaner as she was in a Wall Street financier." A few good-looking male admirers functioned as sentries, keeping at bay those would-be interviewers or fans she preferred not to receive. The visitors permitted backstage found her still in costume and makeup, even two hours after the final curtain. As Thyra Samter Winslow, a writer for the sophisticated *New Yorker*, observed, "A star still in make-up is far more interesting than an overdressed little woman in street clothes."

Winslow, whose interview resulted in a lengthy *New Yorker* profile, limned a portrait of a gutsy, upbeat, singularly self-absorbed actress who had little interest in anything outside the theater. "Clubs and cards and outdoor activities do not amuse her." Even on days when there were no matinees, Winslow reported, Mae West arrived at her dressing room around two or three in the afternoon. (This was one way to escape Timony's watchful eye.) "Her reading is confined usually to *Variety* or the occasional newspaper. She does not even know the names of important theatrical figures unless she had come into direct contact with them. The other night, Ina Claire [a celebrated leading lady on Broadway] came to see *Diamond Lil*. When Mae West was told she was out front she said, 'All right, bring her in. But who is she?'"

Winslow found Mae West "seemingly frank, with a frankness that tells nothing." She picked up an undercurrent of anxiety, born of her subject's new success: "She is afraid of . . . people getting a hold on her, of grafts, of attacks because she has succeeded . . . Old acquaintances wouldn't look her up if they didn't want something . . . Would they?" Apparently Mae's wariness failed to protect her from down-and-out acquaintances seeking handouts, and she lived up to her reputation as a soft touch. Although she netted almost half a million dollars from *Diamond Lil*, at the end of its run she found herself broke, "due to her large gifts and loans to friends." Her legal bills for *Pleasure Man* would soon take a large bite as well.

She found it easier to dispense money than to be forthcoming about her background. Secretive about her family and her history, she pointedly avoided personal disclosure. "Since her prosperity, she is building up a very pleasant past . . . smoothing out events here and there . . . deleting where deletion seems necessary." Her age and her mother's German birth were not revealed, but the family connections to the Copleys and to Harry Thaw were mentioned. She told Winslow her father was a doctor, in the Richmond Hill section of Queens, and admitted to a brother in the automobile business and an actress sister, Beverly Osborne, who was cast as Sally, the disgraced young woman of good family in *Diamond Lil*.

The one outside interest Mae West pursued—beyond her own career, and men—according to Winslow, was "the occult and spiritualism." Actor Jean Hersholt corroborated this. On a trip back to New York from Hollywood, after seeing *Diamond Lil* and coming backstage, he was invited to a séance held in the smoking room of the Royale. They all sat around a big table in a darkened room. He sat next to Mae West and held her hand for four hours. The medium told them they were going to talk to Caruso and Valentino. "Suddenly a voice said, 'Jean.' I answered, 'Yes, Rudy. Where are you and how are you?' Rudy then proceeded to tell me that he was happy . . . Then Rudy called upon Mae. Mae was all aquiver and said, 'Yes, Rudy, I am right here.' Rudy said, 'Mae, you have a lot of enemies and don't trust any of them.' Mae was quick to promise, 'No, I won't, Rudy.' . . . Mae was very much in earnest." This is Mae's second reported attempt to reach Valentino beyond the grave. He must have mattered to her. Perhaps she recognized their kinship—the hyperbolic sexuality, theatricality, cult status, and glamour they shared.

Being told by the disembodied Valentino that she had many enemies only confirmed Mae's natural suspiciousness. There were people out to get her, she believed, even within the *Diamond Lil* family. In addition to the friction with the Linders, she had to handle other backstage struggles. Curtis Cooksey's haughtiness irritated her ("She enjoyed cutting him down to size in a photo"), and her relationship with Wendell Phillips Dodge turned sour. She hired a detective as an extra, to spy on the *Diamond Lil* cast, in particular to check up on the young man who always won in the company crap games. "I knew everything that went on in the company without asking anybody."

She grew increasingly territorial, intolerant of poachers on her turf. She had made no protest, in 1928, right after *Diamond Lil* opened, when Dorothy Sands in the *Grand Street Follies* impersonated her "as she might have done Juliet in a Max Reinhardt version on the steps of the New York Public Library." Again she remained silent after Grace Hayes first brought her impression of Diamond Lil to the stage of the Palace in a vaudeville act. But in time, when Grace Hayes showed no inclination to retire her imitation, she was threatened with a lawsuit unless she dropped her "Lil" act.

Mae had cultivated quite a taste for intrigue; it excited her, heightened the pleasurable feeling that she lived at the edge. "Sly and ruthless as a Borgia princess," Lewis Lapham said of her.

She took refuge, during the first run of *Diamond Lil*, in her room at the West Fifty-fourth Street Harding Hotel, which also housed gangsters Legs Diamond and Hymie "Feet" Edson. Owned in part by Owney Madden, it was not an address you'd choose if you had conventional worries about keeping out of harm's way. Matilda West was reportedly a co-owner, and a rumor circulated that Mae herself had a financial interest.

The Harding housed a series of nightclubs, several of them hosted by Texas Guinan, that were known to be the favorite all-night playgrounds of the gambling and bootlegging mob. It was there, at the Club Abbey, in an early-morning 1931 free-for-all, that Dutch Schultz was shot in the shoulder and Charles "Chink" Sherman, one of Madden's chief lieutenants, was both shot and stabbed in a struggle over Broadway beer-selling rights.

Mae's hyperactive love life kept her talent for covert action in top form. "I was starring in *Lil*, and I was going steady with my lawyer. I was also going with a Frenchman and another guy—but not so steady." The Frenchman, who is called "Dinjo" in *Goodness Had Nothing to Do with It*, would pick her up at the Royale when the last admirer had finally departed. Keeping the possessive Timony in the dark about the Frenchman required skill and imagination. "We met any place we could—dressin' rooms, elevators, the back seat of his car or my limousine. A kind of hit-and-run affair, you might say." She bragged about their stamina as lovers: "One Saturday night we were at it till four the next afternoon. A dozen rubber things. Twenty-two times. I was sorta tired." (Though she told interviewers that only the game mattered to her, not the score, in truth she was always counting. When the ghostwriter of her autobiography expressed skepticism about some of her statistics about the number of rubbers used on a given night, she offered to furnish a signed affidavit.) The affair with the Frenchman ended after his wife showed up, complaining that her husband was neglecting her and their child, and that he beat her.

The "other guy" in the picture must have been George Raft. A friend of Owney Madden's from boyhood days in Hell's Kitchen, his successes as a Broadway hoofer and sometime scout for prizefighters had not closed off shadier avenues. A gambler, he'd rolled the dice with the likes of Al Capone and Lucky Luciano in a garage behind Jimmy Durante's Club Durant. He reportedly held the drunk-rolling concession at the El Fey Club when he was working with Texas Guinan. After hours, armed with a .38 gun, he drove the convoy car for Madden's fleet of beer trucks.

Renowned as a lady-killer, Raft spared no expense dressing for the part. For winter he favored either a black form-fitted coat with a velvet collar or a sporty brown camel wraparound. He borrowed from Owney Madden a predilection for black shirts, white ties, and gray fedoras pulled low over one eye. "He wore fifty buck shoes with pointy toes, shined so bright you could see your face in them."

One of George Raft's extracurricular assignments was to drive to the Royale and pick up Owney Madden's percentage of that night's *Diamond Lil* take. Predictably, he caught Mae's eye, and another affair on the run began, very much along the same energetic lines as the affair with the Frenchman: "The word was—frequent, all the time, and anyplace. Raft and West made love in cars, closets, on the floor, kitchen tables." But where the Frenchman was quickly relegated to history, George Raft would remain Mae's friend and a favorite for the next five decades. It was George Raft whose recommendation brought Mae West to Hollywood, to appear with him in a supporting role in *Night After Night*. (He preceded her to Hollywood by several years and was immediately type-cast as a slick-looking tough-guy/gangster.) They lived for a time in the same Hollywood neighborhood, and stayed in touch. As if by prearrangement, the two died within days of each other in 1980.

After a long run of eight months and 323 performances on Broadway, *Diamond Lil* went on the road, to Pittsburgh, Chicago, Detroit, San Francisco, and Los Angeles. Several original cast members joined the road company: Raphaella Ottiano as Rita, a role she would repeat in the movie; Curtis Cooksey as Cummings, Mae's sister Beverly as Sally, and Jack La Rue, who was smitten with Mae, as Juárez.

In Chicago, where the show ran for eighteen weeks, the first twelve at the Shuberts' newly refurbished Apollo theater, some unsavory types, "gunmen, gangsters, thieves and some lower-class bootleggers," were denied admission on opening night. Detectives at the door turned them away. A few in the crowd that made it inside were scandalized by what they saw onstage—"kisses such as never were kissed on any stage before"—and demanded police intervention. A love scene between Lil and Juárez had to be toned down.

Mae told the ghostwriter of her autobiography that she once spent a night with Al Capone, that he sent flowers to her dressing room and taught her to shoot a machine gun. But their chumminess, if actual, didn't immunize her against a shakedown that occurred a few months into her Chicago stay. A number of performers in the city, including Harry Richman and Roy Rogers, were approached by gunmen demanding "protection" money. She was among them. "Hardest hit victim of backstage racketeers, according to reports at the State Attorney's office, was Mae West, who is said to have turned over $3,000 for 'protection.' "

She paid up, and took the additional step of hiring a bodyguard, a former boxer who had been in the cast, and installing him in her suite at the Sherman Hotel. "We got him a gun, and he was with us constantly."

She supplemented the bodyguard's services with protection of another, less tangible sort. For the first time in her life, physical complaints were plaguing her. She suffered attacks of intense abdominal pain. When the usual diagnostic techniques—X-ray and physical examination by a doctor— turned up nothing conclusive, Timony brought in an Indian healer, Yogi Sri Deva Ram Sukul. The Yogi placed his hands on her waist, prayed in Hindi, and pronounced her cured. The pains vanished, and Mae felt she had "touched the hem of the unknown." She never returned to her old way of thinking, her previous conviction that the material world, "a pleasant world of inanimate objects like money, cars, suites, good reviews, diamonds, clothes, strong lovers"—interesting that she groups her lovers with inanimate objects—was everything. She would continue her spiritual quest, convinced now that "the Forces" had been enlisted to watch over her.

Compared to her other plays, *Diamond Lil* encountered little censorship; in New York, no one cried foul. But in Detroit, where the company traveled after leaving Chicago, the mayor, John C. Lodge, ordered the play closed after Mae West distributed—"in the neighborhood sections and among children"—a mock-up of *The Police Gazette* with her image on the pink-colored front page, over a caption comparing her to Madame Du Barry. The sold-out Detroit run was able to resume under a restraining order.

Mae returned to New York and was about to take her company to the West Coast when the stock market crashed. *Variety* ran its celebrated banner headline, WALL STREET LAYS AN EGG. In smaller print it added: "Drop in Stocks Ropes Showmen/Many Weep and Call Off Christmas Orders— Legit Shows Hit." The Wall Street disaster had a ripple effect. The theater district was renamed the Groaning Forties as nightclubs, speakeasies, and theaters went under. Posh apartments were abandoned, and secondhand markets were flooded with luxury items—Duesenberg cars and Oriental carpets—being offered for quick cash at a fraction of their value. "Actors were ruined, shows closed, backers blew out their brains."

Mae states in her memoir that the crash left her financially unscathed, since her only investments were in show business and diamonds—"I didn't invest in something I couldn't sit and watch." But a Chicago newspaper from 1929 printed a photo of her in an overcoat lined with $21,000 worth of deflated stock certificates, an amount she said she had recently lost. "Miss West, however, has made plenty on Wall Street, she says, and can well afford to smile." This sounds like creative thinking on the part of a publicist for the Shuberts.

The depressed economy had an immediate impact on the imminent West Coast tour of *Diamond Lil*. The company made the costly cross-country move, but profits from the play's three-week run at San Francisco's Curran Theater dwindled disappointingly after a strong start. In Los Angeles, at the Biltmore, the box office was weak from the beginning. *Variety* reported a take of only $8,000 in the second week, "which implies a flop."

Before it closed in California, and the company regrouped in New York for a run on the low-budget subway circuit, the movie colony put out feelers about converting *Diamond Lil* into a film. From San Francisco, Timony had sent a night letter to Lee Shubert: "Have been asking $100,000 picture rights Diamond Lil. Picture People Think Too High. Have told them communicate Direct with You." Both Columbia and Universal Studios expressed interest.

Movie censors were up in arms at the mere possibility. Colonel Jason Joy, head of the Studio Relations Committee of the Hays Office, sounded an alarm after going to see *Diamond Lil* at the Biltmore in Los Angeles, at the request of Universal's Junior Laemmle, the younger Carl. The joyless Joy wrote: "I have advised Mr. Laemmle that because of the vulgar dramatic situations and the highly censorable dialogue, in my opinion an acceptable picture could not be made." He added, "The possibility of employing Mae West as a member of Universal's writing staff was brought to my attention. Of course, I discouraged the idea."

Diamond Lil joined a list of plays and books the Hays Office ruled out for screen adaptation, including two other Mae West titles, *Sex* and *Pleasure Man*, along with *Virtue's Bed, Dishonored Lady, Love, Honor and Betray,* and *Bad Girl*. In 1930 the Hays organization had limited enforcement power, and several titles on the "Banned" list found their way to the big screen nonetheless. *Diamond Lil* had to be scrapped as a title, but there were no constraints on *She Done Him Wrong*. Millions of moviegoers eventually got their chance to see Mae West as the diamond-studded chatelaine of Suicide Hall, "one of the finest women ever walked the streets."

The role became a kind of life preserver, a provider of rescue during professional doldrums. After Mae West's movie career ground to a halt in the

1940s, she took the stage version of *Diamond Lil* out of mothballs and brought it to London for her only appearance outside the United States. She then toured with it, in triumph, on home turf.

She went to court more than once to establish her exclusive ownership of the Lil name and image. The first time, in 1960, she failed; the San Francisco Superior Court found "Diamond Lil" to be "words of common usage in the public domain which were not susceptible to appropriation by a given individual." A woman named Marie Lind was allowed to continue advertising her supper-club act as "Diamond Lil." Mae saw red. She wrote to J. J. Shubert that after so much money had been spent to advertise and exploit the Diamond Lil name, she could not allow another person to "appropriate the name and benefit by the world-wide fame I have created for it." Four years later, a Los Angeles decision reversed the San Francisco ruling. No other performer could thereafter claim to be Diamond Lil. She belonged exclusively to Mae West, who submerged her identity in the character. "Diamond Lil—I'm her and she's me and we're each other."

11

REPEAT OFFENDER

*B*ACK in 1928, while *Diamond Lil* continued to pack them in at the Royale, Mae West and Timony began planning a simultaneous production of a new play to be scripted by Mae, a backstage drama in which she would not perform. In August, *Variety* reported that Mae West was again invading producing ranks "as a side-line to her current tie-up as author-star of 'Diamond Lil.' In the new exploit Miss West will register in dual capacity of author-producer of "Five-A-Day," saga of the coffee and cake circuit masquerading as vaudeville theaters."

Once again, Mae West would be mining her past, this time a more recent chapter in her history: her years of trouping on the Keith and other circuits. By now, supplanted by movies and radio, vaudeville had been consigned to shadowy sideshow status. Mae was indulging in a backward glance at a world that would soon vanish. She hoped to re-create the bustle, high spirits, and tensions of a milieu she knew by heart, taking the audience behind the scenes where trunks are carried in, the orchestra tunes up, hoofers try their routines, acrobats tumble, electricians—when not occupied with spider boxes and olivettes—argue about union cards, small-timers grumble about stands in Peoria and blue laws, costumes come on and off, interlopers from the legitimate stage pull rank, and Irish scrubwomen, as they mop up, kid each other about the number of husbands they've buried.

Mae was able to hire some old-timers whose authenticity would set the tone. Stan Stanley, a former acrobat who became a comedian "with a pugnacious air and a booming voice," was cast as a wisecracking stage manager: "Have you had your cream puff today?" he asks a female impersonator. Stanley had once appeared on the same bill with Mae in a Louisville, Kentucky, vaudeville lineup. Alan Brooks, who played the villain, was a veteran of vaudeville playlets. Herman Lenzen, one of the comic German tumblers, had been an acrobat for more than twenty years.

Before long, word circulated that the new Mae West endeavor would follow in the steps of *The Drag*. The cast of the new play, eventually titled *Pleasure Man*, would include many gay actors, described by *Variety* as "men wearing slave bracelets." Several of these—Leo Howe, Ed Hearn, Charles Ordway—were holdovers, in fact, from the stillborn *Drag*. Both plays feature an outrageous drag party that ends with a murder, and both contain the line, spoken by a drag queen, "I've had so many operations . . . I look like a slot machine."

For Mae, gay characters belonged in a play with a backstage setting: they had long been an integral part of show business, attracted by "its color, its interesting life, and its values beyond accepted society." Besides, she added in an interview, the third sex guaranteed a good time. "I personally get a big kick outta them . . . They're all so talented, so very clever." Once again, she grouped all gays together as effeminate types, female souls trapped in male bodies who sew or make lampshades in their spare time and have names like Peaches or Bunny. "What's normal to them is abnormal to us. Well, who's right—who's gonna say?" Again, she defined homosexuality as a disease, but not a crime: "I think the medical profession should find a cure before they condemn them and throw them into jail."

As in *The Drag*, she provides a showcase for their self-mocking "campin'" and punning, sexually charged banter:

Third Boy: My, what a low cut gown you've got.
Fourth Boy: Why, Beulah, a woman with a back like mine can be as low as she wants to be.

Mae West insisted that *Pleasure Man* was only incidentally about gays; the main plot involves "normal people" whose lives intersect with the villainous Rodney Terrill (Alan Brooks), a preening Lothario—the title's pleasure man—who tries to seduce every young woman in sight, including the female half of "Dolores and Randall," a married dance team. ("The only thing he hasn't made is one of the lions in front of the public library," quips the female impersonator Paradise Dupont.) Terrill, not the drag artists, supplies the most shocking moment in the play: he is murdered by castration. The murderer turns out to be the electrician brother of Mary Ann, one of Terrill's sexual victims, an innocent young thing who was both impregnated and brutalized by Terrill. The brother wants to make sure Terrill will prey upon no other woman as he has Mary Ann.

Terrill's womanizing in some ways mirrors the man-hunting of the character Mae West usually plays. Like her Tira in *I'm No Angel*, he exhibits photographs in his dressing room of all his conquests. But unlike Tira (or Margy LaMont, or Diamond Lil), he's a heavy, an unscrupulous, unfeeling brute who inflicts pain on his partners and totally lacks humor or self-awareness. And while Tira levels with us, if not her conquests, Terrill lies to and deceives all the women he pursues, pretending that each is the sole object of his desire. He's the moral antithesis of Paradise, the female impersonator who rushes to help the young woman Terrill strikes, "a sister in distress," and thanks God he's not a man—if Terrill is representative of that sex.

Mae West liked to present herself as a woman who never met a man she didn't like—"I love 'em all," she'd announce—but her characterization of Terrill betrays an undercurrent of vengeful fury. Karl Fleming, who interviewed her over a period of weeks, came away convinced she held men—both deceivers and the deceived—in contempt.

She risked a great deal when she undertook *Pleasure Man*. Although she hit pay dirt with *Diamond Lil*, she knew the censors might scapegoat it, as they had turned on *Sex* when *The Drag* was about to open in New York. True, the publicity generated by another police raid might spur a box-office bonanza. But it could also backfire. A punitive crusade might ensue. Because she had already served time on a morals offense, she faced severe sentencing as a repeat offender if found guilty a second time.

She gambled with the prospect of spending years in jail for a play she didn't even have the time to write. The producer, Carl Reed (once Lillian Russell's manager, and more recently the producer of *Aloma of the South Seas*), agreed to come on board with nothing more than an outline in hand. He never saw a script, because the script came into being only after rehearsals began. The actors were handed scraps of paper with lines written on them for individual parts. But many lines had to be improvised. Camelia Campbell, who played Dolores, the married dancer smitten with Terrill, told George Eells she hadn't had a clue about what she was supposed to say in the crucial scene where she finds her would-be lover dead and mutilated. Mae coaxed her during rehearsal: "What would you do?" When Campbell said she'd call the police, then hesitate, Mae indicated she was on the right track and should follow her hunches. Everything Campbell said was kept.

The first tryout, at the Bronx Opera House in mid-September 1928, was eyed with suspicion by the borough's district attorney, but escaped police intervention after producer Carl Reed cut "a naughty word and a song." It earned $9,000 in a week—not bad for the Bronx.

Variety's reviewer, Jack Conway, a virtuoso of slang, aped the swishy manner of the drag queens as he urged:

> Oh, my dear, you must throw on a shawl and run over to the Biltmore in two weeks to see Mae West's *Pleasure Man*. Monday night at the Bronx Opera House it opened cold and was adorable . . .
>
> [In the last act] one of the Queens who used to be in show business throws a party for all the performers on the bill. The female impersonators, four strong, and some other queens all go in drag. Are you screaming? . . .

Variety prized this review. After Conway died, they ran it twice more in the course of the lengthy *Pleasure Man* trial.

Conway's good-humored appreciation was seconded by the New York *Evening Post*'s Nunnally Johnson, who reported after seeing a preview in Jackson Heights, Queens, that he had emerged from the show uncontaminated and that he considered the evening "great, with Rabelais only a half-jump or so ahead." But there the cheering stopped.

When the play moved from the outer boroughs to an October 1 opening at the Biltmore, on Forty-seventh and Broadway, invective ruled the day as reviewers from the press hurled one critical brickbat after another: "No play of our time has had less excuse for such a sickening excess of filth," sneered the New York *Sun*. "Three tiresome and unspeakably slimy acts, smeared from beginning to end with such filth as cannot possibly be described in print," snarled the *Post*." *Billboard*'s Wilfred J. Riley seethed: "*Pleasure Man* is prostitution of the rankest sort, a flagrant attempt to capitalize filth and degeneracy and cash in on the resultant cheap publicity." He called the portrayal of show people "libelous and treacherous."

Walter Winchell, now writing about Broadway for *Life*, called this venture "uglier than sewerage." The expression 'Gone West,'" he suggested, "no longer means to die; it now means 'to get filthy, nasty, or vulgar.'" Robert Benchley's tone was less incendiary, but his verdict equally contemptuous: "Besides being gratuitously nasty," he wrote, "[*Pleasure Man*] was as badly written and as cheap as *Sex* and *Diamond Lil*, which gives Miss West a score of 100 . . . The cast included Cases 1 through 28 in Volume Two of Havelock Ellis."

By the time these attacks appeared in print, *Pleasure Man* had already closed, and $200,000 in ticket sales were refunded. Some members of the opening-night audience had left in disgust during the performance; others had signaled their enthusiasm with uproarious laughter; they "howled and snickered and let out degenerate shrieks from the balcony." But after the final curtain, the police stormed the dressing rooms and arrested the entire cast of fifty-five.

Many members of the audience gathered expectantly outside the theater. "Soon Forty-seventh Street from Eighth Avenue half way up the block to Broadway was packed with men and women, many in evening clothes." Some in the crowd "spat upon the pavement and booed and hissed as the 'female impersonators' in the cast [who were still in costume] were brought out of the stage entrance, where here and there was heard a frail falsetto cheer." Camera flashes exploded as news photographers snapped pictures of the cast being loaded into wagons. "Many of the women performers and some of the men carried bunches of flowers, opening night tributes from admirers." The female impersonators, called "temperamentals," were quoted as saying things like "Beat it, Annie" and "Tell Maude to get me out."

After finishing her performance as Diamond Lil, Mae West learned what had transpired at the Biltmore and hurried to the yellow brick 18th Precinct Forty-seventh Street police station to arrange bail and visit cast members, who responded with "much whoopee." There she, too, was arrested—eventually, so were producer Carl Reed and director Charles Edward Davenport—and in the early-morning hours each was released on $1,000 bail.

Once again, Mae West became front-page news, and as before not just in the tabloids. Next to an article about Franklin D. Roosevelt being drafted by the Democrats to run for governor of New York, *The New York Times* ran the story: "RAID MAE WEST PLAY, SEIZE 56 AT OPENING / Police Arrest Entire Cast of 'Pleasure Man' after Last Act at Biltmore Theatre."

Mae West insisted she had done nothing wrong. She denied that she was trying to reprise *The Drag*, as the Hearst press insisted. " 'The Drag' was about a homosexualist," she stated. "This play is about a normal man and women. I have some lady impersonators in the play . . . But what of it? If they are going to close up the play and prevent these people from making a living because they take the part of female impersonators, then they should stop other female impersonators from appearing on the Keith Circuit . . . How many thousand female impersonators do you think there are in this country? Are they going to put them all out of business?"

For her chief lawyer this time out, she chose Nathan Burkan, dean of show-business attorneys, whose list of clients included Chaplin, Ziegfeld, Jolson, ASCAP (American Society of Composers, Authors & Publishers), Actors Equity, and eventually the mayor, Jimmy Walker, his adversary in the present case. It was Mayor Walker who had instigated the *Pleasure Man* raid, telling the police commissioner that "any dastardly drama even slightly odorous" would not be tolerated on Broadway.

The raid had occurred on Monday night, October 1. On Tuesday, Nathan Burkan obtained an injunction, and the play was able to resume that night. But the injunction was set aside by the Appellate Division of the Supreme Court, and during the Wednesday matinee, in the middle of the final act's drag scene, police lieutenant James Coy rushed down the aisle to the orchestra pit, demanding the crowd's attention. He announced that he was a police officer and that he was placing the cast under arrest. Spectators began filing out in orderly fashion, but the players onstage booed. As Lieutenant Coy stepped onstage, Jay Holly, the actor playing Tom Randall, launched into a diatribe against police oppression. Holly had to be ejected forcibly from the stage, and the rest of the cast was arraigned, with makeup still on their faces and costumes on their backs. In the paddy wagons, "the impersonators attracted more attention . . . than they could ever hope to get in the show."

The mayor issued a statement: "This administration is determined to put an end to this kind of salacious performance. The mayor is a liberal and always has been a patron of the theater. But anything so offensive to decency . . . cannot continue while I am mayor."

Cast members were charged with participation in an indecent and immoral production, which "paraded and glorified sex perversion." All pleaded Not Guilty and were released on $500 bail. In court, as the pleas were entered, Mae West appeared to have "lost much of her previous bravado." She seemed worried, as she had good reason to be. According to *Variety*, her conviction and that of her co-defendants would carry a sentence of not more than three years, a $500 fine, or both, at the discretion of the sentencing court.

Expressions of support from the community did not pour forth. Actors Equity, before the second raid, informed its members who were in the cast that they had no obligation to continue performing in *Pleasure Man* unless the injunction became permanent.

George Jean Nathan, the highly regarded theater critic for the *American Mercury*, the very man who would one day praise the movie star Mae West as the only honest-to-God female on the screen, placed himself squarely in the camp of the mayor and the police. "If the shutting down of the exhibition called "Pleasure Man" by the authorities constitutes censorship of the drama," he wrote, "then I go on record as being head, foot and tail for censorship. I have seen a lot of degenerate stuff in my travels . . . but I have never seen perversion, inversion and such physiological idiosyncrasies so brazenly and shamelessly offered to the general public at so much a look . . . There was no trace of playwriting in it. The thing was a mere lifting over to a theatre stage of the kind of Harlem 'drag' that the police peremptorily raid." He attacked not only the play but its creator: "The West woman has now been collared twice by the police for usurping the theatre to her nasty purposes; one may wish that the police will get rid of her for good. She knows no more about playwriting than the colored piano professor in a bawdy house; her sole purpose seems to be to make money out of out-and-out fornicatory and homosexual rodeos. She has done more to bring on theatrical censorship than any hundred persons before her . . . This dollar-itching cow-dirt . . . calls for garbage haulers."

The only contrary note was sounded by actress Peggy Wood, who, in the wake of the second raid on *Pleasure Man*, addressed a group of Methodist ministers and pleaded for a tolerant attitude toward theater morality. True, profanity existed on the stage, she acknowledged; but "I believe there is also an appalling amount of it in private life. We cannot seem to get along without it." To indicate how standards had changed, she mentioned that her father had years ago been dismissed from Ohio Wesleyan University merely for attending a performance of *Othello*.

More than a year passed before the trial of the *Pleasure Man* defendants began. In the interim Nathan Burkan tried unsuccessfully to have the trial moved from New York City to Nassau County, Long Island. To support the change of venue, Mae West charged in an affidavit that the New York newspapers had "so inflamed" the public that a fair trial on home ground would be impossible. That strategy failed, and so did Burkan's opposition to the district attorney's decision to select a "blue ribbon" jury of prominent citizens. "Why can't a jury of laborers and artisans decide this case rather than a jury of the intelligentsia?" Burkan asked. "A special panel jury is not democratic. We are entitled to have the case tried by the kind of people who went to see the play—a regular panel of jurors." The blue-ribbon jury that was ultimately selected included an architect, several real-estate bro-

kers, two manufacturers, a builder, a street railway manager, and the secretary of a fraternal organization. Burkan had a point: these were not the
kind of people likely to have seen *Pleasure Man*.

During the interlude before the trial got under way Mae West went on
tour with *Diamond Lil*, soon after it closed on Broadway. While she was
appearing in Chicago, she published an article in *Parade* magazine, "Sex in
the Theater," which defended her record and attempted to legitimize her
plays as serious and edifying works. "I have been misunderstood," she complained, accused of appealing to the salacious and evil-minded. Could the
ten million Americans to whom she claimed to have played all be salacious?
The theater, she argued, is "one of the greatest educational mediums that
we have. For years I have been devoting my career in the theater to the
education of the masses to certain sex truths . . . Often great teachers, to
preach a right, showed a wrong. The Bible does this too." She begged the
public to view her as separate from the roles she played: "People have said
that I must be bad myself because I play bad parts so well. They fail to
credit me with intelligence and love for my art . . . I repeat that the best
way to teach the right is by showing the results of the wrong." Not only
was she innocent of all charges, she was actually a moral paragon who
opposed companionate marriage: "Marriage, Love and Home should be kept
sacred."

Robert Lewis Shayon told Gerald Weales that he was the ghostwriter of
"Sex in the Theater." Mae did, obviously, have help with it. But she and
her lawyers surely knew the value of damage control; independently of any
ghostwriter, Mae West supposed she might benefit in court if her standing
before the public improved.

While in San Francisco with *Diamond Lil*, Mae received word that her
mother had become seriously ill. Although upset and anxious, she decided
she had to honor her obligation to the rest of the cast and carry on. In Los
Angeles in mid-January 1930, she learned that her fifty-nine-year-old
mother was suffering from cancer of the liver, had contracted pneumonia,
and was not expected to recover. "It was a staggering blow . . . I canceled
all further bookings, chartered a special train, and transported the entire
company of more than sixty people back to New York."

Matilda survived only two days after her beloved daughter's return to
New York. At her death, she was living not with her husband in the
home she owned on Eighty-eighth Street in the Woodhaven section of
Queens—the house was hers, not community property, and it had two

Mae West as a vamp, à la Theda Bara, after her appearance in Ned Wayburn's *Demi-tasse Revue;* cover, *New York Dramatic Mirror*, December 25, 1919 *(Wisconsin Center for Film and Theater Research)*

Bra-less Mae West attempts sleek flapper contours. Sheet music cover for "I Never Broke Nobodys Heart When I Said Good-bye" by Alfred Bryan, Leon Flatow, and Albert Gumble, 1923. Published by Jerome H. Remick & Co. *(Courtesy Lois Cordrey, editor Remember That Song, Glendale, Arizona)*

Around 1920, the shimmy period, Mae West in her late twenties is poised between the flapper and the diva. Note embryonic grand manner *(Eddie Brandt's Saturday Matinee)*

Sheet music cover, "Big Boy!" by Jack Yellen and Milton Ager, 1924. Cover art by
P. Ditzer. In insert photo, note Mae West's lightened hair and plunging neckline
(Courtesy Bob Johnson's Music Library, Oakland, California)

Front page of the tabloid *New York Evening Graphic*, December 30, 1926, shows a daring scene from *Sex* six weeks before the police raid: Mae West with Lyons Wickland as Jimmy Stanton

(Billy Rose Theater Collection, New York Public Library, Astor, Lenox and Tilden Foundations)

This ad, from a Chicago paper in 1929, touts Mae West in the touring company of *Sex*. Ukulele pose anticipates her scene strumming a Chinese stringed pipa in *Klondike Annie*

(Courtesy Shubert Archive)

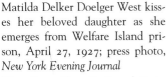

Matilda Delker Doelger West kisses her beloved daughter as she
emerges from Welfare Island prison, April 27, 1927; press photo,
New York Evening Journal
(*Harry Ransom Humanities Research Center,
University of Texas at Austin*)

Mae West with the principals of *Sex* after police
raid, February 9, 1927. Photos of her with a throng
of men would remain a staple. Press photo [origin
unknown]
(*Margaret Herrick Library, Academy of Motion Picture Arts and
Sciences*)

Drawing by Irving Hoffman of Mae West as Diamond Lil, with insert photo; from *Theatre Arts* magazine, September 1928

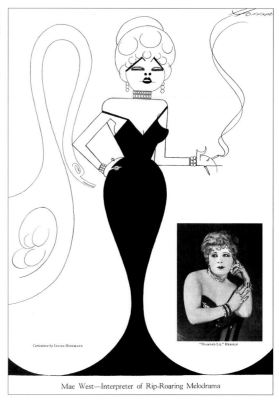

Mae West—Interpreter of Rip-Roaring Melodrama

Mae West as Diamond Lil; weekend newspaper photo section, 1928

Mae West in Swan Bed, Diamond Lil; White Studios photo, 1928

Veiled Mae West departing funeral parlor to attend her mother's funeral, January 27 or 28, 1930. Man behind sedan door, in Persian-lamb-collared coat, is Owney Madden. *New York Evening Journal* photo

(Harry Ransom Humanities Research Center, University of Texas at Austin)

In mourning during the *Pleasure Man* trial, March 1930: Mae West, brother, Jack Junior, Beverly. Press photo

(Harry Ransom Humanities Research Center, University of Texas at Austin)

Attorney J. Rosenthal, Mae, actor Alan Brooks of *Pleasure Man* cast, and nightclub
hostess Texas Guinan; press photo taken March 1930
(Billy Rose Theater Collection, New York Public Library, Astor, Lenox and Tilden Foundations)

Bearcat Delaney, Babe Gordon, and Wayne
Baldwin, characters from *The Constant Sinner*
road company cast, 1931
(Courtesy Shubert Archive)

mortgages on it—but in an apartment at 95 Euclid Avenue, Brooklyn, perhaps the home of a friend or relative who was caring for her. Whether she and Battlin' Jack had been living apart for some time or had only separated when her illness became grave is not known. The brief obituaries that appeared in the press describe her simply as Mae West's mother. Her death certificate, in the space for "Occupation," reads: "Housewife." She left no will.

Mae's grief swept over her like a tidal wave. She fainted, wept, howled that she wanted to die, stopped speaking entirely for three days. A press photograph taken as she emerged from the funeral home to set out for the funeral shows her utterly inconsolable behind a black veil. (Owney Madden, who stands to her left, will presumably help her, along with funeral home employees, into the open-doored black sedan.) This was the supreme crisis of her life, her emotional nadir. Her overwhelming sense that she had lost her closest ally, a wellspring of devotion and support, mingled with remorse over her recent absence, and perhaps over her lack of candor about her long-ago marriage. "I turned my face to the wall. Nothing mattered," she would recall. "When my mother died, it was as though everything had gone with her. Everything!" She had not yet found the faith that promised a chance to meet her mother again in another life.

Mae had always indulged her mother with lavish gifts—hats, dresses, purses. Now she purchased space for her in an expensive mausoleum at the interdenominational Cypress Hills Cemetery in Jamaica, Queens (part of the cemetery is in Brooklyn): a large, granite, aboveground. two-story structure, built in 1926, that has a chapel inside and beautiful stained-glass windows. The composer Paderewski and ex-boxing champion Jim Corbett are among those at rest in the same mausoleum, and baseball player Jackie Robinson lies nearby, outside. Mae was still paying for the crypt after she settled in Hollywood. When she was robbed in September 1932, she was carrying $18,000 in cash—final payment, she later explained, for the monument to her late mother.

Mae decided to plan for family entombment, purchasing spaces for her entire family behind an ornamental iron gate inscribed "West." Matilda's crypt eventually received the bodies of Jack Senior, Jack Junior, Mae herself, and Beverly, the last to die. Mae made all the decisions about spacing. She reserved the top compartment, a marble drawer, for herself, an indication that she saw herself as the head of the family, or at least as its most important member. She reposes directly above her mother, who is separated from her husband in the crypt by the drawer occupied by Beverly.

*   *   *

Perhaps it was a good thing that the *Pleasure Man* trial demanded Mae's time and attention very soon after she lost her mother. The assistant district attorney, James G. Wallace—an adversary from the days of the *Sex* trial—made it very clear that she, Mae West, was the prosecution's target; she had offended decency and would be brought to justice. He announced, in the same courtroom in which Harry Thaw had been tried for murdering Stanford White, that the prosecution would prove "that it would take the most confirmed pervert to write such a play." Miss West, who sat at the counsel's table, "seemed imperturbed." Nathan Burkan was also called to task for having "made more motions in this court than any of Miss West's actors have on stage."

The Police Department's James J. Coy, promoted since the raid to the rank of captain, became the star of the proceedings. "Resplendent in his court costume of form-fitting dark suit, brick dust red tie and hanky to match, and fairly chomping at the bit to expose *Pleasure Man*, he settled himself in the witness chair in General Sessions." He displayed a decided theatrical flair, and it emerged that he had once performed in a play and had toured with the circus.

On October 1, *Pleasure Man*'s opening night, he testified, he had gone to the Biltmore Theater with several other detectives and a police stenographer, Sergeant Powers. He was able to take extensive notes in the dark, he maintained, and could document "at least twelve" instances of indecency. Powers, too, had detailed notes; Coy would nudge him whenever a line or situation struck him as objectionable.

"He gave a magnificent performance," wrote Irene Kuhn of the *Daily News*. "His hipshaking was marvelous, his imitations of the Whoops Sisters convulsing, and his cobra dance brief but artistic." Coy attested: "The curtain rose on a scene backstage. They were scrubwomen and they were conversing. One said 'I've got IT.' Another woman answered her . . . and she walked across the stage like this—shaking her hips from left to right—and adding, 'O, I've had my time,' while the other scrubwoman muttered: 'Sure, with the whole fire department.' " (This is all in the *Pleasure Man* script.)

The second act, Coy continued, showed a cross section of the stage with open dressing rooms, upstairs and down. "Four male characters dressed as female impersonators helped each other off with their dresses. They wore silk bloomers, silk stockings, and brassieres. They all put on kimonos and one of them began to sew on a silk lamp shade."

Most scandalous of all, by his lights, was what transpired at the third-act cast party, given by an ex-showman named Toto. Coy demonstrated a snake dance and referred to a few of Toto's songs: "Officer, Let Me Pat Your Horse" and "I'm the Queen of the Beaches." In the last, the word "beaches" sounded suspiciously like "bitches." He accused the German acrobats of performing "suggestive" acts.

Coy's delivery yielded unintended comic effects. Attempting to add dignity to his testimony, he used the biggest words he could think of. "Nothing ever happened; everything 'transpired.' The ladies and gentlemen of the cast were never dressed; they were always 'attired.' " Asked how he, from his row O orchestra seat, could see the female impersonator sewing with needle and thread, Coy explained, 'It was very illuminous on the stage.' He got a huge laugh from the courtroom assemblage when Burkan asked if he carried his synopsis of *Pleasure Man* around with him. "No," Coy answered, "I don't like to bulge myself out."

Nathan Burkan defended the *Pleasure Man* cast as "respectable men and women, some of them married and with families." He said many of the acts and lines deemed "objectionable" had been performed for years in vaudeville without protest. "The acrobatic stunt objected to is an old act on the Keith Circuit. Most of the gags throughout the show come from vaudeville acts." As for female impersonators, he pointed out that no one had considered them indecent in Shakespeare's day, when female parts were routinely played by males. Moreover, at present "they do it in college shows and at the Lambs Gambol where females are not allowed to appear." Assistant District Attorney Wallace was forced to admit that "female impersonation in itself is no violation of the law."

Burkan succeeded in striking out one count, the Public Nuisance charge, against Mae West. That meant, if found guilty, she would spend a maximum of a year in jail and pay a maximum fine of $1,000, not the $500 reported in *Variety*. His motion to have the entire case thrown out was denied.

The prosecution brought forward witnesses who claimed to be experts in obscenity and street argot, in an attempt to prove that apparently innocent-sounding words can carry dangerous hidden meanings. Burkan protested that it was possible to put an indecent interpretation even on "words sung by children at Sunday School."

All the members of the cast who testified claimed ignorance of any indecent overtones in what they said or did onstage. Both Alan Brooks and May Davis, who played one of the scrubwomen, told the court they had no knowledge of any double meanings in the script. Brooks, "a tall animated figure in spats," said that as Randall Terrill he portrayed "a rake—not a voluptuary. I'd call it . . . the part of a gay Lothario." With a straight face, he asked the court to believe he had no knowledge of the castration by which he was murdered.

Acrobats Herman Lenzen and William Selig did ten minutes of hand-springs, backflips, and balancing stunts "while a black-robed judge and solemn-faced jury looked on." Captain Coy and another police officer protested afterward that the act done by the tumblers in court was not the same as the one in the play.

Chuck Connors, Jr., one of the female impersonators (who was also in the road company of *Diamond Lil*), could only sing his "objectionable indecent" song after the courtroom had been cleared of unofficial spectators. As he sang, "Mae West at the counsel table covered her mouth with a black handkerchief to hide laughter."

After three weeks of testimony in which a total of thirteen witnesses were heard—seven of them friendly to the defense—*Variety* commented that *Pleasure Man* was having a longer run in court than it had on Broadway.

The last days of the trial were enlivened by the presence at the press table of Texas Guinan, "who swished into court with ermine tails and clattering strings of pearls that reached to her knees" and stole the spotlight. "Miss West flashed a tiny smile at the beaming Miss Guinan, whose diamonds outflashed her own and whose furs and make-up outdistanced hers by six pelts and several pounds of paint." Mae's court costumes were subdued: black hat, dress, cloak, and fox furs. She was still in mourning for her mother.

When court adjourned, Miss West and Texas "kissed and greeted each other, 'Hello, dear.' " Writing about Mae West for the New York *American*, Guinan quipped about her friend, "Mae's a good girl at heart, but she's got a bad heart."

In his closing statement before the jury, Nathan Burkan assailed "nightstick censorship" and argued that Mae West and the cast of *Pleasure Man* had been framed. "The police officers went deliberately to the theatre to get Mae West and they got her. Coy sat down later with [police stenographer] Sergeant Powers and deliberately framed the testimony he gave in court . . . You, by your verdict, will put a stop to police frame-ups and officers deliberately committing perjury."

The assistant district attorney concluded by asking the jury for a conviction if the jurors shared his belief that the accused were "cunning, unscrupulous people willing to capitalize filth."

Judge Amadeo Bertini's instructions to the jury marked him as far from impartial. They should find the defendants guilty, he said, if the play "tended to the corruption of the morals of youth or other people . . . The people of the State of New York are anxious to have pure drama. We are anxious to have decent plays."

After deliberating for ten hours, the jury reported a deadlock on April 3, 1930; they could not reach agreement. Seven jurors remained adamant for conviction, five could not be budged from their decision for acquittal. A letter eleven of them sent to Governor Roosevelt expressed dissatisfaction with criminal litigation as a method of censorship; they favored state censorship instead. The jury foreman, Irving Chandler, was the only one opposed to censorship of any kind. He refused to sign the letter, maintaining that state censorship would lower theaters to the same category as speakeasies—"open for raiding by the police at will."

In dismissing the jury, Judge Bertini agreed with the jurors that courts cannot fairly pass judgment on plays they have never seen performed on a stage. "Words, intonations, gestures and actions cannot be easily reproduced secondarily." But he couldn't let them go without a final pitch for stage purity, sounding a warning about the harm inherent in shows "calculated to excite in the spectator impure imagination . . . Such a performance is really more dangerous to public morals than any mere vulgar exhibition of nudity. The latter may arouse impure thoughts, but it is more apt to incite disgust. The greater danger lies in the appeal to the imagination." Although Mae West left the court a free woman, this wasn't exactly the "vindication" she vaunts in her autobiography.

What to do next? Mae was broke. Nathan Burkan had to sue her for the legal fees she owed him, claiming she had paid him only $5,000 of the $15,000 tab. The idea of reopening *Pleasure Man* held no appeal. "The edge was off the show. We had refunded all advance sale money, and when the trial was over, I said, 'It would be like putting on a revival to open again.' "

She made a halfhearted return to vaudeville, signing with the Fox circuit after being rejected by Loew's and RKO, which considered her too bawdy. "Spice is all right, but dirt is out," said the RKO chief. But vaudeville, on its last legs, couldn't support her. It was announced in the summer of 1930 that the Shuberts were going to send her to Chicago in the starring role of a new play she had written, *Frisco Kate*.

Never produced, but used six years later as the basis for the film *Klondike Annie*, *Frisco Kate* packs a wallop despite its crudities. All the action takes place at sea, aboard the freighter *Java Maid*, characterized in the stage directions as a "hell ship" whose "motley crew is an animalistic collection of the dregs of the waterfronts." The entire crew has been shanghaied, forced on board by an alcoholic gorilla of a captain, a kinsman of O'Neill's Hairy Ape: brutish, tyrannical Bull Brackett. The randy crew has yet to discover that an enticing temptress lurks among them, a woman who has been shanghaied, as they have, and sequestered on board, in the cabin adjacent to the captain's. She is the San Francisco Doll, also called Frisco Kate, "the swellest tart in the Barbary Coast . . . the swellest trollop in the Golden Gate."

Initially ignorant of her past life on the Barbary Coast, Bull Brackett has mistaken Kate for a decent woman. All he knows is that she bears an uncanny resemblance to a figurine he keeps on his desk and holds sacred, an eighteen-inch statuette of a nude bacchante endowed, he's convinced, with the supernatural powers of a pagan idol. "See this lady?" he asks a mate. "She's been my pal and good luck for fifteen years . . . See how soft and white she is . . . Look how round she is . . . I've tramped through the hookshops [brothels] of the Seven Seas, tryin' to find one like her. Black, brown, yellow and white. But no one like my doll . . . That's somepin' more than a human bein' . . . She's one o' them kind that the natives down in the Islands *pray* to." Years before Mae West laid legitimate claim to icon status, and before she commissioned the nude statue of herself that became a fixture of her Hollywood apartment, she prophetically drew the blueprint.

Frisco Kate turns on the recurrent Westian theme of the taming of male beasts by a female idol. "Get back into the cage and have a good roar," Kate advises the captain. She is the only woman on board—Mae West's fantasy situation—and the men go berserk when they discover her. But *she* never loses control, promising her favors in return for the release of the man she loves, Stanton (a name carried over from *Sex*), who is first mate and imprisoned in the brig. One of the sailors pronounces her queen of the ship.

In addition to being commanding and irresistible—there's a strip scene where we get a look at her in her lingerie "combination"—she's caring and warmhearted, intervening on behalf of the frightened cabin boy, Buddie, when Bull tries to strike him. "I wish I had a sister like you," says Buddie, who resembles Willie, the innocent boy in *The Wicked Age*.

As in *Diamond Lil* and in her film roles, Mae's Frisco Kate character reduces all men to supporting players, mere accompanists to her solo lead. The scenes between Frisco Kate and Bull Brackett go further than that. Bull is humiliated by her. She has him "eating out of my hand." When he neglects his duties as skipper, allowing the crew to abandon the pumps even though the ship is leaking, Kate goads him: "I thought you were a bruiser. . . . Show them you're a man." Instead, he kneels before her, bandaging her cut foot. When he forces himself on her, he upsets the magic statue, and it comes tumbling down, shattered. Remorseful and seized with foreboding, he turns meek, offering to tidy her cabin for her. She mocks his subservience, but at the same time chides him for trying to force her into an embrace: "Bein' a lady, I got a right to preferences. When I say no, I mean no, and when I say yes, I mean okay. And it's up to you to respect what I mean." Moveover, "I ain't used to maulin' and rushin' tactics. I always take my time." She ends up murdering him as he tries to rape her, plunging a stiletto into his back—the same method used by Diamond Lil on Rita.

The last scene sounds an uncharacteristically domestic note. Calm descends at sea after a mutiny and a hurricane which rescues Frisco Kate from gang rape. Kate boards a lifeboat with Stanton and the cabin boy, Buddie, who has an injured leg (another chance for Frisco Kate to show her maternal side). As a steamer approaches to rescue them, Stanton tells Kate, "If we pull through—no more sea for us. It's solid land and a cottage somewhere." Kate adds, "And a boy—like Buddie." You can almost hear the violins, as "a shaft of sunlight pierces the clouds." This is the only moment in a Mae West script that presents her as a prospective parent, a temporary lapse from the persona Colette would praise for its splendid isolation.

Instead of carrying out their plan to produce *Frisco Kate* in Chicago, the Shuberts decided to revive *Sex*, undoubtedly because *Sex* had proven box-office appeal, and because it is cheaper to mount a production with sets and costumes already in place than to start from scratch with a new play that no one has ever heard of. The Depression had devastated the legitimate theater. Few shows were produced, and those undertaken that survived did so with short runs, low cast salaries, and cut-rate ticket prices. The Shubert organization had lost a million dollars. Although *Sex* pulled off a ten-week run at the Garrick in Chicago, it had only three other plays as competition. A dozen other legit theaters in town were dark.

"Mae West is getting ready to shock the smaller burgs," *Variety* announced near the end of her Chicago run. *Sex* moved on to Detroit, St. Louis, and Cleveland, where a critic wrote: "There is a kind of fascination in its brazenness, a kind of humorous charm in the force of its unblushing, unselfconscious crudity. [Mae West] is a sort of roughhouse Sadie Thompson, walking with undulating hips, speaking devastatingly from the corners of her mouth, emitting from her amply proportioned body the radiance of rhinestones and the fragrance of many bottles of insistent perfume." This was a Margy LaMont enhanced with Diamond Lil glitter and sass.

When touring in a new city, Mae made it a point to visit three kinds of institutions: zoos, prisons, and mental institutions. She loved animals, especially monkeys, and was fascinated by criminology and psychiatry. She told herself she was gathering material for future plays, but in the present depressed economy future plays would have to wait.

In Kansas City, money troubles stole the show. *Sex* was attached [seized by legal process] "for an obligation of $500 by Gus Hill of New York." A writ prevented removal of the production from Kansas City, until two notes signed by Mae West in July were paid in full. The money must have been found, because the play did leave Kansas City and move on to Milwaukee, where it provoked an outraged editorial in a local paper, the *Sentinel*, demanding police intervention.

Mae had learned to turn this kind of negative attention to her advantage. Maybe it would boost sales of her book, *Babe Gordon*. In odd moments, during the trial and on tour, she had dictated a novel and found a publisher for it.

12

BLACK AND WHITE

*E*ARLY in 1930 Mae West had decided to try her hand as a novelist. As she explains in her autobiography, she had several reasons for turning to fiction rather than the stage for her next creative venture, the first having to do with the novel's superior longevity. While "a play is soon finished, remembered only by its photographs and yellowing reviews, a book lasts as long as someone keeps it on a shelf." Second, her mother's recent death had left her drained, "too weak to fight the material as a play." And finally, the threat of censorship and more legal headaches worried her. She was trial-weary and believed no one would go after her for what she published in book form. "A book author had more freedom of expression than the stage permitted at that time."

Not mentioned was the devastation visited upon Broadway by the Depression, which had reduced the number of legitimate productions to a fraction of their number before the crash. Increasingly, actors and comics who could talk effectively—among them James Cagney, George Raft, and some of the Marx Brothers—were being lured from the stage to Hollywood and sound movies. The once Great White Way now functioned as a cheap bargain center, a garish remnant of its pre-Crash exuberance. "Tooth paste ads . . . have crowded out the names of Broadway stars in the incandescents. Probably because there are not enough stars left . . . Broadway has gone cut rate with a vengeance. Anything from barbering to theatre tickets are cuts." There were phony auction rooms, peep shows, miniature golf courses, and "any number of catch penny rackets . . . Cut rate eateries, too." Replacing the parade of finely clad gents and ladies of palmier days were "racket men, dames on the make, shills for speaks, actors at liberty, playboys out for a lark, out of towners bewildered by the bright lights, a legless man . . ."

The novel Mae conceived was to be set in Harlem, like that stage sensation of a few years back *Lulu Belle*, and also like the 1926 Carl Van Vechten bestseller, *Nigger Heaven*. Initially called *Babe Gordon* and later *The Constant Sinner*, it would cater to the white public's fascination with the after-hours amusement center in black Manhattan, where inhibitions could be parked outside, and fantasies of indulgence—in alcohol, drugs, gambling, and mixed-race sex—were allowed free rein. It would perpetuate the image of Harlem as a kind of primitive preserve, vibrant with sensuality and the wildness of the jungle. "Harlem," Mae West would write, "is the Paris of the Western Hemisphere" [never mind that she'd never seen Paris]: "a museum of occult sex, a sensual oasis in the sterile desert of white civilization." There, in the early hours of the morning, as a band poured its soul into every note, you could watch "the bodies of almost naked colored women, wriggling and squirming"; or take in a peep show devoted to "the antics of blacks, and blacks and whites, in tortured postures of cruel . . . soul-naked passion."

Even Mae West was not liberated enough to admit to firsthand experience of Harlem's nightlife or of the tawdry excesses her novel depicts. She makes no mention in her memoir of a "black and tan" jazz club, the Nest, on 133rd Street's Jungle Alley, where she had been spotted frequently in the mid-1920s, accompanied by Johnny Carey, one of the club's co-owners. She never tells us that she numbered among the few whites (Carl Van Vechten was another) allowed into the clubs along 140th Street that presented transvestite floor shows. Nor does she reveal that her great good friend Owney Madden owned a major interest in the famed Cotton Club, where a white clientele was entertained by mocha-skinned chorines and the Duke Ellington Jungle Band blazed its way to international acclaim.

She makes no reference either, in her autobiography, to her own experiences with mixed-race sex. Without question, she was attracted to black men, and many black men were attracted to her. In her Hollywood years, she would form liaisons with William "Gorilla" Jones, whose middleweight boxing career she managed, and with featherweight fighter Chalky Wright, who functioned for a time as her chauffeur. In New York, according to Lorenzo Tucker, a black actor who had a part in *The Constant Sinner* when it became a play, "she had several black lovers." One of them may have been former heavyweight champion Jack Johnson, who once owned the club that became the Cotton Club and who continued to work there as a manager. Johnson, whose defeat of the "Great White Hope" Jim Jeffries in 1910 prompted race riots, had a well-known predilection for white women as lovers. When Robert E. Johnson asked Mae West, in an interview for

Jet, if she had ever seen Jack Johnson in the ring, she answered, "No, but he came up to see me—several times."

Fighters and body-builders, both black and white, always ranked high on her list of preferred lovers, in part because they recalled her father's fitness-conscious milieu. "I've always liked athletes because they don't smoke, don't drink, and understand the importance of keeping their bodies in top working order . . . A hard man is good to find." Like Babe Gordon, the heroine of her novel, she attended prizefights partly to size up the contenders in the ring with an appraising eye. "She could get an idea, from the way a fighter handled himself in the ring, of the way he treated women." Like Babe, she had a fetishistic fondness for rippling biceps and bulging pectorals. The lines "I ain't gonna hurt him. I only want to feel his muscles," spoken by Babe Gordon in the play version of *The Constant Sinner*, and repeated by Tira in *I'm No Angel*, originated in a lifelong Mae West practice.

Although she elsewhere insisted that she wrote about what life had taught her, directly out of her own experience and observation, Mae maintained that her "research" for this novel had been conducted by someone else, a black actor named Howard Merling, who had played Eben in O'Neill's *Desire Under the Elms* and who lived on the outskirts of Harlem. Merling, she says, visited her backstage after a New York performance of *Diamond Lil* and urged her to write something "mixing the black and white theme together." She had to admit it was a hot subject. "Negroes had become the rage of society . . . Their vices charmed thrill-seekers." Merling volunteered to provide detailed information about "the speaks, the numbers rackets, the clip joints, night clubs, the fly characters." After a few months he presented her with a sheaf of hard-to-decipher notes. Afraid she would be able to make no sense of them on her own, she cast him as a Chinese in *Diamond Lil* when it toured the West Coast at the end of 1929, so that he would be on hand to read his notes to her when time permitted.

Working with a dictaphone and a secretary who helped her "piece the different parts together and arrange chapters and things," she fashioned a vivid narrative peopled by whores, pimps, boxers, drug addicts, dealers, slumming socialites, and flashy high rollers. One of its strengths is the authenticity and freshness of its street-smart dialogue—evidence that Mae West had listened well to people like those she wrote about. Prostitutes are a "couple of overtime mamas doin' piece work." They try to pick fighters who win, because "they copped the big end of the dough." A rich black man is "livin' lak a king up dere in Strivers' Row in a palacious apartment." Occasionally the narrator drops out of the vernacular mode, sounding an awkward, inappropriately analytical note: "Bearcat's subconscious yearning for women was having its effect."

Publisher Lowell Brentano read parts of the manuscript early in 1930 and expressed an interest in publishing it under the title *Black and White*. Mae had returned to New York, and Brentano was told to call at the Manhattan apartment on West End Avenue she shared with Beverly. (Beverly wasn't present when he stopped by.) Admitted by "a demure colored maid [Bea Jackson]," he entered the living room, which he surveyed in "pained surprise." There appeared to be no place to sit down. The large room had two levels, separated by a few steps. The lower level contained no furniture; on the high level, "in the exact center of the wall, between the two windows, stood a huge bed, with an elaborate lace spread, posts, a tall and ornamental top and bolster ... Surrounding this bed were four tiny gilt chairs, so fragile in appearance as to make me think they would collapse on first use. I was afraid to sit on the bed, afraid to sit on the chairs, so nervously I paced the room."

Mae West appeared, "gowned in a very beautiful and ... very expensive negligee. She walked with her well-known undulating glide, one hand holding the negligee about her, the other on her hip." Instead of shaking hands, she bowed courteously, then threw herself down on the bed, "her head on the bolster, her hands behind her head, her legs crossed. Then she smiled languidly ... 'Well, Mr. Brentano, what can I do for you?' Without even giving me a chance to reply, she took one hand, patted the bolster, and said, 'Now, Mr. Brentano, don't be bashful, come right over here and sit down.'"

When Brentano had seated himself on the bed, they discussed her novel. He recommended certain cuts and deletions. "Don't try to make me respectable," she advised. "My public expects me to be bad."

Although she signed a contract with Brentano, and he urged his editorial board to accept the novel, they turned it down, no doubt because of its raunchiness. Another publisher, Macaulay, stepped in and brought the book out with the title *Babe Gordon*.

As a publicity gimmick, publisher Macaulay decided to run a contest, advertising in *Publishers Weekly* that it was offering a prize of $100 to the person with the best suggestion for a better title. The judges would be Walter Winchell (a surprise, in view of his attacks on Mae West's plays), Harold E. Williams of the American News Company, and Charles Springhorn of Macaulay. In March 1931, four months and four printings after the initial publication, the winner was announced, again in an ad in *Publishers*

Weekly reporting that "ladies submitted most titles that were furthest south in innuendo," and revealing the retitled book's new cover design showing a smiling brunette with bobbed hair. Effie Mattison of New York had successfully renamed the book *The Constant Sinner*, a title which invited ironic comparison with the play *The Constant Wife*, a Somerset Maugham opus in which Ethel Barrymore had starred in 1926, and perhaps with Dorothy Parker's *New Yorker* column, "Constant Reader."

The Constant Sinner goes further than any previous Mae West text in defying moral conventions. Babe Gordon isn't just "a prize-fighters' tart" who consorts with "trollops, murderers, bootleggers and gambling den keepers"; she is a white woman who works in Harlem and takes a black lover, Money Johnson, an ex-pimp, bookie, and policy king with a magnificent body, while still married to the white fighter Bearcat Delaney. Never before had a self-created Mae West character actually taken wedding vows, only to break them within months, and never previously had she publicly crossed the sexual color line (except in the Jack Yellen lyrics of the song she sang, "Big Boy," about a darktown sheik who drives both pale and brown-skinned ladies wild.)

Babe takes a white lover as well, the aristocratic Wayne Baldwin, who wears evening clothes made in Bond Street and is heir to a chain of dimestores. Baldwin first spots her at the Harlem Breakfast Club. Wrapped in ermine, her diamonds glittering, she sits beside the leonine "colored Apollo," Money Johnson, whose bronze hand rests on her shoulder, "the finger-tips caressing her cream white throat." Baldwin is shocked, but also aroused. The thought of "Babe's white body and Johnson's black body . . . is terrible, and yet it gives him a sensual thrill." Within a matter of months, while Money Johnson serves time in jail, Baldwin has made Babe his own mistress. He maintains her in style in a posh Riverside Drive apartment similar to the one on West End Avenue that Mae and Beverly shared.

The narrator accepts Babe's infidelities as inevitable. Some women are just made that way:

Nature creates different kinds of females and makes them perplexingly contrary to a moral law that assumes all female flesh to be the same. As a matter of fact, there are women so constituted that physically and mentally they have no desire for men and therefore become old maids, or enter nunneries. There are women who live a normal, conventional sex life and enter into marriage and motherhood. And then there are women so formed in body and mind that they are predestined to be daughters of joy. These women whom the French call *"femme amoureuses"* are found not alone among women of the streets, but in every stratum of society.

Babe places herself in the *femme amoureuse* category, as a woman put on earth for men, "not one man but many men." By the end of the novel, Babe has divorced Bearcat and gone off to Paris with Wayne Baldwin. We're assured that she has no expectation of remaining faithful to him. "Even if she decides to marry Baldwin, that would not prevent her having a lover, or lovers, on the side. That is Babe Gordon."

Also accepted as a matter of course and without harsh judgment is Babe's untruthfulness. Although it isn't the case, she tells Bearcat she has been to church—without a scruple. "To Babe, a lie was simply something one told to gain an advantage, to get what one wanted by the shortest route. She never lied just for the sake of lying. When she lied she had a definite reason for doing so. It was for the purpose of creating a valuable impression." Babe has no moral sense. She calls herself "unmoral. For her, morals did not exist."

Babe's eagerness to follow her sensual desires wherever they may lead is matched by a veneration for money. According to her, people are commodities and "the whole world is selling something: goods, ability, personality." Her body, allure, and sexual sophistication carry a high market value. In her past she has used them to "pick clean" any number of fighters, and she knows how to "pluck a hard-boiled racketeer or gambler for every cent he had on him." She longs for "the gorgeous trapping of romance that she saw pictured on the silver screen, and she dreamed that some day all the pleasure and refinements of luxury would be hers."

When Bearcat is a champion in the chips, she sticks with him, resplendent in the fox-collared coat he has bought for her. But when a dissipated life with Babe sentences Bearcat to a losing streak in the ring and a dearth of earnings, when Bearcat trades her fancy roadster for a taxi, she bails out and returns to her old life in Harlem. "The world loves a hero and success, and Babe couldn't be bothered with a fallen idol." To prove she does have heart, she anonymously leaves money for Bearcat to return to training in the Adirondacks. (Anonymous charity was also Diamond Lil's style.)

Babe takes a high-commission job peddling drugs behind a Baldwin's five-and-ten-cent store cosmetics counter; she gets a one-third cut on the morphine, heroin, and coke concealed in gold-plated rouge compacts. The "unmoral" Babe has no qualms about being a pusher, as she later has none about indulging in cooked gum-opium with Money Johnson to help him celebrate his release from jail. In fact, the danger inherent in the enterprise excites her. "Selling dope gave her a great kick, an absolutely new kind of power. The risk of detection only added glamour to the game." Her sole concern is escaping unscathed—which, by manipulating others and dissembling artfully, she always manages to do. She is never punished for her sins (unlike Lulu Belle, who ends up strangled) and never repentant.

If there is a villain, she is Cokey Jenny, an addict who will do anything for money or a fix, and who in a jealous rage ends by ratting on her former friend Babe, tipping off detectives about her dope selling in the five-and-dime, revealing the truth about Babe's sordid past to Wayne Baldwin's family, and disclosing Babe's whereabouts to both Baldwin and Bearcat when Babe is holed up in a Harlem tenement with Money Johnson, enjoying a lovers' spree after his release from jail. Baldwin intrudes and shoots Money Johnson.

Cokey Jenny is too obsessed with drugs to be interested in men, but other black women in Harlem, Money Johnson's ex-lovers, will do anything to get him back. They hate Babe, the white woman who has captured their man. In the world of *The Constant Sinner*, whites hold the sexual trump card. Money Johnson "had the pick of the dusky Harlem girls but no longer found colored women attractive. He craved white women." Only the most seductive blacks can win the trophy of a white partner. Pearl, the black maid who comes with the Riverside Drive apartment Babe shares with Baldwin, tells Babe: "Ah's too ugly to have a white man. Hard enough fo' me to git a colored man."

Although drawn to interracial sex, Mae West accepted many racial and ethnic stereotypes. In *Diamond Lil*, Jacobson, the Jewish landlord, is a grasping, money-obsessed cartoon, and Juárez represents the cliché of the unctuous Latin lover; in the conversation about vaudevillians that opens *Pleasure Man*, a Scotsman is described as a true-to-type penny-pincher. In *The Constant Sinner*, blacks are sexually dynamic primitives, innocent of the kind of moral hypocrisy the white establishment makes its specialty.

A trial scene exposes the pomposity, race hysteria, and dishonesty of whites who have power. Baldwin has killed Money Johnson, but Bearcat takes the rap. Bearcat is acquitted after his expensive lawyer, bankrolled by Baldwin, pleads that a white woman's "honor" (Babe's) was being protected from assault by "a low, lustful, black beast." Bearcat, according to his lawyer, has "upheld the best traditions of the white race, the honor of its womanhood." The all-white jury falls for this racist line. Justice in court turns out to be just another form of manipulation, a matter of pressing the right buttons rather than determining objective guilt or innocence.

According to Mae West, the novel *The Constant Sinner* went through five editions and sold 94,000 copies. She dubbed it a bestseller, but it was never included on *Publishers Weekly*'s bestseller lists, which that year included books by Edna Ferber, Louis Bromfield, Ann Douglas Sedgwick, and Somerset Maugham, and was universally ignored by the reviewing establishment. But *The Constant Sinner* set a respectable sales record, and its financial success helped persuade the wobbly Shubert organization that a play based on the novel would likewise make money. By August 1931, an interracial cast had been chosen and rehearsals were under way.

Mae went up to Harlem in search of talent for her cast. "She was always strong for the colored," Lorenzo Tucker, "the Colored Valentino," remembered. "At the Cotton Club she hired Paul Meers to do the African Strut. Another place she found Robert Rains for Liverlips . . . She hired Rudolph Toombs for Mr. Gay, Hubert Brown as a waiter, and Trixie Smith for the upstairs maid in the whorehouse."

She fought hard to cast Tucker himself in the role of Money Johnson, but the best she could do—overcoming the opposition of Timony, the Shuberts, and director Lawrence Marsden—was to employ him as understudy for that role, doubling as the headwaiter.

Miscegenation remained an explosive theatrical theme. In 1924, white and black children had not been allowed to appear together in Eugene O'Neill's *All God's Chillun Got Wings*. That play's representation of a black man (played by Paul Robeson) married to a white woman incited panic in some quarters. A Hearst paper called the situation "nauseating," and predicted rioting. The license commissioner's threat to close the theater never materialized, but the air hummed with tension. By 1931, African-American performers like Ethel Waters and Paul Robeson had gained acceptance on Broadway, and there had been several shows with all-black casts. Still, a drama showing casual interaction, dancing, and coupling between men and women of different races was guaranteed to produce shock waves, especially at a time when the Scottsboro case, in which nine black youths were sentenced to death for the alleged rape in the South of two white prostitutes, was eliciting protests and garnering enormous attention.

To defuse a potential explosion in response to *The Constant Sinner*, a white, Greek-American actor, George Givot, was cast in the part of Money Johnson. During curtain calls, Givot would remove his wig and makeup, revealing himself as a white man, in the same way that female impersonators like Eltinge would reveal that they were really male after performing in drag. "He walks on for a bow in whiteface at the finish," *Variety* reported, "to square the mixture as much as it possibly could be squared."

When rehearsals for *The Constant Sinner* began, a finished script existed—something new for a Mae West production, as an article in the *Herald Tribune* pointed out:

> In the past there has been some report to the effect that a Mae West drama is a product of spontaneous generation; in other words, that as a playwright Miss West hews to the chip and lets the lines fall where they may . . .
>
> However true this . . . might have been in respect to previous Mae West plays, it certainly does not apply to *The Constant Sinner*. *The Constant Sinner* was a carefully wrought manuscript before the first material step had been taken toward production.

The play is pithier and more epigrammatic than the novel, with Babe copping most of the wisecracking laugh lines. For instance, when she hears that Bearcat is a middleweight, five feet eleven inches tall, she says, "Just fits my bed." When Cokey Jenny complains of poor turnover in the trick-turning business, Babe suggests, "It's the depression. Why don't you cut your prices?" Offered a deal peddling dope at a cosmetics counter, Babe accepts, saying, "I never turn down anything but the bedcovers." At the very end, Babe introduces Bearcat to Baldwin, hinting that a *ménage à trois* may be in the works. She says she knows a poem about faith, and tries to quote it, but "Oh god dam it I forgot it."

One scene that has no counterpart in the novel brings us into Babe's Manhattan hotel room, one wall of which is decorated with pictures of famous women of history: Cleopatra, Du Barry, Catherine the Great, all women Mae West identified with, feeling kinship with them for their success in combining fame, potent sexuality, and power. (Desdemona pictured with Othello completes the group. She doesn't really belong with the others, but finds a place because she serves as an example from the past of a white woman mated with a black man—a Moor, Babe explains, not "a dinge.")

The great ladies of the past provide occasions for quips. Cleopatra, Babe tells a friend, "even went to bed with snakes," and Catherine the Great "kept the biggest standing army in the world. She kept them standing right outside her bedroom." Mae liked this joke so much, she would repeat it many times.

The offstage Mae West was fascinated by these historic heroines, especially Catherine the Great, about whom she would write a screenplay (never produced) and a stage vehicle, *Catherine Was Great*, which was produced in the 1940s. She came to believe she was a reincarnation of the shrewd, sexually insatiable Russian Empress. Never a reader, Mae West nonetheless collected books about female rulers, legendary *femmes fatales*, and powerful courtesans of history, including Elizabeth I, Helen of Troy, Lucrezia Borgia, and Lola Montez.

After opening in Atlantic City and a brief stop at Brighton Beach, Brooklyn, *The Constant Sinner* moved to Manhattan under rush conditions. An earlier than anticipated opening was scheduled, to ensure that the Shuberts would have at least one show on Broadway.

Backstage, according to actor Arthur Vinton, who played Bearcat's feisty manager, Charlie Yates, Mae was all business. The cast always addressed her as "Miss West," never "Mae." "She has the most masculine mind in the most feminine body of any woman alive today . . . Her brain is trigger-quick . . . She was as punctual as an eight-day clock. She worked like a trouper. She was generous in the extreme to other members of her cast . . . extremely tolerant of human failings." Vinton disputed her reputation as a seductress: "I never knew her to do so much as look at a man in any but a friendly and frank way."

But George Givot told George Eells she was always inviting him into her dressing room, and that he resisted her because her mechanical attitude toward sex turned him off and because Timony ran interference—though Mae assured Givot that the romance part of her relationship with Timony had ended.

The theater was the Royale, on Forty-fifth Street, where *Diamond Lil* had flourished. Comparisons with *Diamond Lil*, the last play in which Mae West had performed in New York, were inevitable. Writing in the New York *Evening Post*, Wilella Waldorf declared that *The Constant Sinner* would disappoint fans of Diamond Lil: "In place of Diamond Lil's gaudy costumes of the nineties, the old fashioned bar and the golden swan bed, we now have a series of 1931 Harlem speakeasies and cheap hotel rooms." Instead of singing, as she did as Diamond Lil, Mae West as Babe Gordon "sat sedately at a ringside table while a hired entertainer did an 'African Strut.' " *Variety's* Weintraub concluded, a propos the "bold, at times raw" dialogue, "Diamond Lil was a Mother Goose story compared to this one."

Robert Benchley, now theater critic for *The New Yorker*, suggested that excessive praise for her performance in *Diamond Lil* had turned Mae West's head and had nourished in her "an almost insupportable satisfaction with her own powers and personality. Duse herself could not have filled the stage with such an aura of complete success and confidence."

Praise accrued for set designer Rollo Wayne, whose revolving jackknife stage could accommodate sixteen scenes in three acts, allowing for almost as many punchy finish lines. The "shrewd use of many quickly changing scenes" lent the melodrama "a certain flair, more than a hint of good theater." The elaborate staging took a big bite out of the budget. Twenty-one stagehands were needed to handle the sets. In addition, there were more than forty actors—Mae adored big companies—which made for a hefty payroll.

The grittiness of the dialogue received mixed reviews. "Seldom has fouler talk been heard on the Broadway stage, even in these frank and forward times," *The New York Times* growled. For some, the smutty street argot was redeemed by its sizzle. "It may not be denied," the New York *American* conceded, "that some of the thieves' slang in which the play is written possesses a tang unknown to purer phrases." Straddling the fence, Howard Barnes of the *Herald Tribune* commented: "It is a pity that the actress-playwright is so definitely convinced that art can be profitable only when judiciously mixed with filth. In *The Constant Sinner* . . . she has fashioned a piece of tough and frequently convincing stage realism, and then interrupted it continually with stupidly suggestive lines and situations."

Among the "suggestive situations" was a scene in which Mae West crossed a dimly lit stage in a thin chiffon gown, then changed into a robe. "I wasn't really nude," she explained much later; but apparently she appeared to be. The largely stag opening-night audience enjoyed a "snickering good time," but the New York *Sun's* Stephen Rathbun parted company with them. "No burlesque show strikes a lower level of life and morals," he snarled.

Robert Coleman of the *Daily Mirror* went further, roundly condemning the play as "a three-ring circus of depravity and degeneracy, vulgarity and miscegenation . . . Gomorrah had its corruption and viciousness, Rome had its orgies and mad Emperors—and New York has its Mae West to provide moronic and debasing roles."

To Joseph Wood Krutch, a distinguished critic who published a piece called "In Defense of Mae West" in the liberal weekly The Nation, the audience, not the star and playwright, deserved reprimand. Mae West, "a kind of Lillian Russell gone slightly to seed," possessed "personality" and a "sound if not very subtle idea of stage technique." Her crude and lurid play was livelier than many a Broadway offering, and as respectable as the much-heralded *Lulu Belle*. But the crowd of overgrown boys that came to gape and snicker got the back of his hand. "They greet every suggestive line with giggles, gurgles, shrieks and other strange noises." It would make no sense to punish Mae West and leave her boorish fans unscathed.

Responses to the play ultimately hinged on the viewer's take on Mae West. *Variety* crowned her "still the best bum of 'em all," praising her easy nonchalance. *The New York Times* grew weary of her limited bag of acting tricks: "Her peculiar slouching about the stage, her vocal stunts, her exploitation of blond buxomness—all these grow pretty tiresome through repetition." Heywood Broun of the *World Telegram* found himself liking her and sympathizing with her, while deploring her lack of moral sense. "Her ribald wisecracks do not offend me as they would if mouthed by any one else." And the *Graphic* called the play "mediocre entertainment, but . . . good Mae West. We firmly believe that the public . . . doesn't give a hoot what she appears in as long as they can get a seasonal view of her famous figure and listen to the sensuous drawl that serves as her stage voice."

But Percy Hammond, in a piece titled "Is There No Flit?," voiced revulsion. He considered Mae West a candidate for the zoo who should be plied with peanuts, not proffered jewels: "She is a large, soft, flabby and billowing superblonde who talks through her nostrils and whose laborious ambulations suggest that she has sore feet." By his lights, she possessed craft as a show woman, but as an actress stood out as "the world's worst . . . She is a menace to art, if not to morals."

The opening-night crowd responded with unstinting adulation, applauding wildly and even cheering. "Miss West received many curtain calls . . . and was called upon to make a curtain speech" in which she asked the audience not to confuse Mae West with the character she played. As the *Times* wryly put it, she "confided to her public that she was not really a Babe Gordon offstage . . . but was more the home girl type. She did not, however, confirm reports that she would act next year for the Children's Theatre in 'Snow White and the Seven Dwarfs.' "

When the cheering stopped Mae found herself seized with melancholy, "just sitting" alone and pensive in her dressing room when friends and admirers arrived. " 'There wasn't anyone to play to,' I told them . . . It was the first time I'd opened without my Mother."

The Constant Sinner faced no police raid or censorship demand beyond the deletion of two lines. Perhaps Mayor Walker was too distracted by his own legal problems to spearhead another campaign to clean up Broadway; he was in Europe at the time of the opening, anyhow, doing his best to forget his troubles. He had been charged with malfeasance and negligence of official duties, and would soon resign in disgrace.

In her memoir, Mae West describes *The Constant Sinner* as a hit at the Royale. "We had to operate two ticket offices to take care of the crowds." Here she demonstrates her resemblance to Babe Gordon, who does not scruple to alter the truth if she has a good reason. The reason, in this instance, was Mae West's belief that her public image as a winner should not be defaced. Even while *The Constant Sinner* was still playing, and taking a beating at the box office, Mae West insisted that it was a success. *The New York Times* published her "Apologia Pro Vita Sua," a plea for under-standing, similar to her opening-night curtain speech (and to her earlier piece "Sex in the Theater"), that took exception to the view that her writing proved her own familiarity with "the dregs of humanity." She begins by listing *The Constant Sinner* among "the string of hits I have turned out— my batting average as a playwright still being 1000." She goes on to main-tain that the play depicts "a phase of life which every civic-minded person must understand if there is to be any improvement in the moral tone of the city." She herself understood this "phase," but not because of firsthand knowledge. "Nobody ever saw me in the dives which I am supposed to know so intimately . . . Nobody ever sees me in night clubs and cabarets anywhere . . . I am, in fact, retiring by nature, in my private life, to the point of shyness. I even do all my shopping by telephone, because I cannot stand the attention other shoppers give me in a store . . . On the stage I may dress vividly; but off it I am usually attired in black. I do not drink. I do not smoke. I have my books, my writing, my friends—that is my private life."

By publishing this extraordinary outburst in the *Times* Mae may have hoped to attract some of the upscale and highbrow types that had flocked to *Diamond Lil* and thus broaden her current play's popularity. It didn't happen.

Variety listed *The Constant Sinner* among the failures of the 1931–32 sea-

son. The box office never gathered momentum, and after limping along for
eight weeks, the show closed. The trade weekly referred to dashed hopes at
the cash register and called it a flash in the pan. After hitting a high of
$11,000 a week, the take had dwindled to $5,000. The same issue of *Variety*
revealed that the Shubert organization had gone into receivership and faced
bankruptcy.

With reckless determination, Mae West and a road company set out
with tour dates booked for *The Constant Sinner* in Newark, New Jersey,
Philadelphia, Washington, D.C., and Chicago. In Chicago, she announced, she planned to cast the black Lorenzo Tucker in the Money
Johnson role.

But the play breathed its last after two performances in Washington,
when District Attorney Leo Rover threatened to arrest the entire company
if another show was attempted. An assistant district attorney and two detectives had attended the opening night at the Belasco Theater, and then
characterized the "theme, language and postures" of the play as "lewd and
lascivious." Washington was a segregated city, and according to *The Washington Post*, the most disturbing aspect of *The Constant Sinner* was its "objectionable intermingling of color."

Mae West received news of the close-down "while attending the races at
a nearby Maryland track." Not only did the last leg of the tour, the Chicago
run, have to be scrapped; she faced a company of disgruntled actors who
had been deprived of their promised and contracted salaries. Twenty-two
of them, including Russell Hardie, who played Baldwin, and Arthur Vinton,
filed claims with Actors Equity.

1931 ended grimly, with reports that Broadway had suffered its worst
debacle in two decades. In addition to the Shuberts, producer A. H. Woods
went into bankruptcy, as did Arthur Hammerstein. Theaters were about 45
percent dark. Breadlines formed along Times Square. "There is little scratch
anywhere," Damon Runyon wrote, "and along Broadway many racketeers
are wearing their last year's clothes and have practically nothing to bet on
the races."

An announcement, made in October, that Mae West would have her
own theater, on Eighth Avenue near Forty-eighth Street, in which she
would present her own plays, came to naught. Instead, *Variety* disclosed,
"Mae West will do no more legiting at present. She has started another
novel." While free of performing dates she would turn *Diamond Lil* into a
book.

Within six months, two events of red-letter magnitude in the annals of American womanhood would take place. Amelia Earhart would solo by air across the Atlantic. And, in a reversal of fortune worthy of the corniest melodrama, Mae West would arrive, after an overheated four-day train ride, in Hollywood to appear in her first movie, *Night After Night*. She had no idea how long she would be staying.

13

BIG GIRL IN A LITTLE TOWN

"*M*AE West blew in on the Chief from New York, tired, not cranky, but peeved at the Great American desert for providing her with weather that was too torrid for even Mae." Thus was the Los Angeles public alerted to a new presence in their midst.

When she arrived in Pasadena on June 20, 1932, despite her reputation for brazen worldliness, Mae West was innocent of the craft of moviemaking. Although she had tested for *Daredevil Jack* in the early twenties she had never set foot in a movie studio. "She has never even seen a talkie made— even in Gotham." But she was about to start learning. She had been drafted by Paramount to play a role in the George Raft picture *Night After Night*.

Her departure from New York had been a helter-skelter affair. On June 16, she and Timony boarded the train, after she had hurriedly affixed her name to "the fastest deal she ever closed." She signed a contract with Paramount, negotiated by agent William Morris, Jr., that promised to pay her $5,000 a week for ten weeks. "She signed up Wednesday, left the same night, and as she had negotiated to put on *The Constant Sinner* in Chicago . . . had to stop off in the Windy City" to cancel the production and continue to California, where she would make her screen debut.

Paramount, the most sophisticated and Europeanized of Hollywood studios, had pondered signing Mae West in the past, but nothing came of it. Production chief B. P. Schulberg once suggested her for a movie, in 1928, to Jesse Lasky, a founder of Paramount, for whom Mae West had worked in *A La Broadway*, her first Broadway role, back in 1911. Lasky demurred, on the grounds that Paramount's chief executive, Adolph Zukor, would "have all our heads" if they hired her. Zukor's memoir confirms that the scandalous reputation she had created in New York did not commend her to Hollywood. "No one believed that the Mae West of the stage could be transferred almost intact to the screen."

Three of her plays—*Sex, Pleasure Man,* and *Diamond Lil*—had been specifically judged unsuitable for adaptation to the screen by the Hays Office, and the sort of woman she habitually portrayed, a trollop or a siren with multiple lovers, would be sure to offend moral taskmasters. The Motion Picture Production Code of 1930 categorized sex and passion outside of marriage as "impure love," and insisted that such love, when presented in a movie, must be shown to be wrong and "must not be the subject of comedy or farce or treated as the material for laughter."

However, the Code of 1930 lacked teeth; its enforcement was spotty, its guidelines routinely ignored by producers who were fighting for their economic survival and knew the box-office value of sex. In the early thirties, in fact, movies about promiscuity, adultery, divorce, and prostitution were enjoying a heyday, even though Paramount banned such words as "broads," "floozies," "molls," or "sex." Audiences responded to gritty urban landscapes peopled by tough-talking gangsters and fallen women. "Hollywood wailed for new types—depression types . . . to yank frightened nickel-nursers into movie palaces. Hollywood didn't know exactly what it wanted, but Hollywood knew want."

George Raft was the person immediately responsible for bringing Mae West into motion pictures. The onetime nightclub dancer and driver for Owney Madden had established himself as a leading movie gangster in *Scarface,* where he'd casually flipped a coin while being shot by Paul Muni. He also looked promising as a romantic lead, since his profile and slicked-back patent-leather hair recalled Valentino. One of the perks of his new stardom was the right to be consulted on casting for his current movie, *Night After Night,* to be directed by Archie Mayo. He would play Joe Anton, an ex-fighter now presiding over a Manhattan speakeasy. The role of Maudie Triplett, his former girlfriend, was originally meant for Texas Guinan, in whose clubs Raft had danced. "Guinan's a friend of mine and she'd be great," Raft told Mayo. "But I know a woman who would be sensational": Mae West.

Raft's request for Mae came at a time of national turmoil. In 1932, a quarter of the American workforce was unemployed. Unprecedented numbers of beggars and panhandlers took their places on the streets. Their refrain "Brother, Can You Spare a Dime?" found its way into a popular song of rare social realism. Those with jobs found their hours reduced and their paychecks shrinking. Everywhere banks were closing, businesses failing, farms being foreclosed, and savings accounts going up in smoke. Franklin Roosevelt, nominated for the presidency in July, promised a New Deal that would restore hope to the "forgotten man."

Although millions of Americans continued going to the movies every week, seeking not just distraction and entertainment but reassurance and hope, the audience had dropped by 40 percent, while production costs for the new talkies mounted. Admission prices were reduced, and to lure in viewers, theaters gave away dishes, planned bank nights, and booked double features. Despite the come-ons, 20 percent of the country's movie houses had shut their doors.

Paramount had greeted the advent of sound by dumping its silent stars. "Clara Bow was through at Paramount. I could have her old dressing room if I wanted it," Mae remembered. She didn't. The dressing rooms of ex-stars William Haines, Ramon Novarro, and John Gilbert were also available. The studio hired a new list of players who had theatrical training: Claudette Colbert, Nancy Carroll, Ruth Chatterton, Tallulah Bankhead, Fredric March, Walter Huston. Marlene Dietrich, who had played small parts in Max Reinhardt productions, as well as in feature films, and who had made a sensation in *The Blue Angel*, was brought over from Germany. Prosperity did not accompany the new players. The studio posted record losses in 1932, to the tune of $21 million. Its profits were down two-thirds from 1931, and the value of its stock was plummeting. Five thousand non-contract employees were dropped, and those with contracts were asked to take voluntary pay cuts. Seventeen hundred Paramount theaters faced conversion into office buildings.

In a behind-the-scenes power shuffle, B. P. Schulberg was displaced as Paramount production chief by Emanuel Cohen, a four-foot-eleven dynamo, "crafty and tough-minded," with a background in newsreels, who announced that "arty features" appealing only to a few would be replaced by films with a "strong element of showmanship." Cohen also renounced the studio's past conservatism in favor of a resolve to be "as daring as possible." His ascendancy resulted in Paramount's producing *A Farewell to Arms* (which included an illegitimate pregnancy and a childbirth), purchasing Faulkner's explosive novel *Sanctuary*, and signing Mae West.

Mae West's arrival in the land of orange groves, jasmine, palm trees, swimming pools, and restaurants shaped like derby hats initially left Hollywood underwhelmed. Murray Feil, her West Coast William Morris agent, came to greet her and Timony at the Pasadena train station, but where was the hoopla a star had the right to expect? "Filmtown gave [me] the biggest frozen handshake I'd had in years. Hollywood, when I lifted the toothbrush and the corsets off the overland train, just looked limp. There wasn't even a band to play the girl to her new home. The nearest cameraman was about twenty miles away. Just for a minute, as I hiked to the taxi rack, I reckoned that Mae West stock had taken a Wall Street high ball."

It's been widely reported that Mae West's first words to the press upon detraining were "I'm not a little girl from a little town making good in a big town. I'm a big girl from a big town making good in a little town." The sentiments are entirely in keeping with her mood on arrival. But in fact, no reporters were on hand at the station, and her famous put-down of Los Angeles was made to a journalist in 1934, by a Mae West who had by then achieved international celebrity.

Disappointment at Hollywood's indifferent reception escalated to anger when Mae found herself waiting around several weeks for a script, drawing a salary but not working. Paramount was having script trouble with *Night After Night*. New writers kept being called in. "O. H. P. Garrett, Vince Lawrence, and Kitty Scola have now been assigned to rush *Night After Night* for production. Nine other writers have worked on the script," *Variety* reported. Casting problems were rumored as well. The role of Jerry Healy, "Miss Park Avenue," the socialite down on her luck, originally announced for Nancy Carroll, went instead to Constance Cummings, who had to be borrowed from Columbia.

While she waited, Mae at night attended the fights, where few people in the crowd recognized her; she had seats at the Olympic Auditorium every Tuesday, at the Pavillion in Santa Monica on Wednesdays, and at the Legion Stadium on Fridays. Hollywood was a new scene, but at the fights she fit right in, surrounded by familiar types.

By day she busied herself with the manuscript for the novel *Diamond Lil*, which would be released in the fall. Her reputation as a wellspring of zesty material attracted offers for her to develop scripts for Marlene Dietrich and Jean Harlow. MAE MULLS SOCK YARNS FOR MARLENE AND JEAN. *Variety* alleged she had been asked to come up with "strong stuff" for the rival blond actresses. She never considered accepting these offers; why should she supply gag lines for other stars? "If I thought of something funny, I wasn't about to give it to them." She claimed Louis B. Mayer nourished a grudge against her forever more after she refused either to write or to act for MGM, which aggressively courted her after her first success.

She gave a few interviews, expressing pleasure at the hugeness of her Paramount dressing room and optimism about her future: "I'll either be sensational or nothin' . . . But bein' an optimist I'm sure I'll be sensational. Why shouldn't they like me? Wouldn't you like it if y' were gettin' a Cadillac for the price of a Ford?"

She told Muriel Babcock of the *Los Angeles Times* that she'd come to Hollywood to learn about film acting, which she knew to be different from acting for the stage. "The screen doesn't require as much acting of a certain type. The camera catches the slightest facial movements, the slightest twitch of an eye." Her mastery of nuanced eye movements—appraising up-and-down glances, sideways glimpses, come-hither flutters—would soon become hallmarks of her screen art. "We must do all that only and exclusively with the eyes," she later told Marlene Dietrich. For now she was all ears, a true apprentice. "I got in everyone's hair asking questions. Why this and why that? I was in a strange land and I had to learn the tricks."

At Paramount's publicity office, in her summer print dress topped by a scarlet jacket and ornamented with a black picture hat, diamond collar, ring, and bracelet, she appeared to her interviewer to be at least twenty pounds lighter than she'd looked on her last stop in Los Angeles, when she was playing Diamond Lil. She claimed she merely *appeared* slimmer; people remembered her in the padded costumes of Diamond Lil. Actually, she had been dieting and was trimmer than she'd been in years—a fact overlooked by gossip columnist Louella Parsons, who called her "fat, fair and I don't know how near forty." Mae would soon turn thirty-nine, a secret revealed only to intimates, and had become fairer than before, having dyed her previously golden-colored hair a Harlow-like platinum shade.

She commended the balmy California climate and the outdoor life, but remarked that Los Angeles offered little in the way of nightlife; there was far less to do here than in New York—which was okay with her, she enjoyed living quietly out here in the provinces. "To most people I am off-stage what I am on; a deep dyed hussy without a moral in the world . . . As a matter of fact I live quite a decent, quiet, moral life. I am a showman and I know that the public wants sex in their entertainment and I give it to them."

When it came to sex appeal, she said she found Hollywood stars wanting. Clark Gable had "about as much sex appeal as a dish of left-over potato salad," and Garbo, although a wonderful actress, was "cold—terribly cold." Mae remained diplomatically silent on the subject of Paramount's reigning sex goddess, Marlene Dietrich, and also ignored MGM's about-to-detonate sex bomb, Jean Harlow. Instead, she praised silent star Pola Negri (whose

American career had ended with her return to Europe) as the only "present" female star with sex appeal. Among the men, she lauded Maurice Chevalier, on whom she surely cast bedroom eyes, as "the perfect lover."

Mae settled into the Rossmore Avenue apartment that her agent had found for her, on the sixth floor of the Ravenswood, an Art Deco building in the staid, monied Hancock Park section of Los Angeles. Its lobby welcomed residents grandly with "Moorish touches . . . tapestries, velvet chairs and sofas, gold-painted tables and lamps with statues for bases."

From the start, she considered her apartment at 570 North Rossmore a kind of charm, in part because it connected with her lucky number, eight, and because extreme good fortune came to her while she lived there. The apartment number was 611: "That's lucky. 611 adds up to 8, and 8 is my lucky number. At the studio my dressing room is number 116. That adds up to 8. My motor car license is 3W5. Also my telephone number adds up to 8."

She would remain at the Ravenswood—less than a mile from Paramount's Marathon Street studio—for the next forty-eight years, long after she bought property elsewhere. "Everyone else that gets in the money out here buys a forty-room house, hires a dozen servants and gets ritzy. But not me. I'd be lonesome." Living in an apartment building, on a tree-lined but dense city block, put her at ease; and the front desk, which screened all calls and visitors, provided a sense of security. So did her distance from the street. "I like to live high up and hear people moving about, and listen to traffic noises. A quiet country estate would bore me. I'm a city gal and I like rackets—and I don't mean what you think." George Raft lived right down the street at the El Royale.

For the first few months, the apartment was fitted with colorless hotel furniture and decorated with few flourishes. There were "no books, no flowers, no pictures. Just an apartment like a thousand others in Hollywood, only less pretentious than most," and one in which she kept a woolly monkey as a pet. Timony stayed with her until he rented his own place in the same building. Although he had trouble accepting the fact, Mae had long since lost any interest in him as a lover as he gained weight and acquired chins. Still, she considered him family, and at this juncture he remained vital to her professional life.

At last she received dialogue sheets for *Night After Night*—and "hit the overhead lamps." The lines she was supposed to speak were utterly lifeless and without distinction. "My part had absolutely nothing going for it! It was unimportant to the story and flatly written." She offered to return her salary to Paramount posthaste if they would release her from her contract.

Here the producer of the movie, William La Baron, stepped in. Le Baron remembered Mae West from *A La Broadway*, and knew how successfully she had tinkered with the script and lyrics he'd written for her part in that show. He had a knack for spotting comic talent, having given W. C. Fields his first role in a feature film and been responsible for bringing Fields to Paramount. Le Baron had been around the block a few times since he and Mae West last worked together. He'd served as head of RKO production before returning to Paramount, whose East Coast studio he once supervised, and had produced one rousing success, the Academy Award 1931 choice for Best Picture, *Cimarron*. Recognizing Mae West's gift for dialogue and powerful sense of her own comic identity as assets that could be exploited for everybody's benefit, he consented to allow her to rewrite her part to suit herself.

Night After Night placed Mae West in a milieu she knew intimately and felt completely comfortable in: Prohibition-era Manhattan awash with gangsters, fighters, ex-millionaires, cheap women, drunks, and social climbers. Set in a mansion off Fifth Avenue that has been converted into a speakeasy, it is based on the Louis Bromfield short story "Single Night," in turn based on the real-life experience of Woolworth heiress Barbara Hutton at Club Napoleon, which she recognized tearfully, when stopping there one night, as her former family home.

As Joe Anton, George Raft is an ex-fighter turned club owner who is trying to put his rough past behind him. He dons an elegant silk robe after his bath, which his manservant, also an ex-pug, has drawn for him, and at night sports a boutonniere on his elegant suit jacket. Anton's current girlfriend, Iris (Wynne Gibson), has begun to bore him. She drinks too much, cares too much, and lacks the touch of class that attracts Anton to the melancholy ex-heiress Jerry Healy, played by Constance Cummings, who comes into the club alone to reminisce nostalgically about the golden days when the speakeasy was a luxurious private dwelling, her home before her family lost its money.

Miss Healy's blue blood and sophisticated "classy" background intimidate Joe Anton and awaken in him a desire to better himself. He hires the matronly English teacher Mabel Jellyman (Alison Skipworth) to tutor him in manners, grammar, pronunciation, culture, and current affairs, so that he will be able to hold his own in refined society and impress Miss Healy with his breeding and intelligence. Miss Healy has accepted his invitation to dine with him upstairs at the club tonight; everything hinges on his success in playing the suave gentleman at dinner.

Mae West, as Maudie Triplett, crashes the party in a beaded and sequined white V-neck gown, her hair marceled close to her head, her diamond necklace blazing, and overturns Raft's phony apple cart. She blows his gentlemanly cover and reveals his background for what it is. "Joey, Joey, well, well, come here and kiss me, you doll . . . Who's the dame?" She harks back, slapping her knee, to uproarious old times she and Joe have shared: "You should have seen this kid fight for me . . . We got so plastered, it took five cops to land us in jail . . . When I first met him he was a third rate pug."

Miss Jellyman, who has been invited along to keep Joe in line and raise the dinner conversation to a suitably high level, ends up getting drunk with Maudie and, reversing roles, taking lessons from her, in drinking and spontaneity: "Do you really think I could get rid of my inhibitions?"

The next day, for the first time in her life, Miss Jellyman, hungover, sleeps in and misses a class she was supposed to teach. Maudie tells her not to worry about getting sacked; she can get her a job in her business, "one of the best payin' rackets in the world," which Miss Jellyman assumes is prostitution. Miss Jellyman is incredulous and says she recognizes that "your business" has been a "great factor in the building of civilization" and "thereby protected the sanctity of the home." She evokes the memory of Cleopatra, adding, "Of course, France owes a great deal to Du Barry." At last she sneaks in, "Well . . . don't you think I'm just a little old?"

Maudie puts it to her: Say, what kind of business do you think I'm in? She explains that she owns a chain of beauty parlors, and that Miss Jellyman would make a great hostess at the Institute do Beaut.

Most of Mae West's on-camera moments in this picture are shared with another woman, the dowdy, middle-aged, British-accented Alison Skipworth. Publicity stills pictured her romantically posed alone with George Raft, but they don't correspond to any scene in the movie. This wasn't the way Mae West liked to play, and she would not do it again. But she made the best of the material at hand and appeared, in her first on-screen moments ever, surrounded by a gaggle of male admirers who want to accompany her upstairs to the elegant speakeasy dinner. She tells them, "You know, my father's very strict and he don't let me see boys after nine." This is pure autobiography, a reference to the time, back in Brooklyn when she was twelve, that a cousin tattled about her staying up late with boys and her father threatened her.

In the movie, Maudie tells her corps of worshipful men to go home to their wives—a line that would never have gotten past the post-1934 Production Code censors. (Neither would they have allowed the double entendres in the conversation about Maudie's "business," or the scene in which George Raft and Wynne Gibson sit together, fully clothed, in a double bed. Even George Raft's reference to the flowers he prefers, "anything but pansies," would have been cut.)

One of the most quoted lines in screen history is spoken when diamond-decked Maudie checks her white-fox fur wrap before ascending to dinner. "Goodness, what beautiful diamonds!" the coat-check girl exclaims. Maudie corrects her: "Goodness had nothing to do with it, dearie." (The claim that Texas Guinan originated this line has not been verified. *Screen Play* credited Mae for "placing it [the appropriated line] right.")

In her autobiography, which takes its title from this scene, Mae West describes a conflict about how the follow-up to her wisecrack should be shot. She says she liked Archie Mayo, a director Paramount had borrowed from Warner Brothers, "a ball-bearing shaped bundle of energy and bounce," but felt certain her background in theater made her a better judge of how to milk a laugh than he, who knew only movies. It's evident her moment of humility, her feelings that as a novice in movies she had much to learn, had quickly abandoned her. She was convinced that the camera should focus on her as she sashayed up the staircase, and both Emanuel Cohen, head of production at Paramount, and producer William LeBaron supported her. Since she apparently never saw the entire movie after its release, she did not learn, even after more than twenty-five years, that the final cut of *Night After Night* lacks the shot of her ascending the steps.

In many of her stage appearances Mae West had made a point of moving and speaking languorously, at half the speed of others around her. In *Night After Night*, the opposite occurred. "In this picture I noticed all the scenes that preceded me were shot at a very slow pace . . . If I slowed up too, I'd be in slow motion." She decided to change *her* tempo, and work fast, so fast the audience would wake up and accelerate with her. "I had to come in like a streak of lightning." Not only does she talk a blue streak, she bubbles with animation, smiling more broadly, drinking up, and laughing more giddily than she will in any subsequent movie role.

She does set the tone for future films by establishing her character's independence. No one tells Maudie what to do. Joe Anton in fact tries to put her off, having his butler tell her he's out when she calls. When they try to prevent her from crashing the dinner party, it's "no sale, no sale, I'm gonna see him tonight." She's her own woman, and barges in. Although she likes Joe, she's not shedding any tears over him—unlike both Iris and Miss Healy. No victim she.

When Mae West began shooting this first movie, she expressed amazement and horror at how wasteful and spendthrift the process was, compared to the theater. Actors didn't know their lines, and the director seemed unsure of what he was doing. They would repeat a take over and over. She and Timony agreed that in Hollywood money wasn't real. "It melts like snowflakes."

Where her own earnings were concerned, however, she made no outcry about extravagance. Even though Mae West was billed fourth in *Night After Night*, after George Raft, Constance Cummings, and Alison Skipworth, she received the top salary. The Paramount Production Files disclose that she received $4,000 a week (with possibly another $1,000 for her work on the script); Alison Skipworth was paid $458 weekly, and George Raft, the "star," for some reason earned only $191.69 per week. No wonder George Raft complained about Mae West: "She stole everything but the camera." He found her higher salary, dominating style, and looming stardom threatening. He and Mae had ceased to be lovers, though she always held him dear.

When production of *Night After Night* was almost complete, Mae West, while being driven home from the studio by her temporary chauffeur, Harry Voiler, was held up at gunpoint and robbed of $23,000 in jewelry and cash. Voiler, who although armed offered no resistance, turned out to be in on the job, with two Detroit gangsters, Edward "Happy" Friedman and Morris Cohen. Mae had known Voiler for several years—although not very well— as a Chicago ticket broker who became Texas Guinan's personal manager. She probably did not know that he had been jailed once for armed robbery with intent to kill, and sentenced to fifteen to thirty years in a Michigan penitentiary, but if she did, it would have made little difference to her.

The holdup shocked and frightened Mae. She became less trusting, even more cautious, more insular. She took out a $100,000 insurance policy on her own life, installed a steel front door with a speakeasy-type window in it, allowing visitors to be screened, and took to sleeping with a pistol next to her bed. She eventually hired Mike Mazurki, a burly wrestler who went on to an acting career, as her bodyguard.

Because of her friendships with underworld figures, she had thought of herself as invulnerable to such crimes. "I think it's a terrible thing that I was robbed of my jewels and lots of money as soon as I landed out here. That could never have happened to me in New York or Chicago. I know too many of the boys there. I've befriended them on too many occasions. They're out to protect me always."

Voiler tried to strike a deal with her, telling her he knew where her jewels were and could recover them, for a consideration of $5,000. She refused, and instead went to the police. This was a major switch. In the past, police had been "them," not "us."

When she testified in court, the press commented on her wardrobe: "Mae West, in a clinging black gown that swept the white marble floors of the Hall of Justice, went up and saw the grand jury." All three perpetrators were indicted. The robbery eventually became the subject of a *Calling All Cars* radio program.

Any doubts Mae entertained about whether she should remain in Hollywood were annihilated by the enthusiasm that greeted her debut in *Night After Night*. *Photoplay* gushed: "Wait till you see Mae West. An out-and-out riot, Mae is. It's snappy and you'll love it." Writing in the *Herald Tribune*, Richard Watts, Jr., enthused: "On the screen . . . she brings some of that quality of rowdiness which the increasingly effete cinema needs . . . She is in an engagingly gutter fashion a delight." And *Variety* found much to praise: "Miss West's dialogue is always unmistakably her own. It is doubtful if anyone else could write it . . . It wouldn't be taking a chance to shoot the works on her from now on."

Mae West became a hot property. Paramount immediately offered her a fat contract to make another picture. When *Night After Night* was first released, it was billed as a George Raft vehicle. A few months later, it had a repeat run, this time "being solely played on the Mae West reputation."

Nothing could stop her now.

[14]

SHE DONE HIM WRONG

$\mathcal{W}$HEN production began on *She Done Him Wrong*, the film adaptation of *Diamond Lil*, Mae West had no inkling that after the picture's release she would find herself both hailed and reviled: for instigating a revolution in American social mores, capsizing the traditional image of woman as either Satan's ally or a passive and monogamous sexual vessel who endures, rather than initiates, lovemaking; and for reversing the comic stereotype of the woman over thirty-five as a cranky, sexless old bag. Or that she would be celebrated for replenishing the phrase bank of the American language. "Come up and see me sometime," a misquote of her line "Why don't you come up sometime, see me?," would become one of the most repeated catch-phrases in the English-speaking world, as universally recognized in 1933 as "Who's Afraid of the Big Bad Wolf?" Nor did she suspect that she would inspire a transformation in women's fashions on two continents, and even change the way children play; it turned out they loved imitating her, wiggling their hips and lowering their voices to ape the famous invitation to "come up."

What she did know was that she felt pushed by an irresistible force to bring her signature stage role to the screen, and that Paramount, facing bankruptcy and desperate for a smash hit, would win out.

Before this could happen, formidable obstacles had to be surmounted—or at least dodged. Although Paramount bought the film rights for *Diamond Lil* in 1931—reportedly for less than $30,000—they hesitated. Studios catered to a young audience, and the Paramount story department feared that the college students, teenagers, and children they depended on at the box office would be put off by the Gay Nineties costumes and sets. They also questioned the size of the cast required, and the fact that "little characters bob up here and there and you keep losing them." They had second thoughts, too, about the number of colorful lowlife characters involved: crooked politicians, white slavers, counterfeiters, escaped convicts, gigolos. Gangster pictures that made crime seem glamorous were out of favor with the censors. Mae West argued, "Everywhere I go in life I find [odd little characters], so I like them in my plays. All my life I have been interested in people, all kinds of people, but most of all the unimportant people—hoodlums, they're called. They are real, natural." No way would she remove them from her script. Real and natural, she assured the studio brass, would sell in these Depression-racked hard times.

But the most daunting opposition issued from the Hays Office, which in 1930 had placed *Diamond Lil* on the banned list. Dr. James Wingate, former New York film censor and new head of the Hays Office's Studio Relations branch, wrote to Will Hays in New York that he had learned that Lowell Sherman had been hired by Paramount to direct *Diamond Lil.* "We informed him," Wingate wrote in code, "that according to last advice from your office story was still unusable and on Banned list. Until we receive instructions from you that picture is suitable story material and permitted to be made by your office we feel we should not touch the matter."

The name Lowell Sherman in itself conjured enough dubious associations to make censors squirm in their straight-backed chairs. Sherman, an actor on the stage and in silent films before he became a director, had a reputation for rough living in life and for portraying libertines, dandies, and villainous roués as an actor. It didn't help that he had been present at the notorious wild party hosted by Fatty Arbuckle in San Francisco in 1921 and had seen starlet Virginia Rappe tearing off her clothes and groaning in pain but done nothing to help her. It was that party, and the resulting sensational trial of Arbuckle, that had led to the creation of the Motion Picture Producers and Distributors of America, and the appointment of its chief, movie czar Will Hays, in the first place.

In the fall of 1932, the *Los Angeles Times* printed a story saying that Mae West would be starring in a picture called *Honky-Tonk,* not *Diamond Lil.* "There are reports that the Hays office doesn't approve of the [Lil] yarn." Then they announced a new title: *Honky-Tonk* had been dropped because of "a touch of Hays fever." Instead, Mae West would star in *Ruby Red,* a title that recalls her early play *The Ruby Ring.*

Hays warned Paramount chief Adolph Zukor that merely altering the film's title would do nothing to quash moral objections. "If *Diamond Lil* could be produced merely by changing the title," Hays wrote, "without otherwise respecting the agreement of October 31, 1930 [banning it], then, of course, *Shanghai Gesture*, *Lulu Belle* and others could be produced by merely changing the title." He sternly reiterated that on his watch there would be no production of *Diamond Lil* tolerated, under any title.

Rumors persisted that *Diamond Lil* was being turned into a movie; if true, if the Hays Office really intended to look the other way, it would signal a permissiveness and an indifference to code standards significant for the entire film industry. Harry Warner, one of the Warner Brothers, wired Will Hays: "Please wire immediately whether I can believe my ears that Paramount has arranged to make Diamond Lil . . . Recollect that it was absolutely definite that Diamond Lil was not to be produced. I am not sending this wire as a protest but I want to know how to run our business in the future." Hays assured Warner he had been misinformed. Paramount was abandoning the Lil project. "Believe situation plainly understood by Paramount and that there is no danger of their violation of the agreement."

What Hays didn't know was that his edict was being politely ignored. Instead of abandoning the *Diamond Lil* project, Paramount intended merely to disguise and launder it. Its strategy was to alter the script in minor ways, deleting or recasting the most censorable material to forestall future objections. All the play's references to drugs, for example, had to go. The studio's Harold Hurley dispatched an interoffice memo suggesting that the nationalities of the villainous Rita and her lover, Juárez, be changed, so as not to offend the moviegoers of South America, and that San Francisco's Barbary Coast replace Rio as the scene of their crimes. (Since the Soviets were not importing American films, turning the villains into Russians seemed to make commercial sense. Rio Rita became Russian Rita. Juárez became Serge, the Gilbert Roland role.)

He further recommended that the names of other characters also be changed to minimize associations with the play (hence Lil became Lady Lou), that references to Sunday school and psalm singing be expunged, and that certain lines of dialogue be erased. For instance, he said the curtain line, "I always knew you could be had," could be altered to "retain all of the thoughts implied, but the lines will have to be written more subtly and much more cleverly. It is the plain, rather ugly use of phrases that will get us into trouble."

Finally, he directed that any references to prostitution would have to be scuttled. The saloon set must under no circumstances "take on the atmosphere of a house. We should be very careful with the principal set to show that it is a dance hall, and stay away from private rooms that could be used for immoral purposes." These proscriptions weren't persuasive enough to cause the many scenes shot in Lady Lou's boudoir—including one in which she changes costumes behind a screen, and another in which she wears a negligee—to be edited out of the finished picture. Nor were we denied being introduced to Lou as "one of the finest women ever walked the streets."

Without admitting defeat, the Hays Office began making concessions. After examining the script of what was still called *Ruby Red*, Dr. Wingate telegrammed Hays, assuring him that "while it resembles Diamond Lil in its basic structure [it] may in our opinion with proper treatment become acceptable under the code." At a November 28 meeting in New York, when the picture had already completed its first week of shooting in Hollywood, Zukor prevailed; the picture *would* be made, but he promised the censors that the title "Diamond Lil" would be scotched and never mentioned in advertising or publicity, that only "suitable material" would be used, that the "white slavery" angle would be muted, that Mae West would not be depicting a "kept woman," and that the young missionary would not be connected to the Salvation Army.

While *Variety* misinformed its readers that " 'Lil' is out, whole and in part," the New York meeting actually signaled a green light for the picture, now retitled *She Done Him Wrong*. (*He Done Her Wrong* was briefly considered, but Mae said no—the title had to evoke a woman who acts, not one who is acted upon.) Confirming that the go-ahead had been given, and trying to make the best of a considerable setback, Dr. Wingate wrote Paramount's Hurley, urging the studio to "develop the comedy elements, so that the treatment will invest the picture with such exaggerated qualities as automatically to take care of possible offensiveness."

Exaggeration had been a hallmark of Mae West's comedy since her earliest days in vaudeville, and she didn't need Dr. Wingate's coaxing to make her bring it to the fore now. The glittery padded costumes, plumed picture hats, stiltlike high heels concealed under flowing skirts, and heavy jewelry that made Diamond Lil larger than life on stage were carried over to the screen; their lavishness—fifteen dozen ostrich plumes were used, and two thousand bunches of beads—made an even more emphatic point now, in the depths of the Depression, than they had during the boom of 1928, the time of the stage premiere. On screen, Charles Lang's camera added avoirdupois; lighting made beaded, sequined costumes and diamonds blaze almost blindingly; and close-ups helped to magnify the star's undulating dimensions and stature. "Big" was once more the key word. Costume designer Edith Head, on her own for the first time in *She Done Him Wrong*, recalled: "I designed 30 or 40 pounds of jewelry for Mae to wear . . . I first found pictures of period jewelry to show her. 'Fine, Honey,' she said, 'just make the stones *bigger.*' "

That Lou is an icon of irresistible magnetism and allure is established from the first shot of a huge nude painting of her that adorns Gus Jordan's Suicide Hall saloon, prompting every man to think what one man says: "I never saw a woman so beautiful." ("I gotta admit that's a flash," Lou comments, puncturing her icon status even as she reinforces it, "but I do wish Gus hadn't hung it up over the free lunch.") Lou makes a habit of distributing photos of herself to her admirers, photos we don't see but hear described as suitable for the bedroom, "a little bit spicy, but not too raw." Lou presides, absorbing every scintilla of attention, in part by being *copied*, reproduced in images on canvas and paper. One Lou isn't enough. "The Bowery Bank and Schmidt's Brewery are fightin' to use her picture exclusive on their New Year's calendars." We in the audience ogle her, and constantly see others ogling, and commenting, in rapture. We watch the watchers, and are cued by them how we should respond. When she sings, we see Cummings and others in the bar, transfixed by her magic. She, like subsequent Mae West heroines, keeps being duplicated and reflected, eliciting praise, desire, and tribute.

The set's well-traveled staircase, between the saloon on street level and Lady Lou's upstairs boudoir, made it a literal necessity for any character playing a scene alone with her to have to come *up*. By standing on a stair during dialogue with Cary Grant's Captain Cummings, she appears at least the physical equal of a man more than a foot taller than she. "I taught Cary Grant how to drape himself around my eyes," she would boast. Grant would intimate that she dwarfed everyone around her in a way he found distasteful. Her personality was so dominant that everyone with her became "just a feeder."

Writing in the *Los Angeles Times*, Alma Whitaker remarked on the way Mae West lorded it over Cary Grant. When he first played the lover in pictures, with Dietrich in *Blonde Venus*, with Sylvia Sidney in *Madame Butterfly*, with Nancy Carroll and Carole Lombard, he was able to retain at least a semblance of his "lord-of-the-creation" attributes. But (here she quotes Grant) "with Mae West, well, that word 'chattel' about which the suffragettes of yore would snort, does sort of creep into the picture, what?"

Mae West liked to take credit for discovering Cary Grant. Her story about spotting him, an unknown who "hadn't made a picture yet," on the Paramount lot and announcing, "If he can talk, I'll take him," has entered the annals of Hollywood folklore. Supposedly, in one variant account, she said this when informed that the actor in the white suit was currently filming *Madame Butterfly* with Sylvia Sidney, and prefaced her comment with "I don't care if he's making *Little Nell*." In fact, Grant had been signed by B. P. Schulberg and had already appeared in seven movies when she sighted him, but he was not yet a big name. His potential as a romantic lead had been recognized, but not, so far, his gift for comedy.

Grant, who would eventually express irritation with her egotism and "superficiality," readily conceded that he owed plenty to Mae West, having learned "almost everything" from her. To *Variety*, he heaped praise on her "instinct," her perfect timing, her "so right" grasp of comic situations, and her tempo sense, which in her pictures mattered more than the "sincerity of the characterization." And he confessed no small delight that the audience one reaches in a Mae West picture provided an actor with "a magnificent break."

Grant recognized that one of the things he had going for him as Mae West's romantic lead in *She Done Him Wrong* was his distinctness from her. His dark, youthful good looks complemented her fair ripeness: "She is blond and I am dark and we made a suitable contrast." There are *no* other blond heads in *She Done Him Wrong*, and very few lovely young women, either; only the rather schoolmarmish Rochelle Hudson, who plays the deflowered innocent, Sally. Ann Sheridan, a stock actress at the time, remembered that Mae West preferred to surround herself with older actresses. "Mae would look us over, and all the young ones were weeded out. Nothing mean about that. She was smart. It was her film and she wasn't going to have any distractions from herself."

Exaggeration took the form—standard for Mae West—of highlighting polar extremes: between light and dark, white and black in the scenes between Lady Lou and her maid, Pearl, between the iciness of diamonds and the "soul" Cummings says they mask, between innocence and experience; between the good old days—"when there were handlebars on wheel and lip" and five-cent lager beer flowed like water—and the audience's consciousness of the forced dryness of Prohibition America; between the promise of sensual extravagance and restraint. Cary Grant became the embodiment of the last-named quality, as repressed, British, and buttoned up as Lady Lou is suggestive, American urban, and bursting at the seams.

Her costumes allowed her not a millimeter of breathing room. " 'I like 'em tight, girls,' " she told Edith Head and her seamstresses. "And tight they were, there wasn't a costume in which she could lie, bend or sit." To afford her some relaxation, Head improvised a reclining board: "It had armrests and was tilted at an angle, and there she'd lean between scenes in glittering splendor." A separate, slightly larger version would be made of each gown, for the scenes requiring movement. In the scene in which she fights with Rita (Rafaela Ottiano, who played the same role onstage), she literally over-flows the gown, bazooms bursting from their moorings.

Grant's Captain Cummings is always covered to the nth degree; he wears a high-collared dark uniform while he masquerades as the head of a mission; converts to coat, collar, and tie when he's revealed as the police detective known as the Hawk. "Loosen up," Lou advises him when he sits beside her on a chaise longue. "Unbend. You'll feel better."

As in the play, Lil/Lou's hidden "goodness" shines through when she secretly buys the mission from the grasping Jew, Jacobson, and in her nur-turing of Sally, the shabby young fallen woman who faints after almost taking her own life. "I'll look after her," Lou promises, unaware that Rita and Gus Jordan have plans for Sally involving white slavery on the Barbary Coast. Lou has the girl carried to her room, where she hovers over her, administering a bracing drink and smelling salts. When Sally awakens, Lou comforts her by demolishing Sally's conventional notions about what "bad" means. As long as she hasn't committed murder, Lou assures Sally, she has nothing to worry about. Lou/Lil repeats her line from the play: "Men's all alike, married or single. It's their game. I happen to play it their way." When Sally says she fears no man will ever want her, sullied as she is, Lou responds with a quip that topples the fallen-women conventions which demanded wages for sin: "When women go wrong, men go right after them."

That quip *wasn't* in the play. The movie is far richer in memorable wise-cracks. "Haven't you ever met a man that can make you happy?" Cummings asks Lou. Her oft-quoted answer: "Sure. Lots of times." Later she again sends up marriage, saying he's "the kind a woman would have to marry to get rid of." Mae West considered the infusion of verbal wit a compensation for the loss of the suggestive situations (such as showing Lil/Lou in nothing but her corset, or engaged in "lustful kissing" with several different men) that the Hays Office prohibited. "I didn't start putting in all these wisecracks till I started pictures. When I wrote *She Done Him Wrong* . . . the studios and the censors wouldn't let me do certain things . . . and so with everybody weak-ening my drama, I figured I had to put some other element in." For now, anyhow, censorship had an up side. It forced performers to be clever, to use indirection and suggestion, instead of bald statement.

Mae West wrote her own quips, but the transformation of her stage melo-drama into a workable screenplay required the intervention of two pros, John Bright, who did the bulk of the work, and Harry Thew, who was called in at the very end. Bright, soon to become a founder of the Screen Writers Guild, had successfully collaborated with Thew not long before on the screenplay for one of the great gangster pictures of the thirties, the Jimmy Cagney vehicle *The Public Enemy.* When he was hired by Paramount, John Bright had just been fired by Darryl Zanuck and told he would never work again in the industry. "The reply of my agent . . . was to gain a job for me the next day for more money. It was the screenplay for *Diamond Lil.*"

Bright didn't think much of the play, finding it "creaky and absurd," undermined by "rickety structure" and "clichéd dialogue." Although he rec-ognized in Mae West an "astonishing personality" who sanctioned "pleasure for its own sake, not needing love for its justification," he found working with her a trial. She fought his suggestions for changing the script, con-vinced that she was the ultimate authority on what was best for herself. To win her approval, Bright patronizingly reports, "I had to 'remind' her of lines she had 'forgotten.' " Director Sherman and producer Le Baron would privately support his ideas, then back down when Mae West voiced dis-pleasure. " 'Sorry, baby,' Sherman shrugged over his manicure, 'but I have to handle the bitch-goddess on the set.' "

No love was lost between Mae West and Lowell Sherman. He agreed to her recommendation that the actors be allowed to rehearse for a week before filming began, as they would a play in the theater. But they clashed over her resistance to direction and her habitual lateness. Theater had trained her to be a night person, "a charter member of the Broadway Sun Dodgers" accustomed to leisurely mornings, and he got tired of scolding her for miss-ing her early-morning call on the set. Finally he barred her late arrival by moving equipment to the door and blocking it. She had to push her way in and was not late again.

Sherman died in 1934, but had he lived, they still would not have worked together again. Although Mae kept Le Baron as producer and became de-voted to cinematographer Karl Struss after *Belle of the Nineties,* she never worked with any film director twice. In another era, she would have openly functioned as her own director. "I was really always the director. Nobody could tell me how to be me."

Perhaps because all parties were eager to get the work behind them, *She Done Him Wrong* was completed in an astonishing eighteen days of shooting in December 1932, at a cost of $200,000, more than half of which went to the woman Sherman referred to as "America's wet dream."

Paramount invited Dr. Wingate to a preview early in 1933. He reported to Hays that the studio had toned down the picture, which in its present form would offend only "the most stringent censors." The pasted-on promise of marriage at the end seemed to placate him, though visions of sustained wedded bliss hardly leap to mind when Cary Grant calls Mae West "you bad girl" and she counters, "You'll find out." The audience, responding at the preview with "hearty, if somewhat rowdy amusement," seemed to enjoy the picture, Wingate said.

Released during the bleak "lame duck winter" of 1933, when low farm prices were driving farmers west and Roosevelt hadn't yet supplanted Hoover at the White House, *She Done Him Wrong* became one of the triumphs of the year. Just weeks after Paramount entered receivership, the film began breaking box-office records all over the country, in small towns as well as cities, earning more than $2 million in less than three months. Letters from fans to Mae West were pouring in at the astonishing rate of fifteen hundred a week.

Many theaters brought the film back for repeat runs—contributing to the greatest record of "repeats" since *The Birth of a Nation*. "Not Once but Again and Again" read one ad placed by Paramount. By September, 786 theaters had booked it twice and 108 theaters had played it three times. Mae West was heralded as "Filmdom's Newest Star, Sweeping the Nation in Her First Starring Vehicle, Playing to Capacity Audiences Everywhere." "Yes," says Mae West in an ad, "they kinda went for me."

Another ad, exploiting the supposedly hush-hush link with *Diamond Lil*, hyped the picture as "the red-light, heartbreak and hotcha saga of Gotham's glorious sinner," featuring "Diamond-Decked Lou, the Bowery's Light O' Love, Mistress of the Street Where Beer Was a Nickel—and Love Had a Price Too." It pictured an outsize Mae West in an off-the-shoulder black gown (the same one spoofed by Groucho Marx, depicted in an ad for *Duck Soup*, à la Mae in drag), with her hand on the rump of a miniature man in a suit. Yet another, listing theaters in New York, Chicago, New Orleans, Los Angeles, Houston, Rochester, Boston, Detroit, and Springfield that had done land-office business, announced that Mae West, pictured holding a smoking gun, had done in "Mr. Low Gross," who lies wounded on the floor. THE WHOLE COUNTRY IS GOING "WEST," proclaims a banner headline. Another still featured a full-page close-up of Mae, with lips reddened and cleavage resplendent; both the movie and the décolletage are touted for hitting THE BULL'S-EYE OF LUSTY ENTERTAINMENT.

One publicity angle, dreamed up by Paramount's Bill Thomas, highlighted the connection between uninhibited beer guzzling on the 1890s Bowery and the imminent repeal of Prohibition. Anti-rum evangelist Billy Sunday was summoned to the barroom set during filming, to pose with Mae West for Paramount newsreels; the incongruity between sinner and crusader, and between Sunday and saloons, would surely grab the attention of a public fed up with being prohibited. The Paramount Press Book for *She Done Him Wrong* suggested promoting the picture by sponsoring either beer-carrying ("How many twelve-ounce schooners of beer can you hold in both hands?") or beer-drinking contests, "to be promoted in conjunction with a local hotel which may provide the beer." It recommended a tie-in furniture ad for Philco Wonder-Bar Cellarette, a home bar and radio equipped with trays for glasses and beverage bottles. After repeal, newspapers carried photos of Mae West and Paramount leading man Gary Cooper at a brewery, schooners aloft near a big barrel; the caption urged, "Girls, drink beer. It'll give you those sexy curves." No one—including Mae herself—had any scruples about a conflict between this campaign and her real-life abstinence from alcohol. Drinking had long been part of her live-to-the-hilt public persona.

Publicity came to a head in New York City, where the picture opened. Repeat bookings of *She Done Him Wrong* at the Paramount—first in Manhattan, then in Brooklyn—coincided with a Mae West personal appearance tour that booked her into the same theaters that were showing the movie on its first run. Press photographs pictured Miss West's arrival by train for the New York leg of her tour, being met at Grand Central Terminal in a dashing horse-drawn Victoria, a relic of the 1890s, and conducted up Broadway like British royalty. The New York publicity blitz included a series of biographical articles by Martin Sommers in the *Daily News* that hurled "hot grenades from the Western front."

Variety pointed out that in her second week of personal appearances at the midtown Paramount movie theater, she bested the box-office take of her former *Sometime* co-star Ed Wynn, competing at the Capitol, by more than $5,000. It also reported on a rare Mae West radio date on the Rudy Vallee variety show—Fred Astaire and Claude Rains were other guests— on which, backed by a male quartet, she sang an extended "Frankie and Johnny" that dramatized her role as a murderess.

The live stage show pleased Mae West's fans more than it did reviewers. "Too much is still too much," one wrote, "and there is too much Miss West at the Paramount this week. In the picture Mae has all the boys chasing her. On the stage, they're still chasing, one in the flesh and the others on the telephone." The Paramount show provided a vivid demonstration of how much freer from censorship in-person performance remained, compared to the screen. "She plays a bad, bad lady who gets more applicants than a want ad." In the daring sketch, Mae West enters in a town car, accompanied by a convoy of motorcycle cops. She steps out, dazzling in a clinging black gown all covered with diamonds, sings, "tosses 'em some hot chatter," then moves to her stage boudoir. After in-structing her stage maid not to call her madame, she answers the phone repeatedly, turning down date after date. Then, seated on a chaise longue, she sings a duet with George Metaxa, who tells her he's a gigolo and presents a price list for his services. Having surveyed the list, Mae agrees to sample a kiss. After a long and fervent demonstration, they separate, and Mae crows, "Boy, are you lousy!"

Mae was so pleased with the director of her New York Paramount stage show that she brought him with her to the next city on her personal ap-pearance tour, Chicago, and subsequently had him hired by Paramount in Hollywood as an assistant for her future pictures. They would remain close, both professionally and personally, for several years. He was Boris Petroff, a Russian-born former ballet master. (Mae's sister Beverly had a Russian intimate at this time, too, actor Vladimir Baikoff, soon to become her sec-ond Russian-born husband.)

Although *She Done Him Wrong* did well in Los Angeles, Mae West made no personal appearances there, convinced that in her new hometown she lacked a following strong enough to justify them. Although 30,000 citizens "howled on Hollywood Boulevard" the night of the West Coast premiere, the stars stayed away, making it very clear that they didn't consider it vital to court Mae West's good graces. It would have helped if Mae had sent them free tickets, or if she had ever made an appearance at another star's opening night.

The snub by big-time Hollywood affirmed her "outsider" status—to which she frankly laid claim. Among movie luminaries she remained more talked about than talked *to*. Yes, she knew the people at Paramount, where Mar-lene Dietrich's dressing room adjoined her own. Yes, Emanuel Cohen had given a tea for her on the lot, introducing her to players and crew. But her name appeared on few guest lists. "I don't go in for Hollywood parties," she said. "I go to a fight somewhere every night . . . I've known 'pugs' all my life and they never fail to give me a 'kick.' . . . I hate pose and flub-dub . . . I'm always too busy to go in for a lot of front, and besides, I know too many people who are down and out."

Her identification with down-and-outers, her refusal to attempt to adopt highfalutin speech or airs, only increased and broadened her popular appeal. Adolph Zukor considered her just right for the early thirties. "Neither the sweet ingenue nor the glamour girl fit the depression years. Mae did. She was the strong confident woman, always in command."

More than one observer of Hollywood trends considered her better attuned to the American frame of mind in 1933 than such "languorous, exotic pretenders to the film throne" as Tallulah Bankhead, Garbo, or Marlene Dietrich. The fact that, by the summer of 1933, Mae West had broken all box-office records set by Garbo and Dietrich seemed to confirm her high ranking. "Mae fits the temper of the times," mused a writer for a fan magazine. "This is the day of directness, honesty, 'facing things' . . . Tallulah Bankhead has retreated to the stage, Marlene talks of leaving the U.S." Elza Schallert concurred.

> Mae West [she wrote] is the first real Waterloo of the Garbo and Dietrich schools of sultry, languorous, erotic emotions. Because she has made them appear slightly foolish—as if they didn't know how to get a 'kick' out of life. Her healthy, Amazonian, audacious presentation of the ancient appeal of sex has made the world-weary, secretive charm of Greta and Marlene appear feeble by comparison . . . She spells absolute doom to the hollow-eyed, sunken-cheeked, flat-chested, hipless exponents of the neurotic.

A cartoon in the humor magazine *Life* pictured an emaciated, stick-figured Garbo being encouraged by a bountiful Mae West: "Do your exercises, dearie, you'll get there."

Mae believed that her abundant figure appealed to people because it conveyed optimism and plenitude. The leanness born of scarcity and deprivation gave way, in her person, to a vision of opulent indulgence. "My corseted silhouette," she mused in an article about her impact on fashion that was published in *Vogue*, "what is it but a return to normal, the ladies' way of saying the depression is over?" Trend watchers in Paris and New York took note of a new fashion frenzy. The hourglass figure was "in" again. Hips, busts, and cinched waists made a comeback. "Today everybody is wearing everything à la Mae West, from diamond shoe buckles to false bosoms. She has become a furor."

Every star, Mae West remarked, starts something new: "Garbo and her 'I Won't Talk.' Clara Bow and her 'It.' Marlene Dietrich and her trousers. Katharine Hepburn and her weird mannerisms. Well, curves would be something new in talkies." And Mae West spelled curves that were wedded to wisecracks delivered in a nasal drawl redolent of New York.

She won the day as the perfect Depression diva, a human antidepressant, tough, round, upbeat, funny, financially ascendant, but still in touch with a past that included struggle, hard times. She could make you forget your troubles, without asking you to deny your roots, your sexuality, or how good the lush life looks. Like her Lady Lou, she reminds you that she wasn't always rich; she can remember back to the days when the wolf was not only at the door but "when he came into my room and had pups." With her common touch and air of complete assurance, she encourages: If I could make it, so can you.

She sensed that her unapologetic, self-mocking sinfulness increased her appeal, and that her comic approach to sex defused it of menace. "The very best thing that I have done for the public during this depression has been the humorous manner—even ribald sometimes—in which I have treated sex. My fight has been against depression, repression and suppression." The public preferred funny miscreants to sourpussed goody-goodies, anyhow. She said she admired good women, but you never hear about them. "The only good girl to make history was Betsy Ross, and she had to sew up a flag to do it." There were some who could break the rules yet always come out on top. The worse they behaved, the better you liked them. "No, the wages of sin in all cases is not death."

The only actor in Hollywood she claimed kinship with was screen tough guy Jimmy Cagney, Mr. Public Enemy, another slangy, brash, street-smart New Yorker. "My style and technique are like Jimmy Cagney's," she said. "He's a big hit because he's different. He's fresh and he's got nerve . . . I give them a character with . . . no hooey. A real woman who is honest and fearless and expects no more from life than what she has put into it . . . She's never yellow . . . I deal with the fundamental things in life . . . Love, Life, Sex. That's what I'm talking about."

Mary Pickford, America's former sweetheart and the ex-wife of actor Owen Moore (Chick Clark in *She Done Him Wrong*), made it clear that she walked on the other side of Mae West's street. She took exception to the song Ralph Rainger wrote for Mae West to sing in *She Done Him Wrong*, the one called "A Guy What Takes His Time." Rainger, who wrote "Moanin' Low" for Libby Holman and "Hot Voodoo" for Marlene Dietrich,

may have been thinking of Ida Cox's "One Hour Mama" ("I want a slow
and easy man ... / 'Cause I work on that long time plan") when he wrote
these words for Mae West to torch in Gus Jordan's saloon:

> *A guy what takes his time*
> *I'll go for any time*
> *I'm a fast movin' gal*
> *I like them slow*
> *Got no use for fancy drivin'*
> *Wanna see a guy arrivin' in low.*
> *I'd be satisfied, electrified,*
> *To know a guy what takes his time.*

Mae felt so close to this lyric that when she bought three racehorses, she
named one Take Your Time. She subsequently declined an invitation to
appear before a group called the Los Angeles Minute Men, explaining that
she liked a guy what takes his time.

When Mary Pickford passed by the door to the room of her seventeen-
year-old niece—a young woman who had been raised "oh, so carefully"—
and heard the niece singing bits from "A Guy What Takes His Time"
(which was released on a Brunswick record label soon after the movie's
premiere), she saw, and turned, red. Pickford couldn't even bring herself
to repeat the ditty's name: "I say 'that song' because I blush to quote the
title."

That particular lyric rankled censors as well. Dr. Wingate of the Hays
Office found it "very lowtoned" and anticipated that it would spur "objections ... and censorship difficulties." He proved correct. After several
states—New York, Pennsylvania, Ohio, Maryland, and Massachusetts—
deleted the song, Paramount was moved to cut the two middle stanzas, one
hundred feet of film in the sixth reel: "This reduces the song ... to an
entrance by Mae West, one opening and one closing verse, eliminating the
scene of the woman pickpocket and the pianist ogling the singer."

Great Britain scuttled shots of the nude painting, and most of the celebrated, quotable lines, including: "One of the finest women ever walked the
streets." "A little spicy, but not too raw." "When women go wrong, men
go right after them." And "Why don't you come up sometime, huh? Come
up, I'll tell your fortune."

Pennsylvania made many of these same cuts, adding to the list of outtakes
Lou's line to Rita concerning her new assistant Serge, "Day or night work,

Rita?" And Flynn to Lou: "You can't expect to go around getting men all on fire and think they're going to forget all about it." The Pennsylvania state censors objected to Lou's "Sure, lots of times" in answer to Cummings's question about whether she's ever met a man that can make her happy. And they clipped "Hands ain't everything," a line also scissored out in Kansas and Virginia.

Java, Latvia, and Australia rejected the film outright. Vienna suppressed it, claiming in its semiofficial *Reichspost* that the picture amounted to "nothing but uncouth and clumsy eroticism, appealing to the basest instincts." At the same time, box offices in London and Paris were besieged by eager ticket buyers.

Back in the U.S.A., the picture's phenomenal impact only heightened the dudgeon of bluenoses, some of whom held positions of power within the movie industry. Sidney Kent, a member of the board of directors of the MPPDA (Motion Picture Producers and Distributors of America) and president of Fox Films, dispatched an outraged letter to General Will Hays. "I went last night to see the Mae West picture, *She Done Him Wrong*," it began.

> In my opinion it is the worst picture I have seen. It was the real story of Diamond Lil and they got away with it. They promised that that story would not be made. I believe it is worse than [Jean Harlow in] *Red Headed Woman* from the standpoint of the industry—it is far more suggestive in word and what is not said is suggested in action.
>
> I cannot understand how your people on the Coast could let this get by. There is very little that any of us can do now. I think the place to have done anything was at the source.

Kent's admonition that the place to stop suggestive movies was "at the source"—while the picture was being made, not after its release—sounded an ominous and, as it turned out, prophetic note.

The outcry by Father Daniel Lord, the Catholic priest who had written much of the Production Code, made Kent's salvo seem temperate. Lord charged that *She Done Him Wrong*, "which everybody knows is the filthy Diamond Lil slipping by under a new name," was a total violation of his code.

Hays defended himself, saying he had done his best to keep *Diamond Lil* off the screen. While admitting that the picture "illustrates every one" of the problems his office faced, he voiced some sympathy for Paramount's economic fragility, which had pushed them to gamble on Mae West. He informed Father Lord that *She Done Him Wrong* was breaking box-office records, and that it had been almost "unanimously hailed" as a "splendid comedy" by reviewers.

"Unanimous" isn't quite right. There were some negative reviews, notably from *Variety*, which sourly declared that the "only alternative to a strong drawing cast nowadays, if a picture wants business, is strong entertainment. This one has neither." The review praised director Sherman for holding Mae West in check, keeping her from going too far, "something Mae has never been able to do on her own," but faulted the leading lady for wearing "so much jewelry she looks like a knickerbocker ice house," and hogging "all the lens gravy." Conceding that "Mae West couldn't sing a lullaby without making it sexy," it mocked the pretense that the role she played was anything but that of Diamond Lil: "Nothing much changed except the title, but don't tell that to Will Hays."

The New York Times forgave Mae West for carrying off "a remarkably suspicious impersonation of Diamond Lil," since she managed, in doing so, to "fill the screen with gaudy humor," creating "a hearty and blustering cinematic cartoon."

A review in the trade publication *Motion Picture Herald*, whose publisher and editor, the conservative lay Catholic leader Martin Quigley, had co-authored the code, was surprisingly restrained: "The film is lively, contrives to be amusing . . . but is rather several degrees south of the lower limit of propriety." Instead of condemning the picture outright, it advised discretion. "The individual exhibitor will have to decide for himself whether he can afford to run the film . . . [which] spares the feelings of no Ladies' Aid Society."

Coming from a very different place, Cy Caldwell, in *The New Outlook*, expressed the undiluted delight of a long-time burlesque fan:

I am happy to report that Lil, or Lou, shines with her accustomed brilliance, one of the finest women that ever walked the streets. As an actress Mae West is a refreshing and healthy change from the slinky dopey foreigners and the simpering little home-grown chits to whom we of the older, or early burlesque era have grown accustomed but not resigned. I want to advise youse gents what used to imbibe culture at the fount presided over by Billy B. Watson and his Beef Trust Beauties, that here is something for you to see and enjoy to the limit. As for you, Aunt Effie, I think that you'll love it, but won't admit it.

The Hollywood Reporter actually congratulated Paramount "for whole-heartedly thumbing its nose at Haysiana and going ahead with *Diamond Lil*—which really wears no disguise at all in *She Done Him Wrong*." So long as kids were kept away from the picture, it had no difficulty recommending the film as "swell entertainment—of a very low variety." Sure, it was "steeped in sin and sex—BUT it is plenty funny."

Unstinting praise issued from William Troy of *The Nation*, a Mae West and Diamond Lil enthusiast. "The picture," he put it, "which owes every-thing to Miss West's versatile talents, is astonishing entertainment." Other celebrants included *The New Yorker*, which applauded *She Done Him Wrong* as one of the great comedies from a year in need of "all the laughs one can squeeze out of it," and *The* (London) *Times*, which lauded Mae West's "amazing vitality and air of self-conscious insolence." Critic Rob Wagner pronounced Mae West "as gorgeous as Lillian Russell," with "more IT than Clara at her Bowest." He said if he were king, he'd "show [the film] in the schools as a picture of robust and healthy entertainment that would cheer up the children of these out-of-joint times."

Mae West's victory with *She Done Him Wrong* amounted to more than the sum of glowing reviews, a publicity blitz, and terrific box office. The stardom she achieved brought admission to the celebrity firmament. Mae West became a mythic figure, as she put it, a household word, and "a star seen in the third person, even by myself . . . More people had seen me than saw Napoleon, Lincoln and Cleopatra. I was better known than Ein-stein, Shaw or Picasso." She was compared, appropriately, to a Disney cartoon. "It will not be at all surprising," J. C. Furnas wrote, "when Miss West's name and face are as popular a commercial trademark as Mickey Mouse's."

An animated film turned her into an actual cartoon. In a Krazy Kat short, "Whacks Museum," she's a wax figure (like the one she would shortly in-spire at Madame Tussaud's in London) who goes up in flames and begins to melt while singing "Frankie and Johnny," igniting a fire in the waxworks which Krazy Kat tries to extinguish. Soon she would inspire the Betty Boop cartoon "She Wronged Him Right." In 1935 Disney would use her as the model for ample-breasted Jenny Wren in "Who Killed Cock Robin?" and he would include her caricature in "Mickey's Polo Team" three years later. The *Los Angeles Times* published James Montgomery Flagg's cartoon drawing of an imaginary encounter between Mae West and George Bernard Shaw, a recent visitor to Hollywood; it shows Mae West yanking Shaw's beard.

Mae West was photographed in her diamonds by Steichen for *Vanity Fair*.

Her face was used in an ad selling Lux soap, adjoining images of Carole Lombard and Claudette Colbert. She was marketed to girls as a paper doll. You couldn't escape her.

She Done Him Wrong hatched a mini-craze for movies set in the Bowery, or another city's equally raucous tenderloin, in the 1890s: *The Bowery*, *Barbary Coast*, and *Diamond Jim Brady* followed in rapid succession. Not every studio had a Mae West, but everyone hoped to cash in on her vogue.

Even an anonymous schoolboy in Waldo, Kansas, tried to benefit from the Mae West boom. It was reported in *Photoplay* that, when asked why he had signed his math paper "Mae West," he answered, "Because I done 'em wrong."

Paramount, wanting to ride the crest, sought another Mae West picture before the year's end. They briefly considered attempting a version of *Sex*, but rejected the idea almost immediately when they learned the play had sent Mae West to jail. Trial balloons floated about a picture to be called *Don't Call Me Madame* and another titled *The Golden Soubrette*; both came a cropper.

When Mae turned up at the Barnes Circus in Los Angeles in May, accompanied by photographers and two hundred orphans for whom she was throwing a party, she set off rumors: her next picture, the guessing went, would have something to do with the circus.

15

AT THE TOP OF THE LADDER

*T*HE American countenance brightened in the interval between the release of *She Done Him Wrong* and the filming of Mae West's next feature: Hoover's sour expression was displaced by FDR's infectious grin. The Republican Hoover administration's paralysis gave way as the New Deal declared war on the Depression, and a climate of optimism (punctuated with outbursts of panic), activism, and reform prevailed. The Democratic Roosevelt era began, spearheaded by a take-charge leader determined to banish that greatest of all bugaboos, "fear itself," and pledged to a credo of caring. "We cannot merely take but we must give as well," said Roosevelt as he took office.

People compared Roosevelt to Napoleon sweeping his army across France. In his first hundred days, Roosevelt closed and reopened the banks, took the country off the gold standard, delivered two "fireside chats" over the radio, made ten major speeches, met with his "braintrust," and pushed through fifteen major relief and recovery laws.

In Hollywood and New York, nobody knew quite how the new administration would affect the financially shaky movie industry. A series of Payne Fund Studies, popularized in Henry James Forman's book *Our Movie Made Children*, had alerted concerned parents, women's clubs, educators, editorial writers, and church activists to an alleged link between adolescent moviegoing and subsequent criminal conduct or "sex delinquency." Perhaps, the moguls and others within the industry feared, the present climate of reform under the New Deal would invite government regulation, a Washington-based crackdown on cinema "immorality."

Federal interference was the last thing the industry's own censors at the Hays Office wanted. The evening after Roosevelt's inauguration, Hays, a former Republican national chairman, called an emergency meeting of the

MPPDA Board of Directors, at which he pushed for and got a reaffirmation of the objectives, prohibitions, and constraints of the Production Code. Only by more rigorous enforcement of the code, only by cleaning up its own house, he insisted, could the industry keep government at bay and appease mounting demands for moral rectitude in the movies. Dr. Wingate was asked to tighten the reins of control, and a man named Joseph Breen, an Irish Catholic zealot and former newspaperman destined to become Mae West's arch antagonist, was elevated to a position of prominence on the Hays Office's Studio Relations Committee.

Government regulation seemed imminent with the passage, in June 1933, of the National Industrial Recovery Act. Symbolized by the blue-eagle emblem and popularized with the slogan "We Do Our Part," the NRA empowered each industry in the country to draw up its own code of practices governing hours, wages, working conditions, and the like. In general, hours were to be shortened and wages increased for the lowest paid but leveled off for those at the top.

Under the NRA, the film industry set up a thirty-six-hour production week, tried to curb excessive salaries, prohibited one producer from enticing another's employee, and attempted to establish guidelines for the relationship between artists, agents, and producers. Efforts to reduce the exorbitant salaries some stars received went nowhere; the newly formed Screen Actors Guild saw to that. Guild president Eddie Cantor told the press that Mae West, a recent Guild recruit, was bringing millions to the studio and was certainly worth the $5,000 a week she received.

The NRA code for moviemakers touched on matters of morality and threatened to encroach on Hays Office turf when it proposed a clause pledging industrywide commitment to maintaining "the right moral standards in the production of motion pictures." Although the NRA morals clause for movies remained vague (and in any case was invalidated, along with the entire National Recovery Act, by the Supreme Court in 1935), it intensified the pressure on the Hays Office to crack down.

Paramount had every reason to want to rush Mae West into production and release her next picture before the ax fell.

After the break-the-bank success of She Done Him Wrong, the studio seemed to be eating out of Mae West's hand. Her new picture would be budgeted at $25,000 beyond the amount of her first starrer and would feature a director who had directed Valentino and Clara Bow, and more recently had been nominated for an Academy Award, Wesley Ruggles. Its song lyrics, at

Mae West's insistence, would be written by Ben Ellison (with Gladys DuBois) instead of Paramount's original choice, Sam Coslow. It would benefit from the talents of Paramount's top-drawer costume designer, Travis Banton, who would produce a closetful of luxurious creations for the star. Banton, when designing for Mae West, developed and stuck to a proven formula: "Diamonds—lots of 'em and huge hats, feather boas, fox stoles and vertical panels of light material or brilliants, with darker side panels to slim her down."

Banton had postponed his first meeting with Mae West for as long as possible, out of nervousness about what she might say when she discovered that he was the nephew of her old *bête noire*, Joab Banton, the New York district attorney responsible for sending her to jail for *Sex*. When the dreaded moment arrived, she expressed more amusement than rancor, telling Travis Banton she wished she'd known him "when the fireworks were going off" and praising his uncle as "a fine gentleman" who was "only doing his duty. I don't hold any hard feelings."

Although her contract, drawn up when she signed for *She Done Him Wrong*, kept her salary fixed at about $100,000, of which $25,000 was for her work on the script, the real payoff entailed capitulation to her wishes, letting her have her way. When Mae decided she had a better idea than the one Paramount had already announced for her next movie, a story about the career of Louise Montague titled *Barnum's Million Dollar Beauty*, the studio gave her the nod: anything to keep the lady happy.

Lowell Brentano, the writer and publisher who had once hoped to publish her novel *The Constant Sinner*, showed up backstage at the New York Paramount Theater while Mae was appearing there with *She Done Him Wrong*, and when she told him her next movie would have a circus theme, and reminded him of her lifelong dream of becoming a lion tamer, he gratified her promptly by presenting to her a treatment for a script, *The Lion and the Lady*. Paramount hired two writers, Frank Butler and Claude Binyon, to help develop the script, but Mae had them fired in short order, claiming they were not making her part tough enough. She did accept help from "continuity" writer Harlan Thompson (who actually wrote much of the script and some of the dialogue credited to Mae West), and with him put together a treatment and first draft for what became *I'm No Angel*. Harlan Thompson's wife resentfully commented: "How much she contributed I don't know, but she moved in, as she always moved in on everything, and got credit for the story, the screenplay and dialogue."

Psychologically, and in most other respects, the picture belongs to Mae

West. To put herself at ease on the set, she insisted on the presence of Jim Timony and his current roommate at the Ravenswood, Boris Petroff, who was described as her "style advisor." She hired friends and former associates for acting parts: Dan Makarenko, with whom she'd once appeared on vaudeville bills, took the role of ringmaster at $300 a week, and Ed Hearn, a female impersonator who had appeared in *Pleasure Man*, was cast as a courtroom spectator. Her real-life maid, Libby Taylor, portrayed one of the four black maids with whom she banters and kids on screen. Gregory Ratoff, a cousin of sister Beverly's soon-to-be husband, Vladimir Baikoff, was hired to play the New York lawyer Benny Pinkowitz.

She slipped many references to her own life—some obvious, others coded and disguised—into the dialogue and action; *I'm No Angel*, filmed in the weeks before and after her fortieth birthday, sustains a powerful autobiographical undercurrent. The movie works as a kind of cinematic *apologia pro vita sua*.

Begin with the opening carnival scene: the barker might have been lifted whole from outside Little Egypt's tent at Coney Island during Mae's littlegirlhood. An outdoor crowd of raucous men gets primed to view the beautiful Tira (Mae West), "dancing, singing marvel of the age. Supreme Flower of feminine pulchritude, the girl who discovered you don't have to have feet to be a dancer." The spieler's pitch resembles the one Mae West once used to advertise her suggestive "muscle dances" and the undulating hootchy-kootch effects of her early turns in vaudeville, during the years when Yale students rioted and cranky naysayers urged her, "a wiggly sort of rough soubret," back to burlesque. Burlesque certainly comes to mind as Tira slowly gyrates, clad in a Salome costume with sequined circles and spokes on her breasts, tasseled nipples, a partially sheer midriff, and a fringed, transparent shawl to drape over her lower face and slowly swaying torso. "She'll throw discretion to the winds, and her hips North, East, South and West," the spieler promises, recalling words spoken during the *Sex* trial. "Yes, sir, boys, she can assume shapes that would astonish a chiropractor. Next to her a wiggling worm looks paralyzed . . . And now—Tira! The girl who makes your dreams come true."

Dr. Wingate objected to a few lines in the barker's buildup: "She'd give the old biological urge to a Civil War veteran" and "The only girl who has satisfied more patrons than Chesterfields" had to go. (Mae used the second line years later on a Perry Como radio program.) The band of black musicians indicated in the first script was changed to all white. Although other cuts were demanded or suggested, in general, Wingate told Hays, "the script submitted contained no particularly objectionable sex scenes." Other current movies—like *The Story of Temple Drake*—were considered far more offensive to standards of decency, and provoked more outrage at the Hays Office, at this moment, than *I'm No Angel.*

I'm No Angel's opening sequence of close-ups and wide panning shots of the sweaty stag crowd ogling Tira betrays unmistakable contempt for men in heat. There's a shot of a silly-looking geezer with lust in his eyes (he winks) and the words "Oh Mama" on his lips; another of a man smiling grossly and eating rudely, with something white and disgusting all over his mouth as he pronounces Tira "elegant." These men, neither handsome nor young, muscular nor masterful, offer no competition to the hunky acrobat (Nat Pendleton) who inspires Tira's comment, a carryover from *The Constant Sinner*, "I'm not gonna hurt him; I only want to feel his muscles." Rather, they're randy, childish simpletons who can readily devolve into brutes. (A line cut out of the script has Tira saying, "That's all, boys. Now you can go home and beat your wives.") Tira manipulates and controls her male fans ("Am I making myself clear, boys?") the way she later controls the lions, but with no need for the gun or whip that she uses to subdue the big cats. Her muttered wisecracks, her always moving face and body, as she deploys them, do the trick.

Her conviction that men are beasts gets developed and reinforced later when we see that she keeps a menagerie of ceramic figurines of animals in her room, each one corresponding to the photograph of another man in her life. Her boss at the carnival, Bill Barton, is a skunk; socialite Kirk Lawrence is a stag; pickpocket Slick a snake; an anonymous someone a frog.

As she sings "a lowdown, hot number," "They Call Me Sister Honky Tonk," that tags her as "a devil in disguise," we hear a guy call out, "If I wasn't a married man, I could go for you, baby." Under her breath, Tira calls the whole bunch of leering Toms "suckers."

That epithet echoes Texas Guinan's famous nightclub greeting, "Hello, Suckers," another way for Mae West to covertly summon her own past—although when Guinan breezed through town during the filming of *I'm No Angel* Mae offended her, never stopping by or calling Guinan's hotel to say hello. Guinan had given Mae a party in Chicago, during the personal appearances tour for *She Done Him Wrong*. Now Mae had no time for her old pal, inspiration, and cohort in the wisecrack hall of fame. The fact that Guinan's former manager and boyfriend, Harry Voiler, had robbed Mae of jewelry and cash soon after she arrived in Hollywood did nothing to revive friendly feelings. Had Mae known that she wouldn't have another chance—

that Guinan would be dead in a few months—perhaps she would have made time to see her.

If the men at the carnival are suckers of one sort, the silk-hat types Tira attracts when she plays New York are equally helpless before her, but far more attractive and sympathetic. Aristocratic Kirk Lawrence (Kent Taylor) pursues her with expensive gifts—diamonds, furs, and Paris gowns. His millionaire cousin Jack Clayton (Cary Grant), always elegantly turned out in a tailored suit or a tux, ends up writing her a check for $100,000, which she tears up in a fleeting effort to convince us that love has come to supersede crass material concerns. (An earlier, more believable version of this incident had her pretend to tear up the check, while surreptitiously pocketing it.)

The Cary Grant and Kent Taylor characters don't correspond to types Mae West privately fancied, unless you count her brief fling, after her break with Deiro, with the wealthy and well-connected Chicagoan she called "Rex." Rather, they recycle the patrician, rich-and-handsome suitors in Mae West's imagination—her fantasy plot—and in her plays: Reggie Muchcash in *The Ruby Ring*, Bob Van Sturdivant in *The Hussy*, Jimmy Stanton in *Sex*, Wayne Baldwin in *The Constant Sinner*. In the plays, as in *I'm No Angel*, the prospect of union with a man of high social standing boosts the status of the lowlife Mae West character, who is bent on success that can buy opulence. Contrasts between high and low life— she even sings, "I'm high, I'm low"—lie at the core of both Tira's story and Mae West's own.

Also carried over from the plays is the jealous, hoity-toity female society type who puts down the Mae West character as "common" and has a proprietary interest in a man who falls for Mae. In the plays (*The Hussy*, *Sex*) this ritzy, venomous woman was usually the man's mother; in *I'm No Angel* she's Alicia Hatton (Gertrude Michael), engaged to Kirk Lawrence and about the same age as Tira. Alicia calls Tira "crude" and "ill-bred"; why fuss so, she asks her rich friends, over an "ordinary" circus performer? "She's obviously a person of the commonest sort . . . Men all have low minds and she's low enough to appeal to them." An exchange that was cut has Alicia sarcastically ask Tira if she's from Radcliffe. "No," snarls Tira, "Ninth Avenue."

When Alicia tries to buy her off, Tira shoves her out the door, having already spit water on her back in an earlier scene. (Wingate wanted to cut the spitting, but didn't succeed.) Tira, insisting she's the one who's really a lady (her reference to Alicia as a "tart" was cut), sneers, "A better dame than you once called me a liar and they had to sew her up in twelve different places. You're lucky I'm a little more refined than I used to be." Though she now keeps her violent impulses under wraps (a song that was cut had her singing, "Got my gun in my holster/Got my whip in my hand"), no snob can high-hat her and get away with it.

Just like Mae's, Tira's fortunes rise; she moves "from a tent to a penthouse," a high-class apartment decked out with works of art on the walls, a grand piano, modern furnishings, and gigantic floral arrangements. Socialites seek her out. Maids surround her, unwrap the expensive gifts male admirers have sent, fuss over her hair, fingernails, and wardrobe, as she sings, "Gimme my fine furs and fancy gowns/I found a new way to go to town." Her advice to the lovelorn Thelma, with whom she generously shares some of her bounty, is "Take all you can get and give as little as possible," not exactly a New Deal sentiment. Never look back, she advises. "Find 'em, fool 'em and forget 'em." Climb the ladder of success, as the ads would claim Tira did, "wrong by wrong."

As in *She Done Him Wrong*, the character Mae plays merges moral, as well as social, extremes. She's both bad and good ("I've got the face of a saint"), she-devil and angel with clipped wings. Reversing the meaning of "bad" the way hipster slang does, Tira tells Clayton, "When I'm good I'm very good, but when I'm bad I'm better."

The "bad" Tira, like Diamond Lil, has consorted with criminals. In this instance it's a sneering pickpocket named Slick Wiley (Ralf Harolde). At the time we meet Tira, when she's working as a kootch dancer at Barton's cheap carnival, she and Slick seem to have a long-standing partnership that includes both work and play. He picks pockets as she entertains—and they share the ease that accompanies prolonged familiarity. She baits men who look as if they have things worth stealing, and he robs them. But after enticing a "Chump" named Ernest Brown (William Davidson) who flashes a diamond ring, Tira rips into Slick for busting in on them in her room just when things were getting cozy and the Chump was about to pledge money to her show. Slick knocks the Chump out by slamming his head with a liquor bottle. They take the Chump for dead, and Tira chides Slick for implicating her in a murder and stealing from the dead. Tira gives Slick the slip. She's got her eye on richer game. "Somewhere there's a guy with a million waiting for a dame like me."

Tira's ascent, her upward turn of fortune, has been predicted. Mae's off-screen reliance on spiritual advisers is represented in the movie via Tira's visit to a fortune-teller, Rajah (Nigel de Brulier), who tells her she was born

in August, described by Tira as "one of the hot months." Tira gives August
17 as her birthday, the same as Mae West's, and learns she was born under
the sign of Leo, King of Beasts. Rajah tells her as he gazes into his crystal
ball that she can look forward to a wonderful future; tomorrow will be very
lucky. "I see a man in your life," he foretells. Tira betrays disappointment:
"What, only one?" He then augurs a change of position. "Sitting or reclining?" she quips, but she knows he's speaking of a predicted improvement in
her social and financial standing; she will soon connect with a man of
enormous wealth. Rajah gives her her horoscope, which she says she plans
to take to bed with her.

Initially, Tira mistakes Kirk Lawrence for the dark-eyed millionaire the
Rajah has foreseen as the agent of her future wealth, telling him, "If you're
half the man I think you are, you'll do." Then, after Kirk's cousin Jack
Clayton intercedes, Tira realizes that Clayton's the one for her, not Kirk.
In the course of the movie, she switches partners multiple times: from Slick
to the Chump (that "Dallas man" who displaces a Memphis and a Frisco
man), to Kirk, and finally to her true love, the one she falls for "so hard it
hurts," Jack Clayton. There have been so many men in her life, she tells
one of her maids, she's thinking of putting in a filing system. (In an earlier
script, it was a filling station.) Sure, she's a one-man woman—"one at a
time." When Clayton says, "I wish I could trust you," she reassures him,
"Hundreds have."

She and Clayton become engaged. After she quits the circus, we actually
see Tira/Mae being fitted out in a bridal gown and veil (some fans might
remember that Banton had once designed the wedding gown in which Mary
Pickford married Douglas Fairbanks), although in an early scene she told
the Chump she would marry only as a last resort. When Clayton is tricked
into believing Tira is deceiving him with Slick, he breaks the engagement.
Tira then sues him for breach of promise, a charge he contests. The trial,
an oblique replay of Mae West's many days facing morals charges in New
York courts, turns into a defense of Tira's character and a vindication of
her past, although she protests, "I don't see what my past has got to do with
my present." She admits she's been the love interest in more than one guy's
life: "I'm the sweetheart of Sigma Chi, so what?" Right now "I'm doin' my
best to be legitimate."

She by-passes her lawyer and takes over her own defense, cross-examining
witnesses herself and proving that the men she's been with are the ones at
fault, not she, and that she has the smarts to show them up. Slick is exposed
as a predatory jailbird, the Chump as a man who cheats on his wife, Kirk

Lawrence as an engaged man who freely gave expensive gifts to a woman who was not his fiancée. When Tira's remarks in court, backed by the testimony of her maid Beulah, reveal that she still loves Clayton, Clayton drops the charges and admits defeat. She wins both the case and Clayton. Triumphant, she poses for press photos. Answering a woman reporter who asks about the number of men in her life, Tira sums up her situation with a quip that would become a much-repeated favorite: "It's not the men in my life, it's the life in my men."

The trial, which showcases Tira's quick wit, fearlessness, and mastery and power over men, in some ways parallels an earlier scene of triumph, the one where Tira enters the lions' cage in the circus and risks her life by placing her head in "the jaws of death"—one lion's mouth. As one critic put it, citing the similarity between court and cage, "Tira puts her fair head in a court of law."

When Tira agreed to enter that lions' cage and stick her head in the beast's mouth, an act never attempted "since Nero threw the Christians to the lions," she hit the big time, playing to a roaring crowd in New York's Madison Square Garden. Acting this scene allowed Mae to live out the enduring fantasy that was born during her childhood trips to Coney Island with her father to see Bostock's lions: "My father told me that the lion was the king of animals and the most beautiful and ferocious beast."

Mabel Stark, a real lion tamer in the Barnes and the Ringling Circuses, allowed Mae West to watch her in action and obligingly acted as coach. Another professional stood by on the set. On the day the scene with the lions was to be filmed, the director, the producer, and Paramount VP Al Kaufman all tried to dissuade the star from risking life and limb in the cage. They wanted to use a double. "They weren't gonna let me do it. The professional lion tamer couldn't be there because, just before, a lion had attacked him and he had to be taken to the hospital." She insisted on going ahead, riding into the circus ring on an elephant (Mae was wary of horses, boats, and airplanes, but could ride an elephant boldly) and entering the lions' cage. Marksmen took their places nearby, ready to shoot any lion on the attack.

Dressed in white silk tights, white boots, a tall white plumed hat, and a military jacket trimmed with gold braid, Mae cracks her whip and shoots her pistol (her violent proclivities aren't *that* remote) into the air until the lions settle down on their stands. "The lions were wonderful. They were nervous though . . . but I wasn't. I was thrilled. I was able to stand my ground and dominate those big male lions." Mae's account of how she felt in the cage lends the experience a decided erotic charge: "I could see nothing, hear nothing, feel nothing but an overpowering sense of increasing mastery that mounted higher and higher until it gratified every atom of the obsession that had driven me."

The masculinity of the lions wasn't part of the original idea. An early script has Tira call one "Sheba." Since Tira has to show she tames lions in the same way she does men, "Sheba" became "Big Boy." Tira addresses other lions as "you mug," "Handsome," and "Romeo."

Although several observers insist that Mae really did put her head in the lion's mouth, and publicists quoted her saying, "Now I know how Jonah felt when he slipped down the gullet of that whale," Mae indicated to John Kobal that it was a trick shot involving a stand-in, a sedated beast, or both. "They wouldn't let me put my head in the lion's mouth, though I wanted to."

At times during filming, the set took on the aspect of a zoo. In addition to the elephant Tira rides and the lions she tames, a little South African woolly monkey was present and allowed his moment on screen in one of Tira's boudoir scenes. He was Mae West's pet monkey, Boogey, one of a series of pet monkeys on whom she lavished affection. Stanley Musgrove, who as her publicist became a good friend, said, "She says she never wanted to be a mother, but you should see her with her pet monkeys. She calls them 'baby' and calls herself 'mama' and cuddles them like kids."

Cary Grant's dog, Archibald (Grant's real given name), also frequented the set, and Boogey became attached to the canine. Grant recalled: "Mae held up the entire production while the dog thrust his nose between the bars of the monkey's cage and that monk kissed and fondled my dog." Mae enjoyed the scene and paid scant attention to the huge production costs which were mounting every minute.

Boogey provides the key to one of Tira's most-quoted lines. After Tira slams the door on Alicia Hatton, she coolly saunters back into her penthouse and addresses her maid with words that ratify her new high-class status: "Beulah, peel me a grape." The line works without need of the explanation that Boogey, a fastidious creature, loved grapes but never ate one before peeling it, or having someone else peel it for him.

The set of *I'm No Angel* felt friendlier, less tense than that of *She Done Him Wrong*. Director Wesley Ruggles, in contrast to Lowell Sherman, found positive things to say about his leading lady. Partly because she worked out daily with a trainer, Jim Davies, she astonished him with her vigor, fitness, and physical strength. Ruggles said, "She has twice the energy and physical stamina of any other actress." He praised her perfectionism and high performance standards, which could border on the excessive: "She rehearsed one of her songs eighteen times," although Ruggles had okayed the sixth.

She wowed two of the men who court her in the movie, Kent Taylor, who played Kirk Lawrence, and the actor who played the Chump, William B. Davidson. Davidson said she was "full of dynamite. Sure, I fell for her hook, line and sinker . . . I would almost leave my happy home for her." Kent Taylor seemed equally smitten: "She is even more delicious off the screen than on. I would gladly work for her for nothing." Taylor found her helpful, too, willing to point out how and why a scene could be done better. He added that her screen loving "really gets to you."

Cary Grant, as you might expect, sounded a much cooler, more detached note, announcing that he was not in love with Miss West, nor she with him. He kidded, "Well, it was very pleasant to be done wrong twice in the same place," and again hinted that he found Mae West a somewhat overwhelming presence: "I have never worked with anyone who has as much 'she' as Miss West." He described her as "extremely helpful" in the love scenes, during which it sometimes became difficult to realize that she was only acting. Although some of their scenes together were in fact shot separately, with first Mae West, then Cary Grant sweet-talking the camera at different times, in others they embraced and touched.

Whether because a Paramount publicist told him to, to advance his own career, or out of genuine regard for her, Cary Grant wrote, or at least signed his name to, a series of articles on Mae for the British *Picturegoer*, depicting her as a fighter who had struggled against contumely and a diligent worker totally dedicated to her career. He saw her success in films as a vindication, and the greatest triumph any film actress had known in their generation. And he likened her to such luminaries from the past as Sarah Bernhardt, Lillian Russell, Lillie Langtry, and Modjeska. Today she was "more talked about even than Garbo." He quotes Will Rogers to the effect that "Mae West has taught all these other actresses in Hollywood how to act."

" 'I have never gone hungry,' " he quotes her as saying, " 'or walked the tracks when stranded . . . but I *have* worked twenty hours a day, many times.' " His Mae West is one who has rehearsed for twelve hours at a stretch, and then lain in bed for hours more repeating, improvising, even adding new lines and business. She has "sacrificed everything" for her career, passing up good times and travel, because she found herself on a "fascinating merry-go-round" and wanted to know where it would carry her. She was a believer in fate and destiny, but knew with certainty that her good fortune had not come accidentally. Her whole life had been an orderly sequence of events leading up to it.

Mae's professionalism, savvy, and earthy sense of fun endeared her to Marlene Dietrich, who occupied the adjacent dressing room at Paramount and sometimes watched—joined by Maurice Chevalier on at least one occasion—while Mae rehearsed a song. Dietrich honored her in her memoir as "a teacher, no, a rock to which I clung, an intelligent woman who understood me and divined all my problems." At that time Mae was probably unaware of her importance to Dietrich.

Dietrich surely must have learned about Mae's German mother, but the sense of kinship went beyond nationality. Both performers could comment on themselves as they worked; each could see herself at a remove, as "she." Each recognized the link between vamping and camping, and each flaunted a masculine side, although Mae West didn't like to clothe hers in man-tailored suits or trousers.

Gossip writers for newspapers and fan magazines tried to drum up a jealous rivalry between the two Paramount queens. When Dietrich returned from a trip to Europe and was asked her opinion of Mae West, the press reported that she answered, "Who is she? I never heard of her." Dietrich insisted she had never said these things; that, rather, she had been asked to comment on Mae West's influence on fashion and had professed ignorance of "Mae West fashions." She insisted she harbored only the warmest, most positive feelings toward her sister actress: "When I saw the preview of *She Done Him Wrong*, I was thrilled by this new, arresting, dynamic personality . . . I recognized Miss West as a star before anyone else did. I met her before I left for Europe and we became friends."

Mae West, for her part, denied holding any negative sentiments or impressions. "Miss Dietrich is too intelligent to show any jealousy toward me, even if she felt it—and I know she doesn't. We aren't at all alike on the screen. She used to come into my dressing room and tell me how she and her daughter, Maria, played my songs at home." As for Miss Dietrich's professed ignorance of Mae West fashions, stuff and nonsense. "Why, she wore them herself in her last picture, *Song of Songs*. I even heard that she wore my corset so she could show the Mae West curves." Paramount's wardrobe department insisted that Dietrich's corset had been made especially for Dietrich.

Dietrich's daughter Maria (now Maria Riva), who often joined her mother on the lot, sensed an unusual ease between the two stars and was surprised that they never saw each other outside the studio. Mae West was one of the few who could get away with entering Dietrich's dressing room, knocking as she came in. She'd comment, "Not bad, honey—not bad at ALL," about one of Dietrich's revealing costumes. Mae worked out in her mind a division of the female form, bestowing honors for the upper, bosomy portion on herself, for the lower, leggy half on Dietrich: "You give 'em the bottom and I'll give 'em the top." Riva remembers that Mae once took one of her breasts out of the whalebone corset, for all to wonder at. If we had to worry only about appealing to men, instead of to women as well, she explained, "all I'd have to do is take 'em out."

The bisexual Dietrich may have interpreted the display of a breast as a sexual come-on. If so, she totally misread Mae West, who professed no attraction to women and who extended to lesbians none of the goodwill she showed to male homosexuals. In her book on sex, health, and ESP, Mae evinces shock at the behavior of a Hollywood "glamour girl" who entered her dressing room one morning when she was washing her hair. "I turned off the water and felt a towel being placed on my head, then hands moving it . . . I still didn't know who the hands belonged to, and when I turned around I was surprised to see this girl staring at me, wearing nothing but a flimsy robe. 'You're better button up, dearie,' I said. 'You're going to catch a cold.' " Many have concluded that the "glamour girl" was Dietrich.

Dietrich's efforts to stay in touch in later years were shunned. Robert Duran, a close associate, helper, and friend to Mae West in the last decades of her life, recalled that Dietrich once telephoned, wanting to drop by at the Ravenswood to say hello. Mae answered, pretending to be Beverly, as she often did when she didn't want to talk to someone. "Beverly" said Mae West was away.

It's eerie to think that Mae and her sister traded identities so freely. Beverly went on tour in November 1933 with an all-female troupe and a routine in which she imitated her sister, a task for which she felt herself uniquely qualified: "Who is more familiar with her every little mannerism than I?" Mae urged the public to "come up and see my sister." In truth, they had only one identity between them: Mae West's.

Mae's work schedule left little room for diversions of any kind. She'd brought her brother, Jack, and sister, Beverly, to join her in Los Angeles, and they, with Timony, dominated a private life that left her feeling constricted. "I ain't had time to have a personal life," she complained to Ruth Biery. "My life is just the same routine every day. I see my manager and my brother and my maid and my chauffeur. The studio calls up early in the mornin' and late in the night to see how I'm comin' with my story. I'm like a machine."

Although she took lovers—Gary Cooper, she hinted, was one; bodyguard Mike Mazurki another—Timony kept watch, putting a cap on the degree of attachment permitted and the amount of time she could spend with a particular man. (She never spent the entire night in the same bed with anyone, by her own preference.) Mae had enough insight to recognize that Timony, limping behind her wherever she went like a devoted police dog, now functioned as her mother once had: "My mother wouldn't let me learn to really love . . . and now Timony protects me. It's to his own interest to protect me. But don't you see? First my mother, and now Timony." Because Timony interfered, her assignations had to be arranged and carried out on the sly—which for her added to the delight. She was so good at being secretive that her liaisons mostly stayed out of the scandal sheets. She would never go the way of Clara Bow, whose career was effectively ruined by public scandal.

To another interviewer Mae cheerfully pleaded exhaustion: "Come in, kid. Got an aspirin in your vanity bag? I'd swap my diamonds for a good night's sleep. This writing of scenarios, film acting, giving interviews, posing for pictures, and making gramophone records in time to get to the fights each night is just about killing the old bird."

Most mornings she routinely attended Mass at the Church of Christ the King with Timony, although she did not consider herself a Catholic. "It just does me good to begin the day that way," she explained. "My manager's a Catholic." In addition to attending Mass, she made financial donations to Catholic charities and gave her discarded cars to the nuns. Whether she was motivated by private devotion or a lingering, unacknowledged sense of guilt isn't clear. Chris Basinger, a friend who worked at the Ravenswood switchboard at a much later date, says he recalls seeing a statue of Jesus and a votive candle in an alcove off her bedroom. According to him, "she covered all bases." She was administered last rites by a priest on her deathbed, although the decision to call the priest was probably made by her companion, Paul Novak, not by Mae herself.

But she never could accept the Catholic view that sex for pleasure alone, sex with multiple partners, and sex outside of marriage are sinful. Nor would she accept sole credit or blame for introducing sex into motion pictures. "When were pictures ever without sex? Have we forgotten the vampish writhings of Theda Bara and Valeska Suratt? Sex is considered the strongest instinct next to self-preservation. When will humans lose interest in it?"

Professing confusion about Catholic opposition to her films, she asked the priest at the Church of Christ the King for an explanation. "I've never done anything to harm the Catholic Church," she told him, "why does the Catholic Church start preachin' against me?" He answered, "Well, as you know, the Catholic Church is very wise and knows everything," then indicated that many men of all ages—young, old, and middle-aged—had come to him to confess "sins committed in consequence of spending an evening at a Mae West picture." Reports of such sins made her more proud than ashamed. She liked being known as a turn-on. "I stimulated sex all right."

Deluged with fan mail, some of it asking her to comment on moral issues of the day, she quipped, "Loose morals? Why, after four years of depression you'd be lucky if you could find a loose nickel!" She continued to attack the double standard, wondering aloud why it used to be considered all right for a man to have as many romances as possible, "while a woman had to walk a chalk [line]. But say, there's just one code that the woman of today should adopt, and that's the code of common sense."

Aware that the country's mood seemed again to be swinging away from permissiveness and in the direction of constraint and regulation, Paramount publicists began trying to reshape Mae West's public image. Instead of emphasizing the similarity between the "real" Mae West and the characters she played, they adopted the strategy of the journalistic Mae West of the later twenties and tried to stress differences. She may portray wild women, they hinted, but in private life she's retiring, work-centered, devoted to her family, a stay-at-home who neither smokes nor drinks. *Variety* reduced this tactic to a wry headline: COME UP TO SEE ME SOMETIME IS TEA INVITE—PAR. Picking up the cue, Jean Harlow, in *The Girl from Missouri* (1934), insists, "I'm just an old-fashioned home girl—like Mae West."

At least one observer, Gladys Hall, considered the attempt to tone down and sanitize Mae West's image to be totally misdirected. "If Mae agrees to the prissying process, she will commit suicide," Hall warned in *Motion Picture*. "Sex, unashamed and unabashed, has built her into her present international fame . . . Prudery will slaughter her." Mae West's popularity, Hall maintained, was a by-product of her ability to talk "spicily, straight from the shoulder, without compromise or one eye on the Womans Clubs evasions. You could take her or you could leave her. We all took her . . . Her ideas were so vital, her personality so important that no one bothered about her private life. No one cared. She was hard and brilliant as a faceted diamond. We must have needed hardness in a world that had felt licked and whimpery." Don't disavow your Diamond Lil low-downness, your "un-manicured morals," Hall begged of Mae West. The whole world, "from Mayfair to kindergarten," has wanted to imitate you. "But no one is going to imitate the *expurgated edition* . . . To put Diamond Lil in the kitchen, in gingham, would be like putting Cleopatra in the nursery to change a baby's thingumabob."

Despite Gladys Hall's best efforts to boost the bad-girl image, a flurry of news articles emphasizing Mae West's goodheartedness and generosity appeared. Much was made of her participation in a radio drive promoting the local Community Chest, during which Mae West urged, "Love your neighbor—and by that I don't mean his wife." Her unsolicited check to the Motion Picture Relief fund was reported, as was her participation in an Elks' show to provide aid to the unemployed and destitute. She was praised for supporting the families of prisoners and attempting to help addicts kick their habits. The world heard about her appeal to the governors of California and South Carolina to pardon C. D. Cooper, alias Ben Jones, a motion-picture projectionist who turned out to be an escaped prisoner and murderer. In an effort that may have backfired, Mae vouched for Cooper's good character, asserting that he had reformed himself into a useful citizen. She chummily addressed California Governor Rolph in a letter appealing for mercy for Cooper that was quoted in the *Los Angeles Times*: "Now, Jim, you know that I know men."

Hollywood reporter George Kent, probing the source of her enormous popularity, went so far as to characterize her appeal as maternal, pairing her with Will Rogers as "the Mammy and Daddy of Us All." Mae West's magnetism, he argued, resided in her projected promise as a nurturer. "The shape of her body and the shape of her spirit spell MOTHER." Kids see in her, not a temptress, but "a great sunny gale of sweet temper, kindness and human understanding . . . It was a mother, a better, bigger, rounder, more beautiful mother, one who had time for them, a kind of mother earth on sparkling slippers and able to make wisecracks." In the Depression, her sex appeal counted less than her image as "someone to lean on." According to Kent, "People go to Mae West pictures for the same reason little boys run to their mothers when they faw down and go boom!"

If Mae West seemed motherly to some, she emphatically steered clear of movie roles that would have cast her as a woman with children, because she (unlike Dietrich) felt mothers couldn't be sex symbols. She had a list of shall nots, in fact, and never compromised it. The woman she played could not be, or ever have been, a mother; be or ever have been turned down, stood up, or left flat by any man; ever be tricked, outwitted, or gypped; ever be afraid of anything, stumped or stopped by anything. She must always come up a winner, and the audience must never feel sorry for her. In truth, she played a sort of superwoman. The "real" Mae West needed to be softened and humanized by studio publicists.

Articles began to appear that focused on Mae West's home-loving nature, on her luxurious and sybaritic, but apparently moral, lifestyle:

> Mae never takes showers, preferring tub baths perfumed with rose-scented bath salts. She has more than a dozen fluffy negligees and wears a different one every morning for breakfast, which she eats on a pink satin chaise lounge in her boudoir.
>
> She has twenty-seven bottles of perfume on her dressing table, but the one she uses almost exclusively is of sweet pea scent . . . Her hair-dresser comes to her home every morning to give her a finger wave. Her hair is shampooed weekly. Mae's fingernails are manicured three times a week and always coated with a vivid red polish. She has massages several times a week.
>
> For the sake of her curves she eats rich, creamy foods—likes chocolate candy too.
>
> She is left-handed, naturally, but hides the fact in public. She can't ride a horse, but is proud of her ability to ride an elephant. She likes to motor, but can't drive a car, and is afraid of ocean and air travel. She is a disciple of Yogi, writes in bed, dictating to a secretary.
>
> She's a home girl, and oddly her homework is writing.

In order to market her image as a domestic being, both she and the studio encouraged articles that described and pictured her recently refurbished Ravenswood apartment. Paramount art director Hans Dreier had brought in the white-and-gold furniture, of a style best described as "early French Candy Box." The living room featured polar-bear rugs, a long, fringed sofa, and a white-and-gold baby grand piano. Mae liked to call it her "anteroom," because that's where she negotiated her contracts. "I let 'em sit out there until they raise the ante. That's why I call it the anteroom." The famous nude marble statue of her idealized form by Gladys Bush and the Florence Kinzel painting of her lying on her back, nude, were added in the mid-thirties.

All the coffee tables and consoles were topped with mirrors, and all the mirrors had gold instead of silver backing. Even her china service bore heavy gold decoration. "When you're on a diet," she joked, "you need something to make the food taste rich." Ashtrays in the shape of golden swans—like the celebrated Diamond Lil bed—were scattered about.

She called her bedroom "regal," and thought of it as part of French aristocratic tradition: "Back in the eighteenth century, when everybody had long white hair, great ladies used to receive their callers in the bedroom. It was considered class." Her canopied bed, draped from its crown, was embossed with the initial W, and hung with pale pink brocade edged with lace. The headboard was quilted in pale pink fabric, and the ceiling and wall behind the bed were covered with heavy mirrors, framed with white and gold. The mirror above the bed prompted her much repeated explanation, a variant of one of the catchphrases in *I'm No Angel*, "I like to see how I'm doin.' " (The phrase in the movie was Tira's recurrent question, "How'm I doin'?")

"I made this apartment into a home," she said. "This is all my stuff. I had them take out all that hotel junk. You'll notice the furniture is more white than gold. Out here we're artistic, but more restrained. I like restraint—if it doesn't go too far."

Everything about the place had been designed, as a movie set might be, to offset and flatter the leading lady. Asked about her choice of pale colors, Mae explained, "Gets all the flesh tones, honey—without being vulgar."

Neither Mae West nor Paramount thought twice about the contradiction between her image as a "no hooey," straight-talking, no-nonsense, tough, and bone-honest Brooklyn dame and the frilly, kitschy, pseudo-royal, and highly artificial style in which she decked out both her apartment and her person. The gap between her natural-woman verbal style and the rococo ornateness of her hair, makeup, clothing, and material surroundings would expand to a yawning cavern over the years. Cary Grant ended up roundly condemning her artificiality. "She never told the truth in her life," he generalized, decades after their period of working together. "She dealt in a fantasy world; the heavy makeup she wore was one sign of her insecurity. We were all very careful with her."

*   *   *

By October 1933, when *I'm No Angel* opened, the NRA had become the topic of the day. Paramount lined itself up squarely behind the National Recovery Administration, advertising as a "National Recovery Act" its list of new pictures sure to "Bring Back Business to the Theaters": the Marx Brothers in *Duck Soup*, Miriam Hopkins and Fredric March in *Design for Living*, W. C. Fields in *Tillie and Gus*, Maurice Chevalier in *The Way to Love*, Carole Lombard in *White Woman*, and, at the top of the list, Mae West in *I'm No Angel*. All the current films displayed, along with the credits, the NRA emblem and motto, "We Do Our Part."

The Paramount press book for *I'm No Angel* designates Mae West "screendom's exponent of the New Deal," citing her hearty endorsement of the NRA code and her declaration that it did not go far enough. "She proposed a special code for Bachelor Girls. For example, she shall take no more than she can get . . . [in] jewelry, motor cars, flowers, furs and candy." Mae told the press, "NRA stands for No Regrets After," adding a throwaway line that suggests how out of touch she actually has become: "I kind of like the New Deal . . . But how much is a dollar worth these days, Mac? I've been sort of busy and haven't paid much attention."

It was difficult to kid away fears that a major campaign on movie morals was in the offing. "It's hard to be funny when you have to be clean," Mae worried aloud. FILM MORALS—OR ELSE threatened a headline in *Variety*. "There is direct word that the President and the NRA have already let the business know that administration's attitude on proper standards . . . Immediate and vigorous action will be taken with the first sign of picture indecency under the New Deal, film leaders understand." The box-office success of *Little Women* was cited as an example of how a movie could be both clean and a hit.

In far-off England, an editorial in *Picturegoer* alerted the public to the "dangerous nature" of the new Mae West film ("Who Says I'm a Bad Girl?" she protested to *Picturegoer* readers) and predicted a long-overdue crackdown on Hollywood delinquency: "Under the Roosevelt 'New Deal' . . . it is proposed to supersede the Hays machine with three commissions which will be required to *enforce* the existing Hays moral code."

Christian Century magazine blanched at an ad for *I'm No Angel* that read: "Mae Packs 'Em In. This 1933 Don't Care gal has PERSONALITY—swinging hips—bedroom eyes and the throaty growl of an amorous cat—She just doesn't give a damn."

But it was primarily *after* the release of *I'm No Angel* that the Hays Office began muttering about the "Mae West menace," and Martin Quigley, one of the authors of the 1930 code and the influential editor of *Motion Picture Herald*, branded Tira "a scarlet woman whose amatory instincts are confined exclusively to the physical."

Before the picture's release, the Hays Office's deletions and alterations of *I'm No Angel* had been relatively modest in scope. A scene showing Slick picking pockets was considered too graphic. Some of the spieler's hyperbole regarding Tira's allure was, as we've seen, deleted, as was the word "tart" wherever it appeared. The words "jeez," "punk," and "Lawdy" were also vetoed, and scenes showing Thelma in Tira's bed with Slick and a woman's arm handing the phone to Tira's attorney Pinkowitz in bed had to go. When Tira spells "Pinkowitz" for the telephone operator, she has to say, "W, like in witch" instead of "W for Will he or won't he." "Z like zoftig" was deleted, as well as "I for indecent." Tira's line to Kirk "I like sophisticated men to take me out" originally read, "I like sophisticated men to take me home."

The song lyrics vexed the censors most, especially in the case of a song originally titled "No One Does It Like That Dallas Man." Although Paramount's Russell Holmon did his best to convince the Hays Office that "both the lyrics and the title of this song are perfectly harmless," and that all the Dallas man does is "kiss, hug, tame the ladies and ride a horse," the title had to be changed to "No One Loves Me Like That Dallas Man." As Tira sings them in the movie, the words to this song are hard to make out; they are played on a record, as background in the scene showing Tira and the Chump dancing together.

In "I Found a New Way to Go to Town," Tira sings, "Takes a good man to *break* me," instead of the original "Takes a good man to *make* me."

The title song, "I'm No Angel," is heard over the closing credits, a placement that made cuts easy to accomplish and hard to detect. On most prints, the song is hacked to pieces; the entire first, fourth, and fifth stanzas vanish, and the listener misses out on Tira's invitation to "Take my kisses till your weary heart's at ease." Although she wasn't permitted to promise to make her lover "lose your self-control," she got away with bidding him to "Love me, honey, love me till I just don't care."

Mae West herself altered one line in the song she sings while performing her carnival kootch dance, "They Call Me Sister Honky-Tonk." Lyricist Ben Ellison claimed he originally wrote the song about female impersonator Julian Eltinge. The original lyric went, "I've got the face of a Saint./On the level it's paint." Mae insisted on changing the second line to "On the level it *ain't* paint." She wanted the world to believe her good looks came naturally. It was the Hays Office, not she, however, who cut the lines "I'm not looking for a true man/All you need's the price, come on and pay."

One Hays Office functionary, V. G. Hart, saw dollar signs where he might have seen red. "This picture will be box office to the nth degree," he predicted. "Most of the suggestions are left to the imagination. It is a knockout . . . and I am sure [Mae West's] lines "How am I doin'?" and "When I'm good, I'm very good, but when I'm bad I'm better" will become as famous as "C'm up sometime."

Predictions that the picture would be a box-office smash came true. When *I'm No Angel* opened at Chicago's Oriental Theater, it broke records in both grosses and attendance, earning $50,000 in its first week. It grossed $84,500 in its opening week in New York, with five shows a day, and was held over for four weeks, the only such holdover in the history of the Paramount Theater. In Brooklyn, police reserves had to be called out to keep the fans in order, and continuous performances, beginning at 9 a.m. and ending at 5 in the morning, had to be scheduled to accommodate the crowds. At Boston's Fenway Theater, according to the *Boston Transcript*, "the street outside gave the effect of a run on the neighboring bank, with a line extending in the rain along Massachusetts Ave. . . . The round-up inside was as overwhelming, and when the languid hoyden slithered into view, every inch of seating and standing room was taken."

In Omaha, publicists arranged a midnight show for men only, a morning show for females only. The women were served coffee and rolls and each received a copy of Mae West's "NRA code for bachelor girls." Men at the midnight show were presented with an autographed photo of the star along with a candy kiss.

A film that cost $225,000 to make wound up earning more than $3 million, and nobody doubted that Mae West was the draw, that people paid to see *her*. "Everybody's analyzing the whyfore of her click," *Variety* reported, naming her the "picture-celeb" currently most sought-after for commercial product tie-ins. (Among the offers she turned down were one from a milliner wanting to name a hat after her and three from beer companies dreaming of offering "Mae West brew.") All in all, *Variety*'s review of *I'm No Angel* concluded, Mae West today had emerged "the biggest conversation-provoker, free-speech grabber and all-around box-office bet in the country. She's as hot an issue as Hitler."

*   *   *

Chicago Tribune critic Mae Tinee suspected that Mae West's allure stemmed from the fact that "she really and truly doesn't give a damn." The world was "full of people who would like not to and she provides vicarious easy shoes and relaxed stays for their inhibitions. She's not afraid of the big bad wolf, be he cop, censor or club woman." What was the result? "Cops wink. Censors pass her films, and the ladies, God bless them, are now luxuriously ordering whipped cream with their chocolate."

While *Newsweek* branded her "the world's best bad actress," and the New York *Sun* dismissed her as "primarily a stunt," in the highbrow *New Republic* Stark Young went to the opposite extreme, crowning her, "next to Charlie Chaplin . . . the best actor in Hollywood." What he found most remarkable was her exaggerated quality, her stylized and farcical unreality: "Miss West has created a sort of Lillian Russell–gay-nineties-bad-good-diamond-girl myth or figure, heightened and typified, that is becoming as distinct as Charlie."

There were some who viewed the romantic, happily-ever-after ending of *I'm No Angel* as a sign Mae West was losing her satiric edge. "America's sweetheart, Mae West, shows certain minor but disturbing signs of going respectable on us," groused Richard Watts, Jr., in the New York *Post*. In France, Colette complained: "She has not been sufficiently on her guard against the scenario, which lacks bite," but added, "Happily, the beautiful blond she-devil spirits away all the weakness of the film with a sway of her hips, a glance that undermines morals."

The trade paper *Hollywood Reporter* assigned itself the role of advocate for the movie's underutilized supporting players, everyone in the cast who was not Mae West. "No member of the cast is permitted a crack—they all play straight for Mae." Calling her dominance "downright stupid production tactics," the *Reporter* seemed to be prophesying doom: "There never was a star in this business who ever held his or her place by shoving . . . everyone else off the screen for more than one or maybe two pictures."

Mae West's popularity with the carriage-trade audience surprised some observers, who didn't know that ever since *Sex* and *Diamond Lil*, the monied folk Mae called "silk hats" had been beating a path to her performances. Now, in the Depression, her blue-chip appeal intensified. Word was out that at exclusive parties boring Social Register aristocrats couldn't compete with "nimble-witted life-of-the-party people with no more gentility than a rabbit. Mugs and pugs, really." A society columnist for *Life* reported that "the bluest-blooded hostess would give her right monocle to get Mae West to come calling . . . Schnozzle Durante is another plum society leaders go for, and he's no Little Lord Fauntleroy either." Of course, Mae West and Jimmy Durante weren't just any "mugs and pugs." Their gritty New York accents might have belonged to hash slingers or taxi drivers, but had celebrity cachet. The society columnist was really saying that fame breaks all social barriers.

Mae indicated that she held socialites in high regard—or at least considered those bluebloods who paid homage to her more admirable than movie stars who pretended she didn't exist. At the Hollywood premiere of *I'm No Angel*, she reported, "there weren't so many picture people, but lots of society, and that's my idea of a house. I always try to play to the best."

In fact, the opening at Grauman's Chinese Theater was a glittering event. Mae West was photographed for the newsreels arriving at the theater in a crystal-beaded silver lace gown trimmed with white fox that Travis Banton had created especially for the occasion. Although superstition prevented her from leaving her footprint in the cement, she got a huge laugh from the crowd when, over the microphone, she referred to the theater as the place where stars "leave their fingerprints." She corrected herself, "I mean footprints."

The *Los Angeles Times* reported fewer stars present than usual at the opening, but a "representative congregation" did show: Loretta Young, Paulette Goddard, and Charlie Chaplin. Mae West had to be delighted at the attendance of Chaplin, a man whose range of talents she considered a match for her own. She saw Chaplin as her precursor in the film treatment of sex. "He always had a lot of sex in his pictures, and he never made it obvious either. He kidded it, and that's exactly what I do."

At the Grauman's Chinese premiere, before the movie screening there was a stage circus show, "a novel affair, with animal acts, including dogs and an amazing trained seal. Then the bareback riding act, a clowning musician, trapeze and bicycle acts," iron jaw artists, and stilt walkers. Cary Grant, a onetime stilt walker, got up and thanked Sid Grauman "for using the act with which he made his show biz start."

By the end of 1933, Mae West in *She Done Him Wrong* and *I'm No Angel* had sold about 46 million tickets. She had established herself as Paramount's top attraction, and earned a position as the eighth-ranked star in the nation. If she had not, as she often claimed, single-handedly rescued Paramount from bankruptcy, she had certainly contributed hugely and decisively to the studio's fiscal salvation.

Seizing the moment, she and agent Murray Feil renegotiated her contract with Paramount, turning away rival studios who were offering her $200,000 per picture plus a percentage of the profits. Her new Paramount contract guaranteed her $300,000 per film, and another $100,000 per screenplay, for two films a year. She had the right to approve all scenarios—not a problem so long as she continued contributing to her own scripts and receiving sole credit for writing them. As she said, "At the end, I have all the power, I control everything in the picture."

Like Tira, Mae West had demonstrated her command of almost miraculous rejuvenative powers. "She'll cure sick box-offices, bring dead theaters to life, and cause blood to race in hardened arteries." She shrugged off hints that a potentially lethal assault lay coiled nearby, about to spring.

16

SCANDALIZE MY NAME

IN 1934 Mae West, the fifth most popular star in the country according to theater owners, earned the highest salary of any woman in America. She had acquired a reputation as—among other things—a shrewd business-woman, and keenly appreciated the reality that an actress over forty, even if her name is Mae West and her image ranks near Mickey Mouse's in omnipresence, must look to her financial future. Her mother had taught her, at the knee, that real estate offers the best hope for safe investment, but up until now she had been unable to act on that maternal advice. In the past, many of the dollars she made had been shoveled back into her career. The plays made her name but ate up her earnings. Now, in Holly-wood, she had finally paid off her last debt (a Chicago furrier extracted $206.50 he insisted she owed for some black fox), but had not managed to save much. She needed to be appropriately gowned and jeweled, after all, and she required a staff: maid, chauffeur, bodyguard. Then there were family members to support.

By now, Mae had not only brought her newly remarried sister, her brother, and her father to be with her in California, she had put them on her payroll. Her brother-in-law, Vladimir (Robert) Baikoff, who met Beverly while they were both working at a radio station, was an underemployed actor with a drug problem; he too depended intermittently on Mae's re-sources, in particular her assistance in finding him acting parts. Mae also helped land her brother, Jack, a position as a labor supervisor at Paramount which he managed to keep only a short time, reportedly because he slept on the job; again he became her dependent.

Finally, there was Timony. Her relationship to him was changing; he moved out of the Ravenswood in July and reluctantly relinquished major management responsibilities to Murray Feil of the William Morris Agency.

But even as their day-to-day contact diminished, he never stopped adoring Mae, and she continued to think of him as a member of her family, a permanent fixture whose loyalty and past contribution to her success she could never repay. She went on supporting him until his death in 1954. In her inner circle, as in her performing life, Mae surrounded herself with people who needed her and encouraged her to call the shots.

Despite all these obligations, and her frequent dips into the pot on behalf of friends or even strangers in need, she could at last afford to buy property. Mae liked to relax on chauffeured drives in the back seat of her limousine. Often she would think up plot situations and smart comebacks as she rode. These days, though, she scanned the landscape with an acute speculator's eye, for she had been bitten by the real estate bug. During one drive to the Van Nuys area, a favorite spot for cruising, she spotted "a huge grove of deodar trees—they looked like Ponderosa pines." Without stopping the car, she told Timony to investigate. The next day he discovered that the lot was owned by a Mexican family and all the acreage was about to be sold for $600 back taxes. "I said, 'Give them $6,000 for it.' . . . That was a fortune in those days." The property, at the intersection of Van Nuys and Chandler Boulevards, right in the soon-to-burgeon Van Nuys business district, rapidly increased in value.

Another drive in the same San Fernando Valley resulted in her purchase, for $16,000, of a six-acre orange ranch near Van Nuys, with a ten-room residence and two smaller guest houses. For a short time, Mae considered moving into it herself, explaining that she wanted to "see how it is to wake up and hear a bird singing for a change, instead of listening to taxis and trucks." But once her father arrived on the West Coast, in March 1934, she decided to settle him there, instead. After his death, less than a year later, the ranch became Beverly's domain. Brother Jack moved into a house on an adjacent lot. Both Jack Junior and Beverly's husband, Baikoff, participated in handling the harness racers and saddle horses Mae bought and kept in a stable there.

Mae didn't like to talk in public about money matters; it seemed to her unladylike, and risky too, like counting your cash on a busy street corner. Her evident wealth and celebrity cushioned her in some respects, but made her vulnerable in others. These were paranoid times in Hollywood. The Lindbergh kidnapping left permanent psychological scars, especially among people in the public eye. Threats against Marlene Dietrich's daughter in 1932 brought bodyguards onto the Paramount lot. Some thugs in the underworld had not taken kindly to Mae West's recent cooperation with the district attorney, and her public testimony against the men who had robbed her of jewels and cash resulted in ominous hints that acid would be thrown in her face. MAE WEST LEADS STARS IN WAR ON GANGSTERS, blazoned the *Los Angeles Times*, quoting the star's declaration that racketeers must be stopped. Forgetting for the moment that she remained on warm terms with Owney Madden, had had an affair with Madden's close friend George Raft, and had met Raft's sometime companion at the track, Bugsy Siegel, she stated, "I've got to do it as a citizen. I've got to do it for society . . . They threaten us under penalty of having acid thrown in our faces, and they don't stop at threats either."

The district attorney took the threats very seriously. He appointed two detectives as full-time guards, Jack Chriss and J. C. Southard. They followed her everywhere, even to the fights, where a reporter for the L.A. *Herald* observed, "Mae never looked to left or right. Her eyes looked straight ahead and she looked tense." Her appearance at the fights *without* bodyguards, in March, was considered newsworthy in itself. According to the *Los Angeles Times*, Timony, who sat beside her, appeared to be toting a gun, taking on the role of private security guard. He "was observed sitting all through the bouts with his hand in his pocket, if that means anything."

It was during this period that Mae West, greeting her bodyguards at a train station, famously asked one of them, "Is that a gun in your pocket, or are you just happy to see me?" The line resurfaced often, and made its way into *Sextette* more than forty years later.

Possibly, some time after she gained access to District Attorney Buron Fitts, she took advantage of his affection for her to urge him to intercede on behalf of Owney Madden, who was once arrested during a trip to Los Angeles. Although Madden from the 1930s on resided in Hot Springs, Arkansas, and was involved there with his future wife, Agnes, he was still chummy enough with Mae, according to Madden's biographer, Graham Nown, to be able to hide out in Mae's Ravenswood apartment for a week. Nown dates this episode in 1931, though in fact that was before Mae West had moved to Hollywood or the Ravenswood.

The bodyguard-detectives encouraged Mae to purchase an armored car. Soon she ordered a custom-built bulletproof Duesenberg, like one Madden owned. The long black speedster she commanded could race a hundred miles per hour and was designed to withstand machine-gun attack. It had special locks, and its windshield, mirrors, and windows were made of shatterproof glass. Her driver at the time, Gar Bell, sat in an open front seat, a moving target if there ever was one, while she enjoyed the splendor of the closed five-passenger cab behind, upholstered in beige leather, with sheep-skin rugs on the floor, a built-in, lighted vanity, and an electric speaker system over which she could issue directives.

When production began in March 1934 on the picture tentatively titled *It Ain't No Sin*, for the first time in her filmmaking career Mae West closed the set to all outsiders, even Timony. Instead of "walking in the front door, smiling at autograph seekers," she now entered the studio unobtrusively, through a side gate. Detective Jack Chriss kept watch, packing a pistol he claimed Pancho Villa had presented to him when Chriss was a Texas Ranger. Personal bodyguard Mike Mazurki was given a bit part in the movie. She was protecting all flanks.

Emboldened by the popularity of *She Done Him Wrong* and *I'm No Angel*, she asked for and got an extravagant budget for the new picture, to be set in late-nineteenth-century St. Louis and New Orleans against a *Show Boat*-like backdrop. At a final cost of $800,000, the movie eventually titled *Belle of the Nineties* consumed more dollars than had her last two hits combined. Although two thousand extras, many of them show-business or boxing old-timers, had to be hired, the heftiest sum went directly to the star. In addition to her $300,000 salary, she began collecting double payment, an extra $10,000 a week, when the filming overlapped into the time allotted for her next picture. (Her contract called for two pictures a year, six months apart.) She also received $100,000 for her work on the script. She could well afford the $15,000 worth of gifts she bestowed, by way of thanks, on cast, crew, and director.

Art director Hans Dreier and set designer Bernard Herzbrun spared no ex-pense in creating Ace Lamont's Sensation House, the lavish New Orleans mansion of modified Louis XV style that has been converted into a sumptuous gaming house, in which the Mae West character, Ruby Carter, both resides and performs, and which finally burns up in a fire she helps to start. The man-sion was illuminated by three giant crystal chandeliers; its appointments in-cluded a marble staircase, gold-framed paintings (one of them looked "more like an old mistress" than an Old Master), drapes and upholstery of silk, a nude statue on which Ruby strikes a match, and—a touch of home for Mae—polar-bear rugs. A reporter for *The New York Times*, admitted to the sound stage after convincing the guards "that I was incapable of violence or uttering gangster threats," described the set as a "minor cathedral."

Travis Banton's 1890s costumes for Mae rose to the occasion. We see

Ruby/Mae first as a burlesque queen posing in a shimmering skin-tight sheath for a series of static "living pictures" against highly stylized backgrounds created by stereopticon slides. As a tenor (Gene Austin) croons "My American Beauty," she transforms herself successively into a butterfly, a bat, a rose, a spider—all symbols of beauty or predatory female lust—and finally, arm aloft with a torch, head crowned, torso draped in flag-like stripes, into the Statue of Liberty, or what George Jean Nathan preferred to call the "Statue of Libido."

After Ruby Carter moves from St. Louis to New Orleans, she decks herself out lavishly in Banton-created black lace and tulle, white net embroidered with silver sequins, pink chiffon dotted with rhinestones, neckline and train massed with roses, black velvet trimmed with spiral bands of pearls and brilliants, and gray wool trimmed with ermine tippet. Her hats made a generous contribution to the endangered species list of subsequent decades: they were adorned with the plumes of birds of paradise (a West favorite since the days of *Sex*), white aigrette (egret), and blue-dyed ostrich tips and ostrich feathers. Mae was so pleased with Banton's work that she rewarded him with a Chinese jade figurine.

Cinematographer Karl Struss, aided by makeup artist Dot Ponedel, helped her achieve a luxurious, finished sheen, a high-contrast, porcelain-patina perfection on screen. She looks stunning in this movie, but less touchable, more masked, than in the past. Struss, who immediately became Mae West's cinematographer of choice, had a background in still-portrait photography and had participated in Stieglitz's Pictorialist Photo-Secession Group in New York early in the century. Coming to Hollywood to work with Cecil B. DeMille, he brought with him the soft-focus lens he'd developed as a portraitist. He shot Mary Pickford, Gloria Swanson, and Claudette Colbert through gauze, and had acquired a reputation for delivering soft, romantic, idealizing images. He had been the recipient, in 1927, of the first Academy Award for cinematography.

One of the reasons Mae West liked him so much was that he made her look terrific. He subscribed to the notion of *perfected* actuality or "idealized realism" and saw it as his duty "to minimize . . . physical imperfections. Makeup, diffusion, lighting, and carefully chosen angles are the chief tools."

"I lit Mae depending on the angle," said Struss, who enjoyed working with her, though he never depended on her as she did on him. "If she was looking from right to left, my key light was from the left side and vice versa. That made the narrow side of the face brighter and narrows the whole face.

It also put the chin line in the shade." Struss's camerawork for *Belle of the Nineties* reaches both backward and forward in its techniques. The series of static, statue-like "American Beauty" tableau shots of Mae allowed him to draw upon the portrait style developed in the early twentieth century, although the film portraits use sharp rather than hazy focus. The "Troubled Waters" sequence, in which Mae as Ruby Carter sings a bluesy spiritual accompanied by a torchlit black chorus, experiments with the most advanced process shots, double exposures, superimposed images, and split-screen effects.

The musical score blends the modern with the old-fashioned as well. For the old, we have the spiritual tradition behind "Troubled Waters" and the early blues sounds of W. C. Handy, which are squeezed anachronistically into an 1890s *mise-en-scène*. For the modern, swinging sound of the 1930s, we have Duke Ellington.

Mae fought for, and won, the pricey services of the Duke Ellington band. She wanted the best. Very likely she had known Ellington in New York in the late twenties, when he and his band replaced King Oliver at Owney Madden's Cotton Club and became acclaimed, hugely successful broadcasting and recording artists. She loved his sophisticated, velvety sound. When she asked for Duke Ellington and his orchestra for *Belle of the Nineties*, the studio brass initially balked, saying they had their own orchestra under contract that played for all their pictures and that Ellington would cost too much. She reminded them that the great Duke had made a slew of hit records and would be "just right for our New Orleans setting." Then they said if she insisted that the picture use black musicians, they'd hire extras, have them sit in with instruments, "and fake-play the music, which the studio orchestra would pre-record."

She wasn't having any of it. "I told them . . . you can't take white people and play black music." She finally persuaded Emanuel Cohen that Ellington would be an invaluable asset, and Ellington—who subsequently named Mae West his favorite actress—came on board to back her in the Arthur Johnston–Sam Coslow songs "My Old Flame," "Troubled Waters," "When a St. Louis Woman Comes Down to New Orleans," and in the W. C. Handy classic "Memphis Blues."

Mae exempted herself from her stated opinion that black music should be performed by blacks. The songs she sings in this picture and her belting delivery owe everything to the black blues, ragtime, and jazz idioms that she had drawn upon from the time she shouted the dialect "Movin' Day" in her first Brooklyn amateur contest. With the help of Sam Coslow's lyrics, Arthur Johnston's music, and the mellow sonorities of the Ellington band, she places herself directly in the tradition of Handy's diamond-ringed "St. Louis Woman," with the significant difference that Mae West's St. Louis Woman doesn't suffer. She wastes no tears on a lost love, remaining emphatically upbeat and up-tempo.

The band quotes a refrain from Handy's famous "St. Louis Blues" (to which Mae had performed a belly dance in *Sex*) during an interlude in "When the St. Louis Woman Comes Down to New Orleans"; the lyrics echo both "Frankie and Johnny," associated with Mae West since the first performance of *Diamond Lil*, and West's own most quoted tag line: "Now, he was her man,/But he came up to see me sometime./I lived six flights up,/And he sure was willin' to climb."

Belle of the Nineties also borrows some characters and situations from *The Constant Sinner*, Mae West's 1930 novel and 1931 play set in contemporary Harlem, but moves the setting to the South and the time frame back to the tried-and-true 1890s. Her character's romance with a boxer is carried over (his name is changed from Bearcat to the Tiger Kid, hers from Babe Gordon to Ruby Carter), and so is the fighter's meddlesome manager, who thinks sexy women and boxing don't mix. But where the novel and play daringly represent mixed-race sex, adultery, prostitution, and drug dealing, the only black-white interplay permitted in the movie is between Ruby Carter and her none-too-bright maid, Jasmine (Libby Taylor, also Mae West's offstage maid), between Ruby on a balcony and the black chorus below, or between Ruby the singer in performance with the Ellington band. A lyric that was never used did offer up a Ruby who sings about "puffin' reefer" and yearns for the loving arms of a creole man with "high-brown skin." "I'll make you forget that you're a married man," Ruby's never-used lyric promised. It was dropped immediately.

Instead of miscegenation in Harlem, *Belle* gives us segregation in the South. The character Money Johnson, the lubricious Harlem policy man, has no counterpart in the movie, nor is there anyone like drugged-out Cokey Jenny. The only hint of drug use comes when Ruby slips knockout drops into Tiger's water bottle during a fight. (Knockout drops have figured as a favorite plot device since the days of *Sex*.) In the movie, instead of sensual dancing at a Harlem dive, we see the all-black chorus staging a torchlit revival meeting down by the levee, shouting, gospel-style, swaying, rolling their eyes, and dancing frenetically as Brother Eben, a preacher with white hair, leads them in an exchange about sin and the Devil. Ruby emerges on the balcony of Sensation House and sings the spiritual-like "Troubled Waters":

> They say that I'm one of the Devil's daughters
> They look at me with scorn
> I'll never hear that horn
> I'll be underneath the water Judgment morning
> Oh, Lord, am I to blame?
> Must I bow my head in shame?
> If people go round scandalizin' my name
> I'm gonna drown down in those troubled waters.

This song, which borrows directly from the spiritual "Scandalize My Name," strikes a somber new chord in the career of Mae West. She has never before, in either song or story, sounded guilty, contrite, repentant, or the least bit troubled by the prospect of eternal damnation. In fact, this song's lyrics have little to do with the Ruby Carter otherwise depicted in the final screenplay. The situations that might have explained her remorse—among them her past involvement in a bank robbery and in the murder of a millionaire—were stricken from the script, along with the self-referential line "All that notoriety . . . put her on the stage." Also destroyed were early scenes showing her, through a series of dissolves, shacked up with the Tiger Kid for several days. Mae West's earlier characters would have felt no guilt for any such transgressions.

Ruby, except in the revival meeting scene, looks and sounds a lot like wisecracking, swaggering Lady Lou in *She Done Him Wrong* and brazen Tira in *I'm No Angel*. She's a lavishly costumed performer pursued by several men, one of whom she interrupts as he lists her charms ("your golden hair, fascinating eyes, alluring smile, your lovely arms, your form divine"), with the lines "Wait a minute! Is this a proposal, or are you takin' inventory?" Although she keeps Ace LaMont at arm's length, in general she'd rather be "looked over than overlooked," and would prefer to have a man around her neck instead of at her feet. She won't settle for just admiring glances; she wants action: "A man in the house is worth two in the street." As in the past, her lovers include a rich socialite (played this time by ex-football star John Mack Brown) and a boxer, the Tiger Kid, played by Roger Pryor. (George Raft, initially announced to play Tiger, backed out on the grounds that his part would be too small, and that in a few places in the script, Mae

West would be shown in close-up while his back was turned to the camera. Paramount suspended him for ten weeks as a result of his walkout.)

"I'm in the habit of pickin' my own men," Ruby tells the depraved LaMont, who's so jaded "his mother should have thrown him out and kept the stork." A villain cut from the black-and-white cloth of nineteenth-century melodrama, he sneakily arranges to have Tiger steal Ruby's jewels, instead of adding to her collection. (The jewelry heist borrows directly from Mae West's recent experience.) Like other Mae West heroines, Ruby has a habit of accepting gifts of diamonds from men, although for the first time she makes a show of intending to give the gifts back. (In the last scene, she's still wearing them.) Instead of being nervous about receiving jewels from men, "I was calm and collected." (Mae quoted the last line in her remarks to the press about Owney Madden's fighter Primo Carnera, who was handicapped "by that fiery Latin temperament . . . It has no business in the ring. You've got to keep cool and calm to collect when you're in there trading punches.")

As in the past, the Mae West character shows a generous, openhearted, and fair-minded side that might be called good, despite her boast that she'd be staying in New Orleans, but "not for good." She tells her jealous, dark-haired rival, Molly (played by Katherine DeMille, adopted daughter of Cecil B. and future first wife of Anthony Quinn), that it's her policy not to steal another woman's man: "I ain't took a man from another woman yet, not unless she done me dirt. It's a principle with me." She and the Tiger end up rescuing Molly from the burning Sensation House; Ruby phones the fire department and explains, "I've done all I can."

The song "Troubled Waters" is at odds with the rest of the movie, but not with the intensified uproar about morals in American cinema. In the months between the release of *I'm No Angel* in the fall of 1933 and the start of production for *Belle of the Nineties* in the spring of 1934, rumblings about the need for a cleansing crusade in Hollywood crescendoed to a roar.

Initially, Mae displayed scant awareness of the changes in the works, or their portent for her film career. In an interview with *Variety* conducted just two weeks into the filming of *Belle of the Nineties*, she indicates that she believes her major censorship worries are behind her. Asked to compare Hollywood with Broadway, she states that, in pictures, "you don't even have to worry about censorship—much—once you learn the rules." In Hollywood they tell you what not to do before you do it, while on the New York stage "they let you go ahead and do it and then break in and arrest you." The prescience she took so much pride in abandoned her in this instance.

Just at the time *I'm No Angel* was about to open, Monsignor Amleto Giovanni Cicognani, the Pope's representative in America, addressed a convention of Catholic charities in New York after meeting with Martin Quigley and Joseph Breen, two lay Catholic leaders of the clean-up-Hollywood movement. The Monsignor had been persuaded to sound a rallying cry for concerted Catholic action against sinful movies, and he did so. "Catholics are called by God, the Pope, the Bishops and the priests," he intoned, "to a united and vigorous campaign for the purification of the cinema, which has become a deadly menace to morals." Within a month, church leaders had formed the Episcopal Committee on Motion Pictures, one of whose purposes was to prevent banks from lending money to "the producers of filthy pictures."

On April 11, the Episcopal Committee formed the Catholic Legion of Decency, a national organization dedicated to the annihilation of un-Christian films and pledged to purging the country "of its greatest menace—the salacious motion picture." The Legion set about hurting the movie industry right where it lived—in the pocketbook; it would organize boycotts of indecent pictures. Within ten weeks 11 million people—mostly Catholic, but including some Protestants and Jews—had signed a pledge condemning "vile and unwholesome" movies as "a grave menace to youth, to home life, to country and to religion." "I condemn absolutely those salacious motion pictures which . . . are corrupting public morals and promoting sex mania in our land," the pledge continued. "I hereby promise to remain away from all motion pictures except those which do not offend decency and Christian morality."

Within the Hays Office, the forgiving administration of Dr. James Wingate came to an end. First fiery Joseph Breen became the effective leader of the Studio Relations Office. Then, in June, the Studio Relations Committee vanished, to be replaced by the Production Code Administration, or PCA, headed by Breen.

At last the Production Code of 1930 could be strenuously enforced; it finally grew teeth and meant what it said: "Evil and good [must never be] confused, and evil [must always be] recognized clearly as evil." Seduction "should *never* be treated as comedy." Scenes of passion "must *not* be explicit in action nor vivid in method, e.g., by handling of the body, by lustful and prolonged kissing, by evidently lustful embraces, by positions which strongly arouse the passions." Love that is "impure," not sanctified by human or divine law, must be clearly "known by the audience to be wrong." Dances "designed to arouse passions," like the kootch (one of Mae West's trademarks), are forbidden. Brothels and bedroom scenes must be avoided. "The sanctity of the institution of marriage and the home shall be upheld." Depicting "sex perversion" was out (an effeminate call boy in the first script of *Belle* was excised), and even the suggestion of obscenity by gesture or manner would no longer be tolerated.

From now on, studios were directed by Hays to submit all treatments and scripts to Breen for approval. Each film approved by the Production Code Administration (PCA) would receive a certificate, to be displayed on every print. A fine of $25,000 would be exacted from anyone who released a film in violation of the code. In the past, producers who disagreed with the Hays Office's strictures had recourse to appeal to a Hollywood jury, composed of other producers, that would mediate differences. Now the jury was eliminated. Recommendations changed into edicts. The only appeal possible would be to the New York–based board of the Motion Picture Producers and Distributors of America. Pictures without a seal would be barred from major theaters. *Variety* crowned Breen "supreme pontiff of picture morals from now on." A British periodical, *Film Weekly*, went further. It called Breen "the Hitler of Hollywood."

Will Hays welcomed Breen, the new Production Code Administration, and the Legion of Decency that had helped to put them in place with open arms. "Far from considering the Legion an enemy," he wrote, "I welcomed its cooperation . . . Here was one of the most striking examples of 'let's get together' I ever experienced. To this day the majority of people probably consider the Legion's work an 'attack.' I saw it as a 'defense' of the moral standards we had ourselves adapted."

Even the White House appeared to support the war on indecent motion pictures. The NRA motion-picture code "practically puts Hollywood under government control," an article in *Movie Classic* maintained. Eleanor Roosevelt, the same article claimed, planned to conduct her own investigation of Hollywood, on behalf of the women's clubs. On her maiden radio broadcast, Mrs. Roosevelt hailed the appointment of Breen: "I am extremely happy the film industry has appointed a censor within its own ranks," she said.

The creation of the Production Code Administration and the installation of Breen as its head actually slowed the momentum for direct government intervention. NRA divisional administrator Sol Rosenblatt promised, "Washington will observe a hands-off policy, satisfied that the morals question is purely an industry matter."

Was Mae West responsible for the crackdown on screen immorality? Did she trigger Breen's appointment as the enforcer of the Production Code? Many people have believed so, including Marlene Dietrich, who said, "I like Mae, but it is all her fault that we have the Hays office and this childish censorship." Culture critic Gilbert Seldes called Mae West "in all probability . . . the chief cause of the most violent outbreak of hostility against the movies in the present generation." Writing in *Motion Picture* magazine, William French summed up her situation: "She made amorous dallying appear entirely too funny. And so she was the straw that broke the poor old camel's back." He dubbed Mae West "the alarm clock that awakened the cleaner-uppers."

Certainly there were dozens of pictures having nothing to do with Mae West that raised the hackles of moralists. The Legion of Decency's list of condemned films did include *She Done Him Wrong* and *I'm No Angel*, but it also mentioned a raft of others, among them *Ann Vickers*, *A Farewell to Arms*, *Of Human Bondage*, *The Story of Temple Drake*. A *Newsweek* article on the film boycott cited protests over *The Life of Vergie Winters* for "glorying illegitimacy," *Dr. Monica* for "giving its blessing to illicit love," Garbo's *Queen Christina* for containing a "lurid bedroom scene," and *Tarzan and His Mate* for "glorified nudity." The censors had their work cut out for them, even without Mae West.

The Catholic pressure groups and Joseph Breen targeted Hollywood moguls and producers more than any single performer. Film historian Gregory Black has shown that Breen persuaded himself that the Jews in Hollywood were responsible for indecency in movies. He called the Jews—a group that included both Adolph Zukor and Paramount production chief Emanuel Cohen—"simply a rotten bunch of vile people." Jews were "the scum of the earth," among whom "drunkenness and debauchery are commonplace." He saw America's Christian Main Street "being debauched by Jews and pagans," and proposed "that the Catholic church take up the sword."

Breen did harbor an animus against the highly visible Mae West, or at least against the movies she starred in, and he shared this antipathy with many Catholic groups and women's clubs. Alice Ames Winter, a representative of the Federation of Women's Clubs in Hollywood who did public-relations work for the MPPDA, addressed women's clubs and church groups all over Southern California on the subject of the Mae West menace. She saw Mae West as a threat to "the happiness and the onward movement of our children and our homes. Children represent forty percent of the movie-going public and we want the forces that play on them to be the best . . . They don't need Mae West as a teacher." And Father Daniel Lord, an author of the code who edited the Catholic magazine *Queen's Work*, black-listed all Mae West films.

Breen eventually created three categories for pictures released before his reign. The third category grouped together films that had to be reedited to conform to the Production Code and reclassified. The second included pictures that would be withdrawn after playing out existing contracts. Class I pictures were to be withdrawn at once and never released again; into that group he placed *I'm No Angel* and *She Done Him Wrong*, which would not be taken out of the vault again until the later 1960s.

When Paramount tried in 1935 to rerelease these two huge moneymakers, Breen laid down the law. He told Hays, "I saw both pictures myself, and they are definitely wrong. It would be a tragedy if these pictures were permitted to be exhibited at the present time. I am certain that such exhibitions would seriously throw into question much of the good work which has been done and stir up enormous protest." By his lights, both pictures were "so thoroughly and so completely in violation of the Code that it is utterly impossible for us to issue a certificate of approval."

Martin Quigley went so far as to list *I'm No Angel* as a negative example, "typical of wrong standards," in his book *Decency in Motion Pictures*. "Considered as entertainment for the mass theatre audience of the United States," he wrote, "it is vulgar and degrading. It is morally objectionable because it is generally of low moral tone and because specifically its sportive wise-cracking tends to create tolerance if not acceptance of things essentially evil." If Mae West was telling the joke, purity crusaders tended not to get it.

Her past record of violating the code with relative impunity certainly fueled Breen's overkill responses to *Belle of the Nineties*, the movie being filmed just as the controversy about alleged indecency exploded. He believed Mae West's earlier pictures simply should never have been made, and he would tolerate no more Mae West films of similar illicit tincture. After reading the first submitted script of what was then called *It Ain't No Sin*, Breen roundly condemned it as a glorification of prostitution and violent crime. "The general flavor of the story . . . is highly offensive," he warned Paramount, "and the several story factors based . . . upon seduction, gambling, robbery, and arson, together with the brutal treatment accorded one of the characters . . . suggests to us the kind of picture which we . . . would be compelled to reject."

Breen subscribed to a theory of "moral compensating values" in movies. He demanded that each film must contain "sufficient good" to compensate for any evil depicted. In *It Ain't No Sin* he objected to the criminal backgrounds of both Ruby Carter and the Tiger Kid, and especially to the fact that in the original script they go off "scot free" at the end.

Although Emanuel Cohen did not want either the New York Paramount executives or the Hays Office breathing down his neck, and would have preferred a situation where Breen stated his objections to the picture verbally rather than in writing, Breen came down hard and on paper, sending copies of his letter to New York. He insisted on the following changes:

a. Deleting action and dialogue suggesting that Ruby was a "lady with a past," and by inference a prostitute.
b. Tiger Kid must be depicted only as an ambitious prizefighter, with no suggestion that he is an ex-convict.
c. Removing reference to the five-day affair between Ruby and Tiger; removing shots of violent and lustful kissing.
d. Removing shot of Ruby stealing money from Ace LaMont.
e. Removing scene of Ruby and Brooks Claybourne kissing and showing mutual fondling.

The effect on the finished movie of these wholesale excisions did not concern the Production Code Administration in the slightest. But such changes could not help but inflict damage. Considering the virulence of the assault, it's amazing that *Belle of the Nineties* manages to be as entertaining as it is.

When the film succeeds, it does so as a series of separate shimmering moments rather than as an integrated whole. Predictably, the picture that survived after substantial cutting is full of gaps and glaring inconsistencies, most of them unrelated to Leo McCarey's direction. Ruby, for example, arrives in New Orleans on a paddleboat; we're not allowed to hear that, on board, five men visited her cabin in one day but were never seen coming out. But we are allowed to hear Ruby say, apropos of men gathered around her, "Give them all my address." In the opening sequence, we're told that Ruby Carter is a burlesque queen, but all we see is the tame "American Beauty" performance; her garter dance, in which she removed her garters and tossed them to the men in the audience, has been dropped. Her intimate scenes with Brooks Claybourne have been removed. And, as we've seen, her criminal record, her involvement in a banker's murder, and her dalliance with the Tiger Kid have been deleted. In effect, she's been laundered in Clorox bleach; instead of being a scarlet woman, she's pale pink. Nonetheless, she's inexplicably repentant in the "Troubled Waters" scene.

Joseph Breen approved the flawed re-edited version of the film in early June, but still more roadblocks had to be faced before its release. New York censors rejected the title *It Ain't No Sin* and demanded a new ending. A group of priests had marched on Broadway, under a sign advertising *It Ain't No Sin*, bearing placards that read: IT IS.

Informed of the censors' actions, Mae West took a conciliatory tone and promised, "If they think it's too warm, I'll cool it off." "I want to please them [the censors]," she told the Los Angeles *Herald*. "You never can say I refused to meet anybody half way."

Although Paramount had already spent thousands of dollars in advertising and publicity for the original title—including the expense of purchasing fifty parrots and training them to say, "It Ain't No Sin"—the picture was renamed "St. Louis Woman." As it happened, that title had been used recently on another picture and could not now be reprised. After "Belle of St. Louis" and "Belle of New Orleans" were considered and rejected, the title *Belle of the Nineties* finally passed muster.

Roger Pryor and Mae West were summoned to reshoot the ending. With Paramount's John Hammell serving as in-house moral watchdog, seeing to it that no close-up "got too close for Primville," they filmed a new ending that finds Ruby Carter and the Tiger Kid, cleared of murdering Ace LaMont, getting legally hitched by a justice of the peace. Although prior Mae West pictures had ended with an engagement, this was the first portrayal of an actual wedding. *Variety* interpreted the "benefit-of-clergy" finale as "an obvious curtsey to Joe Breen," although the New York Board of Censors, not Breen, had demanded the cleaned-up denouement. "Mae West," wrote André Sennwald in *The New York Times*, "has graciously permitted the New York censors to make an honest woman of her in her new picture." *Literary Digest* called it "a sort of shotgun wedding."

The expurgated and, by today's standards, completely inoffensive *Belle of the Nineties* appeared on several local Legion of Decency banned lists, and a priest on Long Island picketed the theater at which it played. Nonetheless, the picture did well, grossing over $2 million; a quarter of a million was earned in the first four weeks. In Atlantic City over Labor Day weekend, it played to overflow crowds at twelve screenings a day, and in Baltimore it brought in the biggest grosses in years. The week it opened in St. Louis, it

took the lead over all competition, earning a respectable $22,000. That was
good, *Variety* noted, "but by no means as sensational as either of [Mae
West's] first two."

Although it was subjected to additional cuts in Ohio, Pennsylvania, and
Massachusetts, and was rejected outright by Sweden, Norway, Italy, Java,
and Holland, *Belle of the Nineties* demonstrated that Mae West still enjoyed
immense popularity and that in some places the censorship controversies
actually increased the box office.

The American filmgoing public did not unanimously endorse the purity
campaign. At theaters in Boston, New York, Chicago, Detroit, and Cleveland, audiences booed or hissed the PCA seal when it was displayed on
screen. News weeklies published letters arguing that moviegoers over
twenty-one should be allowed to select movies of their choice. An editor
of *Photoplay* likened the morality crusade to Prohibition and asserted: "No
moral question was ever settled by compulsion. It is proverbial that you
cannot make men good by force. And legal censorship means to attempt
just that."

Richard Watts, Jr., of the New York *Herald Tribune* mocked the pettiness
of the Legion of Decency in light of the looming Nazi threat and the dark-
ening international climate:

With the Western World showing more than an occasional sign of collapse, and everything from German terrorism to strikes and rumors of war
blackening the horizon, you might think that the Legion . . . could find
some more serious matter to fight against than Mae West's terrible influence on the ten-year-old mind.

But such protests could neither dethrone Breen nor defang the code. An
entire generation of moviegoers would grow up convinced that in the best
homes, married couples slept in separate beds and that proper ladies lacked
navels.

Mae West's own view of censorship can't be summarized simply. She
issued contradictory statements about the cuts made in *Belle of the Nineties*,
telling the *Los Angeles Times*: "I had to change some of the wisecracks . . .
yet I don't think it hurt the film," but complaining a few months later, to
another newspaper, that *Belle* was "not a good story because they made me
make it three times before I found out what they wanted." Her outrage was
muted; an overtly hostile or confrontational stance would not have helped
her, and she knew it.

At times, in later decades, she vented anger, although it was always anger tempered with levity: "Imagine censors that wouldn't let you sit in a man's lap. I've been in more laps than a napkin!" At others she recognized that without censorship—particularly without her much publicized imprisonment for *Sex*—she might have missed out on becoming a celebrity. Scandal and controversy generate notoriety, and without notoriety where would Mae West be? "I *believe* in censorship! If a picture of mine didn't get an "X" rating, I'd be insulted." She gloried in her position as a "kind of godmother to the Motion Picture Code."

She did favor limits of some kind. She could be shocked, and she abhorred on-screen nudity and four-letter words. "I've never believed in going haywire on stage or screen. Obviously no medium of mass entertainment can be allowed to throw all restraint out the window. Strict censorship, however, has a reverse effect. It creates resentment on the part of the public. They feel that their freedom of choice is being dictated. They don't want their morals legislated by other than criminal law."

She had known since her early days in vaudeville that censors can delete words but it's much harder for them to apply the shears to manner, tone, insinuation. It's not what you say but the way you say it that makes the difference, she was fond of repeating. "It's the sex personality, it's not the words. The censors could never beat *that*." Insisting that she wanted her movies to be fit for children to see, and acknowledging that censorship had established new ground rules ("I did things a year ago that I wouldn't do at all now"), she again took refuge in the safety of indirection. "I can accomplish a lot more with a scene today, with a little innuendo." Since she found it hard to accept or acknowledge any loss of control, she persuaded herself that she was deceiving the censors and maintaining the upper hand by submitting scripts that included lines that she knew would be cut, to distract from other, less obvious, suggestive passages. "I'd add hot lines and jokes that I knew they'd cut."

She did this—but the censors changed more than words. They altered characters and attitudes, deleted roles, tampered with song lyrics and plots, cut scenes, insisted on "moral" endings. Powerful as Mae West was, the Hays Office, from 1934 on, ruled supreme. She had to meet their standards—not the other way around.

The close of 1934 found Mae West on the defensive. A series of articles had raised questions about her ability to stay on top. "Is Mae West Slipping?" one reporter inquired. Is she a fizzle, another wondered. A column in *Vanity Fair* cattily listed her among old fads, along with nudism and jigsaw puzzles. A fan magazine raised the question, on her behalf, "Will I Last?" It provided a forum for her to take up cudgels in self-defense, seconding her certainty that nothing could deter her. "The popularity of Mae West will continue just as long as Mae West herself wants it to," she insists. "I never let anything stop me, once I set my heart on it. I've never had a wishbone where my backbone should be."

Hollywood watchers feared for the survival of all the reigning sex goddesses: "What's going to happen to Anna Sten, Jean Harlow, Mae West, Marlene Dietrich, Norma Shearer and the other stars who have risen to fame and fortune by being tempting—or tempted—ladies? Can they survive the banning of sexy pictures?" Marlene Dietrich would not be kissing another woman on screen anytime soon.

It was Mae West in particular who troubled George Davis. In a devastating screed for *Vanity Fair* called "The Decline of the West," he made a case for her has-been status. Implying that praise from intellectuals had turned her head, and that Garbo had outstripped her, he lamented the passing of the old Mae West of vaudeville and Broadway fame, the one who didn't pretend to be beautiful but instead offered up "an uproarious take-off of a beautiful dame." The Mae West of the plays didn't pretend to act, either; instead, "she *did an act*." The Mae West he cherishes is the bawdy and gaudy one who parodies herself, who carries the put-on to its campiest extreme; professing his devotion, he gave her credit for having "healed the wound in my heart caused by the death of the one and only Bert Savoy. I love you, Miss West, because YOU are the greatest female impersonator of all times."

"The Decline of the West" appeared before the release of *Belle of the Nineties*. If Davis found the screen Mae West too glamorous and mainstream compared to her outrageous stage presence, others found the new film a comedown compared to *She Done Him Wrong* and *I'm No Angel*, and they had a point. *Belle* is, as released, a much safer and less original picture than the earlier films. William Troy, writing in *The Nation*, said he could discern "all through Miss Mae West's latest challenge to public morals and taste a disturbing and inappropriate note of weariness." He wondered if the audience betrayed signs of weariness as well. Richard Watts, Jr., blamed the censors more than the star, pointing to "the clumsy way the picture has been cut into shreds."

Paramount couldn't fail to notice that in terms of box office, too, the film didn't match its predecessors, in part because it cost so much to produce. Although still the top Paramount star, Mae West was being squeezed by Marlene Dietrich, Shirley Temple, Claudette Colbert, Carole Lombard, Bing Crosby, and Gary Cooper. In 1934 "she did not bring as much bacon home for the company as she did the year before," *Variety*'s Hollywood reporter noted, opining that folks "out here" think "that Miss West must get away from her present type of picture."

To be sure, the picture had its defenders, and so did Mae West. André Sennwald hailed *Belle of the Nineties* in *The New York Times* as one of the best screen comedies of the year and defended its star, likening her to a "cleansing wind." He went on: "She is so sane, so frank, so vigorous, and withal, so uproariously funny that she composes the healthiest influence which has reached Hollywood in years." Otis Ferguson, in *The New Republic*, found her irrepressible: "They made her change this picture all around, but they have probably found since that if you want to censor Mae West, you have got to lock her in a plaster cast."

In England, Hugh Walpole linked her, as a satirist, with Chaplin; they alone in Hollywood "dare to directly attack with their mockery the fraying morals and manners of a dreary world." And actor Cedric Hardwicke offered the opinion that Mae West had actually cleaned up movies: "She took the very thing of which the nastiest sex films were made, and then not only laughed at it herself, but made the public see the jokes also. She killed screen vulgarity by vulgarizing it to the point of absurdity."

In Hollywood defenders were few, but they did exist. Will Rogers called Mae West the most interesting woman in Hollywood. Elizabeth Yeaman, in the Los Angeles *Citizen-News*, griped about the raw deal Mae West was getting. "Most of the Hollywood film colony is venomously jealous of Mae and must have secretly rejoiced over the prospect that Mae would be wiped out by the Church crusade for clean pictures. But Mae accepted the challenge hurled by censors and . . . has turned out a picture that is just as entertaining as either of her previous efforts."

Leo McCarey, a well-seasoned (and often pickled) comedy director who had overseen Laurel and Hardy shorts and directed the Marx Brothers in *Duck Soup* before taking the helm for *Belle of the Nineties*, took pen in hand to salute Mae West: a consummate comedienne who is the soul of rhythm in her playing and who understands the importance of relaxation in acting. He called her "a sleeping leopard, relaxed yet with all her senses fully alert for the big moment." He thought she could branch out into other kinds of roles; she could play Peg O' My Heart with an Irish brogue, or Stella Dallas. Was he subtly suggesting she should diversify, not always play the same character?

*   *   *

Plans that had already been announced for Mae West's next movies had to be scotched. Nothing ever came of reports that she would co-star with boxer Max Baer, despite her admiration for his *sangfroid* in and out of the ring. ("He can hit, he isn't afraid of anything, and he doesn't know the meaning of 'nerves,' she said of Baer.) It had also been reported that she would star in *The Queen of Sheba*, a biblical comedy that would show her "kidding around with Solomon a little," and after that "Me and the King," the story of an American actress who, on a tour of Europe, "almost wins a kingdom from a bedazzled monarch." But with Breen in command, and the necessity for every new picture to carry his seal, other plans had to be made. "One picture that is probably out for the time being is "The Queen of Sheba," the *Los Angeles Times* reported in September. "New rules and regulations would make that too difficult."

She had hoped to mount her Catherine the Great picture, finally, but since Marlene Dietrich had strained the coffers at Paramount with her lavish production of *The Scarlet Empress*, Mae found no takers.

Change was in the wind as a difficult year came to a close. Battlin' Jack West developed a debilitating heart condition and was being looked after in a Ravenswood apartment. Her maid of six years, Libby Taylor, had left to pursue her own acting career. The parting had not been amicable. After coming out from New York to serve faithfully as "watchdog, dresser, personal maid and guardian angel to her famous mistress," Taylor had begun to manifest an unforgivable devotion to her own pursuits. "When she began wanting me to wake her up in the morning I told her she'd better stop being a maid and give all her time to the public."

A picture called "Gentleman's Choice," starring Mae West, had already been advertised, but it went the way of "The Queen of Sheba" and "Me and the King": nowhere. Finding a property for Mae West—something that would please her as well as the censors—had become a major challenge. The trade papers sounded authoritative in October when they reported that Mae West's next feature had been scheduled to begin production soon. It was said to be "a story by Marion Morgan based on an episode in the life of Mrs. Jack Gardner, of Boston's Back Bay social crowd," and would be called *Now I'm a Lady*.

Mae West and George
Raft around the time of
Night After Night (1932);
publicity shot
(Eddie Brandt's Saturday Matinee)

Mae West in dress de-
signed by Edith Head; publicity shot, 1933
(Courtesy Jack Allen Collection)

Groucho à la Mae West;
1933 publicity shot
*(Margaret Herrick Library, Academy
of Motion Picture Arts and Sciences)*

MAE: *Do your exercises, dearie; you'll get there.*

Cartoon of Mae West giving Garbo advice, by Jano Fabry from
the old *Life* magazine, appeared in October 1933
(Courtesy Library of Congress)

Paper-doll Christmas
card made by Buzza
Craftacres, ca. 1933
*(Lilly Library, Indiana
University)*

Mae West behind
costume dummies.
Dummy on left says,
"Kate Smith, Large."
Dummy on right says,
"Miriam Hopkins,
Boyish." Mae West's
dummy says, "Perfect
36." Publicity shot,
1933
*(Margaret Herrick Library,
Academy of Motion Picture
Arts and Sciences)*

On the set of *I'm No Angel*, 1933, with
Paramount honcho Adolph Zukor

Still from *I'm No Angel*, 1933: Mae West with tamed
lion

Still from *I'm No Angel*, 1933: Mae West with Libby Taylor and Gertrude
Howard

Premiere of *I'm No Angel*, October 12, 1933, Hollywood. Mae West
with Sid Grauman, movie theater owner; William Le Baron, Paramount
producer; Paramount vice-president Al Kaufman
(Museum of Modern Art Film Study Center)

Hollywood premiere of *Belle of the Nineties*, September 1934. Left to
right: Jack West, Jr., Jim Timony, Jack West, Sr., Mae, Beverly West
Baikoff, Vladimir Baikoff, Boris Petroff *(Courtesy Chris Basinger Collection)*

Literary Possibilities:

Colette gets a few pointers on love from our American representative.

Cartoon by Selz, "Literary Possibilities," *Life*, January 1934
(Courtesy Library of Congress)

Mae West as the Statue of Liberty; publicity shot, 1934
(Museum of Modern Art Film Study Center)

On the Paramount lot with Marlene Dietrich, 1935
(Museum of Modern Art Film Study Center)

On the *Belle of the Nineties* set with cinematographer Karl Struss and camera, 1934

(Margaret Herrick Library, Academy of Motion Picture Arts and Sciences)

On the rifle range in 1934, with bodyguard Jack Criss of the Los Angeles district attorney's office's Gangster Bureau

(Margaret Herrick Library, Academy of Motion Picture Arts and Sciences)

Still from *Goin' to Town*: Mae West in 1935 as Delilah in scene from Saint-Saëns's opera *Samson and Delilah*

(Copyright © 1997 by Universal City Studios, Inc. Courtesy of MCA Publishing Rights, a division of MCA Inc. All rights reserved. Museum

At the helm of an 1890s-style horse-drawn streetcar to Brooklyn Bridge; publicity shot, 1933

(Private collection)

Charlie McCarthy and Mae West in publicity shot for their radio broadcast on the *Chase & Sanborn Hour*, December 1937

(Harvard Theater Collection, Houghton Library)

Mae West in the bedroom of her Hollywood apartment at the Ravenswood, ca. 1935

(Margaret Herrick Library, Academy of Motion Picture Arts and Sciences)

Salvador Dali, gouache over photographic print, ca. 1934, *Face of Mae West Which Mae Be Used as an Apartment*

(Photograph © 1995, Art Institute of Chicago. All rights reserved. Dali art: copyright © 1997, Demart Pro Arte, Geneva/Artists Rights Society [ARS], New York)

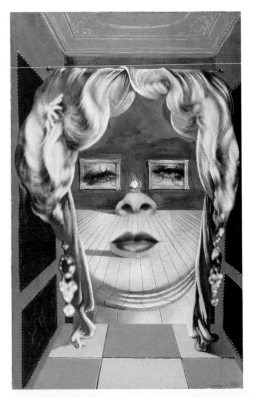

17

DAMAGE CONTROL

*T*HE inner circle—Beverly and her husband, Baikoff, brother Jack, Petroff and Timony—recognized that for Mae West career took precedence over any other claim. Her family attachments, sex life, and ventures into the occult—all high priorities—could not rival her commitment to the job of being a movie star. "She lives for her work . . . Nothing but *success* really matters to her," writer Ruth Biery noted, comparing West to other actresses. "Joan Crawford, now, is a hundred different women . . . Barbara Stanwyck has a stronger personality as a *woman* than she has on the screen . . . But Mae West—there's only one Mae West, and the public knows her better than her so-called friends."

As if to illustrate this point, when her father died of a heart attack while visiting friends in Oakland, in the San Francisco Bay Area, she insisted on continuing to work, missing only half a day's shooting to attend the funeral in Los Angeles on January 8, 1935. She did foot the bill for the private ceremony, which cost $1,491, and arranged to have the body transported to New York for burial near Matilda at Cypress Hills, not far from where he once lived. Mae did not accompany her dead father East; Beverly, Jack, and James Timony, who had always considered Battlin' Jack a buddy, did the honors.

The contrast between Mae's rather matter-of-fact response to her father's death and her complete collapse just five years earlier, at the loss of her mother, speaks volumes about the division in her daughterly emotions. To Jack Senior she behaved with conscientiousness rather than devotion; he profoundly influenced her sense of humor, her body consciousness, her fondness for the ring and the track, her standards of male attractiveness, her whole stance. But at the same time he had sometimes frightened, angered, and even disgusted her. "Pa spent his time reading the sporting editions, one foot on the mantelpiece, and the other tucked under him. I'm obliged to him for the physique he gave me" was the best tribute she could muster. She made it a few days before he died.

With both parents gone, Mae felt herself drawn back into the world of spiritualism, which promised contact with the dead. At a resort called La Quinta, which was frequented by Paramount executives, she met Amelia Earhart, who shared this mystical bent. (Earhart's husband, former publisher George Palmer Putnam, was working for Paramount as head of the company's editorial board.) Mae had long admired Earhart for her courage and her mastery of the sky, "a man's world. She was never afraid and she was smart," Mae said of her. Earhart, in turn, admired Mae West, and the two pioneers—one in aviation, the other in sexuality—talked about their mutual interest in psychic explorations. Earhart took the role of spirit guide, promising to share "some of the mysteries," almost as fascinating to her as flying.

At a table in Mae's resort bungalow, Earhart presided over a séance, instructing those gathered round not to move the table in any way. She informed the group that as the psychic forces were summoned, they would make their presence known by tipping the table so that it rapped the floor in front of the person they wanted to contact. Each rap signified a letter of the alphabet, one rap meaning A, two raps B, and so on.

"Suddenly," according to Mae, "the table began to tip in my direction." A message was being sent her—from her recently deceased father, it turned out. He informed her that one of the men she was seeing—a man who happened to be present at the séance—was "okay" and that she should continue to see him if she wanted to. But she had another admirer at the time. He should be dropped, Battlin' Jack advised. (Possibly the one who got the nod was heavyweight wrestling champion, "handsome brute" Vincent Lopez. At any rate, Mae began seeing Lopez, her future bodyguard, around this period and sustained the relationship for some years. The admirer he warned against may have been Jack Durant, an ex-acrobat and dancer with whom she was briefly seen around town.)

During the séance, Mae's father referred to her as "my kid," which made her suspicious; she had never heard him speak of her in that way. But a Paramount executive included in the séance reported that during visits to the lot Jack Senior used to talk about Mae's antics as a child and, when he told those stories, had consistently referred to her as "my kid."

After the séance with Amelia Earhart, Mae concentrated on developing her psychic powers. Each day she retreated to a dark room, where she sat, meditating, on a straight-back chair, placing her hands on her knees.

During his months in California, Mae had introduced her father to many Paramount stars and officials, sometimes describing him to them as a chiropractor as well as an ex-pugilist. She remained touchy about her background and assertive about her proud lineage. She kept a copy of the West coat of arms and the West genealogy, documenting her descent from Alfred the Great, on the wall in her Ravenswood living room.

The issue of social status arose frequently in a Hollywood where Constance Bennett married a billionaire, Douglas Fairbanks Jr. a Hartford, and Randolph Scott a DuPont; where Gary Cooper kept company with a countess and later married a socialite. Multimillionaire Howard Hughes and John Hay Whitney, an American aristocrat, both participated in moviemaking, and Hollywood social events were attended by Vanderbilts and Kennedys, by the likes of Doris Duke and Barbara Hutton. The boundaries separating celebrity, wealth, and blue blood grew less and less distinct.

Mae West could trundle out her own list of elite social contacts. One of the wealthiest men in the world, the Sultan of Johore, had visited the set of *Belle of the Nineties* with his wife, the Sultana; they and the star had been photographed together on the lot. Cary Grant introduced her to Noël Coward, "as witty as any character in his smart plays." She met Mrs. Reginald Vanderbilt, her sister Lady Furness, and the President's son, Elliott Roosevelt. The head of London's Selfridge's paid a call. Mae gave tea to World War I hero Viscount Byng and Lady Byng. Invited to attend King George's Jubilee in London, she sent regrets: "Sorry George— too busy."

Questions of class, snobbish exclusion, and social mobility dominate the picture Mae began filming in late 1934, titled first *How Am I Doin'*, then *Now I'm a Lady*, before it became *Goin' to Town*. Mae plays Cleo Borden, a dance-hall entertainer in the contemporary American West (the exact location isn't specified, but it could be Texas). Cleo inherits the ranch and oil wells of cattle rustler Buck Gonzales (Fred Kohler), who is shot soon after winning Cleo's hand in a crap game. ("He's a bad man," Cleo sings about Buck, "but he loves me right.") Now an heiress, Cleo falls for an elegant and haughty Englishman, Edward Carrington, who works as a geological engineer on the Gonzales ranch. (The Carrington role, originally scripted for Cary Grant, is played by Paul Cavanaugh.)

Carrington initially spurns Cleo as "rather crude oil." Like Cary Grant's Captain Cummings, who was advised to "loosen up," he has trouble letting go; his British reserve makes him all the more a challenge. Cleo chides him, "Why don't you release those brakes?" Instead of attraction, he at first shows contempt, which she answers by shooting off his hat and roping him like a steer, actions Mae thought would appeal especially to children in the audience. Mae had to master some new skills to play Cleo: she practiced handling a lariat, drawing, twirling, and firing a six-shooter, and dealing cards, and trained her voice to sing opera; she also overcame her fears and learned to ride horseback.

Cleo's British assistant Winslow explains that a man like Carrington wants a woman with "background," someone from his own social stratum. "What's that," Cleo wonders, "something I ain't got?" She tells Carrington he acts as if "I ain't exactly a lady." When he admits that to him she's something new, she comments, "You're used to dames who serve pink tea and stick out their little finger when they drink it." Later, she charges him with disdain for her pedigree: "You'd like to have my ancestors go back and come over on the *Mayflower*."

Naturally, Carrington falls for her. But for the first time in many years Mae West plays a woman in hot pursuit of reluctant quarry, a climber willing to travel to Buenos Aires, even to marry a titled wastrel, just to gain the social cachet she feels she must have to win Carrington. "Find me a guy with blue blood in his veins and I'll put a deposit on him tonight," she tells Winslow. Cleo Borden in time becomes Mrs. Fletcher Colton, of New York, Miami, and Southampton. (The originally announced idea of basing the movie on the saga of Isabella Stewart Gardner of Boston was never developed; only the high-society milieu was retained.)

As in the plays and in *I'm No Angel*, a snobbish, viperish socialite matron tries to prevent the Mae West character from crashing high society. In *Goin' to Town* she's Mrs. Crane Brittony (played by Marjorie Gateson, who despite her broad *a* was actually born in Brooklyn). Mrs. Brittony regards Cleo Borden as a vulgar *arriviste*. "Shocking what sort of people have money nowadays," she sneers, behind Cleo's back. Mrs. Brittony drips disdain. Though she is listed in the *Social Register* and her portrait, in riding gear, adorns the pages of *Town and Country* magazine, she has fewer scruples than an alley cat: she bribes the caddish Russian aristocrat Ivan Valadov (Ivan Lebedeff) to disable Cactus, the American horse Cleo backs in the International Sweepstakes in Buenos Aires, and hires the same mercenary Ivan to compromise Cleo's marriage to Fletcher Colton, Mrs. Brittony's nephew, and drive Cleo out of Southampton.

When Mrs. Brittony, with two other patrician matrons, Mrs. Pillsbury and Mrs. Cranford, call on Cleo at Colton Manor, Southampton, they try to expose Cleo's commonness. Cleo won't be put down. She says she had her ancestors traced, "but they were too smart, they couldn't catch them." A shot showing Cleo's monkey jumping on Mrs. Brittony's head, making a mockery of her phony dignity, was deleted, but even without that scene she's exposed as a sham, a blue-blooded guttersnipe, while Cleo exhibits superior substance beneath a lower-class manner.

Cleo will prove her high-class mettle by singing the role of Delilah ("one lady barber that made good") in the Saint-Saëns opera *Samson and Delilah*. Clad in a black chiffon gown with a long, shimmering trail and diamond-studded pelvic- and breast-plates; crowned with a long-haired blond wig topped by a tiara of diamond leaves, Cleo makes a grand entrance as dark-skinned, half-naked male slaves bow in homage to her. Cleo sings, in French, the mezzo half of the duet "Mon coeur s'ouvre à ta voix" as she fondles her Samson's long curls. Sending up the prima donna had been part of Mae West's vaudeville act in 1922; now she expands it in an elaborate cinema spoof of high culture. Since she is having fun at the expense of the diva, she is also indulging in self-parody. This is Mae West at her best.

As satire, however, *Goin' to Town* sabotages itself. It mocks upper-crust arrogance and pretension—when Ivan tells Cleo he's the backbone of his family, she advises his family to see a chiropractor—but it also shows elite status to be something worth angling for. Cleo goes through with a marriage of convenience to demonstrate her worthiness of Carrington—as if acquiring a fancy last name really did better her. We wonder, if her spendthrift husband, Fletcher Colton, hadn't conveniently been murdered, how she would have managed to snare Carrington, now the Earl of Stratton. Did she marry with a plan to quickly divorce? The silly plot won't bear too close scrutiny.

Paramount tried to sell *Goin' to Town* as a new departure for Mae West. Although the director, Alexander Hall, had been an editor of *She Done Him Wrong*, that picture's 1890s formula was traded in for something contemporary. Instead of playing a Bowery Belle, Mae West was touted as "a gal of the hour." In place of a corset, she sports Western gear; astride a horse, she wears white britches and shirt, a ten-gallon cowgirl hat on her head. "She's left the Bowery days," ads promised, "and the old-fashioned Nineties behind. She's modern now . . . streamlined for speed, slick as a cocktail bar."

Press releases touted Miss West's wish to be introduced to a list of the men of the moment: She wanted to meet John D. Rockefeller, she said, "to find out where he gets all those dimes"; famed baseball pitcher Dizzy Dean, "to find out if he's as good as he says he is"; the Prince of Wales, "who's been looking for the right girl for forty years"; Oliva Dionne, father of the famed quintuplets, just to get a look at him; James Branch Cabell, to learn whether "his books really mean what I think they do"; G-man Melvin Purvis, the agent who tracked down Dillinger, because he must be "fascinatin' "; and Turkey's Mustapha Kemal, because she wanted to thank him personally: "When he took the Turkish women out of harems and out from behind their veils, he did a real service."

But efforts to update the Mae West of *Goin' to Town* had little impact and less staying power. The picture's contemporary Western backdrop lasts only a short time. "I didn't keep the plot in the West too long, because I wanted to wear some fabulous clothes," she explained. When Cleo "goes to town" in Buenos Aires and later in Southampton, Mae West is gowned, sequined, jeweled, be-feathered and be-furred in Travis Banton finery as of old. Although a weight gain has, despite Paramount's "streamlined" claim, swelled her famous hourglass figure, in the latter two-thirds of *Goin' to Town* the new Mae West looks a lot like her predecessors.

In her statements to the press, Mae West promised that her new picture would offend no one's moral sensibilities. She told Edwin Schallert of the *Los Angeles Times*, "The story for my next film, in which I play a cattle queen, was too censorable as they gave it to me, and so I rewrote it. It's going to be funny, but it will also be safe." To demonstrate her uprightness, she pounced on a shocking, recently released nudist picture (one that bypassed the Hays Office because it did not play at major theaters and therefore did not require the MPPDA Seal of Approval) called *Elysia*. "You can't blame people for objecting to the rough stuff," she said. "I went to see *Elysia* myself and it was terrible. All those people running around without any clothes. Adults want to know they can go to the theater with their children, and they have a right to take them." Her efforts to appease the presiding Hays Office powers are unmistakable.

Joseph Breen agreed that, compared to previous Mae West movies, *Goin' to Town* seemed pretty tame stuff. "We are happy to note that a sincere effort has been made to get away from any basically questionable elements," he wrote to Hays midway through production, after he had cut out a sequence in which Cleo does the tango and the rumba with her Native South American assistant Taho (Tito Coral), and deleted another scene showing

Cleo's horse, Cactus, in her bed. (A goat in W. C. Fields's bed was tolerated in *My Little Chickadee*.)

Cleo's song "Now I'm a Lady" was put through the wringer. The original version provoked Breen more than anything else in the picture, and the lyric by Irving Kahal, in its final revision, bears slight resemblance to the original. Before Breen got his hands on it, Cleo's songs revealed her as an unabashed gold digger who had to work for her pennies "to keep my cloud silver-lined." This Cleo had plenty of sugar daddies, "as much as seven or nine,/But now I'm a lady/I see 'em one at a time." The unexpurgated Cleo admits she did "some chiselin' and moochin'/To win a little success." There's more than a hint that she used to sell her body, for she once owned a honky-tonk in El Paso "where every jack was a john./But now she's a lady./She went from saloon to salon." She was a "red-hot Delilah" who "set the prairie aflame."

The original contained some clever wordplay, but Breen was not amused. He interpreted the lyric as "the boasting of a woman of loose morals who has had any number of men in her time, and has climbed over them to the top of the ladder . . . Even in a lyric, this seems to us to be definitely the wrong kind of material for the screen." He urged Paramount to have the song rewritten or risk seeing the picture condemned. Irving Kahal obliged with a new lyric. In the cleaned-up version which is used in the film, Cleo steers clear of the dance called the jelly roll, and has no honky-tonk or gold-digging proclivities in her past, though she does lay claim to "the army/Of my forgotten men."

In a letter to Paramount's John Hammell, Breen specified that there must be no suggestion of prostitution in the dance-hall sequence, but he let stand the scene where Cleo smooches with a cowboy (Grant Withers) before Buck Gonzales wins the promise of her hand. Since the code prohibited unnecessary violence as well as unsanctified sex, Breen also suppressed scenes involving cattle branding.

Breen's objection to a shot showing Cleo silhouetted in a doorway as the light behind discloses her form through her garments was honored. But some of the lines he questioned slipped in. For instance, Cleo's description of herself as "a woman of few words but lots of action," and the following exchanges:

CLEO: For a long time I was ashamed of the way I lived.
YOUNG MAN: You mean to say you reformed?
CLEO: No, I got over being ashamed.

And:

> CLEO: What do you know about me?
> CARRINGTON: Just what I see, and that's quite sufficient.
> CLEO: Hmm, you're easily satisfied.

Italy and Moravia rejected the film outright. England accepted it, but cut "I got over being ashamed" and "a woman of few words, but lots of action." Pennsylvania and Ohio cut "You're easily satisfied." Carrington's description of a "curved portion" of the map, and of "undeveloped territory" didn't survive the shears of censors in Massachusetts and Ohio.

Goin' to Town cost $924,000 to make, of which $300,000 was paid to Mae West, compared to $11,302 for the director, Alexander Hall. Although after taxes she was left with only $155,050, Mae West still ranked eleventh-highest-paid star in 1935, largely because of *Goin' to Town*. The picture did well in Manhattan, Brooklyn, San Francisco, Minneapolis, and Los Angeles, but only moderately well in Pittsburgh, grossing $10,000 in its first week there, "no great shakes for a West picture, all of which have just about doubled that take in the past."

Like *Belle of the Nineties*, *Goin' to Town* suffers by comparison with *She Done Him Wrong* and *I'm No Angel*, two wholly original, refreshing, funny, and bold undertakings. Although *Goin' to Town* boasts some laugh-out-loud lines, gives us the wonderful grand-opera send-up, explores new settings, and highlights a class angle that provides some interest and zip, it breaks no new ground. Its heroine has been corraled. Cleo Borden defies fewer taboos and breaches social and sexual conventions less often than either Lady Lou or Tira. This is only partly the fault of Joe Breen. It's also the consequence of a repressive moral climate at large in the nation, and of Mae West's need to stick with her character's well-established attributes, proven box-office winners. With each new outing she who was once defined by her risk taking becomes more predictable and formulaic.

When the film was released, critics were on the whole unimpressed; for most of them, the bloom was off the Westian rose. *Goin' to Town*, averred the *Hollywood Reporter*, "is the weakest and most slipshod production that Madame West has taken credit for writing. What once looked like hearty bawdiness has palled to the point where it's just the handwriting on the back fence." *Variety* concurred, labeling it "Mae West's poorest." Among the trade papers, only the morally conservative *Motion Picture Herald* proffered a good word, praising the picture's "high moral tone."

The New York critics were equally underwhelmed. Meyer Levin, in *Esquire*, unkindly expressed dismay at a Mae West who looked "like a very ordinary double-chinned dame," and at a movie that offered up "a bad imitation, almost a parody, of the Mae West formula." André Sennwald of *The New York Times*, after identifying himself as "one of Miss West's most abject idolaters," sadly detected "intimations of mortality." She "seems to have gained weight in not altogether discreet localities," he lamented. "Nor has the change to modern dress improved her lure for those of us who loved her as the brewery beauty of her earlier masterpieces." Sennwald found the picture's lampooning of high society to be heavy-handed, betraying in Mae West "a slight feeling of inferiority toward the socially elect." As for the romance between Cleo Borden and Carrington, "whoever heard of Miss West chasing a man?"

The New Yorker loved the Samson and Delilah aria, but rated the film as "very credible West," rather than "sensational West." It recommended the picture, not as a main course, but "by way of a chaser after *The Informer*."

The tepid response to *Goin' to Town* only intensified Mae West's feelings of fatigue, sadness, and confusion. The censorship wars were getting to her, prompting soul-searching about her own values and about what makes something right or wrong. What was really bad? Was she? Social arbiters and organized religion seemed to ignore gray regions and to invite hypocrisy.

Prevailing attitudes about marriage especially baffled her. The world—not just the Hays Office—seemed to demand that couples legitimize their relationships; yet in Hollywood people changed marriage partners readily, breaking their wedding vows as casually as teacups. Mae West continued to believe that sexual morality should be a private matter, to be mediated between individuals; it could not be governed solely by laws or religion. Yet she no longer could scoff at religion as she once had.

Her hard-won sense of security was being tested by changes in the Paramount pecking order that impacted on her directly. Her mentor Emanuel Cohen, the man responsible for signing her to Paramount in 1932, was abruptly fired from his position as vice president in charge of production just as shooting of *Goin' to Town* came to an end. (This was just a month after the death of Battlin' Jack. Father figures were getting scarce.) Studio brass, and Cohen himself, remained mum about the cause of the split and made it appear that Cohen had resigned of his own free will. "Mr. Cohen declined to comment on reports of friction between himself and Adolph Zukor and other executives," the press reported. Rumor had it that Cohen was sent packing for being a "star pamperer." Perhaps the studio believed the exorbitant payments to Mae West, among others, were out of bounds.

Another theory held that Cohen was dismissed when it was discovered that he was covertly signing personal contracts with Paramount stars like Mae West, Gary Cooper, and Bing Crosby. This he certainly did. He signed them all to his independent production company, Major Pictures, arranging later to have his Major films funded and distributed by Paramount. But the formation of Cohen's independent Major Pictures was not announced until July 1935 and Mae West didn't officially sign with Major Pictures until early 1936. Manny Cohen was fired in February 1935. Exactly which cart came before what horse isn't clear. But as of February 6, 1935, the new heads of production at Paramount became lawyer Henry Herzbrun and director Ernst Lubitsch.

Manny Cohen, although widely credited with turning around Paramount's economic fortunes in his two and a half years as production chief, did not enjoy personal popularity. Short in stature, aggressive and conspiratorial by temperament, he was likened by Budd Schulberg to "all the small, darting predatory animals—ferrets, weasels, rats." Betty Lasky blamed him for overthrowing her father, Jesse, in the shakeup in which Cohen came to power in 1932, and Dorothy Parker dismissed him as "a pony's ass." But Mae West remained loyal to him; as far as she was concerned, he had been instrumental in opening doors to her and making her Hollywood triumphs possible. In gratitude, she joined Gary Cooper and Cecil B. DeMille on the planning committee for a huge banquet in Cohen's honor, held shortly before Cohen's sudden dismissal by Paramount, at the Indian Room of the Ambassador Hotel. Among those who entertained that night were Bing Crosby, W. C. Fields, singer Lyda Roberti, and the "College Rhythm" chorus. Guests included Claudette Colbert, Kitty Carlisle, Marlene Dietrich, Charles Laughton, and several of Mae West's past and future co-players: Katherine DeMille, Cary Grant, Alison Skipworth, Randolph Scott, and Kent Taylor. After dinner Mae West made a rare speech, singing Cohen's praises, as she affected an editorial—or was it a royal?—"we." She gushed, "He's the real man in our picture life . . . He made it possible for us to produce pictures which have lifted theater mortgages all over the country and given us an opportunity to cheer up millions of people."

Shortly after Cohen made his unwelcome and anxiety-provoking exit from Paramount, a figure from her past made a disturbing re-entrance into Mae West's life: Frank Wallace. In Milwaukee, a worker for the County Register of

Deeds came upon the 1911 marriage certificate of Mae West and Frank Wallace, and leaked the discovery to the press. Newspapers from coast to coast published photographs of the actual license, along with the wedding photo showing dark-haired Mae and jaunty, straw-hatted Frank smiling within the cradle of a crescent moon. The license gave the bride's age in 1911 as eighteen, adding a year to her actual age at the time. Since Mae West habitually gave the year of her birth as 1900, she was caught in more than one fib.

The New York *Mirror* gave the story front-page coverage, and reproduced a 1927 court document showing that Mae West had answered "Yes" to the question "Married?" To further complicate matters, a diligent reporter in Fort Worth, Texas, came up with the marriage license issued on March 22, 1924, to Mae West and B. A. Burmester.

Mae had long regarded the facts of her biography as a text that could be edited: revised, embellished, and altered at her will. She immediately issued an outraged denial. "I'm not married. I never have been married. Not to Frank Wallace. Not to Jim Timony . . . Not to that fellow in Texas . . . I'm a single gal with a single-track mind—and it doesn't run to matrimony." If she'd been married all this time, why would she have worked so hard to support herself? "A girl might forget matrimony maybe but never alimony or any other kind of money, and all the alimony I ever got wouldn't buy a diamond in a ten cent store." Being known as a single, available woman—a spinster, as she jokingly called herself—was an essential component of the package called Mae West. She wasn't about to repackage herself. She made fun of the sudden run on claimants to the husband title. Appearing with cast members from *Goin' to Town* on the Louella Parsons radio program on station KHJ, Los Angeles, she quipped, "I hope all my husbands are listening in."

The press had a field day. For a brief period there was conjecture that the Frank Wallace who married Mae West was a bit player by that name who'd had a small part in the 1928 production of *Diamond Lil*. But before long the real Frank Wallace, a very eager interviewee, crawled out of the woodwork, admitting in articles quoted nationwide that he had indeed wed Mae West, "a classy little brunette," twenty-four years ago, when touring with her on the Columbia burlesque circuit. "We were playing at the Gaiety in Milwaukee when Mae and I decided to make it a double." He'd met her in Canarsie, he said, and had been invited to her house in Ridgewood to partake of Matilda's pigs' knuckles and sauerkraut. He'd returned often to rehearse songs (like "When My Marie Sings Chiddee Biddee Bee") and dances with Mae in the basement. Neglecting to mention that he had married and divorced another woman since parting with Mae, he professed undying devotion to the star. "If I had the money I would still be sending her flowers every week."

Wallace, "a slender, dark chap of medium height," still made his way as a struggling song-and-dance man, he informed the press, the male half of the team Wallace and Le May, managed by Jack Cornell of the Strand Building, if anyone out there wanted to get in touch. Before long he put together an act duplicating his old one with Mae; he was billed as "Mr. Mae West."

Mae was so distressed by the torrent of unwanted publicity that she went into seclusion for a time. She refused to acknowledge the truth about her early marriage until the courts finally forced her to, in July 1937. After a protracted legal battle over which state—New York or California—held legal jurisdiction, in 1941 Wallace sued in San Bernadino County, California, for $1,000 monthly maintenance; Mae West countersued in Los Angeles, winning a final divorce decree on July 23, 1942. Wallace, who died in 1966, attempted to exploit the situation to the end. On his way back from a trip to Mexico, he wrote a song about divorce, "The Honeymoon's Over on the Mexico Lane," which he promoted as "a hillbilly classic."

Despite mounting evidence to the contrary, Mae persisted in refusing to admit her true age, or that she had ever played in burlesque. Eva Tanguay, now ill, destitute, and almost blind, spoke up in Mae's defense from her Los Angeles home, claiming that Frank Wallace must have married the other Mae West, the tall brunette burlesque queen who headlined at the Columbia Theater in Chicago. But an old-time burlesque comedian, Harry Fields, insisted that the famous movie star was the same woman he'd played with on the Columbia Circuit.

Nor would Mae grant that she had ever had brown hair. If a fan asked her to autograph an old photo of the brunette Mae West, she'd try to take it in exchange for another. "That's not me," she'd insist.

She celebrated her forty-second birthday quietly at a dinner with her brother and sister, brother-in-law, Baikoff (who had been given, at Mae's insistence, a small part in *Goin' to Town,* and would appear in her next film as well), Timony, and Petroff. (Petroff broke from the fold at the end of 1935.) Her gifts included a diamond bracelet and a platinum evening purse studded with diamonds, sapphires, and emeralds. To cheer herself up she bought another car, a Duesenberg roadster with white sidewall tires and skirted fenders. She hadn't yet spoken the line from her next picture: "It isn't what you get that counts, but what you give."

*   *   *

The moral confusion Mae West addresses in her autobiography surfaces in her next, and most uncharacteristic film, *Klondike Annie*, a movie that emits mixed signals. She plays a former kept woman named Rose Carelton, the Frisco Doll, who switches identities with a missionary woman and becomes Soul Savin' Annie, an evangelical do-gooder, in the gold-rush town of Nome, Alaska.

The stories of Jack London created a vogue for tales about the Klondike that flourished early in the century and survived into the twenties and thirties. Chaplin's *The Gold Rush* (1925) had famously exploited the Klondike setting on film. A vaudeville playlet of 1915, "Salvation Sue," set in the Alaskan gold fields, concerned a female Salvation Army leader who works at soul-saving in the town's dance halls and saloons. The Edward Sheldon play and movie based on it called *Salvation Nell* (remade in 1931) was set not in Alaska but in a Lower East Side Manhattan settlement house; it told of a bad girl, mistress of a thief, who turns into a God-fearing woman. Threads from these earlier plots were woven into the script of *Klondike Annie*. The popularity of the charismatic evangelist Aimee Semple McPherson lent fresh topicality to plots involving missionary women.

Several writers helped create the script for the new Mae West vehicle. A story by Frank Mitchell Dazey, set in Alaska and titled "Lulu Was a Lady," had been announced as the next project, then scrapped when Marion Morgan and George Dowell, the team behind *Goin' to Town*, were brought in. Their story was going to be called "Hallelujah I'm a Saint," and it was going to incorporate some of Frank Dazey's Alaska material, as well as characters and settings from Mae West's unproduced play of 1930, *Frisco Kate*. Other titles considered were "How About It, Brother?" and "Klondike Lou." The "Lou" was dropped because it was too reminiscent of Lady Lou in *She Done Him Wrong*, now banned.

In her play *Frisco Kate*, the part Mae West intended for herself was the Frisco Doll, the "sweetest tart in the Barbary Coast," who is shanghaied and brought aboard the ship *Java Maid*, where she is worshipped by its brutish and idolatrous captain, Bull Brackett. When Brackett tries to rape her, she murders him with a stiletto and goes off into the sunset with her true love, Stanton. In the screenplay, the man the Doll murders is her Chinese keeper, the vice lord Chan Lo, who has imprisoned her under his roof, forcing her to entertain guests at his posh San Francisco gambling resort, and jealously curtailing her contact with other men. During her year with Chan Lo she has adapted: she has learned to speak some Chinese and to wear exotic finery. In her first scene she entertains Chan Lo's customers by singing "I'm an Occidental Woman in an Oriental Mood for Love." She accompanies herself on a Chinese stringed instrument which she holds Western style like a guitar or ukulele (returning to a pose she once struck for an old sheet-music cover), and wears a shimmering, Balinese-looking headdress.

She has learned to stand up to Chan Lo, to confront him fearlessly, despite his jealousy and cruelty. (His threats to blind and torture her were deleted by the Hays Office.) She tells him she's tired of being exhibited like one of his curios, and that he stifles her. When he calls her his "pearl of pearls," she counters: "This pearl of pearls is getting unstrung." After she complains that he prevents her from having men friends "of my own race," he tells her he doesn't trust men: "It is written there are two perfectly good men, one dead, one unborn." She jeers, "Which one are you?"

The Hays Office cut the scene showing her knifing Chan Lo in self-defense, but we hear about it. We see her escaping with her Chinese servant Fah Wong, who will join a lover in Seattle, and boarding the *Java Maid* on a foggy San Francisco night. The ship's captain, Bull Brackett (Victor McLaglen), is considerably tamed from his incarnation in *Frisco Kate*. There he was a crude, drunken, out-of-control brute who doltishly worships a female nude statue as an icon. Victor McLaglen's Brackett does drink and does possess a statue, but scenes revealing his worshipful feelings about it were removed. He's gruff but endearing, and he loyally tries to conceal the Doll from the police who come on board to search for her. Although the Doll cares more for the mounted policeman (Phillip Reed) who falls for her than for Brackett, in the end she settles for the sea captain, telling him, "You're no oil painting, but you're a fascinatin' monster."

The character Annie Alden has no counterpart in the play. Angelic Sister Annie Alden, pious, kind, devout, sincere, and selfless to a saintly degree, boards the *Java Maid* at Vancouver and moves into the Doll's cabin. The Doll, a.k.a. Rose Carleton, befriends the missionary and falls under her righteous influence. She "sees things different now." The Doll is deeply moved by Annie's call to good works, by her desire to save the fallen souls in gold-besotted Alaska. Annie tries to find goodness in everybody. When the Doll offers her whiskey, she declines, but thanks her for her charity. Seeing Rose and Bull Brackett embrace, she exhibits shock, then tells Rose, "It must be hard for such a pretty woman to be good." The Doll demonstrates she's capable of selfless kindness by caring for Annie attentively when Annie falls sick. On her deathbed, Annie insists on giving her prayer book to the Doll, thereby passing on to her both piety and a mission. After Annie dies, the Doll switches clothing and identities with the dead woman. She emerges from the cabin—which police are about to search in their quest for the murderess Rose Carleton—transformed, dressed in a nunlike plain black dress and bonnet, with what looks like a prayer book or Bible clutched in her hands.

In Nome, the Doll, disguised as Annie, will raise money for a new settlement house, preach to a full house against the evils of drink, enlist the charitable aid of dance-hall girls (telling their leader, "When you take religion for a joke, the laugh is on you"), and reunite a separated married couple before revealing her true identity and setting out for San Francisco to face murder charges. She proves an effective spiritual leader precisely *because* of her closeness to the sinners; she speaks their language, and she knows how to "wrassle the devil. Tyin' a knot in his tail won't throw him on his back. You gotta grab him by the horns." Like Margy LaMont in *Sex*, she refuses the love of the clean-cut suitor (in this instance, the policeman), falling back on the rough-cut one (in this case, Brackett) because she could not live with herself if she ruined a man's future. She has assuaged "the pain in my conscience" and has learned "that you don't have to go around lookin' sad and wearin' a long face to be good . . . You can do right and still have a good time in this world."

The religious strain in the story sent the Hays Office into a frenzy of anxiety. When Paramount's John Hammell advised Will Hays that Mae West would in her new film impersonate a religious worker, Hays insisted that it must be made evident that "Miss West is not masquerading as a preacher, revivalist, or any character known and accepted as a minister of religion . . . Rather, her assumed character should be that of a social service worker." He also insisted that as Annie, Mae West must play it straight. "There should be no feeling of burlesque in this social worker." References to God and Jesus, to the Lord's Vineyard, to the angel Gabriel, to Christian Evangelists, to preaching, and to missions had to go.

Hymns had to be changed to secular tunes (although "It's Better to Give than to Receive" sounds like a hymn). Joseph Breen reminded Paramount that the British Board of Film Censors had eliminated in toto the spiritual singing sequence in *Belle of the Nineties*, and the prayer meeting that accompanied it. In *Klondike Annie* the word "Hallelujah" was proscribed, and the book Annie carries was changed from a Bible to one called *Settlement Maxims*. Doll's line "I can tell you about what King Solomon knew but didn't tell" was excised, and she was not allowed to appear in flowing white garments, with a diamond Star of Bethlehem in her hair. Despite deletions intended to encourage vagueness, most viewers easily identified the settlement house as a Salvation Army mission.

A scene that caused particular consternation—it was shown in previews but quickly pulled—pictured the Doll making up the dead Sister Annie to look like a strumpet, putting heavy makeup on her face, curling her hair, reclothing her body, and painting a beauty mark on her cheek. The *Hollywood Reporter* singled this scene out as "particularly distasteful," commenting: "It is unnecessary to show the flash of the dead woman with her hair curled and dressed in flimsies." No trace of this lost footage has yet turned up.

Production of *Klondike Annie* seemed to be jinxed from the start. An extortion attempt, a few weeks after shooting started, distracted and upset the star. MAE WEST ACID THREAT BARED; SUSPECT HELD, the headline ran after an arrest was made. An unknown thug was threatening her with disfigurement if she did not cough up $1,000. The extortionist, who turned out to be employed as a busboy at Fox Film Studio, was staked out by a covey of detectives who hid in the background at the designated drop-off location as decoy Harry Dean of the district attorney's office, fitted out in a white fox fur coat, blond wig, and white beret so that from a distance and in the dark he resembled Mae West, emerged from her chauffeur-driven limousine and placed a package of bogus money at the base of a palm tree. The strategy failed for some reason. No one came to pick up the package. Another drop-off appointment was set up by Mae and the would-be extortionist. This time she herself emerged from the limousine and dropped the package. Within a half hour the suspect arrived and picked it up. He was surrounded by the detectives, who wielded rifles and submachine guns. "Were you frightened?" a reporter asked Mae after the miscreant had been arraigned. "Sure," she admitted. "I was afraid of fireworks either from the extortioner or the detectives."

Tensions mounted on the set as well as off. Although Mae West had hand-picked her director, Raoul Walsh, he was threatening to walk by the second week of shooting, and production stopped cold for one week. *Variety* described the conflict as a "three-way scrap," among studio, director, and actress. Mae West was accused of ordering countless retakes, insisting on hiring excessive numbers of bit players, employing 270 dressmakers, and in general ignoring cost overruns at a time when Paramount, reorganized with John Otterson at the helm, had emerged from receivership determined to shave production expenses.

Mae made no secret of her dissatisfaction with cinematographer Victor Milner, demanding that he be replaced by Karl Struss. Struss, however, was busy working on another film, *Anything Goes*, with Bing Crosby, and Crosby stood firm, refusing to release him. A compromise was finally reached when Struss's assistant, George Clemens, agreed to take over the cameras for the Mae West film.

Miss West's habitual lateness caused further stress. She arrived early enough at the studio, but because of her desire to have her hair and costumes appear perfect, she spent many hours being fussed over and gussied up, and would show up at the set a half hour after the 9 a.m. call. Walsh decided not to confront her about her tardiness, "because I knew what a perfectionist she was." But Lubitsch, the new Paramount production chief Mae liked to call a son of a Lubitsch when he was out of earshot, saw fit to reprimand her. When he snapped at her, Mae "started after him with a hand mirror . . . and got in a couple of whacks." Lubitsch tried to retreat, but she pursued him, "swearing like a Portuguese sailor and swinging the mirror like a club." She cursed him until he took cover. As one hundred extras clapped and cheered, she muttered, " 'If that Dutch clown ever comes near me again, I'll wreck him.' "

Although Walsh rated her performance top-notch, script and casting problems plagued the production, and the budget soared. Victor McLaglen agreed to join the cast quite late in the game; playing opposite Mae West was widely considered a difficult assignment, unless the actor in question enjoyed functioning as a feeder. Mae West chose McLaglen in part because of his bulk. Her weight had soared to 142 pounds and she thought that next to McLaglen—"He's not only tall, but wide, a very thick look in his face"—she'd appear thin. Lubitsch regretted that McLaglen—whose performance in *The Informer* would soon win him an Academy Award—was underutilized in *Klondike Annie*, being asked to function as a mere "stooge." "Other actors," Lubitsch told Mae, "don't mind sharing a spotlight. Look at Norma Shearer and Fredric March, or Clark Gable and Jean Harlow, or William Powell and Myrna Loy. Why can't you write a script with two major roles instead of just one? Don't forget that Shakespeare wrote a play called *Romeo and Juliet*." Mae West got in the last word. "Shakespeare had his style," she snapped, "and I have mine."

Lubitsch had had it. In exasperation he turned over all further studio responsibility for the picture to Henry Herzbrun and William Le Baron. When Timony accused him of acting like Hitler, trying to push Mae West around, and of demonstrating that he lacked Mae West's years of show-biz experience, Lubitsch scoffed, "Try to push her around? She's much too heavy . . . Of course she was in show business before I was. She's older than I am." (Lubitsch was really a few months her senior.)

Originally budgeted at $750,000, *Klondike Annie* costs mounted to close to a million and a half, and production finished more than three weeks behind schedule in December 1935. An ending was not agreed on until the last minute, and Paramount came to regret its past indulgences to the star. Henceforth, they informed her, she would have to work out her story at home and not take time out from production. Her $10,000 a week salary was beginning to seem untenable. No wonder her loyalty to the studio began to falter. Paramount didn't feel like home to her anymore.

Klondike Annie stands out as the only Mae West movie in which she deviates from her formula. In place of her past philosophy, "Take as much as you can and give as little as possible," her character now affirms the joy of giving. For the first time, she sheds tears and admits to "a pain in my conscience." For the first time she occasionally doffs her ironic mask, seeming to speak from the heart about her desire to uplift people, to answer for her sins, and to perform good works. Viewers could understandably become confused, have trouble reconciling the new character with Mae West's well-established screen persona, and even with remnants of that persona in the Frisco Doll. The picture, stated one critic, "is neither flesh nor fowl nor good red herring. In this film something has scared [Mae West] stiff. Is it the censors? Is it that she thinks her old style is going out of fashion? Or, horrid thought! has she reformed?" Alberta, Canada, rejected the film outright as "an offensive mixture of religion and immorality."

Advertisements focused on the leading character's steamy, rather than her virtuous, side. ALASKA GOES TROPICAL IN KLONDIKE ANNIE. MAE ANSWERS THE CALL OF THE WILD. SHE MAKES THE FROZEN NORTH RED HOT.

Klondike Annie tries to have it both ways, to show the heroine as a sinner who undergoes a genuine moral transformation, and at the same time to fall back on familiar Mae West shtick. The "new" Mae West resembles the old one in her role as a performer with an eye for multiple men. Even as Soul Savin' Annie she goes for a romantic sleigh ride with the Mountie Jack Forrest, who tells her, "I can't visualize you as anything but the kind of woman to be loved, to be adored." It's the unrepentant Mae West, not earnest Rose Carleton, who observes, when trying to decide which man to follow, "When caught between two evils, I generally like to take the one I never tried." It's Mae West, not Rose, who wonders what good it is resisting temptation, since there'll always be more, and who tells Sister Annie, after Annie has expressed concern about girls who follow the line of least resistance, that a good line is hard to resist. If the censors had let her, Rose would have observed, "Give a man a free hand and he tries to put it all over you."

Breen finally anointed *Klondike Annie* with a Seal of Approval, but he had reached the sorry conclusion that Mae West movies could never be completely cleaned up. They were doomed to offend. "Just as long as we have Mae West on our hands," he thundered in a memorandum, "with the particular kind of story which she goes in for, we are going to have trouble. Difficulty is inherent with a Mae West picture. Lines and pieces of business, which in the script seem to be thoroughly innocuous, turn out, when shown on the screen, to be questionable, at best, when they are not definitely offensive."

Although the Legion of Decency rated *Klondike Annie* a "B"—not recommended for children, "not vicious in its entirety"—vituperative protest issued from a source that had not been actively crusading against Mae West since the days of *The Drag*. William Randolph Hearst sent the managing editors of all Hearst newspapers a tirade denouncing *Klondike Annie* as a filthy picture. "I think we should have editorials roasting the picture and Mae West and the Paramount Company . . . the producer, director and everyone concerned. We should say it is an affront to the decency of the public and the interests of the motion picture profession. Will Hays must be asleep to allow such a thing . . . but it is to be hoped that the churches of the community are awake to the necessity of boycotting such a picture." He urged the papers to publish editorials about the film's indecency, to be followed by a blackout: DO NOT MENTION MAE WEST IN OUR PAPERS AGAIN WHILE SHE IS ON THE SCREEN AND DO NOT ACCEPT ANY ADVERTISING OF THIS PICTURE. In some locations, theaters got around the ad ban by urging the public to phone the theater for the title of "that certain picture."

Hearst's New York *American* soon after ran an editorial headlined THE SCREEN MUST NOT RELAPSE TO LEWDNESS that read the riot act to Mae West, dredging up her past imprisonment on morals charges for *Sex* and concluding with a description of the unnamed film as "basically libidinous and sensual." He especially deplored *Klondike Annie*'s depiction of a white woman as "consort to a Chinese vice lord." Hearst deemed the offenses committed grave enough to justify the intervention of "the churches, the women's clubs, the various state censors, the state legislators and the Congress of the United States."

Hearst, who loved grandstanding, was said to be nursing a grudge against the Hays Office because it had made cuts on *Ceiling Zero*, produced by his Cosmopolitan Pictures. This explanation washes better than either the contemporary press's conjecture that he was punishing Mae West for a slur against his mistress Marion Davies, or the claim that Miss West had enraged him by snubbing Hearst gossip columnist Louella Parsons.

Hearst's call to arms was seconded in the Paul Block dailies, one of which ran a front-page editorial denouncing the film. In San Francisco, where Mae West movies usually flourished, the president of an organization representing eighteen civic, religious, and educational groups wrote to Hays, Breen, and Mae West herself to urge that children be barred from *Klondike Annie*. "Any picture that presents its heroine as a mistress to an Oriental, then as a murderess, then as a cheap imitation of a missionary—jazzing religion—is not in harmony with the other educational forces of our social set-up. And these elements are particularly objectionable when they are interspersed with smutty wise-cracks." The theater marquee of San Francisco's Warfield theater advertised: HERE COMES TROUBLE/KLONDIKE ANNIE.

The widely publicized attacks on *Klondike Annie* caught Mae off guard. She was both surprised and hurt. "She took personal pride in the benevolent quality written into the evangelist role. It was a stinging jolt to have her sincere interpretation of the character branded indecent."

But the controversy only helped the film at the box office. Paramount rushed the movie to theaters, taking the view that any publicity—good or bad—sells tickets. At the New York Paramount, opening-day records were broken, despite the ad ban, "rain, Lent and the elevator man's strike. By one o'clock the picture had played to 9,000 patrons." In Rochester, New York, it was moved from the 1,900-seat Century Theater to the 3,400-seat RKO Palace. Although banned in Lincoln, Nebraska, *Annie* broke records in Boston. All in all, *Variety* reported, the attacks by Hearst and Paul Block newspapers could be counted a boon, and credited with adding "one hundred per cent more than original valuations."

As the damage from Hearst's editorials was being calculated, hearings were held in Washington before a House subcommittee on the Neely–Pettengill bill to abolish block booking. Clubwomen and other supporters of the bill argued that "compulsory block booking forces exhibitors to play

'Mae West pictures' symbolizing a type, or else pay and not play." The distributors, who opposed the bill, submitted evidence "that there had not been a single cancellation by an exhibitor on a Mae West picture, even during the height of the Legion of Decency boycott movement in 1934." But a lawyer for the MPPDA told the subcommittee that even if block booking continued—which it would, until 1947—Mae West's stock would plummet. "Public taste is running away from Mae West so fast it is pathetic."

Despite her continued box-office appeal, no one could deny that Mae West's name had become synonymous with trouble—for now, the wrong kind. Paramount, grappling with skyrocketing costs and internal disarray, was rethinking its allegiance to her, questioning whether she was worth all the controversy she incited. The studio put her on notice that in the future her demands for total control would no longer be countenanced; Paramount would not renew its option unless she agreed to submit to outside direction, and refrained from "interfering" or guiding the casting of her future pictures. "The producer . . . and the front office will have the last say."

By failing to plan for another picture with her as star, Paramount, according to Mae West, had violated and invalidated their contract. In effect, by their inaction, Paramount had fired her. Current Paramount employee Michael Kaplan says his great-uncle Boris Kaplan informed her of the news. She could console herself that she was in excellent company. Ernst Lubitsch was fired as Paramount production chief at roughly the same time, February 1936. Marlene Dietrich would soon be leaving the studio as well. By now Paramount was retreating from its past association with European sophistication and moving toward conventional middle-class and middle-of-the-road values.

Mae West preferred to describe the rupture with Paramount as her decision. MAE WEST QUITS PARAMOUNT/THEY DONE HER WRONG, SHE SAYS, AND, BESIDES, ANOTHER OFFERS HER DOUBLE PAY. Accompanied by Emanuel Cohen and his cohort Ben Piazza, another exile from Paramount, she took off for Chicago in search of new material; she would see, and possibly buy the rights to a play on tour there, *Personal Appearance*. After viewing the play, she suddenly returned to Los Angeles instead of continuing to New York as planned. Through her attorney Loyd Wright she announced in April 1936 that she had signed with Emanuel Cohen's Major Pictures; Cohen would pay her $300,000 per picture, plus a percentage of the gross receipts. Although Cohen had briefly set up shop at Columbia Pictures, he announced that he had worked out a deal with Paramount; the studio would finance and distribute Cohen's Major Pictures productions, and Cohen would take a flat fee for each, plus a percentage of the release profits.

It appeared that, at least for the present, both Mae West and Emanuel Cohen had snatched victory from the jaws of defeat.

18

GOING TOO FAR

$\mathcal{A}$ROUND the time of her signing with Major Pictures, Mae West turned down one offer from RKO and another from MGM that would have cast her opposite Clark Gable. Anita Loos served as conduit for the latter offer; she had an idea for a script about a widow who owns a hockey team whose star player would be Gable. "I can't see myself horsing around with hockey players in a business way," said Mae, rejecting the proposal. "It would make me feel unappealing. Any time I show my authority over the male sex, it's got to be 100 percent emotional." A successful businesswoman in real life, Mae considered portraying such a woman on screen a compromise of her femininity and a risky career move.

Besides, she didn't like what she'd seen of Clark Gable in the movies. "I think he's a fine actor. But Clark pushes 'em around, or anyway he did in his pictures with Jean Harlow, and that's a habit of his." Evidently she hadn't troubled to see him in the 1934 hit screwball comedy *It Happened One Night*, where his behavior toward Claudette Colbert is anything but brutish. Mae had become quite insulated.

If somebody was going to push people around off camera, she wanted to be the one. Henry Hathaway, the director of her next film, *Go West, Young Man*, found her taxing to work with, demanding to be "the director, the star, the photographer, the designer, the architect, the art director." Hathaway, a veteran best known for Westerns and action pictures, disliked having his authority challenged. Mae rejected unconditionally his plan for a shot showing a bulldog emerging from a limousine with her, wiggling its bottom in synch with the star's. "I'm the one who's going to get the laughs," Mae insisted, in her Red Queen tone of voice. "Out!"

Hathaway, fresh from his triumph with the Technicolor *Trail of the Lonesome Pine*, had bailed out of *Pennies from Heaven*, a vehicle for Bing Crosby, to answer an emergency call from Emanuel Cohen to work on the Mae West picture. The director had made money for Paramount before, on Cohen's watch, with *Lives of a Bengal Lancer*, and Cohen was counting on him to work his magic again.

The Broadway hit called *Personal Appearance* had immediately attracted Cohen as a potential vehicle for Mae West, with whom he saw it in Chicago. The play, by Lawrence Riley, was about an affected, insincere, and predatory movie star who gets stranded in a Pennsylvania backwater. It had starred Gladys George and won her a movie contract. But Mae West, not Gladys George, would play the spoiled Hollywood diva in the movie, which the Hays Office had already turned down once as a vehicle for Jean Harlow at MGM.

When Cohen bought rights to *Personal Appearance* for a screen adaptation to star Mae West, he didn't doubt he could get around any censor's objections. Breen had complained that the play glorified adultery, made being a nymphomaniac seem funny, and that the script cast Hollywood in an unflattering light, but Cohen assured him he could and would make it all right. "Mr. Cohen stated," Breen reported in a memo, "that he felt confident that when he came to write the script he could meet any objection which might arise, under the Code." Cohen saw no point in reminding Breen that Mae West herself—not Cohen—would be working on the dialogue.

Variety reported that Cohen got a go-ahead from the Hays Office as soon as he agreed that, in the movie, the leading lady would never have been married to a film producer, as she has been in the play. Breen found the arrangement in *Personal Appearance* especially distasteful, since in the play the actress with the wandering eye is a Hollywood wife. He saw himself as, among other things, protector of the film industry's reputation. Cohen had reassured Breen, the trade paper reported, that in the screen version she wouldn't be married at all.

Breen drew up a long list of quibbles with the script; he reminded Cohen that any talk of code approval was premature. He disliked the character of the Jewish producer and abhorred "the characterization of Mavis [the movie star, whose name in the play had been Carol] as a promiscuous woman." He insisted that the scene between garageman Bud (Randolph Scott) and Mavis Arden (Mae West) in a barn be moved to a workshop, and that Bud "should not indicate he is unduly excited sexually." Professor Rigby, the cantankerous boarder, "should not come out of Mavis' room in the morning, and there should be no rouge on his lips." The publicity portrait of Mavis for theater lobbies should show no cleavage: "Breasts must not be too definitely outlined, nor covered with any thin, gauzy or transparent material."

Perhaps Breen knew that in real life Mae West employed a black chauffeur (Chalky Wright), and maybe he was unhappy with her well-established on-screen tradition of chumminess with black servants and other non-white characters. He demanded that such racial mingling not be repeated in the new film, stipulating to Cohen that "Mavis' maid and chauffeur should not be colored." The only black player in the cast, Nicodemus, once a singer and dancer with Cab Calloway, portrays a racially stereotypic buffoon, slow-moving and simpleminded, who has not a single scene with Mae West. His characterization marks a decided step backward.

Breen made sure that any political satire in the script lost its edge. Instead of being a senator, Francis X. Harrigan's role (played by Lyle Talbot) was changed to that of a mere candidate for Congress. In the original screenplay, when Mavis's manager Morgan (Warren William)—the man entrusted with responsibility for keeping the "susceptible" Mavis single—tips off the press that she's alone with Harrigan, and the press bursts in on them, demanding a statement from Mavis, she says: "A politician is usually a guy that promises the working man a full dinner pail—and then after election, he steals the dinner pail." *Go West, Young Man* was filmed during the 1936 presidential campaign and released right after FDR's landslide re-election. Mavis's line about politicians who break promises never made it to the screen, although the scene with the press bursting in remained. Nor was she permitted to take a swipe at the government, in particular the Public Works Administration, for spending millions on "silly old dams that nobody gives a—." However, her line "A thrill a day keeps the chill away," a variation on Texas Guinan's "An indiscretion a day keeps depression away," stayed in.

On the first day of shooting *Go West, Young Man* in August 1936, Hathaway instantly alienated his star by having the effrontery to suggest that she needed to wear a girdle to conceal a belly bulge. She assured him that her figure need not concern him; in fact, as she liked to remind the press, her measurements improved on those of Venus de Milo—and she reprised her joke that, again besting the famous statue, *she* had arms! But the physical flaws of others in the movie irked Mae and she thought those *should* concern the director. She demanded that the bald spot of Xavier Cugat, who leads the band in the opening sequence, the film within a film called *Drifting Lady*, be covered with a toupee. To make sure that she would not appear dwarfed by the towering Randolph Scott, she had him stand in a hole for close shots, or she and Scott would be filmed separately.

As in the past, she liked to assign some of the roles to actors in her coterie. Jack La Rue, who'd played Juárez onstage in *Diamond Lil* and had been devoted to her ever since, was cast as the heavy in the film within a film, and her brother-in-law, Baikoff, again portrayed a Russian admirer. Lyle Talbot had once auditioned for the Chicago company of *Sex*; although he didn't take that part, he and Mae became chums. Her current trainer and sometime lover, former welterweight champion Johnny Indrisano, was cast as the chauffeur. Arthur Johnston, who'd written the songs for *Belle of the Nineties*, repeated his songwriting assignment, and her favorite cinematographer, Karl Struss, again stood behind the camera.

Several commentators point out that, for a Mae West picture, the finished movie gives an unusually large number of prominent roles to women. The explanation is that the *Personal Appearance* script required the boardinghouse in which Mavis finds herself stranded when her limousine breaks down to be a largely female enterprise. Its proprietor, Mrs. Struthers (Alice Brady), has fallen on hard times; where in the past leading socialites used to call, she's now reduced to renting rooms to paying guests. Mrs. Struthers's daughter Joyce (Margaret Perry), her outspoken maiden aunt Kate (Elizabeth Patterson, who played the same role onstage), and a screen-struck servant named Gladys (Isabel Jewell) all help to run the place. In the screenplay, Mavis tangles with all the women. She makes a play for Joyce's man, Bud, and resents Aunt Kate's intrusion on an amorous evening alone with him. She's patronizing to Gladys, who aspires to be a movie star herself, and rude to her hostess, Mrs. Struthers.

Apparently the conflict with Alice Brady carried over to off screen. Brady, a well-respected Broadway actress before she came to Hollywood, had little regard for Mae West and made no secret of it. Mae retaliated. In an effort to trim Brady's sails, she trimmed her part.

Mae West habitually used self-parody as a way of letting the audience in on the joke. Look, she seemed to be saying about herself, isn't she a stitch? But in *Go West, Young Man* it's not always clear who's being kidded. Mavis Arden resembles Mae West in being a famous, glamorous, American movie star who's vain, highly sexed, enamored of masculine brawn, and has a manager who constantly obstructs her attempts at amorous dalliance. But Mavis's humor is often inadvertent, and she's a phony—something Mae West never was, on or off the screen. Mavis pretends to be at heart "a simple unaffected country girl," a guileless innocent, "a very human person like yourself," who just happens to live in an Italian villa and to travel with a French maid in a chauffeured Rolls-Royce. She tries to butter up her fans, but she privately loathes them, considering them morons.

And in marked contrast to Mae, she's pretty dim herself. Sometimes she does use language, in Mae West's time-honored way, to demonstrate her dominance; when she tells Bud how many men she has helped "to realize themselves," she's aware of the double meaning, but he isn't. She's in charge when she suggests that the way to stop Professor Rigby would be to steal his pants. But in this script the Mae West character misconstrues and misuses words, undercutting her own power. She confuses "ulterior" with "exterior" ("your interior is just as picturesque as your ulterior"), and "commute" with "commune" ("I must commute with myself"). She calls internal organs "infernal organs." These malapropisms were carried over from the play. They simply don't work for Mae West.

In previous movies, the Mae West character has always risen above hardscrabble roots and a questionable past. An early script of *Go West, Young Man* has a line suggesting that Mavis once worked in a cheap Chicago dive—maybe a burlesque house—called the Bucket of Blood. But in the movie, the name of the place she once worked in has been sanitized, changed to the Follies. Her manager jokes that Mavis comes "from one of the finest families in New Guinea." The class angle, a Mae West staple, is present, but has been muted. Here, instead of being one of the ordinary folk, she's cast as a woman who has made it and who considers ordinary folk—at least the ones who lack "large and sinewy muscles"—boring simpletons.

Many in-jokes, references to particular movie stars, were deleted, although Gladys's imitation of Dietrich singing "Falling in Love Again" was kept in, along with Morgan's suggestion that she spoof the four Marx Brothers. Mavis in the early draft tells the curmudgeon Professor Rigby, trying to placate him, that she wants to give him a screen test, and that he reminds her of such fine film actors as George Arliss, Charles Laughton, John Barrymore, Paul Muni. None of these names survived the editing process. It's no accident that the only stars whose names were kept worked for Paramount.

References to Mae West, by name, didn't survive either. In the original script, the servant Gladys has a sister whose favorite movie actresses are Mae West and Marlene Dietrich. Mavis, in that first script, boasts: "Next to Mae West I draw the biggest gross that ever played the Paramount." Perhaps this seemed too transparently self-serving.

*   *   *

Go West, Young Man did adequately, not spectacularly, at the box office when it was released in November 1936, and that was an appropriate response to an unremarkable, amusing picture that plays it pretty safe—although not safe enough for the bluenoses. The picture's best showing was in New York, where it shared the bill with the first-ever Popeye cartoon in color, and a stage show featuring Paul Draper's dancing and the Al Donohue band.

Advance publicity had announced Mae West as the featured live performer at the New York Paramount, which was celebrating its tenth anniversary. She was to come to New York from a personal appearance in Chicago and prior to the screening of *Go West, Young Man* would perform a stage act scripted by Harry Conn, a comedy writer for Jack Benny, Eddie Cantor, and Burns and Allen. Mae would be paid $10,500 per week, plus a 50–50 split above a gross of $53,000. But it was not to be. Rumors circulated that she was dissatisfied with Conn's material. She asked for additional money to pay the salaries for an expanded cast; she planned to appear with Jack La Rue, Lyle Talbot, singer-composer Gene Austin, and a stage maid. She demanded a two-week guarantee as well. Like the fisherman's wife in the fairy tale, she kept on asking for more and more, never satisfied. Exasperated, the Paramount Theatre pulled the plug and booked another show. MAE MADE TOO MANY DEMANDS, SAYS N.Y. PAR. Mae now announced that she was ill and would go to the desert for two weeks of recuperation. The whole episode sounds like an outtake from *Go West, Young Man*, with Mae West taking her cues from Mavis Arden.

Critical opinion about *Go West* divided along predictable lines. Martin Quigley's conservative *Motion Picture Herald* called it "a case of motion picture entertainment gone Minsky. The release of this picture will cause many people to wonder whether Miss West . . . enjoys immunity from the operations of the Production Code." While the General Federation of Women's Clubs reproved its "sly innuendos and daring vulgarities," Robert Garland in the New York *American* commented, "It's difficult to be disapproving when you're in stitches." Kate Cameron, in the New York *Daily News*, failed to pick up Mavis Arden's confusing signals and applauded *Go West* for "giving Miss West a gorgeous chance to kid herself."

Several reviewers expressed wonder and relief that Mae West had survived the assaults she had suffered at the hands of the Legion of Decency and the Hays Office. "We musn't, of course, ever allow anything to curb

Mae West," said *The New Yorker*, "so it is a relief that we find her in this
film no more shy than before."

A few critics ominously sensed a certain lack of freshness; the swagger
was becoming old news. Graham Greene, in the British *Spectator*, found to
his sorrow that "the wisecracks lack the old impudence" and the story was
"quite incredibly tedious."

An entire year passed before work began on a new Mae West film. In the
interim, a strike by the motion-picture craft guilds—scenic artists, costum-
ers, makeup artists, and the like—curtailed production. Mae was apprised
of the unwelcome ruling by the Superior Court that she was indeed the
legal wife of Frank Wallace, and the newspapers made this item public. She
witnessed the film community's shock and grief at the death at age twenty-
six of Jean Harlow, considered by the Hays Office to be her cohort in moral
waywardness on the screen. Within weeks of Harlow's death, which occurred as Harlow was making yet another film with Clark Gable, Mae
learned that her spirit-guide Amelia Earhart had disappeared on a flight to
Howland Island in the Central Pacific. It was a season of losses.

Two interests—horses and boxers—distracted her. She purchased another
ten-acre patch in the San Fernando Valley for her brother to use to tend
her horses and ready them for the Santa Anita track. In October 1937, Jack
West was hauled into court, charged with neglecting his stock, and dismissed with a warning from the judge to clean up his corral and make peace
with the neighbors.

Mae broke in a new chauffeur, Speedy Dado, a Mexican bantamweight
boxer, and helped him out when he faced charges for threatening two men
with a gun during a traffic altercation. She sponsored the return of her
former chauffeur and lover, Chalky Wright, to boxing, backing him, through
bouts set up by promoter Morrie Cohen, in his quest to became world
featherweight champion. And in an effort to help Joe Louis, she leaned on
Owney Madden, manager of Slapsy Maxey Rosenbloom, phoning Madden
in Hot Springs, Arkansas, to urge him to arrange for Joe Louis to fight Jim
Braddock instead of slap-happy Rosenbloom. Madden did just that, and
Louis became heavyweight champion in June 1937.

One reason for the long wait between pictures was that Mae West kept
trying in vain to convince Emanuel Cohen to produce her Catherine the
Great script. She had no success thinking up something new. "I was tired

and didn't have the vaguest idea for a story. Paramount was upset, and I wasn't very happy either."

In May 1937, Eddie Sutherland—a proven comedy director who'd worked with W. C. Fields and Carole Lombard and who became Mae West's favorite, "so tasteful, so enthusiastic"—was announced as the director for the next Mae West film, which might or might not be a musical set in the 1890s. Emanuel Cohen wanted her to return to the nineties, not only because the public had proven its willingness to pay for seeing her in turn-of-the-century roles, but also because he had already spent a lot of money on a replica of Rector's, the famous old-time Broadway restaurant. George Rector himself would be available for a cameo appearance.

Mae claimed that a song called "Mademoiselle Fifi" by Sam Coslow magically inspired her to invent the plot and characters for *Every Day's a Holiday*. Coslow had come to her bungalow to try out some song ideas. After hearing "Fifi," Mae asked him to play the chorus a second time. He did, triggering a mental explosion in her. She visualized herself in nineties gowns as Peaches O'Day, the lady sharpie who became Mlle Fifi, a supposedly French *chanteuse* wanted by the police. She imagined the black wig she'd don as part of her transformation from Peaches to Fifi. "I saw the whole story, heard lines and saw the supporting characters," all in less than a minute. The Forces, as she called them, had come to her aid. She immediately dictated the story to a secretary and took full credit for the screenplay.

The screenwriting credit properly belonged at least in part to Allan Rivkin, usually a writer for Warner Bros. Rivkin reported to George Eells and Stanley Musgrove that he agreed to take a $5,000 bonus and a three-month vacation as payment for relinquishing screen credit and allowing it to go solely to Mae West. Any dealings with Rivkin were conducted completely under the table. The Paramount Production files for *Every Day's a Holiday* list Jo Swerling (later a co-author of *Guys and Dolls*) as the writer; he was paid $64,999 for his contribution. Mae West received $280,000 as star, her old buddy Joe Frisco (also uncredited) was paid $1,000 to consult on the dance numbers, and Elsa Schiaparelli received $7,825 for designing gowns and accessories that proved troublesome. Schiaparelli, based in Paris, had worked from the wrong measurements and her costumes for Mae required much alteration. The total cost for the film ran to more than a million dollars.

The plot of *Every Day's a Holiday* retreads familiar Mae West turf. She's back in New York at the turn of the century (the narrative begins on New

Year's Eve, 1899), back on the Bowery as a performer in a raucous nightspot, and back on the wrong side of the law as Peaches (a name from Mae's past) O'Day, an amiable con artist who totes tools for picking locks, cutting glass, and prying open safes, and who now and then sells the Brooklyn Bridge to gullible immigrants. Once again she cracks high society, winning the friend-ship of Van Doon (Charles Winninger), an addlepated aristocrat, and his deadpan butler, Graves (Charles Butterworth), and celebrating with both of them in a palatial mansion with marble floors.

The elegantly gowned Peaches prefers to live dangerously. Her motto, a tilt to Oscar Wilde, is "keep a diary and some day it'll keep you." More mischievous than evil, her lawbreaking is shown to be not very threatening. The money she took for the Brooklyn Bridge is restored to the naïve German (Herman Bing) who paid it, and despite her record of twenty-five arrests, Peaches insists, "I may crack a law, but I ain't never broke one." After cutting through the glass of a department store window and removing from the manikins an ermine cape, a gown, and a hat, she shrugs off her crime by promising to compensate the store later. She tells her accomplice, "Larceny nothin', you'll send 'em a check in the mornin'."

Peaches is cast as the lead in a glittering New York variety show, which the wealthy, bibulous reformer Van Doon will back; but because she's wanted by the New York police, her producer, Nifty Bailey (Walter Catlett), comes up with a scheme: she will leave town and return to New York from Boston wearing a black wig, disguised as a French singer named Fifi, a temperamental prima donna out of vaudeville—in fact, out of Mae West's own French-prima-donna turn with Harry Richman.

The villain of the piece is the police chief, "so crooked he uses a cork-screw for a ruler," Honest John Quade (Lloyd Nolan). Quade cares only for his own power. Rebuffed by Fifi, he fires the good cop McCarey (Edmund Lowe) who stands up to him when he tries to close down the theater in which Fifi performs. McCarey decides to oppose Quade in the upcoming mayoral election. Naturally, he's sweet on Peaches. Naturally, she helps him win the election, engaging the services of Louis Armstrong to lead a jubilant campaign parade in which she herself plays the drums.

Lloyd Nolan privately admitted he found Mae West stunningly attrac-tive—"She'd really lost weight, and she's got a gorgeous complexion"—but "strange." For her, "for a thing to be funny, it's got to be dirty." He recalled a relaxed set, with lots of laughs.

In pitching his new Mae West production to Joe Breen, Emanuel Cohen advised him, "There are no sex situations that could possibly arouse the criticism that her pictures previously received." After reading the script, Breen lodged objections to numerous suggestive lines, to "excessive drinking and drunkenness," and to the tenor of the political satire, which he characterized as "extremely dangerous." He insisted that the nationality of the sucker who buys the Brooklyn Bridge be changed from Greek to German, presumably because he wasn't concerned about offending moviegoers in Nazi Germany, who would have no opportunity to view the picture. And he urged a consultation with the Paramount legal department about the depictions of New York politicians at the turn of the century as dishonest. "These people or their next of kin may take serious objection."

The Legion of Decency also requested changes. It promised to upgrade its rating of the picture from B to A if two lines were deleted: "I wouldn't lift my veil for that guy" and "He couldn't touch me with a ten-foot pole." The lines were duly excised.

Although *Every Day's a Holiday* infects us with its festive, celebratory spirit—it begins with New Year's Eve fireworks and ends with an election-eve street rally—its comedy is both overly broad and overly familiar. The jokes about horseless carriages, temperamental divas, and crooked politicians are wearing thin, and we're reminded too many times of the star's irresistible allure. Mae West neither sings the best song—Louis Armstrong gets to perform Hoagy Carmichael's "Jubilee"—nor utters the most quotable line: "Get out of those wet clothes and into a dry martini" is spoken by the manservant Graves.

Sheilah Graham voiced a minority opinion when she called *Every Day's a Holiday*, released in mid-January 1938, "a better picture than *She Done Him Wrong*—and clean." Howard Barnes in the New York *Herald Tribune* more typically found it "clean and dull." Frank Nugent in *The New York Times* pronounced it "a witless period comedy," and concluded: "Sex ain't what it used to be, or maybe Miss West isn't." All in all, judged the critic for the New York *Sun*, "it would probably seem much funnier to someone who had never heard of Mae West."

As if to remind the world how much Mae West's stock had plummeted, the New York Paramount Theatre coupled *Every Day's a Holiday* with an applause-stealing stage show featuring the Benny Goodman Band, with Gene Krupa on drums, Teddy Wilson at the piano, and Lionel Hampton on vibes. Mae West's appearance on screen was greeted with "only half-hearted applause," though the audience perked up, "singing and beating time," when Louis Armstrong emerged. When the live band began to play after the movie, the young crowd went wild, dancing in the aisles and raiding the stage. The police had to be called in to restore order. It was the King of Swing, not Mae West, who created mayhem—an irony not lost on observers from the press, who agreed that the West film played second fiddle. "It was like old times yesterday with a new Mae West show opening and a squad of patrolmen marching down the aisles. The joker is that the police weren't after Mae West, but had been called in to restore order when a personal appearance of Benny Goodman and his band threatened to turn the Paramount into a playground." As an expression of "that thing called sex," Howard Barnes crushingly observed, "swing has more or less supplanted Mae West."

At a time when her ability to shock movie-goers was flagging, Mae West proved herself still incendiary in another medium, radio. She managed to provoke a national hullabaloo via the airwaves with her appearance with ventriloquist Edgar Bergen, his dummy Charlie McCarthy, and actor Don Ameche on the Chase and Sanborn show on Sunday, December 12, 1937. The show, the most popular radio program of the time, was organized something like a vaudeville bill. There were several comedy sketches interspersed with songs. Nelson Eddy harked back to the early part of the century by singing Victor Herbert, and the band struck a contemporary note with "Swing Is Here to Stay." Dorothy Lamour, an up-and-coming Paramount glamour queen, anticipated the guest appearance of Mae West by singing the theme song from *Every Day's a Holiday*. It was the holiday season, two weeks before Christmas, and a party atmosphere prevailed, helped along by lots of jokes about gift giving.

Mae West appeared in two sketches. In one, she recycled as many of her famous lines—especially those from *She Done Him Wrong*—as she could, while playing up the absurdity of having a partner who is made of wood. She's in a championship match with "short, dark and handsome" Charlie McCarthy, and she's "in great form." She says Charlie came up to her apartment to see her etchings and show her his stamp collection. That's all that happened, Bergen insists, and Charlie stage-whispers, "He's so naïve." Has she ever met one man she could really love? Sure, lots of times. Edgar Bergen? He can be had. Her favorite perfume is Ashes of Men. (This line was appropriated from an early *Every Day* script; it never made the final cut.) She likes a man what takes his time. She's got a man for every mood, and she changes her men "like I change my clothes." Although Charlie is "all wood and a yard long," and despite the fact that his kisses give her splinters, he's welcome to come home with her: "I'll let you play in my woodpile." Photos published as advance publicity showed the negligeed Mae West in bed with the monocled dummy.

In the hubbub that followed the broadcast, that sketch—which was briefly cut off the air—went unmentioned. It was the one about Adam and Eve that sent Catholic Church leaders, women's groups, and editorial writers into high dudgeon, and threw NBC, the J. Walter Thompson advertising agency, the head of the Federal Communications Commission, and a few members of Congress into a tailspin.

The script by Arch Oboler, written specifically for Mae West, depicts Adam (played by Don Ameche) as a laid-back and complacent husband, "long, lazy and lukewarm," and Eve (Mae West) as his bored and discontented wife. Adam has no complaints about Eden, where the temperature's perfect, the sun always shines, and everything is "peaceful, quiet and safe." But Eve finds the place stultifying, a "dismal dump." "A couple months of peace and security and a woman's bored all the way down to the bottom of her marriage certificate." She yearns for excitement and a chance to expand her "personality"; the fact that she and Adam have signed a lease obligating them to stay in Eden doesn't trouble her at all. When she learns that the lease stipulates that she and Adam will be thrown out of the garden if they eat forbidden fruit, she's set on her course. A snake (Edgar Bergen) happens by; he's "long, dark and slinky," skinny enough to squeeze through the fence around the apple tree. Egged on by Eve, he promises to pick forbidden apples. "Get me a big one," Eve commands; "I feel like doin' a *big* apple." (At this point, the studio audience howls.) Eve crowns herself "the first woman to make a monkey out of a snake."

When Eve converts the apples into "forbidden applesauce," she feeds the sauce to Adam, just back from a fishing trip, and consumes some herself. There is a sudden crash of thunder, a wail of wind, and a loud boom: Eve and Adam have been dispossessed, expelled from Eden. Adam is accusing, but Eve crows: "I've just made a little more history, that's all. I'm the first woman to have her own way—and a snake'll take the rap for it!" She and Adam may have lost one form of paradise, but they've found another: sex. Adam looks at Eve as if for the first time. She's beautiful, and he wants to hold her closer. There's another crash. "That," explains Eve, "was the Original Kiss."

In composing this sketch for Mae West, Arch Oboler gave the familiar story of Adam and Eve a feminist twist. "Instead of going on the premise that the snake tempted Eve," he explained, "it occurred to me, since Miss West was such a dominant woman, to have Eve tempt the snake." Another scriptwriter, Joan Storm, went to court to claim Oboler had plagiarized her skit "Love and Applesauce." The judge ruled against Storm, citing her characterizations of Adam and Eve as distinctly different from Oboler's. In Storm's treatment, Adam was strong and domineering, his wife a clinging vine. Oboler, in writing for Mae West, put it the other way. His Eve is the "central figure . . . a highly sophisticated, clever female who . . . induces the snake to do her bidding."

The announcer on the Chase and Sanborn program characterized the Adam and Eve skit as a "light-hearted travesty," but there was nothing lighthearted about the diatribes it inspired. As Don Ameche pointed out, several years after the episode, it was the Adam and Eve story's biblical origin, coupled with the fact that the travesty was broadcast on a Sunday, that many listeners found so offensive. Ameche had anticipated trouble during rehearsals and had tried to change certain lines, but to no avail.

The Adam and Eve uproar reopened the wounds *Klondike Annie* had inflicted on religious sensibilities when it mingled the sacred and the profane. NBC was besieged with letters of protest. Among them was one from the chairman of the FCC, Frank McNinch, describing the Adam and Eve sketch as "offensive to the great mass of right-thinking, clean-minded American citizens." He demanded to see a transcript of the skit, labeling the broadcast "a serious offense against the proprieties and a rather low form of entertainment."

"Mae West Pollutes Homes" announced an editorial in the Catholic *Monitor* as the Legion of Decency pondered launching a campaign to clean up radio. A statement by Dr. Maurice Sheehy, professor of religion at Catholic University, was introduced into the *Congressional Record*. It charged that Mae West had "introduced her own sexual philosophy into the Biblical incident of the fall of man." Dr. Sheehy called Mae West "the very personification of sex in its lowest connotation," tagged the radio program "indecent, scurrilous and irreverent," and declared: "To have this lewd and filthy take-off on the Bible's Adam and Eve was a disgrace."

A Massachusetts congressman demanded an investigation of the FCC, which had allowed a "foul and indecent broadcast" to invade millions of American homes. "The American people are clean of mind, and naturally they resent the intrusion into their homes of any blasphemous, sensuous, obscene or profane utterance." Senator Clyde Herring of Iowa proposed the establishment of a board of review for radio programs, "to prevent the recurrence of such broadcasts as the Adam and Eve skit."

"Radio is badly scared and will lock the barn door," *Variety* predicted.

Chase and Sanborn apologized, and the J. Walter Thompson advertising agency promised their mistake would not be repeated. Charlie McCarthy turned dumb: "Ho hum, this is one time I'll let Mr. Bergen do all the talking, thank you." Mr. Bergen too remained close-mouthed. As ratings soared on the Chase and Sanborn hour, NBC duly issued an order forbidding even the mention of Mae West's name on the air, an action praised by the Hearst press as "proper protection for the homes of decent Americans." Jailed in New York and banned on the radio, "Mae West finds refuge only in motion pictures." It was high time that film producers learned that Americans would not tolerate "impropriety."

Breaking a deafening silence on the part of Mae West supporters, a group of her fans pointed out that the sketch was typical of her comedy, and highly enjoyable to boot. And Mae defended herself: "Did they expect a sermon? Why weren't they in church if they were so religious? Forty million people listened to that broadcast. That's more people than listened to the abdication of King Edward, even." She swore she would never participate in another broadcast on a Sunday.

In the past, Mae West's public clashes with the police and with guardians of morality had always translated into bigger box office for her current endeavor. Paramount hoped that the same pattern would again prevail and rushed *Every Day's a Holiday* into release right on schedule, instead of waiting for the din to die down. "The star is news right now and . . . most any publicity is box office. Company is putting on a national campaign in the newspapers and magazines, and will spend $35,000 to $40,000 on the splurge."

But this time the publicity backfired and the rush to buy tickets never happened. *Every Day's a Holiday* failed to make money—a first in Mae West's movie career. The picture got buried in the landslide response to Disney's first animated feature, *Snow White and the Seven Dwarfs*, which Mae said would have made even more money if she'd played Snow White. "I used to be Snow White," she'd quip, "but I drifted."

Within weeks of *Every Day*'s release, Paramount severed its connection with Emanuel Cohen's Major Pictures, and Cohen decided to drop Mae West. She was just too much trouble. Standing behind her made sense while she packed them in at the box office, but not, the studio brass reasoned, when the moviegoing public seemed to be losing interest in her. Five and a half years and eight movies after her arrival in Hollywood, the forty-four-year-old star found herself without a contract.

Gamely she went to New York for a series of personal appearances at

Loew's theaters. She had not been to New York since her triumphant appearances with *She Done Him Wrong*, but she felt confident of an enthusiastic response. She got one. Her live performances were jammed. She informed a columnist for the New York *Post* that her popularity was undiminished, and well-nigh universal. "I'm the first personality since Chaplin that's got the masses. I've got all classes and all ages. My pictures are a terrific success in Europe. The foreign people understand me."

Returning to her roots, she made a nostalgic trip to Brooklyn, revisiting scenes from her childhood. At Coney Island, she returned to the place where, with her father, she first saw Bostock's Lions and Little Egypt. Now she stopped at the Steeplechase, the Cyclone, and some shooting galleries, advising the locals to "keep exhibits arty, boys," and reminding the reporters who gathered that she was a Brooklyn native, born, she said, on Willoughby Avenue between Greenpoint and Bushwick, and that her father hailed from Greenpoint.

For her stage act, performed successively in Manhattan at the Loew's State, at the Fox in Brooklyn, and in Newark and Connecticut, she was accompanied by an orchestra led by Lionel Newman, singer Milton Watson, and a male chorus line, seven handsome young men in top hats and tails. "They always put pretty dames on the stage for the men, but how about the women? Don't women like to look at somebody handsome sometimes?" Six times a day, for a record salary of $12,000 a week, plus half the gross over $38,000, she draped herself in diamonds and ostrich plumes, put over songs like "Come Up and See Me" and the steamy "Slow Motion," and tried out some dialogue she would use in subsequent nightclub and stage appearances. When a stage maid informs her there are four hundred men waiting for her in the lobby, Mae says, "Well, I'm a little tired today, so one of those guys will have to go."

Several times after the last show, battered-looking ex-fighters limped into her dressing room, claiming to be former buddies of her father, now down on their luck. She unfailingly handed each suppliant a wad of bills, enough for a new suit.

Before her tour ended, she sustained another body blow, this time delivered by Harry Brandt, president of the organization of Independent Theater Owners. An article in the *Independent Film Journal* that led to an ad in *The Hollywood Reporter* and became the subject of an article in *Time* came down hard on a list of stars deemed more expensive than they were worth. Whereas Shirley Temple, Myrna Loy, and Gary Cooper were sure earners, Mae West, along with Katharine Hepburn, Joan Crawford, Edward Arnold,

Greta Garbo, Fred Astaire, and Marlene Dietrich, were labeled "box-office poison." Although she had certainly been placed in classy company, she must have found it painful to be named a "poisonality."

Always the fighter, Mae immediately shot back that the poor earnings were the result of a general market decline, not the fault of the individual stars. "The box office business in the entire industry has dropped off 30 per cent in the past four months," she pointed out. But it was clear that her place in the world of entertainment needed to be reassessed. As the Spanish Civil War raged, polarizing continents, nations, and families, world war seemed more and more inevitable. Tastes were changing, the European market for American films was closing down, and "new types of film, especially film noir, were being generated to suit the changing national mood." In the new era, pinup girls and "girls next door" would reign supreme. Sentimental comedy, Betty Grable musicals, and other family films would displace screwball comedy and rout Mae West's brand of wisecracking, sexually charged humor.

The most dynamic phase of her career had come to an end. Although she'd helped the world learn that women—even after the age of forty— possess libidos, that power isn't an exclusively male prerogative, and that sex can be openly kidded and enjoyed, she hadn't shouted down repressive voices that kept her from doing the work she wanted and needed to do. Nor had she learned that replaying a single role can pall. Famous and wealthy, credited with enriching the language and praised as well as blamed for loosening moral stays, the owner of California acres, a stable of horses, heaps of diamonds, dozens of pairs of false eyelashes, closets packed with furs, and many blond wigs, she would continue to perform and record, to write, and to repeat her most celebrated lines, but not to change. She resembled the character in a song Bert Williams used to sing, a number she may have performed back in Brooklyn as Baby Mae: "All Dressed Up with No Place to Go."

EPILOGUE

*I*T could be argued that by the time Mae West and Paramount parted company her career had been damaged beyond repair. But by another reckoning she had no reason to worry. Her status as a cultural icon had become so securely ensconced by the late thirties that it remained invulnerable, safe in a place where no Joseph Breen or William Randolph Hearst could dislodge it. From the movies she had already made, the world knew what she looked like, how she walked and talked. Many could quote at least one of her signature lines. "More than being a person or an institution, she has entered the language and taken her place in the underworld of the present's mythology," John Mason Brown wrote in 1949, and what he said then still holds true. Her bons mots continue to be quoted and enshrined between book covers, insinuating themselves into a collection called *The Wit and Wisdom of Mae West* and more recently into the august pages of the *Oxford Dictionary of Modern Quotations*: "Goodness had nothing to do with it, dearie." "Beulah, peel me a grape." "When caught between two evils I generally like to take the one I never tried before." It's even possible to quote her in French: *"La bonté divine n'a rien à voir la-dedans, ma chérie."* "Come up and see me sometime" could be heard, in the mid-thirties, on the lips of citizens as far off as Canton, China.

As a mythic personality, she takes her place within the American tall-tale tradition, exalted as a rowdy braggart of humble origin and superhuman dimension, a bulwark against the highfalutin and the pretentious, a giantess right up there with doughty Paul Bunyan, downer of tall trees, brawling Davy Crockett, and Mike Fink, the audacious riverboatman. Like her larger-than-life forebears, she flaunts a bottomless appetite—in her case, for diamonds and men. If Catherine the Great had three hundred lovers, Mae West did the best she could (as she boasted in her curtain speech for *Cath-*

erine Was Great) in a couple of hours. Like other creatures of legend, she always triumphs in any contest. "I'm in a class by myself. I star in everything and I break records all over the world. My *ego's* breakin' records."

The monuments to her include—in addition to an unending stream of suggestive jingles and dirty jokes, at least one pornographic video send-up and droves of flamboyant, whiskey-tenor drag-queen imitators—World War II Royal Air Force life jackets nicknamed "Mae Wests"; a "Mae West Curve" on the road to Yellowstone Park; a magnet shaped like her torso designed by Princeton scientists; a bottle for Schiaparelli's perfume Shocking that copied her shape. Willem De Kooning drew her in 1964 as a resplendent bosom attached to an asymmetrical face, with a wandering eye.

Salvador Dali in the mid-thirties boosted her iconic standing by painting his extraordinary *Face of Mae West Which May Be Used as an Apartment.* In it, Mae West's image is literally where she lives. Her photographed visage, superimposed on a room, becomes the ultimate object, a formal and imposing painted façade, a set designed for show in which the placement of every artifact has been meticulously prearranged and nothing is left to chance: steps form the chin line of a room in which her nose serves as a fireplace, her hair becomes curtains, her eyes are framed paintings (they can't look out, being opaque), and the full, shapely lips become a satin sofa. Dali's lip-shaped sofa design was turned into actual furniture in the studios of Green and Abbott, London, and Jean-Michel Frank in Paris. (The Parisian sofas were made for Elsa Schiaparelli, who rejected them after a viewing.) There are renditions of the lip-shaped sofa to be viewed in England: one with pink satin upholstery at the Victoria and Albert, London, and renderings in outrageous red at the Brighton museum and at the Ashmolean in Oxford. The entire room was realized as a tableau for the Dali Museum in Figueras, Spain, in 1974. There one can literally step up to see her.

The Mae West legend shows no sign of mortality.

What became of the flesh-and-blood woman?

Before her death at the Ravenswood in 1980, at age eighty-seven, Mae West appeared in four more movies. The first and best of these, *My Little Chickadee* (Universal, 1940), co-starring W. C. Fields, still attracts millions on television. It's a Western that pits her character, Flower Belle Lee, against rigid town bluenoses, and pairs her in an unconsummated marriage with Fields's Cuthbert J. Twillie. On the set Fields's ego clashed with hers, and his drinking infuriated her. The two highly verbal comics and connivers, despite parallel backgrounds in vaudeville and a common indebtedness to William Le Baron, could not share the spotlight with equanimity. Each rebelled against the very premise of co-starring. During and after the shoot, Mae bad-mouthed Fields for coming on the set drunk and stealing writing credit from her; but on his part, he expressed nothing but admiration for her comedic and writing talents, praising her as "the only author that has ever known what I was trying to do."

The Heat's On (Columbia, 1943), an out-and-out disaster that prompted the critical comment "The heat is definitely off," induced a drought in Mae West's filmmaking career that would last more than twenty-six years. Directed by Gregory Ratoff, who had played Benny Pinkowitz in *I'm No Angel*, *The Heat's On* was Mae West's only film written entirely by others, and the mistake of appearing in it convinced her she would rather retire from films altogether than ever again relinquish script control. In the 1940s, director Andrew Stone tried to cast her in a spy thriller but was not able to put a deal together.

Later, after the Hays Office had been supplanted by the rating system, and her earlier Paramount pictures had finally been rereleased, she made two frankly raunchy movies: the X-rated *Myra Breckinridge* (Twentieth Century–Fox, 1970) and *Sextette* (Crown International, 1978) capitalize on her campy absurdity; in both films her insistence, at ages seventy-seven and eighty-five, on playing an irresistible siren desired by every man who sets eyes on her makes us laugh at, not with, her. She did retain a remarkable youthfulness, her famous complexion still smooth, her good teeth still gleaming, her cleavage intact, though the waistline by now suggested a highball glass more than a wine stem. But her conviction that she had successfully and completely thwarted time, remaining forever twenty-six, could not be universally shared.

Interviewed in connection with *Myra*, she'd insist, "I'm not making a comeback. I never went away!" She'd made every effort to keep her legend alive, quoting her best lines at any opportunity and performing when conditions met her specifications. With her movie career on hold, she'd resurrected her roadshow past, renewing acquaintance with live audiences. Between stretches of inactivity she returned to the theater, turning the script she never managed to transform into a movie into her play *Catherine Was Great* and touring with it. She then toured with her own adaptation of a play she titled *Come On Up, Ring Twice*, in which she played an FBI agent tracking Nazis. In the late forties she took *Diamond Lil* on the road, first to England—her sole outing overseas—and then across the United States. In London she was called "a Restoration comedy rolled into one body" and was entertained by the Sacheverell Sitwells. In the London as in all *Diamond Lil* productions, she insisted that the other actresses darken their teeth, so that hers would shine most brightly and there could be no debate about who was fairest of them all.

Aided by ghostwriters, she completed and published her autobiography, *Goodness Had Nothing to Do with It,* a novelization of *Pleasure Man,* and a book on sex, health, and ESP, released in England, that dispenses advice on nutrition, colonics, positive thinking, spiritualism, and staying sexy; she recommends meditation, bottled water, fresh vegetables, indirect lighting, fantasy, separate bedrooms, and enemas—not necessarily in that order.

Her interest in psychic phenomena grew as she allied herself with two successive spiritual advisers, Jack Kelly—who, according to her, predicted the Japanese invasion of Pearl Harbor—and Richard Ireland. Acquaintances would be invited to attend séances or ESP demonstrations at the Santa Monica beach house she bought in the fifties. With the help of her advisers, she insisted she could remain in contact with her mother, father, and, eventually, after his death, her brother, Jack, whose lack of ambition, she assured him from the other side, she accepted.

When Mae was in residence, the beach house was kept shuttered and dark; likewise the Ravenswood apartment. She considered the sun an enemy, as were houseplants: they consumed too much oxygen.

The beach house featured murals depicting naked men with golden phalluses and disembodied testicles "floating like pink clouds across blue skies." Diane Arbus interviewed Mae and was somewhat aghast that the two pet monkeys housed there "are as unhousebroken as can be all over the carpet." Arbus found Mae West "imperious, adorable, magnanimous, genteel and girlish . . . There is even, forgive me, a kind of innocence about her."

Some time after Timony's death in 1954, a loss Mae mourned profoundly, she created a hugely popular nightclub act featuring herself, Louise Beavers in a maid's uniform, and a clutch of musclemen in loincloths. Ann Sheridan recalled seeing the act at Ciro's. Mae West, she said, "had a tremendous, tough, wonderful quality. Cary Grant said to go see her. He said everybody must see this woman, because she's the only one of her kind."

One of her male pinups, Paul Novak, a.k.a. Chester Ribonsky and Chuck Krauser, became Mae's live-in companion, chauffeur, bodyguard, and trainer, remaining her devoted lover and helpmate for the rest of her life. A butler, a male secretary, and an ever-changing circle of worshipful acolytes all danced attendance. Cecil Beaton, in a visit to the Ravenswood, observed that what she asked of the adoring men around her was not in-timacy but obeisance.

The list of roles turned down by Mae West divulges at least as much about her as the tally of parts she accepted. Cole Porter, who'd used Mae West's name in the lyrics to "Anything Goes" and "You're the Top," wanted her for two of his Broadway musicals: *You Never Know* and *DuBarry Was a Lady*. Because she insisted that the recently immobilized Porter visit her in Hol-lywood to discuss the roles and hear her sing, no deal was cut.

She was offered the role of Vera Simpson, the bewitched, bothered, and bewildered rich socialite of a certain age in the film adaptation of Rodgers and Hart's *Pal Joey*, opposite Marlon Brando, "but I turned it down. Joey makes a sucker out of this dame and that's against my whole concept of handling men." Another account has it the other way around: Mae West, in this version, was nixed by Harry Cohn, head of Columbia Pictures. The role of Vera, in any case, went against the Westian grain. "I like movies about strong women," Mae West explained. "I was the first liberated woman, y'know. No guy was gonna get the best of me, that's what I wrote all my scripts about." In the 1957 movie of *Pal Joey* that was finally made, Rita Hayworth played Vera to Frank Sinatra's Joey.

Around 1964, Mae was offered the part of Maude, a carnival owner, in an Elvis Presley vehicle called *Roustabout*. She lost interest when she learned her character would be an older woman faced with losing her business and tied to a sloshed lover. No way could she take such a fall. (Barbara Stanwyck took it.) She left the door open, however, to the possibility of starring in a future picture in which Elvis would play a small part opposite her.

Fellini courted her for roles in *Juliet of the Spirits* and *Satyricon*. For the latter, he wanted her to play an erotic witch (which was fine), who was a mother (which wasn't). Mae felt no inclination, either, to make the long trip to Rome which would have been required. (She avoided air travel as much as possible.) Fellini never told her that he found her entirely won-derful but anti-erotic. "She always seemed to be anti-sex, because she made a joke of sex and made you laugh, and that is anti-erotic. I think that her work was really her sex."

The most celebrated of her rejected offers, extended to her when she was in her mid-fifties, in the late 1940s, was the role of Norma Desmond, the fading and deluded former diva of the silent screen, in *Sunset Boulevard*. Billy Wilder was shocked to find Mae West more insulted than flattered at being considered. Far from being a faded flower who lived in the past, she would have him know, Mae West was enjoying the best years of her life, thank you very much. She wanted him to know that she had no affinity whatever with Norma Desmond, and moreover had never played in silent pictures. Gloria Swanson, who accepted the part of Norma Desmond and played it so memorably, was actually several years younger than Mae West, but had begun her film career much earlier, and of course had made her name in silent movies.

Billy Wilder, after talking with Mae West about portraying Norma Desmond, decided to withdraw the offer anyway. He felt she would turn the production into a "kind of Laurel and Hardy picture"—not quite what he had in mind. It's hard to imagine Mae West, rather than Gloria Swanson, saying, "I'm ready for my close-up, Mr. DeMille," though not at all difficult to envision her saying, "I *am* big. It's the pictures that got small."

Eager to keep in step, Mae West released rock-and-roll recordings and made appearances on television with Red Skelton and the talking horse, Mr. Ed. With Rock Hudson, she sang "Baby, It's Cold Outside" and gave him a long, juicy, nationally televised kiss on the mouth at the 1958 Academy Awards ceremony. The Academy of Motion Picture Arts and Sciences had never nominated Mae West for a single one of her movie roles or, for that matter, bestowed its honors on anyone who participated in any way in her pictures; this invitation to perform one of the nominated songs was its sole nod in her direction.

Censorship no longer plagued her—Jane Russell had supplanted her as the Hays Office whipping girl, more for her cleavage than for her words—until the banning of *Diamond Lil* in Atlanta in 1951. A better-known set-to arose in consequence of the cancellation by CBS of her 1959 appearance with Charles Collingwood on television's *Person to Person*. The public could read about but never see and hear her telling Collingwood she kept a mirror over her bed because she liked to see how she was doing, or that she'd always had a weakness for foreign affairs. The TV audience never had a chance to enjoy her answer to Collingwood's question: "Have you any advice for teenagers?" "Yes," she offered: "Grow up."

She perpetuated her long association with the law courts by successfully suing a woman named Marie Lind who had the temerity to bill herself as "Diamond Lil" on the nightclub circuit. The name "Diamond Lil," Mae crows in an afterword to her autobiography, "is mine, all mine." In another court action, she sued *Confidential* magazine for libeling her in an article called "Mae West's Open Door Policy." She extracted from them a published retraction of their claims—which in this case happened to be true—about her sexual liaisons with Chalky Wright, Johnny Indrisano, Speedy Dado, and Watson "Gorilla" Jones.

Mae continued to display her talons to females she perceived as rivals, like Raquel Welch in *Myra Breckinridge*, and Marilyn Monroe, who was attractive, she conceded, but a pale imitation of herself. She remained wary toward strangers of unproven mettle. Subdued and reticent in the company of new acquaintances, she impressed one interviewer as "a cautious person of a rather serious turn of mind." Beneath her show of optimism, her air of contentment, complete self-confidence, and jocular good humor lurked an abiding mistrust. "I'm sorry that I can't have faith in people as a whole," she once wrote to a functionary of the Shubert organization in Boston. "I wish I could, but unfortunately (or fortunately) for me, I have in the past had certain people presumably reputable and trustworthy exposed as not doing as they were supposed to do." But she knew she could rely on herself. Concentrating on yourself was the only way a person could hope to become a true star.

Alert to the last about the public's perception of her, she never told the press, once the diagnosis was made, that she had diabetes—sex symbols don't get sick—but delighted in spreading the news that doctors had discovered she had a double thyroid; she thought that explained her hypersexuality.

In the 1970s, it was rumored that Mae West had amassed one of the largest fortunes in Hollywood. Her estimated worth was said to be between five and fifteen million. But by the time of her death, her estate had dwindled to about one million. She sold the beach house before she died, and the ranch, in Beverly's hands, fell into neglect. To speak for the record about money matters remained taboo for as long as she lived. "I've spent a lot of money," Mae told Karl Fleming. "I used to play the horses pretty bad, and then I owned a string of horses. I've got a lot of property, but I don't like to talk about my investments in public."

Beverly, who divorced Baikoff, continued to be a thorn in her sister's side, but Mae remained loyal to her, even more so after their brother's death in 1964. Mae paid for her drying-out stays in sanatoriums, helped her record and release a disk, and named her the chief beneficiary in her will. (Beverly survived her by less than two years.) Paul Novak, bequeathed only $10,000 in the will, had to go to court to win a more generous settlement for himself.

The Mae West whose star still glistens so brilliantly is not the private woman devoted to her family or the monumentally self-absorbed personality who, when introduced a single time to Greta Garbo, could find no more fascinating subject for conversation than her own career. Neither is she the celebrity who would sometimes sit in absolute silence at a restaurant, moving the lamp at hand to make the light more flattering. Rather, the eternal Mae West is the self-created persona: the cooing, self-mocking "sex personality" exaggerated into a cartoon with perfect timing, projected from stage or screen with equal portions of attitude, wit, glitz, and nonchalance. She survives as a daring crosser of borders: between 1890s honky-tonk and the age of RuPaul, Roseanne, and Madonna; between gay and straight, masculine and feminine, black and white, raunchy and respectable, artificial and authentic. In an era intrigued with blurred margins, Mae West continues to stop traffic at the risky intersection of Vamp and Camp.

NOTES

ABBREVIATIONS

The following abbreviations are used in the notes:

AFI: American Film Institute, Los Angeles
AMPAS: Margaret Herrick Library, Academy of Motion Picture Arts and Sciences, Beverly Hills
BFI: British Film Institute, London
BHS: Brooklyn Historical Society, Brooklyn
BPL: Brooklyn Public Library, Grand Army Plaza, Brooklyn
Harvard: Harvard Theater Collection, Cambridge, Massachusetts
HRC: Harry Ransom Humanities Research Center, Austin, Texas
Iowa: Keith/Albee Collections, University of Iowa, Iowa City
L of C: Library of Congress, Washington, D.C.
Lilly: Starr Sheet Music Collection, Lilly Library, Indiana University, Bloomington
MCNY: Museum of the City of New York, New York City
Muni: Municipal Archives, New York City
MW: Mae West
NYPL: Billy Rose Theater Collection, Lincoln Center New York Public Library, New York City
NYU: Wagner Labor Archives, Tamiment Institute Library, New York University, New York City
PCA: Production Code Administration
SFPALM: San Francisco Performing Arts Library and Museum
Shubert: Shubert Archive, New York City
SMU: Oral History Collection, De Golyer Library, Southern Methodist University, Dallas, Texas
USC: Stanley Musgrove Collection, University of Southern California, Los Angeles
Wisc: Wisconsin Center for Film and Theater Research, Madison

INTRODUCTION

  6 "Sorry, Mae": Quoted in *Mae West on Sex, Health and ESP* (London and New York:
     W. H. Allen, 1975), p. 3.
  9 "From nothing in the movies": Unattributed clip, May 20, 1934, AMPAS.
 13 George Davis: "The Decline of the West," *Vanity Fair* (May 1934):46, 82.
 14 John Mason Brown: "Mae Pourquoi?" in *Dramatis Personae: A Retrospective Show*
     (New York: Viking, 1963), p. 258.
 14 Colette: *Colette and the Movies*, eds. Alain and Odette Virmaux, trans. Sara W. R.
     Smith (New York: Frederick Ungar, 1980), p. 63.

1. HER CHRISTIAN NAME WAS MARY

 17 "When she dances": Quoted by Robert C. Toll, *On with the Show: The First Century
     of Show Business in America* (New York: Oxford University Press, 1976), p. 225.
 18 "the most outrageous assault": Anthony Comstock, quoted by Heywood Broun and
     Margaret Leech, *Anthony Comstock, Roundsman of the Lord* (New York: Albert &
     Charles Boni, 1927), p. 227.
 18 a woman had been arrested: *National Police Gazette*, November 25, 1893.
 18 "Poor Little Country Maid": "Streets of Cairo" (1895) by James Thornton, in *Fa-
     vorite Songs of the Nineties*, ed. Robert A. Fremont (New York: Dover, 1973),
     pp. 272ff.
 18 Coney Island: John F. Kasson, *Amusing the Million: Coney Island at the Turn of the
     Century* (New York: Hill & Wang, 1978), p. 53.
 19 "Her Christian Name Was Mary": Quoted in *Brooklyn Eagle*, November 20, 1949,
     Brooklyn Eagle Scraps, BHS, Vol. 83, pp. 164–66.
 19 "I don't like anything downbeat": MW to Charlotte Chandler, *The Ultimate Seduction*
     (Garden City, N.Y.: Doubleday, 1984), p. 51.
 19 "full moon" face: Alexander Walker, *Sex in the Movies: The Celluloid Sacrifice* (Bal-
     timore: Penguin Books, 1968), p. 65.
 20 sister: MW to Chandler, p. 47.
 20 Katie West: Born August 23, 1891; birth certificate, Muni.
 20 home births: Henry Collins Brown, *In the Golden Nineties* (Freeport, N.Y.: Books for
     Libraries Press, 1970 [1927]), pp. 92–3.
 20 "I was born": MW in Paramount Press Book for *Belle of the Nineties*, AMPAS.
 20 "Since lions travel in prides": *Mae West on Sex, Health and ESP* (London and New
     York: W. H. Allen, 1975), p. 37.
 20 "like a jewel": MW to Chandler, p. 47.
 20 "I'd pose as I'd walk along": MW to Richard Meryman, "Mae West," *Life* (April 18,
     1969): 68.
 20 her photograph appeared: MW to Helen Ormsbee, New York *Herald Tribune*, Feb-
     ruary 19, 1949.
 20 "I was different": MW to Ruth Biery, "The Private Life of Mae West," Part One,
     Movie Classic (January 1934):56.
 21 "Mother knew how": MW to Denis Hart, *London Daily Telegraph*, August 21, 1970.
 21 a blond doll: MW, *Goodness Had Nothing to Do with It* (New York: Manor Books,
     1976), p. 12.

21 if her father . . . voiced regret: MW to Ruth Biery, Part One, p. 58.

21 "Mother dressed me": MW, *Goodness*, p. 14.

21 chocolates were *verboten*: Chandler, p. 46.

21 massaging with baby oil: *Ibid.*, p. 49.

21 family forbade it: John Kobal, *People Will Talk* (New York: Knopf, 1985), p. 161.

22 "a lasting appreciation": *Mae West on Sex*, p. 66.

22 "Aubrey Beardsley might have drawn": Cecil Beaton, *Beaton in Vogue*, ed. Josephine Ross (London: Thames & Hudson, 1986), p. 191.

22 marriage certificate: Muni.

23 Peter Doelger's estate: *The New York Times*, December 16, 1912.

23 "My father had swept her": MW, quoted in *Newark Star Ledger*, August 25, 1938.

23 parents' interactions: MW, *The Hussy* (1922), pp. 18–19, L of C, Manuscripts Division.

23 Doelger brewery: Will Anderson, *The Breweries of Brooklyn* (Croton Falls, N.Y. 1976), p. 41.

23 part Jewish: George Eells and Stanley Musgrove, *Mae West* (New York: William Morrow, 1982), p. 21; Maurice Leonard, *Mae West: Empress of Sex* (New York: Birch Lane, 1992), p. 9.

24 married "outside": Tim Malachosky to author, January 3, 1994.

24 Brooklyn street: U.S. Census, 1900.

24 "secretive": Thyra Samter Winslow, "Profiles: Diamond Mae," *The New Yorker* (November 10, 1928):26.

24 "that shrewd . . . woman": Biery, Part Two, *Movie Classic* (February 1934):20.

24 "the Jewish publications claim": Winslow, p. 26.

24 Harry Thaw: Gerald Lang Ford, *The Murder of Stanford White* (Indianapolis and New York: Bobbs-Merrill, 1962), p. 26.

25 "Just because I was born in Brooklyn": "Mae West Gives All the Answers," *Movie Classic* (February 1937):36.

25 "We were descended": MW to John Kobal, "Mae West," *Films and Filming* (September 1983):25.

25 "one of a long line": MW, *Goodness*, p. 1.

25 the midwife aunt: Stanley Musgrove, Myra Breckinridge Diary, p. 6, carton 4, Musgrove Collection, USC.

25 Sunday school: Kobal, *People*, p. 164.

25 a whaling captain: MW to Denis Hart, August 21, 1970.

25 Civil War: U.S. Census of Union Veterans, 1890.

25 the only one who did not go to college: MW, *Goodness*, p. 10.

25 speculated in real estate: Fergus Cashin, *Mae West: A Biography* (London: W. H. Allen, 1981), p. 28.

26 "Prize-fighting is an evil": *The New York Times*, October 21, 1893.

26 "men who hover": Quoted by Elliott J. Gorn, *The Manly Art: Bare-knuckle Prize-fighting in America* (Ithaca, N.Y.: Cornell University Press, 1986), p. 196.

26 "all knobby": MW, *Goodness*, p. 10.

26 recoiling against confinement: John Higham, "The Reorientation of American Culture in the 1890s," in *The Origins of Modern Consciousness*, ed. John Weiss (Detroit: Wayne State University Press, 1965), p. 23.

26 he once beat: MW, *Goodness*, p. 23.

26 knocking his rival out: *Ibid.*, p. 10.

26 "He'd go to a drawer": MW to Meryman, p. 69.

26 "all had 'Family Entrances' ": Willie "the Lion" Smith, quoted by Kathy Ogren, *The Jazz Revolution* (New York: Oxford University Press, 1989), p. 73.

26 liquor licenses issued: Cited by Grace Mayer, *Once Upon a City: New York from 1890 to 1910* (New York: Macmillan, 1956), p. 401.

27 employed as a bartender: Walter Kaner, *Brooklyn Daily News*, November 26, 1980.

27 John L. Sullivan: Gorn, p. 208.

27 "He came home": MW to Steven Roberts, "76—And Still Diamond Lil," *The New York Times Magazine* (November 2, 1969):80.

27 "I was always more like my father": MW to Chandler, p. 48.

27 a stranger to the kitchen: Meryman, p. 69.

28 "banging physical action": MW, *Goodness*, p. 10.

28 what kind of man: MW to Mead, "If I Were a Man," *Movie Classic* (August 1934):28.

28 livery stable: MW, *Goodness*, p. 11.

28 ride the elevator: Musgrove diary, p. 3, carton 4, USC.

28 "I was crazy about my mother": MW to Kobal, *People*, p. 161.

28 "a big detective agency": MW to Karl Fleming and Anne Taylor Fleming, *The First Time* (New York: Simon & Schuster, 1975), pp. 313–14.

28 King's *Handbook*: *King's Handbook of New York City* (Boston: Moses King, 1893), p. 528.

29 "He's a doctor": MW to Winslow, p. 26.

29 Feet Samuels: Damon Runyon, "A Very Honorable Guy," *Guys and Dolls* (New York: American Reprint Company, 1976 [1931]), p. 77.

29 spends his days at the track: MW, *The Hussy*, I, p. 40.

29 Meeker Avenue: *Brooklyn Daily News*, November 26, 1980.

29 six family house: BHS scraps, vol. 106, p. 41.

29 Linden Street: Records of P.S. 81, Ridgewood; supplied by Rosemarie Russell.

30 new ethic: Lewis A. Erenberg, *Stepping Out: New York Nightlife and the Transformation of American Culture, 1890–1930* (Westport, Conn.: Greenwood Press, 1981), p. 200.

30 "I was a child": MW, *Goodness*, p. 10.

31 more Irish than Dublin: W. A. Swanberg, in *The Nineties*, ed. Oliver Jensen (New York: American Heritage, 1967), p. 128.

31 Shop girls craved: Kathy Peiss, *Cheap Amusements: Working Women and Leisure in Turn-of-the-Century New York* (Philadelphia: Temple University Press, 1986), p. 35.

31 New York women: Rupert Hughes, *The Real New York* (New York: The Smart Set, 1904), pp. 29–31.

32 Tenni's Arab Acrobatic Troupe: Ruth Biery, "The Private Life of Mae West," Part Three, *Movie Classic* (March 1934):32.

32 "saying everything": MW to Biery, Part Two (February 1934):21.

32 burlesque of Sarah Bernhardt: John Kobal, *People Will Talk* (New York: Knopf, 1985), p. 157.

32 a "dingy spot": John E. Di Meglio, *Vaudeville USA* (Ohio: Bowling Green University Popular Press, 1973), p. 132.

33 "The actor ahead of me": MW in unattributed clip, Harvard.

33 "like the strongest man's arms": MW to Charlotte Chandler, *The Ultimate Seduction* (Garden City, N.Y.: Doubleday, 1984), p. 51.

33 "Movin' Day": Words by Andrew B. Sterling, music by Harry Von Tilzer, 1906.

33 "I had a deep, rough voice": MW, *Goodness Had Nothing to Do with It* (New York: Manor Books, 1976), p. 17.

33 skirt dance: Robert W. Snyder, *The Voice of the City: Vaudeville and Popular Culture in New York* (New York: Oxford University Press, 1989), p. 137.

34 Herbert Kenwith: *Los Angeles Times*, May 21, 1981.

34 a sword swallower: *Variety*, January 16, 1919.

34 prizefighters in show biz: Oliver Pilat and Jo Ransom, *Sodom by the Sea: An Affectionate History of Coney Island* (Garden City, N.Y.: Doubleday, 1941), p. 86; Russell B. Nye, *The Unembarrassed Muse: The Popular Arts in America* (New York: Dial, 1970), p. 158.

34 "Philadelphia Jack" O'Brien: *New York Dramatic Mirror*, October 26, 1907.

34 He built her a stage: *New York Tribune*, October 5, 1928.

35 "Mother was always talkin' ": MW to Ruth Biery, Part Two, p. 20.

35 Matilda kept herself apart: Eric Concklin to author, August 29, 1994.

35 "Miss West made her professional debut": Paramount Press Book, *Night After Night*, AMPAS.

35 Lillian Gish: Obituary, *Los Angeles Times*, March 1, 1993.

35 Sophie Tucker: Tucker, *Some of These Days* (Garden City, N.Y.: Doubleday, 1945), p. 12.

35 Clara Bow's mother: David Stenn, *Clara Bow: Runnin' Wild* (New York: Doubleday, 1988), p. 13.

35 "the very offal": Quoted by Claudia D. Johnson, *American Actress: Perspectives on the Nineteenth Century* (Chicago: Nelson-Hall, 1984), p. 7.

35 "somewhere between that of a gypsy": Groucho Marx, *Groucho and Me* (New York: Manor Books, 1974), p. 91.

36 "by their saffron hair": Quoted by Benjamin McArthur, *Actors and American Culture, 1880–1920* (Philadelphia: Temple University Press, 1984), p. 57.

36 "I don't see why": Dora (Ranous) Knowlton, *Diary of a Daly Debutante* (New York: Benjamin Blom Inc., 1972 [1910]), p. 105.

36 "are but leaders in the vast army": Quoted by Parker Morell, *Lillian Russell: The Era of Plush* (New York: Random House, 1940), p. 259.

36 They "lose all modesty": Elbridge T. Gerry, "Children of the Stage," in *American Vaudeville as Seen by Its Contemporaries*, ed. Charles Stein (New York: Knopf, 1984), pp. 141–42.

36 " 'lust palaces some fun' ": Quoted by Timothy J. Gilfoyle, *City of Eros: New York City, Prostitution and the Commercialization of Sex, 1790–1920* (New York: Norton, 1992), p. 225.

36 Tony Pastor's theater: Sophie Tucker, pp. 46–47.

37 "Vaudeville theaters": Rupert Hughes, p. 94.

37 "shills of the consumer culture": McArthur, p. 165.

37 silk top hats: *Ibid.*, p. 57.

37 a gold-plated bicycle: Morell, p. 221.

37 Eva Tanguay: Tucker, p. 81.

37 Florodora girls: Allen Churchill, *The Great White Way* (New York: Dutton, 1962), p. 9.

38 photographs of actresses: McArthur, p. 148.

38 "Ned Wayburn's Training School": Ad in *New York Dramatic Mirror*, March 9, 1907.

38 he drilled his chorines: Unattributed clip, 1915, Harvard.

38 the American *girl*: Richard Kislan, *Hoofing on Broadway: A History of Show Dancing* (New York: Prentice-Hall, 1987), p. 53.

38 he had learned ragtime's rhythms: Unattributed clip, 1904, Harvard.

38 "I was always imagining": MW to Chandler, pp. 51–52.

38 "I was so carried away": MW to Kobal, *People*, pp. 161–62.

39 "I hated school": MW to W. H. Mooring, "Mae West Talks," *Film Weekly* (September 28, 1934):8.

39 "How do you expect?": Mrs. Joanna Franz to *Brooklyn Eagle*, October 7, 1955, in BHS scraps, vol. 106, p. 41.

39 Buster Keaton: Keaton, in *American Vaudeville*, p. 148.

39 "She was terribly sensitive": Anonymous statement by a member of the cast of the 1928 *Diamond Lil*, Harvard.

39 "talkin' Brooklyn": MW in New York *Sun*, March 27, 1934.

39 amateur contests: Di Meglio, p. 67.

39 there would be a chord: *Ibid.*, p. 19; Luc Sante, *Low Life: Lures and Snares of Old New York* (New York: Farrar, Straus & Giroux, 1991), pp. 92–93.

40 "Mariutch Make-a the Hootch-a-ma-kootch": Words by Andrew B. Sterling, music by Harry Von Tilzer, 1907.

40 "Even as a little girl": Beverly West to Hester Robison, "Mae West Isn't Diamond Lil," *The New Movie Magazine* (May 1933):94.

40 Brooklyn police raided: *Popular Music: 1900–1919*, ed. Barbara Cohen-Stratyner (Detroit: Gale Research, 1988), p. 294.

40 *Mrs. Warren's Profession*: Heywood Broun and Margaret Leech, *Anthony Comstock: Roundsman of the Lord* (New York: Albert & Charles Boni, 1927), p. 232.

40 Salome dance craze: Abel Green and Joe Laurie, Jr., *Show Biz: From Vaude to Video* (New York: Holt, 1951), p. 9.

41 "discouraged shoulders": Ann Charters, *Nobody: The Story of Bert Williams* (New York: Macmillan, 1970), pp. 19–20.

41 incipient race war: *The New York Times*, February 19, 1903.

41 "It's not! It's not!" Chandler, p. 52.

41 "Mother took me": MW to Biery, Part Two (February 1934):21.

41 "I used to visit her": Eva Tanguay to Louella Parsons, *Los Angeles Examiner*, April 26, 1935.

42 "She screams": Quoted by Robert C. Toll, *On with the Show: The First Century of Show Business in America* (New York: Oxford University Press, 1976), p. 279.

42 two pearls: *Ibid.*, p. 280.

42 "personalities": MW, *Goodness*, p. 14.

42 Hal Clarendon: Questionnaire, NYPL.

43 eighteen dollars: MW, *Goodness*, p. 19.

43 average working-class family: Peiss, p. 12.

43 "anything like secure": MW, quoted by Kirtley Baskette, "Mae West Talks About Her 'Marriage,' " *Photoplay* (August 1935):38.

43 Clarendon's company: *The Brooklyn Eagle*, April 15, 1907.

43 "I had gotten too mature": MW to Kobal, *People*, p. 162.

44 "Matinee girls": *American Theater Companies, 1888–1930*, ed. Weldon B. Durham (Westport, Conn.: Greenwood Press, 1987), p. 426.

44 so roundly hissed: *Ibid.*, p. 426.

44 FOOL BOYS: *New York Telegraph*, June 9, 1907.

44 "I played . . . the moonshiner's daughter": MW, *Goodness*, p. 20.

44 "No actress ever had": *Ibid.*, pp. 9, 21.

44 using greasepaint: Paramount Press Release, 1933, BFI.

44 "They used to tell me": MW to Helen Ormsbee, New York *Herald Tribune*, February 19, 1949.

44 dividing long words: Alexander Walker, *Sex in the Movies: The Celluloid Sacrifice* (Baltimore: Penguin Books, 1968), p. 67.

45 "Father, dear father": Quoted by Toll, p. 151.

45 Melodramas: Frank Rahill, *The World of Melodrama* (University Park: Pennsylvania State University Press, 1967), p. 93.

45 A fallen woman: Lea Jacobs, *The Wages of Sin: Censorship and the Fallen Woman Film, 1928–1942* (Madison: University of Wisconsin Press, 1991), p. 11.

46 "high class royalty plays": *New York Dramatic Mirror*, February 16, 1907.

46 "wave daggers": MW, *Goodness*, p. 21.

46 Lady Macbeth: MW, quoted in *San Francisco Chronicle Datebook*, August 5, 1979.

47 "After I read it": MW to John Kobal, *People Will Talk* (New York: Knopf, 1985), p. 161.

47 "She'd drop her clothes": George Hurrell to Kobal, *Ibid.*, p. 269.

47 nonchalantly lifting: Maria Riva, *Marlene Dietrich* (New York: Knopf, 1993), p. 142.

47 "feel these": Stephen Longstreet to author, August 18, 1994.

47 "Sex is no more vulgar": MW to James Fidler, "Mae West Answers Twenty Personal Questions," *Movie Classic* (September 1933):71.

47 "My mother thought": MW to C. Robert Jennings, "Mae West: A Candid Conversation with the Indestructible Queen of Vamp and Camp," *Playboy* (January 1971): 80.

48 "because she really didn't like women": Edith Head in *Los Angeles Times*, May 21, 1981.

48 "I always went with the boys": MW, *Goodness Had Nothing to Do with It* (New York: Manor Books, 1976), p. 21.

48 Mae considered women: Rona Barrett to author, August 11, 1994.

48 "Boys could hold me up": MW, *Goodness*, p. 21.

48 "I was liberated": MW to Karl Fleming, *The First Time* (New York: Simon & Schuster, 1975), p. 312.

48 "Even as a child": *Mae West on Sex, Health and ESP* (London and New York: W. H. Allen, 1975), p. 6.

49 helped break down reticence: Ellen Chesler, *Woman of Valor: Margaret Sanger and the Birth Control Movement in America* (New York: Simon & Schuster, 1992), p. 71; Nathan G. Hale, Jr., *Freud and the Americans: The Beginnings of Psychoanalysis in the United States, 1876–1917* (New York: Oxford University Press, 1971), pp. 154–55.

49 Magazines began publishing articles: James McGovern, "The American Woman's Pre–World War I Freedom in Manners and Morals," *Journal of American History*, 55 (September 1968): 316.

49 Havelock Ellis: John D'Emilio and Estelle B. Freedman, *Intimate Matters: A History of Sexuality in America* (New York: Harper & Row, 1988), p. 224.

49 Emma Goldman: Hale, p. 270; Richard Drinnon, *Rebel in Paradise: A Biography of Emma Goldman* (Boston: Beacon Press, 1961), p. 153.

49 "For the first time": Quoted by Lewis A. Erenberg, *Steppin' Out: New York Nightlife and the Transformation of American Culture, 1890–1930* (Westport, Conn.: Greenwood Press, 1981), p. 70.

49 nickelodeons closed down: Lary May, *Screening Out the Past: The Birth of Mass Culture and the Motion Picture Industry* (New York: Oxford University Press, 1980), p. 43.

49 people fainted: Brooks McNamara, *The Shuberts of Broadway* (New York: Oxford University Press, 1991), p. 69.

49 *The Easiest Way*: W. David Sievers, *Freud on Broadway: A History of Psychoanalysis and the American Drama* (New York: Hermitage House, 1955), p. 41.

49 double entendre songs: MW, *Goodness*, p. 31.

50 "Evenings the gang": *Ibid.*, p. 21.

50 it also included: MW to Jennings, p. 76.

50 "Oh, let her go": Ruth Biery, "The Private Life of Mae West," Part Two, *Movie Classic* (March 1934):62.

50 "People are always talking": MW, *The Hussy*, p. 20, L of C.

50 "But when one of 'em": MW to Biery, Part Two, p. 62.

50 "She would point out": MW to Charlotte Chandler, *The Ultimate Seduction* (Garden City, N.Y.: Doubleday, 1984), p. 57.

50 "I never used bad language . . . functions": Fleming, pp. 314–15.

51 Joe Schenck: MW, *Goodness*, p. 27.

51 Otto North: *Ibid.*, p. 29.

51 first orgasm: *Mae West on Sex*, p. 9.

51 telling Karl Fleming: Fleming, pp. 316–17.

51 postponed intimate sex: Jennings, p. 78; Kobal, *People*, p. 162.

51 "It didn't wash": Karl Fleming to author, May 11, 1993.

51 Sis Hopkins type: MW, *Goodness*, p. 26.

51 A New York theatrical manager: *Los Angeles Examiner*, April 25, 1935.

52 chaperons: Kobal, *People*, p. 161.

52 "The fan was big": Biery, Part Two, p. 70.

52 "A swell looking woman": Frank Wallace in New York *Mirror*, May 15, 1935; *Los Angeles Herald*, April 23, 1935.

52 Mrs. Szatkus: New York *Evening Journal*, April 2, 1935.

53 "The public of the nineties": Edward B. Marks, quoted by Robert C. Toll, *The Entertainment Machine: American Show Business in the Twentieth Century* (New York: Oxford University Press, 1982), p. 105.

53 " 'Rag' strains will empty the tables: *Variety*, August 9, 1912.

53 "I Love It": words by E. Ray Goetz, music by Harry Von Tilzer, 1910.

53 "It was the black man's sound": MW to John Kobal, *Gotta Sing, Gotta Dance: A Pictorial History of Film Musicals* (New York: Hamlyn, 1970), p. 190.

54 past practices in social dancing: Alice Duer Miller, "The New Dances and the Younger Generation," *Harper's Bazaar* 46 (May 1912):225.

54 "Honey Man": Words by Joe McCarthy, music by Al Piantadosi; published by Leo Feist, 1911.

54 "I learned to dance": MW, *Goodness*, p. 49.

54 "a reversion to the grossest practices": "The Revolt of Decency," quoted in *Literary Digest* (April 19, 1913): 894.

54 "book" shows: Abel Green and Joe Laurie, Jr., *Show Biz: From Vaude to Video* (New York: Holt, 1951), p. 76.

54 "A Florida Enchantment": *Variety*, June 3, 1911; *Clipper*, September 2, 1911.

55 "I told him": MW to Fleming, pp. 312, 317.

55 a venerable method: Linda Gordon, *Woman's Body, Woman's Right: A Social History of Birth Control in America* (New York: Viking, 1976), pp. 26, 44.

55 "little silk sponge": MW to Fleming, p. 316.

56 stepping out on him: George Eells and Stanley Musgrove, *Mae West* (New York: Morrow, 1982), p. 31.

56 "My dear husband": Frank Wallace, *Los Angeles Daily News*, November 28, 1936.

56 "My Darling Sister": Letter from Jack to Beverly West, Jack Allen Collection.

56 "I was born to be a solo performer": *Mae West on Sex*, p. 28.

56 "I saw what it did": MW to Jennings, p. 80.

56 "Mae's heart was broken": Rona Barrett to author, August 11, 1994.

56 no family should be without: Kirtley Baskette, "Mae West Talks About Her 'Marriage,'" *Photoplay* (August 1935):38.

56 "I'm not the cottage apron type": MW to Jennings, p. 80.

56 "What do you think I am?" MW, *Sex*, p. 4, L of C.

57 "The Times Square section": *Variety*, February 24, 1911.

58 "The house will have": *Clipper*, April 15, 1911.

58 "An expanding stage": Jesse Lasky with Don Weldon, *I Blow My Own Horn* (Garden City, N.Y.: Doubleday, 1957), pp. 82–84.

58 "It's too big": MW, *Goodness Had Nothing to Do with It* (New York: Manor Books, 1976), p. 35.

58 "to provide an added spice": Unattributed clip, April 20, 1912, Locke Collection, NYPL.

58 playlets: Lasky, p. 75.

58 "small smile": "Paramount Pictures," *Fortune* (March 1937): 92.

58 "a peppy, vivacious 'tomboy'": Le Baron, quoted by Edward Churchill, "So You Think You Know Mae West," *Motion Picture* (July 1935): 49.

59 "As for those curves": Frank Wallace to James Whittaker, New York *Daily Mirror*, April 24, 1935.

59 "a flip, fresh, lazy character": MW, *Goodness*, p. 38.

59 *Evening World*: Quoted in *Ibid.*, 39.

59 Orientalism: Valerie Steele, *Fashion and Eroticism: Ideals of Feminine Beauty from the Victorian Era to the Jazz Age* (New York: Oxford University Press, 1985), p. 232.

59 "The Philadelphia Drag": Words by M. H. Hollins, music by Harold Orlob, 1911.

59 "that in order to break even": Lasky, p. 86.

60 "The legitimate houses . . . are complaining": *Variety*, November 4, 1911.

60 *The Fascinating Widow*: Gerald Bordman, *American Musical Theatre: A Chronicle* (New York: Oxford University Press, 1986), p. 270.

60 *The Never Homes: Ibid.*, p. 272.

60 *Undine: Variety*, November 25, 1911.

60 Gaby Deslys: Brooks McNamara, *The Shuberts of Broadway* (New York: Oxford University Press, 1991), p. 67.

61 "You married?": *Vera Violetta* (1911), by Leo Stein, adapted by Leonard Liebling and Harold Atteridge, Prompt Book, Shubert.

61 "Outside of Mlle. Deslys": *Variety*, September 16, 1911.

61 "When she came out": MW to Kevin Thomas, *Los Angeles Times*, August 31, 1969.

61 "stricken with pneumonia": *Variety*, November 25, 1911.

61 I believe I'll go to Paris": MW, in unattributed clip, NYPL.

61 "After seeing Vera Violetta": *Variety*, November 25, 1911.

61 "It is said Mae was right in the middle": *Ibid.*, March 9, 1912.

62 HER WRIGGLES: MW, *Goodness*, pp. 44–45.

62 "Miss West exhibits": *Variety*, January 20, 1912.

62 "Mae West Monday evening": *Ibid.*, March 9, 1912.

63 gowns: MW, *Goodness*, p. 47.

63 "generous, vital, and adoring": *Ibid.*, p. 44.

63 "by winning three games": *Variety*, May 18, 1912.

63 "I learned that one man": Mae West to Ruth Biery, "The Private Life of Mae West," Part Three, *Movie Classic* (March 1934):62.

63 he brought suit: *Variety*, March 13, 1914; February 11, 1916.

64 "Just another of those composites": *The New York Times*, April 12, 1912.

64 skaters on real ice: Charles Higham, *Ziegfeld* (Chicago: Henry Regnery, 1972), p. 86.

64 "The tunes won't last long": New York *Globe*, April 12, 1912.

64 "All curls and wiggles": Charles Darnton, New York *World*, April 12, 1912.

64 "Mae West assaults the welkin vigorously": *New York Dramatic Mirror*, April 17, 1912.

64 " 'Piccolo': Sime, in *Variety*, April 20, 1912.

64 "abruptly left the cast": *Ibid.*

64 vaudeville audience: Albert F. McLean, Jr., *American Vaudeville as Ritual* (Lexington: University of Kentucky Press, 1965), p. 46; Robert W. Snyder, *The Voice of the City: Vaudeville and Popular Culture in New York* (New York: Oxford University Press, 1989), p. 105.

65 "It may be a kind of lunch-counter art": Quoted by Rhea Foster Dulles, *America Learns to Play: A History of Popular Recreation, 1607–1940* (New York: Appleton-Century, 1940), p. 219.

65 "whizzed before the audience": Robert C. Toll, *On with the Show: The First Century of Show Business in America* (New York: Oxford University Press, 1976), p. 277.

65 "gives way to the trapeze artist": *Theatre Magazine* (May 1927):62.

65 "Vaudeville suits the American nature": E. F. Albee, New York *Telegraph*, December 15, 1912.

65 "Within fifteen minutes": McLean, p. 112.

65 city slang: *Ibid.*, p. 119.

65 "examined the front": Fred Allen, *Much Ado About Me*, in *American Vaudeville as Seen by Its Contemporaries*, ed. Charles Stein (New York: Knopf, 1984), p. 254.

66 "coming under the wire": *Billboard*, January 11, 1913.

66 It was a thrill: Sophie Tucker, *Some of These Days* (Garden City, N.Y. Doubleday, 1945), p. 96.

66 "a big, tinkling pearl box": Alan Dale, quoted by David Ewen, *All the Years of American Popular Music* (Englewood Cliffs, N.J.: Prentice-Hall, 1977), p. 180.

66 when Mae brags: MW, *Goodness*, p. 57.

67 shared billing: based on vaudeville routes published in *Variety* and *Billboard*.

67 "so filthy": MW to George Christy, "Mae West Raps," *Cosmopolitan* (May 1970), reprinted in Carol M. Ward, *Mae West: A Bio-Bibliography* (Westport, Conn.: Greenwood Press, 1989), p. 127.

67 Travis Banton: Julie Lang Hunt, "Trials and Triumphs of a Hollywood Dress Designer," *Photoplay* (June 1936):88.

68 "I would try": MW, *Goodness*, p. 53.

68 Mrs. Ripley Hetherington: MW, *Pleasure Man*, pp. 23–24. L of C.

68 "How did you get on stage?": *Ibid.*, p. 15.

69 The most sought-after spots: George Gottlieb, "Psychology of the American Vaudeville Show from the Manager's Point of View," in *American Vaudeville as Seen*, pp. 179–81.

69 "some of her very good material": *Variety*, December 13, 1912.

69 "Mae West, 'The Scintillating . . . ' ": *Ibid.*, May 18, 1912.

69 "registered a most emphatic hit": *Billboard*, June 1, 1912.

69 she should not be billed: Manager's Report Book 15, Philadelphia, week of November 3, 1913, p. 251, Iowa.

69 "This hunk of humanity": Manager's Report Book 16, Cleveland, week of March 15, 1914, p. 175, Iowa.

70 cut out the crown: MW, *Goodness*, p. 54.

70 "some clothes that give Valeska Suratt": *Variety*, November 14, 1913.

70 chosen by Matilda: Beverly West to Hester Robison, "Mae West Isn't Diamond Lil," *The New Movie Magazine* (May 1933):41.

70 "Mae West is nearly an Eva Tanguay": *Billboard*, February 21, 1914.

70 "The girl is of the eccentric type": Sime, *Variety*, May 25, 1912.

71 "that Cohanesque, Tanguayish president of the female 'nut' club": New York *Morning Telegraph*, October 1, 1913.

71 "She is doing less 'singing' ": Jolo, *Variety*, October 3, 1913.

71 Tommy Gray songs: George Eells and Stanley Musgrove, *Mae West* (New York: William Morrow, 1982), p. 36.

71 He sued . . . she promptly coughed up the cash: *Variety*, August 22, 1913; September 26, 1913.

71 "Miss West can't sing": New York *Morning Telegraph*, October 1, 1913.

71 "A Muscle Dance in a Sitting Position": *Variety*, July 26, 1912.

71 "It isn't what you do": MW, *Goodness*, pp. 53–54.

72 "It's easy for 'em to . . . I used to take": MW to C. Robert Jennings, "Mae West: A Candid Conversation with the Indestructible Queen of Vamp and Camp," *Playboy* (January 1971): 76.

72 "The Nell Brinkley Girl": Words by Harry B. Smith, music by Maurice Levi, Cohan and Harris Publishing Co., 1908.

72 "The Brinkley Girl is lithe": Unattributed clip on Annabelle Whitford, Robinson Locke Collection, NYPL.

73 "The men like her better": Manager's Report Book 16, Philadelphia, week of November 10, 1913, Iowa.

73 "Vaudeville has started on the downward path": *Variety*, September 27, 1912; October 17, 1913.

73 "A wave of sex hysteria": "Sex O'Clock in America," *Current Opinion*, 55 (August 1913): 113–14.

73 a rush of "vice plays": John Burnham, "The Progressive Era Revolution and American Attitudes Toward Sex," *Journal of American History*, 59 (March 1973): 906.

73 Theda Bara: Lary May, *Screening Out the Past: The Birth of Mass Culture and the Motion Picture Industry* (New York: Oxford University Press, 1980), p. 106.

73 "are meeting the dance craze . . . floor": *Billboard*, March 21, 1914.

74 A New York grand jury: McGovern, p. 331.

74 *A Night Out*: *Variety*, March 12, 1915.

74 National Board of Censors: John Collier, "Censorship and the National Board," in *The Movies in Our Midst*, ed. Gerald Mast (University of Chicago Press, 1982), p. 149.

74 Supreme Court: *Mutual Film Corp. v. Industrial Commission of Ohio*, in Mast, pp. 136 ff.; David Nasaw, *Going Out: The Rise and Fall of Public Amusements* (New York: Basic Books, 1993), p. 204.

74 Blue envelopes: Tucker, pp. 148–49.

74 "chicken": Manager's Report Book 16, Cleveland, week of March 15, 1914, p. 175, Iowa.

75 " 'My God . . . my way' ": *Mae West on Sex, Health and ESP* (London and New York: W. H. Allen, 1975), p. 3.

75 "He'd read it": MW to William Scott Eyman, *Take One* (September 1972):21.

75 "And Then": Words by Alfred Bryan, music by Herman Paley, Paley Music Co., 1913. Thanks to Sue Presnell, Lilly Library.

75 "The big hit": *Detroit News*, August 26 [1913?], Locke Collection, NYPL.

75 "overstep the line": *Variety*, November 28, 1913.

76 "repressed her exuberance": *Ibid.*, January 9, 1915.

77 "Since the death of William Hammerstein": *Billboard*, August 8, 1914.

77 salary reductions: *Variety*, October 17, 1914.

78 "girl members": *Ibid.*, October 3, 1914.

78 "far away and still remote": MW, *Goodness Had Nothing to Do with It* (New York: Manor Books, 1976), p. 49.

78 "With Russia, Germany": *Variety*, July 31, 1914.

78 "you boys down there in the trenches": Quoted by Abel Green and Joe Laurie, Jr., *Show Biz: From Vaude to Video* (New York: Holt, 1951), p. 165.

78 "helping to lift the rigging": *Variety*, October 24, 1914.

78 *Lusitania* in vaudeville: *Ibid.*, August 20, 1914.

79 Mr. D.: MW, *Goodness*, p. 55. George Eells and Stanley Musgrove first identified Deiro as Mr. D. in *Mae West* (New York: Morrow, 1982), p. 53.

79 a plate of spaghetti: MW, *Goodness*, p. 59.

79 "There was never a bill": MW, *Pleasure Man* (New York: Dell, 1975), p. 135.

79 "a New York favorite": *New York Dramatic Mirror*, April 23, 1913.

79 "the classiest classic": *Variety*, July 2, 1910.

80 "The sex thing was terrific": MW to Karl Fleming with Anne Taylor Fleming, *The First Time* (New York: Simon & Schuster, 1975), p. 313.

80 "very deep": MW to C. Robert Jennings, "Mae West: A Candid Conversation with the Queen of Vamp and Camp," *Playboy* (January 1971):80.

80 "the Eva Tanguay of vaudeville": San Antonio *Light*, September 8, 1914. Locke Collection, NYPL.

80 "the applause hit": *Variety*, January 9, 1915.

80 "came near stopping the show": *Ibid.*, February 20, 1914.

80 "engaged jointly": Ad, *Ibid.*, December 25, 1914.

80 writes in his memoir: Nils T. Granlund, with Sid Feder and Ralph Hancock, *Blondes, Brunettes and Bullets* (New York: David McKay, 1957), p. 42.

81 an earlier complaint: *Variety*, February 25, 1914.

81 "My mother didn't like it": MW to Ruth Biery, "The Private Life of Mae West," Part Two, *Movie Classic* (February 1934):71.

81 "It almost killed the poor guy": MW to Fleming, p. 313.

81 "None of those Italian knife tricks": *Goodness*, p. 63.

82 "Waiting until she could forget *love*": Biery, p. 71.

82 "I felt that Mother": MW, *Goodness*, p. 63.

82 "racial and sexual tolerance": Ronald L. Morris, *Wait Until Dark: Jazz and the Underworld, 1880–1940* (Ohio: Bowling Green University Press, 1980), p. 60.

82 "low husky blues": MW, *Goodness*, p. 64.

82 "big black men": *Ibid.*, pp. 65–66.

82 "They got up": MW to Robert E. Johnson, "Mae West: Snow White Sex Queen Who Drifted," *Jet* (July 1974):44.

83 "it like to tore the house down": MW to Malcolm Oettinger, "Literary Lil," *Picture Play* (September 1933):26.

83 "Do not wriggle": Quoted by Marshall and Jean Stearns, *Jazz Dance: The Story of American Vernacular Dance* (New York: Macmillan, 1968), p. 96.

83 linked to Little Egypt's hootchy-kootchy: *Ibid.*, p. 105.

83 the first "jass" band: Samuel B. Charters and Leonard Kunstadt, *Jazz: A History of the New York Scene* (New York: Da Capo Press, 1981), p. 53.

83 Joe Frisco: MW, *Goodness*, p. 68; *Variety*, February 8, 1918.

83 "You can't tell": *Variety*, November 1, 1918.

83 Shelton Brooks: Dempsey J. Travis, *Autobiography of Black Jazz* (Chicago: Urban Research Institute, 1983), p. 64.

84 Tucker's girth: Robert C. Allen, *Horrible Prettiness: Burlesque and American Culture* (Chapel Hill: University of North Carolina Press, 1991), p. 272.

84 "I had graduated from ragtime": MW, *Goodness*, p. 64.

84 Jules Stein: Joyce Haber, *Los Angeles Times*, July 2, 1970.

85 "backward, low-class form": Quoted by Morris, p. 60.

85 "The word jazz": F. Scott Fitzgerald, *The Crack-Up*, ed. Edmund Wilson (New York: New Directions, 1993), p. 16.

85 Victoria Burlesquers: *Pittsburgh Leader*, April 9, 1916. NYPL.

85 at Sing Sing: *Variety*, June 2, 1916.

85 a childhood injury: Tim Malachosky to author, January 3, 1994.

86 "But we never did much of a sister act": MW, *Goodness*, p. 49.

86 "You can't get a man": MW, *The Ruby Ring*, I, p. 2. L of C.

86 Frank Bohm had died: *Variety*, March 17, 1916.

86 a "show house": Fred Allen, *Much Ado About Me* (Boston: Little, Brown, 1956), p. 206.

86 tore off the old-fashioned dress: Eells and Musgrove, p. 38.

87 "Miss Hamlet": *Variety*, June 9, 1916.

87 President Wilson: *Ibid.*, August 4, 1916.

87 " 'I am very pleased' . . . Unless Miss West can tone down": *Ibid.*, July 7, 1916.

88 told her mother: Eells and Musgrove, p. 38.

88 an assumed name: *Variety*, November 16, 1916.

88 Beverly's marriage: Reported at the time of her divorce, *The New York Times*, April 16, 1927.

88 a major clean-up order: *Variety*, October 27, 1916.

89 a campaign to rid: *Billboard*, March 31, 1917.

89 blacklist: *Variety*, September 15, 1916.

89 "Actors do not work": Reprinted in *Ibid.*, December 15, 1916.

89 he resigned as counsel: *Ibid.*, January 5, 1917.

89 when he died: Obituary of James A. Timony, *The New York Times*, April 6, 1954.

89 Timony's ads: *Variety*, May 4, May 11, 1917.

90 "he owned a baseball club . . . in 1915": MW, *Goodness*, p. 65.

90 "the guys with busted noses": MW quoted by Martin Sommers, undated *Daily News* clip, MCNY.

90 "His overcoat": Elza Schallert, "Go West—If You're an Adult," *Motion Picture* (May 1933):33.

90 he had won several murder cases: Tim Malachosky, *Mae West* (Lancaster, Calif.: Empire, 1993), p. 4.

90 visited San Quentin: Andrew Stone to author, September 29, 1993.

91 "Your power": MW, *The Ruby Ring*, I, p. 10. L of C.

91 "He said I ought to realize": Frank Wallace, New York *American*, June 30, 1935.

91 "I didn't like to travel": MW, *Goodness*, p. 73.

92 "I'm dying for one little dance": "I'm Going to Follow the Boys," quoted in *Variety*, November 16, 1917.

92 "Broadway was wearing a grouch": *Billboard*, December 22, 1917.

92 "She took her coat off": Quoted by Charles and Louise Samuels, *Once Upon a Stage: The Merry World of Vaudeville* (New York: Dodd, Mead, 1974), pp. 101–2.

93 Isadora at the Met: Victor Seroff, *The Real Isadora* (New York: The Dial Press, 1971), p. 215.

93 "I put some flag waving": MW, *Goodness*, p. 63.

93 "Mary had a little voice": Tommy Gray, *Variety*, June 22, 1917.

94 purge of German propaganda: *Ibid.*, June 28, 1918.

94 at the Jefferson theater: *Ibid.*, November 16, 1917.

94 "She chirped about heaving balls at the Hun's head": *Ibid.*, August 2, 1918.

94 at the Palace: *Ibid.*, May 25, 1917.

94 Douglas Fairbanks: David Nasaw, *Going Out: The Rise and Fall of Public Amusements* (New York: Basic Books, 1993), p. 212.

94 "the greatest white slaver": Lewis A. Erenberg, *Steppin' Out: New York Nightlife and the Transformation of American Culture, 1890–1930* (Westport, Conn.: Greenwood Press, 1981), p. 234.

94 *Patria*: *Ibid.*, p. 171.

94 "A French spy": Lewis Jacobs, "Movies in the World War," in *Movies in Our Midst*, ed. Gerald Mast (University of Chicago Press, 1982), p. 171.

95 "You're a real girl": MW, *Ruby Ring*, I, p. 10. L of C.

95 "absence from home": *Variety*, June 28, 1918.

95 "This is no time to make jest": *Ibid.*, June 28, 1918.

95 Federal officials in Chicago: *Ibid.*, March 15, 1918.

95 "Mother, dear Mother": *Life* (August 22, 1918):260.

95 Mary Pickford: Green and Laurie, p. 146.

95 "What Women Can Do": *Variety*, January 31, 1919.

96 *Midnight Frolic: Ibid.*, April 27, 1917.

96 a nurse just back: *Ibid.*, September 27, 1917.

96 "Making love lightly": Quoted by James McGovern, "The American Woman's Pre–World War I Freedom in Manners and Morals," *Journal of American History*, 55 (September 1968):326.

96 *Suppressed Desires: Variety*, February 22, 1918; Fred Matthews, "The New Psychology in American Drama," in *1915, The Cultural Moment: The New Politics, the New Woman, the New Psychology, the New Art and the New Theater in America*, eds. Adele Heller and Lois Rudnick (New Brunswick, N.J.: Rutgers University Press, 1991), p. 151.

96 "a specimen to be stuck on pins": Kevin Brownlow, *Behind the Mask of Innocence* (New York: Knopf, 1990), p. 31.

96 Leo Feist ad: *Variety*, September 15, 1916.

96 Lois Weber: Marjorie Rosen, *Popcorn Venus: Women, Movies and the American Dream* (New York: Coward, McCann & Geoghegan, 1973), p. 395.

96 *Birth Control: Variety*, April 13, 1917.

97 "flubdubs" and "mollycoddles": Quoted by Mark Sullivan, *Our Times*, vol. V, *Over Here: 1914–1918* (New York: Scribner's, 1933), p. 205.

97 Even little boys: Peter G. Filene, *Him/Her/Self: Sex Roles in Modern America* (Baltimore: Johns Hopkins University Press, 1986), p. 98.

97 "As show girls": Mary Vida Clark, "Sauce for the Gander and Sawdust for the Goose," *The Dial* (December 14, 1918):542.

97 "the cleanest group of young men": Quoted from *The Delineator* by Filene, p. 102.

97 DISEASE SPREADERS: Quoted by John D'Emilio and Estelle B. Freedman, *Intimate Matters: A History of Sexuality in America* (New York: Harper & Row, 1988), p. 211.

97 "A German Bullet": Quoted by David M. Kennedy, *Over Here: The First World War and American Society* (New York: Oxford University Press, 1980), p. 185.

97 "Fellers, this ain't a war": John Dos Passos, *1919* (New York: Penguin Books, 1969 [1932]), p. 114.

97 the VD rate soared: Filene, p. 102.

97 "The availability of contraceptives": Linda Gordon, *Woman's Body, Woman's Right: A Social History of Birth Control in America* (New York: Viking, 1976), pp. 64, 205.

97 to "lose their heads": Quoted by Filene, p. 105.

97 Del, a young wife: *1919*, p. 181.

98 "the French in crayon blue": MW, *Goodness*, p. 48.

98 she performed gratis: *Variety*, June 6, 1919.

98 "You know, I always liked a man in uniform": MW, *Diamond Lil*, (1928) I, p. 28, L of C.

6. THE SHIMMY TRIAL

99 "Well bred people": Quoted in *American Heritage* (August 1965):8.

100 "Diamond Daisy": *Variety*, November 9, 1917.

100 Mark Linder skit: *Ibid.*, June 22, 1917.

100 "Until the 1920 census": Ethan Mordden, *That Jazz: An Idiosyncratic Social History of the American Twenties* (New York: Putnam's, 1978), p. 18.

100 the "tough girl": Bernie Bookbinder, *City of the World: New York and Its People* (New York: Abrams, 1989), p. 160; Shirley L. Staples, *Male-Female Comedy Teams in American Vaudeville* (Ann Arbor, Mich.: UMI Research Press, 1984), p. 96.

101 "takes her sweetie buy-buy": Quoted by Irving Lewis Allen, *The City in Slang: New York Life and Popular Speech* (New York: Oxford University Press, 1993), p. 80.

101 "Mae West, known in vaudeville": *Variety*, May 24, 1918.

101 "No female impersonators": *Ibid.*, August 2, 1918.

101 Bert Savoy quips: *Ibid.*, January 21, 1921; March 5, 1920.

102 "I used to be an acrobat": "The Rottenest Job." Lyric by Rida Johnson Young, [music by Rudolf Friml]. *Sometime* typescript, I, p. 38, Shubert. © 1919, by G. Schirmer Inc.

102 "He helped me the most": MW to Danton Walker, New York *News*, April 15, 1938.

103 "I wonder why these dames": "What Do You Have to Do?" Lyric by Rida Johnson Young, [music by Rudolf Friml] *Sometime*, Chorus Book #438, Shubert.

103 "I don't talk spaghetti": *Sometime* typescript, I, p. 39, Shubert.

103 "I was born a scamp": "Send Me Any Kind of Man." Lyric by Rida Johnson Young, [music by Rudolf Friml] *Sometime*, Chorus Book #438, Shubert.

104 "A whippet tank": Leonard Hall, New York *Telegram*, April 18, 1928.

104 "Mae West gave a capital characterization": New York *Tribune*, October 6, 1918.

104 "stopped the show": Sime, *Variety*, October 11, 1918.

105 Ed Wynn demanded: *Ibid.*, January 10, 1919.

105 she wrote to President Harding: Milton Berle, *"B.S." I Love You: Sixty Funny Years with the Famous and Infamous* (New York: McGraw-Hill, 1988), pp. 241–42.

105 Armistice Day in New York: Frederick Lewis Allen, *Only Yesterday: An Informal History of the 1920s* (New York: Harper & Row, 1964 [1931]), p. 14; Brooks Atkinson, *Broadway*, rev. ed. (New York: Limelight Editions, 1985 [1974]), p. 173.

105 "I was happy we won": MW, *Goodness Had Nothing to Do with It* (New York: Manor Books, 1976), p. 67.

105 "PUBLIC TURNING AWAY . . . Weary Nation": *Variety*, November 22, 29, 1918.

105 "Squibb's Dental Cream": Atkinson, p. 174.

105 "Prohibition appears to be": *Variety*, July 11, 1919.

106 "Honey baby, won't you come": "Everybody Shimmies Now." Words by Eugene West, music by Joe Gold and Edmund J. Porray, Fisher Music Corp., © 1918, renewed 1945. Administered by Sony/ATV Music, Nashville, Tenn.

106 "to saxophone-shrill foxtrots": Abel Green and Joe Laurie, Jr., *Show Biz, from Vaude to Video* (New York: Henry Holt, 1951), p. 228.

106 "The Skirt": *Variety*, October 10, 1919.

106 *her* shimmy: MW, *Goodness*, p. 66.

107 not a "ladylike way": Quoted in *Variety*, December 13, 1918.

107 "shameless evidence": *Ibid.*, July 11, 1919.

107 Chicago: *Ibid.*, November 21, 1919.

107 "The evil genius": *Ibid.*, February 3, 1922.

107 "either cut the wiggle": *Ibid.*, January 10, 1919.

107 "that if the shoulder": *Ibid.*, December 6, 1918.

107 monitors of stage morals: *Ibid.*, December 19, 1919.

107 "There is less psychology than physiology": Quoted in *Ibid.*, December 12, 1919.
108 "before we had a National Board": MW, *The Ruby Ring*, I, pp. 6, 16. L of C.
108 "giving the cold shoulder": *Variety*, August 8, 1919.
108 "packed from pit to dome . . . in vaudeville": *Ibid.*, September 19, 1919.
109 at the Capitol: *Ibid.*, August 13, 1920.
109 she "scored as a single": *Ibid.*, October 31, 1919.
110 "Who wants to make a career": MW, *Goodness*, p. 25.
110 "In nominating": *Variety*, June 25, 1920.
110 as it "flashed through": *Ibid.*, November 5, 1920.
110 at the Colonial . . . big time feature.": *Ibid.*, August 13, 1920.
111 upstate New York: *Ibid.*, October 8, 1920.
112 "Most men value you": MW, *The Hussy*, II, p. 34. L of C.
112 "I take diamonds": *Mae West on Sex, Health and ESP* (London and New York: W. H. Allen, 1975), p. 51.
112 "She's got too damned many clothes": MW, *The Hussy*, I, p. 20. L of C.
113 "I don't want to be": *Ibid.*, I, p. 17.
113 "The more men": MW, *The Ruby Ring*, I, p. 2.
114 Fred Allen said: Fred Allen, *Much Ado About Me* (Boston: Little, Brown, 1956), p. 217.
114 "Stringent Methods": *Variety*, February 18, 1921.
114 Slang expressions: *Ibid.*, November 18, 1921.
114 Groucho Marx: Cited by John E. Di Meglio, *Vaudeville USA* (Ohio: Bowling Green University Press, 1973), p. 25.
114 The "flip style of act . . . where liberties are allowed": *Variety*, February 18, November 18, 1921.
114 Irving Berlin's song: *Ibid.*, March 3, 1921.
114 "The public likes its dirt": *Ibid.*, February 18, 1921.
115 "There was one outstanding feature": Meakin, in *Ibid.*, March 11, 1921.
115 "All these girls are afraid": Quoted in MW, *Goodness*, p. 70.
115 "The Trial of Shimmy Mae": In *Whirl of the Town* [later *The Mimic World of 1921*], by Harold Atteridge, James Hussey, and Owen Murphy, script, Shubert.
115 "The Bridal Suite": *Variety*, March 11, April 22, 1921.
115 several vaudeville acts: *Ibid.*, August 26, 1921.
116 "a plumber's idea of Cleopatra": Quoted by Ron Fields to author, March 28, 1994.
116 Madelon and Shifty Liz: *Mimic World of 1921* program, Shubert.
116 Shifty Liz skit: *Whirl of the Town* [1921] script, Shubert.
116 a hodge-podge: *The New York Times*, August 18, 1921.
116 "They give ample opportunity": *Billboard*, August 27, 1921.
117 "pretty snappy": *Variety*, August 26, 1921.
117 "looked more as if": New York *World*, undated clip, Shubert.
117 "not only décolleté": *Women's Wear*, August 24, 1921, Shubert.
117 "the leading woman": *Theatre Magazine* (November 1921):308.
117 Jack Dempsey: MW, *Goodness*, p. 70.
117 At the Dempsey–Carpentier fight: *Variety*, July 8, 1921.
117 today's ideal man: MW, *The Ruby Ring*, I, p. 9.
118 "hoisting up his bellbottoms": Alexander Walker, *Rudolph Valentino* (New York and London: Penguin Books, 1976), p. 54.
118 Grantland Rice: Quoted by Jack Dempsey with Barbara P. Dempsey, *Dempsey* (New York: Harper & Row, 1977), p. 122.

118 Timony . . . didn't think: MW, *Goodness*, p. 70.

119 they made love often: Milton Berle, p. 241.

119 "Falling in love. . . . fabrics": Harry Richman, with Richard Gehman, *A Hell of a Life* (New York: Duell, Sloan & Pearce, 1966), pp. 38–40.

119 her telephone disconnected: *Ibid.*, p. 41.

119 casting her eyes upward: *Ibid.*

120 "how different types of vamps": *Variety*, June 23, 1922.

120 "alarmingly legitimate": *Ibid.*, July 7, 1922.

120 "delineator of character songs": *Ibid.*, June 23, 1922.

120 "she took to the track": Undated [July 1922], *Zitt's Vaudeville Weekly* clip, NYPL.

120 "just as long as the shimmy lasts": Unattributed clip, NYPL.

120 "let that blonde baby": *Variety*, July 14, 1922.

120 "She made a world of friends": Undated clip, *Zitt's Vaudeville Weekly*, NYPL.

120 She told Albee: MW, *Goodness*, pp. 73–74.

122 Bert Savoy: Robert Baral, *Revue: A Nostalgic Reprise of the Great Broadway Period* (New York: Fleet, 1962), p. 129; Robert Toll, *On with the Show: The First Century of Show Business in America* (New York: Oxford University Press, 1976), p. 255; Edmund Wilson, *The American Earthquake: A Documentary of the Jazz Age, the Great Depression and the New Deal* (Garden City, N.Y.: Doubleday, 1958), p. 60.

123 "I'm steel and steam . . . She don me doit!": Eugene O'Neill, *The Hairy Ape*, I, iv, in *Twenty-Five Best Plays of the Modern American Theater*, Early Series, ed. John Gassner (New York: Crown, 1949).

123 "Eugene O'Neill, You've Put a Curse On Broadway": Program, *Ginger Box Revue*, Stamford, Conn., July 28, 1922; NYPL; *Variety*, August 4, 1922.

123 Dave Apollon: MW, *Goodness Had Nothing to Do with It* (New York: Manor Books, 1976), p. 75.

124 "wiseacres": *Variety*, August 4, 1922.

124 "GINGER REVUE NOW A PEPLESS . . . the salaries they wanted": New York *Daily News*, August 13, 1922.

124 thirteen Equity actors: *Variety*, September 1, 1922.

125 "The electric sign": New York *Daily News*, August 13, 1922.

125 "There he was with a show house": MW to Wood Soanes, undated clip, *Oakland Tribune*, SFPALM.

125 "Mae West always triumphs": MW to Larry Sloan, quoted by George Eells and Stanley Musgrove, *Mae West* (New York: William Morrow, 1982), p. 17.

125 She and Richman were booked: *Billboard*, August 28, 1922.

126 Richman confided: Eells and Musgrove, p. 42.

126 MAE WEST, AUTHOR, LOSES . . . : *Variety*, September 8, 1922.

126 "the little touch of finesse": *Ibid.*, January 19, 1923.

126 Conway reported . . . prima donna": *Ibid.*, April 26, 1923.

127 Mae fumed: Nils T. Granlund, with Sid Feder and Ralph Hancock, *Blondes, Brunettes and Bullets* (New York: David McKay, 1957), p. 91.

128 "Hula Lou": Words by Jack Yellen, music by Wayne King, and Milton Charles, © 1924. Renewed, © Warner/Chappell Music, Inc. Sheet Music Source: Jack Allen Collection.

128 throughout the twenties: Barry Singer, *Black and Blue: The Life and Lyrics of Andy Razaf* (New York: Schirmer, 1992), pp. 172, 258.

129 "Down by the Winegar Woiks": Words and music by Don Bestor, Roger Lewis, and Walter Donovan, © 1925, Shapiro-Bernstein. Renewed, © Hal Leonard Corp. Quoted by permission. Sheet Music Source: Sandy Marrone Collection.

129 bit parts in burlesque: Jon Tuska, *The Films of Mae West* (Secaucus, N.J.: Citadel Press, 1973), p. 30; *Billboard*, March 5, 1923, through January 12, 1924; Marybeth Hamilton, "Mae West Live: SEX, The Drag, and 1920s Broadway," *The Drama Review* 36, No. 4 (Winter 1992):83.

129 how young and inexperienced: *Billboard*, January 12, 1924.

130 Burmester: Maurice Leonard, *Mae West: Empress of Sex* (New York: Birch Lane, 1992), p. 59. A copy of the marriage license was shown to the author by Chris Basinger.

130 "He's a wild horse trainer": Rejected draft of "No One Does It Like That Dallas Man," which became "No One Loves Me Like That Dallas Man," words by Gladys DuBois and Ben Ellison, music by Harvey Brooks. Hays Office file, *I'm No Angel*, AMPAS.

130 "a distorted publicity gag": Los Angeles *Examiner*, April 25, 1935.

130 "business jumped smartly": *Variety*, November 19, 1924.

130 more "booze joints": *Ibid.*, April 8, 1924.

130 BOOTLEG DRUGS: *Ibid.*, September 10, 1924.

131 hotels: George Chauncey, Jr., "The Policed: Gay Men's Strategies of Everyday Resistance," in *Inventing Times Square: Commerce and Culture at the Crossroads of the World*, ed. William R. Taylor (New York: Russell Sage Foundation, 1991), p. 319.

131 cabarets: Laurence Senelick, "Private Parts in Public Places," in *ibid.*, p. 332.

131 Dutch Schultz: Cited by Carl Sifakis, *Encyclopedia of American Crime* (New York: Facts on File, 1982), p. 642.

131 "Legs Diamond . . . like baseball": MW, *Goodness*, p. 88.

132 "Citizen's Jury": Allen Churchill, *The Theatrical Twenties* (New York: McGraw-Hill, 1975), p. 121.

132 "No woman was ever ruined": Quoted in *The New York Times*, May 3, 1923.

133 "the fact that he went to sea": MW in *The Brooklyn Eagle*, August 23, 1931.

133 "Mr. O'Neill always takes": *Variety*, November 11, 1921.

133 "a mulatto courtesan": *The New York Times*, February 10, 1926.

133 "Jeanne Eagels in *Rain*": John Mason Brown, "The Theatre of the Twenties," in *Dramatis Personae: A Retrospective Show* (New York: Viking, 1963), p. 9.

134 The Committee of Fourteen: *Variety*, July 20, 1927.

134 "For the first time": Marjorie Rosen, *Popcorn Venus: Women, Movies and the American Dream* (New York: Coward, McCann & Geoghegan, 1973), p. 108.

134 Gloria Swanson's "Seven Deadly Whims": Displayed at the Museum of the Moving Image, London.

135 "working roadhouses . . . money": Rosen, p. 108.

135 "When I went home": MW to Richard Meryman, "Mae West," *Life* (April 18, 1969):66.

136 "There's a chance of rising": MW, *Sex*, I, p. 8. L of C.

136 "Don't think I'm afraid": *Ibid.*, I, p. 7.

137 "the leading character in *Rain*": MW in unattributed clip, NYPL.

137 Byrne testified: *The New York Times*, July 29, 1926.

137 "palpably designed for salacious appeal": *Ibid.*, March 31, 1927.

137 She did squawk: *Variety*, April 27, 1927.

138 "My mother had watched me": MW to Meryman, p. 62.

138 "a paper bag maybe": *Ibid.*, p. 66.

138 "When the play is put in rehearsal": George Halasz, *The Brooklyn Eagle*, June 24, 1928.

139 "Which do I throw?": MW, *The Ruby Ring*, I, p. 12. L of C.

140 "She did none of the writing": Stephen Longstreet to author, August 6, 1994.

140 "I'm fast as a thinker": MW to W. H. Mooring, *Film Weekly* (September 28, 1934): 8.

140 a comic and risqué version of *Peter and the Wolf*: Thomas Day to author, July 28, 1994.

141 she created "a category": John Mason Brown, "Mae Pourquoi?" in *Dramatis Personae*, p. 259.

141 "I'm too nervous": MW to Karl Fleming with Anne Taylor Fleming, *The First Time* (New York: Simon & Schuster, 1975), p. 312.

141 "Good reviews": MW to C. Robert Jennings, "Mae West: A Candid Conversation with the Indestructible Queen of Vamp and Camp," *Playboy* (January 1971):80.

141 "I had one with me": MW to Malcolm Oettinger, "Literary Lil," *Picture Play* (September 1933):62.

141 "everything about books": MW, *The Ruby Ring*, I, p. 16.

141 "I write in my books": MW to Ruth Biery, "The Private Life of Mae West," Part One, *Movie Classic* (January 1934):58.

141 "I've never studied": MW to W. H. Mooring.

141 "People come to my plays": MW typescript on *Sex*, Shubert.

142 "In vaudeville you learn . . . what they want": MW in *The Brooklyn Eagle*, August 23, 1931.

142 "People want dirt": MW to Thyra Samter Winslow, "Profiles: Diamond Mae," *The New Yorker* (November 10, 1928):26.

142 "Get close to me!": Quoted at USC tribute to MW, March 21, 1982. Pamphlet published by Friends of the USC Library (Los Angeles, 1983), unpaged. USC.

142 "Mae West herself": New York *American*, April 27, 1926.

143 "She undresses before the public": New York *Mirror*, April 30, 1926.

143 Zora Neale Hurston: "Characteristics of Negro Expression," in *Negro Anthology*, ed. Nancy Cunard (Colchester, London, and Eton: Ballantyne Press, [1934]), pp. 45–46.

143 "That's more like you": MW, *Sex*, III, p. 22. L of C.

143 "You've got a sex quality": Quoted in MW, *Goodness*, p. 83; Meryman, p. 66.

143 "If I didn't have": MW, *Sex*, III, p. 26.

144 "People . . . can be dull at home": MW to Winslow, p. 26.

144 "Blessed are the prurient in heart": *Life*, May 6, 1926.

144 New York *Evening Graphic*: December 30, 1926, front page.

144 "I sent boys all over town": MW to Charles Higham, in *Celebrity Circus* (New York: Delacorte, 1979), p. 23.

145 Among the titles Hays cited: *Variety*, July 2, 1924.

145 "Let 'em close the show": Timony, quoted by Ruth Biery, "The Private Life of Mae West," Part Three, *Movie Classic* (March 1934):62.

145 "Timony used to lock her up": Ruth Waterbury, quoted by Stanley Musgrove, Myra Breckinridge Diary, typescripts, box 4, USC.

145 Matilda's roadhouses: Danton Walker, New York *Daily News*, April 15, 1938.

146 Owney Madden: Edward Jablonski, *Harold Arlen, Happy with the Blues* (New York: Doubleday, 1961), p. 65; Sifakis, p. 460; Herbert Asbury, *The Gangs of New York* (Garden City, N.Y.: Doubleday, 1927), p. 345; Lewis Yablonsky, *George Raft* (San Francisco: Mercury House, 1989), p. 36.

146 "So sweet": Quoted by Kevin Thomas, *Los Angeles Times Calendar*, December 23, 1984.

146 "They were open and genuine": Graham Nown, *The English Godfather* (London: Ward & Lock, 1987), p. 18.

147 "Gangsters, as a rule": MW in *Movie Classic* (September 1933):70.

147 "It was like knowing the mayor": Quoted by James Robert Parish and Steven Whitney, *The George Raft File: The Unauthorized Biography* (New York: Drake, 1973), p. 52.

147 "all had plenty of parking space": Jimmy Durante with Jack Kofoed, *Night Clubs* (New York: Knopf, 1931), p. 233.

147 "She favored picture hats": Allen Churchill, *The Year the World Went Mad: 1927* (New York: Crowell, 1960), p. 56.

148 "the World's most charming Hostess": Ad, *Variety*, September 16, 1925.

148 "Exaggerate the world": Quoted by Louise Berliner, *Texas Guinan: Queen of the Nightclubs* (Austin: University of Texas Press, 1993), p. 25.

Page   8. PRISONER'S SONG

149 Previews: *Variety*, March 31, April 14, June 16, 1926; MW, *Goodness Had Nothing to Do with It* (New York: Manor Books, 1976), p. 86.

150 "how anything so undressed": G.W.G. in *The New Yorker*, May 8, 1926:26.

150 "the cheapest, most vulgar": *Billboard*, May 8, 1926.

150 "Never has disgrace . . . filth": *Variety*, April 21, 1926.

150 "A more flaming": New York *American*, April 27, 1926.

150 "[It] ranges from": New York *Sun*, April 27, 1926.

150 "She has an amazing degree": Walter Winchell in New York *Evening Graphic*, April 28, 1926.

151 "Chick, Mae is hot": Jack Conway, *Variety*, May 5, 1926.

151 "Miss West has been in vaudeville": *Ibid.* June 30, 1926.

152 "At first we thought . . . 'lark' ": Robert Benchley in *Life*, May 20, 1926:23.

152 "Hamlet without the Dane": *Variety*, May 9, 1928.

152 a volunteer Play Jury: *Ibid.*, June 9, 1926.

152 *Variety* hinted darkly: *Ibid.*, June 30, 1926.

153 State Penal Law: *Theatre Magazine* (April 1927):23.

153 a séance: *Philadelphia Inquirer*, May 4, 1969. USC clip.

154 "Pink Powder Puffs": Quoted by Marjorie Garber in *Vested Interests: Cross-Dressing and Cultural Anxiety* (New York: Routledge, 1991), p. 361.

154 gay subculture: George Chauncey, Jr., *Gay New York: Urban Culture and the Making of a Gay Male World, 1890–1970* (New York: Basic Books, 1994), pp. 245–58.

154 "an increasing number": *Variety*, March 7, 1928.

154 "The fairy's most obvious attribute": Chauncey, p. 61.

155 "the man who frequents night clubs": Quoted by Kaier Curtin, *"We Can Always Call Them Bulgarians": The Emergence of Lesbians and Gay Men on the American Stage* (Boston: Alyson Publications, 1987), p. 86.

155 DON'T RELAX: New York *American*, January 26, 1927.

155 THREE SHOWS HALTED: New York *Herald Tribune*, February 10, 1927.

155 front page spot: *The New York Times*, February 10, 1927.

155 "There were faint cheers": *Ibid.*, February 10, 1927.

156 "The police were perfectly lovely to us": MW, *The Drag*, III, i, p. 2, L of C.

156 released on bail: *The New York Times*, February 10, 1927.

156 *The Virgin Man*: *Ibid.*, February 13, 1927.

156 "an affront to American womanhood": Quoted by Curtin, pp. 44–45.

156 "You may think I'm kidding": MW, quoted by Allen Churchill in *The Theatrical Twenties* (New York: McGraw-Hill, 1975), p. 235.

156 "Well, anyhow we're normal": MW, quoted by Martin Sommers, New York *Daily News* undated clip, MCNY.

156 "Some homosexuals are not to be blamed": MW, "Sex in the Theater," *Parade* (September 1929):13.

157 "about forty young men": *Variety*, January 12, 1927.

157 "a realistic drama": MW, *Goodness*, p. 90.

157 "liked her sexes stable": MW to C. Robert Jennings, "Mae West: A Candid Conversation with the Indestructible Queen of Vamp and Camp," *Playboy* (January 1971): 74.

157 "I read Freud": MW, *Goodness*, p. 92.

157 "Remember, when you're hitting": *Mae West on Sex, Health and ESP* (London and New York: W. H. Allen, 1975), p. 40.

158 "caused the sudden. . . . censured": *The New York Times*, February 1, 1927.

158 "I'm one of those damned creatures": MW, *The Drag*, I, p. 6.

158 "One man is born white": *Ibid.*, I, p. 8.

158 "born with inverted sexual desires": *Ibid.*, I, p. 13.

158 "A judge's son": *Ibid.*, III, p. 6.

158 "permit[ted] the 'our sex' members": *Variety*, January 26, 1927.

158 "The characters in West's scripts": Pamela Robertson, " 'The Kinda Comedy That Imitates ME' ": MW's Identification with the Feminist Camp," *Cinema Journal* 32, no. 2 (Winter 1993):61.

159 "Ride me around": MW, *The Drag*, I, p. 6.

159 "So glad to have you meet me": *Ibid.*, II, p. 8.

159 "a succinct, epigrammatic language . . . invulnerability": Wayne Koestenbaum, *The Queen's Throat: Opera, Homosexuality and the Mystery of Desire* (New York: Poseidon Press, 1993), p. 132.

159 "All my life": *Variety*, April 17, 1968.

159 "bein' funny and dishy": MW to Jennings, p. 76.

159 "only by staging it": Koestenbaum, p. 133.

159 "I guess he meant it as a compliment": MW, quoted in *Los Angeles Times* obituary, November 23, 1980.

159 "I wanted to show": MW to Jennings, p. 78.

160 "has a moral": Quoted by Curtin, p. 83.

160 angling for endorsements: *Variety*, February 9, 1927.

160 WENT TO BE SHOCKED: New York *Evening Graphic*, February 1, 1927.

160 "laughed immoderately": *Variety*, February 2, 1927.

160 in Paterson: Curtin, p. 87.

160 "a deliberate play . . . a calamity": *Variety*, February 2, 1927.

161 "We see where the lack of censorship": New York *American*, February 2, 1927.

161 "The men who ran New York": *Mae West on Sex*, p. 39.

161 "Perversion is a horror": Letter to *The New York Times*, January 21, 1927.

161 offered to withdraw: *Variety*, February 2, 1927.

161 "We are going forward": *The New York Times*, February 10, 1927.

161 "If they are right now . . . straw": *Ibid.*, February 11, 1927.

162 RAIDED SHOWS PLAY TO CROWDED HOUSES: *Ibid.*, February 13, 1927.

162 Morganstern announced: *Ibid.*, February 13, 1927.

162 "It is necessary": *Ibid.*, February 19, 1927.

162 a lively debate . . . Mayor Walker: *Ibid.*, February 11, 13, 17, 19, 28, 1927.

163 "He produced a sheaf": Undated [February 16, 1927], unattributed clip, Harvard.

163 "changing 'joint' . . . trial": *The New York Times*, February 16, 1927.

163 "What we have here": New York *World*, January 26, 1927.

164 "Twenty years ago": Quoted in *The New York Times*, March 30, 1927; *Variety*, March 30, 1927.

164 A member of the Play Jury: *The New York Times*, April 1, 1927.

164 "was nothing more . . . west": MW, *Goodness*, p. 95.

164 He pointed out: *The New York Times*, March 30, 1927.

164 "STAR . . . Hotel": *Ibid.*, March 21, 1927.

165 the actors rejected: *Variety*, March 23, 1927.

165 "Had the public exhibited": *Ibid.*, April 6, 1927.

165 "He showed a remarkable memory": *The New York Times*, March 30, 1927.

165 "We've got red lights": *Ibid.*, April 5, 1927.

165 Wales Padlock Act: Jonathan Katz, *Gay American History* (New York: Crowell, 1976), p. 90.

166 "Mae West is being readied": *Variety*, May 25, 1927.

166 Wallace protested: *The New York Times*, April 2, 1927.

166 "You've made enough speeches": New York *Herald Tribune*, April 6, 1927.

166 reactions of Timony, cast, crew: *The New York Times*, April 6, 1927.

167 "Assuming the hard-boiled manner": *Variety*, April 20, 1927.

167 "We are not through . . . art": MW in *The New York Times*, New York *Herald Tribune*, April 6, 7, 1927.

167 Judge Donnellian praised the guilty verdict: *The New York Times*, April 20, 1927.

168 Timony was marched off: *Ibid.*, April 21, 1927.

168 "a spinster type": MW, "Ten Days and Five Hundred Dollars," *Liberty* (August 20, 1927):53.

168 "The other inmates": *Ibid.*, p. 54.

168 she downed a breakfast: Unattributed, undated clip, BPL.

168 MAE WEST GOES TO WORKHOUSE: Unattributed, undated clip, BPL.

168 "a place of quiet": Quoted by Carol von Pressentin Wright, *New York Blue Guide* (New York: Norton, 1991), p. 574.

168 "I expect it will be": MW in unattributed, undated clip, Harvard.

168 "about the most profitable days": MW to Jay Brien Chapman, "Is Mae West Garbo's Greatest Rival?" *Motion Picture* (July 1933): 28.

168 "A matron took my purse": MW, "Ten Days," p. 54.

168 "MAE WEST WEARS. . . . hardened offenders": *The New York Times*, April 21, 1927.

169 prisoners: MW, "Ten Days," pp. 55–56.

170 "If I hadn't started writing plays": MW to Richard Meryman, "Mae West," *Life* (April 18, 1969):68.

170 song: MW, "Ten Days," p. 56.

171 "Mae West is a fine woman": Quoted by Ruth Biery, "The Private Life of Mae West," Part Three, in Carol M. Ward, *Mae West: A Bio-Bibliography* (Westport, Conn: Greenwood Press, 1989), p. 115.

171 "I expected to find": MW in New York *American*, April 28, 1927.

171 "She announced that hereafter . . . 61st Street": *The New York Times*, April 28, 1927.

172 "Stars with Stripes": *Variety*, May 25, 1927.

Page   9. PLUMP FLAPPER

173 an unprecedented number of shows: Daniel Blum, *A Pictorial History of the American Theatre, 1860–1976*, enlarged and revised by John Willis, 4th ed. (New York: Crown, 1977), p. 231; Brooks Atkinson, *Broadway*, rev. ed. (New York: Limelight, 1985), p. 179.

173 Radio could claim: Barbara H. Solomon, Introduction, *Ain't We Got Fun? Essays, Lyrics and Stories of the Twenties* (New York: New American Library, 1980), pp. 6–7.

174 sobbing women: Arnold Shaw, *The Jazz Age: Popular Music in the 1920s* (New York: Oxford University Press, 1987), p. 77.

174 "a very plump flapper": New York *Sun*, November 7, 1927.

174 "rather a misguided move": New York *Telegram*, November 5, 1927.

175 Actors Equity document: Equity Folder SC43, Wagner Labor Archives, Tamiment Institute Library, NYU.

176 "Costumes worn by Mae West": Program, *The Wicked Age*, NYPL.

176 glossy postcards: *Variety*, November 23, 1927.

176 "While his voice did carry": Letter, Scibilia to Mr. Searles of Actors Equity, November 1, 1927, NYU.

176 "The set proved": *Variety*, November 9, 1927.

177 "felt their way": *Billboard*, November 12, 1927.

177 "somewhat dark": New York *Herald Tribune*, November 5, 1927.

177 "greasy gathering": *Time*, November 14, 1927.

177 "needs the talents": Quoted by James Robert Parish, *The Paramount Pretties* (New Rochelle, N.Y.: Arlington House, 1972), p. 300.

177 "a hit and a headache": MW, *Goodness Had Nothing to Do with It* (New York: Manor Books, 1976), p. 98.

177 "a choice piece of limburger": *Variety*, November 9, 1927.

177 "She stands alone": New York *Telegraph*, November 6, 1927.

177 "Some of our best people": Quoted in *Variety*, November 9, 1927.

177 "The clinches . . . $1.65": *Ibid.*, September 9, 1927.

177 "She throws out": New York *Herald Tribune*, November 5, 1927.

177 "throughout the performance": *Variety*, September 28, 1927.

178 "gross, disgusting": *Long Branch Daily Record*, quoted in *The New York Times*, October 2, 1927.

178 "tawdry morons": *Billboard*, November 12, 1927.

178 "incredibly cheap": *The New York Times*, November 5, 1927.

178 "This as a play": Dana Reed, typed reader's report on *The Wicked Age*, NYPL.

178 An explanation: *Variety*, November 16, 1927.

178 "Babe, you certainly can neck": MW, *The Wicked Age*, I, p. 33. L of C.

179 "I want to be filthy low": *Ibid.*, I, p. 39.

179 "Success today": *Ibid.*, I, ii, p. 4.

180 "You can't ride two horses": *Ibid.*, III, p. 10.
180 "the older generation": *Ibid.*, I, p. 10.
180 "seems to have taken": *Ibid.*, III, p. 16.
180 the divorce action: *The New York Times*, April 16, 1927.
181 "Have me married": MW, *The Wicked Age*, III, p. 2.
181 "Drink . . . something": *Ibid.*
181 "There is always someone": *Ibid.*, p. 22.
182 He thought she'd certainly witnessed: Karl Fleming to author, May 11, 1993.
182 "I analyzed it": MW to Richard Meryman, *Life* (April 18, 1969):62c.
183 hosting a nightclub: *Variety*, January 11, 1928; Allen Churchill, *The Year the World Went Mad: 1927* (New York: Crowell, 1960), p. 299.

184 "If you've found a magic": Quoted by Edith Head and Paddy Calisto, *Edith Head's Hollywood* (New York: Dutton, 1983), p. 21.
184 "voice like a kazooka": Alexander Walker, *Sex in the Movies [The Celluloid Sacrifice]* (Baltimore: Penguin Books, 1968), p. 66.
185 "the heightened unreality": Unattributed fragment about *Diamond Lil*, NYPL.
185 "Rasping and undulating": John Mason Brown, "Mae Pourquoi?" in *Dramatis Personae: A Retrospective Show* (New York: Viking, 1963), p. 259.
185 "sullenly about the stage": Gilbert Seldes, *The Dial* (June 1928): 531.
185 "that audacity of leisure": Review by Stark Young, *The New Republic* (June 27, 1928): 145.
185 "You'd have thought": Robert Garland, New York *Evening Telegram*, April 5, 1928.
185 "Mae West . . . is more admired": Quoted by MW in *Goodness Had Nothing to Do with It* (New York, Manor Books, 1976), p. 108.
185 "She makes Miss Ethel Barrymore": *Ibid.*, p. 107.
185 "Flaming Mae": New York *Evening Telegram*, April 18, 1928.
186 Linder's script: Richard Helfer, *Mae West on Stage: Themes and Persona* (unpublished Ph.D. dissertation, City University of New York, 1990), pp. 257–58.
186 "I only go into a play": Quoted in *Variety*, July 4, 1928.
186 "heavy cream lace": *Ibid.*, May 23, 1928.
187 The female audience would love: MW to Richard Meryman, "Mae West," *Life* (April 18, 1969):62c.
187 "This scene can be worked": Stage direction by MW in script of *Diamond Lil* (1928), III, p. 1, L of C.
187 "looked well by appearing mannish": MW in unattributed clip, MCNY.
187 nostalgia for the 1890s: Luc Sante, *Low Life: Lures and Snares of Old New York* (New York: Farrar, Straus and Giroux, 1991), p. xii; Roger Burke Dooley, *From Scarface to Scarlett: American Films in the 1930s* (New York: Harcourt Brace Jovanovich, 1981), pp. 109–10.
187 tour operators: Irving Lewis Allen, *The City in Slang: New York Life and Popular Speech* (New York: Oxford University Press, 1993), p. 84.
188 "I recall all the famous places": MW in Paramount Press Book for *She Done Him Wrong*, 1933, AMPAS.
188 "à la Chuck Connors": MW, *Diamond Lil*, I, p. 1.
188 "She hired real bums": Anonymous memo, Harvard.
188 the days of Tony Pastor: Helfer, p. 267.

189 a diamond set in one of her teeth: *Variety*, April 4, 1928.

189 "wise comebacks": *Ibid.*, November 9, 1917.

189 "a gaudy, blazing thing": MW, *Diamond Lil*, II, p. 1.

189 "a mother image": Walker, p. 71.

189 "While her look": Pamela Robertson, " 'The Kinda Comedy That Imitates Me':
     Mae West's Identification with the Feminist Camp," *Cinema Journal* 32, No. 2
     (Winter 1993):64.

190 "Married or single": MW, *Diamond Lil*, I, p. 20.

190 "can be had": The line occurs in I, p. 27 of the Shubert Archive's stage manager's
     script of *Diamond Lil*, dated November 5, 1929, indicating that it was added during
     the course of the play's first run.

190 "you have to do somethin' ": MW, *Diamond Lil* (1928), I, p. 19.

190 "I don't kid myself": *Ibid.*

190 "I ain't afraid": *Ibid.*, p. 28.

190 "Who the hell": MW, *Diamond Lil* [novel] (New York: Macaulay, 1932), p. 148.

190 "All I'm interested in": *Ibid.*, p. 161.

190 "She liked the stalwart David": *Ibid.*, p. 141.

190 "What was the harm": *Ibid.*, p. 179.

191 "True enough . . . lookin' at them": *Ibid.*, pp. 107, 127.

191 "plaster saints": *Diamond Lil* [play, 1928], II, p. 22.

191 "Would God masquerade?": *Ibid.*, p. 24.

192 "Take the ball and chain": *Ibid.*, III, p. 8.

192 "wore a large diamond horseshoe": Fred Allen, *Much Ado About Me* (Boston: Little,
     Brown, 1956), pp. 236–37.

192 "A performer": Sophie Tucker, *Some of These Days* (Garden City, N.Y.: Doubleday,
     1945), p. 108.

192 "Naturally any doll": Damon Runyon, "A Very Honorable Guy," in *Guys and Dolls*
     (New York: American Reprint Co., 1976), p. 108.

192 "Men would wither": MW, *Diamond Lil* [novel], p. 15.

192 she decked her arms: *Variety*, July 4, 1928.

192 "I had never before seen": Anonymous memo, Harvard.

192 in August: *Variety*, August 15, 1928.

192 salaries: Actors Equity file on *Diamond Lil*, NYU.

192 Half that: *Variety*, July 11, 1928.

193 "Did you write . . . didn't I?": Quoted in *ibid.*

193 Jack Linder issued a statement: *The New York Times*, July 10, 1928.

193 Linder withdrew the complaint: Unattributed clip, July 18, 1928, NYPL.

193 "They had her name": Quoted in *Variety*, December 26, 1928.

194 Linder sued: *The New York Times*, February 20, 1940.

194 "Sitting side by side": Jack La Rue to Gladys Hall in "Three Men—and All Kissed
     by Mae West," *Motion Picture* (November 1933):86.

194 "to greet the swanky mob": *Variety*, May 9, 1928.

194 "There's enough that's funny": *Ibid.*, June 27, 1928.

194 "fine . . . entertaining": *The New York Times*, April 10, 1928.

194 David Belasco, Carl Van Vechten, John Colton: MW, *Goodness*, p. 107.

195 "the play would be": Thyra Samter Winslow, "Profiles: Diamond Mae," *The New
     Yorker* (November 10, 1928):28.

195 "one-man show": *The Brooklyn Eagle*, June 24, 1928.

195 Sterling interpreted this: *Variety*, November 18, 1928.

195 "She would get a regular boned corset": Anonymous memo, Harvard.

195 "I prefer to talk to men": MW, *Diamond Lil* [play, 1928], II, p. 14.

195 "Well, if you don't like it": Anonymous memo, Harvard.

195 "People of every kind": Jack La Rue to Gladys Hall, p. 86.

196 "A star still in make-up . . . who is she?' ": Winslow, p. 26.

196 "She is afraid": *Ibid.*, p. 29.

196 "due to her large gifts": Dana Rush, "Back of the West Front," *Photoplay* (February 1934):109.

196 "Since her prosperity": Winslow, p. 26.

197 They all sat around: Jean Hersholt in *Variety*, July 11, 1928.

197 "I knew everything": MW to Meryman, p. 68.

197 "she enjoyed cutting him down": Anonymous memo, Harvard.

197 "as she might have done Juliet": Gerald Bordman, *American Musical Theatre: A Chronicle* (New York: Oxford University Press, 1986), p. 439.

197 Grace Hayes: *Variety*, October 23, 1929.

197 "Sly and ruthless": Lewis H. Lapham, "Let Me Tell You About Mae West," *The Saturday Evening Post* (November 14, 1964):78.

197 a rumor circulated: *Variety*, October 3, 1928.

198 early-morning 1931 free-for-all: *Ibid.*, January 28, 1931.

198 "I was starring in *Lil*": *Mae West on Sex, Health and ESP* (New York and London: W. H. Allen, 1975), p. 19.

198 "We met any place": MW to C. Robert Jennings, "Mae West: A Candid Conversation with the Queen of Vamp and Camp," *Playboy* (January 1971):80.

198 "One Saturday night": MW to Charlotte Chandler, *The Ultimate Seduction* (Garden City, N.Y.: Doubleday, 1984), p. 58.

198 when the ghostwriter: Stephen Longstreet to author, August 6, 1994.

198 he'd rolled the dice: Lewis Yablonsky, *George Raft* (San Francisco: Mercury House, 1989), p. 31.

198 the drunk-rolling concession: James Robert Parish and Steven Whitney, *The George Raft File: The Unauthorized Biography* (New York: Drake Publishers, 1973), p. 62.

198 For winter he favored: Graham Nown, *The English Godfather* (London: Ward Lock, 1987), p. 68.

199 "The word was": Milton Berle, *"B.S." I Love You: Sixty Funny Years with the Famous and Infamous* (New York: McGraw-Hill, 1988), p. 242.

199 "gunmen, gangsters, thieves," *The New York Times*, January 25, 1929.

199 "kisses such": Ashton Stevens in *Chicago Herald and Examiner*, January 21, 1929.

199 a love scene had to be toned down: *The New York Times*, January 25, 1929.

199 Al Capone: Stephen Longstreet to author, August 6, 1994.

199 "Hardest hit victim": *Variety*, June 12, 1929.

200 "We got him a gun": *Mae West on Sex*, p. 20.

200 "touched the hem . . . lovers": MW, *Goodness*, p. 129.

200 in Detroit: *Variety*, June 12, 19, 1929.

200 WALL STREET LAYS AN EGG: *Variety*, October 30, 1929.

200 "Actors were ruined . . . sit and watch": MW, *Goodness*, p. 130.

201 "Miss West, however": Unattributed clip, Shubert.

201 "which implies a flop": *Variety*, January 8, 1930.

201 "Have been asking": Timony to Lee Shubert, November 25, 1929, Shubert.

201 "I have advised": Jason Joy résumé, April 22, 1930, *She Done Him Wrong*, Hays Office files, AMPAS.

201 Hays Office ruled out: Wingate to Joy, April 22, 1930, *She Done Him Wrong*, Hays Office files, AMPAS.

202 "words of common usage": *Mae West v. Marie Lind, California Reporter* 288, p. 564.

202 after so much money: MW to J. J. Shubert, November 4, 1959, Shubert.

202 "Diamond Lil—I'm her": MW, *Goodness*, p. 110.

Page   11. REPEAT OFFENDER

203 "as a side-line": *Variety*, August 9, 1928.

203 "Have you had your cream puff?": MW, *Pleasure Man* (1928), I, p. 10, L of C.

204 "men wearing slave bracelets": *Variety*, August 29, 1928.

204 "I've had so many operations": *The Drag*, III, i, p. 3; *Pleasure Man*, III, i, p. 1.

204 "its color, its interesting life": MW, *Goodness Had Nothing to Do with It* (New York: Manor Books, 1976), p. 123.

204 "I personally get a big kick . . . jail": Undated [1928?], unattributed clip, MCNY.

204 "My, what a low cut": MW, *Pleasure Man*, III, i, p. 1.

204 "The only thing he hasn't made": *Ibid.*, II, ii, p. 24.

205 "a sister in distress": *Ibid.*, II, p. 24.

205 she held men in contempt: Karl Fleming to author, May 11, 1993.

205 Camelia Campbell: Cited by George Eells and Stanley Musgrove, *Mae West* (New York: Morrow, 1982), p. 83.

206 "a naughty word": *Variety*, September 26, 1928.

206 "Oh, my dear . . .": Jack Conway, *Ibid.*, September 19, 1928.

206 "great, with Rabelais": New York *Evening Post*, September 30, 1928.

206 "No play of our time": New York *Sun*, October 2, 1928.

206 "Three tiresome": New York *Evening Post*, October 2, 1928.

206 "*Pleasure Man* is prostitution": *Billboard*, October 13, 1928.

206 "uglier than sewerage": Walter Winchell, "Along the Main Stem," *Life* (October 26, 1928):6.

206 "Besides being gratuitously nasty": Robert Benchley, "The Theatre," *Life* (October 19, 1928):19.

207 "howled and snickered": New York *Evening Post*, October 2, 1928.

207 "Soon Forty-seventh Street": *The New York Times*, October 2, 1928.

207 "spat upon the pavement": New York *Sun*, October 2, 1928.

207 "Many of the women performers": *The New York Times*, October 2, 1928.

207 "Beat it, Annie": *Variety*, October 10, 1928.

207 RAID MAE WEST PLAY: *The New York Times*, October 2, 1928.

207 "'The Drag' was about a homosexualist": MW in New York *World*, October 3, 1928.

208 "any dastardly drama": Mayor Walker, quoted by Kaier Curtin in *"We Can Always Call Them Bulgarians": The Emergence of Lesbians and Gay Men on the American Stage* (Boston: Alyson Publications, 1987), p. 136.

208 "the impersonators attracted": *Variety*, October 10, 1928.

208 "This administration": Quoted in *The New York Times*, October 4, 1928.

208 "lost much": *Variety*, October 10, 1928.

209 "If the shutting down . . . haulers": George Jean Nathan in *American Mercury* (December 1928): 500–2.

209 Peggy Wood: Quoted in *The New York Times*, October 9, 1928.

209 change of venue: *The Brooklyn Eagle*, November 14, 1928.
209 "Why can't a jury": Nathan Burkan in *The New York Times*, February 6, 1930.
209 the jury: *Brooklyn Eagle*, March 18, 1930.
210 "I have been misunderstood": MW, "Sex in the Theater," *Parade* (September 1929): 12–13.
210 that he was the ghostwriter: Gerald Weales, *Canned Goods as Caviar: American Film Comedy of the 1930s* (University of Chicago Press, 1985), p. 51.
210 "It was a staggering blow": MW, *Goodness*, p. 135.
210 the house was hers: *Los Angeles Times*, January 13, 1937.
211 death certificate: Filed January 28, 1930, Bureau of Records, Muni.
211 "I turned my face": MW, *Goodness*, p. 135.
211 "When my mother died": MW to Ruth Biery, "The Private Life of Mae West," Part One, in *Mae West: A Bio-Bibliography* by Carol M. Ward (Westport, Conn.: Greenwood Press, 1989), p. 106.
211 final payment: Unattributed clip, January 17, 1934, MCNY.
212 "that it would . . . on stage": *The New York Times*, March 20, 1930.
212 "Resplendent in his court costume": New York *Daily News*, March 21, 1930.
212 performed in a play: *The New York Times*, March 22, 1930.
212 Coy would nudge him: New York *Evening Journal*, March 24, 1930.
212 "He gave a magnificent . . . suggestive": New York *Daily News*, March 21, 1930.
213 "Nothing ever happened": *Ibid.*, March 22, 1930.
213 Nathan Burkan: *The New York Times*, October 19, 1928; March 21, 1930.
213 "female impersonation in itself": *Ibid.*, March 27, 1930.
213 striking out one count: *Variety*, March 26, 1930.
213 "words sung by children": Quoted in *The New York Times*, March 29, 1930.
213 Alan Brooks and May Davis: *The New York Times, New York World*, April 2, 1930.
214 acrobats: *The New York Times*, April 1, 2, 1930.
214 "Mae West at the counsel table": *Ibid.*, March 29, 1930.
214 *Pleasure Man* was having: *Variety*, April 2, 1930.
214 Texas Guinan: Unattributed clip, April 2, 1930, Harvard.
214 "Hello, dear": *New York World*, April 2, 1930.
214 "Mae's a good girl": Quoted by Louise Berliner, *Texas Guinan: Queen of the Nightclubs* (Austin: University of Texas Press, 1993), p. 165.
214 closing statements: Quoted in *The New York Times*, April 3, 1930.
215 Irving Chandler: *Variety*, April 23, 1930.
215 "Words, intonations": *The New York Times*, April 4, 1930.
215 "vindication": MW, *Goodness*, p. 124.
215 had to sue her: *Variety*, January 19, 1932.
215 "The edge was off": MW, *Goodness*, p. 124.
215 "Spice is all right": Quote by Abel Green and Joe Laurie, Jr., *Show Biz, from Vaude to Video* (New York: Holt, 1951), p. 374.
216 "hell ship": MW, *Frisco Kate* (1930), I, p. 1, L of C.
216 "the swellest tart": *Ibid.*, II, p. 18.
216 "See this lady?": *Ibid.*, I, ii, p. 13.
216 "Get back into the cage": *Ibid.*, II, p. 9.
216 "I wish I had a sister": *Ibid.*, I, ii, p. 24.
217 "I thought you were a bruiser": *Ibid.*, p. 29.
217 "Bein' a lady": *Ibid.*, II, p. 14.
217 "I ain't used to maulin' ": *Ibid.*, III, p. 8.

217 "If we pull through": *Ibid.*, ii, p. 31.
217 The Shubert organization had lost a million dollars: Jerry Stagg, *The Brothers Shubert* (New York: Random House, 1968), p. 276.
217 only three other plays: *Variety*, September 3, 1930.
217 "Mae West is getting ready": *Ibid.*, October 29, 1930.
217 "There is a kind of fascination": Unattributed Cleveland clip, Shubert.
218 zoos, prisons: MW, *Goodness*, p. 131.
218 *Sex* was attached: *The New York Times*, November 13, 1930.
218 an outraged editorial: *Variety*, December 10, 1930.

219 "a play is soon finished": MW, *Goodness Had Nothing to Do with It* (New York: Manor Books, 1976), p. 133.
219 "A book author": *Ibid.*, p. 136.
219 "Tooth paste ads": *Variety*, April 29, 1931.
220 "Harlem is the Paris": MW, *The Constant Sinner* [*Babe Gordon*] (New York: Macaulay, 1930; reprint, Sheridan House, 1949), p. 164.
220 "the bodies of almost naked colored women": *Ibid.*
220 "the antics of blacks": *Ibid.*, p. 160.
220 spotted at the Nest: Barry Singer, *Black and Blue: The Life and Lyrics of Andy Razaf* (New York: Schirmer, 1992), p. 172.
220 transvestite floor shows: David Levering Lewis, *When Harlem Was in Vogue* (New York: Oxford University Press, 1989), p. 209.
220 "she had several black lovers": Lorenzo Tucker, quoted by George Eells and Stanley Musgrove, *Mae West* (New York: Morrow, 1982), p. 100.
220 Jack Johnson: Jim Haskins, *The Cotton Club* (New York: New American Library, 1977), p. 30.
221 "No, but he came up": MW to Robert E. Johnson, "Mae West: Snow White Sex Queen Who Drifted," *Jet* (July 25, 1974):45.
221 "I've always liked athletes": *Mae West on Sex, Health and ESP* (London and New York: W. H. Allen, 1975), pp. 12, 18.
221 "She could get an idea": MW, *The Constant Sinner* [novel], p. 17.
221 Howard Merling: MW, *Goodness*, pp. 133–34.
221 "piece the different parts together": MW to Malcolm Oettinger, "Literary Lil," *Picture Play* (September 1933):62.
221 "couple of overtime mamas": MW, *The Constant Sinner* [novel], p. 14.
221 "they copped the big end": *Ibid.*, p. 227.
221 "livin' lak a king": *Ibid.*, p. 172.
222 "Bearcat's subconscious yearning": *Ibid.*, p. 39.
222 Brentano's visit: Lowell Brentano, "Between Covers—II," *Forum* (February 1935): 98.
222 the contest: *Publishers Weekly* (October 25, 1930): 1953 (March 7, 1931):1136.
223 "trollops, murderers, bootleggers," MW, *The Constant Sinner* [novel], p. 9.
223 "the finger-tips caressing": MW, *The Constant Sinner* [novel], p. 168.
223 "Babe's white body": *Ibid.*, p. 313.
223 "Nature creates . . . men": *Ibid.*, p. 15.
224 "Even if she decides": *Ibid.*, p. 313.
224 "To Babe, a lie": *Ibid.*, p. 51.

224 "the whole world is selling something": *Ibid.*, p. 16.

224 "pluck a hard-boiled racketeer": *Ibid.*, p. 10.

224 "the gorgeous trapping": *Ibid.*, p. 55.

224 "The world loves a hero": *Ibid.*, p. 124.

225 "Selling dope gave her": *Ibid.*, p. 159.

225 "had the pick": *Ibid.*, p. 168.

225 "Ah's too ugly": *Ibid.*, p. 250.

225 "a low, lustful, black beast": *Ibid.*, p. 305.

226 five editions: MW to Charles Hammond, New York *Evening Post*, February 18, 1933.

226 never on bestseller lists: Richard Helfer, *Mae West on Stage: Themes and Persona* (unpublished Ph.D. dissertation, City University of New York, 1990), p. 299.

226 "She was always strong": Quoted by Eells and Musgrove, p. 100.

226 *All God's Chillun*: James Weldon Johnson, *Black Manhattan* (New York: Da Capo Press, 1991 [1930]), pp. 193–94.

227 "He walks on for a bow": *Variety*, September 9, 1931.

227 "In the past": New York *Herald Tribune*, September 13, 1931.

227 "Just fits my bed": *The Constant Sinner* [play], 1931, I, p. 5, Shubert.

227 "It's the depression": *Ibid.*, I, iii, p. 5.

227 "I never turn down anything": *Ibid.*, II, i, p. 4.

227 "Oh, god dam it": *Ibid.*, III, vii, p. 6.

227 famous women: *Ibid.*, I, iii, pp. 1ff.

228 "kept the biggest standing army": *Ibid.*, I, iii, p. 6.

228 book collection: New York *Evening Journal*, July 17, 1933.

228 "She has the most masculine mind . . . way": Arthur Vinton to Gladys Hall, "Three Men—and All Kissed by Mae West," *Motion Picture* (November 1933):34, 86.

228 Wilella Waldorf: New York *Evening Post*, September 15, 1931.

229 "Diamond Lil was a Mother Goose": *Variety*, September 1, 1931.

229 "an almost unsupportable satisfaction": Robert Benchley, *The New Yorker* (September 26, 1931):26.

229 "shrewd use": Howard Barnes, New York *Herald Tribune*, September 14, 1931.

229 Twenty-one stagehands: MW, *Goodness*, p. 138.

229 "Seldom has fouler talk": *The New York Times*, September 15, 1931.

229 "It may not be denied": Undated New York *American* clip, Shubert.

229 "It is a pity": Howard Barnes, New York *Herald Tribune*, September 15, 1931.

229 "I wasn't really nude": MW in *Boston Herald*, August 18, 1973.

229 "snickering good time": John Chapman, New York *Daily News*, September 15, 1931.

229 "No burlesque show": Stephen Rathbun, New York *Sun*, September 15, 1931.

229 "a three-ring circus": Robert Coleman, New York *Daily Mirror*, September 15, 1931.

230 Joseph Wood Krutch: "In Defense of Mae West," *The Nation* (September 30, 1931): 344.

230 "still the best bum": *Variety*, September 22, 1931.

230 "Her peculiar slouching": *The New York Times*, September 15, 1931.

230 "Her ribald wisecracks": Heywood Broun in undated *World Telegram* clip, Shubert.

230 "mediocre entertainment": Bob Grannis in New York *Evening Graphic*, September 15, 1931.

230 "She is a large": Percy Hammond, "Is There No Flit?," New York *Herald Tribune*, October 4, 1931.

230 "Miss West received many curtain calls": New York *Sun*, September 15, 1931.

230 "confided to her public": *The New York Times*, September 15, 1931.

231 "There wasn't anyone": MW to Ruth Biery, "The Private Life of Mae West," Part One, in *Mae West: A Bio-Bibliography*, by Carol M. Ward (Westport, Conn.: Greenwood Press, 1989), p. 106.

231 beyond the deletion: Helfer, p. 335.

231 "We had to operate": MW, *Goodness*, p. 137.

231 "Apologia Pro Vita Sua": *The New York Times*, October 4, 1931.

231 among the failures: *Variety*, June 7, 1932.

232 dashed hopes: *Ibid.*, November 3, 1931.

232 "theme, language and postures": *The Washington Post*, November 25, 1931.

232 "while attending the races": *The New York Times*, November 26, 1931.

232 filed claims: Actors Equity File SC6, NYU.

232 about 45 percent: Abel Green and Joe Laurie, Jr., *Show Biz, from Vaude to Video* (New York: Holt, 1951), p. 379.

232 "There is little scratch": Quoted by Ronald L. Morris, *Wait Until Dark: Jazz and the Underworld, 1880–1940* (Ohio: Bowling Green University Press, 1980), p. 169.

232 her own theater: *Variety*, October 20, 1931.

232 "Mae West will do no more legiting": *Ibid.*, December 22, 1931.

234 "Mae West blew . . . Windy City": Eleanor Barnes, *Illustrated News*, June 20, 1932, AMPAS.

234 B. P. Schulberg: I. G. Edmonds and Reiko Mimura, *Paramount Pictures and the People Who Made Them* (San Diego and New York: A. S. Barnes, 1980), p. 189.

235 "No one believed": Adolph Zukor with Dale Kramer, *The Public Is Never Wrong* (New York: Putnam, 1953), p. 267.

235 judged unsuitable: Hays Office memo, March 27, 1930, *She Done Him Wrong*, Hays Office files, AMPAS.

235 Production Code of 1930: Reprinted in *Movies in Our Midst: Documents in the Cultural History of Film in America*, ed. Gerald Mast (University of Chicago Press, 1982), pp. 321ff.

235 enjoying a heyday: Gregory D. Black, *Hollywood Censored: Morality Codes, Catholics and the Movies* (New York and Cambridge: Cambridge University Press, 1994), p. 56.

235 banned words: *Variety*, September 6, 1932.

235 "Hollywood wailed": Martin Sommers, New York *Daily News*, February 26, 1933.

235 "Guinan's a friend": Quoted by Lewis Yablonsky, *George Raft* (San Francisco: Mercury House, 1989), p. 89.

235 a quarter of the workforce: Tino Balio, *Grand Design: Hollywood as a Modern Business Enterprise, 1930–39* (New York: Scribner's, 1993), p. 13.

236 not just distraction: Arthur Schlesinger, Jr., "When the Movies Really Counted," *Show* (April 1963):77.

236 the audience had dropped: Leonard J. Leff and Jerold L. Simmons, *The Dame in the Kimono: Hollywood, Censorship and the Production Code from the 1920s to the 1960s* (New York: Grove Weidenfeld, 1990), p. 28.

236 "Clara Bow was through": MW, *Goodness Had Nothing to Do with It* (New York: Manor Books, 1976), p. 139.

236 record losses: Steven Bach, *Marlene Dietrich* (New York: Morrow, 1992), p. 156.

236 non-contract employees: Edmonds and Mimura, p. 184.

236 "crafty and tough-minded": Budd Schulberg, *Moving Pictures* (New York: Stein & Day, 1981), p. 459.

236 Cohen renounced: Balio, p. 53.

236 "Filmtown gave [me]": MW in Los Angeles *Sunday Dispatch*, January 6, 1935.

237 "I'm not a little girl": MW to George Daws, New York *World Telegram*, August 9, 1934.

237 "O. H. P. Garret": *Variety*, August 2, 1932.

237 casting problems: *Ibid.*, August 23, 1932.

237 attended the fights: *Los Angeles Times*, December 12, 1932.

237 MAE MULLS SOCK YARNS: *Variety*, July 5, 1932.

237 "If I thought of something funny": Sunday London *Times*, December 28, 1969, BFI.

237 "I'll either be sensational": MW to Hedda Hopper, quoted by George Eells, *Hedda and Louella* (New York: Putnam, 1972), p. 143.

238 "The screen doesn't require": MW to Muriel Babcock, *Los Angeles Times*, July 17, 1932.

238 "We must do all that": MW to Dietrich, quoted by Marlene Dietrich, *My Life*, trans. Salvador Attanasio (London: Pan Books, 1989), p. 119.

238 "I got in everyone's hair": MW to George Daws, New York *World Telegram*, August 9, 1934.

238 "fat, fair": Quoted by George Eells and Stanley Musgrove, *Mae West* (New York: Morrow, 1982), p. 104.

238 "To most people . . . perfect lover": MW to Clark Warren, "Dynamite Lady," *Screen Play* (November 1932):30.

239 "Moorish touches": Helen Lawrenson, "Mirror, Mirror, on the Ceiling: How'm I Doing?," *Esquire* (July 1967):72.

239 "That's lucky": MW in *The New York Times*, June 9, 1935, IX.

239 "Everyone else that gets": MW to George Daws, New York *World Telegram*, August 9, 1934.

239 "I like to live high up": "Mae West Gives All the Answers," *Movie Classic* (February 1937):36.

239 "no books, no flowers": Elza Schallert, "Go West—If You're an Adult," *Motion Picture* (May 1933):84.

239 "hit the overhead lamps": MW to William Scott Eyman, *Take One* (September 1972):20.

240 responsible for bringing Fields: Leonard Maltin, *The Great Movie Comedians: From Charlie Chaplin to Woody Allen* (New York: Harmony Books, 1982), p. 147.

240 Barbara Hutton: John Mosedale, *The Men Who Invented Broadway: Damon Runyon and Walter Winchell and Their World* (New York: Richard Marek, 1981), pp. 24–25.

240 *Night After Night* (Paramount, 1932) is currently owned by Universal MCA.

242 "placing it right": *Screen Play* (January 1934):64.

242 "a ball-bearing shaped": MW, *Goodness*, p. 144.

242 "In this picture": *Ibid.*, p. 147.

242 "I had to come in": MW to John Kobal, *People Will Talk* (New York: Knopf, 1985), p. 163.

243 "It melts": MW, *Goodness*, p. 145.

243 salaries: Paramount production files, *Night After Night*, AMPAS.

243 he had been jailed: Louise Berliner, *Texas Guinan: Queen of the Nightclubs* (Austin: University of Texas Press, 1993), p. 161.

243 a pistol: Andrew Stone to author, September 29, 1993.

244 "I think it's a terrible thing": MW to Schallert, p. 84.

244 "Mae West, in a clinging black gown": Los Angeles *Herald*, December 5, 1933.

244 *Calling All Cars*: Broadcast on March 18, 1935. A recording exists at the Motion Picture, Broadcasting and Recorded Sound Division, L of C.

244 "Wait till you see": *Photoplay* (February 1933):14.

244 "On the screen": Quoted by James Robert Parish, *The Paramount Pretties* (New Rochelle, N.Y.: Arlington House, 1972), p. 302.

244 "Miss West's dialogue": *Variety*, November 1, 1932.

244 "being solely played": *Ibid.*, June 13, 1933.

Page   14. SHE DONE HIM WRONG

245 the Paramount story department: MW, *Goodness Had Nothing to Do with It* (New York: Manor Books, 1976), p. 149.

246 lowlife characters: W. H. Mooring, "Mae West Talks," *Film Weekly* (September 28, 1934):9.

246 "We informed him": Wingate to Hays, November 1, 1932. This letter and all subsequent letters and memos quoted in this chapter, unless otherwise noted, come from the Hays Office file for *She Done Him Wrong*, AMPAS.

246 he had been present: Leonard S. Leff and Jerold L. Simmons, *The Dame in the Kimono: Hollywood, Censorship, and the Production Code from the 1920s to the 1960s* (New York: Grove Weidenfeld, 1990), p. 25.

246 "There are reports": *Los Angeles Times*, October 31, 1932.

246 "a touch of Hays fever": *Ibid.*, November 4, 1932.

246 "If *Diamond Lil* could be produced": Hays to Zukor, October 18, 1932.

247 "Please wire": H. M. Warner to Will Hays, October 19, 1932.

247 "Believe situation": Hays to Warner, October 19, 1932.

247 Hurley memo: November 9, 1932.

248 "while it resembles": Wingate to Hays, undated night letter.

248 Zukor promised: Notes to November 28, 1932, MPPDA board meeting.

248 " 'Lil' is out": *Variety*, November 29, 1932.

248 *He Done Her Wrong*: I. G. Edmonds and Reiko Mimura, *Paramount Pictures and the People Who Made Them* (San Diego and New York: A. S. Barnes, 1980), p. 191.

248 "develop the comedy elements": Wingate to Hurley, November 29, 1932.

248 "I designed 30 or 40 pounds": Edith Head with Jane Ardmore, *The Dress Doctor* (Boston: Little, Brown, 1959), p. 53.

249 *She Done Him Wrong* (Paramount, 1933) is now owned by Universal MCA.

249 By standing on a stair: Gerald Weales, *Canned Goods as Caviar: American Film Comedy of the 1930s* (University of Chicago Press, 1985), p. 37.

249 "I taught Cary Grant": MW to George Christy, "Mae West Raps," reprinted in *Mae West: A Bio-Bibliography*, by Carol M. Ward (Westport, Conn.: Greenwood Press, 1989), p. 127.

249 Her personality was so dominant: According to Cary Grant in *Variety*, November 21, 1933.

249 When he first played the lover: Alma Whitaker, *Los Angeles Times*, II, November 5, 1933.

250 "If he can talk": MW, *Goodness*, p. 151.

250 "I don't care": Quoted by Albert Govoni, *Cary Grant: An Unauthorized Biography* (Chicago: Regnery, 1971), pp. 98–99.

250 "superficiality": Charles Higham and Roy Moseley, *Cary Grant: The Lonely Heart* (San Diego and New York: Harcourt Brace Jovanovich, 1989), p. 322.

250 "almost everything": Cary Grant in *Variety*, November 21, 1933.

250 "She is blond": Cary Grant, quoted by Jon Tuska, *The Films of Mae West* (Secaucus, N.J.: Citadel Press, 1973), p. 69.

250 "Mae would look us over": Ann Sheridan to John Kobal, "Mae West," *Films and Filming* (September 1983):25.

250 "I like 'em tight": Quoted by Edith Head, p. 53.

251 "I didn't start": MW to Richard Meryman, "Mae West," *Life* (April 18, 1969):62D.

252 "The reply of my agent . . . set' ": John Bright, "One of a Kind," *L.A. Weekly* (July 16–22, 1982):18.

252 he barred her: Undated, unattributed clip, BFI.

252 "a charter member": Martin Sommers in undated *Daily News* [1933] clip, MCNY.

252 "I was really always the director": MW to Charlotte Chandler, *The Ultimate Seduction* (Garden City, N.Y.: Doubleday, 1984), p. 64.

253 "America's wet dream": Lowell Sherman, quoted by Bright, p. 18.

253 "hearty, if somewhat rowdy amusement": Wingate to Hays, January 13, 1933.

253 letters from fans: Frank Rose, *The Agency: William Morris and the Hidden History of Show Business* (New York: Harper Business, 1995), p. 66.

253 the greatest record of repeats: *Philadelphia Inquirer*, September 2, 1933.

253 "Not Once . . . went for me": Ads, *Variety*, February 14, September 12, 1933.

254 beer-drinking contests: Paramount Press Book, *She Done Him Wrong*, AMPAS; Bill Thomas in USC Friends of the Library Pamphlet, "A Tribute to Mae West, March 21, 1982" (Los Angeles, 1983), p. 16.

254 she bested the box-office take: *Variety*, February 21, 1933.

254 radio date: *Ibid.*, February 7, 1933.

254 New York stage show: Bige. review, *Variety*, February 14, 1933; Eileen Creelman in undated clip *re She Done Him Wrong*, NYPL.

255 in her new hometown: *Variety*, December 20, 1932.

255 the stars stayed away: Frank Condon, "Come Up and Meet Mae West," *Colliers* 93 (June 16, 1934):26, 42.

255 "I don't go in for Hollywood parties": MW to Elza Schallert, " 'Go West'—If You're an Adult," *Motion Picture* (May 1933):84.

256 "Neither the sweet ingenue": Adolph Zukor with Dale Kramer, *The Public Is Never Wrong* (New York: Putnam, 1953), p. 267.

256 "languorous, exotic pretenders": Jay Brien Chapman, "Is Mae West Garbo's Greatest Rival?" *Motion Picture* (July 1933):29.

256 broken all box-office records: Gregory D. Black, *Hollywood Censored: Morality Codes, Catholics and the Movies* (New York: Cambridge University Press, 1994), p. 78.

256 "Mae fits the temper": Jay Brien Chapman, "Is Mae West Garbo's Greatest Rival?" *Motion Picture* (July 1933):76.

256 "Mae West is the first real Waterloo": Schallert, p. 32.

256 "Do your exercises": Caption of a cartoon by Jano Fabry, *Life* (October 1933):46.

256 "My corseted silhouette": MW, quoted by Cecelia Ager, "Mae West Reveals the Foundation of the 1900 Mode," *Vogue* (September 1, 1933):67.

256 "Today everybody": Alice Hughes, New York *World Telegram*, July 31, 1933.

257 "Garbo and her": MW to Ruth Biery, "The Private Life of Mae West," Part Four, *Movie Classic* (April 1934):40.

257 "The very best thing": MW to Maude Latham, " 'Will I Last?' Asks Mae West," *Motion Picture* (June 1934):92.

257 "The only good girl": MW to Cecelia Ager, *Variety*, January 31, 1933.

257 "My style and techniques": MW to Schallert, p. 84.

257 "A Guy What Takes His Time," words and music by Ralph Rainger, © 1932 and 1933 by Famous Music Corp., renewed 1959 and 1960. Quoted by permission.

258 Take Your Time: New York *World Telegram*, February 20, 1933.

258 Minute Men: Cited by Stanley Walker, "Sex Comes to America," in *Mrs. Astor's House* (New York: Frederick Stokes, 1935), p. 253.

258 Mary Pickford: Quoted by Lewis Jacobs, *The Rise of the American Film* (New York: Harcourt, Brace, 1939), p. 533.

258 "very lowtoned": Wingate to Vincent Hart, telegram, February 3, 1933.

258 "This reduces the song": Hays to Wingate, February 27, 1933.

258 cuts: Hays Office files.

259 "nothing but uncouth": *Los Angeles Examiner*, March 10, 1934.

259 London and Paris: Black, p. 78.

259 "I went . . . source": Sidney Kent letter, undated, in Dr. Wingate's file.

259 "which everybody knows": Lord to Hays, Quigley Papers; quoted by Leff and Simmons, p. 30.

259 "illustrates . . . splendid comedy": Hays to Lord, Lord Papers; quoted by Black, p. 78.

260 "only alternative . . . Hays": Bige. in *Variety*, February 14, 1933.

260 "a remarkably suspicious impersonation": *The New York Times*, February 10, 1933.

260 "The film is lively": Aaronson in *Motion Picture Herald*, February 18, 1933.

260 "I am happy to report": Cy Caldwell, *New Outlook* (March 1933):49.

261 "for whole-heartedly thumbing": *The Hollywood Reporter*, January 10, 1933.

261 "The picture, which owes everything": William Troy in *The Nation* (March 1, 1933):242.

261 "all the laughs one can squeeze": J. C. M. in *The New Yorker* (February 18, 1933): 34.

261 "amazing vitality": Quoted by Leff and Simmons, p. 36.

261 "as gorgeous as Lillian Russell": Rob Wagner in *Selected Film Criticism, 1931–1940*, ed. Anthony Slide (Methuen, N.J.: Scarecrow Press, 1982), p. 227.

261 "a star seen in the third person": MW, *Goodness*, p. 152.

261 "It will not be at all surprising": J. C. Furnas, New York *Herald Tribune*, September 17, 1933.

261 Flagg cartoon: *Los Angeles Times*, April 4, 1933, III, p. 6.

261 Steichen: *Vanity Fair* (May 1933):48.

262 "Because I done 'em wrong": Quoted by June Sochen, *Mae West: She Who Laughs, Lasts* (Arlington Heights, Ill.: Harlan Davidson, 1992), p. 72.

262 considered *Sex*: *Variety*, February 28, 1933.

262 trial balloons: *Ibid.*, April 11, 1933; *Los Angeles Times*, April 9, 1933.

Page   1 5. AT THE TOP OF THE LADDER

263 "We cannot merely take": Quoted by Robert S. McElvaine, *The Great Depression: America, 1929–1941* (New York: Times Books, 1993), p. 140.

263 an emergency meeting: Richard Maltby, "The Production Code and the Hays Office," in *Grand Design: Hollywood as a Modern Business Enterprise, 1930–1939*, ed. Tino Balio (New York: Scribner's, 1993), p. 57.

264 NRA code for moviemakers: Louis Nizer, *New Courts of Industry* (New York: Longacre Press, 1935).

264 Eddie Cantor told the press: Frank Rose, *The Agency: William Morris and the Hidden History of Show Business* (New York: Harper Business, 1995), pp. 64–65.

264 "the right moral standards": Article V, Film Industry Code, in *Variety*, August 29, 1933.

265 "Diamonds—lots of 'em": Quoted by David Chierichetti, *Hollywood Costume Design* (New York: Harmony Books, 1976), p. 52.

265 telling Travis Banton: Julie Lang Hunt, "Trials and Triumphs of a Hollywood Dress Designer," *Photoplay* (June 1936):88.

265 not tough enough: *Variety*, May 16, 1933.

265 "How much she contributed": Marian Spitzer Thompson, quoted by George Eells and Stanley Musgrove, *Mae West* (New York: Morrow, 1982), p. 121.

265 *I'm No Angel*, Paramount 1933, is now owned by Universal MCA.

266 "the script submitted": Wingate to Hays, June 26, 1933. *I'm No Angel*, Hays Office files, AMPAS. Unless otherwise noted, subsequent letters quoted in this chapter are from this file.

267 other current movies: See Gregory D. Black, *Hollywood Censored: Morality Codes, Catholics and the Movies* (New York: Cambridge University Press, 1994), pp. 96–97.

267 "That's all, boys": *I'm No Angel*, first script, June 19, 1933, AMPAS.

267 Mae offended her: Louise Berliner, *Texas Guinan: Queen of the Nightclubs* (Austin: University of Texas Press, 1993), p. 186.

268 an earlier version: *I'm No Angel* treatment, April 1933, AMPAS.

269 "Gimme my fine furs": "I Found a New Way to Go to Town," music by Harvey Brooks, lyrics by Gladys Du Bois, and Ben Ellison, © 1933, Shapiro Bernstein. Renewed. Hal Leonard Corp. Quoted by permission.

271 "Tira puts her fair head": Mourdant Hall, *The New York Times*, October 14, 1933.

271 "My father told me": MW to John Kobal, *People Will Talk* (New York: Knopf, 1985), p. 160.

271 "They weren't gonna . . . lions": MW to Charlotte Chandler, *The Ultimate Seduction* (Garden City, N.Y.: Doubleday, 1984), p. 51.

272 "I could see nothing": MW, *Goodness Had Nothing to Do with It* (New York: Manor Books, 1976), p. 157.

272 "Now I know how Jonah felt": MW in Paramount Press Book for *I'm No Angel*, AMPAS.

272 "They wouldn't let me": MW to Kobal, p. 160.

272 "She says she never wanted": Stanley Musgrove to Steven Roberts, "76—and Still Diamond Lil," *The New York Times Magazine* (November 21, 1969):82.

272 "Mae held up": Cary Grant to Gordon Crowley, "Cary Grant Wins with Four Queens," *Motion Picture* (January 1936):61.

273 "She had twice . . . eighteen times": Wesley Ruggles to Cary Grant, "Making Love to Mae West," *Picturegoer* (December 30, 1933):13.

273 "full of dynamite . . . gets to you": Quoted by Alma Whitaker, *Los Angeles Times*, November 5, 1933.

273 "Well, it was . . . helpful": Cary Grant in *Picturegoer* (December 30, 1933); and to Alma Whitaker, *Los Angeles Times*, November 5, 1933.

273 shot separately: Maurice Leonard, *Mae West: Empress of Sex* (New York: Birch Lane, 1992), p. 30.

273 "more talked about . . . many times' ": Cary Grant in *Picturegoer* (December 10 and 30, 1933; January 6, 1934).

274 "a teacher, no, a rock": Marlene Dietrich, *My Life*, trans. Salvador Attanasio (London: Pan Books, 1989), p. 117.

274 "Who is she?": Marlene Dietrich in *Variety*, October 3, 1933.

274 "When I saw the preview": Marlene Dietrich to Sonia Lee, "Dietrich Isn't Afraid of Mae West," *Motion Picture* (January 1934):49.

274 "Miss Dietrich is too intelligent": MW to Kenneth Baker, "War Clouds in the West?" *Photoplay* (December 1933):47, 109.

275 "Not bad, honey . . . out": Quoted by Maria Riva, *Marlene Dietrich* (New York: Knopf, 1993), p. 142.

275 "I turned off the water": *Mae West on Sex, Health and ESP* (London and New York: W. H. Allen, 1975), p. 42.

275 Dietrich once telephoned: Robert Duran to author, September 12, 1994.

275 "Who is more familiar": Beverly West to Edward R. Sammis, "The Strange Career of Mae West's 'Kid Sister,' " *Screen Play* (December 1933):21, 67.

275 "come up and see my sister": *Variety*, November 28, 1933.

275 "I ain't had time . . . now Timony": MW to Ruth Biery, "The Private Life of Mae West," *Movie Classic* (March 1934):62; (April 1934):90; (January 1934):56.

276 "Come in, kid": MW to Iris Foster, "The World Goes West," *Film Weekly* (October 13, 1933):10.

276 "It just does me good": MW to Alma Whitaker, *Los Angeles Times*, April 16, 1933.

276 donations to Catholic charities: Tim Malachosky, *Mae West* (Lancaster, Calif.: Empire Publishing, 1993), p. 165.

276 "she covered all bases": Chris Basinger to author, October 19, 1994.

276 "When were pictures": MW to James Fidler, "Mae West Answers 20 Personal Questions," *Movie Classic* (September 1933):71.

277 "I've never done anything": MW to Denis Hart, *London Daily Telegraph*, August 21, 1970.

277 "Loose morals?": MW, quoted in *Los Angeles Times*, October 18, 1933.

277 TEA INVITE: *Variety*, October 3, 1933.

277 Jean Harlow: Quoted by Gerald Weales, *Canned Goods as Caviar: American Film Comedy of the 1930s* (University of Chicago Press, 1985), p. 31.

277 "If Mae agrees": Gladys Hall, "The Crime of the Day in Hollywood," *Motion Picture* (January 1934): 28ff.

278 "Love your neighbor": *Los Angeles Times*, December 14, 1933.

278 unsolicited check: *Hollywood Reporter* (December 2, 1933):74.

278 support to families of prisoners: *Film Weekly* (October 13, 1933):10.

278 C. D. Cooper: *Los Angeles Times*, October 10, 1933.

278 George Kent: "The Mammy and Daddy of Us All," *Photoplay* (May 1934):32, 33, 101.

279 list of shall nots: Jack Lait, New York *American*, September 24, 1933.

279 "Mae never takes showers": Unattributed BFI clip.

279 "For the sake of her curves": Paramount Press Release, BFI.

279 "She's a home girl": *Screen Play* (January 1934):20.

279 Hans Dreier had brought: Charles Higham, *Celebrity Circus* (New York: Delacorte, 1979), p. 21.

279 "I let 'em sit. . . . go too far": MW in *The New York Times*, June 9, 1936, IX.

280 "Gets all the flesh tones": MW, quoted by Stephen Longstreet to author, August 22, 1994.

280 "She never told the truth": Cary Grant, quoted by Warren G. Harris, *Cary Grant: A Touch of Elegance* (New York: Doubleday, 1987), p. 265.

281 "National Recovery Act": Paramount ad in *Variety*, October 10, 1933.

281 "screendom's exponent": *I'm No Angel* Paramount Press Book, AMPAS.

281 "NRA stands for": MW in *Shadowplay* (April 1934):76.

281 "It's hard to be funny": MW to Malcolm Oettinger, "Literary Lil," *Picture Play* (September 1933):82.

281 "FILM MORALS:" *Variety*, November 21, 1933.

281 "dangerous nature . . . moral code?" *Picturegoer*, November 25, December 23, 1933.

281 *Christian Century*: Cited by Leonard J. Leff and Jerold L. Simmons, *The Dame in the Kimono: Hollywood, Censorship and the Production Code from the 1920s to the 1960s* (New York: Grove Weidenfeld, 1990), p. 42.

282 "a scarlet woman": Martin Quigley, "Decency in Motion Pictures" [1937], in *Movies in Our Midst: Documents in the Cultural History of Film in America*, ed. Gerald Mast (University of Chicago Press, 1982), p. 343.

282 "both the lyrics": Russell Holmon to Maurice McKenzie, June 21, 1933.

282 "I'm No Angel": Words by Gladys DuBois and Ben Ellison, music by Harvey Brooks, © 1933, Shapiro Bernstein. Renewed. Courtesy Hal Leonard Corp. Quoted by permission.

282 Ben Ellison claimed: Quoted by Jack Allen to author, March 29, 1995.

282 "They Call Me Sister Honky-Tonk": Music by Harvey Brooks, words by Ben Ellison, and Gladys DuBois, © 1933, Shapiro Bernstein, courtesy Hal Leonard Corp. Quoted by permission.

283 "This picture will be box office": Hart to McKenzie, October 4, 1933.

283 at Chicago's Oriental Theater: *Variety*, October 10, 1933.

283 in New York: *Los Angeles Times*, November 5, 1933.

283 in Brooklyn: Unattributed BFI clip.

283 "the street outside": *Boston Transcript*, November 8, 1933.

283 In Omaha: *Variety*, October 24, 1933.

283 "Everybody's analyzing": *Ibid.*, November 14, 1933.

283 offers she turned down: *Ibid.*, September 5, 1933.

283 "the biggest conversation-provoker": *Ibid.*, October 17, 1933.

284 "she really and truly": Undated *Chicago Tribune* clip, BFI.

284 "the world's best": *Newsweek* (October 21, 1933):30.

284 "primarily a stunt": John S. Cohen, Jr., New York *Sun*, October 21, 1933.

284 "next to Charlie Chaplin": Stark Young, "Angels and Ministers of Grace," *The New Republic* (November 29, 1933):75.

284 "America's sweetheart": New York *Post*, October 14, 1933.

284 "She has not been sufficiently": Sidonie Gabrielle Colette, *Colette and the Movies*, eds. Alain and Odette Virmaux, trans. Sarah W. R. Smith (New York: Frederick Ungar, 1980), p. 62.

284 "No member of the cast": *Hollywood Reporter* (September 29, 1933):3.

284 "nimble-witted . . . either": Alice Hughes, "The Woman's Slant," *Life* (December 1933):46.

285 "there weren't so many picture people": Unattributed AMPAS clip, May 20, 1934.

285 "leave their fingerprints . . . congregation": Edwin Schallert, *Los Angeles Times*, October 13, 1933.

285 "He always had a lot of sex": MW in unattributed AMPAS clip, May 20, 1934.

285 "a novel affair . . . start": *Los Angeles Times*, October 13, 1933.

285 about 46 million: Black, p. 80.

286 rival studios: *Variety*, October 17, 1933.

286 new contract: James Robert Parish, *The Paramount Pretties* (New Rochelle, N.Y.: Arlington House, 1972), p. 306.

286 "At the end, I have all the power": Quoted by David Ray Johnson, "Biographical Study of Mae West," Appendix, *Mae West on Sex, Health and ESP*, p. 226.

286 "She'll cure sick box-offices": Jay Brien Chapman, "Is Mae West Garbo's Greatest Rival?" *Motion Picture* (July 1933):76.

287 the highest salary: Tino Balio, "Selling Stars," in *Grand Design: Hollywood as a Modern Business Enterprise*, ed. Tino Balio (New York: Scribner's, 1993), p. 162.

287 a drug problem: Stanley Musgrove, *Myra Breckinridge* Diary, USC.

287 because he slept: George Eells and Stanley Musgrove, *Mae West* (New York: Morrow, 1982), p. 145.

288 she went on supporting him: Andrew Stone to author, September 29, 1993.

288 "a huge grove . . . those days": James Bacon, Los Angeles *Herald Examiner*, November 25, 1980.

288 "to see how it is to wake up": MW in New York *Evening Post*, February 28, 1934.

289 "MAE WEST LEADS STARS . . . threats either": *Los Angeles Times*, March 15, 1934.

289 "Mae never looked": Harrison Carroll, Los Angeles *Herald*, February 19, 1934.

289 "was observed sitting": *Los Angeles Times*, March 15, 1934.

289 "Is that a gun": Cited by John Kobal, "Mae West," *Films and Filming* (September 1983): 22.

289 able to hide out: Graham Nown, *The English Godfather* (London: Ward Lock, 1987), pp. 119–20.

289 armored car: Paramount Press release, April 1934, AMPAS.

290 "walking in the front door" . . . Pancho Villa: Kirtley Baskette, "Has Mae West Gone High Hat?" *Photoplay* (July 1934):110.

290 *Belle of the Nineties*, Paramount 1934, is now owned by Universal MCA.

290 her contract: *Variety*, June 19, 1934.

290 $15,000 worth of gifts: *Los Angeles Times*, August 27, 1934.

290 "that I was incapable": Idwal Jones, *The York Times*, September 23, 1934, X.

291 all symbols: Carol M. Ward, *Mae West: A Bio-Bibliography* (Westport, Conn.: Greenwood Press, 1989), p. 56.

291 costumes: *Picturegoer* (October 27, 1934):13.

291 Karl Struss: Scott Eyman, *Five American Cinematographers: Interviews* (Metuchen, N.J.: Scarecrow Press, 1987), p. 1; Charles Higham, *Hollywood Cameramen: Sources of Light* (Bloomington: University of Indiana Press, 1970), p. 128; Charles Hagen, "A Man Who Defied Labels in the Messy 1910s," *The New York Times*, August 11, 1995.

291 "to minimize . . . physical imperfections": Karl Struss, "Photographic Modernism and the Cinematographer," *American Cinematographer* (November 1934):296.

291 "I lit Mae": Quoted by Eells and Musgrove, p. 139.

292 process shots: Jon Tuska, *The Films of Mae West* (Secaucus, N.J.: The Citadel Press, 1973), p. 93.

292 Mae asked for Ellington . . . pre-record": MW to Robert E. Johnson, "Mae West: Snow White Sex Queen Who Drifted," *Jet* (July 1974):44–45.

292 "I told them": Quoted by Tim Malachosky, *Mae West* (Lancaster, Calif.: Empire Publishing, 1993), p. 59.

293 "Now, he was her man": "When the St. Louis Woman Comes Down to New Orleans," words and music by Sam Coslow, Arthur Johnston, and Gene Austin, © 1934, renewed 1961, Famous Music Corp.

293 "Creole Man": Banned lyric by Mack Gordon, PCA *Belle of the Nineties* file, AM-PAS.

294 "Troubled Waters": Words and music by Sam Coslow and Arthur Johnston, © 1934, renewed 1961, Famous Music Corp. Quoted by permission.

294 "All that notoriety": *It Ain't No Sin*, March 5, 1934, script, AMPAS.

294 George Raft backed out: *Variety*, March 13, 1934; *The New York Times*, March 10, 1934.

295 "by that fiery Latin temperament": MW in *Los Angeles Times*, November 18, 1934.

295 "you don't even have to worry": *Variety*, April 3, 1934.

296 "Catholics are called by God": Quoted by Gregory D. Black, *Hollywood Censored: Morality Codes, Catholics and the Movies* (New York: Cambridge University Press, 1994), p. 162.

297 "the producers of filthy pictures": Cited by Leonard J. Leff and Jerold L. Simmons, *The Dame in the Kimono: Hollywood, Censorship and the Production Code from the 1920s to the 1960s* (New York: Grove Weidenfeld, 1990), p. 43.

297 Legion of Decency: *Ibid.*, p. 47.

297 Production Code: Reprinted in *Movies in Our Midst: Documents in the Cultural History of Film in America*, ed. Gerald Mast (University of Chicago Press, 1982), pp. 321ff.

297 "supreme pontiff": *Variety*, June 15, 1934.

297 "the Hitler of Hollywood": Quoted by Leff and Simmons, p. 57.

297 "Far from considering": Hays, quoted by Richard Corliss, "The Legion of Decency," *Film Comment* (Summer 1968):28.

297 "practically puts Hollywood": Dorothy Calhoun, "Hollywood Starts a Big Clean-Up," *Movie Classic* (March 1934):44.

297 "I am extremely happy": Quoted by Leff and Simmons, p. 53.

297 "Washington will observe": *Variety*, July 31, 1934.

298 "I like Mae, but": Quoted by Maria Riva, *Marlene Dietrich* (New York: Knopf, 1993), p. 367.

298 "in all probability": Gilbert Seldes, "The Movies in Peril," *Scribner's* (February 1935):83.

298 "She made amorous dallying": William French, "What Price Glamour?" *Motion Picture* (November 1934):29.

298 list of condemned films: Black, p. 103.

298 *Newsweek* article: *Newsweek*, July 7, 1934.

298 "simply a rotten bunch": Quoted by Black, p. 169.

298 "being debauched by Jews": Quoted by Richard Maltby, "The Production Code and the Hays Office," in *Grand Design*, p. 54.

298 "the happiness": Quoted by Edith Head and Paddy Calistro, *Edith Head's Hollywood* (New York: Dutton, 1983), p. 23.

298 Father Lord: Kenneth Anger, *Hollywood Babylon* (New York: Dutton, 1983), p. 23.

299 three categories: Leff and Simmons, p. 59.

299 "I saw both pictures . . . approval": Breen to Hays, October 7, 1935; October 1, 1935, *Belle of the Nineties* PCA file, AMPAS. Subsequent quotes from letters and memos come from this file.

299 "typical of wrong standards": Martin Quigley, "Decency in Motion Pictures [1937]" in Mast, p. 343.

299 "The general flavor": Breen to A. M. Botsford, February 23, 1934.

299 "moral compensating values": Black, p. 173.

300 the following changes: Breen memo, June 6, 1934.

300 five men visited her cabin: *Ain't No Sin* script, February 6, 1934.

301 IT IS: Anger, p. 260.

301 "If they think": MW in *Newsweek*, July 7, 1934.

301 "I want to please them": MW in Los Angeles *Herald*, June 29, 1934.

301 "got too close": John Mack Brown with Jack Smalley, "Making Love to Mae West Is Like a Football Game," *Motion Picture* (September 1934):62.

301 "an obvious curtsey": *Variety*, September 25, 1934.

301 "has graciously permitted": *The New York Times*, September 22, 1934.

301 "a sort of shotgun wedding": *Literary Digest* (October 6, 1934):32.

301 grossing over $2 million: Tuska, p. 92.

301 first four weeks: James Robert Parish and William T. Leonard, *Hollywood Players: The Thirties* (New Rochelle, N.Y.: Arlington House, 1976), p. 449.

301 in Atlantic City: *Film Weekly*, October 18, 1934.

301 in Baltimore, *Variety*, October 2, 1934.

301 in St. Louis: *Ibid.*, September 18, 1934.

302 "by no means as sensational": *Variety*, September 18, 1934.

302 audiences booed: Black, p. 190.

302 "No moral question": Kathryn Dougherty, "Do We Want Censorship?" *Photoplay* (October 1934):96.

302 "With the Western World": Richard Watts, Jr., *Herald Tribune*, July 15, 1934.

302 "I had to change": MW in *Los Angeles Times*, September 23, 1934.

302 "not a good story": MW in *The New York Times*, February 3, 1935.

303 "Imagine censors . . . Code": MW to Charlotte Chandler, *The Ultimate Seduction* (Garden City, N.Y.: Doubleday, 1984), p. 68.

303 "I've never believed": MW, quoted by James Robert Parish, *The Paramount Pretties* (New Rochelle, N.Y.: Arlington House, 1972), p. 308.

303 "It's the sex personality": Quoted by Leonard Maltin, *The Great Movie Comedians: From Chaplin to Woody Allen* (New York: Harmony Books, 1982), p. 161.

303 "I can accomplish": MW to Edwin Schallert, *Los Angeles Times*, September 23, 1934.

303 "I'd add hot lines": *Mae West on Sex, Health and ESP* (London and New York: W. H. Allen, 1975), p. 4.

303 "Is Mae West Slipping?": *Los Angeles Times*, May 20, 1934.

303 among old fads: *Vanity Fair* (May 1934): 56.

304 "The popularity of Mae West": Maude Latham, " 'Will I Last?' Asks Mae West," *Motion Picture* (June 1934):28.

304 "What's going to happen": William French, "What Price Glamour?" p. 28.

304 "an uproarious . . . of all times": George Davis, "The Decline of the West," *Vanity Fair* (May 1934):46, 82.

304 "all through Miss Mae West's": William Troy in *The Nation* (October 10, 1934):420.

304 "the clumsy way": Richard Watts, Jr., New York *Herald Tribune*, September 22, 1934.

305 "she did not bring": *Variety*, January 1, 1935.

305 "cleansing wind": André Sennwald, *The New York Times*, September 30, 1934, IX.

305 "They made her change": Otis Ferguson, *The New Republic* (October 24, 1934): 310.

305 Hugh Walpole: Quoted by Parish, *Pretties*, pp. 307–8.

305 "She took the very thing": Cedric Hardwicke in *Los Angeles Times*, April 4, 1935.

305 Will Rogers: Cited by Frank Condon, "Come Up and Meet Mae West," *Colliers* 93 (June 16, 1934):42.

305 "Most of the Hollywood film colony": Elizabeth Yeaman, Los Angeles *Citizen News*, August 18, 1934.

305 "a sleeping leopard": Leo McCarey, "Mae West Can Play Anything," *Photoplay* (June 1935):30ff.

306 that she would co-star: *Boston Herald*, January 14, 1934.

306 "He can hit": *Los Angeles Times*, November 18, 1934.

306 "The Queen of Sheba": New York *Evening Post*, May 5, 1934.

306 "One picture that is": *Los Angeles Times*, November 23, 1934.

306 "watchdog, dresser": *Picturegoer* (October 27, 1934):13.

306 "When she began": MW to John Moffitt, *The New York Times*, June 9, 1935, IX.

306 "a story by Marion Morgan": *Variety*, September 25, 1934.

307 "She lives for her work": Ruth Biery, "The Private Life of Mae West," Part Two, *Movie Classic* (February 1934):20.

307 foot the bill: Christie's East catalogue, December 6, 1994, Item No. 63.

307 did not accompany: *The New York Times*, January 7, 1935; *Variety*, January 8, 1935.

307 "Pa spent his time": MW in Los Angeles *Sunday Dispatch*, January 6, 1935.

308 "a man's world": MW to Charlotte Chandler, *The Ultimate Seduction* (Garden City, N.Y.: Doubleday, 1984), p. 66.

308 Earhart séance: *Mae West on Sex, Health and ESP* (London and New York: W. H. Allen, 1975), p. 145.

309 Hollywood socialites: Michael Bruno, *Venus in Hollywood: The Continental Enchantress from Garbo to Loren* (New York: Lyle Stuart, 1970), p. 104.

309 "as witty as" . . . tea to Viscount Byng: MW, *Goodness Had Nothing to Do with It* (New York: Manor Books, 1976), p. 170.

309 *Goin' to Town*, Paramount 1935, is now owned by Universal MCA.

309 "He's a Bad Man": Words and music by Sammy Fain and Irving Kahal, © 1934, 1935 by Famous Music Corp., renewed 1961 by Famous Music Corp. Quoted by permission.

310 new skills: MW, *Goodness*, p. 169.

311 "She's left the Bowery days": Paramount Press Book for *Goin' to Town*, AMPAS.

312 list of men: *Ibid.*

312 "I didn't keep the plot": Quoted by Tim Malachosky, *Mae West* (Lancaster, Calif.: Empire Publishing, 1993), p. 85.

312 "The story for my next film": Edwin Schallert, *Los Angeles Times*, September 23, 1934.

312 "We are happy to note": Breen to Hays, January 2, 1935, PCA *Goin' to Town* file, AMPAS. Unless otherwise noted, subsequent quotes from letters in this chapter are from this file.

313 "Now I'm a Lady": Original lyric by Irving Kahal in PCA file.

313 "the boasting of a woman": Breen to Hammell, January 16, 1935.

313 "Now I'm a Lady": Completed lyric by Irving Kahal, music by Sammy Fain, © 1934 and 1935, renewed 1961 and 1962, Famous Music Corp. Quoted by permission.

314 costs: Paramount production files, AMPAS.

314 after taxes: Jon Tuska, *The Films of Mae West* (Secaucus, N.J.: Citadel Press, 1973), p. 106.

314 "no great shakes": *Variety*, May 29, 1935.

314 "is the weakest and most slipshod production": *Hollywood Reporter*, April 23, 1935.

314 "Mae West's poorest": *Variety*, May 15, 1935.

314 "high moral tone": *Motion Picture Herald*, May 11, 1935.

315 "like a very ordinary": Meyer Levin, *Esquire* (July 1935):152.

315 "one of Miss West's most abject": André Sennwald, *The New York Times*, May 11, 1935.

315 "very credible West": *The New Yorker* (May 18, 1935):67.

315 prompting soul-searching: MW, *Goodness*, p. 172.

315 "Mr. Cohen declined: *The New York Times*, February 6, 1935.

315 "a star pamperer": "Paramount Pictures," *Fortune* (March 1937): 198.

316 another theory: Budd Schulberg, *Moving Pictures* (New York: Stein and Day, 1981), p. 487.

316 "all the small": *Ibid.*, p. 459.

316 Betty Lasky: "The Moguls," *The Hollywood Reporter: The Golden Years*, eds. Tichi Wilkerson and Marcia Borie (New York: Coward-McCann, 1984), p. 20.

316 "a pony's ass": Quoted by Steven Bach, *Marlene Dietrich* (New York: Morrow, 1992), p. 163.

316 "He's the real man": MW in undated Paramount press release, AMPAS.

316 in Fort Worth: *Los Angeles Times*, April 24, 1935.

316 "I'm not married": MW to Kirtley Baskette, "Mae West Talks About Her 'Marriage,' " *Photoplay* (August 1935):39.

316 "A girl might forget": MW to Dorothy Calhoun, "There Are Mae Wests—and There Is Mae West," *Motion Picture* (November 1935):39.

316 "I hope all my husbands": Quoted in *Variety*, May 1, 1935.

316 "a classy little brunette . . . every week": Frank Wallace in Los Angeles *Herald*, April 23, 1935.

318 Wallace sued: Unattributed NYPL clip, October 29, 1941.

318 he wrote a song: Earl Wilson in New York *Post*, February 1, 1944.

318 Eva Tanguay: New York *Mirror*, April 27, 1935.

318 if a fan asked her: Jack Allen to author.

318 her gifts: New York *Daily News*, August 18, 1935.

318 another car: Malachosky, p. 95.

319 "Salvation Sue": *Variety*, February 16, 1915.

319 Their story was going to be called: *Ibid.*, May 8, May 15, 1935.

319 *Klondike Annie*, Paramount 1936, is now owned by Universal MCA.

321 "Miss West is not masquerading": Hays to Hammell, July 2, 1935, *Klondike Annie* PCA file, AMPAS. For the remainder of this chapter, quotes from letters and memos come from this file.

321 Joseph Breen reminded Paramount: Breen to Hammell, September 26, 1935.

322 "particularly distasteful": *Hollywood Reporter*, February 5, 1936.

322 "MAE WEST ACID THREAT . . . detectives": Los Angeles *Daily News*, October 8, 1935; Los Angeles *Post-Record*, October 8, 1935.

322 a "three-way scrap": *Variety*, September 25, 1935.

322 ordering countless retakes: *Ibid.*, September 25, November 6, 1935.

323 "because I knew . . . 'I'll wreck him'": Raoul Walsh, *Each Man in His Time: The Life Story of a Director* (New York: Farrar, Straus & Giroux, 1974), pp. 276–77.

323 "He's not only tall": Mae West to John Kobal, *People Will Talk* (New York: Knopf, 1985), p. 160.

323 "Other actors don't mind": Lubitsch, quoted by Frank S. Nugent, *The New York Times*, March 15, 1936, X.

324 "Try to push her around?": Ernst Lubitsch in *Time* (March 9, 1936):46.

324 she would have to work out her story: *Variety*, November 6, 1935.

324 Paramount didn't feel like home: MW, *Goodness*, p. 178.

324 "is neither flesh nor fowl": *The Times* (London), May 17, 1936.

324 "an offensive mixture": PCA file.

324 Advertisements: Paramount press book for *Klondike Annie* (February 1936), AM-PAS.

325 "Just as long as we have Mae West": Breen memo, February 10, 1936.

325 "I think we should have editorials": William Randolph Hearst, undated typescript, PCA *Klondike* file.

325 THE SCREEN MUST NOT RELAPSE: New York *American*, February 29, 1936; *Time* (March 9, 1936):44.

326 nursing a grudge: *Variety*, March 18, 1936.

326 a slur against his mistress: *Time* (March 9, 1936):44.

326 snubbing Lovella Parsons: *Motion Picture Herald*, March 7, 1936.

326 "Any picture that presents": San Francisco Motion Picture Council to PCA, et al., May 1, 1936.

326 "She took personal pride": *Hollywood* (August 1936), quoted by Tuska, p. 117.

326 "rain, Lent": *Hollywood Reporter* (March 2, 1936):1.

326 "one hundred per cent more": *Variety*, March 4, 1936.

326 "compulsory block booking": *Motion Picture Herald*, March 7, 1936.

327 "Public taste is running away": New York *Herald Tribune*, March 10, 1936.

327 Paramount put her on notice: *Variety*, January 15, 1936.

327 Boris Kaplan informed her: Michael Kaplan to author, April 1, 1993.

327 retreating from its past association: Ramona Curry, "Mae West as Censored Commodity: The Case of *Klondike Annie*," *Cinema Journal*, 31, no. 1 (Fall 1991): 73.

327 MAE WEST QUITS PARAMOUNT: Unattributed MCNY clip, March 6, 1936.

327 Major Pictures: Los Angeles *Examiner*, April 22, 1936; *Variety*, April 22, 1936.

Page   18. GOING TOO FAR

329 "I can't see myself": MW, quoted by Anita Loos, *Kiss Hollywood Goodbye* (New York: Viking, 1974), p. 169.

329 Clark Gable: MW in unattributed clip, NYPL.

329 "the director . . . Out!": Henry Hathaway interview, Oral History Program Collection A80.154, SMU. Quoted by permission.

330 turned down once: *Variety*, February 26, 1936.

330 "Mr. Cohen stated": Breen Memo, February 19, 1936, *Go West* PCA file, AMPAS. Unless otherwise noted, quotes from letters and memos in this chapter refer to this file.

330 Cohen had reassured Breen: *Variety*, June 16, 1936.

330 quibbles: Breen to Cohen, June 3, 17, 1936.

331 "Mavis' maid": *Ibid.*, June 3, 1936.

331 original *Go West* script: Dated June 25, 1936. AMPAS lacks a copy of the very early "yellow script."

331 had him stand in a hole: George Eells and Stanley Musgrove, *Mae West* (New York: Morrow, 1982), p. 161.

332 conflict with Alice Brady: *Variety*, September 2, 1936.

332 *Go West, Young Man*, Paramount 1936, is now owned by Universal MCA.

334 an act scripted by Harry Conn: *Variety*, November 4, 1936.

334 MAE MADE TOO MANY DEMANDS . . . ill: *Ibid.*, November 18, 1936.

334 "a case of motion picture entertainment": *Motion Picture Herald*, November 14, 1936.

334 "sly innuendos": Quoted by Jon Tuska, *The Films of Mae West* (Secaucus, N.J.: Citadel Press, 1973), p. 127.

334 "It's difficult to be disapproving": Robert Garland, New York *American*, November 19, 1936.

334 "giving Miss West a gorgeous chance": Kate Cameron, New York *Daily News*, November 19, 1936.

334 "We mustn't, of course": *The New Yorker* (November 21, 1936):81.

335 "the wisecracks lack": *Graham Greene on Film*, ed. John Russell Taylor (New York: Simon & Schuster, 1972), p. 124.

335 Jack West was hauled into court: *Variety*, October 13, 1937.

335 threatening two men: *Ibid.*, October 21, 1936.

335 phoning Madden: MW, *Goodness Had Nothing to Do with It* (New York: Manor Books, 1976), p. 285.

335 "I was tired": MW to William Scott Eyman in *Take One* (September 1972):21.

336 "so tasteful, so enthusiastic": *Ibid.*, p. 20.

336 "I saw the whole story": *Mae West on Sex, Health and ESP* (London and New York: W. H. Allen, 1975), p. 111.

336 Rivkin reported: Eells and Musgrove, p. 164.

336 Paramount Production files: AMPAS.

336 costumes: David Chierchetti, *Hollywood Costume Design* (New York: Harmony Books, 1976), p. 52.

336 *Every Day's a Holiday*, Paramount 1938, now belongs to Universal MCA.

337 "She'd really lost weight": Lloyd Nolan interview, Oral History Program, Collection A80.154, SMU.

337 "There are no sex situations": Cohen to Breen, August 31, 1937, *Every Day's* PCA file, AMPAS. The remaining quotes from letters and memos in this chapter are from this file.

338 "These people or their next of kin": Breen to Cohen, August 6, 1937.

338 if two lines were deleted: *Variety*, December 29, 1937.

338 Sheilah Graham: Quoted by David Ray Johnson, "Biographical Study of Mae West," Appendix, *Mae West on Sex*, p. 217.

338 Howard Barnes: New York *Herald Tribune*, January 27, 1938.

338 Frank Nugent: *The New York Times*, January 27, 1938.

338 "All in all": New York *Sun*, January 27, 1938.

339 "It was like old times": *The New York Times*, January 27, 1938.

339 "that thing called sex": Howard Barnes in New York *Herald Tribune*, January 27, 1938.

339 The December 12, 1937, Chase and Sanborn Hour broadcast containing the Arch Oboler "Adam and Eve" sketch is available on Radiola cassette MR-1126, 1981.

340 "Instead of going on the premise": Arch Oboler Deposition, *Joan Storm v. Mae West et al.*, U.S. District Court of the Southern District of California, No. 1317-H.

341 Eve is the "central figure": Judge Hollzer Memo of Conclusions, *Storm v. Mae West et al.*

341 Ameche pointed out: Undated Ameche interview on Radiola Chase and Sanborn Hour tape.

341 "offensive to the great mass": Frank McNinch in New York *Journal*, January 14, 1938.

341 "Mae West Pollutes Homes": Quoted in *Variety*, December 22, 1937.

341 Dr. Sheehy: Quoted by David Ray Johnson, p. 219.

341 "The American people": *Congressional Record*, vol. 83 (January 14, 1938):560.

341 a board of review: New York *Sun*, February 15, 1938.

341 "Radio is badly scared": *Variety*, December 22, 1932.

342 "Ho hum": Bergen in unattributed clip, PCA *Every Day's* file, AMPAS.

342 "proper protection": Los Angeles *Examiner*, January 4, 1938.

342 "Did they expect a sermon?" MW in New York *Post*, April 25, 1938.

342 "The star is news": *Variety*, December 29, 1937.

342 would have made even more: New York *Sun*, May 5, 1938.

343 "I'm the first personality since Chaplin": MW to Michael Mok, New York *Post*, April 25, 1938.

343 "keep exhibits arty": MW in unattributed, undated [1938] clip, BPL.

343 "They always put pretty dames": New York *Post*, March 15, 1938.

343 "Well, I'm a little tired today": MW in unattributed clip, April 21, 1938, BPL.

343 unfailingly handed each suppliant: Irwin F. Zeltner, *What the Stars Told Me: Hollywood in Its Heyday* (New York: Exposition Press, 1971), pp. 56–57.

344 "box-office poison": New York *Journal American*, May 4, 1938.

344 "The box office business": MW in New York *Sun*, May 5, 1938.

344 "new types of film": Carol M. Ward, *Mae West: A Bio-Bibliography* (Westport, Conn.: Greenwood Press, 1989), p. 36.

Page   EPILOGUE

345 "More than being a person": John Mason Brown, "Mae Pourquoi?" in *Dramatis Personae: A Retrospective Show* (New York: Viking, 1963), p. 259.

345 as far off as Canton, China: St. Paul *Daily News*, December 8, 1935.

345 tall-tale tradition: See Robert C. Toll, *Blacking Up* (New York: Oxford University Press, 1974), p. 8.

346 "I'm in a class by myself": MW to C. Robert Jennings, "Mae West: A Candid Conversation with the Indestructible Queen of Vamp and Camp," *Playboy* (January 1971): 76.

346 The Dali *Face of Mae West* is held by the Art Institute of Chicago.

346 realized as a tableau: Meredith Etherington-Smith, *The Persistence of Memory: A Biography of Dali* (New York: Random House, 1992), pp. 188, 208. Thanks to Elizabeth Crews for information about the room at the Spanish Dali Museum.

347 "the only author that has ever": W. C. Fields letter to Cliff Work, September 28, 1939, in *W. C. Fields by Himself*, ed. Ronald J. Fields (New York: Warner Books, 1973), p. 441.

347 "the heat is definitely off": Quoted by George Eells and Stanley Musgrove, *Mae West* (Morrow, 1982), p. 200.

347 "I'm not making a comeback": MW to Betty Burton, *Movie Stars* (December 1970): 70.

347 "a Restoration comedy": Quoted by Jon Tuska, *The Films of Mae West* (Secaucus, N.J.: Citadel Press, 1973), p. 173.

348 contact with the dead: *Mae West on Sex, Health and ESP* (London and New York: W. H. Allen, 1975), p. 148.

348 "floating like pink clouds": Jennings, p. 73.

348 "as unhousebroken as can be": Diane Arbus, "Mae West: Once Upon a Time," in *Arbus Magazine Work*, eds. Doon Arbus and Marvin Israel (Millerton, N.Y.: Aperture, 1984), p. 58.

348 "a tremendous, tough, wonderful quality": Ann Sheridan to John Kobal, *People Will Talk* (New York: Knopf, 1985), p. 419.

349 not intimacy: Cecil Beaton, *Beaton in Vogue*, ed. Josephine Ross (London: Thames & Hudson, 1986), p. 192.

349 Cole Porter: Gerald Bordman, *American Musical Theatre: A Chronicle* (New York: Oxford University Press, 1986), p. 518; George Eells, *The Life That Late He Led: A Biography of Cole Porter* (New York: Putnam, 1967), p. 176.

349 "but I turned it down": MW to James Bacon in unattributed clip, December 6, 1957, SF PALM.

349 nixed by Harry Cohn: Maurice Leonard. *Mae West: Empress of Sex* (New York: Birch Lane, 1992), p. 284.

349 "I like movies about strong women": MW in *The New York Times*, July 25, 1976.

349 Elvis Presley vehicle: Frank Rose, *The Agency: William Morris and the Hidden History of Show Business* (New York: Harper Business, 1995), pp. 270–71.

349 "She always seemed to be anti-sex": Federico Fellini to Charlotte Chandler, *The Ultimate Seduction* (Garden City, N.Y.: Doubleday, 1984), p. 117.

349 more insulted than flattered: Leonard, p. 276.

350 a "kind of Laurel and Hardy picture": Billy Wilder, quoted by Gerald Clarke, "Portrait: Billy Wilder," *Architectural Digest* (April 1994): 406.

350 banned in Atlanta: Richard Helfer, *Mae West on Stage: Themes and Personae* (unpublished Ph.D. dissertation, City University of New York, 1990), p. 406.

350 "Have you any advice": Charles Collingwood, quoted in *Variety*, October 21, 1959.

350 "mine, all mine": MW, *Goodness Had Nothing to Do with It* (New York: Manor Books, 1976), p. 272.

351 "a cautious person": Cynthia Lowry, *Oakland Tribune*, August 17, 1952.

351 "I'm sorry that I can't have faith": MW letter [dictated to a secretary] to M. J. Kavanaugh, February 8, 1945, Shubert.

351 concentrating on yourself: MW to Jennings, p. 80.

351 her estimated worth: *Ibid.*, p. 73.

351 "I've spent a lot of money": MW to Karl Fleming and Anne Taylor Fleming, *The First Time* (New York: Simon & Schuster, 1975), p. 319.

ON SOURCES

MAE WEST'S WRITINGS

The Roger Richman Agency of Beverly Hills, California, representing Mae West's re-ceivership estate, governs rights to her writings, including unpublished playscripts.

Mae West's autobiography, *Goodness Had Nothing to Do with It*, first released in 1959 (Prentice-Hall), was republished by Manor Books in 1976 as a paperback with the added postscript "Still the Queen of Sex." I quote from the 1976 edition throughout, because it is the most complete. Both the 1959 and the 1976 editions include photographs and excerpts from reviews. The ghostwriter of *Goodness*, Stephen Longstreet, thanked in Mae West's acknowledgments for his "editorial assistance," is writing his own memoir.

The most interesting novels by Mae West are *The Constant Sinner* (set in Harlem, and originally published by Macaulay in 1931 as *Babe Gordon*) and *Diamond Lil* (Macaulay, 1932). In 1995 Virago republished both in the United Kingdom, the latter under the movie title, *She Done Him Wrong*.

Another novel, *Pleasure Man* (Dell, 1975), relies heavily on the writing skills of Mae West's then-secretary, Lawrence Lee. It jettisons the most fascinating part of the 1927 play of the same name: the female-impersonator subplot.

Mae West's 1975 advice book *Mae West on Sex, Health and ESP*, published by the British house W. H. Allen, also betrays the unmistakable hand of a ghostwriter; none-theless, the anecdotes, memories, and tidbits of wisdom are authentic Mae West. *Mae West on Sex*, including a well-researched biographical essay by David Ray Johnson, offers plenty of facts and revelations.

Most of the manuscripts for the pre-Hollywood plays—*The Ruby Ring* (1921), *The Hussy* (1922), *Sex* (1926), *The Drag* (1927), *The Wicked Age* (1927), *Pleasure Man* (1928), *Diamond Lil* (1928), and *Frisco Kate* (1930)—reside in Washington, D.C., at the Library of Congress, Manuscript Division. One script, *Chick* (1924), although copy-righted by Mae West, is adapted from *Kuecken* by Carl M. Jacoby and Sydney Rosenfeld; it seems highly derivative. Several of Mae West's plays—*Sex, The Drag*, and *Pleasure Man*—have been published by Routledge in a book titled *Mae West's Plays*, edited by Lillian Schlissel.

One Mae West script that is not at the Library of Congress, *The Constant Sinner* (1931, based on the published novel), is housed at the Shubert Archive in New York City. The Shubert Archive also possesses scripts of some of the Broadway plays or revues in which Mae West performed, photographs, a couple of letters to and from her, and clippings of press reviews.

FILMS

Mae West made eight movies originally produced and/or distributed by Paramount: *Night After Night* (1932), *She Done Him Wrong* (1933), *I'm No Angel* (1933), *Belle of the Nineties* (1934), *Goin' to Town* (1935), *Klondike Annie* (1936), *Go West, Young Man* (1936), and *Every Day's a Holiday* (1938). The last two were produced by Major Pictures. Universal-MCA, Universal City, California, now owns all of them.

The screenplays are variously credited. *Night After Night*, based on a story by Louis Bromfield, was adapted and written by Vincent Lawrence. The *She Done Him Wrong* writing credits went to Harry Thew and John Bright, based on "Original Play and Dialogue by Mae West." *I'm No Angel* screenplay and dialogue credit went to Mae West, with "continuity" credit to Harlan Thompson. Mae West received full writing credit for *Belle of the Nineties* and *Every Day's a Holiday*. For *Goin' to Town*, the screenplay credited to Mae West is based on "an original story by Marion Morgan and George B. Dowell," who are also credited with "story ingredients" incorporated into *Klondike Annie*. Mae West used her own unproduced play *Frisco Kate* as the kernel for *Klondike Annie*. *Go West, Young Man* gave Mae West credit for a screenplay "based on a play" [*Personal Appearance*] by Lawrence Riley. She generally wrote her own dialogue.

I read the scripts of all these films (except *Night After Night*, whose script I did not locate) at the Paramount Collection at the Margaret Herrick Library of the Academy of Motion Picture Arts and Sciences in Beverly Hills, California.

Before the Mae West films from the 1930s were released on video by Universal, I watched them at the Film Archive of the University of California at Los Angeles.

BIOGRAPHICAL MATERIAL

I am not the first biographer of Mae West, and am one of many writers about her celebrated movie career. Her work in vaudeville and on the legitimate stage has garnered much less comment. In a book by Jon Tuska called *The Films of Mae West* (Citadel Press, 1973), her vaudeville and theatrical work receive close but incomplete scrutiny; the whereabouts of the manuscripts of Mae West's plays at the Library of Congress hadn't been discovered in the 1970s, when *The Films of Mae West* was written. Tuska is reliable on the films.

Carol M. Ward's outstanding scholarly book *Mae West: A Bio-Bibliography* (Greenwood Press, 1989) does consider the playscripts, and comments astutely on them, the screen career, and Mae West the woman. In addition, Ward includes a chronology and bibliography, and reprints some important interviews. Her book belongs on any shelf of essential Mae West references.

There have been some short, popular Mae West biographies—with varying degrees of reliability. One, by Fergus Cashin (1982), is farfetched and not to be trusted. David Hanna's (1976) is brief but sound.

The first substantial biography, *Mae West*, by George Eells and Stanley Musgrove, was published by Morrow in 1982, two years after Mae West's death. Benefiting from Musgrove's personal and professional association with Mae West, and enlivened by colorful prose, it's a must-read; Eells and Musgrove quote Mae West extensively, and also quote interviews with some of her associates and contemporaries who are no longer alive. But their book cites no sources, doesn't shed much light on Mae West's childhood and fledgling career, and often skewers chronology.

A subsequent British HarperCollins biography by Maurice Leonard, *Mae West: Empress of Sex* (1991), republished in the United States by Birch Lane, uncovers facts about Mae West's flirtation with marriage to a Texan in 1924. Leonard also gives us chauffeur-fighter Chalky White's story about his affair with Mae West.

Tim Malachosky's self-published coffee-table book, *Mae West* (Lancaster, California: Empire Publishing, 1993), has beautiful, in some instances rare, photographs from the Hollywood years. The adulatory text draws on stories Mae West told Malachosky.

Mae West's playscripts are exhaustively and well examined by Richard Helfer in a fine unpublished 1990 City University of New York Ph.D. dissertation.

Marybeth Hamilton's 1990 Princeton dissertation, revised and published by U.S. HarperCollins in 1995 as *When I'm Bad I'm Better: Mae West, Sex, and American Entertainment* (and by Pandora in Britain with the title *Queen of Camp*), also intelligently discusses some of the plays, the New York trials resulting from charges of indecency, and the later censorship struggles in Hollywood with Joseph Breen and the Hays Office. Hamilton focuses on Mae West's Broadway and screen career and its impact on American entertainment, rather than on the life of the child named Mary Jane West who became the woman and actress-writer Mae West. *When I'm Bad I'm Better* was published late in 1995, after I had completed the manuscript for this book. But previews of Hamilton's book—her published articles "Mae West Live: *Sex, The Drag,* and 1920s Broadway" (in *The Drama Review* [Winter, 1992] and " 'I'm the Queen of the Bitches,' " on drag queens in *Pleasure Man* (in the book edited by Lesley Ferris, *Crossing the Stage: Controversies on Cross-Dressing*, Routledge 1993)—appeared while I was researching. I read and learned from both.

Alexander Walker's chapter on Mae West in *Sex in the Movies* (Penguin, 1968) is my favorite essay-length take on Mae West, and John Mason Brown's "Mae Pourquoi?" in his collection *Dramatis Personae: A Retrospective Show* (Viking, 1963) runs a close second. The pithiest published Mae West interviews in periodicals are by Thyra Samter Winslow (*The New Yorker*, November 10, 1928); Ruth Biery in *Movie Classic* (January through April 1934); Diane Arbus (*Show*, January 1965); Richard Meryman (*Life*, April 18, 1969); C. Robert Jennings in *Playboy*, January 1971; Scott Eyman in *Take One* (September 1972); and Robert E. Johnson (in *Jet*, July 1974). Among the substantial interviews included in books are those by Karl Fleming (*The First Time*, New York: Simon & Schuster, 1975); Charlotte Chandler (*The Ultimate Seduction*, New York: Doubleday, 1984); and John Kobal (*People Will Talk*, New York: Knopf, 1985).

Ann Jillian's 1982 portrayal of Mae West in a made-for-TV biopic on ABC Television (written by E. Arthur Kean, directed by Lee Philips) is amazingly persuasive, sensual, and telling. The script's version of her relationship to Jim Timony, however, offers more imagination than accuracy. Consolidating West's ties to gay male performers by incorporating them into a single character (played by Roddy McDowall) works well, as fiction.

The 1994 Wombat Productions biographical documentary *Mae West and Her Men*, produced by Gene Feldman, includes rare footage of Mae West with Texas Guinan, and showcases interesting, often insightful interviews with some of the Hollywood men—actors, fans, gurus, directors, observers, columnists—who knew Mae West. However, the most important men in her life remain silent, some undoubtedly for excellent reasons.

Paul Novak, Mae West's companion in her later decades, does not appear in the video, and the other men who at one time held places in the innermost circle either opted for silence or no longer are living.

SOURCES ON POPULAR MUSIC AND DANCE, VAUDEVILLE, BURLESQUE, AND THEATER HISTORY

A good survey of American popular culture is Russell Nye's *The Unembarrassed Muse: The Popular Arts in America* (New York: Dial, 1970).

For songs, I have relied on the Starr Sheet Music Collection of Indiana University's Lilly Library, on the monthly publication *Remember That Song*, and on the reference resources of ASCAP and BMI. I often consulted David Ewen's *All the Years of American Popular Music* (Prentice-Hall, 1977) and Sigmund Spaeth's *A History of Popular Music in America* (Random House, 1948). Philip Furia's *The Poets of Tin Pan Alley* (Oxford, 1990) and *The Jazz Age: Popular Music in the 1920s*, by Arnold Shaw (Oxford, 1987), were inspirations.

The Smithsonian recordings of American popular songs through the decades preserve original performances of some of the major popular songs of their day. Vernacular dances like the shimmy are engagingly discussed by Marshall and Jean Stearns in *Jazz Dance* (Macmillan, 1968). On Broadway dance, I used Richard Kislan's excellent *Hoofing on Broadway: A History of Show Dancing* (Prentice-Hall, 1987).

The main repositories of newspaper clippings on Mae West's vaudeville and stage career are at the Museum of the City of New York and, most important, the Billy Rose Theatre Collection at Lincoln Center's New York Public Library for the Performing Arts. *The Clipper, The New York Dramatic Mirror, Variety,* and *Billboard*—American periodicals devoted to show business—contain reviews and some detailed information about vaudeville performances, routes, controversies, and box-office receipts. Hometown newspapers in the towns and cities on the circuit often ran local reviews. The Keith/Albee Collection at the University of Iowa has Managers' Reports.

Book sources for information about vaudeville and/or female impersonators include Robert Toll's pathbreaking *On with the Show: The First Century of Show Business in America* (Oxford, 1976); Abel Green and Joe Laurie, Jr.'s insiders' look, *Show Biz: From Vaude to Video* (Holt, 1951); Anthony Slide's informative *The Vaudevillians: A Dictionary of Vaudeville Performers* (Arlington House, 1981) and the same author's *Great Pretenders: A History of Female & Male Impersonators* (Wallace-Homestead, 1986); Charles Stein's compendious anthology, *American Vaudeville As Seen by Its Contemporaries* (Knopf, 1984); John Di Meglio's *Vaudeville USA* (Bowling Green University, 1973); Albert McLean, Jr.'s *American Vaudeville as Ritual* (University of Kentucky, 1965); and Robert W. Snyder's *The Voice of the City: Vaudeville and Popular Culture in New York* (Oxford, 1989).

I read Fred Allen's *Much Ado About Me* (Little, Brown, 1956) and Sophie Tucker's *Some of These Days* (Doubleday, 1945); also books by or about Groucho Marx, Bert Williams, George Burns, Milton Berle, Harry Richman, and W. C. Fields. Bert Savoy and Eva Tanguay should each be the subject of a published book, but so far neither has been.

The classic article on Mae West's resemblance to a female impersonator is George Davis's "The Decline of the West," in the May 1934 *Vanity Fair*. Parker Tyler also addressed the subject in his introduction to Tuska's *The Films of Mae West* and in *Screening the Sexes* (Holt, 1972); and Pamela Robertson's essay on West and camp, in the Winter 1993 *Cinema Journal*, focuses exclusively on the topic. Mae West is mentioned by Wayne Koestenbaum in his insightful *The Queen's Throat: Opera, Homosexuality and the Mystery of Desire* (Poseidon, 1993). Marjorie Garber is interesting on cross dressing in general and on Rudolph Valentino in particular in her *Vested Interests: Cross Dressing and Cultural Anxiety* (Routledge, 1991).

American burlesque is the subject of too few good books. Irving Zeidman's *The American Burlesque Show* (Hawthorn, 1967) and Robert C. Allen's *Horrible Prettiness: Burlesque and American Culture* (University of North Carolina, 1991) begin to fill the void.

Both the Harvard Theater Collection and the Billy Rose Theatre Collection house treasure troves of material on individual performers, productions, and plays.

Books on American or New York theater history that I consulted over and over again were: Benjamin McArthur's *Actors and American Culture, 1880–1920* (Oxford, 1984), Brooks Atkinson's *Broadway* (Limelight, 1985), Robert Baral's hard to find *Revue: A Nostalgic Reprise of the Great Broadway Period* (Fleet, 1962), Allen Churchill's several books on Broadway and the 1920s, Daniel Blum's *A Pictorial History of the American Theatre* (Crown, 1977), and Gerald Bordman's essential *American Musical Theatre: A Chronicle* (Oxford, 1986). Mary C. Henderson's *The City & the Theatre: New York Playhouses from Bowling Green to Times Square* (Preston, 1973), in tracking the history of individual theaters, tells much about the growth of New York City.

SOCIAL HISTORY AND NEW YORK HISTORY

For American social history in the 1920s and earlier, I often consulted the volumes that make up Mark Sullivan's *Our Times: The United States, 1900–1925* (Scribner, 1929–35). I also used the American Heritage series on particular decades.

The Local History collection at the Brooklyn Public Library, Grand Army Plaza, has clippings from *The Brooklyn Eagle* and other publications. The Brooklyn Historical Society has name and street directories going back to the 1870s, and information on neighborhoods and theaters. New York's Municipal Archives has birth, death, and wedding certificates, lists of those arrested in police raids, and documents from the district attorney's office. Los Angeles Superior Court has court records for the Hollywood years. *The New York Times, New York Daily News, New York American, New York Evening Telegram, New York World, New York World-Telegram, New York Daily Mirror, New York Evening Graphic*, and other newspapers, or clippings drawn from them, proved invaluable.

For Manhattan history, I turned to the New-York Historical Society's photo and street files, and the Fifth Avenue New York Public Library collection of old New York guidebooks. Some of the early Byron photographs, accompanied by a knowing, animated narrative, appear in Grace Mayer's *Once Upon a City: New York from 1890–1910* (Macmillan, 1956). Robert Hughes's *The Real New York* (Smart Set, 1904) describes the city at the turn of the century. I took many a cue from Alvin F. Harlow's treasure, *Old Bowery Days* (Appleton, 1931); and from Luc Sante's *Low Life* (Farrar, Straus and Giroux, 1991), Timothy Gilfoyle's *City of Eros: New York City, Prostitution and the Commercialization of Sex* (Norton, 1992), and the jam-packed compendium edited by William R. Taylor, *Inventing Times Square: Commerce and Culture at the Crossroads of the World* (Russell Sage, 1991). *The Encyclopedia of New York City*, edited by Kenneth T. Jackson and published by Yale, came out in 1995 as I was completing my manuscript.

George Chauncey, Jr.'s *Gay New York: Urban Culture and the Making of a Gay Male*

World (Basic Books, 1994) is exemplary as a study of both gay subcultures and New York City. On homosexuality in the theater, Kaier Curtin's *We Can Always Call Them Bulgarians: The Emergence of Lesbians & Gay Men on the American Stage* (Alyson, 1987) is fascinating, detailed, and well documented.

Lewis A. Erenberg's *Steppin' Out: New York Nightlife and the Transformation of American Culture, 1890–1930* (Greenwood, 1981) and Kathy Peiss's *Cheap Amusements: Working Women and Leisure in Turn-of-the-Century New York* (Temple University, 1986) both set many wheels turning in my head about cultural changes as entertainment reflects and shapes them. Irving Lewis Allen's *The City in Slang: New York Life and Popular Speech* (Oxford, 1993) taught me about more than slang. I also learned about New York from books by or about Walter Winchell, Damon Runyon, Cab Calloway, Fanny Brice, Al Jolson, Carl Van Vechten, George Jean Nathan, Gilbert Seldes, Clara Bow, Duke Ellington, Ethel Waters, Louise Brooks, Texas Guinan, George Raft, and Dorothy Parker, all sometime New Yorkers.

On the Jazz Age, I relied on F. Scott Fitzgerald's *The Crack-Up* (first published in 1931), Nils Y. Granlund's out-of-print *Blondes, Brunettes & Bullets* (McKay, 1957), and Stanley Walker's *The Night Club Era* (Stokes, 1933). I consulted Edmund Wilson's *The American Earthquake* (Doubleday, 1958) and the anthology *Ain't We Got Fun? Essays, Lyrics and Stories of the Twenties* (NAL, 1980), edited by Barbara H. Solomon. I referred to Ann Douglas's *Terrible Honesty: Mongrel Manhattan in the 1920s* (Farrar, Straus and Giroux, 1995), and the classic *Only Yesterday: An Informal History of the 1920s* (Harper & Row, 1931, 1964), by Frederick Lewis Allen. I also learned from Jimmy Durante's and Jack Kofoed's *Nightclubs* (Knopf, 1931), Kathy Ogren's *The Jazz Revolution: 20s America and the Meaning of Jazz* (Oxford, 1989), Ronald L. Morris's *Wait Until Dark: Jazz and the Underworld, 1880–1940* (Bowling Green University, 1980), Ethan Mordden's *That Jazz: An Idiosyncratic Social History of the American Twenties* (Putnam's, 1978), and Simon Michael Bessie's *Jazz Journalism: The Story of the Tabloid Newspapers* (Dutton, 1938).

Recordings, long-ago trips to the Apollo, and books by or about Duke Ellington, Bessie Smith, and other blues singers helped shape my impressions of 1920s and early thirties Harlem, as did Barry Singer's riveting *Black and Blue: The Life and Lyrics of Andy Razaf* (Schirmer, 1992). I read Jim Haskins's *The Cotton Club* (NAL, 1977), James Weldon Johnson's *Black Manhattan* (1930, Da Capo 1991), Zora Neale Hurston's "Characteristics of Negro Expression," in *Negro Anthology* (1934), and Jervis Anderson's cultural portrait *This Was Harlem* (Farrar, Straus and Giroux, 1982).

On gangsters, I consulted Herbert Asbury's *The Gangs of New York* (Doubleday, 1927), Dean Jennings's *We Only Kill Each Other* (Prentice-Hall, 1967), and books on Al Capone and Chicago crime. I relied on Graham Nown's British biography of Owney Madden, *The English Godfather* (Ward Lock, 1987), and referred to Carl Sifakis's *Encyclopedia of American Crime* (Facts on File, 1982).

Something of Depression America's history came to me through documentaries that include newsreels and recordings of original performances of thirties songs; through weeklies like *The New Republic*, *Life*, and *The New Yorker*; and through books like T. H. Watkins's *The Great Depression: America in the 1930s* (Little, Brown, 1993) and Robert S. McElvaine's *The Great Depression: America, 1929–1941* (Times, 1993). I found interesting incidentals in J. C. Furnas's chatty *Great Times: An Informal Social History of the U.S.* (Putnam's, 1974).

On bare-knuckle boxing and the prototypical American he-man, I read Elliott Gorn's *The Manly Art: Bare-knuckle Prize-fighting in America* (Cornell University, 1986). To scope out the world of boxing at a later date, I read newspapers, Jack Dempsey's 1977 autobiography, and Budd Schulberg's novel *The Harder They Fall* (Bantam, 1947). I even watched some fights.

For the history of American women's fashion and ideals of beauty, I used Lois Banner's *American Beauty* (Knopf, 1983), Martha Banta's *Imaging American Women: Ideas and Ideals in Cultural History* (Columbia University, 1987), and Valerie Steele's *Fashion and Eroticism: Ideals of Feminine Beauty from the Victorian Era to the Jazz Age* (Oxford, 1985). Michael and Ariane Batterberry's *Mirror Mirror: A Social History of Fashion* (Holt, 1977) has copious illustrations and a spirited text.

I learned about changing American sexual mores from many sources, including such books as *Intimate Matters: A History of Sexuality in America* (Harper, 1988), by John D'Emilio & Estelle B. Freedman; Peter G. Filene's *Him/Her Self: Sex Roles in Modern America* (Johns Hopkins, 1986), and books on Emma Goldman and Margaret Sanger. Linda Gordon's *Woman's Body, Woman's Right: A Social History of Birth Control in America* (Viking, 1976) is crammed with fascinating facts. W. David Sievers's *Freud on Broadway: A History of Psychoanalysis and the American Drama* (Hermitage House, 1955) discusses O'Neill's impact and sexuality in the performing arts. *1915: The Cultural Moment* (Rutgers, 1991), edited by Adele Heller and Lois Rudnik, ties together cultural strands in politics, feminism, and the New Psychology as they intersected with the New Theater and New Art. Its focus is more high culture than pop.

ON MOVIES, HOLLYWOOD, MOVIE CENSORSHIP

The British Film Institute in London has intact American movie magazines and clippings on films and performers. The (Madison) Wisconsin Center for Research on Film and Theater, the Billy Rose Theatre Collection, and the Margaret Herrick Library of the Academy of Motion Picture Arts and Sciences all have slews of Mae West photographs and articles on Mae West; the latter two libraries also have extensive holdings on Paramount films. New York City's Museum of Modern Art Film Study Center has stills, clippings, and a complete collection from *Photoplay*. Stanley Musgrove left his intriguing notes for the Eells and Musgrove *Mae West* to the Doheny Library of the University of Southern California. Southern Methodist University's Oral History Collection has interviews with many former Hollywood studio craftspeople; Ronald L. Davis draws on these interviews in his book *The Glamour Factory: Inside Hollywood's Big Studio System* (SMU, 1993).

David Thomson's *A Biographical Dictionary of Film* (Knopf, 1994) and Ephraim Katz's *The Film Encyclopedia* (Crowell, 1979) are chock-a-block with information on people who have worked in the movies. Halliwell's and Leonard Maltin's film reference books were consulted regularly.

Out of the vast library of nonfiction books on film history, I found these especially informative on the pre-talkie years: Lary May's *Screening Out the Past: The Birth of Mass Culture and the Motion Picture Industry* (Oxford, 1980), David Nasaw's *Going Out: The Rise and Fall of Public Amusements* (Basic Books, 1993), and Kevin Brownlow's essential *Behind the Mask of Innocence* (University of California, 1990). Budd Schulberg's 1981 memoir *Moving Pictures* (Stein & Day) supplied a guided tour of twenties and early thirties Hollywood, and profiles of Paramount personalities like producer Emanuel Cohen.

For Hollywood in the 1930s, nothing beats Nathanael West's novel *Day of the Locust*

(1939), Budd Schulberg's *What Makes Sammy Run* (1941), or F. Scott Fitzgerald's *The Last Tycoon* (1941).

I read *Platinum Girl* (Abbeville, 1991), Eve Golden's book on Jean Harlow; David Stenn's flavorful biographies of Jean Harlow and Clara Bow; the prolific Charles Higham on Ziegfeld, Cary Grant, and other celebrities (including Mae West) in *Celebrity Circus* (Delacorte, 1979). I read or consulted biographies of Hedda Hopper, Tallulah Bankhead, Bette Davis, and Ernst Lubitsch, among others. Anita Loos's *Kiss Hollywood Goodbye* (Viking, 1974) tells about the movie she tried to get Mae West to make with Clark Gable. *On the Other Hand*, a 1989 memoir by Fay Wray, illuminates early talkies. Wray never knew Mae West, but she told me something about her own experiences with the 1920s and thirties, about the Hollywood craze for blond hair, Cary Grant, and co-existing with the Hays Office.

On the place of movies in 1930s America, Arthur Schlesinger, Jr.'s "When the Movies Really Counted," in *Show*, April 1963, taught me a lot, succinctly. I relied on Andrew Bergman's *We're in the Money: Depression America and Its Films* (New York University, 1971) and a serviceable British picture book, Allen Eyles's *That Was Hollywood: The 1930s* (B. T. Batsford, 1987). Tino Balio's 1993 *Grand Design: Hollywood as a Modern Business Enterprise, 1930–39* (Scribner's) provided a survey of the period, both wide and deep. Gerald Mast's collection *The Movies in Our Midst: Documents in the Cultural History of Film in America* (University of Chicago, 1982) contains the Production Code and excerpts from Martin Quigley's *Decency in Motion Pictures*. Kenneth Anger's *Hollywood Babylon* (Dell, 1981) filled me in on screenland's opulent tawdry side. Roger Dooley's survey *From Scarface to Scarlett: American Films in the 1930s* (Harcourt, 1981) proved helpful. And I enjoyed and learned from Gerald Weales's *Canned Goods as Caviar: American Film Comedy of the 1930s* (University of Chicago, 1985).

The Los Angeles Times, *The Hollywood Reporter*, the British *Film Weekly*, and *Variety* supplied all kinds of details, usually not imagined or prepackaged, about the movie business's personalities, wheels, and deals.

On censorship in the movies, I relied on the Production Code files at the Margaret Herrick Library of the Academy of Motion Picture Arts and Sciences. Richard Maltby's "The Production Code and the Hays Office," in the book *Grand Design*, taught me much. So did Raymond Moley's *The Hays Office* (Bobbs-Merrill, 1945), Lea Jacobs's *The Wages of Sin: Censorship and the Fallen Woman Film, 1928–1942* (University of Wisconsin, 1991), *The Dame in the Kimono: Hollywood, Censorship and the Production Code* by Leonard J. Leff and Jerold L. Simmons (Grove Weidenfeld, 1990), Gregory D. Black's *Hollywood Censored: Morality Codes, Catholics and the Movies* (Cambridge University, 1994), and Frank Miller's *Censored Hollywood: Sex, Sin & Violence On Screen* (Turner, 1994).

Mae West's particular predicament as a target of the Hays Office is the subject of Ramona Curry's *Cinema Journal* (Fall 1991) article, "Mae West as Censored Commodity: The Case of *Klondike Annie*." W. A. Swanberg's *Citizen Hearst* (1961) lets us share the view of Hollywood from San Simeon and probes one of Mae West's most virulent and powerful attackers, William Randolph Hearst.

Recordings of performances by Mae West of much-censored songs from her movies (I know of no Mae West recordings from the 1910s or twenties) are available on cassette and CD. The album with the best selection of songs, complete with good notes by Rosetta Reitz, dates from 1990 (Rosetta Records).

On women in film, a vast subject, I particularly trusted Molly Haskell's astute *From Reverence to Rape* (Holt, 1973) and Marjorie Rosen's history, *Popcorn Venus: Women, Movies and the American Dream* (Coward, McCann, 1973); Rosen sees Mae West as a woman uncomfortable with her femininity. I also found Jeanine Basinger's more recent *A Woman's View* (Knopf, 1993) fun to read and enlightening.

The memoir of Paramount Pictures' co-founder Adolph Zukor, *The Public Is Never Wrong* (Putnam's, 1953), gives a guarded, sanitized, personal account of the studio's history. Books that make a stab at covering the subject are: John Douglas Eames, *The Paramount Story* (Crown, 1985) and *Paramount Pictures and the People Who Made Them* (A. S. Barnes, 1980), by I. G. Edmonds and Reiko Mimura. An unsigned article, "Paramount Pictures," in *Fortune* (March 1937) has details about finance and management. James Robert Parish's well-researched *The Paramount Pretties* (Arlington House, 1972) offers much information but no index. Maria Riva's unforgettable, authoritative book about her mother, *Marlene Dietrich* (Knopf, 1993), and Stephen Bach's 1992 exemplary *Marlene Dietrich* (Morrow, 1992) shed much light. Too little is known about Mae West's first and most enduring producer at Paramount, William Le Baron. Interviews with Betty Lasky and Andrew Stone, both of whom knew him well, helped me fill in some of the blanks.

Paramount did not open its legal files or other archival holdings to me. Neither did the William Morris Agency (well chronicled in a 1995 book by Frank Rose), which represented Mae West during the Hollywood years. I wish both had been hospitable, not only to me, but to other biographers or historians of American culture. Individual studios own individual films, estates have executors, specific agents represent particular performers. But mass-entertainment movies from Hollywood's Golden Age—and in some ways, their stars—belong to all of us.

INDEX

189; roadhouses run by, 145–47, 180;
séances and, 348; sister act
encouraged by, 85, 86; as stage
mother, 32, 35, 38; Tanguay and, 41–
42, 52, 70; Timony and, 90, 145;
Woodhaven house purchased by, 66
Western Vaudeville circuit, 80, 82
Where Are My Children? (film), 96
Whirl of the Town, The (revue), 111,
114–15
Whitaker, Alma, 249
White, Frances, 107
White, George, 122
White, Stanford, 24, 37, 49, 212
White Rats, 77–78, 85, 89; Colored
Branch of, 84
White Woman (film), 281
Whitford, Annabelle, 72
Whitney, John Hay, 309
Why Change Your Wife? (film), 134
Wicked Age, The (West), 12, 143, 147,
173–82, 186, 194, 216
Wicked Queen, The, see Drag, The
Wickland, Lyons, 144, 156
Wilde, Oscar, 22, 139, 337
Wilder, Billy, 349–50
Wilhelm, Kaiser, 94, 105
William, Warren, 331
Williams, Bert, 15, 41, 42, 64, 107,
110, 344
Williams, Harold E., 222
Wilson, Edmund, 122
Wilson, Teddy, 338
Wilson, Woodrow, 78, 87, 88, 93
Winchell, Walter, 110, 132, 147, 148,
150, 206, 222
Wingate, James, 246, 248, 253, 258,
264, 266–68, 296
Winninger, Charles, 337
Winslow, Thyra Samter, 196
Winsome Widow, A (revue), 63, 64, 101

Winter, Alice Ames, 298
Winter Garden (New York), 60, 61,
109
Wit and Wisdom of Mae West, The, 345
Withers, Grant, 313
Woman of Fire, A (film), 145
Women's National Democratic Club,
171
Women's Wear, 117
Wood, Peggy, 209
Woods, A. H., 232
Woods, Etta, 55
World's Columbian Exposition, 17–18
World War I, 78, 79, 84, 88, 92–99,
105, 118, 153
World War II, 10, 149, 346
Worm, A. Toxen, 60
Wright, Chalky, 8, 220, 335, 351
Wright, Loyd, 327
Wynn, Ed, 102, 104–5, 184, 254

Yeaman, Elizabeth, 305
Yellen, Jack, 128, 223
You Never Know (musical), 349
Young, Loretta, 285
Young, Rida Johnson, 100, 102, 103
Young, Stark, 185, 284

Zanuck, Darryl, 252
Ziegfeld, Florenz, Jr., 17, 38, 57–59, 63,
64, 69, 70, 96, 100, 107, 109, 122,
208
Ziegfeld Follies, 38, 41, 54, 57, 72, 93,
106
Zimmerman, Katharine, 174
Zukor, Adolph, 164, 234, 246, 248,
256, 298, 315